W9-CDT-498

THE LATINS IN THE LEVANT

"Nach Elis ziehn der Franken Heere,
Messene sei der Sachsen Loos,
Normanne reinige die Meere
Und Argolis erschaff' er gross."

GOETHE, *Faust*, Part II.

THE LATINS IN THE LEVANT

A HISTORY OF FRANKISH GREECE

(1204-1566)

BY WILLIAM MILLER, M.A.

AUTHOR OF "THE BALKANS," "TRAVELS AND POLITICS IN THE NEAR EAST," "GREEK LIFE IN TOWN AND COUNTRY"
ASSOCIATE OF THE BRITISH SCHOOLS AT ATHENS AND ROME

CAMBRIDGE: SPECULUM HISTORIALE
NEW YORK: BARNES & NOBLE, INC

ORIGINALLY PUBLISHED BY JOHN MURRAY IN 1908;
REPRINTED, BY ARRANGEMENT, IN 1964 FOR
SPECULUM HISTORIALE
42 LYNDEWODE ROAD, CAMBRIDGE, ENGLAND

PRINTED IN GREAT BRITAIN BY
LOWE AND BRYDONE (PRINTERS) LTD., LONDON

PREFACE

PROFESSOR KRUMBACHER says in his *History of Byzantine Literature*, that, when he announced his intention of devoting himself to that subject, one of his classical friends solemnly remonstrated with him, on the ground that there could be nothing of interest in a period when the Greek preposition ἀπό governed the accusative instead of the genitive case. I am afraid that many people are of the opinion of that orthodox grammarian. There has long prevailed in some quarters an idea that, from the time of the Roman Conquest in 146 B.C. to the day when Archbishop Germanós raised the standard of Independence at Kalavryta in 1821, the annals of Greece were practically a blank, and that that country thus enjoyed for nearly twenty centuries that form of happiness which consists in having no history. Forty years ago there was, perhaps, some excuse for this theory: but the case is very different now. The great cemeteries of mediæval Greece—I mean the Archives of Venice, Naples, Palermo, and Barcelona—have given up their dead. We know now, year by year—yes, almost month by month—the vicissitudes of Hellas under her Frankish masters, and all that is required now is to breathe life into the dry bones, and bring upon the stage in flesh and blood that picturesque and motley crowd of Burgundian, Flemish, and Lombard nobles, German knights, rough soldiers of fortune from Cataluña and Navarre, Florentine financiers, Neapolitan courtiers, shrewd Venetian and Genoese merchant princes, and last but not least, the bevy of high-born dames, sprung from the oldest families of France, who make up, together with the Greek *archons* and the Greek serfs, the persons of the romantic drama of which Greece was the theatre for 250 years. The present volume is an attempt to accomplish that delightful but difficult task.

Throughout I have based the narrative upon first-hand authorities. I can conscientiously say that I have consulted all the printed books known to me in Greek, Italian, Spanish, French, German, English, and Latin, which deal in any way with the subject; and I have endeavoured to focus all the scattered notices concerning the Frankish period which have appeared in periodical literature, and in the documents of the epoch which have been published. These I have supplemented by further research in the archives of Rome and Venice. My aim has been to present as complete an account as is possible in the existing state of our knowledge of this most fascinating stage in the life of Greece. I have also visited all the chief castles and sites connected with the Frankish period, believing that before a writer can hope to make the Franks live on paper, he must see where they lived in the flesh. Enormous as is the debt which every student of mediæval Greek history owes to the late Karl Hopf, it was here that he failed, and it was hence that his Frankish barons are labelled skeletons in a vast, cold museum, instead of human beings of like passions with ourselves.

One word as to the arrangement of the book. The historian of Frankish Greece is confronted at the outset with the problem of telling his tale in the clearest possible manner. He may describe, like Finlay, the history of each small state separately—a course which not only involves repetition, but prevents the reader from obtaining a view of the country as a whole; or he may, like Hopf, combine the separate narratives in one—a policy which inevitably leads to confusion. I have adopted an intermediate course. The three states of the Morea and continental Greece—the principality of Achaia, the duchy of Athens, and the Despotat of Epiros—were so closely connected as to form a fairly homogeneous whole; and with them naturally go the island county of Cephalonia and the island of Eubœa. The duchy of the Archipelago and the Venetian colony of Corfù, on the other hand, form separate sections, for their evolution differed widely from the other states. I have therefore treated them apart. Crete I have omitted for two reasons: it is not yet a part of the Greek kingdom, and it so happens that Frankish Greece almost exactly coincided with the area of modern Greece; moreover, the history of Venetian Crete cannot be written till the eighty-seven volumes of the "Duca di Candia" documents at Venice are published.

I owe thanks to many friends for help and advice, especially to K. A. M. Idroménos of Corfù.

W. M.

ROME, *December* 1907.

CONTENTS

CHAPTER I

GREECE AT THE TIME OF THE FRANKISH CONQUEST

CHAPTER II

THE FRANKISH CONQUEST (1204-1207)

CHAPTER III

THE ORGANISATION OF THE CONQUEST (1207-1214)

CHAPTER IV

THE ZENITH, OF FRANKISH RULE (1214-1262)

CHAPTER V

THE GREEK REVIVAL (1262-1278)

CHAPTER VII

THE CATALAN GRAND COMPANY (1302-1311)

CHAPTER VIII

THE CATALANS AND THEIR NEIGHBOURS (1311-1333)

PAGE

CHAPTER IX

THE RISE OF THE ACCIAJUOLI (1333-1373)

CHAPTER X

THE NAVARRESE COMPANY (1373-1388)

CHAPTER XI

FLORENTINE AND VENETIAN ATHENS (1388-1415)

CHAPTER XII

THE GREEK RECONQUEST OF ACHAIA (1415-1441)

CHAPTER XIII

THE TURKISH CONQUEST (1441-1460)

CHAPTER XIV

THE VENETIAN COLONIES (1462-1540)

CHAPTER XV

CORFÙ (1214-1485)

THE LATINS IN THE LEVANT

CHAPTER I

GREECE AT THE TIME OF THE FRANKISH CONQUEST

THE history of Frankish Greece begins with the Fourth Crusade—that memorable expedition which influenced for centuries the annals of Eastern Europe, and which forms the historical basis of the Eastern question. We all know how the Crusaders set out with the laudable object of freeing the Holy Sepulchre from the Infidel, how they turned aside to the easier and more lucrative task of overturning the oldest empire in the world, and how they placed on the throne of all the Cæsars Count Baldwin of Flanders as first Latin emperor of Constantinople. The Greeks fled to Asia Minor, and there, at Nice, the city of the famous council, and at Trebizond, on the shores of the Black Sea, founded two empires, of which the former served as a basis for the reconquest of Byzantium, while the latter survived for a few years the Turkish Conquest of the new Rome.

At the time of the Latin Conquest, most of Greece was still nominally under the authority of the Byzantine emperor. The system of provincial administration, which had been completed by Leo the Isaurian early in the eighth century, was, with some alterations, still in force, and the empire was parcelled out into divisions called Themes—a name originally applied to a regiment, and then to the district where it was quartered. Continental Greece, from the Isthmus to the river Peneios in the north and to Ætolia in the west, composed the Theme of Hellas, which thus included Attica, Bœotia, Phokis, Lokris, part of Thessaly, and the islands of Eubœa and Ægina; the Peloponnese gave its name to a second Theme, but at this time these two Themes were administered together by the same official.[1] Nikopolis, the Roman colony which Octavian had founded to commemorate the battle of Actium, formed a third Theme, which included Akarnania, Ætolia, and Epiros. Of the islands, the Cyclades, or Dodekanesos, as they were then called, were included in the Ægean Theme, the Northern Sporades in that of Salonika, while Crete, since its restoration to the Byzantine Empire from the Saracens two-and-a-half centuries earlier, was governed by an imperial viceroy. But most of the Ionian islands no longer formed part of the emperor's dominions. Five years before the Latins conquered Constantinople, a bold Genoese pirate named Vetrano had made himself master of the then rich and fertile island of Corfù, which he may have still held; while Cephalonia, Zante, and Ithaka had been permanently severed from the empire by the invasion of the Normans from Sicily twenty years before, and had been occupied by their admiral, Margaritone of Brindisi.[2] At the time of the Fourth Crusade, they were in the possession of a Count Maio, or Matthew, a member of the great Roman family of Orsini, who seems to have been a native of Monopoli in Apulia and to have married the daughter of the admiral, acknowledging the suzerainty of the king of Sicily. A considerable Italian colony from Brindisi had settled in Cephalonia under the auspices of these Apulian adventurers.[3]

In Thessaly, too, the imperial writ no longer ran. Benjamin of Tudela,[4] who travelled through Greece about forty years before the Latin Conquest, found a part of that province in the possession of the Wallachs, whose confines extended as far south as Lamia. Whatever may have been the origin of this mysterious and interesting race, which still dwells in summer on the slopes of Pindos and on the banks of the Aspropotamos, migrating in winter to the plains of

[1] Lámpros, *Μιχαὴλ Ἀκομινάτου*, i., 157, 160; *Αἱ Ἀθῆναι περὶ τὰ τέλη τοῦ δωδεκάτου αἰῶνος*, 25-6.

[2] Benedict of Peterborough, *Gesta Regis Ricardi*, ii., 199, in *Rolls Series.*

[3] *Libro de los fechos*, 53-4; *Epistolæ Innocentii III.*, vol. ii., pp. 16, 73; A. Dandolo *apud* Muratori, *Rerum Italicarum Scriptores*, xii., 336; *Archivio Veneto*, xx., 93.

[4] Asher, *The Itinerary of Benjamin of Tudela*, i., 45-9.

Bœotia, they had firmly established themselves in Northern Greece by the middle of the twelfth century, and the district where they lived already bore the name of Great Wallachia.[1] That the Wallachs are of Roman descent scarcely admits of doubt. At the present day the Roumanians claim them as belonging to the same family as themselves; but the worthy Rabbi of Tudela argued, from their Jewish names and the fact that they called the Jews "brethren," that they were connected with his own race. They showed, however, their brotherly love by contenting themselves with merely robbing the Israelites, while they both robbed and murdered the Greeks, when they descended from their mountains to pillage the plains. A terror to all, the Vlachi would submit to no king; and, twenty years before the fall of the Byzantine Empire, the foolish attempt of Isaac II. Angelos to place a tax upon their flocks and herds caused a general rising, which led to the formation of the second Bulgarian, or Bulgaro-Wallachian Empire, in the Balkans. Their disaffection and readiness for revolt was further proved, only three years before the Conquest of Constantinople, when an ambitious Byzantine commander, Manuel Kamýtzes, made himself master of Thessaly with the aid of a Wallachian officer, and disturbed the peace of both continental Greece and the Peloponnese, till the revolt was suppressed.[2]

The population of Greece at this time was not exclusively Hellenic. Besides the Wallachians in Thessaly, another alien element was represented by the Slavs of the Arkadian and Lakonian mountains, descendants of those Slavonian colonists who had entered the Peloponnese several centuries before. No one now accepts the once famous theory of Fallmerayer, that the inhabitants of modern Greece have "not a single drop of genuine Greek blood in their veins." No unbiassed historian can, however, deny the immigration of a large body of Slavs into the Peloponnese, where such names as Charvati (the village near Mycenæ) and Slavochorio still preserve the memory of their presence. But the wise measures of the Emperor Nikephóros I. in the ninth century and the marvellous power of the Hellenic race for

[1] So Nikétas Choniátes (p. 841) calls it.

[2] Nikétas Choniátes, 708-9.

absorbing and Hellenising foreign races—a power like that of the Americans in our day—had prevented the Peloponnese from becoming a Slav state—a Southern Servia or Bulgaria. At this time, accordingly, they were confined to the mountain fastnesses of Arkadia and Taygetos (called in the *Chronicles* "the mountain of the Slavs"),[1] where one of their tribes, the Melings, is often mentioned as residing. In the Peloponnese, too, were to be found the mysterious Tzákones—a race which is now only existing at Leonidi, in the south-east of the peninsula, and in the adjacent villages, but was then apparently occupying a wider area. Opinions differ as to the origin of this tribe, which has, to this day, a dialect quite distinct from that spoken anywhere else in Greek lands, and which was noticed as a "barbarian" tongue by the Byzantine satirist, Mázaris, in the fifteenth century. But the first living authority on their language, who has lived among them, regards them as descendants of the Lakonians and calls their speech "New Doric,"[2] and both Mázaris and the Byzantine historians, Pachyméres and Nikephóros Gregorâs, expressly say that their name was a vulgar corruption of the word "Lákones." Scattered about, wherever money was to be made by trade, were colonies of Jews. We read of Jews at Sparta in the tenth century, and I have myself seen numbers of later Jewish inscriptions at Mistrâ. Benjamin of Tudela found the largest Hebrew settlement at Thebes, where the Jews were, in his day, "the most eminent manufacturers of silk and purple cloth in all Greece." Among the 2000 Jewish inhabitants of that ancient city there were also "many eminent Talmudic scholars," indeed, the

[1] *Libro de los fechos*, 48-9; Τὸ Χρονικὸν τοῦ Μορέως, ll. 3040, 4605; *Le Livre de la Conqueste*, 95, 100.

[2] Dr Deffner of Athens, who has written a Tzakonic grammar. See his *Zakonisches* in *Monatsbericht der k. Akademie der Wissenschaften zu Berlin*. Features of their language are the Doric α for the ordinary Greek η, and the digamma in some words. Dr Deffner regards Τζάκωνας as a corruption of τοὺς Λάκωνας, and Mázaris says the Lakonians "are now called Tzákones." Constantine Porphyrogenitus (i., 696) mentions Τζέκωνες in the tenth century, Pachyméres (i., 309) and Nikephóros (i., 98) Τζάκωνες in the thirteenth. It is difficult, in the face of this evidence, to understand how Hopf could have believed them to be Slavs. The name is still common as a proper name, *e.g.* the leading surgeon at Athens is so called.

enthusiastic Rabbi says that "no scholars like them are to be met with in the whole Grecian Empire, except at Constantinople." Next came Halmyros with "about 400 Jews," Corinth with "about 300," Negroponte with 200, and Crissa, now the squalid village of Chryso, on the way up to Delphi, with the same number, who "live there by themselves on Mount Parnassos and carry on agriculture upon their own land and property"—an example of rural Judaism to be paralleled to-day near Salonika. Naupaktos and Ravenika had 100 Jews apiece, Patras and Lamia, or Zetounion, as it was then called, about half that number, and there were a few in Ætolia and Akarnania. The present large Jewish colony at Corfù was then represented by only one man.

The Italian element had become prominent commercially long before the Latin Conquest made the Franks territorial masters of Greece. A century earlier, Aléxios I. had conceded immense, and, as it proved, fatal privileges to the Venetians, in return for their aid against the Norman invaders; and Manuel I., in order to counteract the embarrassing Venetian influence, gave encouragement to the trading communities of Pisa, Genoa, and Amalfi. The Genoese asked in particular for the same privileges as their Venetian rivals in the Theban silk market. Benjamin of Tudela had found Venetian, Pisan, Genoese, and many other merchants frequenting "the large commercial city" of Halmyros in Thessaly,[1] and the commercial treaty of 1199 between Venice and Aléxios III. granted to the subjects of the republic free-trade not only at Halmyros, but at numerous other places in Greece. Among them we notice the Ionian islands of Corfù, Cephalonia, Zante, and Ithaka (called in the document by its classical name); the towns of Patras, Methone, Corinth, Argos, and Nauplia in the Peloponnese; Thebes and "the district of Athens" in continental Greece; the towns of Domokó, Larissa, and Trikkala in the north; and the islands of Eubœa, Crete, and the Archipelago.[2] But there cannot have been much love lost between the Greeks and these foreigners from the west. Old men would still remember the sack of Thebes and Corinth

[1] Asher, *loc. cit.*
[2] *Fontes Rerum Austriacarum*, Abt. II., B. xii., 264-7.

by the Normans of Sicily; middle-aged men would have heard of the horrors of the sack of Salonika by a later Sicilian force; and the children of the islands or coasts must have shuddered when they were told that the dreaded Genoese pirates, Vetrano or Caffaro, were coming. Moreover, ever since the final separation of the Greek and Latin churches in the middle of the eleventh century, a fanatical hatred had been kindled between west and east, which is not wholly extinguished to-day.

But even the rule of the Franks must have seemed to many Greeks a welcome relief from the financial oppression of the Byzantine Government. Greece was, at the date of the Conquest, afflicted by three terrible plagues: the tax-collectors, the pirates, and the native tyrants. The Imperial Government did nothing for the provinces, but wasted the money, which should have been spent on the defences of Greece, in extravagant ostentation at the capital. One emperor after another had exhausted the resources of his dominions by lavish expenditure, and Byzantine officials sent to Greece regarded that classic land, in the phrase of Nikétas,[1] as an "utter hole," an uncomfortable place of exile. The Themes of Hellas and the Peloponnese were at this time governed by one of these authorities, styled *prætor*, *protoprætor*, or "general,"[2] whose headquarters were at Thebes. We have from the pen of Michael Akominátos, the last metropolitan of Athens before the Conquest, and brother of the historian Nikétas, a vivid, if somewhat rhetorical, account of the exactions of these personages. Theoretically, the city of Athens was a privileged community. A golden bull of the emperor forbade the *prætor* to enter it with an armed force, so that the Athenians might be spared the annoyance and expense of having soldiers quartered upon them.[3] Its regular contribution to the imperial exchequer was limited to a land-tax, and it was expected to

[1] P. 78.

[2] *Πραίτωρ*, *πρωτοπραίτωρ*, *στρατηγός*, all occur on two leaden seals of governors of Hellas and the Peloponnese at this period. Lámpros, Αἱ Ἀθῆναι, 25.

[3] Professor Lámpros (*op. cit.*) points out that the idea that the *prætor* might not visit Athens at all is erroneous; his infraction of the city's privilege consisted in coming with an armed following.

send a golden wreath as a coronation offering to a new emperor. When the Byzantine Government, too, following a policy similar to that which cost our King Charles I. his throne, levied ship-money on the Greek provinces, really for the purpose of its own coffers, nominally for the suppression of piracy, Athens expected to be assessed on a lighter scale than the far richer communities of Thebes and Chalkis, and the number of sailors whom it had to furnish was fixed by a special decree. But, in practice, these privileges were apt to be ignored. The Athenians were compelled to contribute more ship-money than either of those cities, not only to the *prætor*, but to Léon Sgourós, the powerful magnate of Nauplia;[1] while the Thebans, who were less exposed to piracy, managed, no doubt by judicious bribery at Constantinople, to obtain a golden bull releasing them from naval service, and the reduction of their pecuniary contributions below those of Athens. The indignant metropolitan complains that the *prætor*, under the pretext of worshipping in the church of "Our Lady of Athens,"[2] as the Parthenon was then called, visited the city with a large retinue. He laments that one of these imperial governors had treated the city "more barbarously than Xerxes," and that the leaves of the trees, nay almost every hair on the heads of the unfortunate Athenians, had been numbered. The authority of the *prætor*, he says, is like Medea in the legend: just as she scattered her poisons over Thessaly, so it scatters injustice over Greece—a classical simile which had its justification in the hard fact that it had long been the custom of the Byzantine Empire to pay the governors of the European provinces no salaries, but to make their office self-supporting—a practice still followed by the Turkish Government. Thus, as we learn from the addresses of the worthy metropolitan, the sufferings of the Greeks depended

[1] Lámpros, Μιχαὴλ Ἀκομινάτου, i., 308.

[2] Lámpros (Αἱ Ἀθῆναι, 35-9) deduces this title from two leaden seals, one of which was probably that of Michael. Moreover, a bull of Isaac Angelos in 1186 mentions *τῆς δεσποίνης Θεοτόκου τῆς ἐν Ἀθήναις τιμωμένης*. Miklosich und Müller, *Acta et Diplomata Græca Medii·Ævi*, vi., 121. A. Mommsen (*Athenæ Christianæ*, p. 33) has shown that there is no authority for the theory that the Parthenon was dedicated by the Christians to the Divine Wisdom.

very much upon the personality of the *prætor*. Worse, however, than the presence of this high official was that of his underlings; so that the Athenians came to regard his coming in person as much the minor of two evils. Yet, we must make some deduction for the rhetorical and professional exaggeration of the ecclesiastical author. At that time the bishops were, as they still are in Turkey, the representatives of their flocks, and Akominátos was naturally anxious to make out as good a case as possible for his clients. He admits to his brother's connections that the annual ship-money extracted from Athens amounted to no more than £320 of our money—which may be taken as a proof of either the poverty of the place or of the exaggeration of his complaints; and he boasts that he had "lightened, or rather eradicated, the taxes."[1] But, at the same time, taxation had become so oppressive in the Theme of Nikopolis, that the people arose and killed their tyrannical governor, and we are expressly told that the Corfiotes had welcomed the Normans half a century earlier because of the heavy taxation of their island.[2]

Piracy was then, as so often, the curse of the islands and the deeply indented coast of Greece. We learn from the English chronicle ascribed to Benedict of Peterborough,[3] which gives a graphic account of Greece as it was in 1191, that many of the islands were uninhabited from fear of pirates, and that others were their chosen lairs. Cephalonia and Ithaka, which now appears under its mediæval name of Val di Compare—first used, so far as I know, by the Genoese historian Caffaro,[4] in the first half of the twelfth century—had a specially evil reputation, and bold was the sailor who dared venture through the channel between them. Near Athens, the islands of Ægina, Salamis, and Makronesi, opposite Lavrion, were strongholds of Corsairs, before whom most of the Æginetan population had fled, while those who

[1] Lámpros, Μιχαὴλ 'Ακομινάτου, ii., 107; 'Ιστορία τῆς πόλεως 'Αθηνῶν, ii., 729.

[2] Nikétas Choniátes, 97.

[3] *Gesta Regis Ricardi*, ii., 197-200; 203-5.

[4] *Liberatio Orientis*, *apud* Pertz, *Monumenta Germaniæ historica*, xviii., 46.

remained had fraternised with the pirates. Attica was full of persons mutilated by these robbers, who feared neither God nor man. They injured the property of the Athenian church, and dangerously wounded the nephew of the metropolitan, who found it almost impossible to collect the ecclesiastical revenues of Ægina.[1] The dangers run by the venerable Akominátos himself on an ecclesiastical visitation to Naupaktos long remained celebrated, and we find allusions to that venturesome journey years after his death. The remedy for piracy was, as we have seen, almost worse than the disease. The Lord High Admiral, Michael Stryphnós, protected by his close relationship with the Empress Euphrosyne, sold the naval stores for his own profit; and a visit, which he paid to Athens for the ostensible purpose of laying an offering in the church of Our Lady, was regarded by Akominátos with ill-concealed alarm. Well might the anxious metropolitan tell his unwelcome guest that the Athenians regarded their proximity to the sea as the greatest of their misfortunes.[2]

Besides the Byzantine officials and the pirates, the Greeks had a third set of tormentors, in the shape of a brood of native tyrants, whose feuds divided city against city, and divided communities into rival parties. Even in those parts of Greece where the emperor was still nominally sovereign, the real power was often in the hands of local magnates, who had revived, on the eve of the Latin Conquest, the petty tyrannies of ancient Greece. Under the dynasty of the Comneni, who imitated and introduced the usages of western chivalry, feudalism had made considerable inroads into the east. At the time of the Fourth Crusade, local families were in possession of large tracts of territory, which they governed almost like independent princes. We find a great part of fertile Messenia belonging to the clans of Branâs and Cantacuzene; Léon Chamáretos, whom a modern Greek writer[3] has made the hero of an historical novel, owned much of Lakonia; the impregnable rock of Monemvasia, the

[1] Miklosich und Müller, *op. cit.*, iii., 61.

[2] Lámpros, Μιχαὴλ Ἀκομινάτου, ii., 42, 43, 68, 75, 170, 238; Ἱστορία τῆς πόλεως Ἀθηνῶν, ii., 702-8; Αἱ Ἀθῆναι, 56, 57, 86, 97.

[3] A. Rhangabês, Ὁ *αὐθέντης τοῦ Μορέως*.

Gibraltar of Greece, which had enjoyed special liberties since the time of the Emperor Maurice, belonged to the three great local families of Mamonâs, Eudaimonoyánnes, and Sophianós, the first of which is not yet extinct in Greece,[1] and Léon Sgourós, hereditary lord of Nauplia, had extended his sway over Argos of the goodly steeds, and had seized the city and fortress of Corinth, proudly styling himself by a high-sounding Byzantine title, and placing his fortunes under the protection of St Theodore the Warrior.[2] North of the Isthmus, the family of Petraleiphas, of Frankish origin, hailing, as its name Petrus de Alpibus implies, from the Alps, held its own in the mountains of Agrapha; while in Crete, the scions of those Byzantine families which had gone there after its reconquest, had developed into hereditary lords, whose fiefs were confirmed to them by the emperor's representative.[3] In addition to these local magnates, members of the imperial family owned vast tracts of land in Greece. The extravagant Empress Euphrosyne, wife of Aléxios III., had huge estates in Thessaly, and Princess Irene, daughter of Aléxios III., owned property near Patras.[4] The manners of these local magnates were no less savage than those of the western barons of the same period. Sgourós, the most prominent of them, on one occasion invited the metropolitan of Corinth to dinner, and then put out the eyes of his guest, and hurled him over the rocks of the citadel of Nauplia. The contemporary historian Nikétas,[5] who was no friend of the Franks, has painted in the darkest colours the character of the Greek *archons*, upon whom he lays the chief responsibility for the evils which befell their country. He speaks of them as "inflamed by ambition against their own fatherland, slavish men, spoiled by luxury, who made themselves tyrants, instead of fighting the Latins." Thus, on the eve of the

[1] Phrantzês, 398.

[2] A leaden seal of Sgourós has been preserved, showing St Theodore on one side and invoking his protection for σεβαστοϋπέρτατον μὲ Λέοντα Σγουρόν on the other. Lámpros, Αἱ Ἀθῆναι, 99, and plate.

[3] Document of 1182, quoted by Hopf *apud* Ersch und Gruber, *Allgemeine Encyklopädie*, lxxxv., 179; Miklosich und Müller, *op. cit.*, iii., 235-7.

[4] The deed of partition specially mentions the *villæ Kyrcherinis*, *filie Imperatoris Kyrialexii*. *Fontes Rerum Austriacarum*, Abt. ii., B. xii., 470.

[5] Pp. 840-2; Lámpros, Μιχαὴλ Ἀκομινάτου, ii., 170.

Frankish Conquest, Greece presented the spectacle of a land oppressed by the Central Government, and torn asunder by the jealousies of its local aristocracy.

The Church still occupied an important place in Greek society. Greece at this time was ecclesiastically under the jurisdiction of the œcumenical patriarch, and contained twelve metropolitan sees, of which Corinth and Athens were the two most important, while Patras, Larissa, Naupaktos, Neopatras, Thebes, Corfù, Naxos, Lacedæmonia, Argos, and the Cretan see of Gortyna completed the dozen.[1] Besides these, the islands of Leukas and Ægina, and the town of Arta were archbishoprics, and each metropolitan see had numerous bishops under it. Such was the arrangement which, with a few alterations, had been in force since the days of Leo the philosopher, three centuries earlier. There were still among the higher clergy distinguished men of learning, who bore aloft the torch of literature, which the Greek Church had received from the last writers of antiquity. Of these the most eminent then living was Michael Akominátos, the metropolitan of Athens, to whom allusion has already been made. Brother of the statesman and historian, Nikétas of Chonae, or Colossæ, he had sat at the feet of the great Homeric scholar, Eustáthios, afterwards archbishop of Salonika, from whom he imbibed that classical culture which inspires all his numerous productions. In the year 1175, or, according to others, in 1180 or 1182, he was appointed to the see of Athens, and from that time to the Frankish Conquest he never ceased to plead the cause of the city, to write to influential personages in Constantinople, and to address memorials to the emperor on

[1] To these should be added Monemvasia, if we may trust the story of the fifteenth century historian Phrantzês (pp. 398-9), himself a Monemvasiote, accepted by Finlay, that it became a metropolitan see under the Emperor Maurice. But an ecclesiastical document of 1397 (Miklosich und Müller, *op. cit.*, ii., 287) states that it was a suffragan bishopric of Corinth down to the Latin Conquest. We know from Phrantzês (*loc. cit.*), and from the Golden Bull of Andrónikos II. in the National Library and the Christian Archæological Museum at Athens, that he raised it to be the tenth metropolitan see of the empire in 1293, and gave it other privileges. *Cf.* Dorótheos of Monemvasia, Βιβλίον ἱστορικόν, p. 397 ; Le Quien, *Oriens Christianus*, ii., 216.

its behalf. But he was not the only literary light of the Church in Greece. Among his contemporaries were Euthýmios, the metropolitan of Neopatras, the modern Hypate, near Lamia, who wrote on theology; Apókaukos of Naupaktos, who composed tolerable iambics and better letters;[1] George Koupharâs of Corfù, whose letters to the Emperor Frederick Barbarossa and other eminent personages of his day have been preserved in translation, and the latter's successors, the controversialist, Pediadites, and the theologian and poet, George Bardánes.[2] Somewhat earlier, Nicholas, bishop of Methone in Messenia, had issued a refutation of neo-Platonism, two polemics against Catholic doctrines, and a life of Melétios, the reviver of monasticism in Greece; a Lacedæmonian abbot had written a biography of St Nikon, the evangelist of Crete and the patron of Sparta, where his memory is still held in honour; and Gregory, metropolitan of Corinth, had published a grammatical work, which still survives. But Akominátos has left us a sordid picture of the Athenian clergy of his time, and it is to be feared that the priests of the great church on the Akropolis were but little inspired by the majesty of their surroundings. The metropolitan found the keeper of the sacred vessels both blind and illiterate, while another of these divines had cheated his brother out of his property, and allowed him to starve. If such was the state of the clergy, "the wicked Athenian priests," as he calls them, it was not to be supposed that the monks were much better.[3] The number of monastic houses in Greece had greatly increased under the dynasty of the Comneni. It was then, according to tradition, that the still existing Chozobiótissa monastery was founded on the island

[1] Lámpros, *op. cit.*, ii., 25-30; 35-8; Ἱστορία τῆς πόλεως Ἀθηνῶν, ii., 730-7; Βυζαντινὰ Χρονικά, iii., 240 *sqq.*

[2] Mustoxidi, *Delle Cose Corciresi*, 417-22, xl.-xlix.; *Illustrazioni Corciresi*, ii., 181-4. The theory of Dr Kurtz (*Byzantinische Zeitschrift*, xv., 603-13) that all these letters were written by the later metropolitan of Corfù, George Bardánes, and that Frederick is therefore not Barbarossa but Frederick II., and Manuel not the emperor but the Despot of Epiros, seems to me disproved by the phrase in which the writer speaks of Manuel as *cognato Imperii tui*. The emperors Manuel I. and Conrad III. married sisters.

[3] Lámpros, Μιχαὴλ Ἀκομινάτου, ii., 30, 240, 417.

of Amorgos;[1] it was then, too, that the Bœotian monastery of Sagmatâs received a piece of the true cross and the lake of Paralimni, into which the waters of the Copais now drain.[2] A Cappadocian monk, Melétios, whose monastery may still be seen from the road between Athens and Thebes, had revived monasticism by his miracles in Greece towards the end of the eleventh century, and had enjoyed the patronage of the Emperor Aléxios I., who assigned him an annuity out of the taxes of Attica. To him was largely due the plague of monks, often robbers in disguise, of whose ignorance Eustáthios, the learned archbishop of Salonika, drew up such a tremendous indictment.[3] Then, as now, the thoughts of the Greek monks centred mainly on mere externals; obeisances in church, the care of their gardens, and such political questions as arose, occupied their ample leisure; while scandals were no less frequent then than at the present day. Akominátos rebukes the abbot of the famous monastery of Kaisariané, at the foot of Hymettos, for misappropriating other people's bees.[4] Yet the same Akominátos has left a funeral oration over an Athenian archimandrite of that period, which shows that, even on the eve of the Frankish Conquest, there were men of conspicuous piety and self-sacrificing life in the Athenian monasteries.[5] The Athenians of that day, however, seem to have taken their religion lightly, comparing unfavourably with the pious folk of Eubœa, though nowhere else in Greece was the service so elaborate. Their spiritual pastor found them irregular in their attendance at church, even though that church was that "heavenly house," the Parthenon—a cathedral of which any bishop and any congregation might have been proud. Even when they did attend, they spent their time in unseasonable conversation, or in thinking about the cares of their daily lives. Moreover, the metropolitan himself had mundane cares in plenty. Besides his task of defending his flock against rapacious governors, whom he addressed on behalf of

[1] Meliarákes in Δελτίον τῆς Ἱστ. καὶ Ἐθν. Ἑταιρίας, i., 598-9; *Byzantinische Zeitschrift*, ii., 294-6.

[2] Miklosich und Müller, *op. cit.*, v., 253.

[3] Ἐπίσκεψις βίου μοναχικοῦ in *Eustathii Opuscula* (ed. Tafel).

[4] Lámpros, *op. cit.*, ii., 311.

[5] *Ibid.*, i., 259.

the city at their arrival, besides missions and memorials to Constantinople, he had to guard the revenues of the see from the clutches of the imperial treasury officials, whom its agent at the capital, the so-called *mystikós*, could not always keep at a distance.[1]

There was some excuse for the preoccupation of the Athenians with their worldly affairs, when we consider the material condition of their city at this period. From the silence of almost every authority, it would seem that the Norman Invasion of 1146, which fell with such force upon Thebes and Corinth, had spared Athens.[2] The Athenians, perhaps, owed their immunity on that occasion to their insignificance. Their only manufactures at the time of the Frankish Conquest were soap and the weaving of monkish habits. They were no longer engaged in the dyeing trade, of which traces have been found in the Odeion of Herodes Atticus, but the ships of the Piræus still took part, with those of Chalkis and Karystos, in the purple-fishing off the lonely island of Gyaros—the Botany Bay of the Roman Empire. There was still some trade at the Piræus, for when the Byzantine admiral, Stryphnós, visited Athens, he found vessels there, and Akominátos tells us of ships from Monemvasia in the port; while we may infer from the mention of Athens in the commercial treaties between Venice and the Byzantine Empire, that the astute republicans saw some prospect of making money there. But the "thin soil" of Attica was as unproductive as in the days of Thucydides, and yielded nothing but oil, honey, and wine, the last strongly flavoured with resin, as it still is, so that the metropolitan, wishing to give a friend some idea of its flavour, wrote to him that it "seems to be pressed from the juice of the pine rather than from that of the grape." The harvest was always meagre, and famines were common. On one occasion, only two or three of the well-to-do inhabitants could afford to eat bread; on another, the Emperor Andrónikos I. ordered a grant of corn to be distributed among the starving people, and we find Aléxios II. remitting arrears of

[1] Lámpros, *op. cit.*, i., 310; Pitra, *Analecta Sacra*, vi., 619.

[2] Otto von Freising (*De Gestis Friderici*, *apud* Muratori, *Rerum It. Script.*, vi., 668) alone mentions Athens.

taxation to Athens, Thebes, and Corinth, so great was their distress. Even ordinary necessaries were not always obtainable in the Athens of the last years of the twelfth century. Akominátos could not find a good carriage-builder in the place; and, just as most Athenian coaches are now built at Thebes, so he had to beg the bishop of Gardiki, which Benjamin of Tudela had described as a "ruined place," to send him some coach-builders. In his despair at the absence of blacksmiths and workers in iron, he was constrained to apply to Athens the words of Jeremiah: "The bellows are burnt." The general poverty of the city was made more striking by the selfishness of the few who were comfortably off, who composed a "rich oligarchy," and who ground down the face of the poor. Under these circumstances, it is not remarkable that emigration was draining off the able-bodied poor, so that the population had greatly diminished, and the city threatened to become what Aristophanes had called "a Scythian wilderness."[1]

Externally, the visitor to the Athens of that day must have been struck by the marked contrast between the splendid monuments of the classic age and the squalid surroundings of the new town. The walls were lying in ruins; the houses of the emigrants had been pulled down, and their sites had become ploughed land; the streets, where once the sages of antiquity had walked, were now desolate. Even though Akominátos had built new houses, and restored some of those that had fallen, Athens was no longer the "populous city, surrounded by gardens and fields" which the Arabian geographer Edrisi had described to King Roger II. of Sicily half a century before the coming of the Franks.[2] But the hand of the invader and the tooth of time had, on the whole, dealt gently with the Athenian monuments. Although the Odeion of Periklês had perished in the siege of the city by Sulla, it had been restored by the Cappadocian king, Ariobarzanes II., and his son; but Sulla had carried off a few columns of the temple of Olympian Zeus, while the pictures of Polygnotos, which the traveller Pausanias had

[1] Lámpros, *op. cit.*, i., 174, 178, 307; ii., 12, 25, 26, 29, 42, 54, 65, 137, 275, 311.

[2] Jaubert, *Géographie d'Édrisi*, ii., 295.

seen in the Painted Porch, had excited the covetousness of an imperial governor under Theodosius II. The temple of Asklepios had fallen a victim to Christian fanaticism; the gold and ivory statue of Athena, the work of Phidias, had long ago vanished from the Parthenon, and Justinian had adorned the new church of the Divine Wisdom at Constantinople with pillars from Athens.[1] Akominátos laments that the closest investigation could not discover a trace of the Heliæa, the Peripatos, or the Lyceum, and found sheep grazing among the few remains of the Painted Porch. "I live in Athens," he wrote in a poem on the decay of the city, "yet it is not Athens that I see." But still Athens possessed many memorials of her former greatness at the close of the twelfth century. The Parthenon, converted long before into the cathedral of Our Lady of Athens, was then almost as entire, and as little damaged by the injuries of time, as if it had only just been built. The metopes, the pediments, and the frieze were still intact. On the walls were the frescoes, traces of which are still visible, executed by order of the Emperor Basil II., "the slayer of the Bulgarians," when he had offered up thanks at that shrine of the Virgin for his victories over the great enemies of Hellenism, nearly two centuries earlier. Within, in the treasury, were the rich gifts which he had presented to the church. Over the altar was a golden dove representing the Holy Ghost, and ever flying with perpetual motion. In the cathedral, too, was an ever-burning lamp, fed by oil that never failed, which was the marvel of the pilgrims. Every year people flocked thither from the highlands and islands to the feast of the Virgin, and so widely spread was the fame of the Athenian minster, that the great folk of Constantinople, in spite of their supercilious contempt for the provinces and dislike of travel, came to do obeisance there—personages of the rank of Stryphnós, the Lord High Admiral, with his wife,[2] the sister of the empress, and Kamaterós, brother-in-law of the emperor; while, as we saw, the *prætor* made a pilgrimage to St Mary's on the Akropolis an excuse for raising money out of the city. Akominátos was intensely proud, as well he might be, of his

[1] Lámpros, *op. cit.*, i., 160; ii., 398.
[2] *Ibid.*, i., 319, 325, 332; Παρνασσός, vii., 23.

cathedral. He tells us that he "further beautified it, provided new vessels and furniture, increased its property in land and in flocks and herds, and augmented the number of the clergy."[1]

Of the other ancient buildings on the sacred rock, the graceful temple of Nike Apteros had been turned into a chapel; the Erechtheion had become a church of the Saviour, or a chapel of the Virgin; while the episcopal residence, which is known to have then been on the Akropolis, was probably in the Propylæa, where the discovery of a fresco of St Gabriel and St Michael seventy years ago indicates the existence in Byzantine times of a chapel of the archangels.[2] The whole Akropolis had for centuries been made into a fortress, the only defence which Athens then possessed, strong enough to have resisted the attack of a Greek magnate like Sgourós, but incapable of repulsing a Latin army.

Like the Parthenon, the Theseion had become a Christian church, dedicated to St George. Akominátos calls it "St George in the Kerameikós," and at the time of the Frankish Conquest it was entrusted to the care of a monk named Luke. In the eleventh and twelfth centuries a monastery and a nunnery seem to have stood there, for the names of various abbots and nuns with dates of that period have been scratched on some of the pillars, just as we learn the names of Akominátos's three immediate predecessors, Nicholas Hagiotheodorites, George Xerós, and George Boúrtzes, from similar scrawls on the pillars of the Parthenon.[3] Under the splendid ruins of the temple of Zeus Olympios had grown up a chapel of St John, surnamed "at the columns," and Byzantine inscriptions on some of the huge pillars still preserve the prayers of the priests. On one of them in the Middle Ages an imitator of St Simeon

[1] Lámpros, Ἱστορία τῆς πόλεως Ἀθηνῶν, ii., 729.

[2] *Ibid.* Μιχαὴλ Ἀκομινάτου, ii., 12. The inscription, invoking the Virgin, found in the Erechtheion (Neroûtsos in Δελτίον τῆς Ἱστ. Ἑταιρίας, iii., 25), may, however, only prove that "the humble chorister of the cathedral of Athens," who invokes her aid, resided with other members of the clergy in the Erechtheion. *Cf.* A. Mommsen, *op. cit.*, 40-1.

[3] *Ibid.*, Μιχαὴλ Ἀκομινάτου, ii., 238, and Αἱ Ἀθῆναι, 21. Kampoúroglos, Ἱστορία τῶν Ἀθηναίων, ii., 308-9, 293. *Byz. Zeitschrift*, ii., 589.

Stylites had taken up his aërial abode. Already strange legends and new names had begun to grow round some of the classical monuments. The choragic monument of Lysikrates was already popularly known as "the lantern of Demosthenes,"[1] its usual designation during the Turkish domination, when it became the Capuchin convent, serving in 1811 as a study to Lord Byron, who from within its walls launched his bitter poem against the filcher of the Elgin marbles—and the credulous West was told that Jason had founded the Propylæa. But even at the beginning of the thirteenth century, many of the ancient names of places, sometimes names and nothing more, lingered in the mouths of the people. The classically cultured metropolitan was gratified, as a good Philhellene, to hear that the Piræus and Hymettos, Eleusis and Marathon, the Areopagos and Kallirrhoe, Psyttaleia, Salamis, and Ægina were still called by names which the contemporaries of Periklês had used, even though Eleusis and Ægina were devastated by pirates, the Areopagos was nothing but a bare rock, the plain of Marathon yielded no corn, and the "beautifully-flowing" fountain had ceased to flow. But new, uncouth names were beginning to creep in; thus, the partition treaty of 1204 describes Salamis as "Culuris" (or, "the lizard"), a vulgar name, derived from the shape of the island, which I have heard used in Attica at the present day.[2]

Besides the remains of classical antiquity, Athens was then rich in Byzantine churches, of which not a few have still survived the storms of the War of Independence and the Vandalism of those who laid out the modern town. Tradition has ascribed to the two Athenian Empresses of the East, Eudokia and Irene, the foundation of many churches in their native city, and the modern inscription inside the curious little Kapnikaræa church embodies the popular belief that the former had been its founder. The charming little Gorgoepékoos church, wrongly called the Old Metropolis, may have been the work of the latter, and was probably standing at this period. We know for certain, however,

[1] Lámpros, Μιχαὴλ Ἀκομινάτου, i., 98.

[2] *Ibid.*, ii., 13, 14, 26, 44; *Fontes Rerum Austriacarum*, Abt. ii., B. xii., 469.

from the inscription over the door of St Theodore's, that that church had been erected a century and a half before the Frankish Conquest, and there then lay just outside the city the church of the Athenian martyr Leonidas, who had died upon the cross.[1] Attica possessed, too, many monasteries, built in pleasant spots, as Greek monasteries always are. There was the beautiful abbey of Kaisarianè, with its plenteous springs of water, in a leafy glen at the foot of Hymettos; there was the monastery of St John the Hunter, still a white landmark on the spur of the mountain visible from all parts of Athens, and founded or restored by the above-mentioned monk Luke at this very time.[2] Finer than all, there was that gem of Byzantine art, the monastery of Daphni in the pass between Athens and Eleusis, of which we find mention about the end of the eleventh century,[3] and which a later popular tradition connected with the romantic story of the fair Maguelonne and her lover, Pierre de Provence.

Of the intellectual condition of Athens we should form but a low estimate, if we judged entirely from the lamentations of the elegant Byzantine scholar whom fate had made its metropolitan. Akominátos found that his tropes and fine periods and classical allusions were far over the heads of the Athenians who came to hear him, and who talked in his cathedral, even though that cathedral was the Parthenon. He wrote, like Apollonios of Tyana before him, that his long residence in Greece had made him a barbarian. Yet he was able to add to his store of manuscripts in this small provincial town, where a copyist of theological treatises was probably then working. Moreover, that Athens still produced persons of some culture, is evident from the fact that one of Akominátos's own correspondents, John, metropolitan of Salonika, was an Athenian; while the future metropolitan of Corfù, Bardánes, if not an Athenian by birth, may have owed his surname of Atticus to the Attic eloquence which he had learned from Akominátos—a surname already applied

[1] Lámpros, *op. cit.*, i., 151.

[2] *Ibid.*, ii., 247; Kampoúroglos, *op. cit.*, ii., 204-15.

[3] Millet, *Le Monastère de Daphni*, 18; Kampoúroglos, Μνημεῖα, ii. 230; Spon, *Voyage*, ii., 211.

to the scholarly Kosmâs of Ægina, who half a century earlier had mounted the patriarchal throne at Constantinople.[1] There is, too, some evidence to prove that, even at this late period, Athens was a place of study, whither English came from the West to obtain a liberal education. Matthew Paris[2] tells us of Master John of Basingstoke, archdeacon of Leicester in the reign of Henry III., who used often to say that whatever scientific knowledge he possessed had been acquired from the youthful daughter of the Archbishop of Athens. This young lady could forecast the advent of pestilences, thunderstorms, eclipses, and earthquakes. From learned Greeks at Athens Master John professed to have heard some things of which the Latins had no knowledge; he found there the testaments of the twelve patriarchs, now in the Cambridge University library, and he brought back to England the Greek numerals and many books, including a Greek grammar which had been compiled for him at Athens. The same author[3] tells us, too, of "certain Greek philosophers"—that is, in mediæval Greek parlance, monks—who came from Athens at this very time to the court of King John, and disputed about nice sharp quillets of theology with English divines. The only difficulty about these statements is that Akominátos expressly says that he had no children, while he might have been expected to mention any adopted daughter of such talent. An eminent Paris doctor of this period, John Ægidius, is also reported to have studied at Athens[4]; but it is possible that this is merely a repetition of the story that a much earlier Ægidius, or Gislenus, had imbibed philosophy in its ancient home during the seventh century.[5] One is tempted to believe the romantic story that the Georgian poet, Chota Roustavéli, together with others of his countrymen spent several years there at the end of the twelfth century; and that, two or three generations earlier, the enlightened Georgian monarch, David II., prompted by

[1] Lámpros, Μιχαὴλ Ἀκομινάτου, ii., 118, 289; Παρνασσός, vi., 159; Nikétas, 105, 106.

[2] *Chronica Majora*, v., 285-7, in *Rolls Series.*

[3] *Historia Minor*, ii., 194; iii., 64.

[4] Leyser, *Historia Poetarum Medii Ævi*, 499.

[5] *Acta Sanctorum*, October; iv., 1030.

his Greek wife, Irene, founded a monastery "on a mountain near Athens," and sent twenty young people every year to study in the schools there.[1] But neither the thirteenth century Armenian historian, Wardan, nor Tschamtschian makes any mention of Georgians at Athens, and the story seems to have arisen through a confusion between Athens and Mount Athos, where there were many Iberian monks two hundred years earlier, and where the "Monastery of the Iberians" still preserves their name.[2]

While such was the material and the intellectual condition of Athens, there were other places in Greece far more prosperous. Thebes, the residence of the Byzantine governor, had recovered from the ravages of the Normans from Sicily half a century before, when they had ransacked the houses and churches, and had dragged off the most skilful weavers and dyers to Palermo. Benjamin of Tudela, as we saw, had found the Theban silk manufacture still flourishing even after the Norman invasion; Akominátos specially says that the luxurious inhabitants of Constantinople obtained their silken garments from Theban and Corinthian looms; and the forty pieces of silk, with which Aléxios III. purchased the friendship of the Sultan of Angora, were made by his Theban subjects. Even to-day though there are no silks manufactured there, I have seen mulberry-trees growing in the little Bœotian town, and the memory of the silk-worms, which fed upon their leaves, lingers on in the name of *morókampos* ("the mulberry plain"), still applied by the peasants to the flat land near Thebes. The population of the city was numerous, and the castle, the ancient Kadmeia, was strong, if resolutely defended. Nor was Thebes the only important commercial town in Northern Greece. Both Benjamin of Tudela and Edrisi describe Halmyros as a big emporium; Larissa produced figs and wine; the fertile plain of Thessaly to which Horace had alluded in his day, and which now yields splendid harvests, provided the capital of the empire with bread; and the even richer Lelantian plain of Eubœa, and the vineyards of Pteleon at the entrance of

[1] Freygang, *Lettres sur le Caucase*, 109.

[2] Kindly communicated by Mr F. C. Conybeare of Oxford, our leading authority on that subject. *Cf.* Neroûtsos in Δελτίον, iii., 52-3.

the Pagasæan gulf sent it cargoes of wine.[1] Negroponte, as the Italians called first the town of Chalkis and then the island of Eubœa, from a corruption of the word Euripos, the fitful channel which separates the island from the mainland, was "a large city to which merchants resorted from all parts," and whose seamen were engaged in the purple-fishery of the Ægean. Thirty-five years before the Conquest, the island was rich enough to equip six galleys for the imperial fleet, and the fortifications of Chalkis strong enough to resist the attack of the Venetians. Akominátos pays a tribute, which every modern visitor must endorse, to the beauty of its situation, and he contrasts the strength of the island capital, united to the continent by a narrow bridge, which could easily be defended, with the defenceless condition of the city of Athens. "I admired," he told the islanders, "your numbers and your devotion to your spiritual pastor," who was one of his suffragans.[2]

The Peloponnese, half a century before the Conquest, had contained thirteen cities and many fortresses, but we are told that the Franks found only twelve castles in the whole peninsula. At the time of the Norman raid, the strength of Akrocorinth had excited the wonder of the Sicilian admiral, and the lower town, "the emporium" as it was then called, had yielded him an even richer booty than Thebes, for its two harbours made it doubly prosperous, while the ancient tramway was still used for dragging small ships across the isthmus. Its silk manufactories still existed, and, at the date of the Frankish invasion, it was defended by walls and towers. The noble citadel was held by the dread *archon* of Nauplia, Léon Sgourós, whose enormities Akominátos, his deadly enemy, has depicted with all the resources of Byzantine eloquence. Of

[1] Nikétas, 608; Lámpros, *op. cit.*, i., 315; ii., 83.

[2] *Ibid.*, i., 181, 182, 315; ii., 106. Euripos appears as a name for Chalkis in Akominátos and Nikétas. This was corrupted into Egripos ("Ægripons" in Innocent III.'s *Letters*, vol. ii., 267), then from the accusative εἰς τὸν Ἔγριπον was formed Negripon, which popular etymology, from a supposed connection with the bridge at Chalkis over the Euripos, converted into Negroponte. Similarly, εἰς τὰς Ἀθήνας became Setines, εἰς τὴν πόλιν Stamboul, εἰς τὴν Λῆμνον Stalimene. Villehardouin, *La Conquête de Constantinople* (I., 80, ch. lxii.) calls Eubœa "Nigre" and Chalkis "Nigrepont." *Cf.* Bury, *The Lombards and Venetians in Euboia*, i., 5.

the other two cities which owned the tyrant's sway, Argos lay spread out "like a tent" in the rich plain at the foot of the imposing castle, the mighty Larissa on the hill above; while Nauplia, across the beautiful bay, was strongly protected against attack, though the lofty eminence of Palamidi, where the convict-prison now stands, was then unfortified; the modern town was then covered by the shallow water, and the city consisted of the rocky peninsula of Itsh Kaleh alone. Farther to the south, and stronger still, lay the "sacred city" of Monemvasia, the Malmsey of our ancestors, accessible by the narrow causeway alone (μόνη ἔμβασις) to which it owed its name. Thanks to its natural position, to the wisdom of its three *archons*, and to the liberties which its inhabitants enjoyed, it had repelled the Norman attack; its trading vessels were seen in the Piræus, and its chief artistic treasure, the famous picture of Christ being "dragged," which gave its name to the Ἑλκόμενος Church,[1] had attracted the covetousness of the Emperor Isaac II. On the west of the Peloponnese, Patras, whose wealth had been almost fabulous three centuries before, must still have had considerable commerce to attract a Jewish colony and to make it worth while for the Venetians to secure trading facilities there in their last treaty with the Byzantine Empire. In the fertile plain of Elis the finest place at the time of the Conquest was the unwalled town of Andravida, now only a squalid village which the traveller passes on the railway to Olympia. On the west coast, farther to the south, Kyparissia, then called Arkadia, was in Edrisi's time a large place with a much-frequented harbour—a position which it is now recovering since the new railway has connected it with Kalamata and Patras. The Franks considered the anchorage bad; but on the hill, which commands the whole rich plain of Triphylia, and enjoys a prospect of the sea as far as Zante, Cephalonia, and the islands of the Harpies, "the giants," so the country-folk said, had built the strong Hellenic tower, which forms the nucleus of the present castle.

[1] Τὸ Χρονικὸν τοῦ Μορέως, ll. 1406, 1462, 1525-6; Nikétas, 97-100, 581-2; Lámpros, *op. cit.*, ii., 83, 137, 171; Phrantzês, 397-8; of course, the remarkable pictures in the present Ἑλκόμενος church, which was restored in 1697, are of Venetian origin and workmanship.

The Messenian port of Methone, or Modon, destined to play so important a part in Frankish times as a half-way house between Venice and the East, then lay deserted, for in 1125 the Venetians had destroyed this nest of corsairs who had preyed on their merchantmen homeward-bound from the Levant, and the Sicilian admiral had again made it a heap of ruins. The other Messenian station of Korone, or Coron, which we shall find always associated with it under the rule of Venice, produced such a quantity of olive oil that no other place in the world, so it was said, could compare with it. In the far south of the peninsula, the people of Maina had a bad reputation among the Crusaders, whom the waves cast on their iron-bound coast; while the fertility of the rich Messenian plain, in which Kalamata lies, was no less extraordinary than now, though the fortress which should have defended the place was weak. At the other end of the picturesque Langada gorge, on the low hills near the right bank of the Eurotas, stood the large city of Lacedæmonia, the Byzantine town which had succeeded the classic Sparta; in the tenth century Venetian merchants had frequented this prosperous mart, and the efforts of St Nikon to expel the Jews from the community afford a further proof of its commercial importance at that period. The excavations of the British school have brought to light curious pieces of Byzantine pottery and Byzantine coins, and the traveller may still see the remains of the fine walls and towers, which, as the *Chronicle of the Morea* tells us, surrounded Lacedæmonia at the time of the Frankish Conquest. Towards the centre of the peninsula, "the middle land," or Mesarea, as Arkadia was then called, there had arisen near the site of the classic Tegea the important and well-fortified Byzantine town of Nikli, a trace of which may still be found in a Christian font in the little museum of the squalid village of Piali; while, due south of Megalopolis, the city of Veligosti, now a mere name, was then sufficiently flourishing to be coupled by the chronicler with Nikli as one of the "chief places in all the Morea."[1]

[1] Τὸ Χρονικὸν τοῦ Μορέως, ll. 1426-9, 1680, 1690-4, 1712, 1740-1, 1753, 2052-3; *Le Livre de la Conqueste*, 44; Benedict of Peterborough, *loc. cit.* I accept the derivation of Mesarea, given by the Italian version of the *Chronicle* (p. 428) and by Hatzidákis, as more probable than that of Meliarákes (Δελτίον, iv., 262) from the Italian *massa*

Of the islands, Corfù is described as "rich and fertile" by everyone who visited it at that period. We are told in 1191 that it paid "15 quintals" (or 1500 lbs.) "of the purest gold" into the imperial treasury every year, the equivalent of about 9,000,000 *drachmai*, or more than the total amount raised by the present Greek exchequer from all the Ionian islands. Dotted about the beautiful hillsides were various towns and many strong castles. But what most interested returning Crusaders was the local legend that the deserted castle of Butentrost, or Butrinto, on the opposite coast of Epiros, which scholars associate with the voyage of Æneas, was the birthplace of Judas Iscariot—a legend which we find at Corfù centuries later, and which may have arisen out of a popular etymology, connecting the surname of the traitor with Scheria, the Homeric name of Corfù, still enshrined in the Corfiote village of Skaria.[1] The Cyclades, or Dodekanesos, had suffered so much from pirates, that many of them had been abandoned, while in some fortified positions, like the Byzantine castle of Apaliri at Naxos, corsairs had established themselves. The "Queen of the Cyclades," however, even then raised cattle, as she still does; Andros, the second island of the group, was very populous, though it had been recently overrun by the Crusaders on their way to Constantinople, and the ancient Panachrántou monastery, ascribed by tradition to Nikephóros Phokâs, the conqueror of Crete, together with the beautiful little Byzantine church of the Archangel Michael at Messaria, the Byzantine capital of the island, which dates from the time of Manuel I., are evidence of its importance in the last two centuries before the Conquest. Its geographical position on the direct course of ships on their way from Italy to Constantinople made it also a good place for hearing news. But the school of philosophy for which Andros had been celebrated much earlier, and which was revived within the memory of many now living in the person of Kaïres, had long ceased to exist.[2] Another island, then populous, was Amorgos, the ancient home of Simonides; while Keos, the birthplace of his namesake, was, as we shall

[1] Villehardouin, *op. cit.*, i., 74, ch. lviii.; Benedict of Peterborough, *op. cit.*, ii., 204; Romanós, Γρατιανὸς Ζιώρζης, 120-1.

[2] Lámpros, *op. cit.*, ii., 145.

presently see, by no means a luxurious exile for an educated man accustomed to live even in the Athens of the twelfth century.

Such was the condition of Greece when the Latin conquerors of Constantinople entered the land which the strangest of accidents had placed at their mercy. Such was the El Dorado which was to provide principalities and duchies, marquisates and baronies, for the adventurous younger sons of the Western nobility.

CHAPTER II

THE FRANKISH CONQUEST (1204-1207)

WHEN, in October 1204, the Crusaders and their Venetian allies sat down at Constantinople to partition the Byzantine Empire, they paid as little heed as any modern congress of diplomatists to the doctrine of nationalities, or to the wishes of the peoples whose fate hung upon their decisions. It had been agreed by a preliminary compact, that a fourth part of the Byzantine dominions should be first set aside to form the new Latin Empire of Romania, of which Baldwin, Count of Flanders, was elected Emperor. The remaining three-fourths were then to be divided in equal shares between the Venetian Republic and the Crusaders, whose leader was Boniface, Marquis of Montferrat, the rival of Baldwin for the throne of the East. The Greek provinces in Asia and "the isle of Greece," as the French chronicler calls the Peloponnese, had originally been intended as the portion of the unsuccessful competitor, who was to do homage to the emperor for his dominions.[1] But this arrangement did not suit the plans of the crusading chief, who wished to exchange the promised land of Asia Minor for a compact extent of territory nearer home. His marriage with the Dowager Empress Margaret, widow of Isaac II., and daughter of the King of Hungary, made him the more desirous to be established somewhere in the Balkan peninsula, within easier reach of her native land.[2] His brother, Rainer, had

[1] Villehardouin, *op. cit.*, i., 178, ch. cxxxiii. A various reading is *l'isle de Crète;* but that already belonged to Boniface. (Del Carretto and Sangeorgio in *Historiæ patriæ Monumenta*, v., 1141; 1322.)

[2] *Ibid.*, i., 182, ch. cxxxvii.; Robert de Clary *apud* Hopf, *Chroniques gréco-romanes*, 76.

received from Manuel I., twenty-five years before, the title of King of Salonika, after his marriage with that emperor's daughter Maria, and the marquis now sought to convert his dead brother's empty title into a living reality.[1] Baldwin I. was, however, in no mood to accept an arrangement which effectually severed the connection between the Empire of Romania and Greece proper at the very outset. He had actually occupied Salonika, and civil war menaced the Latin dominion in the Levant before its foundations had been securely laid. But the intervention of the old doge Dandolo, assisted by influential nobles of the crusading army, men like Ravano dalle Carceri of Verona, the Burgundian Othon de la Roche, the Fleming Jacques d'Avesnes, and Guillaume de Champlitte, styled "of Champagne," who are described as being "most highly esteemed in the councils of the marquis," succeeded in preventing this catastrophe. Boniface took an oath of allegiance to the Latin emperor for his kingdom of Salonika, which was to include a large part of Greece, as yet unconquered. "I am your man in respect of it," he said, "and I hold it from you."[2]

The deed of partition, which was obviously based on the last commercial treaty between Venice and the Emperor Aléxios III., assigned to Boniface and his army of Crusaders in Greece "the district of Larissa, the province of Wallachia (*i.e.* Thessaly), with the private and monastic property which they contained, the estates of the ex-Empress Euphrosyne, viz., Vessena (near Pelion), Pharsala, Domokó, Ravenika, Upper and Lower Halmyros, and Demetrias." It also awarded them "the territory of Neopatras" (the modern Hypate), Velestino, the village near the modern battlefield, and "the district of Athens with the territory of Megara." But the Venetians, with their shrewd commercial instincts and their much more intimate knowledge of the country,

[1] Robertus de Monte in *Rerum German. Scriptores*, iii., 924; *Memoriale Potestatum Regiensium;* and B. de S. Georgio, *Historia Montisferrati*, *apud* Muratori, *Rerum Ital. Scriptores*, viii., 1165; xxiii., 373; which prove that this grant was not a subsequent invention to justify Boniface's title, as Finlay (iii., 149) imagined.

[2] Villehardouin, *op. cit.*, I., 183, 192, 198, 358, chs. cxxxvii., cxlv., cl., cclxxiii.

had secured in the partition treaty all the best harbours, islands, and markets in the Levant. Their share included in the Peloponnese "the province of Lacedæmonia, Kalavryta, the districts of Patras and Methone with all their appurtenances, viz., the territory of the Branâs family, the territory of the Cantacuzene family, and the towns belonging to Princess Irene, daughter of Aléxios III." In Epiros the republic had obtained "Nikopolis, with the territory of Arta;" in Ætolia "Acheloos and Anatoliko." The Ionian islands of Corfù, Cephalonia, Zante, and Leukas had also fallen to her share. Oreos in the north, and Karystos in the south, of Eubœa were to belong to Venice; in the Saronic Gulf, Ægina and "Culuris," as Salamis was described in the partition treaty, were marked as hers; and finally, "the province of Sunium with the Cyclades," among which Andros, and perhaps Naxos, are specially mentioned, rounded off the Venetian possessions. In addition, the Marquis of Montferrat, by a solemn "deed of Refutation," signed August 12, 1204, had sold Crete, which had been "given or promised" to him by Aléxios IV. during his stay at Corfù fifteen months earlier, to the Venetians for 1000 marks of silver down and the promise of possessions in the western part of the empire sufficient to bring him in an income of 10,000 gold hyperpers (£4480). The only items of the emperor's share which concern our subject are the islands of Lemnos, Tenos, and Skyros; the rest of his portion was outside the limits of Greece proper.[1]

Besides these territorial acquisitions, the careful republic had stipulated that all the commercial privileges which she had enjoyed in the time of the Byzantine Empire should be

[1] *Fontes Rerum Austriacarum*, Abt. ii., B. xii., 468-73, 476-7, 486-8, 513-15; Da Canal, *La Chronique des Veniciens* in *Archivio Storico Italiano*, viii., 340-4. *Colonie* would seem to be Sunium (Cape Colonna). The chief difficulty is whether the Cyclades fell to the Venetians or to the Crusaders. The text of the deed assigns the *Dodecanisos* to the latter, and Spruner-Menke (*Handatlas für die Geschichte des Mittelalters*, p. 40) and Mr Fotheringham accept this statement. But the *Dodecanisos* occurs in the midst of places in Macedonia, next to Prespa. Can it be a corruption for the island on Ochrida, the former Bulgarian capital? I follow Tafel and Thomas, who conjectured *cum Cycladibus* for *Conchilari* in the Venetian portion, to which the Cyclades would naturally belong.

continued to her. Thus, the Venetian lion had secured the lion's share. Well might the doge describe himself, as he did for the next century and a half, "ruler of one quarter and half a quarter of the whole Empire of Romania."[1] Long after that ephemeral empire had fallen, the Venetians kept their hold on the Levant, and to-day many a fortress, from Candia to Chalkis, from Nauplia to Corfù, preserves on its walls the winged lion of the evangelist. But, for the moment, the lion had obtained more than he could digest. Imposing as the Venetian share looked on paper, much of it required to be conquered. Besides the places which were still occupied by the Byzantine garrisons or by local Greek magnates, Corfù was in the hands of the Genoese pirate Vetrano, while Zante and Cephalonia belonged to Count Maio, or Matteo, Orsini. In short, it soon became evident, that the allies had partitioned the empire much as mediæval popes drew lines of demarcation on the map of Africa.

Having settled his differences with the Emperor Baldwin, Boniface set out in the autumn of 1204 to conquer his Greek dominions. The new King of Salonika belonged to a family which was no stranger to the ways of the Orient. One of his brothers, as we saw, had married the daughter of the Emperor Manuel I. Another brother and a nephew of Boniface were kings of Jerusalem—a vain dignity which has descended from them, together with the marquisate of Montferrat, to the present Italian dynasty. Married to the affable widow of the Emperor Isaac II., Boniface was a sympathetic figure to the Greeks, who had speedily flocked in numbers to his side,[2] and several of them accompanied him on his march through Greece, among them his stepson, Manuel Angelos, and a much more dangerous member of the same family, the bastard Michael, first cousin of Isaac II.[3] With the King of Salonika there went, too, a motley crowd of Crusaders in quest of fiefs, men of many nationalities, Lombards, Flemings, Frenchmen, and Germans. There were Guillaume de Champlitte, Viscount of Dijon, who derived his name from the village of Champlitte in Franche-

[1] Akropolita, 15; X. τ. M., ll. 1025, *sqq.*, *L. d. C.*, 21.
[2] Villehardouin, *op. cit.*, i., 194, 196, chs. cxlviii., cxlix.
[3] *Ibid.*, i., 210, ch. clix.

Comté, but who was surnamed *le Champenois* after his grandfather, the Count of Champagne; Othon de la Roche, son of a Burgundian noble, Ponce de la Roche-sur-Ognon,[1] a castle which still commands the rolling plains of the Haute-Saône; Jacques d'Avesnes, son of a Flemish Crusader who had been at the siege of Acre, and his two nephews, Jacques and Nicholas de St Omer; Berthold von Katzenellenbogen, a Rhenish warrior who had given the signal for setting fire to Constantinople; the Marquis Guido Pallavicini, youngest son of a nobleman from near Parma who had gone to Greece because at home every common man could hale him before the courts; Thomas de Stromoncourt, and Ravano dalle Carceri of Verona.[2] To record his deeds, the king of Salonika took with him Rambaud de Vaqueiras, a troubadour from Provence, who afterwards boasted in one of the letters in verse, which he addressed to his patron, that he "had helped to conquer the empire of the East and the kingdom of Salonika, the island of Pelops, and the duchy of Athens."[3]

There was one man still left in Greece who might have been expected to offer a determined resistance to the invaders. Léon Sgourós, the proud lord of Nauplia, Argos, and Corinth, was the strongest of the native *archons*, but he showed more desire to profit by his country's misfortunes than to fight against its enemies. He had long cast covetous glances at Athens, whence he had once already levied blackmail, and he availed himself of the general confusion, consequent on the invasion of the capital by the Franks, to attack the Athenians by land and sea. The noble metropolitan proved himself at this crisis a worthy representative of those classic heroes whose lives he had so carefully studied; and his brother, the historian Nikétas, might well interrupt his stilted narrative to express his pride at being the near kinsman of such a man. From the sacred rock of the Akropolis he solemnly warned the selfish magnate of the

[1] Buchon, *Nouvelles Recherches*, i., lxxxiv.-lxxxix.

[2] Litta, *Le famiglie celebri Italiane*, vol. v., plate xiv.

[3] Schultz-Gora, *Le Epistole del Trovatore Rambaldo di Vaqueiras*, p. 6.

"Ai vos aiudat
"A conquerre emperi e regnat
"d'aquesta terra e l'*isla e'l dugat*."

double iniquity of a Greek fighting against Greeks, a Christian against Christians. He made a personal appeal to an assailant, whom he had counted among his spiritual children, who had never refused him the titles of father and pastor. But the *archon* of Nauplia was unmoved by these spiritual arguments; he cynically replied that, at the time when the capital of the empire was in the hands of the foe, it behoved everyone to look after his own interests; and, as an excuse for his attack, demanded the surrender of an Athenian youth of notoriously bad character. The metropolitan refused to give up even the least worthy of his flock, and defended the walls of the Akropolis with engines of war. His material proved better than his spiritual weapons, and Sgourós had to content himself with setting fire to the houses of the town, and carrying off a nephew of the metropolitan as a page, whom he afterwards murdered in a fit of passion for his clumsiness in breaking a glass cup. From Athens he marched upon Thebes, which, though a stronger position, afforded an instance of the truth of Thucydides' saying, that it is not walls, but the men who man them that make a city. The chief town in Greece yielded to the first attack, and the victor continued his march unchecked to Larissa. There he met the fugitive Emperor Aléxios III., who bestowed upon him the hand of his daughter Eudokia, a lady who had already been thrice married to one monarch after another.[1]

It was at this moment that Boniface and his army traversed the classic vale of Tempe and entered the fertile plain of Thessaly. At the news of his approach Sgourós—"Lasgur," as the Franks called him—retreated to Thermopylæ,[2] allowing the invaders to occupy Larissa. The king of Salonika bestowed that ancient city upon a Lombard noble, who henceforth styled himself Guglielmo de Larsa from his Thessalian fief, and who also received the important town of Halmyros where the Venetian and Pisan colonies continued to flourish. Velestino, the ancient Pheræ, the scene of the legend of Admetos and Alkestis, fell to the share of Count Berthold von Katzenellenbogen, whose name

[1] Nikétas, 799-807; Lámpros, Μιχαὴλ Ἀκομινάτου, ii., 162-87; *Libro de los fechos*, 15.

[2] Villehardouin, *op. cit.*, i., 210, ch. clix.

must have proved a stumbling-block to his Thessalian vassals.[1] The army then took the usual route by way of Pharsala and Domokó—names familiar in the ancient and modern history of Greek warfare, down to Lamia, and thence across the Trachinian plain to Thermopylæ, where Sgourós was awaiting it. But the memories of Leonidas failed to inspire the *archon* of Nauplia to follow his example. Nikétas[2] tells us that the mere sight of the Latin knights in their coats of mail sufficed to make him flee straight to his own fastness of Akrocorinth, leaving the pass undefended. Conscious of its strength—for Thermopylæ must have been far more of a defile then than now—Boniface resolved to secure it permanently against attack. He therefore invested the Marquis Guido Pallavicini, nicknamed by the Greeks "Marchesopoulo," with the fief of Boudonitza, which commanded the other end of the pass. Thus arose the famous marquisate of Boudonitza, which was destined to play an important part in the Frankish history of Greece, and which, after a continuous existence of over two centuries, as guardian of the northern marches, has left a memory of its fallen greatness in the ruins of the castle and chapel of its former lords, of whose descendants, the Zorzi of Venice, there are still living some thirty representatives in that city. Following the present carriage-road from Lamia to the Corinthian Gulf, Boniface established another defensive post at the pass of Gravia, so famous centuries afterwards in the War of Independence, conferring it as a fief on the two brothers, Jacques and Nicholas de St Omer.[3] At the foot of Parnassos, on the site of the ancient Amphissa, he next founded the celebrated barony of Salona, which lasted almost as long as the marquisate of Boudonitza. Upon the almost Cyclopean stones of the classic Akropolis, which Philip of Macedon had destroyed fifteen centuries before, Thomas de Stromoncourt built himself the fortress, of which the majestic ruins—perhaps the finest Frankish remains in Greece—still stand among the corn-fields on the hill above the modern town. According to the local tradition, the

[1] *Epistolæ Innocentii III.*, vol. ii., pp. 214, 464-5, 549; *Documenti sulle relazioni toscane coll'Oriente*, pp. 88-90.

[2] P. 799.

[3] *L. d. C.*, 413.

name of Salona, which the place still bears in common parlance, despite the usual official efforts to revive the classical terminology, is derived from the King of Salonika, its second founder. The lord of Salona soon extended his sway down to the harbour of Galaxidi, and the barony became so important that two at least of the house of Stromoncourt struck coins of their own, which are still preserved.[1]

Boniface next marched into Bœotia, where the people, glad to be relieved from the oppression of Sgourós, at once submitted. Thebes joyfully opened her gates, and then the invaders pursued their way to Athens. The metropolitan thought it useless to defend the city, and a Frankish guard was soon stationed on the Akropolis. The Crusaders had no respect for the great cathedral. To these soldiers of fortune the classic glories of the Parthenon appealed as little as the sanctity of the Orthodox Church. The rich treasury of the cathedral was plundered, the holy vessels were melted down, the library which the metropolitan had collected was dispersed. Unable to bear the sight, Akominátos, like his colleague of Thebes, quitted the scene of his long labours, and after wandering about for a time in Salonika and Eubœa, perhaps in the hope of coming to terms with the Papal Legate, finally settled down in the island of Keos, one of the eleven suffragan bishoprics, which had, in happier times, owned his benevolent sway. From there he could at least see the coast of Attica—that Attica which he had once described as "a Scythian wilderness," but which he now lamented as "a garden of Eden."[2]

Thebes with Bœotia, and Athens with Attica and the Megarid were bestowed by the King of Salonika upon his trusty comrade in arms, Othon de la Roche, who had rendered him a valuable service by assisting to settle the dispute between him and the Emperor Baldwin, and who

[1] Sáthas, Τὸ Χρονικὸν τοῦ Γαλαξειδίου, 201. This chronicle, compiled in 1703 from old documents, ascribes to Thomas I. the title of Count, whereas the *Chronicle of the Morea* (ll. 3294, 3633), describes Thomas II. of Salona as simply "lord," ἀφέντης. Sáthas (*op. cit.*), gives a coin of Thomas II., and another of Thomas III.

[2] Nikétas, 805; Lámpros, Μιχαὴλ Ἀκομινάτου, i., 357, ii., 146, 178, 259, 295, 312.

afterwards negotiated the marriage between Boniface's daughter and Baldwin's brother and successor on the throne. Thus, in the words of a monkish chronicler, "Othon de la Roche, son of a certain Burgundian noble, became, as by a miracle, Duke of the Athenians and Thebans."[1] The chronicler was only wrong in the title which he attributed to the lucky Frenchman, who had thus succeeded to the glories of the heroes and sages of Athens. Othon modestly styled himself *Sire d'Athènes*, or *Dominus Athenarum*, in official documents, which his Greek subjects magnified into "the *great* Lord" (Μέγας κύρ, or Μέγας κύρης), and Dante, who had probably heard that such had been the title of the first Frankish ruler of Athens, transferred it by a poetic anachronism to Pisistratos.[2] Contemporary accounts make no mention of any resistance to the Lord of Athens on the part of the Greeks. Later Venetian writers, however, actuated perhaps by patriotic bias, propagated a story, that the Athenians sent an embassy to offer their city to Venice, but that their scheme was frustrated, "not without bloodshed, by the men of Champagne under the Lord de la Roche."[3]

Meanwhile, the soldierly Fleming, Jacques d'Avesnes, leaving the main body of the Franks, had received the submission of Eubœa—an island where they had already stopped on their way to Constantinople. After building a fortress in the middle of the Euripos and garrisoning the place,[4] d'Avesnes hastened to join the King of Salonika and the Lord of Athens in their attack upon the strongholds of Sgourós in the Peloponnese. The Franks routed the

[1] Albericus Trium Fontium, *Chronicon*, ii., 439; Henri de Valenciennes, ch. xxxv.

[2] Χ. τ. Μ., ll. 1555, 2595, 3194 *sqq.*, 4365. *Epistolæ Innocentii III.*, bk. xi., No. 244; bk. xiii., No. 16. Buchon, *Recherches*, ii., 385 *sqq.* Dante, *Purgatorio*, xv., 97. Ducange, *Histoire de l'Empire de Constantinople*, i., 436-7.

[3] Andrea Dandolo, *Chronicon Venetum*, *apud* Muratori, *Rerum Italicarum Scriptores*, xii., 335. Laurentius de Monacis (*Chronicon*, 143), and Stefano Magno, *apud* Hopf, *Chroniques gréco-romanes*, 179, repeat him. Out of this, and a misunderstanding of Othon's title the historian Fanelli, who wrote his *Atene Attica* soon after Morosini's victories, states (p. 278) that the embassy was imprisoned by a certain "Magaduce Tiranno"!

[4] Nikétas, 806.

Greek army at the Isthmus, and, while Boniface marched on to besiege Nauplia, Jacques d'Avesnes and Othon de la Roche attacked Corinth. The lower town, though strongly fortified, was taken by escalade, but Akrocorinth proved, in the hands of Sgourós, an impregnable fortress. In vain the Franks built two castles to coerce it into submission, one on the hill to the south of Akrocorinth, which they called Montesquiou, a name now corrupted into the modern Penteskouphia ("Five Caps"), the other to the north. Sgourós succeeded in making a night sortie and in surprising the Franks in the lower town; many of the besiegers were slain, and their leader, d'Avesnes, was wounded.[1]

But the Greek *archon's* resolute defence of Akrocorinth could not prevent the conquest of the Peloponnese, for the attack upon that peninsula came from a wholly unexpected quarter. It chanced that, a little before the capture of Constantinople, Geoffroy de Villehardouin, nephew of the Marshal of Champagne and quaint chronicler of the Fourth Crusade, had set out on a pilgrimage to Palestine. On his arrival in Syria, he heard of the great achievements of the Crusaders, and resolved without loss of time to join them at Constantinople. But his ship was driven out of her course by a violent tempest, and Geoffroy was forced to take shelter in the harbour of Methone on the coast of Messenia. During the winter of 1204, which he spent at that spot, he received an invitation from a local magnate to join him in an attack on the lands of the neighbouring Greeks. Villehardouin, nothing loth, placed his sword at the disposal of the Greek traitor, and success crowned the arms of these unnatural allies. But the Greek *archon* died, and his son, more patriotic, or more prudent than the father, repudiated the dangerous alliance with the Frankish stranger. But it was too late. Villehardouin had discovered the fatal secret that the Greeks of the Peloponnese were an unwarlike race, and that their land would fall an easy conquest to a resolute band of Latins. At this moment tidings reached him that Boniface was

[1] Nikétas, 807; Villehardouin, *op. cit.*, i., 210, 226, 232, chs. clix., clxxiv., clxxix.; X. τ. M., ll. 1528-38, 2805-8. The last passage gives the name of the fort, but places its construction at a later period erroneously, as Hopf has shown. *Cf. L. d. C.*, 37, 87.

besieging Nauplia, and he at once set out on a six days' journey across a hostile country to seek his aid. Boniface endeavoured to detain him in his own service by the offer of lands and possessions, but in the camp Villehardouin found an old friend and fellow-countryman, Guillaume de Champlitte, who was willing to assist him, for Villehardouin came from a village of Champagne, in the domain of Champlitte's ancestors, a place between Bar and Arcis-sur-Aube. He described to Champlitte the richness of the land which men called "the Morea"—a term which now occurs for almost the first time in history, and which seems to have been originally applied to the coast of Elis and thence extended to the whole peninsula, just as the name Italy, originally confined to a part of Calabria, has similarly spread over the whole country.[1] He professed his willingness to recognise Champlitte as his liege lord in return for his aid, and Boniface finally consented to their undertaking. With a hundred knights and some men-at-arms, the two friends rode out from the camp before Nauplia to conquer the ancient land which had once given birth to Spartan men.[2]

The fate of the Morea, like that of Saxon England, was decided by a single pitched battle. The city of Patras was captured at the first assault, whereupon the castle at once surrendered on terms; from the defenceless town of Andravida, the capital of Elis, the magnates and the community issued forth, with the priests bearing the cross and the sacred eikons, and did homage to Champlitte on con-

[1] The derivation of the word "Morea," which is first found in a MS. of 1111, is much disputed. The traditional explanation, now returning to favour, was that it came from *μορέα* ("mulberry-tree"), either because of the trees grown there, or because of the shape of the peninsula. The Slavonic *more* ("sea"); a former town on the coast of Elis near Katakolo; and a transformation of the word *Romaia* have all been suggested. Both the Greek (*e.g.* ll. 1427, 1610, 1642, 5708) and the French (p. 359) versions of the *Chronicle of the Morea* at times use it in the restricted sense of "Elis." Sáthas, Μνημεῖα Ἑλληνικῆς Ἱστορίας, i., pp. xxx.-xxxviii.; Paparregópoulos, Ἱστορία τοῦ Ἑλληνικοῦ Ἔθνους, v., 88-92; Hopf *apud* Ersch u. Gruber, *Allgemeine Encyklopädie*, lxxxv., 264-7; Finlay, iv. 24; Hatzidákis in *Byz. Zeit.*, ii., 284.

[2] I have here followed Villehardouin (i., 226-32), who is naturally a better authority for what concerns his nephew than is the much later *Chronicle of the Morea*, which narrates these events differently.

dition that he respected their property; the *archons* of the rest of Elis and of Mesarea, "the middle land," as Arkadia was then called, followed the example of Andravida; the low-walled fortress of Pontikokastro, or "Mouse Castle," the ruins of which still stand on the hill above the harbour of Katakolo, was easily taken and garrisoned. The tower of "the giants" at Arkadia (or Kyparissia) and the castle of Kalamata did indeed hold out for a time; but of the two forts on either side of the Messenian promontory, Modon was after all these years still lying deserted, while the garrison of Coron soon surrendered when their houses and property were guaranteed to them. The more patriotic and energetic of the natives did, indeed, succeed in collecting an army some four to six thousand strong, consisting of the Greeks of Nikli, Veligosti, and Lacedæmonia, the warlike Slavonic tribe of Melings, who had been so troublesome to the old Imperial Government, and a detachment under Michael Angelos, who had quitted Boniface and had established himself as Lord, or Despot, of Epiros, and who crossed over the Gulf of Corinth to attack the common enemy. The Hastings of the Morea was fought in the olive-grove of Koundoura, in the north-east of Messenia. The little Frankish force, numbering between five and seven hundred men, completely routed the over-confident Greeks; the Despot retired to his mountains, and one place after another fell into the hands of the Franks. One heroic warrior, Doxapatrês, seems to have held manfully the small but strongly situated castle of Araklovon, which commanded a defile of the Arkadian mountains, and his rare heroism, dismissed in a few lines of the Greek *Chronicle*, made a lasting impression on romantic minds. The compilers of the Aragonese version say that no man could lift his mace, and that his cuirass weighed more than 150 pounds; a local legend has kept alive the splendid courage of his daughter, who allowed herself to be hurled to death from the castle tower rather than become the conqueror's mistress; and a modern Greek dramatist has made Maria Doxapatrê the heroine of one of his tragedies.[1] Though the three strong-

[1] Χ. τ. Μ., ll. 1410-41, 1641-3, 1661-1790; *L. d. C.*, 34-5, 38-44; Villehardouin, *loc. cit.*; Muntaner, *Cronaca*, ch. cclxi.; *Libro de los fechos*, 27; Bernardákes, Μαρία Δοξαπατρῆ.

holds of Sgourós, Corinth, Nauplia, and the Larissa of Argos, still held out; though Veligosti, Nikli, and Lacedæmonia were unconquered; though the isolated rock of Monemvasia, whose sailors had often manned the imperial navies, whose soldiers had repelled a Latin host before, still preserved its traditional liberties; though the Tzákones of Leonidi and the Slav tribe of Melings in the fortresses of Taygetos as yet acknowledged no master, Innocent III., not without reason, already styled Champlitte "Prince of all Achaia."[1]

The new prince rewarded Villehardouin, the real author of this daring scheme of conquest, with the town of Coron.[2] But, at this point, a new competitor appeared on the scene. It will be remembered, that, by the deed of partition, large portions of the Peloponnese, including the haven of Modon, had fallen to the share of Venice. So vast were the dominions which had been assigned to the republic, that she had been slower than the other parties to the deed in occupying her portion of the former Byzantine Empire. Many places, indeed, she never effectively occupied at all. But the twin stations of Modon and Coron were valuable stepping-stones on the way to Crete and Egypt, while there was always danger that the former, in foreign hands, might once more become a refuge of corsairs. Accordingly, in 1206, a fleet was despatched under Premarini and the son of Dandolo, which, after a struggle captured both places from the weak garrisons left there by the Franks. Opinions were divided as to the policy of maintaining the two places; but Dandolo's son offered to keep them up at his own cost, and thus saved them for the republic. The walls of Modon were again destroyed, as a measure of precaution; but Coron seems to have been made a provisioning station, where all passing ships could receive a month's rations—a custom maintained, we are told, when the place became a regular Venetian colony.[3] Thus began the long Venetian occupation of these two spots, the first territorial acquisition

[1] *Epistolæ*, bk. viii., Lett. 153 (Nov. 19, 1205).

[2] Villehardouin, *loc. cit.*

[3] Martin da Canal in *Archivio Storico Italiano*, viii., 348-50; A. Dandolo *apud* Muratori, xii., 335; E. Dandolo, "Cronaca Veneta" (MS.), fol. 43; Sáthas, Μνημεῖα, i., 318.

of the republic in the Greek peninsula, which came to be "the receptacle and special nest of all our galleys, ships, and vessels on their way to the Levant," as a Venetian document quaintly says, and about which there is a whole literature in the Venetian archives.

Thus, almost without effort, a small body of Lombards, Burgundians, and Germans had over-run continental Greece and the Morea. The local leaders had, with one or two exceptions, preferred to cringe to the conquerors rather than to fight; there was no hope of succour from other nations; the people were disused to warfare, oppressed by burdens, and indifferent, or even agreeable, to a change of masters. It was remarked by a Byzantine historian[1] that the European Greeks were weak defenders of fortresses, and ready to fall at the feet of every tyrant, and in the Morea fortresses were few. Moreover, the conquerors seem to have shown a great amount of tact towards the conquered, when once they had convinced the latter that they had come to stay. Thus, Champlitte promised the magnates of Elis and Arkadia to respect the privileges which they had received from the Byzantine Emperors and to recognise their titles to their estates, while the residue, consisting of the old imperial domains and other vacant lands, should be divided among the Franks.[2] Six Greek *archons* were accordingly invited to join the same number of Franks in a preliminary commission for the purpose of defining these lands and liberties of the native and the Frankish aristocracy. Still, the poet of the Conquest, Rambaud de Vaqueiras, was scarcely exaggerating, when he wrote that neither Alexander nor Charlemagne had achieved such feats as the men of the Fourth Crusade.

But fortune, so favourable to the Franks in Greece, had already deserted them in Macedonia. The first Latin emperor, within a year of his coronation, had fallen into the hands of the Bulgarian Tsar, whose aid the Macedonian Greeks had invoked, and vanished in the dungeons of the Bulgarian capital. Boniface, on hearing the news, had abandoned the siege of Nauplia to defend his Macedonian dominions from this new enemy, and had endeavoured to

[1] Akropolita, 178; *L. d. C.*, 58.

[2] X. *τ*. M., ll. 1649-50; *L. d. C.*, 39.

strengthen the Frankish cause by doing homage for his kingdom to the new Emperor Henry and by bestowing upon him the hand of his daughter—a union arranged by his trusty friend, Othon de la Roche, Lord of Athens.[1] But the chivalrous King of Salonika shortly afterwards met his fate in an obscure skirmish with the Bulgarians, and his kingdom passed, at this critical moment, to his infant son Demetrios, under guardianship of Oberto, the ambitious Count of Biandrate, a town between Vercelli and Novara.

Meanwhile, in three other directions, the Byzantine monarchy had shown signs of revival. At Nice, the scene of the famous council, Theodore Láskaris, son-in-law of the Emperor Aléxios III., founded an empire which, fifty-five years later, absorbed the ephemeral Latin realm of Romania; at Trebizond, on the shores of the Black Sea, another Aléxios, the grandson of the Emperor Andrónikos I., established another empire, which survived the Turkish capture of Constantinople; while in Europe, the bastard Michael Angelos, first cousin of the Emperor Isaac II., created a Greek principality, the Despotat of Epiros, Hellas, or Arta, as it was variously called, which played a great part in the history of Frankish Greece. The founder of this new Greek dynasty in Epiros was no ordinary man; son of a former governor of that province, he had been given as a hostage in earlier life to the Emperor Barbarossa, when that monarch was on his way to the Holy Land, and he had received the post of governor of the Themes of Hellas and the Peloponnese shortly before Constantinople fell. After that catastrophe, he had attached himself, as we saw, to Boniface in the hope of obtaining some advantage from him. The discontent of the Greeks of the province of Nikopolis, which included Akarnania, Ætolia and Epiros, with the tyranny of their Byzantine governor, Senacherim, at this moment reached his ears; he slipped away from the Frankish camp, went to Arta, and, finding the governor dead, married his widow, a daughter of the great family of Melissenós, and established himself as an independent Greek sovereign, whose sway extended from his capital of Arta to Joannina in the north, to Naupaktos on the Gulf of Corinth in the south,

[1] Villehardouin, *op. cit.*, i., 274, 358, chs. ccx., cclxxiii.

and apparently included the island of Leukas in the Ionian sea.[1] Ere long, Durazzo became his northern, and part of Thessaly his eastern, boundary, and he succeeded in enlisting the sympathies of the three different races—Greeks, Albanians, and Wallachians, who formed the population of his dominions. The Greeks naturally welcomed a man whose wife was a native of the country and whose father had been its governor. The Albanians were ready to serve a ruler who paid them well and regarded their predatory habits as a positive benefit when they were exercised at the cost of his foes. The Wallachians of Thessaly sought protection against the Franks, and all three races recognised his ability and experience. Moreover, the machinery of the Byzantine administration lay ready to his hand. There was merely a change of name but not of system, except in so far as the taxes were now expended in the country instead of being sent to the distant capital. The configuration of Epiros has always made it a difficult land to conquer; and in the first years of his reign, Michael's enemies were busy elsewhere. He felt so secure, that he crossed into the Peloponnese to assist the Greeks in their stand against the Franks at Koundoura, as we saw above; even though he was defeated with considerable loss, he accepted the *damnosa hereditas* of Nauplia, Argos, and Corinth, when, in 1208, Sgourós at last in despair leapt on horseback from Akrocorinth and perished a formless mass of broken bones on the rocks below. Henceforth, Michael was the sole champion of Hellenism in Europe; he was styled "the lord of Corinth," and his brother Theodore governed the heritage of Sgourós in his name.[2]

The Greek islands had been, for the most part, allotted to Venice by the partition treaty, the Cyclades among them.

[1] Villehardouin, *op. cit.*, I., 210, ch. clix.; Akropolita, 15-16; Nikétas, 841; Nikephóros Gregorâs, I., 13; Buchon, *Nouvelles Recherches*, II., i., 401-2. There is no direct evidence as to Leukas, except that it was ecclesiastically under the Despots' influence; but its inclusion in the Despotat at this period is probable. *Cf.* Romanós, Γρατιανὸς Ζώρζης, 297; Blantês, Ἡ Λευκὰς ὑπὸ τοὺς Φράγκους, 4; Βυζαντινὰ Χρονικά, iii., 270, 276.

[2] Lámpros, Ἱστορία τῆς πόλεως Ἀθηνῶν, i., 421, *n.* 1; Henri de Valenciennes, *apud* Buchon, *Recherches et Matériaux*, ii., 209. Only one MS. adds the title *le signour de Chorynte*.

But the Venetian Government, with its usual commercial astuteness, soon came to the conclusion that the conquest of that large group of islands would too severely tax the resources of the state. It was therefore decided to leave the task of occupying them to private citizens, who would plant Venetian colonies in the Ægean, and live on friendly terms with the republic. There was no lack of enterprise among the Venetians of that generation, and it so happened that at that very moment the Venetian colony at Constantinople contained the very man for such an undertaking. The old doge Dandolo had taken with him on the crusade his nephew, Marco Sanudo, a bold warrior and a skilful diplomatist, who had signalised himself by negotiating the sale of Crete to the republic, and was then filling the post of judge in what we should now call the Consular Court at Constantinople. On hearing the decision of his government, Sanudo quitted the bench, gathered round him a band of adventurous spirits, to whom he promised fiefs in the El Dorado of the Ægean, equipped eight galleys at his own cost, and sailed with them to carve out a duchy for himself in the islands of the Archipelago. There was no one to dispute his claim, though Léon Gabalâs, the Greek *archon* of Rhodes and Karpathos, styled himself "Lord of the Cyclades," and even "Cæsar."[1] Seventeen islands speedily submitted, and at one spot alone did Sanudo meet with any real resistance. Naxos has always been the pearl of the Ægean: poets placed there the beautiful myth of Ariadne and Dionysos; Herodotos describes it as "excelling the other islands in prosperity"; even to-day, when so many of the Cyclades are barren rocks, the orange and lemon groves of Naxos entitle it, even more than Zante, to the proud name of "flower of the Levant." This was the island which now opposed the Venetian filibuster, as centuries before it had opposed the Persians. A body of Genoese pirates had occupied the Byzantine castle before Sanudo's arrival; but that shrewd leader, who knew the value of rashness in an emergency, burnt his galleys, and then bade his companions conquer or die. The castle surrendered after a five weeks' siege, so that by 1207 Sanudo and his comrades had conquered a duchy,

[1] Akropolita, 49, 92; Nikétas, 842.

which lasted between three and four centuries. His duchy included, besides Naxos, where he fixed his capital, the famous marble island of Paros; Antiparos, with its curious grotto; Kimolos, celebrated for its fuller's earth; Melos, whose sad fortunes had furnished Thucydides with one of the most curious passages in his history; Amorgos, the home of Simonides, Ios or Nio, the supposed tomb of Homer: Kythnos, Sikinos, and Siphnos; and Syra, destined at a much later date to be the most important of all the Cyclades. True to his promise, Sanudo divided some of the islands among his companions; thus Marino Dandolo, another nephew of the great doge, who had captured Andros, held that fine island, the second largest of the group, as a sub-fief of his cousin's duchy; Leonardo Foscolo received on similar terms the distant island of Anaphe; the volcanic island of Santorin, as the classic Thera was called in the Middle Ages, from the martyrdom on its rocks of one of the many St Irenes in the Greek calendar, fell to the share of Jacopo Barozzi, and Astypalaia, or Stampalia, to that of the Quirini with whose name it is still associated in that of a street, a bridge, and a palace at Venice. The brothers Andrea and Geremia Ghisi, both enterprising men, not only acquired Tenos and Mykonos, but extended their conquests to the northern Sporades, occupying Skyros, Skopelos, and Skiathos, regardless of the fact that two of these islands Tenos and Skyros, belonged to the Emperor of Romania, according to the deed of partition. With the aid of Domenico Michieli and Pietro Giustiniani, they added to their island domain little Seriphos, the Botany Bay of the early Roman Empire, and Keos, the refuge of Akominátos, which a few years earlier had repulsed the Italian tax-gatherers from Eubœa.[1] Patmos, doubtless by reason of its religious associations, was not only allowed to be independent, but the monks received many privileges from the Venetians. Lemnos, which had been included in the imperial share at the partition, became the fief of the Navigajosi, who

[1] A. Dandolo, M. Sanudo, and Navagero *apud* Muratori, *op. cit.*, xii., 334; xxii., 545; xxiii., 986; Enrico Dandolo, *Cronaca Veneta*, fol. 45; Laurentius de Monacis, *Chronicon*, 143; Lámpros, Μιχαὴλ Ἀκομινάτου, i., 389-90.

received from the emperor the title of Grand Duke, borne in Byzantine days by the Imperial Lord High Admiral. The remote island of Kythera, in later times strangely reckoned as one of the Ionian group, was claimed by Marco Venier, on the ground that the birthplace of Venus belonged of right to a family which boasted its descent from her, while the Viari became marquises of tiny Cerigotto.[1]

The long island of Eubœa, which belongs rather to continental Greece than to the Archipelago, had various vicissitudes. It had been taken in 1205, as we saw, by Jacques d'Avesnes, who was too much occupied with the siege of Corinth to concern himself greatly with the island, and as he died without heirs a few years later, he founded no dynasty in Negroponte, merely bestowing lands there upon the Templars for the repose of his soul.[2] Boniface, however, divided Eubœa into three large fiefs, which were granted to three gentlemen of Verona—Ravano dalle Carceri, his relative Giberto, and Pegoraro dei Pegorari. The Dalle Carceri family, long ago extinct, was at that time influential at Verona. One of the two town councillors in 1178 was a member of the clan; and, of Ravano's two brothers, Redondello was *Podestà* in 1210, and built the old wooden *Casa dei Mercanti*, as a modern inscription on the later building still reminds the traveller, while Henry was bishop of Mantua.[3] Ravano himself had rendered signal service to the King of Salonika by assisting Marco Sanudo in arranging the sale of Crete, while the names of the other two appear as witnesses to the deed of sale. Ignoring the assignment of Oreos and Karystos to Venice by the treaty of partition, Boniface invested Pegoraro with the north, Giberto with the centre, and Ravano with the south of the island, and the three lords assumed the name of *terzieri*, *terciers*, or triarchs, of Eubœa. With the southern barony of Karystos seems to have been united the island of Ægina, likewise on paper a Venetian possession.[4] Ere long, by the return of Pegoraro

[1] Romanós, *op. cit.*, 228.

[2] *Epistolæ Innocentii III.*, bk. xiii., lett. 146.

[3] *Antiche Cronache Veronesi*, i., 388; Panvinius, *Antiquitatum Veronensium*, 153, 189; Turresanus, *Elogium historicarum nobilium Veronæ Propaginum*, 76-7; *Fontes Rerum Austriacarum*, xiii., 90.

[4] A. Dandolo *apud* Muratori, xii., 334; E. Dandolo, *Cronaca Veneta*,

to Italy and the death of Giberto, Ravano became sole lord of Eubœa.

The republic adopted in the case of Corfù much the same plan as that which she employed in the Cyclades. It was, however, first necessary to dislodge the Genoese pirate, Leone Vetrano, who had made the island his headquarters a few years before the Crusade.[1] It is not clear whether his men were actually occupying the castle, or whether the islanders had temporarily reverted[2] to the Byzantine Empire at the time when the Crusaders halted there on their way to Constantinople. But in either case the hardy Genoese captain, as his compatriots called him, had no intention of abandoning an island at once so rich and so splendidly situated for the purposes of his profession. To the Venetians, on the other hand, Corfù was naturally a position of importance, the first link in the chain of their newly-acquired Greek possessions; least of all did they desire it to fall into the hands of a pirate who was—what was worse—a Genoese. Accordingly, the fleet which bore the first Latin patriarch to Constantinople in 1205 formally took possession of Corfù in the name of the republic, after considerable resistance on the part of the inhabitants. A Venetian bailie was left in the island, which was placed at first under the direct authority of the Commune of Venice. But scarcely had the fleet sailed than Vetrano reappeared upon the scene; the Corfiotes gladly gave him provisions and admitted his men, thereby calling down upon themselves a second Venetian visitation. In 1206, a large fleet under the command of the old doge Dandolo's son arrived in the harbour; the castle, in spite of a spirited defence, was taken by escalade, and the capture of Vetrano on the high seas and his execution at Corfù, together with some sixty of his partisans, was intended as a salutary lesson to the rest of the islanders. The castle, whose twin summits (*κορυφώ*) gave the island its mediæval and modern name, was fortified and a governor appointed. But the republic realised, as in the case of the Cyclades, that she had

fol. 44; Magno *apud* Hopf, *Chroniques*, 179; Hopf, *Karystos* (tr. Sardagna), 33; *Urkunden und Zusätze zur Geschichte der Insel Andros*, 225.

[1] Serra, *Storia della antica Liguria*, i., 465.

[2] As Romanós and Idroménos maintain.

not the requisite strength for the direct government of so troublesome a possession. Accordingly, in 1207, Corfù, together with the islets belonging to it, was transferred to ten Venetian nobles, for themselves and their heirs, on consideration that they maintained the defences and made an annual payment of "500 good gold pieces of the Emperor Manuel." The republic reserved special trade privileges to her subjects in the colony, and great care was taken to protect the Greeks, who were to be made to swear fealty to her. The colonists were enjoined to exact from the natives no further dues than they had been accustomed to pay in Byzantine times, and pledged themselves to respect the existing rights of the Greek Church. This arrangement, it was fondly hoped, would secure the possession of the island.[1] At any rate, the fate of Vetrano was not without its effect in other parts of the Ionian group. Alarmed at his fellow-pirate's end on the gallows, Count Maio, or Matthew, Orsini, who ruled over Cephalonia and Zante, discovered that he had qualms about the state of his soul, and, in 1207, placed his territories under the authority of Pope Innocent III., whose interest in Greek affairs strikes every reader of his correspondence. Two years later, however, the count thought it wiser to acknowledge the overlordship of Venice, which accordingly left him in undisturbed possession of his islands, although they were hers by the letter of the partition treaty.[2]

Lastly, there remained to be occupied the largest of all the Greek islands, that of Crete, which Boniface had sold so cheaply to the Venetians. Even before that transaction, the great rivals of Venice, the Genoese, had established a colony there, so that it was clear from the outset that the island would be an apple of discord between the two commercial commonwealths. The Venetians began their occupation by landing a small garrison at Spinalonga in the east of the

[1] Martin da Canal, *La Chronique des Veniciens* in *Archivio Storico, Italiano*, viii., 346, 348, 720; A. Dandolo and Sanudo *apud* Muratori xii., 335; xxiii., 535; E. Dandolo, *Cronaca Veneta*, fol. 43; Tafel und Thomas, *Fontes Rerum Austriacarum*, xii., 569; xiii., 55-9; Mustoxidi, *Delle Cose Corciresi*, vi.-viii.

[2] *Epistolæ Innocentii III.*, vol. ii., pp. 16, 73; A. Dandolo *apud* Muratori, xii., 336

island; but, before the rest of it could be annexed, a Genoese citizen, Enrico Pescatore, Count of Malta, and one of the most daring seamen of that adventurous age, set foot in Crete, at the instigation of Genoa, and received the homage of the Cretans and the submission of the helpless and isolated Venetian garrison.[1] A larger force was then despatched from Venice, which drove out the Maltese corsair, and appointed Tiepolo as the first Venetian governor, or duke, as he was styled, of Crete. But Venice was not yet to have undisputed possession of her purchase. The Count of Malta appealed, as a faithful son of the Church, to Innocent III.; Genoa espoused his cause as her own, and five years elapsed before the count was finally defeated and an armistice with Genoa permitted the Venetians in 1212 to make the first comprehensive attempt at colonising the island and organising its administration. Thus early the merchants of San Marco began to learn the lesson that Crete, though it cost little to buy, was a most expensive possession to maintain.[2]

[1] Nikétas, 843.

[2] Laurentius de Monacis, *Chronicon*, 153. This chronicler, who wrote in 1413, and was Venetian Chancellor of Crete, is the best authority for the island's history down to 1354. Gerola (*La Dominazione Genovese in Creta*) gives the best modern account of these first years.

CHAPTER III

THE ORGANISATION OF THE CONQUEST (1207-1214)

HAVING thus described the manner in which the Franks occupied the various portions of Greece, let us see how they proceeded to organise their conquests. The usual tendency of the desperately logical Latin intellect, when brought face to face with a new set of political conditions, is to frame a paper constitution, absolutely perfect in theory, and absolutely unworkable in practice. But the French noblemen, whom an extraordinary accident had converted into Spartan and Athenian law-givers, resisted this temptation, nor did they seek inspiration from the laws of Solon and Lycurgus. They simply transplanted the feudal system, to which, as we saw, the Greeks had not been altogether strangers under the dynasty of the Comneni; and they applied the legal principles, embodied a century earlier in the famous "Assizes of Jerusalem," and much more recently borrowed by Amauri de Lusignan for his kingdom of Cyprus, to the new Frankish states in Greece.[1] We have, however, a detailed account of the political organisation of only one of these principalities — that of Achaia, the largest and the most important at this stage of Frankish history.

It was not the lot of Champlitte to do more than lay the foundations of his principality. While he was engaged in this work of organisation, he received the news that his eldest surviving brother Louis had died without heirs—an event which necessitated his return to France to claim his Burgundian inheritance. But before he set out, he appointed a commission, consisting of two Latin bishops, two bannerets,

[1] X. τ. M., ll. 2611-14, *L. d. C.*, 79.

and four or five leading Greeks, under the presidency of Villehardouin, for the purpose of dividing the Morea into fiefs, and of assigning these to the members of the conquering force according to their wealth and the number of their followers. Champlitte approved the commission's report, and bestowed upon Villehardouin the baronies of Kalamata and Arkadia (or Kyparissia) as compensation for the loss of his original fief of Coron, now in the hands of the Venetians. He then appointed his nephew Hugh as his deputy or bailie in Achaia, and sailed in 1209 for the West. But on the journey through Apulia he died, and, as his nephew did not long survive him, Villehardouin carried on the government as bailie till the next-of-kin should arrive from France to claim it.[1]

Villehardouin's first act was to summon a parliament at Andravida, then the seat of government, where the book, or "register" as the chronicler calls it, containing the report of the commission was produced. According to this Achaian Doomsday Book, twelve baronies, whose number recalls the twelve peers of Charlemagne, had been created, their holders, with the other lieges, forming a high court, which not only advised the prince in political matters, but acted as a judicial tribunal for the decision of feudal questions. In the creation of these twelve baronies, due regard was paid to the fact that the Franks were a military colony in the midst of an alien and possibly hostile population, spread over a country possessing remarkable strategic positions. Later on, after the distribution of the baronies, strong castles were erected in each, upon some natural coign of vantage, from which the baron could overawe the surrounding country. The main object of this system may be seen from the name of the famous Arkadian fortress of Matagrifon[2] ("Kill-Greek," the Greeks being usually called *Grifon* by the French chroniclers), built near the modern Demetsana by the baron of Akova,

[1] The *Chronicle of the Morea* says that Champlitte appointed Villehardouin as his bailie. But Innocent III., a contemporary extremely well informed in Greek affairs, specially mentions "Hugo de Cham" as the bailie. (*Epistolæ*, bk. xiii., lett. 170).

[2] Or "Stop-Greek" from *mater*. The name of Matagrifon existed also at Messenia.

Gautier de Rozières, to protect the rich valley of the Alpheios. The splendid remains of the castle of Karytaina, the Greek Toledo, which dominates the gorge of that classic river, which the Franks called *Charbon*, still mark the spot where Hugues de Bruyères and his son Geoffrey built a stronghold out of the ruins of the Hellenic Brenthe to terrify the Slavs of Skortá, the ancient Gortys, and the special importance of these two baronies was demonstrated by the bestowal of twenty-four knights' fees upon the former, and of twenty-two upon the latter. The castle-crowned hill of Passavâ, near Gytheion, so called from the French war-cry "Passe Avant," still reminds us how Jean de Neuilly, hereditary marshal of Achaia and holder of four fees, once watched the restless men of Maina; and, if earthquakes have left no mediæval buildings at Vostitza, the classic Aigion, where Hugues de Lille de Charpigny received eight knights' fees, his family name still survives in the village of Kerpiné, now a station on the funicular railway between Diakophtó and Kalavryta. At Kalavryta itself, Othon de Tournay, and at Chalandritza, to the south of Patras, Audebert de la Trémouille, scion of a family famous in the history of France, were established, with twelve and four fiefs respectively. Veligosti, near Megalopolis, with four, fell to the share of the Belgian Matthieu de Valaincourt de Mons, and Nikli, near Tegea, with six, to that of Guillaume de Morlay. Guy de Nivelet kept the Tzákones of Leonidi in check and watched the plain of Lakonia from his barony of Geraki with its six fiefs; and Gritzena, entrusted to a baron named Luke,[1] with four fiefs depending on it, guarded the ravines of the mountainous region round Kalamata. Patras became the barony of Guillaume Aleman, a member of a Provençal family, whose name still exists at Corfù, and the bold baron did not scruple to build his castle out of the house and church of the Latin archbishop. Finally, the dozen was completed by the fiefs of Kalamata and Arkadia, which the bailie had received from Champlitte. In addition to these twelve temporal peers, there were seven ecclesiastical barons,

[1] Dorótheos of Monemvasia (Βιβλίον Ἱστορικόν, 464) alone gives his surname as Τουντετζέπρουντε, an obvious corruption of "de Charpigny."

whose sees were carved out on the lines of the existing Greek organisation, and of whom Antelme of Clugny, Latin archbishop of Patras and primate of Achaia, was the chief. Under him were his six suffragans of Olena (whose bishop took his title from a small village near the modern Pyrgos, but who resided at Andravida), Modon, Coron, Veligosti, Amyklai, and Lacedæmonia. The archbishop received eight knights' fees, the bishops four a-piece, and the same number was assigned to each of the three great military orders of the Teutonic Knights, the Knights of St John, and the Templars. The headquarters of the Teutonic Knights were at Mostenitsa, near Kalamata, while the Knights of St John were established in the neighbourhood of Modon. When, a century later, the Templars were dissolved, their possessions in Achaia and Elis went to the Knights of St John. In Elis, too, was the domain of the prince, and his usual residence, when he was not at Andravida (or Andreville), was at Lacedæmonia, or La Crémonie, as the Franks called it. The knights and esquires who received one fief each, were too numerous for the patience of the chronicler. The serfs living on the baronies were assigned, like so many chattels, to their new lords.

After the distribution of the baronies came the assignment of military service. All the vassals were liable to render four months' service in the field, and to spend four months in garrison (from which the prelates and the three military orders were alone exempted); and even during the remaining four months, which they could pass at home, they were expected to hold themselves ready to obey the summons of the prince, who could fix what months of the year he chose for the performance of their military duties. After the age of sixty (or, according to a less probable reading, forty), personal service was no longer required, but the vassal must send his son, or, if he had no son, someone else in his stead. Those vassals who held four fiefs, the bannerets as they were called, had each to appear with one knight and twelve esquires mustered beneath the folds of his banner, while the holder of more than four was bound to equip, for every additional fief that he held, two mounted esquires or one knight; every knight or esquire, "sergeants of the conquest" as they were called, must render service with his own body for his single fief. Thus, the Franks were on a constant war footing; their whole organisation was military—a fact which explains the ease with which they held down the unwarlike Greeks, so many times their superiors in numbers. This military organisation had, however, as the eminent modern Greek historian Paparregópoulos has pointed out, the effect of making the Greeks, too, imbibe in course of time something of the spirit of their conquerors.

Besides the twelve barons and the other lieges, the ecclesiastical peers had the right of taking part in the proceedings of the High Court, except when it was sitting to try cases of murder; and the bishop of Olena, in particular, as being nearest to the capital of Andravida, whither his residence was ere long transferred, is mentioned by the chronicler as being present at its deliberations.[1] According to the usual Frankish system, there was a second court of burgesses, presided over by the prince's nominee, who bore the title of viscount. We hear on several occasions of an assembly of the burgesses in the *Chronicle of the Morea*,[2] and towards the close of the Burgundian dynasty at Athens, the viscount is specially mentioned.[3] Before this lower court came the legal business of plain citizens; and, at least in the fourteenth century, the prince had two tribunals, at the important towns of Glarentza and Androusa. Each of the great baronies seems also to have had a court of its own; we are specially told, on one occasion, how "the elders" of the barony of Akova were summoned, and how they were bidden to bring "the minutes" (τὰ πραχτικά) of their proceedings with them.[4] Round the prince there grew up a hierarchy of great officials, with high-sounding titles, to which the Greeks had no difficulty in fitting Byzantine equivalents. We hear of the hereditary marshal (πρωτοστ-

[1] Canciani, *Barbarorum Leges Antiquæ*, iii., 511, 513. X. τ. M., ll. 1903-2016, 3145-72; *L. d. C.*, 50-6; *L. d. F.*, 28-32. The Aragonese version gives details, derived from a later date, of the distribution of lands to the knights, and mentions the serfs.

[2] Ll. 3209, 5848, 8632; *L. d. C.*, 297.

[3] *L. d. C.*, 409.

[4] X. τ. M., ll. 7682-3.

ρατορας); of the chancellor (*λογοθέτης*), who presided over the High Court when the prince wished to argue a case before it, and who represented his master as a plenipotentiary abroad and signed treaties on his behalf; of the chamberlain (*πρωτοβιστιάρης*, or *πρωτοβιστιάριος*); of the great constable (*κοντόσταυλος*); of the treasurer (*τριζουριέρης*); and of the inspector of fortifications (*προβεούρης τῶν καστρῶν*). The prince himself bore a sceptre as the insignia of his office, when he presided over the sessions of the High Court.

We learn from the *Book of the Customs of the Empire of Romania*—a codification of the Assizes made apparently in the first quarter of the fourteenth century under Angevin auspices and still extant in a Venetian version of a century later—something about the way in which the feudal system worked in the principality of Achaia. Society was there composed of six main elements—the prince, the holders of the twelve great baronies, or *bers de terre* in feudal parlance; the greater and the lesser vassals (called respectively *ligii* and *homines plani homagii*), among whom were some members of the conquered race; the freemen; and the serfs. The prince, at his accession, had to swear on the gospels to observe all the franchises and usages of the Empire of Romania, to which the barons tenaciously held, and then he received the homage of the barons and the lieges, signified by a kiss, and the oath of his inferior subjects. The prince and his twelve peers (who, at the time when the Assizes were codified, consisted of the Dukes of Athens and of Naxos, the triarchs of Negroponte, the Marquis of Boudonitza, the Count of Cephalonia, and the Moreote barons of Karytaina, Patras, Matagrifon, and Kalavryta, together with the hereditary marshal of the principality) alone possessed the power of inflicting life and death; but not even the prince himself could punish one of his feudatories without the consent of a majority of the lieges. If he were taken prisoner, as happened to the third Villehardouin, he could call upon his vassals to become hostages in his place until he had raised the amount of his ransom. No one, except the twelve peers, was permitted to build a castle in Achaia without his leave; and any vassal who quitted the principality and stayed abroad without his consent, was liable to lose his fief. Leave of absence was, however, never refused, if the vassal wished to claim the succession to a fief abroad, to contract a marriage, or to make a pilgrimage to the Holy Sepulchre, to the churches of St Peter and St Paul in Rome, or to that of St James at Compostella; but in such cases the absentee must return within two years and two days. On the other hand, the prince could neither demolish nor surrender a frontier fortress without the consent of the lieges—a clause which we shall find invoked by Guillaume de Villehardouin in 1262. It was his bounden duty to provide for the support of a feudatory whose fief had been captured by the enemy; and his powers were further restricted by the provision that he could arrest one of his lieges for homicide or high treason alone. Nor could he levy any taxes on the feudatories, the freemen, or their serfs, without the consent of the lieges, feudatories, and freemen. A liege could in theory, and did in practice, bring what we should call a petition of right against the crown. In such cases, of which we have a striking example, it was the duty of the prince to leave his seat as president of the High Court, and to hand his sceptre to a substitute, in order that he might argue the case for the crown in person—a remarkable proof of the equality of the sovereign before the feudal law. Again and again we shall see in the course of this history that a prince of Achaia was not an autocrat, but merely *primus inter pares*, whose will was limited by the feudal code and by the proud and powerful barons, its living personification. One further provision tended above all else to weaken the central authority. Except in the duchy of Naxos, under the Crispo dynasty, the Salic law did not obtain in the Latin states of the Levant, and, by an unfortunate freak of nature, many of the most important baronies, and the principality itself, passed into the hands of women. There are few other periods of history in which they have played so prominent a part, and this participation of the weaker sex in the government of a purely military community, while adding immensely to the romance of the subject, had disastrous effects upon the fortunes of the Latin orient and especially of Achaia. Nor was it the princely dignity alone which suffered by being entrusted to a weak woman, whose sex and position made her the object of dynastic and matrimonial intrigue, and whose husband was always a foreigner and therefore exposed to the contempt which a proud aristocracy usually feels for a prince consort. It happened on one occasion that almost the entire baronage of Achaia was annihilated on the field of battle or detained in the prisons of the enemy, and the fate of the principality was accordingly decided by the votes of its ladies. Most of the misfortunes of that warlike state may be traced directly or indirectly to the remarkable lack of male heirs in most of the great Frankish families, and to the absence of the Salic law—a law admirably suited to the government of a purely military community, surrounded by enemies.

It was vital to the success of the feudal system that the feudatories should be persons well-affected to the prince, and great care was accordingly taken to prevent fiefs falling into the hands of strangers. The greater vassals could not sell their fiefs without the prince's consent; but if the liege were a widow, she might marry whom she pleased, on payment of one-third of a year's income, provided that her intended husband were not an enemy of the prince. On the death of her husband, she was entitled to a moiety of his fiefs and castles, as well as one-half of all the property which he had acquired during their marriage. When a fief fell vacant, the successor must needs appear to advance his claim within a year and a day if he were in Achaia, within two years and two days if he were abroad. Failure to put in such an appearance cost him his prospective fief. All freemen enjoyed the right of testamentary disposition, and everyone was allowed to sell his produce in, or out of the principality. But no feudatory, however eminent, might give his land to the church, to a community, or to a villain, without the leave of the prince, who was alone entitled to make such a grant to the ecclesiastical establishment. This salutary rule, intended to ensure the maintenance of feudal land in the possession of those able and liable to render the full feudal services, came, however, to be seriously infringed at an early period in the history of Achaia.

The lower ranks of this feudal society were composed almost entirely of the Greeks, for on the one hand the number of French soldiers and camp-followers who had entered Achaia at the conquest was not numerous, and on the other, the "Greek feudatories," of whom the *Book of the Customs* speaks, must have formed a small class, as compared with the vast mass of their countrymen. The Greek *archons* of Elis and Arkadia, as we saw, had made special terms with Champlitte, that they should retain their ancient privileges, their lands, and their serfs; and similar concessions were obtained by the citizens of places which surrendered, such as Coron, Kalamata, Arkadia, Nikli, and Lacedæmonia; but the bulk of the native population lived and died in a state of serfdom.

The position of the serf was not to be envied. He could neither marry, nor give his daughter in marriage, without the consent of his lord; if he died without heirs, his lord succeeded to all his possessions; during his lifetime, he had no motive to be industrious, for his lord was entitled to take all his goods and give them to another serf, provided that he was left with just enough to keep body and soul together. Even his body was regarded as a mere chattel, for, if a liege killed his neighbour's serf by mistake, he must give the dead man's master another serf as compensation, and he could at all times give away his own serfs to whomsoever he pleased. If a female vassal married a serf, not only she, but her children also, descended into the rank of serfdom. There were only two ways in which the serf could become a freeman: by the act of the prince; or, in the case of a female serf, by marrying a freeman. No serf might receive a gift of feudal land without the prince's leave; and, if the serf were a Greek, his evidence could not be tendered in criminal cases against a liege. Still, even in feudal Achaia, the serf had some rights. He could sell his animals, if he chose; he could pasture his pigs on the acorns that covered the ground of the oak-forests, where, like everyone else, he might cut firewood indiscriminately, to the great detriment of the country; and his lord could not imprison him for more than a single night. In practice, too, if we may believe the Aragonese version of the *Chronicle of the Morea*, the conquerors did not disturb the serfs in the possession of their goods. But, save for some few privileges, the serf was almost a slave, who worked for the prince, for the prince's vassals, or for the alien church of the Franks, in the pregnant words of Pope Innocent III., "without pay and without expenses."[1]

Having thus established the feudal constitution of the principality, Villehardouin proceeded, with the assistance of the Greeks, to attack Veligosti and Nikli, which, though already granted as fiefs, were still unconquered. The low hill of Veligosti was soon taken; the high walls of Nikli proved a more serious obstacle; but, when the besieger vowed that he would put the garrison to the sword, their Greek relatives in his camp urged them to surrender on terms. These two places were then handed over to their appointed feudal lords. The large walled town of Lacedæmonia now yielded after a five days' siege, and became one of Villehardouin's favourite residences. Thence a raid was effected into the country inhabited by the Tzákones, and the French troops penetrated as far as the causeway which leads to the impregnable fortress of Monemvasia. At the request, however, of the Lacedæmonian *archons* who had lands in that district, Villehardouin recalled the raiders, and set about the conquest of those places which still refused him homage. With his usual tact, he called the leading Greeks to his councils, and consulted with them how he could reduce to his authority the strong Peloponnesian quadrilateral of Corinth, Argos, Nauplia, and Monemvasia. They pointed out what the Franks had already discovered, that those four strongholds were difficult to take by force; but they expressed their willingness to assist him, on condition that he swore in writing that neither they nor their children should be forced to change their faith and their ancient customs. The French conqueror willingly consented, for, like the other Frankish rulers of Greece, he was not a religious enthusiast.[2] It was true that the invaders had seized the Greek bishoprics, that the metropolitan of Patras had disappeared in nameless exile,[3] that a Latin prelate occupied

[1] *Epistolæ*, bk. xiii., lett. 159; Canciani, *Barbarorum Leges Antiquæ*, iii., 493-534; X. τ. M., ll. 7587-9, 7669-70, 7876-87, 7880-95; *L. d. C.*, 399, 436; *L. d. F.*, 31-2.

[2] X. τ. M., ll. 2017-97.

[3] Lámpros, Μιχαὴλ Ἀκομινάτου, ii., 356; Meliarákes, Ἱστορία τοῦ Βασιλείου τῆς Νικαίας, 114.

his see, and that more than a century elapses before we hear of another Greek metropolitan of that diocese, and then only in name.[1] But, fortunately for the success of the Frankish settlement, these extremely shrewd crusaders were neither bigots nor fanatics. The greatest of the popes might desire the union of the churches; but he received little assistance from the mundane barons who had founded "a new France" in the Levant. On the contrary, they were usually more disposed to oppress the Latin Church than to help it in the hopeless task—hopeless then as now—of proselytising among a people, so wedded, at least to the forms of their own religion, as the Greeks, whose leaders cared far more for their religious freedom than for their political independence, and were willing to barter the latter for the former. Thus, aided by the Greek *archons*, and seconded by Othon de la Roche of Athens, Villehardouin proceeded to resume the siege of Akrocorinth, now held by Theodore, brother of the Despot of Epiros. But a summons to attend the parliament which the Emperor Henry had convened at Ravenika in the spring of 1209, temporarily interrupted the siege. The two friends, attended by sixty well-appointed knights, appeared at the gathering; Villehardouin became "the man of the Emperor," and received as the reward of his allegiance the office of Seneschal of Romania.[2]

His next step was to come to terms with Venice, which he saw that he could not dislodge from the two Messenian stations of Modon and Coron. The republic had just sent out a new governor of her Peloponnesian colony, and Villehardouin, hastening back from Ravenika, met him in the summer on the island of Sapienza off Modon. The two high contracting parties there executed a deed, by which Villehardouin relinquished all claim to Modon and Coron, whose territory was to extend as far north as the little stream which falls into the bay of Navarino exactly opposite the classic islet of Sphakteria. The two bishoprics were, however, still to remain under the jurisdiction of the primate of Achaia. He further did homage to the republic for all

[1] Miklosich und Müller, *op. cit.*, i., 5, 8.

[2] Henri de Valenciennes, ch. xxxiii.; Buchon, *Recherches et Matériaux*, i., 89, *n.* 2.

the land which had been assigned to her in the treaty of partition as far as Corinth, "without prejudice, however, to his fealty to his lord, the Emperor of Romania;" and in token thereof, he undertook to send three silken garments to Venice every year, one for the doge, the others for the church of St Mark. He promised to conquer all that portion of Lakonia which was not already his, to hand over one-quarter thereof to the doge, and to do homage for the remaining three-fourths. Finally, he pledged himself to grant to all Venetian citizens free-trade throughout the land, and a church, a warehouse, and a law-court of their own in every town, while he himself and his successors were to become Venetians, and own a house at Venice. By these wise concessions, he secured the support of the republic for his scheme of making himself lord of "Maureson," as the deed quaintly styles the Morea. It was not long before he required it.[1]

The news soon reached the Morea, that a cousin of Champlitte, Robert by name, was on his way to claim the succession. It had been stipulated on the departure of Champlitte for France, that any lawful claimant must appear to put forward his claim within the term of a year and a day, otherwise the claim would lapse. Villehardouin, accordingly, resolved to place every obstacle in the way of young Robert's arrival. He wrote to the doge, asking his assistance, and that crafty statesman managed to detain the passing guest on one excuse or another for more than two months at Venice. When at last Robert put to sea, the ship's captain received orders to leave him on shore at the Venetian colony of Corfù, and to apprise Villehardouin of what had occurred. With difficulty Robert obtained a passage on board an Apulian brig from Corfù to the port of St Zacharias, in the Morea, the usual landing-place from Europe, better known by its later name of Glarentza. In spite of the time thus wasted on the journey, he had not yet exceeded the term appointed, for he had twelve days still to spare. He at once enquired where the bailie was, and, on being informed that he was at Andravida, sent a messenger thither to request

[1] *Fontes Rerum Austriacarum*, Abt. ii., B. xiii., 97-100; Dandolo *apud* Muratori, xii., 336.

that horses might be sent for his journey. The messenger found the crafty Villehardouin absent, but the captain of the town, with the leading citizens, came down to the coast in person to escort the claimant to his capital. There Robert was told that the bailie was at Vlisiri, or La Glisière, a castle near Katakolo. His suspicions were now aroused, and before proceeding thither, he obtained from the captain of Andravida a certificate showing the date of his arrival in the country. But Villehardouin, by moving from one place to another, managed to avoid meeting him until the full period had elapsed. Then at last he awaited Robert at Lacedæmonia, where a parliament was summoned to examine into the claimant's title. The parliament reported that the term had expired a fortnight before, and that Robert had accordingly forfeited his claim. The latter had no course open to him but to acquiesce in this decision; his wounded pride prevented him from accepting his rival's flattering offers, if he would remain in the country; and he returned to France, leaving Geoffrey, to the great joy of his subjects, lord (ἀφέντης) of the Morea. Thus, according to the *Chronicle of the Morea*,[1] did Villehardouin obtain the principality for himself by fraud and legal quibbles. But behind these quibbles lay the hard fact that the barons, who had borne the burden and heat of the conquest, were reluctant to receive as their prince an inexperienced youth accompanied by a horde of needy followers. In the beginnings of all dynasties a prince must be able; and Geoffrey possessed that combination of courage and craft, which both the bold barons and the wily Greeks admired. Moreover, his tact and his fairness towards them had particularly endeared him to the latter.

No attempt was made to dispute the decision of the Achaian parliament, and the family of Champlitte henceforth vanishes from the history of Greece. Innocent III.,[2] who usually recognised accomplished facts, hastened to style Villehardouin "Prince of Achaia"; but the prince considered

[1] X. τ. M., ll. 2096-437; *L. d. C.*, 59-69; *L. d. F.*, 34-43. The "Assizes of Jerusalem" confirm the account of the *Chronicle*. Beugnot, *Recueil des historiens des Croisades*, *Lois*, ii., 401.

[2] *Epistolæ*, bk. xiii., lett. 23; X. τ. M., ll. 2770-2.

himself unworthy of the title, so long as he was not master of the Peleponnesian quadrilateral. Accordingly, with the assistance of the Greek *archons*, whom his tolerance had won to his side, he now resumed the long-drawn siege of Corinth. Othon de la Roche of Athens again supported him; and, in 1210, the citadel at last surrendered, though its defender, Theodore Angelos, succeeded in conveying the treasures of the Corinthian Church to Argos, while many of the inhabitants sought and found a home on the impregnable rock of Monemvasia, which now became a metropolitan see and a place of exceptional importance as the last refuge of Hellenism. For the other two Greek strongholds did not long survive the fall of Corinth. Thanks to the maritime assistance of his Venetian friends at Coron, Villehardouin was able to reduce Nauplia, on condition that the lower and westernmost of the two castles on Itsh Kaleh remained in the hands of the Greeks—an arrangement which gave rise to the local names of "Greeks' castle" and "Franks' castle," still current in the seventeenth century. Finally, in 1212, the Larissa of Argos was taken, and the Athenian and Moreot rulers, with a disregard for ecclesiastical property which scandalised the pope,[1] seized the treasures of the Corinthian Church, which they found there, and divided its goods among their followers. As a still more substantial reward for his aid, Othon de la Roche received Argos and Nauplia as fiefs of the principality of Achaia, and an annual charge of 400 *hyperperi* (£179, 5s.) upon the tolls of Corinth.

The capture of Corinth led to the completion of the ecclesiastical organisation of the principality. That city now became the see of a second Latin archbishop, whose cathedral bore the name of St Theodore the warrior, the patron of its late defender, and under whom Innocent III. placed the seven bishoprics of Argos, Damalâ (near the ancient Trœzen) Monemvasia, "Gilas" (or Helos), "Gimenes" (or Zemenó)—both former Greek bishoprics, the one in Lakonia, the other near Sikyon—and the two Ionian dioceses of Cephalonia and

[1] *Epistolæ*, bk. xiii., lett. 6, xv., 77; Miklosich und Müller, ii., 287; X. τ. M., 2860-81; *L. d. C.*, 89-91; *C. d. M.*, 436; Sanudo, *Istoria del Regno di Romania*, 100; Dorótheos of Monemvasia, 471.

Zante.[1] But this arrangement was largely theoretical, and was soon modified. Monemvasia was still, and long remained, in the hands of the Greeks; Helos was so poor that a bishop was never appointed, and in 1223 was fused with the diocese of Lacedæmonia; Zemenó, a year earlier, was amalgamated with Corinth; and at the same time, Damalâ, which had never had a Latin bishop because it contained no Frankish settlers, was divided between Corinth and Argos; while Cephalonia and Zante, which had been transferred in 1213 to the nearer archbishopric of Patras, were made into a single diocese. In 1222, also, Honorius III.,[2] by the light of the experience which he had then gained, reorganised the suffragan bishoprics of Patras, dividing the diocese of Veligosti, or Christianopolis, as it was called in ecclesiastical parlance, by an adaptation of the classic name Megalopolis, between the Messenian sees of Modon and Coron, and amalgamating Amyklai with Lacedæmonia—an arrangement confirmed by Innocent IV.[3] Meanwhile, Lacedæmonia had been transferred to the jurisdiction of Corinth, and a new bishopric, that of Maina, arose in the place of Helos, so that in the middle of the century, when the Frank principality was at its zenith, the Roman Church in Achaia consisted of the archbishopric of Patras, with its suffragans of Olena, Cephalonia, Coron, and Modon (the last exempted, however, by Alexander IV.[4] from the jurisdiction of the primate), and of that of Corinth, with its suffragans of Argos, Monemvasia, Lacedæmonia, and Maina.

The organisation of the Church was a fruitful source of quarrels. The Venetians had obtained the right to the newly-created Latin patriarchate of Constantinople, and the patriarch, as the representative of the pope in the Empire of Romania, had the right of conferring the pallium upon archbishops. But the primate of Achaia, a Frenchman, fretted

[1] *Epistolæ*, bk. xv., lett. 58, 61; Buchon, *Recherches historiques*, i., pp. xxxix., lxi., lxxxiii.; Eubel, *Hierarchia Catholica Medii Ævi*, i., 188, 218. Albericus Trium Fontium (ii., 558) says, however, that in 1236 Argos was a suffragan bishopric of Athens, to which it belonged politically. The golden bull of Andrónikos II. in 1293, mentions both Helos and Zemenó, which Neroûtsos (Δελτίον, iv., 95 *n.* 2) places near Sikyon.

[2] *Regesta*, ii., 50, 163. [3] *Registres*, i., 212. [4] *Registres*, i., 188.

at being placed under the jurisdiction of a Venetian patriarch, who had promised his government to appoint none but Venetians to archbishoprics. He was not satisfied till his assertion of independence, which Innocent III. refused to sanction, was at last ratified by that great pope's successor. His suffragans had inherited from their Greek predecessors time-honoured but tiresome quarrels as to the boundaries of their dioceses; the clergy disputed with the bishops, the Templars with the primate. Most of the French canons, whom Champlitte had installed in the cathedral church of St Andrew at Patras, where the relics of the saint were then preserved, soon began to experience the usual French malady of home-sickness, and sailed for "Europe." Many of the Latin priests were absentees who drew the incomes, without doing the work, of their livings; many more were mere adventurers who tried to obtain benefices under false pretences. The primate himself was suspended by Honorius III. for squandering the goods of the Church, and Archbishop Walter of Corinth sent back to his monastery for misconduct by Innocent III. The correspondence of Innocent, who took the keenest interest in the establishment of Catholicism in the realm of Romania, is full of complaints against the hostile attitude of the Franks towards the Latin clergy. Nowhere were his complaints better grounded than in Achaia, and nowhere was the Catholic Church in so pitiful a plight. The primate was not safe even in his own palace. Aleman, who, as we saw, had received Patras as a fief, considering the archiepiscopal plan of fortifying the town against pirates amateurish, carried the archbishop off to prison, cut off the nose of his bailie, and hastily converted his residence and the adjacent church of St Theodore into the present castle, using the drums of ancient columns and pieces of sculpture with all the Franks' scorn for archæology. Fragments of ecclesiastical architecture, and what was apparently once the archiepiscopal throne, may still be seen built into the walls. Villehardouin himself was not much better. He neither paid tithes himself, nor compelled his Greek and Latin subjects to pay them, though he and his barons had sworn on the Holy Sacrament to do so, if they returned safe from battle against the Despot of Epiros;

he forced the clergy to plead disputed cases before his secular tribunals, "making no difference between the priests and the laity," as the pope exclaimed in horror; he not only curtailed the ancient possessions of the metropolitan see of Patras, but forbade the pious to grant it more, and, in pursuance of his philhellenic policy, he relieved the Greek priests and monks from the jurisdiction of the archbishop, bidding them pay dues to him alone, while the Greek serfs were not allowed to show due obedience to the Latin Church. Moreover, most of the Greek bishops who had been placed under the archbishop's jurisdiction, had fled at the outset from fear of the conquerors, and declined to return. The archbishop's suffragans told much the same story, though things were better in the Venetian possessions in Messenia. Yet even there, the governor of Coron forbade the bishop to enter his cathedral or to reside in the castle. Innocent III. might well write that "the new plantation of Latins, which the hand of God has transported to the parts of Achaia, seems to have less firm roots in consequence of the recent change."[1]

Meanwhile, the Burgundian Lord of Athens had been engaged in transplanting the feudal system to his classic state. But there was a considerable difference between feudal society in Attica and in the Morea. While in the latter principality the prince was merely *primus inter pares* among a number of proud and powerful barons, at Athens the "Great Lord" had, at the most, one exalted noble, the head of the great house of St Omer, near his throne. It is obvious from the silence of all the authorities, that the Burgundians, who settled with Othon de la Roche in his Greek dominions, were men of inferior social position to himself—a fact farther demonstrated by the comparative lack in Attica and Bœotia of those baronial castles, so common in the Morea. He had, therefore, less necessity for providing important fiefs for personages of distinction than had the princes of Achaia. Indeed, it is probable that in one respect the court of Athens under the De la Roche resembled the

[1] *Epistolæ Innocentii III.*, bk. viii., lett. 153; xii., 143; xiii., 26, 50, 51, 56, 143, 161-5, 171-3; xv., 44, 46, 47, 55; *Regesta Honorii III.*, ii., 85, 255; *Les Registres d'Innocent IV.*, iii., 61; Eubel, i., 218.

present court of King George, namely, that there was no one, except the members of his own family, with whom the ruler could associate on equal terms. But, as in modern, so in Frankish Athens, the family of the sovereign was soon numerous enough to form a coterie of its own. Not only did Othon marry, soon after his arrival in Greece, Isabelle, heiress of Guy de Ray, in Franche-Comté, by whom he had two sons, but the news of their adventurous relative's astounding good fortune attracted to Attica several members of his clan from their homes in Burgundy. They doubtless received their share of the good things which had fallen to Othon; at any rate, we know that one of his nephews, Guy, who had undergone with him the risks of the Crusade, divided with his uncle the lordship of Thebes, and that a little later the other half was bestowed upon a niece named Bonne, who, after marrying young Demetrios, King of Salonika, brought her share of the Bœotian barony to her second husband, Bela de St Omer. Another nephew, William, settled in Greece, and ultimately became by marriage Baron of Veligosti; a sister of Othon became the mother of the future Baron of Karystos, Othon de Cicon; while a more distant relative, Peter, was appointed governor of the Castle of Athens.[1] Other Burgundians will have followed in their wake; for in the thirteenth century Greece was to the younger sons of French noble houses what the British Colonies were fifty years ago to impecunious but energetic Englishmen.

There was yet another marked distinction between Attica and the Morea. Nikétas mentions no great local magnates as settled at Athens or Thebes in the last days of the Byzantine Empire, and those were the most important places of the Frankish state. We hear, indeed, of Theban *archons* in 1209; but, with that exception, during the whole century for which the Frankish sway existed over Athens, not a single Greek of eminence is so much as named by any writer.[2]

[1] *Epistolæ Innocentii III.*, bk. xi., lett. 244; Guillaume, *Histoire des Sires de Salins*, i., 67, 83; *L. d. F.*, 44.

[2] The treaty between Ravano dalle Carceri and Venice and the deed of 1216 (see below) specially mention "Græci Magnates" in Negroponte. Lámpros, Μιχαὴλ Ἀκομινάτου, ii., 277, 280. Michael Láskaris, the Athenian

Thus, whereas Crete, Negroponte, and the Morea still retained old native families, which, in the case of Crete, furnished leaders for constant insurrections against the foreigner, and in that of Negroponte showed a tendency to emigrate to the court of Nice, nothing of the kind occurred in Burgundian Athens. It is only at a much later period that we hear of a Greek party there. That the sway of Othon was mild, may be inferred from the fact that friends of Michael Akominátos, and even his own nephew, returned from their exile to Athens, and were quite content to remain there under the Latin sway.[1] As for the peasants, their lot must have been the same as that of their fellows in Achaia.

Othon's dominions were large, if measured by the small standard of classical Greece. Burgundian Athens embraced Attica, Bœotia, Megaris, the fortresses of Argos and Nauplia, and the ancient Opuntian Lokris. The Marquis of Boudonitza on the north, the Lord of Salona on the west, were the neighbours, and the latter, later on, the vassal, of the Sire of Athens, his bulwarks against the expanding power of the Greek Despot of Epiros. Thus situated, the Athenian state had a considerable coast-line and at least four ports—the Piræus, Nauplia, the harbour of Atalante opposite Eubœa, and Livadostro, or Rive d'Ostre, as the Franks called it, on the Gulf of Corinth—the usual port of embarkation for the West. Yet the Burgundian rulers of Athens made little attempt to create a navy, confining themselves to a little amateur piracy. The strictly professional pirate availed himself of this lack of sea-power to ply his trade in the early Frankish, as in the late Byzantine days; Latin corsairs, named Capelletti, regardless of the fact that Attica was now a Latin state, rendered its coast unsafe, a sail down the Corinthian Gulf was called "a voyage to Acheron," and the bishop of Thermopylæ had to move his residence farther inland to escape these sea-robbers.[2]

We are not told where Othon resided; but it is probable that, like his successor, he held his court at Thebes, the most

patriot of the fourteenth century, in K. Rhangabês play, "The Duchess of Athens," is unhappily a poetic anachronism.

[1] Lámpros, Μιχαὴλ 'Ακομινάτου, ii., 267, 301.

[2] *Regesta Honorii III.*, ii., 167; Miklosich und Müller, iii., 61.

important town of his estates. Both the Akropolis at Athens, the "Castle of Sathines," as it came to be called, and the Kadmeia at Thebes, were under the command of a military governor, and both places were the residences of Latin archbishops. In the room of Akominátos, in the magnificent church of Our Lady of Athens, a Frenchman, Bérard, perhaps Othon's chaplain, was installed as archbishop, with the sanction of Innocent III., who took the church and chapter of Athens under his protection. "The renewal of the divine grace," wrote the enthusiastic pope to Bérard, "suffers not the ancient glory of the city of Athens to grow old. The citadel of most famous Pallas has been humbled to become the seat of the most glorious Mother of God. Well may we call this city 'Kirjathsepher,' which, when Othniel had subdued to the rule of Caleb, 'he gave him Achsah, his daughter to wife.'"[1] Cardinal Benedict, the papal legate who was sent to arrange ecclesiastical affairs in the East, fixed the number of the canons, and the pope granted the request of the archbishop and chapter, that the Athenian Church should be governed by the customs of the Church of Paris. He also confirmed the ancient jurisdiction of the archbishop, derived from the days of the Greek metropolitans, over the eleven sees of Negroponte, Thermopylæ, Daulia, Avlonari,[2] Oreos,[3] Karystos, Koronea, Andros, Megara, Skyros, and Keos—an arrangement which was modified by his successor, who merged the three Eubœan sees of Avlonari, Oreos, and Karystos, with that of Negroponte, and placed Salona and Ægina under Archbishop Conrad of Athens.[4]

Innocent mentions among the possessions of the Church of Athens, and confirms to its use, Phyle, Menidi, and

[1] *Epistolæ*, bk. xi., lett. 111-13, 238, 240, 252, 256, quoting Judges, i., 12-13.

[2] So Neroûtsos (Δελτίον, iv., 59) and Prof. Bury (*The Lombards and Venetians in Euboia*, 11) interpret the papal adjective *Abelonensem*, putting this see at Avlonari, south of Kyme. A bishop of Avalona is mentioned in 1343. (Predelli, *Commemoriali*, ii., 123, 126.)

[3] The most probable interpretation of the word *Zorconensem*, as Oreos in North Eubœa is known to have been a Greek bishopric. Neroûtsos and Prof. Bury (ll. cc.) identify the place with Zarka, near Karystos.

[4] *Mélanges de l'école française de Rome*, 1895, p. 74; *Regesta Honorii III.*, ii., 50, 163; *Registres de Grégoire IX.*, ii., 40-1, 629.

Marathon; the monasteries of Kaisariané (*Sancti Siriani*), St John (the Hunter), St Nicholas of the Columns (probably near Cape Colonna or Sunium), St Mary of Blachernai, St Nicholas of Katapersica, St Kosmâs and St Damian (whom the Greeks call the Ἅγιοι Ἀνάργυροι), St George of the Island,[1] and St Luke. To the Athenian Church belonged, too, "the markets of Negroponte and Athens, and the rivers," not very full of water, it is to be feared, "whence the gardens are watered." The Church was to enjoy its ancient exemption from all exactions of the secular authorities; no man was "to lay rash hands upon it or its possessions," no one was "to harass it with vexations of any kind." Such was the privileged position of the Church of Athens, which Innocent[2] confirmed, obviously from the documents of the former Greek metropolitan see, in 1208. But the theory was very different from the reality. Othon de la Roche was, indeed, at times inclined to further the interests of the Church. Thus, we find him begging the pope to appoint a Catholic priest in every castle and town of his estates where twelve Latins had fixed their abodes, and he was willing to hold the important Bœotian fortress of Livadia as a fief of the Holy See, and to pay two silver marks a year as rent for it.[3] But, when it suited his purpose, he did not hesitate to infringe the privileges of his Church. Soon after his marriage, possibly to provide a place for one of his wife's relatives, he compelled Bérard to give him the appointment to the post of ecclesiastical treasurer—an appointment which the pope revoked. Both he and other feudal lords of continental Greece, like Villehardouin in the Morea, forbade their subjects to give or bequeath their possessions to the Church, levied dues from the clergy, and showed no desire either to pay tithes themselves, or to make the Greek and Latin population pay them. At Thebes matters were worse than at Athens. Othon and his nephew Guy, the joint owners of that city, seized the greater part of the archbishop's revenue under the guise of

[1] Makronesi, opposite Lavrion—the monastery mentioned above as a lair of pirates in the time of Akominátos. Neroûtsos, however (Δελτίον, iv., 70), identifies it with St George (Belbina), off Sunium, and Our Lady of Blachernai with Daphni.

[2] *Epistolæ*, bk. xi., lett. 256. [3] Muratori, *Antiquitates Italiae*, v., 234.

land-tax, so that the Theban Church found its income thus arbitrarily reduced from 900 to 200 *hyperperi* (from £403 to £90); later on, however, the lords of Thebes relented, and contented themselves with an annual contribution of £72 from the Theban chapter. But out of his income the archbishop was requested by the pope to assist his two wretchedly poor suffragans of Zaratoria and Kastoria—places which have been identified with Zagora on Helicon and Kastalia. Instead of doing so, the dean and canons of Thebes, assisted by the captain of the Kadmeia and other laymen, broke into the house of the bishop of Zaratoria, and carried off a man from his very arms. In short, the domestic quarrels of the Latin Church, whose best representatives did not come to Greece, must have been edifying to the Greeks. Now we find the Theban archbishop harassing and excommunicating his canons; now it is the canons of Athens, who are too proud to serve personally in the noblest of all cathedrals—the majestic Parthenon, where, later on, a descendant of Othon himself was glad to find a modest stall.[1]

As in the Morea, so in continental Greece, the military orders and the monks from the west obtained lands and monasteries. The splendid monastery of the Blessed Luke between Delphi and Livadia, the gem of all Byzantine foundations in Greece, was given to the prior and chapter of the Holy Sepulchre. The Knights of St John held property near Thebes, and seized the goods of the Thessalian bishopric of Gardiki, and even the episcopal residence, heedless of its inmate's thunders. The Templars held "the church of Sta. Lucia," outside Thebes, Ravenika, and the neighbouring town of Lamia, where they built a castle, probably that which still stands on the hill there.[2] Othon de la Roche gave the beautiful Athenian monastery of Daphni, which still bears the marks of his followers' lances on its splendid cupola, to the Cistercians of the Burgundian Abbey of Bellevaux, to

[1] Neroûtsos in Δελτίον, iv., 59; Innocent III., *Epistolæ*, bk. xi., lett. 116, 118, 121, 153, 244, 246; xiii., 15, 16, 110; xiv., 110; xv., 26, 30.

[2] *Ibid.*, xiii., 114, 115, 120, 136, 143, 144; xv., 69. I believe that the *ecclesia Sanctæ Luciæ quæ Fotæ nuncupatur* is none other than the famous church of St Luke, outside Thebes, containing his spurious tomb. The papal orthography is very shaky.

which he was devotedly attached, and at Dalphino, or Dalphinet, as the Franks called it, the last Athenian duke of his house found his grave. The Cruciferi, or "Crutched Friars," of Bologna had a hospice at Negroponte. The Minorites followed Benedict of Arezzo to Greece in 1216, and established their monasteries in various parts of the country. A century later their abbey near Athens, probably "the Frankish monastery" at the foot of Pentelikon, figured in the will of Duke Walter of Brienne, and in 1260 their "province of Romania" embraced the three districts of Negroponte, Thebes, and Glarentza, where their church of St Francis is mentioned in the *Chronicle of the Morea* as a place where the High Court of the principality met. At the end of the fourteenth century they had twelve monasteries in Greece, two of which still survive under another form—the church of Sta. Maria delle Grazie at Zante, and the orthodox monastery of Sisia in Cephalonia, which still bears the emblem of the Franciscans and preserves in its name the memory of Assisi, whence St Francis came.[1]

The Greek Church had been better treated than might have been expected from the way in which St Mary's minster on the Akropolis had been seized. It is true that from the time of Akominátos no Greek metropolitan of Athens fixed his residence in that city till the close of the fourteenth century, but the titular metropolitan resided at Constantinople, after its recapture by the Greeks, and is often mentioned in the fourteenth century as a member of the Holy Synod. But the Greek bishop of Negroponte, who had done obeisance to the Latin archbishop of Athens, was allowed by Innocent III. to retain his see.[2] Akominátos himself even ventured over once from Keos to the scene of his former labours, but he hastened his return, "from fear of becoming a morsel for the teeth of the Italians," as he calls the Burgundians of Athens.[3] Yet, though he was too honest

[1] Wadding, *Annales Minorum*, i., 202 ; ii., 206 ; iv., 350 ; *Regesta Honorii III.*, i., 59, 60, 61, 168 ; Χ. τ. Μ., ll. 2659, 7518 ; Romanós, Γρατιανὸς Ζώρζης, 38, 39 ; D'Arbois de Jubainville, *Voyage paléographique*, 336 ; Meliarákes, Γεωγραφία πολιτικὴ τοῦ νομοῦ Κεφαλληνίας, pp. 36, 178.

[2] *Epistolæ*, bk. xi., lett. 179 ; Miklosich und Müller, i., 453, 456, 459, 476, 477, 488, 498, 558, 564.

[3] Lámpros, Μιχαὴλ 'Ακομινάτου, ii., 327.

or too proud to recognise the authority of the Frenchman who sat on his metropolitan throne, he recommended the abbot of Kaisarianè, who had come to terms with the Franks, to render obedience to the powers that be. Even in his island he was not long free from Latin rule, for the brothers Ghisi and their allies occupied Keos soon after his arrival, and suspected him of secret intrigues with the Greek Despot of Epiros. Age crept on, one after another his old friends died; worst blow of all, his brother, Nikétas, the historian, died also, commemorated by the exile in a touching monody, still preserved, which is, however, a less enduring monument than his own valuable history. A few books, saved by friends from the wreck of his library, occasional presents from his old admirers at Athens, now and then a letter from one of his former flock, may have cheered a little the long days of his solitude. Above all, he found distraction in the theorems of Euclid. More than once a message came from the imperial court of Nice, bidding him join the Greek patriarch there, and offering him the vacant post of metropolitan of Naxos. At another time the Despot Theodore of Epiros invited him to his court at Arta; but he was practically a political prisoner in his cell; his strength was failing; he could not, in that uncivilised spot, carry out the treatment prescribed by his doctor; he could scarcely cross his own threshold. He had but one pleasure left—to gaze across the sea at the coast of Attica.[1] At last the end came, and about 1220 the grand old ecclesiastic died, alone in his humble cell of the monastery of St John the Baptist, founded by one of the Comneni. One of his nephews pronounced a monody over him, which has survived. The monastery, however, has disappeared, but a modern Greek geographer found that its church had become a public school.[2] It is to be hoped that the pupils learn something of the life of the last metropolitan of Byzantine Athens, a man worthy to take his place beside the patriots of classical days.

Meanwhile, the Franks of Northern Greece were by

[1] Lámpros, *op. cit.*, i., 345 *sqq.*; ii., 154, 219, 236, 242-43, 295, 301, 311, 326, 328; Ἁρμονία, III., 273-284.

[2] Meliarákes, Κέως, 225.

no means unitedly striving to develop their newly-won dominions. After the death of Boniface, the relations between the kingdom of Salonika and the empire of Romania, which had been strained in his lifetime, had become hostile in the extreme. The Count of Biandrate and the Lombard nobles of Salonika were resolved to shake off the feudal tie which bound them to the empire, and most of the great lords of northern Greece, the baron of Larissa, the Marquis of Boudonitza, Ravano dalle Carceri of Eubœa, and two brothers from Canossa, who seem to have owned lands near the *skála* of Oropos,[1] joined their party. Their attempt to secure the aid of Othon de la Roche failed, but his espousal of the emperor's cause cost him the temporary loss of Thebes, which Albertino of Canossa attacked, and of which that Italian rebel styled himself "Lord." The Count of Biandrate now openly claimed in the name of the infant king of Salonika, or of his half-brother, William, Marquis of Montferrat, all the land from Durazzo to Megara, the Peloponnese, and the suzerainty over Epiros. The emperor replied by marching into Salonika to suppress the revolt. Biandrate was imprisoned in the castle of Serres, which was bestowed upon his gaoler, the loyal Count Berthold von Katzenellenbogen of Velestino; but the other Lombard leaders withdrew to the castle of Larissa, whither Henry followed them. Like the Greeks in the war of 1897, they had neglected to destroy the bridge over the Peneios, the *pont de l'Arse*, as the chronicler calls it; the imperial force crossed it, and forced the adjoining castle on the old Akropolis to surrender. The kindly, tactful emperor showed a wise clemency to the rebels, and allowed the baron of Larissa to retain his fiefs. The Greeks, whom Henry had "treated as his own people,"[2] everywhere received him with enthusiasm; at Halmyros, his next stopping-place, they met him with the eikons, and wished him "many years" of life (πολλὰ χρόνια). But the rebellion was not yet quelled. The Marquis of Boudonitza, Albertino of Canossa, and Ravano dalle Carceri were still up in arms, and the triarch of Eubœa,

[1] *Epistolæ Innocentii III.*, ii., 480, 482, 636; Cairels *apud* Buchon, *Histoire des Conquêtes*, 449.

[2] Akropolita, 31.

who as an island-baron could dispose of a flotilla, tried to capture a vessel from before the emperor's eyes in the harbour of Halmyros. Henry's advisers prudently suggested negotiations, with the object of stopping the fratricidal war. Summonses were issued to a parliament, to be held in May 1209, in the valley of Ravenika, near Lamia, which, as we saw, Othon de la Roche and Villehardouin attended, and at which the latter became the emperor's vassal, and received as the reward of his allegiance the office of Seneschal of Romania. But if the ambitious bailie of Achaia had good reasons for supporting the emperor, who might be expected in turn to sanction his projected usurpation of the principality, the Lombard barons, instead of attending the parliament, remained defiantly behind the walls of the Kadmeia at Thebes. Thither Henry now set out by way of Thermopylæ, sleeping a night at the rebel castle of Boudonitza on the way. The native population bowed before him; at Thebes, Greek priests and *archons* came out to greet him with such a glad sound of drums and trumpets that the ground shook, while the Latin archbishop and clergy escorted him to the minster of Our Lady, where he fell on his knees and returned thanks to God for his past successes. The castle was, however, strong, and its defenders stubborn, so that it was not till he had ordered long scaling ladders to be applied to the walls, that Ravano and Albertino asked for an armistice. Once again the emperor was merciful; Thebes, indeed, he restored to his trusty Othon de la Roche, its legal owner; but he ordered Biandrate to be released, and allowed the rebels to retain their fiefs. Then Henry was able to proceed to Athens, the first emperor who had visited the city since Basil, "the Bulgar-slayer," nearly two centuries earlier, had come there in triumph. Like Basil II., Henry ascended to the Akropolis, and "offered up prayers in the minster of Athens,[1] which men call Our Lady, and Othon de la Roche, who was lord thereof—for to him the Marquis (of Montferrat) had given it, paid him every honour in his power." After two days' stay, he set out for Negroponte, accompanied by the "Great Lord"; on

[1] Henri de Valenciennes (ed. P. Paris), ch. xxxv. Buchon in his two editions reads *Thebes* for *Athaines*.

the way he was warned that his arch-enemy, Biandrate, had preceded him thither, and was plotting to have him assassinated in his bed. The plot, however, failed, owing to the chivalry of the emperor's late foe, Ravano. "The city of Negroponte," quoth the triarch, "is mine; my head shall answer for your safety there." The gentleman of Verona was as good as his word; he bitterly reproached Biandrate with his treachery; the emperor spent three days in Negroponte as his guest, enthusiastically welcomed by the Greeks, who even escorted him to the Latin church of Notre Dame, and then returned safe and sound to Thebes. The Lombard rebellion was at an end. So great was his prestige at this moment, that the crafty Despot of Epiros did him homage. The silvery eloquence of the emperor's envoy, Conon de Béthune, one of the most distinguished poets of the day, as well as one of the best fighters in the crusading army, had such an effect on the Greek ruler, that he presented his daughter's hand and a third of his lands to the emperor's brother.[1]

We have seen how constant were the conflicts between the Frankish barons and the Latin clergy. During his progress through Thessaly and his visit to Eubœa, the emperor must have heard much about the question, for the two Thessalian archbishops of Larissa and Neopatras had both caused public scandals—the one by unjust exactions from his suffragans and the monasteries in his diocese, the other by helping Sgourós to defend Corinth and by slaying his fellow-Latins. Moreover, in both Thessaly and Eubœa, the barons maltreated the Church, occupying monasteries and churches and molesting the religious orders.[2] Henry accordingly thought it a favourable moment to come to an agreement with the Roman hierarchy, and therefore summoned a second parliament at Ravenika in May 1210, for the purpose of arranging ecclesiastical affairs. All the chief feudal lords of Northern Greece were present—Othon de la

[1] Henri de Valenciennes, chs. xviii., xxix.-xxxviii. The author, obviously an eye-witness, was, according to some, the emperor himself. *Epistolæ Innocentii III.*, bk. xiii., lett. 184.

[2] *Ibid.*, bk. xi., lett. 117, 154; xiii., 104, 109, 136, 137, 192, 299; xiv., 94, 98.

Roche and Ravano dalle Carceri; the Marquis of Boudonitza and Thomas de Stromoncourt of Salona; Nicholas de St Omer and Albertino of Canossa; the two great Thessalian barons, William of Larissa and Count Berthold of Velestino; and Rainer of Travaglia, owner of the spot where the parliament met, to whom the emperor had also transferred the Templars' castle of Lamia. There came, too, three out of the four archbishops of the north—their graces of Athens, Neopatras, and Larissa, with eight of their suffragans—a thoroughly representative assembly of Church and State. A *concordat*, subsequently approved by Innocent III., was then drawn up, by the terms of which all churches, monasteries, and other ecclesiastical possessions, "from the boundary of the kingdom of Salonika to Corinth," were entrusted, free of all feudal services, to the Latin patriarch of Constantinople, as representing the pope. On the other hand, it was stipulated that the clergy, whether Greek or Latin, should pay the old Byzantine *akróstichon*, or land-tax, to the temporal authorities; and that, in default of payment, their goods might be siezed; but the family of a Greek priest could not be imprisoned, if he failed to pay. His sons, if unordained, were, however, liable to render feudal services; but after ordination they were to enjoy the same privilege as the Roman clergy.[1] The *concordat* of Ravenika was not, however, signed by the ruler of the Morea, who continued to pursue his anti-clerical policy, seizing the goods of the Archbishop of Patras, and annulling all gifts to his see. Even in continental Greece, to which it specially applied, the *concordat* often remained a dead letter. Thus, both Othon de la Roche and Villehardouin were subsequently excommunicated by their respective archbishops for appropriating church property, and also placed under an interdict by the Latin patriarch of Constantinople, who laid claim to the monasteries and ecclesiastical jurisdiction in the diocese of Thebes.[2]

The Lombard rebellion had a more lasting result than the summoning of the parliaments at Ravenika—the intro-

[1] Text in *Honorii III.*, *Opera*, iv., 414-16, and *Epistolæ Innocentii III.*, ii., 835-7.

[2] *Ibid.*, bk. xvi., 98.

duction of Venetian influence into the island of Eubœa. Ravano dalle Carceri, before he had made his peace with Henry, had been so much alarmed at his isolated position, that he had offered, through his brother, the bishop of Mantua, to become the vassal of Venice. His offer gave the Venetians the opportunity of making good their claims to the island, which the partition treaty had given them, but which they had not yet advanced. Ravano accordingly, in 1209, recognised the republic as his suzerain, promising to send every year 2100 gold *hyperperi* (£940, 16s.) and a silken garment woven with gold to the doge, as well as an altar-cloth for St Mark's. The Venetians were to have the right of trading wherever they wished, and a church and a warehouse in all the towns of the island. With their usual care for the interests of the natives, of which we have already seen an instance at Corfù, they made Ravano promise to keep the Greeks in the same state as they had been in the time of the Emperor Manuel. The republic of St Mark thus obtained, without trouble, most of the practical advantages which would have accrued from a conquest of the island. A Venetian bailie was soon appointed to govern the Venetian settlements in the island of Negroponte,[1] and the history of Eubœa from that date till the Turkish Conquest shows the gradual spread of his authority over the whole of it. The first step in this direction was taken after the death of Ravano in 1216. The Venetian bailie, acting on the system of *divide et impera*, then intervened between the six claimants to the island—Ravano's widow and daughter, two nephews whom he had adopted, and the two sons of Giberto, the former triarch. The bailie divided the island into sixths, giving two-sixths to each pair of claimants, with the proviso that if one hexarch, or *sestiere*, died, his fellow, and not his heir, should succeed to his share. This system left the bailie the real arbiter of the island. Though its capital remained common to all the hexarchs, who usually resided there and had their own judge, "the *Podestà* of the

[1] *Fontes Rerum Austriacarum*, Abt. ii., B. xiii., 89-96; Laurentius de Monacis, 143-4; A. Dandolo *apud* Muratori, xii., 336. The first bailie is mentioned in 1216, but one may have been appointed as early as 1211; he is styled "in totâ insulâ bajulus."

Lombards," and only the part near the sea was subject to Venetian jurisdiction, the bailie's authority became predominant, and Ravano's former palace was soon converted into his official residence. The hexarchs and the Greek magnates swore fealty to him as the representative of the republic, and the value of his services may be estimated from the amount of his salary—at first 450 gold *hyperperi* (£201, 12s.), and then, after the capture of Constantinople by the Greeks, increased, as his position became more important, to 1000 *hyperperi* (£448)—as compared with the 250 *hyperperi* (£112), paid to each of the *castellani*, or captains, of Coron and Modon. Venetian weights and measures were introduced into all the towns of the island,[1] two Venetian judges and three councillors (afterwards reduced to two, and entrusted with levying the dues) had already been appointed, and the church of St Mark at Chalkis, which belonged to the church of San Giorgio Maggiore in Venice, was endowed by the hexarchs, and was subsequently supported by death-duties of 2½ per cent. on all the property of deceased members of the Venetian colony. A considerable number of Venetian settlers now arrived, and there also flocked to the island impecunious "gentlemen of Verona," relatives of the feudal lords, so that it soon contained quite a large and fairly harmonious western society, for the Lombard character harmonised better than that of the warlike French with the mercantile Venetians. Castles rose all over the long island, the imposing ruins of which still remain to tell of the days of Lombard rule. On the way to Eretria the traveller passes at the village of Basilikó a large, square tower, whose only entrance is a hole 25 feet from the ground; on a hill behind the village stands the large castle of Filla, while two tall towers, close together on another eminence, dominate the Lelantian plain, no less fertile now than in the days of Theognis, and still called Lilanto in the Lombard times.[2] A large mediæval castle still rises to the right of Aliveri, and the author has seen another between Achmetaga and Limne. We often hear of La Cuppa, near Avlonari, of

[1] Magno *apud* Hopf, *Chroniques*, 179-80; Predelli, *Liber Communis*, pp. 34, 97; Bifrons, fol. 71; *Fontes Rerum Austriacarum*, xiii., 175-84.

[2] *Ibid.*, xiv., 132; Sanudo *apud* Hopf, *Chroniques*, 127.

Larmena, near Styra, and of La Clisura, which commanded the gorge or *clisura*, between Chalkis and Achmetaga, while, if little remains of the once famous fortress of Oreos in the north, Karystos in the south still boasts its Castel Rosso. From these strongholds the Lombard barons would issue forth to scour the seas in quest of rich booty; and, in the intervals of piracy, met in each others' palaces in the common capital, where brilliant balls were often held. There, too, besides Lombards and Venetians, was the Jewish colony, which Benjamin of Tudela had found there, and which naturally continued to exist under the auspices of Venice. A large proportion of the taxation was placed upon it; in 1355 it was confined in a ghetto on the southern side of the town, and the public executioner was selected from its ranks. It was, however, attracted to the island, as to Thebes, by the manufacture of silk, from which the Venetian bailie was expressly not debarred. Otherwise Venice, unlike Great Britain, did not wish her Levantine consuls to be men engaged in business. Hence she was well served and well informed.

In yet another part of the Greek world the Venetians succeeded in gaining substantial advantages without the expense of annexation. We have seen how the crafty Despot of Epiros had done homage to the Emperor Henry, then at the summit of his good fortune. But that "most potent traitor," as the emperor called him, aided by Franks whom he had taken into his pay, again and again broke his solemn vows to his suzerain, and in 1210 recognised the overlordship of Venice over all his dominions, from Durazzo to "Nepantum" or Naupaktos, promising to give the Venetians a quarter in every town and the right of exporting corn, to protect their young colony in Corfù against Albanians or Corfiotes, and to pay to the republic a tribute of 42 lbs. of *hyperperi* (£2063, 12s.) every year. Thus the republic became the suzerain of those territories in Epiros and Ætolia which had been assigned to her in the partition treaty,[1] while the Despot felt at liberty to carry out his

[1] Innocent III., *Epistolæ*, bk. xiii., lett. 184. *Fontes Rerum Austriacarum*, xiii., 119-23. This is, so far as I know, the earliest use of "Nepantum"—the transition form between "Naupaktos" and "Lepanto." In the accounts of this treaty by A. Dandolo (Muratori, xii., 336), and

ambitious designs in other directions. The fall of the Argive fortresses, which his brother held for him in the Peloponnese, ended, however, any plans which he might have had for the extension of his rule to the south of the Gulf of Corinth; but he penetrated eastward into the territory of the French Lord of Salona. With the aid of the men of Galaxidi, the little town which the traveller passes as he steams into the bay of Itea, and which rendered such noble services to the Greek cause in the War of Independence, the Despot routed the Franks in a pitched battle at Salona, in which Thomas de Stromoncourt was slain. Faithless to all his engagements, the victor next turned westward, and, in spite of his solemn pledges, conquered the fine island of Corfù, where the Venetian colony had scarcely taken root, and where the natives gladly welcomed a ruler of their own race and religion. The local tradition ascribes to him the castle of Sant' Angelo, built to repel the attacks of Genoese pirates, which still stands, an imposing ruin, high above the western shore of the island, near the monastery of Palaiokastrizza. The Greek clergy long afterwards cited his golden bull confirming their privileges. Possessed of such wide dominions, he might well coin his own money. A bronze coin, attributed to him, bearing his effigy and that of St Demetrios on one side, and the figure of the Archangel Michael on the other, has been found in Epiros; one of his leaden seals, also showing the Archangel Michael, was discovered in Corfù.[1] But his triumph was not for long. He was murdered in bed by a slave in 1214,[2] and it was reserved for his brother Theodore, an abler general, and an even more unscrupulous statesman, to prosecute his policy of expansion. Partisan hatred still obscures the history of these two reigns. The latest Greek historian of Epiros regards the first two Despots as patriots

Laurentius de Monacis (p. 144) we find "Neopantum" and "Neopatum." The *Livre de la Conqueste* (p. 323) calls it "Nepant," and it so figures on the coins of Philip of Taranto.

[1] Sáthas, *Χρονικὸν τοῦ Γαλαξειδίου*, 201; Romanós, *Περὶ τοῦ Δεσποτάτου τῆς Ηπείρου*, 23; Barone, *Notizie Storiche di Re Carlo III. di Durazzo*, 61; Marmora, *Historia di Corfù*, 210; Buchon, *Recherches et Matériaux*, ii., 211, and *Nouvelles Recherches*, II., i., 403; Mustoxidi, *Delle Cose Corciresi*, 400-1; Schlumberger, *Numismatique*, 373.

[2] Akropolita, 27.

and heroes; the Latin authorities, and the Byzantine historians, who drew their inspiration from the rival Greek court at Nice, describe them as monsters and barbarians. The truth probably lies between the two extremes.

We have thus described the conquest and organisation of Greece by the Franks. We have seen a Lombard kingdom established at Salonika, a Burgundian nobleman invested with Athens, a French principality carved out of the Peloponnese. The Venetians have founded and lost a colony at Corfù, occupied Crete, sent forth a swarm of adventurers to seize the Cyclades, made themselves the real masters of Eubœa, and gained a footing at two valuable stations in Messenia. Over the Morea and Epiros they have acquired a shadowy suzerainty, with the practical advantages of free trade. But the Greek flag still waves over Monemvasia, and the tribes of Leonidi and Taygetos still own no lord. In the mountains of Epiros and the plains of Bithynia two independent Greek states have arisen out of the ashes of Byzantium, to keep alive the torch of Hellenic freedom. We shall see in the next chapter how the ephemeral Lombard kingdom fell before the vigorous attack of the Epirote Greeks, how Thessaly felt the force of the same strong arm, how the Latin Empire of Constantinople began to shake, as the generation of the bold crusaders passed away and the power of its rivals revived, and how, after reaching its zenith, the principality of Achaia received its first shock.

CHAPTER IV

THE ZENITH OF FRANKISH RULE (1214-1262)

THE new Despot of Epiros had not been long on the throne, when the Latin Empire of Romania received a blow, which was severely felt throughout continental Greece. The Emperor Henry suddenly died in 1216, perhaps poisoned by the relentless Count of Biandrate, still in the prime of life, "a second Ares" in war, a friend to the Greeks, the ablest among the Latins of Constantinople. As he left no heirs, Peter of Courtenay, the husband of his sister Jolanda, succeeded him as emperor, and from that moment the fortunes of the empire began to decline. Peter never lived to reach his capital. After receiving his crown from the hands of Pope Honorius III. in the church of S. Lorenzo, outside the walls of Rome, he crossed over to Durazzo with the intention of marching along the classic Via Egnatia, which so many a Latin commander had trod, to Salonika and the East. Albania was even then a dangerous country, and the crafty ruler of Epiros saw a splendid opportunity of destroying the emperor of his natural enemies, the Franks. The Epirote troops fell upon the unfortunate Peter in the defiles near Elbassan; the emperor and the papal legate who accompanied him were captured; and, while the latter was ultimately released, the former died in prison, perhaps by the sword.[1] His death, as the historian Akropolita says, was "no

[1] There is great difference of opinion among the authorities as to the death of Peter. The continuation of William of Tyre (*Recueil des Historiens des Croisades*, ii., 291-3), which gives the most detailed account, says that he was treacherously captured at a banquet, and died in prison; so, too, Dandolo (*apud* Muratori, xii., 340); the *Chronicle of Fossa Nova* (*ibid.*, vii., 895-6) says that he was imprisoned; Mouskés (*Chronique*

slight aid to the Greek cause," for both the Latin Empire and the kingdom of Salonika were now in the hands of women, as regents—the Empress Jolanda and Margaret, the widow of Boniface, whose chief adviser was the Marquis of Boudonitza.[1] The victorious Despot of Epiros, energetic and ambitious, followed up his success by extending his dominions at the expense of his Frankish and Bulgarian neighbours in Thessaly and Macedonia; soon Larissa alone survived of the Thessalian baronies, for the doughty Katzenellenbogen, who might have resisted him, had returned to his home on the Rhine, and, in 1222, Theodore's career of conquest culminated with the acquisition of Salonika and the extinction of that ephemeral Lombard kingdom. Thus, after only eighteen years of existence, it fell ingloriously—the first of the creations of the Fourth Crusade to succumb. For the conqueror of a kingdom the title of Despot seemed too humble. So, with a fine disregard for the oath which he had once sworn to recognise no other emperor than him of Nice, Theodore had himself crowned at Salonika, assumed the imperial title, the purple mantle, and the red sandals of Byzantine royalty, and appointed all the great officials of an imperial court. The metropolitan of Salonika, faithful to the œcumenical patriarch whose seat was at Nice, refused to perform the coronation ceremony; but his place was taken by the Archbishop of Ochrida and all Bulgaria.[2] The result was a deadly feud between the rival Greek Empires of Nice and Salonika, which had the effect of giving the Latin Empire of Constantinople a brief respite. The ecclesiastics of the two Greek capitals espoused with all the zeal of their profession the quarrel of the respective sovereigns—for the political schism at once affected so essentially political an institution as the Greek Church. An emperor whose sway extended from the Adriatic to the Ægean, and from Macedonia to the Gulf

rimée, ll. 23,019-31) that he died there; Akropolita (p. 28) that he "perished by the sword"; the Aragonese version of the *Chronicle of the Morea*, that he was poisoned in prison. *Cf.* Meliarákes, Ἱστορία τοῦ Βασιλείου τῆς Νικαίας, 125; Romanós, Περὶ τοῦ Δεσποτάτου τῆς Ἠπείρου, 27.

[1] Raynaldus, *Annales Ecclesiastici*, i., 492.

[2] Akropolita, 27-8, 36; Nikephóros Gregorâs, i., 25-6; Pachyméres, i., 82.

of Corinth, might consider himself the heir of Constantinople with as much reason as "the true Emperor of the Romans" at Nice; his clergy, who looked to him for the advancement of themselves and of the Greek idea, could easily meet the Nicene theologians with plausible arguments for ecclesiastical autonomy. One of these apologies for Salonika and its ruler has been preserved in the shape of a verbose and long epistle from George Bardánes, metropolitan of Corfù, to Germanós, the œcumenical patriarch. The Corfiote divine, who also composed theological treatises against the Minorites, on the use of leavened bread in the Sacrament, and on the procession of the Holy Ghost from the Father alone, had received the epithet of *Atticus* from his literary skill, and some tolerable iambics, the sole relic of the old cathedral at Corfù, have been ascribed to him.[1] We learn from his letter that his beloved emperor "imitated the mildness of David," and that at his court "learning lacked not arms, nor yet the armed man learning." The metropolitan had his reward. Theodore, who signed himself "King and Emperor of the Romans," confirmed by a golden bull of 1228, all the privileges of the church of Corfù, granted by Aléxios I. and Manuel I.[2] Among the gifts of the latter emperor were 220 serfs, the living chattels of the church, such as we saw in the possession of the Latin archbishopric of Patras, and a number of "sacred slaves" (*ἁγιόδουλοι*), whose task it was to till the glebe and do other work, and whose name still survives in that of a Corfiote village.

The capture of Salonika made a great impression in the west. Pope Honorius III. ordered the two bulwarks of Northern Greece, the castles of Salona and Boudonitza, to be put in a thorough state of defence; bade the rulers of Athens and Achaia to be of good cheer and to attack the conquered city, and endeavoured to organise a new crusade for its recovery.[3] The prelates and clergy generously sub-

[1] Marmora, *Della Historia di Corfù*, 198-200; Mustoxidi, *Delle Cose Corciresi*, 423 *sqq.*, l.-lvi.

[2] Miklosich und Müller, v., 14-15; Mustoxidi, 439, 689, lvi.-lvii. The pillar containing the inscription is now in the *Magazzino Archeologico*, on the Cælian at Rome.

[3] *Regesta*, ii., 164, 207, 286, 304, 333.

scribed money for the defence of Boudonitza, and Demetrios, the ex-king of Salonika, and his half-brother, the Marquis William of Montferrat, did, indeed, head an expedition against the usurper Theodore, which penetrated as far as Thessaly. There the marquis died, poisoned it was said, and the feeble Demetrios[1] then returned to Italy, where he too died, soon afterwards, in 1227. No further attempt was made to recapture his kingdom; but for another century one person after another was pleased to style himself titular king of Salonika. The Emperor Frederick II., the marquises of Montferrat, and one of the triarchs of Eubœa bore the empty title, which passed by marriage with a princess of Montferrat to the Greek Emperor Andrónikos II., who thus combined in his own person the real and the nominal sovereignty. Even then there continued to be titular kings of Salonika among the members of the ducal House of Burgundy, which had received the barren honour from the last Latin emperor of the East. Their shadowy claim was finally sold to Philip of Taranto in 1320, after which this phantom royalty vexed court heralds no more.[2]

The fall of the kingdom of Salonika separated the Frank states in the south from the Latin Empire at Constantinople, and the fate of the latter had therefore comparatively little influence upon the much stronger dynasties of Athens and Achaia. There Geoffroy de Villehardouin had crowned his successful career by marrying his elder son and heir to Agnes, daughter of the Emperor Peter of Courtenay. Before that ill-fated monarch had started for Constantinople by land, he had sent his wife and daughter on by sea. On the way, the imperial ladies put into the port of Katakolo, at which the traveller now lands for Olympia, and which owes its name to the great Byzantine family of Katakalón.[3] Geoffrey chanced to be in the neighbourhood, and, hearing of their arrival, hastened down to greet them, and invited them up to the adjoining "Mouse Castle," Pontikokastro,

[1] S. Georgio, *Historia Montisferratis*, *apud* Muratori, xxiii., 374, 381, 382.

[2] Ducange, *Histoire de l'Empire de Constantinople*, i., 454-5; Buchon, *Recherches et Matériaux*, i., 69.

[3] Sáthas, Μνημεῖα Ἑλληνικῆς Ἱστορίας, i., p. xxxiii.

which the Franks had appropriately christened Beauvoir from the splendid view of the sea and the islands which it commands. During their visit, at the suggestion of Geoffrey's advisers, and by the mediation of the Bishop of Olena, a marriage was arranged between young Geoffrey and the daughter of the Empress Jolanda, to the advantage of both parties, for the empress saw that her child would be well married, while in all Achaia there was no daughter worthy of the ruler's son. One result of this alliance was that, later on, the Emperor Robert, son and successor of Peter, officially recognised his brother-in-law as "Prince of Achaia"—a title which, though applied by Innocent III., as we saw, to both Champlitte and Geoffrey I., and used by the latter in documents, had not previously received the imperial sanction.[1]

A year later, in 1218, Geoffrey I. died, and great was the grief throughout the Morea. "All mourned," we are told, "rich and poor alike, as if each were lamenting his own father's death, so great was his goodness."[2] An able, if unscrupulous, statesman, he had shown great skill in conciliating the Greeks, and we may endorse the judgment of a modern Greek historian, that he was "perhaps the ablest of all the Frank princes of the East."

The prosperous reign of his son and successor, Geoffrey

[1] *Recueil des Historiens des Croisades*, ii., 291; Albericus Trium Fontium, ii., 497. The *Chronicle of the Morea* twice tells the story of Geoffrey II. and the daughter of the Emperor Robert, who was on her way to marry the King of Aragon. Χ. τ. Μ., ll. 1185-98, 2472, *sqq.*; *L. d. C.* 23, 74-7; *L. d. F.*, 44-6 (which correctly makes the bride Robert's sister). Hopf has shown that this is an anachronism, for (1) Robert had no daughter; (2) the King of Aragon was then aged nine. The prologue of the *Liber Consuetudinum Imperii Romaniæ* (Canciani, *op. cit.*, iii., 499) copies and quotes the *Chronicle—lo libro della Conquista*. *Cf.* also Magno *apud* Hopf, *Chroniques*, 180. Both the *Chronicle* and the *Book of Customs* wrongly ascribe to this occasion the appointment of the prince as Seneschal of Romania (really made at Ravenika in 1209), the permission to coin money (really granted to Guillaume de Villehardouin much later), and the suzerainty over the duchy of the Archipelago (really conferred upon Geoffrey II. by Baldwin II. in 1236). Geoffrey I. styles himself "Prince of Achaia" in a document of 1210. Ducange, *op. cit.*, i., 425; so, too, does Geoffrey II. in one of 1219 (*ibid.*, i., 426), *i.e.*, before the date of Robert's accession.

[2] Χ. τ. Μ., ll. 2461-4; *L. d. C.*, 73.

II., whom the Venetian historian, Sanudo the elder, calls, with technical accuracy, "the first Prince of Achaia," was of great benefit to the principality. "He possessed a broad domain and great riches; he was wont to send his most confidential advisers from time to time to the courts of his vassals, to see how they lived and how they treated their subjects. At his own court he constantly maintained eighty knights with golden spurs, to whom he gave all that they required besides their pay; so knights came from France, from Burgundy, and, above all, from Champagne, to follow him. Some came to amuse themselves, others to pay their debts, others because of crimes which they had committed at home."[1] The only difficulty which the prince had to face was the unpatriotic conduct of the Latin clergy, who, in the snug enjoyment of nearly one-third of the land, declined to assist him in driving the Greeks out of the still unconquered stronghold of Monemvasia. As we saw, by the constitution of the principality, the fiefs of the clergy depended upon the performance of certain military services; so that when they refused to serve, on the ground that they owed obedience to the pope alone, Geoffrey was strictly within his rights in confiscating their fiefs. But, in order to show his own disinterested patriotism, he spent the funds which thus accrued to his exchequer in building a great fortress at Glarentza, in the west of Elis, then the chief port of the Morea, and now recovering some of its mediæval importance. This castle, the ruins of which still stand out like the boss of a shield from a round hill—a landmark for miles around—took three years to construct, and was then called Clermont, or Chloumoûtsi, to which the later name of Castel Tornese was added, when it became the mint for the coins known as *tournois*, so called because they had been originally minted at Tours.[2] The prince proceeded calmly with his building, regardless of interdicts and excommunications; but when the castle was finished, he laid the whole matter before the pope, who had hitherto taken the side of the clergy, and had described Geoffrey as "more inhuman than Pharaoh"

[1] *Apud* Hopf, *Chroniques*, 100-1; *L. d. C.*, 23, 79.

[2] Χ. τ. Μ., ll. 2631-57; *Cronaca di Morea* (*versione italiana*) *apud* Hopf., *op. cit.*, 435.

in his treatment of them. He pointed out that, if the Latin priests would not help him to fight the Greeks, they would only have themselves to blame if the principality, and with it their Church, fell under the sway of those schismatics. Honorius III. saw the force of this argument; the ecclesiastical thunders ceased, and a *concordat* was drawn up in 1223 between Church and State, on the lines laid down for Northern Greece at the second parliament of Ravenika. It was arranged that all Achaian sees should have, free from all secular dues and jurisdiction, all the estates which were or had been theirs from the coronation of the Emperor Aléxios Moúrtzouphlos,[1] that is to say, all the estates of the Greek Church in the Peloponnese on the eve of the Latin Conquest. The prince was to keep the treasures and moveable property of the Church, on condition that he, his barons, and other Greek and Latin subjects, paid a tithe estimated at 1000 *hyperperi* (£448) a year—a sum which was apportioned between the two archbishoprics of Patras and Corinth, and the six bishoprics of Lacedæmonia, Amyklai, Coron, Modon, Olena, and Argos. The *concordat* farther regulated the position of the Greek priests, whom the prince had been accused of treating as his own peasants. The number of the country popes who were allowed exemption from all secular jurisdiction was fixed in proportion to the size of the village—two in a hamlet of from 25 to 70 households, four in a village of from 70 to 125 families, six in places of a still larger population. Where the number of households was less than 25, that number was made up out of the scattered dwellings of the neighbourhood. The exemption was extended to the wives and families of the priests, provided that their children lived at home. All the other country popes were bound to perform the usual services to the secular authorities, but their temporal lord might not lay hands upon their sacred persons, and the clergy of the towns were to be accorded similar treatment.[2] This system was

[1] So Prof. Lámpros interprets the *Alexii Bambacoratii* of the text. Ἱστορία τῆς πόλεως Ἀθηνῶν, i., 439, *n.*

[2] Χ. τ. Μ., l. 2658 *sqq.*; *Epistolæ Innocentii III.*, ii., 835-7; *Honorii III.*, *Opera*, iv., 409-16; *Regesta*, ii., 158, 159, 161, 163; Raynaldus, *Annales Ecclesiastici*, i., 501-2.

based upon a just principle. It limited the number of idle priests; while it exempted the poor and fully-occupied country clergy from all services and dues. Henceforth peace usually reigned between the ecclesiastical and civil authorities of the Morea. Ten years later, however, we find Geoffrey complaining to Gregory IX.[1] that the Archbishop of Patras, to whom the prince had entrusted that important castle, apparently on the death of Walter Aleman, had made a truce with the Greeks, the prince's enemies, and had allowed them to enter the principality—an incident which would seem to indicate a Greek invasion from Epiros, to which Patras would be naturally exposed.

But, when the Latin Empire was menaced by the attacks of the Greek Emperor of Nice and the Bulgarian Tsar in 1236, both prince and clergy alike responded to the papal appeal, urging them to contribute money towards its maintenance. The tithe of all ecclesiastical revenues was to be devoted to the cause, while Geoffrey, in whose land the Emperor Robert,[2] his brother-in-law, had ended his wretched existence in 1228, offered a yearly subsidy of 22,000 *hyperperi* (£9856) to his successor, Baldwin II., for the defence of Constantinople—a striking proof of the excellent state of his finances. He also proceeded to Constantinople with a considerable force, including six vessels, although Venice was so jealous of another Latin sea-power arising in the near East, that she had taken proceedings against one of her subjects who had sold him a galley. With this fleet he broke the Greeks' line, and entered the harbour, after destroying fifteen of their ships.[3]

[1] *Registres*, i., 902; ii., 538.

[2] *Recueil des Historiens*, ii., 295; Dandolo *apud* Muratori, *Rerum It. Script.*, xii., 343. Akropolita (p. 47) makes him die in Eubœa; the Aragonese Chronicle places the death of a Latin emperor at Patras. Buchon (*La Grèce Continentale*, 244) thought that the two tombs in the crypt of Hósios Loukâs were those of Robert and his father Peter of Courtenay. The tradition ascribes them to the Emperor Romanós II. and his wife. The Hegoúmenos expressed to me, when I visited the monastery, a disbelief in the latter theory; the former is a mere conjecture. Sir Rennell Rodd (*The Princes of Achaia*, i., 142) surmises that Robert's tomb is to be found in the monastery of Blachernai, near Chloumoûtsi.

[3] Albericus Trium Fontium, ii., 558, who says that he had 120 ships; Mouskés, *Chronique rimée*, ll. 29,238-41, 29,602-9, 31,191-8; *Registres de Grégoire IX.*, ii., 506, 521, 860; Predelli, *Liber Communis*, p. 128.

As a reward for this service, Baldwin conferred upon him the suzerainty over the duchy of the Archipelago, which had been a fief of the Latin Empire since the time of the Emperor Henry, and over the island of Eubœa, which was in reality under the overlordship of Venice, but which the Latin Emperor might consider as his to bestow in virtue of its former dependence on the extinct kingdom of Salonika. The three lords of Eubœa were bound by this investiture to supply a galley, or eight knights, to their new suzerain, who also received a grant of land in their island. Nor did the imperial marks of favour stop here. The prince, who, like his sire, was Seneschal of Romania, also became suzerain of Boudonitza,[1] and received, as the price of further aid, the emperor's family fief of Courtenay, which, however, Louis IX. of France declined to permit. A second papal appeal found him willing to equip ten galleys for Baldwin's service, and on a false rumour of the emperor's death, he proceeded to Constantinople with ships and a large retinue to act as regent. Once again, in 1244, Innocent IV. urged him to defend the capital of the Latin Empire, and allowed him to deduct from the annual revenues of the Peloponnesian Church sufficient for the maintenance of 100 archers. He was justly regarded as the strongest Frank prince of his time, the leading man in "New France," where the Empire of Romania grew yearly weaker. Such was his prestige, that the Despot Manuel of Epiros and the Count of Cephalonia and Zante voluntarily became his vassals, and the latter was henceforth reckoned, like the three barons of Eubœa and the Duke of the Archipelago, among the peers of the principality of Achaia.[2] Now that the Venetians had lost Corfù, the crafty count had no longer the same motive for acknowledging their supremacy.

[1] Sanudo *apud* Hopf, *op. cit.*, 99-100; Hopf, *Andros* (tr. Sardagna), 167. The *Chronicle of the Morea*, by an anachronism, says that Boniface of Montferrat conferred upon Champlitte the suzerainty over Eubœa and Boudonitza, and that Robert gave to Geoffrey II. that over the Archipelago (ll. 1553-67, 2603-4). The last statement is repeated by the *Liber Consuetudinum* (Canciani, *op. cit.*, iii., 499).

[2] Albericus Trium Fontium, ii., 558; *L. d. F.*, 53-4. Romanós, Γρατιανὸς Ζώρζης, 132-4.

Although he had resolved to be master in his own house, Geoffrey II. was no enemy of the Church, when it did not neglect its duties to the State. He invited the Cistercians, already established, as we saw, at Athens, to send some of their order to the Morea, where both they and the Dominicans founded monasteries; the *Chronicle* tells us that when he felt himself dying he bade his brother, William of Kalamata, carry out a vow which he had himself omitted to fulfil, that of building a church in which his body and that of his father could repose.[1] But we learn from the correspondence of Pope Gregory IX. that it was his father who founded the church and hospital of St James at Andravida, where in due course the bones of the three first Villehardouin rulers of Achaia were laid. The two accounts are not, however, inconsistent, if we suppose that Geoffrey I. built no more than a modest chapel, leaving it to his sons to erect a more ambitious memorial church, "the glorious minster of Monseigneur St James," as the French *Chronicle* calls it. Little now remains of this famous mausoleum of the Villehardouin family; like its founder, it has passed into history. But a Norman arch near the little railway station still testifies to the past glories of Sta. Sophia, the cathedral of the Frankish capital.

Meanwhile, the next most important French state in Greece, that of Athens, had passed into the hands of a new ruler. Othon de la Roche, like Berthold von Katzenellenbogen and several other doughty barons of the Conquest, felt, as age crept on, that he would like to spend the evening of his days in his native land, which he had never forgotten in his splendid exile. Almost to the end of his reign, we find him under the ban of the Church; in 1225, soon after he had made his peace with the pope, he departed for Burgundy with his wife and his two sons, leaving his Greek dominions to his nephew Guy, who had already enjoyed the ownership of half Thebes.[2] If the Burgundian noble, whom chance had

[1] Χ. τ. Μ., ll. 2735-47, 7790-4; *Registres de Grégoire IX.*, ii., 770. I owe the suggestion in the text to Sir Rennell Rodd.

[2] *Regesta Honorii III.*, ii., 304 (Feb. 12, 1225)—the last allusion to Othon in Greece.

made the successor of Kodros at Athens, of Agamemnon at Argos, had the least imagination, or had enjoyed the classical culture of the Greek divine whom he had driven from the Akropolis, he must have been stirred by the thought that it was his lot to rule over the most famous land of the ancient world. But classical allusions did not appeal to the Frank conquerors of the thirteenth century, who looked upon Greece much as we look upon Africa. Cultured men there were among them; Conon de Béthune was a poet and an orator; even the first Geoffroy de Villehardouin wrote verses which have been preserved; Elias Cairels is a poetic authority for the Lombard rebellion; but the most inspired of them all, the troubadour Rambaud de Vaqueiras, though rewarded for his songs by honours and lands in Greece, sighed for the days when he made love to a fair dame in the Far West, when *cantò pur Beatrice in Monferrato.*[1] Home-sickness, the special malady which prevents the French from being colonists, seems to have afflicted many of the founders of "New France."

Othon passed the rest of his life in his beloved Franche-Comté, where he lived at the most some nine years more, and where his descendants became extinct only in the seventeenth century. His sepulchre is doubtful; but the archives of the Haute-Saône contain his seal bearing the arms of his family—*azur equipollé à quatre points d'échiquier d'or.* The counter-seal, consisting of an ancient gem of Hellenic workmanship, which Othon may have picked up at the sack of Constantinople or in some shop at Thebes, represents three naked children teasing a large dog. This is the sole relic of the *Megaskyr.*[2] Guy I., his successor, resided at Thebes, the most flourishing town in his dominions. Half of that city now passed, by the second marriage of Othon's niece, to Bela de St Omer, a member of that famous Flemish family whose name still survives, after the lapse of centuries, in the Santameri tower at Thebes and in the Santameri mountains of the Peloponnese. Thus, as the residence of

[1] Buchon, *Recherches et Matériaux*, i., 419-26; *Recherches historiques*, ii., 376; *Histoire des Conquêtes*, 29, 206, 449; *Giornale Ligustico*, v., 241-71.

[2] *Académie de Besançon* (1880), pp. 140-4; plate iii.

two such important and allied clans, the old Bœotian capital attained to great celebrity. The silk manufacture still continued there, and the Jewish colony was tolerated, for we hear of Hebrew poets at Thebes under Othon—bards whose verses, so a rival singer tells us, were a mass of barbarisms. Besides the Jews, there was also a Genoese settlement there, which already had its own consul. In 1240 he negotiated a commercial treaty with Guy, by which "the Lord of Athens" granted Genoese merchants freedom from all taxes, "except the usual duty paid on all silk stuffs woven in his land." He also permitted them to have not only their own consul, but also their own court of justice for all except criminal cases and appeals, which were reserved for the tribunals of the country. Both at Athens and Thebes, an open space and consular buildings were assigned to them.[1] In return for these favours, the Genoese were to protect "the Lord of Athens," his land, and his subjects. The Greeks, too, as well as the Jews and the Genoese, enjoyed the protection of this enlightened ruler. When the Archdeacon of Athens insisted on levying marriage-fees in money, instead of the hen and the loaf, which the Athenian bridegrooms had paid from time immemorial, he was made to disgorge. Every traveller to Marathon has seen by the side of the road, nearly seven miles out of the city, a Byzantine column with an inscription in iambics. The inscription tells us how "the servant of the Lord, Neóphytos by name," made a road to the monastery of St John the Hunter, of which he was probably the abbot. Those who have visited the famous fort of Phyle may have turned aside to rest at the quaint little monastery of the Virgin of the Defile (*Παναγία τῶν κλειστῶν*). I was there informed by the abbot that the more modern of the two churches was founded in 1242, that is to say, under the rule of Guy. These two examples show that the Greek monks were usually unmolested by the Franks of Athens in his time. Once, indeed, we find him begging the pope to turn out the inmates of a monastery near the frontier, suspected of betraying state secrets to his enemies. For his capital, we are told, was exposed to "frequent devastations" by the Greeks. But Guy was no

[1] *Liber Jurium Reipublicæ Genuensis*, i., 992-3.

lover of adventures, and turned a deaf ear to the papal appeal, urging him to join the Prince of Achaia and Count Matthew of Cephalonia, in defending Constantinople.[1]

While Athens thus enjoyed comparative peace, the new Greek Empire of Salonika had been shaken to its foundations. Theodore Angelos was not the man to be content with the vast dominions which he had conquered. He was now at the zenith of his power; his Italian neighbour, Count Matthew of Cephalonia, was glad to purchase his friendship and secure immunity from attack by marrying his sister—the first of the matrimonial unions between the Greeks of Epiros and the Franks. Even the Emperor Frederick II., the most remarkable ruler of the Middle Ages, did not scorn an alliance with his brother of Salonika, brought about by the good offices of the count, the brother-in-law of one party, the vassal of the other. Copper coins are still extant, showing Theodore and St Demetrios, the patron saint of Salonika,[2] supporting the imperial city, which might claim to have taken the place of Byzantium as the seat of the Greek Empire. But ambition urged Theodore to attack the powerful Bulgarian Tsar, John Asên II., in spite of the treaty of peace which existed between them. The tsar advanced to meet him, bearing aloft on his standard the written oath of the perjurer, and at Klokotinitza, on the Maritza, he routed the Epirote army, and took his adversary prisoner. The Bulgarian, less savage than his kind, treated his captive well, till he detected him plotting fresh schemes of conquest. To unfit him for further political adventures, the tsar ordered his eyes to be put out—the traditional punishment of the Byzantine Empire. Profiting by Theodore's misfortunes, his younger brother, Manuel, seized the remains of his empire, styling himself Despot and Emperor, striking gold and silver coins with the effigy of St Demetrios, and counting upon the toleration of the Bulgarian Tsar, whose illegitimate

[1] *Registres de Grégoire IX.*, i., 636; ii., 108, 421, 607; *Registres d'Innocent IV.*, i., 112; Kampoúroglos; Ἱστορία τῶν Ἀθηναίων, ii., 213-15; 238-9. He gives the date of the church as 1204. The older church, I was told, was built in 742.

[2] Albericus, ii., 558; Ricardus de S. Germano, *apud* Muratori, vii., 1015; Mionnet, *Description de Médailles*, Supp. III., 172.

daughter he had married. Determined to reign at any cost, the new emperor first endeavoured to pacify the court and Church of Nice by ecclesiastical re-union. He wrote to the œcumenical patriarch, apologising for the consecration of his bishops by the Metropolitan of Naupaktos, and suggesting that, as pirates made the journey to Nice too dangerous for the ecclesiastics of Epiros, the patriarch should either allow the present system to continue, or should permit some Nicene divine to run the risks of the voyage. Naturally, the patriarch did not see the force of this argument; "when," he said, "had piracy not existed? All this talk is a mere excuse." Having thus failed to conciliate the patriarch, Manuel promised submission to the pope, sending the ever-useful metropolitan Bardánes on a mission to Rome, and even took an oath of homage to the powerful Prince of Achaia.[1] But meanwhile, the heart of the Bulgarian monarch had been touched by the beauty of blind Theodore's daughter. She accepted his offer of marriage on condition that he released her father, and the latter was no sooner free than he resumed his schemes. Entering Salonika in disguise, he quickly won over a considerable party by his skilful intrigues; his friends aided him in driving out his usurping brother; and, though his physical infirmity prevented him from re-occupying the throne himself, he was able to exercise the real power in the name of his son John, who received the nominal dignity of emperor. The independent Greek Empire of Salonika was, however, not destined to survive the attacks of its stronger rival at Nice, where the powerful emperor, John Vatátzes, was bent on restoring the unity of the free Greeks under his sceptre. Thus, the exiled Manuel not only found a welcome at his court, but by his assistance was enabled to invade Thessaly, where he rapidly made himself master of the principal towns, and became the ally of the triarchs of Eubœa as well as of the Prince of Achaia. In vain Theodore tried to keep the empire in the family by making terms with his brother. Vatátzes crossed over into Macedonia, and compelled the feeble Emperor John, whom

[1] Akropolita, 44-7; Nikephóros Gregorâs, i., 28; Albericus, p. 558. Sabatier, *Description générale des monnaies byzantines*, ii., 303-4; Miklosich und Müller, iii., 59-66; *Registres de Grégoire IX.*, i., 491.

nature had meant for a monk and his father had placed on the throne, to abandon the coveted title of emperor, the red sandals, and the ruby-topped "pyramid" of pearls, and resume the less dignified style of Despot. On these terms, he was allowed to keep his possessions; but, on his death, his brother and successor, Demetrios, so greatly irritated his subjects by his debaucheries that they were glad to welcome the troops of Vatátzes. No opposition was to be feared from the Bulgarians, for their great tsar was dead, so, in 1246, the Emperor of Nice annexed the short-lived Greek Empire of Salonika to his dominions. These rival and scattered Greek forces were thus combined, and their fraternal divisions, which had given the tottering Latin Empire of Constantinople a respite, ceased for the present.

Even yet, however, Hellenism was not united against the foreign foe. The Despotat of Epiros, thanks to the energy of another member of the house of Angelos, had survived the untimely fall of the less stable, but more pretentious, Empire of Salonika. Ten years before that event, a bastard son of the first Despot, styling himself "Michael II., Despot of Hellas," had made himself master of Epiros, Ætolia, and Corfù. Circumstances favoured his usurpation, for the Empire of Salonika had not recovered from the blow which the Bulgarians had dealt it, Theodore was still a prisoner, and the Epirotes saw that they must have a strong man to rule over them. Michael II. won over the Corfiotes by following the traditional policy of his family towards them. Just as Michael I. and Manuel had guaranteed the privileges of the metropolitan church and people of the island, so Michael II., by four successive bulls, exempted them from practically all taxes and duties, relieved the clergy from all forced labour, and granted the Ragusan traders equal rights with the islanders. On the death of his uncle, Manuel, in 1241, he succeeded to the latter's Thessalian dominions, while old blind Theodore, with whom the love of power was still the ruling passion, managed to retain, even after the fall of Salonika, a small piece of territory round Vodena in Macedonia.[1]

[1] Akropolita, 65-73, 75-6, 85-91; Nikephóros Gregorâs, i., p. 47; Χ. τ. Μ., ll. 3061, 3561, 3815; Mustoxidi, *Delle Cose Corciresi*, 401;

Michael II. was at first anxious to remain on good terms with the powerful Emperor of Nice. He had married a saintly woman, whose life,[1] written by a monk in the seventeenth century, is one long record of ill-treatment patiently borne, of Christian forgiveness, and of a devotion to her husband, ill-requited by that passionate man. The Blessed Theodora was the daughter of John Petraleiphas, a member of a distinguished Frankish family from Provence, Pierre d'Aulps (or de Alpibus), established even before the Conquest in the mountainous region of Agrapha. The legend tells us that her husband, tempted by the devil and enchanted by the charms and spells of a fair Greek, called Gangrené, drove his lawful wife into the wilderness and received his paramour into the palace. Remorse, or the remonstrances of his councillors, at last prevailed upon him to recall Theodora, and, as a sign of his repentance, he founded, at her request, the monastery of the Saviour at Galaxidi, on the Gulf of Corinth, which, though now ruined by earthquakes, was still inhabited in the eighteenth century, when it produced the short, but interesting *Chronicle of Galaxidi*,[2] which is one of our authorities for the history of Frankish and Turkish Greece. But Theodora united the usually incompatible qualities of a saint and a diplomatist; she readily went on a mission to arrange a match between her son Nikephóros and the grand-daughter of the Greek Emperor Vatátzes. The emperor consented, and it seemed as if peace were firmly cemented between Nice and Epiros. Indeed, the Emperor Frederick II. actually wrote to the Despot in 1250, begging him to grant a free passage across Epiros to the troops, which his own son-in-law, Vatátzes, was sending him to assist in his struggle against Pope Innocent IV.[3]

Such was the condition of Northern Greece when, in 1246, Geoffroy de Villehardouin died,[4] and his brother William

Barone, *Notizie Storiche di Re Carlo III. di Durazzo*, 61-6; Δελτίον τῆς Ἱστορικῆς Ἑταιρίας, ii., 594-6; *Byz. Zeitsch.*, i., 336.

[1] Job *apud* Buchon, *Nouvelles Recherches*, I., i., 401-6.

[2] Pp. 136, 198-200; Δελτίον τῆς Χριστ. Ἀρχ. Ἑταιρείας, iii., 69.

[3] Miklosich und Müller, iii., 68-9.

[4] He is last mentioned as alive in a letter of May 6, 1246. *Registres d'Innocent IV.*, i., 275.

became Prince of Achaia in his stead. During his long reign of over thirty years, he is the central figure in Greek history, for he intervened in the affairs of nearly every state in Greece, in Eubœa, in Attica, and in Epiros. The new prince was the first of his race born in the country—for his birthplace had been the family castle of Kalamata, which had been his father's fief, and he spoke Greek as his native tongue.[1] In cleverness and energy he surpassed all his subjects ; he was the most adventurous and knightly figure of Frankish Greece, combining at times the chivalrous spirit of France with the wiles of the Homeric Odysseus. He, too, has been made the hero of a poem, *The Chronicle of the Morea*, which in jog-tot "political" verse that is almost prose extols the deeds of this prince "who toiled more than all who were born in the parts of Romania." But his reign was, thanks to his love of fighting, an almost unbroken series of wars ; and if he was able for a brief space to effect the complete conquest of the peninsula, it was in his days that its reconquest by the Greeks began.

His first enterprise was the subjugation of Monemvasia, the last Greek stronghold, which had defied his three predecessors, and which was in uninterrupted communication with the Emperor of Nice.[2] No one who has seen that picturesque spot can wonder at its continued independence in the face of such arms as the Franks could bring against it. The great rock of Monemvasia, the Gibraltar of Greece, stands out defiantly in the sea, and is only accessible from the land by a narrow causeway, the "single entrance," to which it owes its name. It had long enjoyed special privileges from the Byzantine emperors, and was governed by three local magnates, who styled themselves *archons*—Mamonâs, Daimonoyánnes, and Sophianós. William made elaborate preparations for the siege. He summoned to his

[1] X. τ. M., l. 4130.

[2] *Ibid.*, ll. 2765-9, 2946-7. All the three families were still living there when the *Chronicle* was composed ; throughout the Frankish period we hear of them, and the Mamonádes are even now extant. Their history from 1248 to the present day was written by Meliarákes. *Οἰκογένεια Μαμωνᾶ. Ἱστορικὴ μελέτη τῆς οἰκογενείας Μαμωνᾶ ἀπὸ τῆς ἐμφανίσεως αὐτῆς ἐν τῇ Ἱστορίᾳ μέχρι σήμερον.* Like many archontic families, they bore the imperial eagle.

aid the great vassals of the principality—Guy I. of Athens, who owed him allegiance for Argos and Nauplia; the three barons of Eubœa; Angelo Sanudo, Duke of Naxos, with the other lords of the Cyclades; and the veteran Count Matteo Orsini of Cephalonia.[1] But he saw that without the naval assistance of Venice, which had taken care that his principality should not become a sea-power, he could never capture the place. He accordingly obtained the aid of four Venetian galleys, and then proceeded to invest the great rock-fortress by land and water. For three long years or more the garrison held out, "like a nightingale in its cage," as the chronicler quaintly says—and the simile is most appropriate, for the rock abounds with those songsters—till all supplies were exhausted, and they had eaten the very cats and mice. Even then, however, they only surrendered on condition that they should be excused from all feudal services, except at sea, and should even in that case be paid. True to the conciliatory policy of his family, William wisely granted their terms, and then the three *archons* of Monemvasia advanced along the narrow causeway to his camp, and offered him the keys of their town. The conqueror received them with the respect of one brave man for another, loaded them with costly gifts, and gave them fiefs in the district of Vatika, near Cape Malea. A Frankish garrison was installed in the coveted fortress, a Latin bishop at last occupied the episcopal palace there; but the traveller searches in vain among the picturesque Byzantine and Venetian remains of the rock for the least trace of the French prince's brief rule of thirteen years over the Gibraltar of the Morea. Local tradition, however, still indicates the spot on the mainland where his cavalry was left. The surrender of Monemvasia was followed by the submission not only of Vatika, but of the Tzákones also, whose lands had been ravaged by Geoffrey I., but who, even if they had promised to obey him, had never really acknowledged the Frankish sway till now.[2] To com-

[1] X. τ. M., ll. 2891-6; Romanós, Γρατιανὸς Ζώρζης, 136. The French version of the *Chronicle* omits the Naxian and Cephalonian contingents. The *Chronicle* by an anachronism, makes the surrender of Coron and Modon to Venice, really surrendered in 1209, the price of the Venetians galleys, ll. 2783-5, 2854-9.

[2] *Ibid.*, ll. 2064-72, 2960-5.

plete the subjugation of the Morea, William built three strong castles, specially intended to overawe the Slavs of Taygetos and the mountaineers of Maina. Three miles from Sparta, on a steep hill which is one of the spurs of Taygetos, and was perhaps the site of the "dove-haunted Messe" of Homer, he erected the fortress of Mizithrâ, or Mistrâ, the ruins of which are still one of the mediæval glories of the Morea, and which played a great part in the history of the next two centuries. One wonders, on visiting Villehardouin's castle to-day, how the ancient Spartans can have neglected a strategic position so incomparably superior to their open village down in the plain by the Eurotas, and even now, when it is abandoned to the tortoises and the sheep, the hill of Mistrâ looks down, as it were, with feudal pride upon the brand-new streets and hideous cathedral of the modern Sparta. Scholars differ as to the origin of its name, but whether it be of Slavonic derivation,[1] or whether it be Greek, Mizithrâ stands, more than any other spot, except Constantinople, for the preservation of mediæval Hellenism against the Franks. But the French prince was not content with Mistrâ alone. Down in the direction of Cape Matapan, he built the castle of Old Maina, and on the western side of the promontory, near Kisternes, he constructed yet a third fortress, which the Greeks called Levtro and the French Beaufort.[2] The immediate result of this policy was the submission of the Slavonic tribe of Melings, who had given so much trouble to the Byzantine authorities in earlier days, but who now saw that the new forts confined them to the barren mountains, where they could not find subsistence. Accordingly, they promised to be the prince's vassals, and to

[1] Μυζίθρα in modern Greek means a sort of cheese, but Hopf thinks the name Slavonic. *Cf.* Hatzidákis in Βυζαντ. Χρονικά, ii., 58.

[2] X. τ. M., ll. 2985-3042; *L. d. C.*, 91-5; *L. d. F.*, 48-9. The site of Old Maina is placed by Finlay (iv., 198-9) and Sir Rennell Rodd (ii., 277) near Cape Matapan, which tallies with the description in the X. τ. M., which speaks (l. 3005) of a "Cape," and with the description of Nikephóros Gregorâs (i., 80). Leake (*Peloponnesiaca*, 142) thinks it is the castle still so called above Porto Quaglio. Mr Traquair informs me that there is no Frankish work now visible there. A Venetian document of 1278 (*Fontes Rer. Aust.*, xiv., 232, 234) mentions *Castrum de Belforte in partibus Sclavonie.*

serve in his army on the same terms as in the time of the Byzantine emperors, on condition that they were held exempt from dues and other feudal service. The last two castles also shut in the Mainates, so that William's sway was now acknowledged all over the Morea, save where the lion banner of St Mark floated over the two Messenian stations of Modon and Coron. In their own barren land, however, the Mainates continued to indulge in warfare, for, a few years later, the Catholic bishop of Maina was allowed by Pope Alexander IV. to reside in Italy, because the prevailing strife prevented him from living in his own see.[1]

The principality had now reached its zenith. The barons had built themselves castles all over the country, whence they took their titles, and where they lived "the fairest life that a man can." The prince's court at Lacedæmonia, which the Franks called La Crémonie, and of which an Englishman, William of Faversham, was then bishop, was considered as the best school of chivalry in the East, and "more brilliant than that of a great king." The sons of his great vassals and of the other Frank rulers of the Levant came there to learn war and manners; and personages like Marco II. Sanudo, afterwards Duke of Naxos, from whom our chief authority, Marino Sanudo the elder, derived his information, and Hugh, Duke of Burgundy, were his honoured guests. Never since the days of the ancient Spartans had such splendid warriors been seen on the banks of the Eurotas, and Louis IX. of France, the mightiest Latin sovereign of the age, might well wish that he had the giant knights of Achaia to assist him in his crusade against the infidel. From 700 to 1000 of these horsemen always attended the prince, and William was able to fit out a fleet of about 24 vessels and sail with 400 knights to meet the King of France in Cyprus, and to leave behind in Rhodes "more than a hundred noble men and good cavaliers," to assist the Genoese in defending that fine island, which they had recently captured, against the Empire of Nice. We are told that the Morea was at this time the favourite resort of the chivalry of France, and the French soldiers, who had been collected for the defence of Constantinople in 1238, had been content to stop short in Achaia and remain there. But all

[1] *Registres*, i., 184.

this brilliance was not merely on the surface. Trade flourished, and "merchants," says Sanudo, "went up and down without money, and lodged in the houses of the bailies, and on their simple note of hand people gave them money."[1] Commercial travellers from Florence and Siena visited Andravida, and Urban IV. could write to the bishops of Achaia to send him some of those silken garments for which Greece was still famed. For a prince so martial and a state so important, where commercial transactions were constant, a local coinage had become a necessity. William therefore availed himself of his meeting with the King of France in Cyprus to obtain the right of coining money from that sovereign. "Sire," said the soldierly prince, "you are a mightier lord than I, and can lead as many men as you like where you please without money; I cannot do so." The king thereupon permitted him to coin *tournois*, such as circulated in France. The Achaian mint was established in the castle of Chloumoûtsi, which thus obtained its Italian name of Castel Tornese, and ere long coins bearing the princely title, the church of St Martin of Tours, and the inscription *De Clarenciâ*, were issued from it.[2] For more than a century it continued working, and many thousands of its *tournois* have been found in Greece.

Unfortunately, William's ambition, not content with ruling over a realm compared with which that of ancient Sparta was small, soon plunged the country into another, and this time a fratricidal, war. Geoffrey II. on his deathbed had urged his brother to marry again, and secure the succession in the family; and William had hastened to follow his advice. His second wife, Carintana, was one of the Dalle Carceri of Eubœa, and baroness in her own right in the northern third

[1] Sanudo *apud* Hopf, *Chroniques gréco-romanes*, 102. The historian visited his ducal relative several times, and probably wrote in 1328, making additions in 1333, while living in Constantinople. Joinville, *Vie de St Louis* (ed. de Wailly) 53, 151 ; Akropolita, 94 ; *L. d. C.*, 101 ; *Registres d'Urbain IV.*, i., 15-16 ; Mouskés, *Chronique rimée*, ll. 29,602-9, Eubel, i., 302.

[2] Sanudo, *loc. cit.;* Schlumberger (*Numismatique*, 312) thinks, however, that some coins with *G. Princeps Achaie* on them had been struck before this date at Corinth—a name which appears on most of them—probably by William. One coin, not a *tournois*, was struck at "Clarencia" (*Supplément*, 15).

of that island. When she died in 1255, her husband claimed her barony as her heir, and actually had coins minted with the superscription "Triarch of Negroponte." Although the Prince of Achaia was suzerain of the island, neither the other triarchs nor the Venetian bailie were desirous that so restless a man should become their neighbour. One of the triarchs, Guglielmo da Verona, was, indeed, the prince's kinsman, for he was married to Villehardouin's niece; but he could not forget that, by a former marriage, he was titular king of Salonika, and therefore a great personage in heraldic lists, and he was rich enough to keep 400 knights at his court. Accordingly, he and his fellow-triarch, Narzotto dalle Carceri, placed his nephew Grapella in possession of the disputed barony. They then concluded treaties with the Venetian bailie, promising to wage "lively war" against the Prince of Achaia,[1] and to make no peace with him without the consent of the republic, which, in return, was to consult them before ceasing hostilities. The castle on the bridge of Negroponte was to be entrusted to the Venetians, who were also to receive a strip of land from St Mary of the Crutched Friars down towards the castle and two other strips in the vicinity. The former pacts of 1209 and 1216 were renewed, with the exception that, instead of the payment of 700 *hyperperi* from each of the triarchs, Venice should take all the tolls, the triarchs being, however, exempt from paying them. A further treaty localised the war to the Empire of Romania.

The Prince of Achaia was not the man to be deterred by coalitions. Using his late wife's Eubœan barony as a base of operations, he summoned the two triarchs, Narzotto and Guglielmo, to appear before him, their suzerain, at Oropos; and, so strong was the feudal tie which bound a vassal to his lord, that they obeyed his summons, and were at once arrested, remaining in captivity till after the capture of their own captor. Their wives, accompanied by many knights of the Dalle Carceri clan, now numerous in the island, went weeping to the Venetian bailie, with dishevelled hair and clothes rent, and implored his aid. The bailie, moved alike

[1] *Ibid.*, 356; Bury, *The Lombards and Venetians in Euboia*, i., 13-21; *Fontes Rer. Austr.*, xiv., 1-16.

by policy and sympathy, at the spectacle of the two noble dames, consented; but the energy of the Achaian prince had already secured the town of Negroponte. Thrice the capital changed hands, till finally, after a siege of thirteen months, the Venetians succeeded in re-occupying it, and then inflicted a crushing defeat on the famous cavalry of Achaia. Meanwhile, in spite of the wise warnings of Pope Alexander IV., who urged the prince to release his prisoners and make peace "lest the Greeks should become more powerful in the Empire of Romania," the war had spread to the Morea and continental Greece. Guillaume de la Roche, brother of the "Great Lord" of Athens, though by marriage he had become baron of Veligosti and Damalâ (the ancient Trœzen), and therefore a vassal of the Prince of Achaia, had actively assisted the Venetians at the siege of Negroponte, and they had granted him lands in their territory, and had promised him an annuity in case his Peloponnesian barony was confiscated. He had set his name as a witness to the arrangements between Venice and the triarchs, and one of those treaties had actually been "done at Thebes," in the capital of his brother, Guy I. On the other hand, the Prince of Achaia had summoned the "Great Lord" of Athens, his vassal for Argos and Nauplia, to assist him in the conflict against the Eubœan barons and their Venetian allies. It was even pretended that Attica and Bœotia, the marquisate of Boudonitza, and the three Eubœan baronies, had been placed by Boniface of Salonika under the suzerainty of the first Frank ruler of Achaia at the time of the Conquest. The result of such a claim, recorded by the author of the *Chronicle of the Morea*, perhaps for the glorification of his favourite hero William, perhaps by an anachronism pardonable in one who wrote in the following century, would have been to establish the supreme authority of that ambitious prince over all the Frankish states of Greece. But, as we have seen, the suzerainty over the three Eubœan baronies and Boudonitza had been given much more recently to William's brother by the Emperor Baldwin II., while the Sire of Athens owed him allegiance for Nauplia and Argos alone. Although Guy I. had married one of William's nieces, he not only refused to assist him, but aided his enemies, despatching troops to Negroponte and Corinth, and sending out his galleys from Nauplia to prey upon any passing ships, without regard for the rights of neutrals. Another Frank potentate, also married to a niece of William, Thomas II. de Stromoncourt, Lord of Salona, joined the Sire of Athens and Ubertino Pallavicini, Marquis of Boudonitza, against the Prince of Achaia, while Geoffroy de Bruyères, baron of Karytaina, "the best soldier in all the realm of Romania," who had fought for his prince in Negroponte, after a struggle between conflicting ties of kinship, deserted his liege lord and uncle, William, for the side of his father-in-law, Guy. Thus a baron's league was formed against the prince, whose pretensions were doubtless resented and feared by all the Frank states of Northern Greece.[1] William was not, however, without allies. The Genoese, ever ready to injure their great commercial rivals the Venetians, and grateful for the assistance which the knights of Achaia had rendered them in Rhodes, manned his galleys, which darted out from behind the rock of Monemvasia when the lion-banner was seen out at sea; while Othon de Cicon, though a relative of the Sire of Athens, held the fine castle of Karystos and made the difficult passage of the Doro Channel even still more difficult for Venetian vessels. William displayed his restless activity in all directions. At one moment he was besieging the Venetians in Coron; at another, he was nearly captured on a rash raid into Attica. Then he resolved on a regular invasion of the Athenian state. Accordingly, in 1258, he mustered all the forces of the principality at Nikli, near the classic Tegea, crossed the isthmus, and, forcing the narrow and ill-famed road which leads along the rocky coast of the Saronic Gulf towards Megara, the *κακὴ σκάλα*, as it is still called, met Guy's army at the pass of Mount Karydi, "the walnut mountain," which lies three hours from Megara on the way to Thebes. There took place the first battle between Frankish Athens and Frankish Sparta; the Sire of Athens was routed; and, leaving many of his warriors dead

[1] Sanudo, 103-4; Dandolo and Navagero *apud* Muratori, xii., 363; xxiii., 997-8; *Fontes Rer. Austr.*, xiv., 29-31; X. *τ.* M., ll. 1553-67, 3185-7; *L. d. C.*, 102, 110; Muntaner (ch. cclxi.) expressly says that Athens was originally free of all suzerainty.

on the field, took refuge with his allies behind the ramparts of Thebes. Thither William followed him, but the prayers of the archbishop and the arguments of his own nobles, who pleaded for peace between relatives and old comrades-in-arms, prevailed upon him to desist from an assault upon his enemy's capital. Guy thereupon promised to appear before the High Court of the barons of Achaia and to perform any penalty which it should inflict upon him for having borne arms against the prince.

The High Court met at Nikli, and the Sire of Athens appeared before it, escorted by all his chivalry—a brave sight to all beholders. If William had expected that his barons would humiliate his rival, he was disappointed. They decided that they were not Guy's peers, and therefore were incompetent to be his judges. They accordingly proposed to refer the matter to Louis IX. of France, the most chivalrous and saintly monarch of that age, and the natural protector of the French barons of the East, many of whom had seen him in Cyprus a few years before. William, a powerful prince, but still only *primus inter pares* by feudal law, felt bound to accept their decision, and, summoning Guy to his presence and that of his great lords, bade him go in person for judgment to the King of France. Then came the turn of the traitor Geoffroy de Bruyères. With a halter round his neck, the proud baron of Karytaina came before his prince. Moved by the sad spectacle of so famous a warrior in the guise of a criminal, his fellow-barons flung themselves on their knees, and implored William's mercy for his erring vassal and kinsman. The prince was long obdurate, for Geoffroy was his undoubted subject, and had been guilty of the gravest of all feudal offences, that of aiding the enemies of his liege lord. At last he yielded, and restored to the culprit his forfeited fief, but only for life, unless he left direct heirs of his body. Then the parliament broke up with jousts, tourneys, and tilting at the ring on the fair plain of Nikli.[1]

When the spring came, Guy started for Paris, leaving his brother Othon as his deputy at Thebes, and stopping some

[1] Sanudo, 105-6; X. τ. M., ll. 3207-370; *L. d. C.*, 101-12; *L. d. F.*, 49-52.

time on the way in his native Burgundy to see his relatives and borrow money "for the needs of his land."[1] Louis IX. received him graciously, and also the messenger of Prince William, who bore the written statement of the case. The king referred the matter to a parliament at Paris, which decided that Guy, being a vassal of William, had been guilty of a technical offence in taking up arms against his lord, but that as he, in fact, had never paid homage to the Prince, he was not liable to the forfeiture of his fief. Moreover, it was considered that his long and costly journey to France was a quite sufficient punishment for any offence he might have committed. The king then told him that he must not return empty-handed, and asked what mark of royal favour he desired. Guy replied that he would prize above all else the title of "Duke of Athens," for which, he told the king, there was an ancient precedent. Neither Guy nor his predecessor had ever borne it, but the Byzantine historian, Nikephóros Gregorâs, writing in the next century, tells a fabulous story, that in the time of Constantine the Great the governor of the Peloponnese had received the rank of "Prince," the commander of Attica and Athens, the title of "Grand-Duke," and his fellow of Bœotia and Thebes that of "First Lord" (*πριμμικήριος*); this last name, he adds, "has now been corrupted by an alteration of the first syllable into 'Great Lord' (*μέγας κύριος*), while the ruler of Athens has dropped his adjective and become 'Duke,' instead of 'Grand-Duke.'"[2] There is, however, no trace of such an official at Athens in Byzantine times; though the Latin word "Duke" was sometimes used, even by Greek writers, as the equivalent of their own word "General" (*στρατηγός*). But it is quite natural that the Sire of Athens, in asking for a title which would put him on a level with the Duke of Naxos, should, after the manner of the newly-ennobled in all ages, seek for some venerable precedent for it. Louis IX. willingly conferred it upon him, and the title, borne by his successors for two centuries, has become famous in literature,

[1] Two documents of his, dated 1260 (new. style), printed by Ducange, *Histoire de l'Empire de Constantinople*, i., 436-7.

[2] X. τ. M., ll. 3458-61; *L. d. C.*, 112-17, Nikephóros Gregorâs, i., p. 239.

as well as in history, from its bestowal, by a pardonable anacronism, upon Theseus by Dante, Boccaccio, Chaucer, and Shakespeare, and upon Menelaos by the Catalan chronicler, Ramón Muntaner.[1] All of these authors, except Shakespeare, were the contemporaries, one of them—Muntaner—the friend, of Athenian dukes. Accordingly, they transferred to the legendary founder of Athens the style of its mediæval rulers, whose names were well known in Italy, and thence passed to England.

During Guy's absence in France, great events had happened in Greece. The success of William at Karydi, coupled with another victory of his forces over the Venetians at Oreos, in North Eubœa, had induced the doge to authorise the bailie of Negroponte to make terms with the victor.[2] But suddenly, by a turn of fortune and his own rashness, the victorious prince had himself become a prisoner of war. Since the death of his wife, Carintana, William had been looking out for a third consort, who would give him an heir, and in 1259, his choice fell upon Anna, daughter of Michael II., the ambitious Despot of Epiros. The alliance involved him in the politics of that troubled state.

The peace between the two Greek states of Nice and Epiros had been of short duration. Abetted by that restless intriguer, blind old Theodore, Michael had, in 1251, once more resumed hostilities. But the rapid successes of Vatátzes in Macedonia, and the defection of his own supporters, convinced him that he had better temporise. His enemy accepted the suggestion that they should come to terms, and sent the historian George Akropolita as one of his envoys to Larissa to arrange conditions of peace. The historian returned to his master with old Theodore in chains, and the varied career of that versatile and ambitious man closed in the dungeons of Nice. But Michael II. was only waiting for a favourable opportunity to renew the attack, and

[1] Dante, *Inferno*, xii., 16-18; Boccaccio, *Decamerone*, Novel 7, Day 2; and *La Teseide*, i., 13-14; Chaucer, *Canterbury Tales*, ll., 862-3; Shakespeare, *Midsummer Night's Dream*; Muntaner, ch. ccxiv. (ed. Lanz.). Buchon's translation is here quite misleading.

[2] *Fontes Rer. Austr.*, xiv., 25-8.

it was not long in coming. After the death of Vatátzes, in 1254, his son and successor, Theodore II. Láskaris, had invested the worthy Akropolita with the chief civil command in his European provinces. The historian soon found that his post was no sinecure. The Despot of Epiros had been further incensed by being compelled to cede the valuable fortress of Durazzo, on the Adriatic, which his predecessors had taken and strengthened, as the price of his son's tardy and long-delayed marriage with the daughter of the new emperor. He accordingly excited the Albanians to rise, and blockaded the historian in the strong castle of Prilap. The treachery of the garrison opened the gates to the besiegers, and the historian, in his turn, was led off in chains to the prison of Arta, where he had ample leisure for meditating that literary revenge, which colours his history of his own times. Michael was now master of all the country to the west of the river Vardar, and the death of the Emperor Theodore II., in 1258, and the succession of a child to the throne of Nice, might well encourage his aspirations to displace the tottering Latin Empire of Romania and reign at Byzantium. An alliance between so important a ruler and the powerful Prince of Achaia seemed to both parties to have much to commend it. William doubtless thought that a Greek marriage would please his own Greek subjects, whom it was the traditional policy of his dynasty to conciliate; Michael II. was anxious to have the assistance of the famous chivalry of Achaia in his coming struggle with the Nicene Empire for the hegemony of the Greek world. Determined to make himself doubly sure, the Despot, whose daughters, like Montenegrin princesses in our own day, were a valuable political asset, had given Anna's lovely sister, Helene, to Manfred the ill-fated king of the two Sicilies, who received as her dowry several valuable places in Epiros, which had once belonged to his Norman predecessors, and the splendid island of Corfù, which he entrusted to his admiral, Filippo Chinardo, a Cypriot Frank of distinguished bravery. Indeed, it is probable, as a Byzantine historian suggests, that Michael's two sons-in-law were both scheming to carve out for themselves a vast domain in Northern Greece at his expense. William may well have aspired to revive the Lombard kingdom of Salonika, and rule from Macedonia to Matapan.

It was not long before the wily Despot had to invoke the aid of his new allies. The real power of the Nicene Empire was now wielded by a strong man, Michael Palaiológos, scion of a family which is first mentioned about the middle of the eleventh century, and which was connected by marriage with the imperial house of Comnenos. The great-grandson of Aléxios III. on his mother's side, Michael Palaiológos had been more than once accused of aiming at the purple, and his strong character and great experience of affairs quite overshadowed the child in whose name he ruled. He had already held command in Europe, like his father before him, and was therefore well acquainted with the character and designs of his namesake of Epiros. One of his first acts as regent was to despatch his brother John with a force against the Despot, while, by the agency of a special envoy, he gave the latter the option of peace on very favourable terms. But Michael of Epiros, relying on the two great alliances which he had contracted, replied with insolence to the proposals of Palaiológos, who had now mounted, as Michael VIII., the imperial throne of Nice. The envoy returned to his master after a sinister threat that ere long the Despot should feel the force of the imperial arm. Embassies sent from Nice to the Sicilian and Achaian courts proved equally futile. Accordingly the emperor ordered his brother to march without delay against the rival who dared to reject his offers. Meanwhile, Manfred had responded to his father-in-law's appeal by sending him 400 German knights in full armour, and William came in person at the head of a force, mainly consisting of Franks, but also containing a contingent of Moreot Greeks. So great was the prince's prestige after his recent successes, that the troops of Eubœa and of the Archipelago, Count Richard of Cephalonia, Thomas II. of Salona and Ubertino of Boudonitza, and a body of soldiers from Thebes and Athens under the command of Guy's brother and deputy Othon, did not fail this time to rally round the flag of Achaia. Never had the prince commanded so fine an army, gathered from every quarter of Frankish Greece.

After spending some time in plundering, the allied army met the imperial forces on the plain of Pelagonia, in Western Macedonia, in 1259—a spot where, centuries before, the Spartan Brasidas had encountered the Illyrian hosts. The imperial general had wisely hired foreign troops to contend against the dreaded Frankish chivalry—300 German horsemen under the Duke of Carinthia, 1500 mounted archers from Hungary, and 600 more from Servia, a detachment of Bulgarians, a large number of Anatolian warriors accustomed to fight against the Turks, 500 Turkish mercenaries, and 2000 light Cuman bowmen on horseback. Various devices were adopted to exaggerate the size of his army, and a scout was sent privily to spread discord between the Franks and Greeks. The lack of harmony between the unnatural allies was increased by a private quarrel between the Prince of Achaia and John, the Despot's bastard, who complained that some of the Frank knights had paid unwarrantable attentions to his beautiful wife, and received for reply from the prince, instead of justice, an insulting allusion to his birth. The bastard, in revenge, deserted to the enemy at a critical moment; the Despot, warned of his son's intended treachery, fled in the night, and the Franks were left alone to face the foe. For an instant even William's courage seems to have failed him; but the reproaches of that stalwart baron, Geoffroy de Bruyères, prevailed on him to lead his diminished but now homogeneous army against the heterogeneous host of Greeks, Hungarians, Germans, Slavs, and Turks. The Franks fought with all the courage of their race; picking out the Germans as their most dangerous enemies, they fell upon them with lance and sword; Geoffroy de Bruyères slew the Duke of Carinthia in single combat, and the German knights dropped before the sweep of his blade "like grass upon a meadow." The Greek commander then ordered his Hungarian and Cuman bowmen to shoot at the horses of the Frankish knights now inextricably mingled with his German mercenaries, whose lives he cheerfully sacrificed. The archers did their work well; horseman after horseman fell; Geoffroy de Bruyères, "the flower of the Achaian chivalry," was taken prisoner, and the prince, while charging to the rescue of his nephew, was unhorsed. The prince tried to conceal himself under a heap of straw, but was discovered and identified by his prominent front teeth. Only the rank and file escaped, and of those, only some evaded the clutches of the predatory Wallachs of Thessaly, who were devoted to the person of the treacherous bastard, and made their way back to the Morea. William and the other principal prisoners were led to the tent of the Greek commander, where the prince's knowledge of the Greek tongue, which he spoke with native fluency, enabled him to hold his own against the reproaches of his conqueror. Sending his prisoners to his brother's court at Lampsakos, the Greek general followed up his victory in Epiros and Thessaly. While one detachment of his army besieged Joannina and occupied Arta, the two chief towns of the Despotat, releasing the unhappy Akropolita from prison, he marched with the Despot's bastard through Thessaly to Neopatras, and thence to Thebes. He was engaged in plundering that city, when the bastard again turned traitor and fled to his father, who had taken refuge with his family in the islands of Leukas and Cephalonia. The house of Angelos was popular in Epiros, where the natives regarded the Greeks of Nice as interlopers, and the tactless conduct of the victors soon aroused the discontent of the vanquished; Arta declared for its old Despot, the siege of Joannina was raised, and the imperial commander thought it prudent to abandon Bœotia and return home.[1]

The versatile Despot of Epiros speedily recovered from the results of this campaign. A year after the battle of Pelagonia he received a fresh contingent of troops from his son-in-law Manfred, with which his eldest son, Nikephóros, severely defeated the imperial general, Aléxios Strategópoulos, and took him prisoner. A brief truce followed, Strategópoulos was released, and was thus enabled to cover himself with glory by capturing Constantinople from the Latins in the

[1] Akropolita, 95-9, 141-2, 148-53, 156-61, 167-8, 171, 174-84; Nikephóros Gregorâs, i., 47-9, 71-5; Pachyméres, i., 81-6; Sanudo, 106-7; Miklosich und Müller, iii., 240; X. τ. M., ll. 3060-137, 3469-4191; *L. d. C.*, 96-100, 117-42; *L. d. F.*, 53-63; M. Palaiológos, *De vitâ suâ*, 6-7. The *Chronicle*, though it contains historical matter, traces the war to a family quarrel between the sons of Michael II., Nikephóros and John, whom it calls Theodore.

following year. But the captor of Constantinople, by a sudden change of fortune which astounded the Byzantine historians and led them to compare him with Cyrus, Hannibal, and Pompey, again became the captive of the crafty Despot, whom he had a second time attacked, and was sent to the custody of Manfred, where he remained till he was exchanged for the King of Sicily's sister, Anna. Three years later, the emperor's brother John, the victor of Pelagonia, once more attacked his old enemy with such success that Michael II. had to invoke the diplomatic aid of his saintly wife, who went to Constantinople with her second son John, and left him there as a hostage for her husband's good behaviour. The expostulations of the patriarch, who rebuked the emperor for making war against a fellow-Christian—that is to say, a member of the Orthodox Church—combined, with the expense and difficulty of these Epirote campaigns, to bring about peace; and the Despot's eldest son, Nikephóros, now a widower, received the emperor's niece as a wife and a pledge of union between the two Greek states.[1]

But, while the battle of Pelagonia had thus only a passing effect upon the fortunes of Epiros, it was a fatal blow to the Frankish principality of Achaia. It was the primary cause of all the subsequent disasters, for the capture of the prince gave the astute Emperor Michael the means of gaining a foothold in the Morea, from which, little by little, Byzantine rule was extended once more over the whole peninsula. Such was the result of Villehardouin's rashness. Well, indeed, might the troubadours of France lament the captivity of their hero, and mournfully prophesy the loss of Achaia after that of Constantinople.

When the prisoners had arrived, the emperor summoned them before him, and offered them money for the purchase of broad lands in France, on condition that William should cede to him the Morea. The prince replied that it was not in his power to cede that, in which he had only a qualified share. He explained that the land had been conquered by his father and his father's comrades, that the Prince of Achaia was no absolute monarch, but was bound in all matters to

[1] Pachyméres, i., 89, 106-7, 137, 185, 205-7, 214, 242. Nikephóros Gregorâs, i., 83, 90-2, 98.

consult the opinion of his peers, and to observe the agreements made at the time of the Conquest. The emperor, irritated at this plain statement of the principles of feudalism, ordered his Varangian guards, among whom there may have been some of our Anglo-Saxon forefathers, to take the prince and his companions back to their prison. For three long years they remained prisoners, while their captor dealt the Latin Empire of Romania its death-blow, and restored the Greek throne from Nice to Constantinople.[1]

The capture of the prince and so many of his barons had deprived the principality of all its leading men. Accordingly, the princess and those Franks who remained, in order to prevent a threatening rising of the Greeks, wrote to the Duke of Athens,[2] who was still in France, offering him the post of Bailie of Achaia. Rarely had the wheel of fortune turned with such rapidity; the victor of Karydi was now a prisoner, the vanquished whom he had haled before the High Court at Nikli as a rebellious vassal was now a Duke of Athens and administrator of his conqueror's estates. He had been detained in France owing to the troublesome complaints of some French merchants and pilgrims to King Louis, that they had been injured by the Athenian privateers which issued from the port of Nauplia, and had not received compensation from the duke.[3] Guy now settled this matter, and started for the Morea. His first act on landing was to order the liberation of the two imprisoned triarchs of Eubœa; and he commemorated his governorship of Achaia and his acquisition of the ducal title by striking a coin at the mint of Glarentza—the earliest coin of an Athenian duke which we possess.[4] He was engaged in administering the country to the general satisfaction, when the startling news of the recapture of Constantinople by the Greeks and of the flight of the last Latin emperor, Baldwin II., reached him. The fugitive first stopped at Negroponte, where his wife had stayed to raise money from the wealthy citizens thirteen

[1] X. τ. M., ll. 4217-323; *L. d. C.*, 141-6.

[2] *L. d. F.*, 65, 66; Sanudo, 107. [3] *Ibid.*, 106.

[4] Schlumberger, *Numismatique*, 337, 340, who thinks that this coin is a forgery. Buchon, *Atlas*, plate xxv. One of his coins is in the Archæological Museum at Venice; his previous currency bears the title *Dominus*.

years before, and where the three barons received him with the magnificent honours due to his exalted rank. Thence he proceeded to Thebes and Athens, where he found the duke waiting to greet him. In the Castle of the Kadmeia and on the ancient Akropolis, which, fifty years earlier, had welcomed another Latin emperor in his hour of triumph, there gathered round their feudal chief, now a landless exile, the barons who had survived the fatal day of Pelagonia and the prisons of Palaiológos. The Duchess of Naxos came with her ladies to offer presents to him, and Othon de Cicon, lord of Karystos and Ægina, who had played so active a part in the Eubœan war, and had lent him 5000 *hyperperi* (£2240) in his sore need. Baldwin had nothing but barren titles and a few relics, the remnant of the Byzantine sacristies, to bestow. But he was generous of knighthoods, and he liquidated his debt to the baron of Karystos with an arm of St John the Baptist, which the pious Othon subsequently presented to the Burgundian Abbey of Cîteaux. Thus, on the venerable rock of Athens was played the last pitiful scene in the brief drama of the Latin Empire of Constantinople. Then Baldwin sailed from the Piræus for Monemvasia; and, leaving behind him not a few of his noble retinue in the Morea, set out for Europe, to solicit aid for his lost cause and to play the sorry part of an emperor in exile.[1]

The "new Constantine," as Michael Palaiológos styled himself after the recovery of Constantinople, was now doubly anxious to restore Greek rule in the Morea also. Three years of confinement had somewhat broken William's Frankish pride; some of his fellow-captives had died in prison; and, as Michael VIII. was now more moderate in his demands, a compromise was possible. The emperor desired Argos and Nauplia to be included among the places to be ceded to him; but his prisoner could plead that they were the fief of the Duke of Athens. William might, however, conscientiously agree to the surrender of the three castles of Monemvasia, Maina, and Mistrâ, which he had either captured or built himself, and which were therefore his to bestow. The

[1] Sanudo, 115, 172; X. τ. M., ll. 1301-32; *L. d. C.*, 27-31; Ducange, *Histoire de l'Empire de Constantinople*, i., 432; Dandolo *apud* Muratori, xii., 369; *Exuviæ Sacræ Constantinopolitanæ*, ii., 144-8.

contemporary Greek historian, Pachyméres, anxious to magnify the emperor, adds that the prince was to become Michael's vassal for the rest of the principality and received from his suzerain the title of Grand Seneschal—an obvious attempt at explaining, in a way flattering to Greek vanity, the origin of an office which the Latin emperors had conferred upon the rulers of Achaia. In return for the three castles, William and his comrades were to be set at liberty, and the prince swore a most solemn oath over the baptismal font of the emperor's infant son that he would never levy war against Michael again. Geoffroy de Bruyères, who was a special favourite of the emperor, was released from prison and sent to arrange for the transference of the castles to the imperial authorities.[1]

Guy of Athens received the message with grave misgivings. He saw that the three castles would be a lever with which the emperor could shake the Frankish power in the peninsula, and that Monemvasia in particular would provide him with an admirable landing-place for his troops. As was his duty, he convened the High Court of the principality at Nikli, the same spot where he had himself stood to await his sentence. But this time it was a ladies' parliament which met on the plain to decide the future of the state—for all the men of mark had been slain at Pelagonia or were in prison at Constantinople, and their wives or widows had to take their places at the council. Only two of the stronger sex were present, the Chancellor of Achaia, Leonardo of Veroli in Latium, and Pierre de Vaux, "the wisest head in all the principality." It was only natural that with an assembly so constituted sentiment should have had more weight than reasons of state. In vain the Duke of Athens argued in scriptural language, that "it were better that one man should die for the people rather than that the other Franks of the Morea should lose the fruit of their fathers' labours"; in vain, to show his disinterestedness, he offered to take the prince's place in prison or pledge his own duchy to provide a ransom. The men were, we are told, unwilling to cede the castles,

[1] Sanudo, 108; X. τ. M., ll. 4324-48; *L. d. C.*, 146-7; Pachyméres, i., 88; Nikephóros Gregorâs I., 79-80. Pachyméres adds Geraki, and the Aragonese version of the *Chronicle* (p. 67) Corinth, to the list of castles.

justly surmising that this might be the ruin of the country. But the conjugal feelings of the ladies who formed the majority found a convenient legal excuse for the surrender of the three castles in the technical argument that they were the prince's to give or to keep, and Guy, anxious not to lay himself open in Greece and at the French court to the charge of cherishing malice against his late enemy, finally yielded. The castles were forthwith surrendered, and two noble dames, Marguerite, daughter of Jean de Neuilly, Marshal of Achaia, and the sister of Jean de Chauderon, the Grand Constable of the principality and nephew of the prince, were sent as hostages to Constantinople.[1]

As soon as he was released, William set out for Negroponte, where he was received with great honour, and where the Duke of Athens met him and escorted him to Thebes. There, in the house of the Archbishop Henry, a treaty of peace between the Prince of Achaia of the one part, and Venice and the triarchs of the other part, was concluded. The treaty of Thebes practically restored the *status quo* before the death of Carintana, which had been the occasion for the war. William recognised Guglielmo da Verona, Narzotto dalle Carceri, and Grapella as triarchs, and they, in turn, recognised him as their suzerain, and promised to destroy the castle of Negroponte at their own expense, retaining its site for themselves. Venice kept the strips of land conceded to her by the triarchs in 1256, as well as the right of levying the tolls; but the prince, as well as the triarchs with their Greek and Latin retainers, and all clerics were exempted from paying them, and the house of his agent at Negroponte was restored to him. Finally, the republic engaged to cancel all fiefs granted by her bailie since the death of Carintana, and received from the prince the right of free trade and personal security for all her subjects throughout his estates. Thus, of all the parties, Venice had gained least by the Eubœan war. She had incurred great expense for no special result, and the island had suffered from the ravages of the soldiers. The Venetian Government felt the failure of its Eubœan policy so strongly, that it prohibited its bailies in Eubœa from interfer-

[1] Χ. τ. Μ., ll. 4360-512; Sanudo, 108; *L. d. C.*, 148-53; *L. d. F.*, 67-8.

ing in questions of feudal rights—a salutary provision, which long remained in force.[1]

The combatants had good reason for making up their differences. They were all alarmed at the restoration of the Greek Empire in Constantinople, and Venice feared even more than the Greeks her ancient rival Genoa, which had just become their ally. A year earlier, shortly before the Latin Empire fell, the Genoese had concluded a treaty with the Emperor Michael VIII. at Nymphaion in Lydia, which by a stroke of the pen transferred from Venice to themselves the monopoly of the Levantine trade. The Ligurian republic, which had taken no part in the labours of the Fourth Crusade, was now granted, in return for its pledge to make war against Venice, free trade throughout the Greek empire and in the Venetian islands of Crete and Negroponte, which the emperor hoped to conquer. The Genoese received permission to found colonies at Anæa, Lesbos, and in the rich mastic-island of Chios, which had been captured from the Latin Empire by Vatátzes fourteen years earlier; they obtained the city of Smyrna, and were assigned after the conquest of Constantinople, the suburb of Galata as their special quarter.[2] Finally, the Black Sea was closed to their enemies. From the treaty of Nymphaion in 1261 dates the growth of Genoa as a Levantine power; from that moment she became an important factor in the Eastern question.

The Prince of Achaia might reasonably imagine that he had nothing to fear from the Genoese, for they had been his allies against Venice, and they had expressly stipulated at Nymphaion that they should not be called upon to make war upon him. But he knew full well that he would ere long have to grapple with the Byzantine Empire in his own land. The Emperor Michael VIII. attached much importance to the new Byzantine province in the Morea, which not only furnished him with excellent light troops, whom he settled at Constantinople and employed as marines on his

[1] *Fontes Rer. Austr.*, xiv., 46-55; Sanudo, 108, 111.

[2] *Liber Jurium Reipublicæ Genuensis*, i., 1345 *sqq.*: a better text is that given in *Atti della Società Ligure*, xxviii., 791-809; X. τ. M., ll. 1277-84; Nik. Gregorâs, i., 97; Hopf, *Les Giustiniani*, 5; Ducange, i., 438-53.

ships,[1] but was also a stepping-stone towards the reconquest of the whole peninsula. An imperial viceroy, called "Captain (κεφαλή) of the Territory in the Peloponnese and its Castles," was appointed, at first for an annual term; a marshal (πρωτοστράτωρ, πρωτοαλλαγάτωρ) was instituted, as in the Frankish principality; and a Byzantine hierarchy grew up around the viceregal residence at Mistrâ.[2] It was therefore obvious that ere long war must ensue between the prince and the imperial viceroy. From 1262, the date of the cession of the fortresses, began the decline of Frankish power in the Peloponnese. Henceforth the rivalry between the Franks of the principality and the Greeks of the adjoining Byzantine province led to almost constant conflicts, which devastated the country, especially as mercenaries were usually employed on both sides, who, in default of their pay, pillaged the hapless inhabitants without mercy. Moreover, in the neighbouring Byzantine districts the discontented Greek subjects of the Franks found support and encouragement; the unity of the Morea was destroyed almost as soon as it had been established, and by the same wilful ruler, and the way was thus ultimately prepared for the Turkish conquest.

In 1263, a year after the peace had been signed in his capital of Thebes, Guy I. of Athens died. During his long reign he had experienced various extremes of fortune, and had enjoyed the privilege of heaping coals of fire upon the head of the foe who had defeated him. He had emerged from his defeat with honour, and he was able to leave to his elder son John, not only a ducal title, but a state which was more prosperous than any other in Greece.

Thus the seventh decade of the thirteenth century marks the close of an era in the history of the Latins in the Levant. The Latin Empire has fallen; a Greek emperor rules once more on the Bosporos, and has gained a foothold in the Morea; a rival of his own race faces him in Epiros, but he has learned the art of dividing the Latins against each other, and has found in Genoa a makeweight against Venice.

[1] Pachyméres, i., 188, 309.

[2] These titles occur in the Mistrâ inscriptions. *Bulletin de Corresp. hellénique*, xxiii., 115, 123.

CHAPTER V

THE GREEK REVIVAL (1262-1278)

It was not to be expected that either Villehardouin or the emperor would long desist—the one from the reconquest of his three lost castles, the other from an extension of his power. On his return to the Morea, the prince set out on a tour of inspection, accompanied by a brilliant retinue. From the rock of Mistrâ the imperial garrison could see the tall Frankish knights and their gallant lord pricking across the fertile plain of the Eurotas to the prince's favourite residence of Lacedæmonia. Not unnaturally, their suspicions were aroused, and they regarded this brave display as a hostile demonstration against themselves. Without delay they called upon the warlike Melings to quit the gorges of Taygetos and rally round the double eagle of Byzantium, and messengers were sent post-haste to apprise the imperial governor of Monemvasia of what seemed to be a breach of the peace. Pope Urban IV., who, as a Frenchman, felt special interest in the prosperity of the "New France" which his countrymen had created oversea, and furnished William with money for its defence,[1] salved any qualms of conscience that the Prince of Achaia might have felt, by telling him that his solemn oath to the emperor had been wrung from him when he was a prisoner, and was therefore not binding; and the Franks might pretend that the Greek garrisons had committed acts of pillage and received the prince's discontented Greek subjects. The news was speedily communicated from Monemvasia to the emperor, who sent thither an army under his brother Constantine, assisted by Philês and Makrenós, two high officials. He had engaged for the campaign a body of 1500 Turks and a number of

[1] *Les Registres d'Urbain IV.*, ii., 47; *Fontes Rer. Austr.*, xiv., 57.

warlike Greeks from Asia Minor, and he strongly enjoined upon his commander to win as many allies as possible in the Morea by the gift of privileges under the imperial seal. Meanwhile, a fleet was despatched under Philanthropenós, mostly manned with Tzakonians from the Peloponnese and with the so-called *Gasmoûloi*, or "bastards," the offspring of mixed marriages between Franks and Greek women, who were particularly valuable soldiers, because they combined Greek caution with Latin courage.[1] This fleet operated against the islands of the Ægean, of which the Prince of Achaia was suzerain, and the south coast of the Morea. The Genoese, unmindful of his services, assisted his enemies by landing a great number of the imperial troops at Monemvasia, and by joining in the attack upon the islands.

The arrival of the imperial force, and the prompt secession of the Melings, the Tzakonians, and the restless inhabitants of the two promontories of Malea and Matapan, whose chiefs were easily won by the promise of privileges and the gift of high-sounding titles, had caused William to summon his great vassals to his aid. They seem to have been somewhat slow in responding to his appeal, but one of them, his old enemy, Guglielmo da Verona, the richest and most powerful of the Eubœan barons, rendered him such great services, that the prince was inclined to reward him with the overlordship over his fellow-triarchs and over the Duke of Athens. An Athenian contingent came to aid in defending the Morea,[2] but the fine flower of all the Achaian chivalry, the doughty Geoffroy de Bruyères, had been ensnared by the charms of a beautiful woman, and had gone with his mistress to Apulia, under the pretext of a visit to the famous shrines of St Nicholas at Bari and of St Michael, on one of the spurs of Monte Gargano. No longer kept in check by the great castle of Karytaina, in the absence of its master, the Slavs of Skortá soon joined those of Taygetos against the Franks.

[1] *Les Registres d'Urbain IV.*, ii., 100, 341. The latter part of the word, μοῦλος, is Moreot Greek for a "bastard"; the first part may be the French *gars*. See Prof. Karolides' note to Paparregópoulos, Ἱστορία τοῦ Ἑλληνικοῦ Ἔθνους, v., 130.

[2] Sanudo, 116. The *Chronicle* says that it did not come.

Meanwhile, William was waiting for his great vassals at Corinth, and the imperial commander, who had so far met with no opposition, and had taken Lacedæmonia and other towns, boasted to the emperor that a third of the Morea was already his, and that if he had more men, he could conquer the whole. Michael VIII. sent him reinforcements, and a distinguished soldier, Michael Cantacuzene, grandfather of the subsequent emperor and historian, and member of an old family which we saw settled in Messenia at the time of the Frankish Conquest, also arrived in the Morea. The imperial commanders had now 6000 cavalry and a large force of infantry at their disposal; they accordingly divided the cavalry into eighteen squadrons, and ordered a march on Andravida, the Frankish capital. Leaving the mart of Veligosti a smoking ruin, they marched past Karytaina, and, guided by some of the Slavs of Skortá, reached Prinitsa, not far from Olympia, having burnt on the way the Latin monastery of Our Lady of Isova, whose Gothic windows still survey the valley of the Alpheios, the Charbon, as the Franks called it.[1] At Prinitsa they were met by a small body of 312 Franks, under the command of Jean de Catavas, husband of the lady with whom Geoffroy de Bruyères had eloped, and a valiant but rheumatic warrior whom the prince had left in charge during his absence at Corinth. Despite the smallness of his forces and his own physical infirmity, which prevented him from holding sword or lance, he ordered the prince's standard—the anchored cross of the Villehardouins—to be tied fast to his hand, and, reminding his men that they were Franks and their enemies men of many nations, bade them win fame which would endure "so long as the ark remains on Ararat." The little band of Franks seemed lost among the Greeks, but they cut down their foes with their swords, "as a scythe mows the meadow grass," while their leader, as he made straight for the tent of Constantine Palaiológos, dressed all in white, seemed to the superstitious Greeks to be none other than St George, guiding the Franks to victory. Some cried that this was the vengeance of the Virgin for the sacrilege at Isova, others that it was retribution for the perjury of the emperor, and

[1] Buchon, *La Grèce Continentale*, 497.

Constantine was glad to mount his swift Turkish horse and ride for his life by devious paths to Mistrâ, leaving his men to escape to the woods.

The season of 1263 was now far advanced, and it was not till the following spring that Constantine re-assembled his Slav and Tzakonian allies, and marched again upon Andravida. Near the chapel of St Nicholas at Mesisklin, a spot not far from the Frankish capital, the two armies met. A Frank had warned the Byzantine general, that one horseman of Achaia was worth twenty Greeks, and that he must use artifice rather than force if he wished to conquer. Despite this warning, Cantacuzene, who was possessed of that boastful spirit which the Greeks usually regarded as a peculiarly Frankish characteristic, insisted upon showing off his horsemanship in front of the enemy's line, and paid with his life for his rashness. At this disaster the Greeks retired without giving battle, and the Prince of Achaia was persuaded to act with prudence and refrain from pursuing them. Dissensions now broke out between Constantine and his Turkish mercenaries. Six months' pay was already owing to them, and as he refused to give it to them, they offered their services to William, whom they believed to be a man of his word. On the banks of the river of Elis the first unholy alliance was made between a Frank ruler of Greece and its future masters. Ancelin de Toucy, a great noble who had settled in the Morea after the fall of Constantinople,[1] and who spoke Turkish, acted as go-between, and William gladly accepted the offer of the Turkish chiefs, Melik and Salik, who were eager to punish their late employers. The Franco-Turkish forces accordingly marched southwards in the direction of Kalamata, and then ascended the beautiful pass of Makryplagi, "the broad hillside," up which the present railway climbs. When Ancelin, who was in command of the van, reached the ridge, the Greeks sprang up from their ambuscade, and fell upon him. Twice the Franks were beaten back, but their commander bade them cease "playing hide-and-seek" with their enemies;[2] they stormed the ridge; the Turks, coming up behind, completed the discomfiture of the Greeks, and the Greek commanders, who had sought

[1] X. τ. M., ll. 1321-4.

[2] *Ibid.*, l. 5395.

refuge in the grotto of Gardiki—a place celebrated two centuries later for two appalling massacres—were discovered by the Turks, and led prisoners before the prince. The emperor's brother had, fortunately for him, returned home before the battle,[1] but his two surviving colleagues, Makrenós and Philês, and many of their followers, were now at William's mercy. The two principal captives were sent to the strong castle of Chloumoûtsi, where Philês died, and his fellow-prisoner, though subsequently exchanged, was accused on his return to Constantinople of collusion with William, who was said to have promised him, as the reward of his treachery, the hand of the widowed daughter of the late Emperor Theodore II., Láskaris, who was living on her Moreot barony of Veligosti.[2] The suspicions of the usurper, Michael VIII., were easily aroused, and he put out the eyes of a general, who might have espoused the claims of the dethroned dynasty.

The victory of Makryplagi had removed all fear of a further attack by the Greeks, and William was able to proceed to his beloved Lacedæmonia, the Greek population of which had fled to Mistrâ. He supplied their places with trusty Franks, whom he bade restore the deserted town, sent his forces to ravage Tzakonia and the country round Monemvasia, and ordered the Turks to plunder the Slavs of Skortá, who, though lately pardoned, had again risen in the absence of the baron of Karytaina. Soon after, Geoffroy de Bruyères, stung by the reproaches of King Manfred, returned penitent to the Morea. He flung himself down before the prince, with his girdle round his neck, in the church of Santa Sofia at Andravida, and, thanks to the good offices of Manfred and the intercession of the nobles, he was a second time forgiven. From that time to his death he loyally served his uncle and prince.

The fighting was now over, and the Turks asked permission to return to their homes in Asia. In vain William pressed their chief to stay; but some of his followers con-

[1] Pachyméres, i., 207; the *Chronicle*, less likely to be well-informed, represents him as one of the captives.

[2] Her first husband had been the baron. Pachyméres, i., 180; Nikephóros Gregorâs, i., 92.

sented to settle in the Morea. All who remained there were baptised; the prince knighted two of them, and gave them fiefs and wives; one of them seems to have married a noble damsel, the lady of Pavlitsa (near Bassæ); and, when the *Chronicle of the Morea* was composed, their posterity was still living at two places in the peninsula. Thus a new element was added to the mixed population of the Morea.[1] The land, indeed, was in danger of becoming desolate, owing to the loss of life in the war; Urban IV. received from the prince and the barons a gloomy picture of its depopulation; and one woman, so Sanudo informs us, lost seven husbands, one after the other, all of whom died in battle.

Disappointed of winning the Morea by force, Michael VIII. now proposed to William that his son and heir, the future Emperor Andrónikos II., should marry the prince's elder daughter, Isabelle, and that Andrónikos should succeed as Prince of Achaia. This arrangement would have not only re-united the Morea with the Greek Empire, and thus spared it much bloodshed, but, by welding Moreot Greeks and Franks closely together, might have so strengthened the principality that it could have offered a better resistance to the Turks later on. But the Frank barons, proud of their nationality, were not willing to accept a Greek as their future sovereign. In spite of the prince's marriage with a Greek princess, the Frank nobles continued to select their wives from the best families in France, and the difference of religion combined with the pride of race to make them disdainful of the connection with Byzantium. As the historian Nikephóros Gregorâs[2] remarked, they despised marriages with Greeks, even with those of imperial blood. Isabelle was destined to make a marriage which united the principality to the fortunes of the great house of Anjou.

Charles of Anjou, the most ambitious prince of his time, had now appeared upon the stage of Italian politics. Summoned by Urban IV. to the throne of the Two Sicilies, he routed Manfred at the historic battle of Benevento; and,

[1] X. τ. M., ll. 4513-5921; *L. d. C.*, 153-99; *L. d. F.*, 69-84; Sanudo, 116-18, 135; *Les Registres d'Urbain IV.*, ii., 292-4; Pachyméres, i., 88, 205-9; Nikephóros Gregorâs, i., 80.

[2] *Ibid.*, i., 237.

not content with having seized the Italian possessions of the Hohenstaufen, he considered himself the heir of those places beyond the sea which Manfred had received as his wife's dowry from the Despot of Epiros. Though the fair Helene of Epiros was now languishing with her children in an Italian dungeon, Filippo Chinardo continued to hold Corfù and the Epirote fortresses, either for her or for himself, a few months longer. But the treacherous Despot, who had first tried to conciliate the bold Frank by giving him his sister-in-law in marriage, together with Corfù, which he was pleased to regard as once more his own to bestow, had him assassinated in 1266, intending to seize Helene's former dowry and re-unite it with his dominions. But Chinardo, short as his rule in Corfù had been, had granted fiefs there to brave knights, such as the brothers Thomas and Garnier Aleman, members of a Provençal family, already settled at Patras, and whose name is still borne by one of the Corfiote deputies. Garnier Aleman undertook the defence of the island against the Despot, till he was able to invoke the aid of his countryman and co-religionist, Charles of Anjou, who, as a reward for his services, named him his vicar and captain-general. Thus, in 1267, the finest of the Ionian islands became a possession of the Angevins of Naples, under whom it remained for more than a century.[1]

Charles was anxious to make Corfù and Epiros a stepping-stone to the conquest of the rest of Greece, and desired, like most conquerors, to have some legal claim to his proposed conquests. There was at that time in Italy the deposed Latin Emperor of Romania, Baldwin II., who, after in vain besieging the reluctant ears of western potentates, thought that he had found in the victor of Benevento the man who would assist him. The exiled emperor and the king of the Two Sicilies met on May 27, 1267, in the presence of Pope Clement IV., in a room of the papal residence at Viterbo—a building recently restored—and there concluded a treaty, which gave the house of Anjou the legal right to intervene in the affairs of Greece. Baldwin II. ceded to Charles the suzerainty held by himself and his predecessors over "the

[1] Pachymeres, i., 508. Buchon, *Nouvelles Recherches*, I., i., 195-201; II., i., 309-11; Minieri Riccio, *Alcuni fatti riguardanti Carlo I.*, 24.

principality of Achaia and Morea, and all the land which William de Villehardouin holds by any title whatsoever from the Latin Empire." William, who was represented by his chancellor, Leonardo of Veroli, one of the witnesses to the treaty, was pledged to recognise Charles and his heirs as his lords, and the famous knights of Achaia were to form part of the 2000 horsemen whom Charles promised to provide for the recovery of the Latin Empire within the space of six, or, at the most, seven years. Baldwin also considered himself entitled to bestow upon Charles the lands which had formed the dowry of Helene of Epiros, and "which had been held by Manfred and Filippo Chinardo," and transferred to him, on paper, all the islands which had belonged to the Latin Empire, except the four most important. The alliance between them was to be cemented by the marriage of Charles's daughter Beatrice and Baldwin's son Philip, which was celebrated six years later. The other provisions of the treaty are of no importance, because the course of Italian politics frustrated the hopes of the high contracting parties that the Empire of Romania would be restored by the strong arm of the Angevin.[1]

The Angevin connection could not fail to please the Prince of Achaia. Charles of Anjou was a Frenchman, and Achaia was practically a French colony; he was the brother of the saintly Louis IX., whom Villehardouin had met in Cyprus, and to whose decision the punishment of Guy of Athens had been deferred, and he was King of Naples, and therefore a powerful neighbour, whose troops could reach Glarentza from Brindisi in three days. Venice, too, ever an uncertain ally, had recently, for selfish reasons, concluded an armistice with the Greek emperor, who had thus a free hand against the Franks of Achaia and the Lombards of Eubœa. The wily Palaiológos swore to observe a "pure and guileless truce"[2] with the Venetians, to confirm them in their existing possessions at Coron and Modon, in Crete and Eubœa, while they promised not to help the Lombards of the latter

[1] Ducange, *Histoire de l'Empire de Constantinople*, i., 455-63; Buchon, *Recherches*, i., 30-7; Nikephóros Gregorâs, i., 98, 123.

[2] The word used, ἀγάπη, mediæval Greek for a "truce," is still the technical expression in Maina for the cessation of a blood-feud.

island, but to remain neutral while the Greeks invaded it, and to allow Michael to retain temporarily the Thessalian port of Halmyros, so that he might prevent the export of provisions for the use of the islanders. As a further reward for this absolutely selfish policy, eminently characteristic of Venetian statesmanship and worthy of modern German diplomacy in the near East, the republic was to receive that valuable Thessalian port and to keep her quarters in Negroponte after the war was over, while the Genoese were to be expelled the Greek Empire, which was to be thrown open to Venetian trade. Those Ægean islands which had acknowledged the suzerainty of the Prince of Achaia during the latter years of the Latin Empire, were now to be transferred to Michael. The armistice, originally made in 1265, was in 1268 confirmed, with one or two modifications, for the term of five years.[1] Thus Venice, in order to checkmate her Genoese rivals and recover her Levantine trade, calmly sacrificed the French and the Lombards.

Before the Prince of Achaia had received assistance from his new suzerain, the latter summoned him to his aid against the luckless Conradin, who had crossed the Alps to claim the heritage of the Hohenstaufen. In spite of the fact that Manfred's widow was his wife's sister, William hastened in response to the appeal of her gaoler. The feudal tie was stronger for him than that of sentiment, and a prince so fond of fighting for fighting's sake was probably not sorry to exhibit his prowess before the most successful sovereign of southern Europe. Together with his two nephews, the redoubtable Geoffroy de Bruyères and Jean de Chauderon, grand constable of the principality, and other barons and knights, 400 in number, the fine flower of the renowned Achaian chivalry, William was present at the fatal battle of Tagliacozzo

> "Ove senz' arme vinse il vecchio Alardo."

Indeed, the defeat of Conradin, which Dante ascribed to the craft of Érard de Valeri, is by the author of the *Chronicle of*

[1] *Fontes Rer. Austr.*, xiv., 66-89, 92-100. Dandolo and Navagero *apud* Muratori, xii., 369; xxiii., 1000.

the Morea, attributed to the Prince of Achaia.[1] According to him, the prince advised Charles of Anjou to use cunning, after the fashion of Greeks and Turks, against an enemy numerically his superior. The King of Naples allowed himself to be guided by William's unrivalled experience of Eastern warfare; and the latter's plan of alluring Conradin's predatory Germans into the king's richly furnished camp, and then closing in upon them while they were intent on plunder, proved to be completely successful. But an unprejudiced authority, the Florentine historian Villani,[2] records how "William de Villehardouin, a knight of great importance," was with Charles and Érard on that memorable day, while Clement IV. urged the appointment of so seasoned a soldier as commander against the rebellious Saracens of Lucera.

After the battle, William accompanied his suzerain to Naples, whence he returned, laden with gifts, to the Morea. He had now been a quarter of a century on the throne; and, as he had no son, he was anxious that his elder daughter, Isabelle, should marry Philip, the second son of Charles of Anjou, and thus strengthen the connection which had existed since the treaty of Viterbo between the Angevins of Naples and the French principality of Achaia. The proposed alliance met with the approval of both the Neopolitan court, which saw that it might favour its designs upon Greece, and the leading men of the Morea, who were glad that the husband of the young princess should be of their own race and speech. But the marriage-contract was extremely favourable to the Angevins, for it stipulated that whether the Prince of Achaia left heirs or not, the principality should belong to the house of Anjou. William also undertook to make all the barons and commanders swear to hand over their castles peaceably to his successor, and to obtain from the Princess Agnes a ratification of these conventions. Thus Charles had secured no mere phantom suzerainty, but the real possession of Achaia after the prince's death, and thereby a convenient basis for the prosecution of his schemes

[1] X. τ. M., 6870-7072; *L. d. C.*, 228-33; *L. d. F.*, 88-9. He also confuses Tagliacozzo with Benevento.

[2] *Apud* Muratori, *op. cit.*, xiii., 249; Del Giudice, *Codice Diplomatico*, ii., 140.

against the Greek Empire. Isabelle was still a mere child, but she was torn from her home, a sacrifice to the *raison d'état*. Four noble ladies and the son of her old nurse, who had probably been her playmate in the castle of Kalamata, went with her; and amidst the greater glories of Naples, they must often have talked of her native land of Achaia. In 1271 the wedding took place in the beautiful cathedral at Trani, and Isabelle and her husband went to live in the Castel dell' Uovo at Naples, the selfsame spot where, sixty years later, her daughter was destined to die a prisoner.[1]

Michael VIII. had meanwhile renewed his attempt to conquer the Morea. A fresh expedition, largely composed of Turkish and Cuman mercenaries, under a commander closely connected with the emperor, landed at Monemvasia, and William was obliged to invoke the aid of his suzerain. Charles sent him corn, money, and men, and appointed his marshal, Dreux de Beaumont,[2] to take command of them. But the operations on both sides were unimportant. The Greeks had learnt wisdom from their defeats at Prinitsa and Makryplagi, and abstained from giving battle in the open, while the Franks had not sufficient supplies for a prolonged blockade of Mistrâ. Thus, after a punitive expedition against the rebellious Tzakonians, the campaign closed, and the emperor was in no hurry to renew it. The artful Michael, alarmed at the marriage of Baldwin II.'s son with Charles's daughter, was at this time endeavouring to gain the support of the papacy and so avert the danger of a fresh attack upon Constantinople by professing his willingness to accept the union of the Eastern and Western Churches. The Prince of Achaia was requested by Gregory X. to allow the imperial delegates to pass through his dominions on their way to attend the Council of Lyons; but the plenipotentiaries, of whom the historian Akropolita was one, were so rash as to make the journey round, instead of across, the Peloponnese

[1] Sanudo, 118-19; Minieri Riccio, *Alcuni Fatti*, 122, 140, 141; *Della Dominazione Angioina*, 3; *Il Regno di Carlo I.*, 19, 20; *L. d. F.*, 91; Muntaner, ch cclxii.; d'Esclot, *Cronaca*. ch. lxiv.; *C. d. M.*, 438.

[2] Buchon, *Nouvelles Recherches*, I., i., 221-6; II., i., 326-7, 329. The *Chronicle of the Morea* confuses De Beaumont with Galeran d'Ivry, who was sent after William's death.

in the month of March. Off Cape Malea, one of the storms so common at that place and season, a *fortuna*, as the sailors call it, got up; one of the two ships foundered with all hands, and the other, which contained Akropolita, with difficulty managed to put into the Venetian port of Modon. The much-suffering historian thence continued his journey to Lyons, and the services which he there rendered to the cause of ecclesiastical union were rewarded, when fanaticism gained the ascendency after the death of Michael VIII., with a second term of imprisonment, which must have reminded him of his previous confinement in the dungeons of Epiros.[1]

Nowhere did the cause of orthodoxy find warmer defenders than in that rival Greek state. In 1271, the Despot of Epiros,[2] Michael II., had ended his long and stormy reign. Amidst all the vicissitudes of fortune, he had contrived to hold his heritage in the mountain fastnesses of his native land against the Greek Empire of Constantinople. Despite the vagaries of his married life, the builder of three monasteries and churches was invested by monkish chroniclers with the odour of sanctity, and the memory of his pious wife, the Blessed Theodora, still lingers in Epiros, where her religious foundations perhaps compensated for some of the misery which her husband's restless ambition had brought upon his country. After his death, she became a nun, and her tomb, with her effigy and that of her husband, is still shown in the monastery of St George, which she founded at Arta, and which now bears her name. Many were the miraculous cures ascribed to her relics, and it was not unnatural that one who had healed a case of cancer should be beatified by a grateful Church.[3]

The death of Michael led to a complete division of the Despotat. His eldest son, Nikephóros I., succeeded to Old Epiros and the island of Leukas. Corfù, as we saw, had already passed into the hands of the house of Anjou, and its

[1] Pachyméres, i., 396-7; *Les Registres de Grégoire X.*, 124.

[2] Hopf (*apud* Ersch und Gruber, lxxxv., 298) fixes his death in 1271, Finlay in 1267.

[3] Buchon, *Nouvelles Recherches*, I., i., 398; II., i., 405-6; Δελτίον τῆς Χριστ. Ἀρχ. Ἑταιρείας, III., 81.

history is henceforth separate from that of the mainland. In Epiros itself, the same strong house had acquired, by the treaty of Viterbo, the former possessions of Manfred; and, though Charles had not yet had leisure to occupy all of them, the Greeks had been unable to recover them from Chinardo's sons, while Joannina was held by an imperial garrison. Still, the sway of Nikephóros extended over the rest of Epiros and over Akarnania and Ætolia, while the bastard John I., who had played so treacherous a part at the battle of Pelagonia, was established at Neopatras, or La Patre as the Franks called it, beneath the rocky walls of Mount Oeta, and thence ruled over a mixed population of Wallachs and Greeks, the successors of those Myrmidons, whom Achilles had led to the siege of Troy. His boundaries were Olympos on the north, and Parnassos on the south; while to the east of the latter mountain they ran down to the Gulf of Corinth, at Galaxidi, and included much of the ancient Lokris Ozolis; from the emperor he received the title *Sebastokrátor*: the Franks, by a misunderstanding of his family name of Doúkas, styled him "Duke" of Neopatras; and, in that splendid and healthy spot where the moderns seek the baths in summer, he had built a strong castle, the ruins of which still attest his sovereignty.[1] Married to a daughter of Taronâs, a Wallach chief, he had enlisted the sympathies of that race; and his opposition to the subjection of the Orthodox Church to the pope, if it drew upon him and his feebler but no less orthodox brother the anathemas of the time-serving patriarch of Constantinople, made him the leading representative of that fanatical Hellenism which arrogated to itself, as it still does to-day, the sole right to the Christian name. Beneath his standard, many rigidly orthodox families of the imperial capital found shelter, some of whose descendants are still living in his old dominions. Among the fugitives there were sufficient ecclesiastics to hold a council, which excommunicated the emperor, the pope, and the œcumenical patriarch, with all the combined bitterness of theologians and exiles. Two of the Thessalian bishops, their Graces of Trikkala and Neopatras, did indeed venture

[1] Nikephóros Gregorâs, i., 109 *sqq.*; Romanós, Γρατιανὸς Ζώρζης, 153, 297; Sáthas, Τὸ Χρονικὸν τοῦ Γαλαξειδίου, 140; X. τ. M., l. 3098.

to protest against this new schism; but the one was put in prison, and the other was stripped of all his garments except his shirt, and then turned out of doors on a freezing December night.[1] After this there could be no doubt of the bastard's orthodox zeal.

His restless character was well known at Constantinople; but the emperor's past experience of the difficulties which his troops had met in their Epirote campaigns, and the state of his Asiatic provinces, made it desirable that he should pacify a rival whom he would find it hard to subdue. Accordingly, he endeavoured to flatter the bastard's vanity by arranging a marriage between his own nephew, Andrónikos Tarchaneiótes, and John's beautiful daughter, and by conferring upon the Duke of Neopatras the high dignity of *Sebastokrátor*. But Tarchaneiótes, who had received an important command in the Balkans, believing himself to have been passed over in the bestowal of honours, threw up his post and fled to the court of his father-in-law, who was not sorry to have an excuse for war with the emperor. The shelter given to his treacherous official, and the violation of his territory by the bastard, forced the emperor to despatch a large army, including both Turkish and Cuman auxiliaries, against him under the command of his own brother John, the victor of Pelagonia, a commander well acquainted with the enemy and the enemy's country. Many places in Thessaly submitted to the imperial commander, and the bastard sought refuge behind the strong walls of Neopatras, which he had recently fortified. The lofty position, and the artificial defences of his capital, enabled him to defy the efforts of the imperial engineers. But the size of the garrison led the bastard to fear that his supplies would fall short, and he was doubtless aware that the besiegers were using threats to induce his followers to betray him. Accordingly, choosing a dark night, he had himself lowered by a rope from the ramparts, and, disguised as a groom, traversed the enemy's camp, crying out in the Greek of the stables that he was looking for a horse which he had lost. Once out of the camp, he proceeded by way of Thermopylæ to Thebes, the

[1] Pachyméres, i., 83; *Les Registres de Nicholas III.*, 134-7; Sáthas, *op. cit.*, 144.

court of his namesake, John, Duke of Athens, "Sir Yanni," as the Byzantine historian calls him, and implored his aid against the emperor. As an inducement to the Duke, he offered him the hand of his daughter Helene. John of Athens declined the proposed match for himself, pleading his delicate health and his gouty disposition, but suggested his younger brother William as a husband for the lady. The bastard consented, but it was agreed that the allies should first attack the enemy. The Duke of Athens, at the head of from 300 to 500 picked Athenian horsemen, accompanied the fugitive back to some rising ground near Neopatras, from which it was possible to see the imperial army, estimated at 30,000 cavalry. This huge disparity of numbers did not, however, daunt the chivalrous duke. In Greek, and in a phrase borrowed from Herodotos,[1] which seems to have become proverbial in Greece, he remarked to his companion that they were "many people, but few men." He then addressed his Athenian knights, and told them that if any feared to face such enormous numerical odds, they were free to go home. Two alone availed themselves of his permission, and then the rest fell upon the imperial camp. The besiegers were completely taken by surprise; their great host, composed of incoherent elements and various races, was thrown into confusion by the compact body of Franks; one of those panics, so common with Balkan armies, seized them; the cry was raised that the Duke of Athens, or even the terrible Prince of Achaia was upon them, and they fled in disorder, and the bastard re-entered his capital in triumph. Byzantine piety ascribed the defeat to the vengeance of Heaven upon the Cuman auxiliaries, who had plundered Thessalian monasteries, and eaten their rations off the holy eikons; a modern historian may say that here, as in so many battles between Greeks and Franks, Providence was on the side of the small but homogeneous and well-horsed battalions. For once, the bastard kept faith with his Frankish ally. His daughter married William de la Roche, and the important town of Lamia, together with Gardiki, the ancient Larissa Kremaste, Gravia on the route from Lamia to Salona, and Siderokastro, or Sideroporta, the ancient

[1] vii., 210.

Herakleia, not far from Thermopylæ, were her dowry.[1] Thus, the influence of the Athenian duchy extended as far north as Thessaly.

The news of the victory at Neopatras soon spread to Eubœa, where the Lombard barons recognised in the bastard a serviceable ally against the Greek emperor, who was his and their enemy alike. Simultaneously with the despatch of his army against the Duke of Neopatras, Michael VIII. had sent a large fleet under his admiral, Philanthropenós, to prevent the Franks of the islands from co-operating with the bastard. This fleet was now stationed off Demetrias, in the Gulf of Volo, and the Eubœan barons, excited by the success of the Franks on land, resolved to repeat it at sea. They manned a flotilla of Eubœan and Cretan vessels, armed with wooden towers, which made them resemble floating towns, and placed it under the command of the son of the late Venetian bailie. The flower of the Lombard nobility took part in an enterprise which, shortly before, would have seemed as hopeless as "shooting arrows against the sky." But for an accident, however, it would have proved successful. The rival fleets joined battle in the beautiful gulf, where the navies of the world could easily lie, and, despite the superior numbers of the Greek ships, the besiegers, from their wooden towers—for the conflict "resembled a siege rather than a naval battle"—severely pressed their opponents. Philanthropenós was seriously wounded, many of his vessels were driven ashore, and his flagship was being towed off by the victors, when John Palaiológos suddenly arrived with the remnant of his defeated army on the scene. Manning the empty ships with the best of his soldiers, he attacked the exhausted Lombards with such vigour that all but two of their ships fell into his hands, one of the triarchs, Guglielmo II. da Verona, who was also in virtue of his wife, the Lady of Passavâ, Marshal of Morea, was slain, and many of the Eubœan nobles and their Venetian commander were taken prisoners. Guglielmo's brother, Giberto, managed to escape on a light armed vessel to Chalkis, which, thanks to the energy of the Venetian bailie and colony, who abandoned their neutrality at the alarm of an attack, and to the prompt

[1] *L. d. C.*, 408, 413; Sanudo, 136.

despatch of reinforcements by the Duke of Athens, was saved from the Greeks.[1]

The Emperor's brother did not, however, attempt to follow up his victory, returning instead with his captives to Constantinople, and then retiring from the public service in disgust. But the Lombards of Eubœa had now to cope with a more serious enemy, who had arisen in their midst, and whom their overweening pride had converted into a valuable tool of Michael VIII. Some time before the battle of Demetrias, there was living in Eubœa a knight of Karystos, named Licario, whose ancestors had come from Vicenza, apparently soon after the Lombard settlement.[2] Licario, a penniless adventurer of great ambition, was, when we first hear of him, attached to the court of Giberto II. da Verona, who succeeded as triarch of central Eubœa after the death of Guglielmo II. in the naval engagement. In Giberto's house was also residing Dame Felisa, widow of the triarch Narzotto, who acted as guardian for her infant son. Felisa was still charming, Licario was ambitious; he dared to avow his love, was told that it was requited, and secretly married her. The fury of her relatives at this *mésalliance* knew no bounds; Licario's endeavours to obtain the intervention of various persons of influence in the Franco-Greek world on his behalf failed; so he returned to Karystos and established himself in a rocky fastness of the island, called, from its exposed position, Anemopylæ, or, "the gates of the wind." Taking unto him other adventurous spirits, in which feudal Eubœa was not lacking, he created such a reign of terror by his frequent descents upon the surrounding fields and villages, that the peasants went to live within the walls of the nearest town, and durst not resume their agricultural pursuits by day without first stationing watchmen to tell them when Licario was coming. But he soon grew tired of plundering peasants, and still thirsted for revenge on the haughty barons who had spurned him. He therefore entered into negotiations with

[1] Pachyméres, i., 307-9, 322-36; Nikephóros Gregorâs, i., 109-20; Sanudo, 120-2; *Les Registres de Nicholas III., loc. cit*; M. Palaiológos, 8.

[2] Sanudo, 119—a passage which effectually disproves the idea of Finlay (iv., 141) that Licario was a Genoese of the famous Zaccaria family. The Byzantine historians call him Ikários.

the emperor; and, finding his overtures welcomed, proceeded to Constantinople, where he placed his services at Michael's disposal. He told the emperor that he would undertake to subdue the whole of the island, if he were given sufficient forces, and offered to hand over his own fortress, so that it might serve as a basis of attack. His plan was accepted, soldiers were put at his disposal, and he carried on a guerrilla warfare against the Lombards, which inflicted great harm on the island; Oreos was taken, and he seized and fortified the castle of La Cuppa. The triarchs received, however, valuable assistance from their suzerain, the Prince of Achaia, who availed himself of a lull in the war against the Greeks in the Morea to come over to Negroponte with as many men as he could collect, and wrested La Cuppa from its Greek garrison. A more voluble but less useful ally was Dreux de Beaumont, the marshal of Charles of Anjou, who accompanied the prince with 700 men. To judge from his boasts, he was going to drive the Greeks into the sea, but his obstinacy brought upon him a signal rout under the walls of Oreos.

After the defeat of the Lombards' fleet off Demetrias, Licario prosecuted his campaign in Eubœa with still greater success. Many of the islanders had now flocked to his standard, and he ventured to besiege the strong "red castle" of Karystos, his own birthplace. Othon de Cicon, the Burgundian baron of Castel Rosso, held out for long against a combined attack by land and sea, but he was at last compelled to surrender, and Licario was richly rewarded by his imperial master for his capture of this great prize. Michael VIII., like the Comneni before him, had adopted the principles of feudalism, and he, accordingly, invested his faithful henchman with the whole island as a fief, on condition that he kept 200 knights for the service of his liege lord. He also bestowed on him the hand of a noble and rich Greek lady, who took the place of the fair Felisa. These marks of favour spurred Licario to further efforts; the important castles of La Cuppa, Larmena, and La Clisura were all taken and re-fortified. Even beyond the shores of Eubœa his hand was felt. The neighbouring island of Skopelos was regarded as impregnable by its inhabitants;

even if all the realm of Romania were lost—so they boasted—they would escape in safety, and Filippo Ghisi, the proud island baron, was fond of applying to himself the line of Ovid, "I am too big a man to be harmed by fortune." But Licario, who knew that Skopelos lacked water, invested it during a hot summer, forced it to capitulate, and sent its haughty lord in chains to Constantinople. Far to the south we find Licario in the Bay of Navarino, "the port of rushes,"[1] as it was called, and he drove the Venieri from their island of Cerigo, the Viari from theirs of Cerigotto. Venice became naturally alarmed at these successes; she did not desire the system of triple government in Eubœa to be superseded by the establishment of a strong, centralised administration in the hands of an able man, who might found a dynasty. So, when she renewed her truce with the emperor in 1277, she expressly stipulated that she should be allowed "to help and defend the island of the Evripos and those in it against your majesty."[2]

The emperor continued to make use of his corresponding right to levy war against the island, and Licario, supported by the Greek fleet at Oreos, and by a body of Catalan mercenaries, who now make their first appearance in Greek history, resolved upon nothing less than an attack upon its capital. Knowing from bitter experience "the superciliousness of the Latins," who were sure to make the mistake of despising, and rushing out to attack a foreign enemy, he laid an ambuscade for the impetuous garrison, and then appeared in sight of the town. Duke John of Athens, the hero of Neopatras, was then in Negroponte, and, gouty as he was, he mounted his horse and rode out of the gate with the triarch Giberto da Verona and their followers along the road in the direction of Oreos and the north. The rival forces came to close quarters at Varonda, the modern village of Vathondas; the Catalan knife and the generalship of Licario were too much for the impetuous Franks; the Duke of Athens was wounded, and, unable to keep his gouty feet in the stirrups, fell to the ground and was taken prisoner with Giberto and many others. The town of Negroponte now seemed to lie

[1] *Fontes Rer. Austr.*, xiv., 237.

[2] *Ibid.*, xiv., 133-49; Miklosich und Müller, iii., 84-96; Dandolo *apud* Muratori, xii., 393.

at the mercy of Licario, but a crushing defeat of the imperial forces on the mainland, and the energy of the Venetian bailie, combined to save it. Simultaneously with the despatch of the Greek fleet to Oreos, another army had been sent, under the two imperial generals, Synadenós and Kavallários, to attack the redoubtable bastard of Neopatras. The bastard met them on the historic plain of Pharsala, famous alike in the struggles of Roman against Roman and of Greek against Turk. His clever strategy, and the rush of his Italian auxiliaries, decided the day; one of the Greek commanders was captured; the other fled, only to die of his injuries. Meanwhile, at Negroponte, Morosini Rosso, known as "the good bailie" for his lavish expenditure on the improvement of the town, had taken prompt measures for its defence, and the news of its danger had at once been sent to Jacques de la Roche, who governed Argos and Nauplia for his cousin, the Duke of Athens. By forced marches, the governor reached Negroponte in the incredibly short space of twenty-four hours, and the city was saved. Licario contented himself with occupying the fine castle of Filla, and then set out with his prisoners in chains to Constantinople. His revenge was complete; his haughty brother-in-law, Giberto, in whose train he had once been a humble knight, was now his prisoner, while he stood high in the confidence of his sovereign, and received the dignity of Great Constable of the Empire as a further mark of imperial favour. A Byzantine historian has depicted the final scene of Licario's triumph in dramatic language, worthy of the best days of Hellenic literature. He shows us Giberto waiting as a prisoner at the door of the audience-chamber, while the emperor is seated on his throne, surrounded by his councillors. Then Licario enters, but yesterday Giberto's servant, now arrayed in all the splendour of his official robes, and showing by his haughty manner how great a man he had become. The prisoner's pulse beats faster and faster, the fellow is actually whispering into the imperial ear! This was more than Lombard pride could bear; Giberto burst a blood-vessel, and fell dead upon the floor.

Michael VIII. might well be proud of his triumphs. He had not only recovered the capital of the empire, but had

had the rulers of the two strongest Frankish states in Greece in his power. He did not, however, avail himself of Duke John's captivity to extort territory from the Franks of Athens as he had done in the similar case of Villehardouin. It might have been expected that he would have rounded off the Byzantine province in the Morea by insisting on the cession of the Athenian fief of Argos and Nauplia as the price of the duke's freedom. On the contrary, he did not ask for a single stone of the Athenian fortresses. He even thought of giving his prisoner his daughter in marriage and so converting him into an ally. John's state of health, however, was such that a marriage was inadvisable, and the emperor accordingly released him on payment of 30,000 gold *solidi* (£13,440).[1] We may be sure that it was policy and not generosity which prompted this act of forbearance. Michael VIII. knew that at that moment Charles of Anjou, a man whose ambitious designs he dreaded, was at last preparing his long-expected expedition against the Greek Empire. Nearer home he had a restless and victorious rival in the person of the Duke of Neopatras, who was bound by ties of marriage to the ducal house of Athens, by ties of friendship and commerce to the royal house of Naples.[2] Finally, in the midst of his own capital, there was a body of discontented ecclesiastics, who regarded as a schismatic the man who had sent envoys to the pope and had endeavoured to prevent the dismemberment of his empire by uniting the churches. Michael was a cautious statesman, and he saw that the policy adopted in 1262 would not answer in 1279. Duke John of Athens did not long survive his release from captivity; in 1280 he died, and his brother William, baron of Livadia, reigned in his stead.[3]

Licario returned to his native island after his signal triumph over his own and the emperor's enemies at Constantinople, and took up his abode in the great castle of Filla, whose imposing ruins still look down upon the

[1] Nikephóros Gregorâs, i., 95-7; Pachyméres, i., 205, 410-13; Sanudo, 119-20, 122-7, 136; Magno, 181-2.

[2] Del Giudice, *La Famiglia di Re Manfredi*, 393-7; *Arch. Stor. Ital.*, Ser. III., xxii., 16, 19; xxiii., 237.

[3] *Arch. Stor. Ital.*, Ser. IV., iii., 162.

Lelantian plain. Outside the walls of Chalkis he was now master of the island, and he maintained such a reign of terror that no one could go in safety to attend to the vineyards in the plain, nor could the priests "bless the waters" of the classic fountain of Arethusa at Epiphany.[1] Beyond Eubœa, he continued to make the Franks rue the day when he had gone over to the enemy. Ere long, he succeeded Philanthropenós as Byzantine admiral, with the usual style of "Grand Duke," attached to that high official, and in that capacity ravaged the islands of Seriphos and Siphnos, which he captured from their Latin lords, took many castles on the mainland, and made an annual raid with the fleet upon the dominions of Duke William of Athens. Then his name disappears from history; we know not how he ended, nor what became of the children whom his rich Greek wife had borne him. His strange and romantic career strikes the imagination, and even in that age of adventurers he stands out above his fellows. No renegade Latin had inflicted so much injury on his fellow-countrymen. He had wrested almost all Eubœa from the Lombards; he and his Byzantine allies had captured almost all the Ægean islands from their Italian lords, and some of them remained henceforth part of the imperial dominions. Even as far east as Paphlagonia, he had won laurels by defeating the Turks.[2] Another Latin succeeded him in the post of Lord High Admiral, the pirate captain John de lo Cavo of Anaphe, who continued, though in less dramatic fashion, the destruction wrought by the low-born knight of Karystos.

Meanwhile, the long reign of William de Villehardouin in the Morea had drawn to a close. After 1272 the war between Franks and Greeks in the peninsula languished, owing to the negotiations between Michael VIII. and the papacy, and William and Dreux de Beaumont were able, as we saw, to go over to help the Lombards of Negroponte against Licario. Three years later, however, the Greeks

[1] I take this to be the meaning of Sanudo's phrase, *batizar la Croce al Fonte*—a ceremony I have myself seen in Greece. The *Fonte* is, of course, the famous Arethusa, which one passes in going from Chalkis to Filla and the Lelantian plain.

[2] Pachyméres, i., 413; Sanudo, 127, 144; Nikephóros Gregorâs, i., 98.

renewed hostilities, and the prince ordered his nephew, Geoffroy de Bruyères, to take the Angevin auxiliaries, whom Charles had placed at his disposal as his captain-general, and garrison the southern frontier of Skortá. Geoffroy accordingly proceeded with his men to a place to which the Slavs of Skortá had given, from its numerous walnut-trees, the name of Great Aráchova, and which, still known under that Slavonic designation, may be found to the left of the road between Tripolitza and Sparta.[1] There the French soldiers contracted a fatal gastric fever from rash indulgence in the cold water, with which the place abounded, and, though their leader pluckily led the remnant of them against the Greeks, he succumbed himself to the disease, thus ingloriously closing his varied career. In the Greek *Chronicle of the Morea* he has found his funeral epitaph: "All, great and small, mourned his loss, even the very birds, which have no speech; for he was the father of the orphan, the husband of the widow, the lord and defender of the poor." But his Greek foes could not refrain from rejoicing at the death of "the best knight of all Romania."[2]

The rest of Prince William's reign was mainly occupied by feudal disputes, which do not always reflect very highly on the character of that warrior, who is a finer figure leading his knights to battle than when relying on technicalities in the High Court. The double desertion by Geoffroy of his liege lord had been punished, as we saw, by the restriction of his barony of Skortá to himself and the heirs of his body, so that, as he left no children, it escheated, on his death, to the prince, who allowed Geoffroy's widow, Isabelle de la Roche, to retain one-half of it as her portion, according to the usual custom of the country. Against this a certain knight, named Pestel, protested as next-of-kin, and appealed from the prince to Charles of Anjou, as suzerain of Achaia. Charles ordered his vassal to invest Pestel with the barony; but William

[1] The "cold fountain" near this spot, and two other passages of the *Chronicle* (*L. d. C.*, 379, 385) favour this identification, though this Aráchova is rather far to the south to be included in Skortá. Buchon hence put it near Demetsana. (*La Grèce Continentale*, 492). The name is very common.

[2] Χ. τ. Μ., ll. 7177-232; *L. d. C.*, 236; *L. d. F.*, 92.

disregarded his orders, and there for the present the matter rested. Isabelle, on her part, did not long remain a widow. Two years after her late husband's death, she married Hugh, Count of Brienne and Lecce, an old friend of her father, Duke Guy I. of Athens, and member of a family destined to be even more celebrated in the history of Greece, than it had been in that of France, Italy, and the Holy Land. The family came, like that of Champlitte, from Champagne, where it first appears in the reign of Hugh Capet. In the early part of the thirteenth century two brothers of this adventurous house had won fame, the one in Italy, the other in the East. Walter, the elder, was invested by Innocent III. with the dignity of Count of Lecce, near Brindisi, while John, the younger, became King of Jerusalem and Emperor of Constantinople. Walter's son, fourth of the name, was created Count of Jaffa by the King of Cyprus, and died, after excruciating tortures, in the prisons of the paynim. His son, Hugh, who now became connected with the affairs of Athens and Achaia, was already well known to the prince and the barons of the Morea. An hereditary enemy of the Hohenstaufen in Southern Italy, he had fought against Manfred at Benevento, and had stood by the side of Prince William and Charles of Anjou at Tagliacozzo. The reward of his services was the restoration to him of his forfeited possessions at Lecce. In 1277 his marriage with Isabelle was celebrated at Andravida, in the presence of the bride's brother, Duke John of Athens. Hugh received his wife's half of the great barony of Skortá, and, after arranging its affairs and appointing bailies to look after his interests, he sailed with her to Apulia. Not long afterwards, Isabelle died, leaving a son, who was destined to be the last French Duke of Athens.[1]

Another feudal case caused the prince considerably more trouble than that of the barony of Skortá. It will be remembered that, when he had been released from imprisonment at Constantinople in 1262, one of the hostages sent there on his behalf was the Lady Marguerite, daughter of Jean II. de Neuilly, baron of Passavâ, and hereditary Marshal of Achaia. While Marguerite was still a hostage at

[1] X. τ. M., ll. 7240-60, 237-9; *L. d. C.*, 237-9; *L. d. F.*, 92; Sanudo, 117; Buchon, *Nouvelles Recherches*, I., i., 231-3.

Constantinople, her uncle Gautier II. de Rozières, baron of Akova or Matagrifon, as the Franks called it, died without heirs of his body. As the Salic law did not prevail in Frankish Greece, Marguerite was entitled to the barony as the next-of-kin; but her compulsory absence from the Morea prevented her from making her claim within the term of two years and two days, provided by feudal law for claimants abroad. The prince thereupon declared the barony forfeited to the crown, and, when Marguerite was at last released and claimed her inheritance, he ungenerously raised the technical plea that the time for making such a claim had expired—a piece of chicanery similar to that by which his father had won the principality. In vain the lady pleaded that she had been absent on his service, William ungallantly stuck to the letter of the law. Unprotected and helpless, for both her husbands had been killed in battle—Guibert de Cors at Karydi, and Guglielmo II. da Verona in the sea-fight off Demetrias—she was advised by her friends to marry some influential man, who would espouse her cause. The idea met with her approval, and her choice lighted upon Jean de St Omer, brother of Nicholas II., who was hereditary lord of half Thebes, where he built the magnificent castle, of which the Santameri tower is the sole surviving fragment. By this marriage Jean became hereditary Marshal of Achaia, and his family thus extended its authority south of the Gulf of Corinth. Jean de St Omer did not allow his wife's claim to be neglected, and demanded to be heard before the court of the principality. The prince convened the court in the church of the Divine Wisdom at Andravida, and Jean, his wife, and his two brothers, Nicholas and Othon, appeared before it. Then the lord of Thebes arose, proud of his lineage—for his grandmother had been widow of Boniface of Salonika, and daughter of the King of Hungary, while the Duke of Athens was his first cousin—and stated his sister-in-law's case. The prince, nettled at his arrogant demeanour, asked him whether he demanded the barony of Akova for her as a right or begged it as a favour, and when the Theban baron replied that he asked no favour, but only what was justly due, William summoned all the barons, prelates, and vassals of the principality to consider the question thoroughly.

This second parliament was held in the Minorite church of St Francis at Glarentza, and the prince, handing his sceptre to the chancellor, Leonardo of Veroli, descended himself into the arena to plead the cause of the crown in person. In lawyer-like fashion he called for the Book of Customs, and cited the chapter relating to the obligation of a vassal to become a hostage for his lord. The Court seemed at first decidedly in favour of the claimant, but when the prince again called its attention to the letter of the law, it gave its judgment against her. William thanked the Court for its decision, but Jean de St Omer was so much offended that he refused even to go through that usual form.

Having thus obtained a confirmation of his legal position, William could afford to be generous. He called for the chancellor, told him that he had been irritated by the arrogance of the barons of St Omer, but that, now that he had gained the case, he wished to give one-third of the barony as a favour to the Lady Marguerite. Accordingly Colinet, the Lord Chamberlain of the principality, and the elders of the barony, who knew its boundaries and history, were ordered to come with the minutes of the baronial court, and eight of the twenty-four fiefs of Akova were selected for her. A deed was at once drawn up and sealed by the chancellor; it was placed under the coverlet of the prince's bed, and Marguerite was summoned to the presence of her lord. Then the chancellor drew back the coverlet, and disclosed the document. The prince handed it to her, and invested her with his glove, while the remaining two-thirds of the barony were bestowed upon her namesake, the prince's younger daughter, Marguerite.[1]

Not long after this William died. When he felt his end approaching, he retired to his beloved castle of Kalamata, the family fief of the Villehardouins, where he had been born. To his bedside he summoned the nobles of the principality, and asked their counsel in making his will. His wife, his two daughters, and his subjects, great and small, he com-

[1] Χ. τ. Μ., ll. 7301-752; *L. d. C.*, 240-54; *L. d. F.*, 85-7; *Liber Consuetudinum*, *apud* Canciani, *op. cit.*, III., 505; *Les Registres de Nicholas III.*, 26. Both he and Clement IV. (*Registres*, i., 101) call her Catharina.

mended to the care of King Charles I. of Naples, and appointed Jean de Chauderon, the Great Constable, Archbishop Benedict of Patras, and the Bishop of Modon, as his executors. The first of them was to administer the affairs of the principality, until Charles had had time to appoint a bailie. He begged that all his gifts, whether to Latin and Greek monasteries, or to private individuals, should be respected, and directed that his body should be buried in the memorial church of St James at Andravida, which he had built and presented to the Templars, beside those of his father and brother. Then on 1st May 1278 he died. The last of the Villehardouin princes was laid to rest as he had ordered, and four chaplains were appointed, in accordance with his wishes, to pray for the souls of the three departed in the church of St James. The outline of the church can still be traced, but no archæologist has disturbed the long repose of the French rulers of the Morea. *Requiescant in pace!* [1]

It was a great misfortune for the principality that William left no son to inherit it. With him the male stock of the Villehardouins came to an end, for the "Prince of the Morea," mentioned by the Byzantine historian Pachyméres [2] as having become patriarch of Antioch, and being at one time a likely candidate for the œcumenical throne, cannot be proved to have been a brother of Prince William. Nor was the latter's son-in-law, Philip of Anjou, alive at the time of his death. The young prince had overstrained himself in bending a crossbow, and never got over the effects of the injury. A year before his father-in-law he died, and in the beautiful cathedral at Trani, where, six years earlier, his marriage had been celebrated, he found a grave.[3] Thus the Villehardouin family was now reduced to William's two daughters, of whom Isabelle, according to the Catalan

[1] X. *τ*. M., ll. 7757-810; *L. d. C.*, 254-6; *L. d. F.*, 92; Buchon, *La Grèce Continentale*, 509-10; *Arch. Stor. Ital.*, Ser. IV., i., 436, which fixes the true date to 1278.

[2] i., pp. 402, 437. The story may have arisen from the fact that there was a *Giufridus*, *clericus*, *consanguineus principis Achaiæ*, who had a cure of souls at Olena, and whom Gregory IX. ordered to be presented to a better living. (*Registres*, ii., 851.)

[3] Sanudo, 119; *Arch. Stor. Ital.*, Ser. III., xxvi., 11, 211.

chronicler Muntane;[1] was only fourteen years old, though already a widow, and Marguerite was two years younger. Their Greek mother, Anna of Epiros, or Agnes as the Franks called her, who received the castles of Kalamata and Chloumoûtsi for her life, soon afterwards married Nicholas II. of St Omer, the proud baron who had treated her first husband with such arrogance. Henceforth, in the hands of women, the principality naturally declined. There was no strong man to keep the unruly barons in check; the bailies whom the kings of Naples appointed were sometimes foreigners, ignorant of the country and its conditions, and after the time of Villehardouin only four princes of Achaia ever resided in the land, whence they took their title. Moreover, by this time a change had come over the feudal society of the Morea. Of the twelve original baronies, two alone—Vostitza and Chalandritza—remained in the families of the old barons. Two—Kalavryta and probably Geraki—had been lost to the Greeks since the fatal re-establishment of the imperial power in the peninsula; Patras had early passed from the Aleman family to the archbishop; and, though it seems to have returned to its secular lords, William Aleman had more recently pledged it to the primate for 16,000 *hyperperi* (£7168), and had left the country;[2] the baron of Gritzena has never been mentioned again, and had, therefore, probably died without heirs; the families of Karytaina, Akova, Veligosti, Passavâ, and Nikli were all extinct in the male line, and those great baronies passed by marriage either altogether or in part to the houses of Brienne, St Omer, De la Roche, and De Villiers. Of the two Villehardouin family fiefs, Arkadia had been bestowed by the late prince upon Vilain d'Aunoy, Marshal of Romania, one of the French nobles who had emigrated from Constantinople to the Morea after the fall of the Latin Empire;[3] while Kalamata was temporarily in the hands of the Princess Agnes, not only a woman but a Greek, and was soon exchanged, together with Clermont, the rest of her widow's portion, for other lands in less important strategic positions.[4] Nothing is more remarkable in the history of Frankish Greece than the rapidity with

[1] Ch. cclxii. [2] *L. d. F.*, 88. [3] X. τ. M., ll. 1325-7.
[4] *Arch. Stor. Ital.*, Ser. IV., iv., 176-7.

which the race of the conquerors died out. Only two generations had passed since they first set foot in the Peloponnese, yet already many of their families were extinct. The almost ceaseless wars of Prince William, and the racial suicide which the Franks committed by keeping themselves as far as possible a caste apart from the Greeks, had had the natural results, and where they intermarried with the natives, the children were almost always more Greek than French, serving on the emperor's ships and fighting the emperor's battles. One of the few exceptions to this tendency was where, for reasons of state, a French prince married a Greek princess, as in the case of William of Achaia and his namesake of Athens. But in mediæval Greece, as in modern Europe, mixed marriages between sovereigns bear no resemblance to those between private individuals; in almost every instance, the offspring of a royal union sympathises with the nationality with which his interests are identified; whereas, the *Gasmoûlos*, despised by the haughty Franks, found a welcome and a career in the service of the Greek Empire.

No contemporary authority informs us what became of the Franks who had lands in that part of the Morea which was reconquered by the Greeks after 1262. We know, indeed, that one prominent man, Jean de Nivelet, baron of Geraki, settled down at a place near Vostitza, to which he gave his family name.[1] No doubt some others followed his example, and it is probable that several of the smaller persons found a new home within the Venetian colonies of Modon and Coron. But those twin trading settlements were circumscribed, the conditions of life there would scarcely appeal to the fighting chivalry of France, and, as the Frank principality grew less, it must have become harder for them to find even small estates, where they could live the life to which they had been accustomed down in the south. To return to France was difficult; for two whole generations spent in the East must have unfitted them for the West, just as to-day, the Levantine who is happy at Smyrna is miserable in London or Berlin. The only course open to many of them was to remain in the Byzantine province, where fusion

[1] *L. d. F.*, 137; Schmitt, *The Chronicle of Morea*, liv.

with the Greek race awaited them, and, as its natural corollary, the adoption of the orthodox religion by themselves or their children—a phenomenon which meets us in the case of the Franks of Arkadia sixty years later. Where the Italian element in Greece has been strong and compact, and where Latin rule has endured, as in the Ionian and Ægean islands, for many centuries, it has been possible for the descendants of the Venetians to keep their own religion, and even their own speech. But that has not been the case in the Peloponnese, in continental Greece, or in Eubœa. On the other hand, the Moreot Franks were never fanatical Catholics; Prince William endowed Greek monasteries; his brother appropriated Catholic revenues; the rank-and-file may therefore have thought that the omission of the *filioque* clause from the creed was a small price to pay for their undisturbed residence among the Greeks of the Byzantine province, where, as time went on, they became merged in that extraordinary nationality which has assimilated one race after another upon the soil of Hellas.

All over Frankish Greece an era seemed to have closed with the death of the foremost Frank ruler of his time. Across the Gulf of Corinth, Thomas II. of Salona, who had married one of William's nieces, and had stood by his side on the stricken field of Pelagonia, had lately died, and his son William held the noble castle in his stead.[1] His fellow-warden of the marches, Ubertino, Marquis of Boudonitza, another of the combatants of Pelagonia, had been succeeded by his sister Isabella.[2] In Thessaly, on the ruins of the baronies which Boniface had distributed among his German and Lombard followers,[3] and of which that of Larissa was now the sole, and perhaps merely nominal, survivor, there had arisen, under the vigorous Despots of Epiros, a Greek

[1] We know of the existence of this man from the notice in the Angevin archives of the marriage of his daughter Agnes to Dreux de Beaumont, Charles of Anjou's marshal, in 1275. (Hopf *apud* Ersch und Gruber, lxxxv., 292). The bride's father is there described as "Guglelmo domino de Salona." Sáthas, Τὸ *Χρονικὸν τοῦ* Γαλαξειδίου, 237).

[2] Riccio, *Nuovi Studii*, 11.

[3] A baroness, Beatrice de Larissa, is mentioned as late as 1280 (*ibid.*, 5); but she had probably lost her estates, while retaining her ancestors' title, and doing homage for her phantom barony to Princess Isabelle.

feudal system, which closely imitated that of the Franks. At this time the most important of these Greek feudal lords was the great family of Melissenós, which we found connected by marriage with the Epirote dynasty at the time of the Frankish Conquest. The Melissenoí received from Michael II. monastic lands in the district of Halmyros, recovered from "the Greek-eating Latins." They were a family of conspicuous piety; they founded the monastery of Our Lady at the picturesque village of Makrinitza, which peeps out of one of the folds of Pelion, "the mountain of the defile,"[1] as it is called in the Greek of the period, and endowed that of St John Baptist at Nea Petra, near Demetrias—institutions which both received charters from the Emperor Michael VIII.; while two of the Melissenoí renounced the pomps of the world, left behind them their splendid coat-of-arms, the double-eagle,[2] the bees, and the bells, and retired into monastic cells. Another local magnate, Michael Gabrielópoulos, styled himself in 1295 "lord of Thessaly," and made Phanari, near Trikkala, his headquarters, promising the citizens that he would never introduce Albanian colonists or a Frankish garrison there. Thus, Thessaly was already being prepared, under Greek auspices, for the introduction of the *timariot*, or Turkish feudal system, a little more than a century later—a system of which we may still see the traces in the large estates which characterise that latest addition to the modern Greek kingdom. There, under mediæval Greek rule, the system of cultivation by serfs prevailed, as in Corfù and the Morea, and a golden bull of the Emperor Michael enumerates the villains of the monastery of Makrinitza in the same category as its mills, both equally its property. Thessaly, like Thebes, was at this time celebrated for its silk, and many thousand pounds of that commodity were exported thence to Apulia by the Duke of Neopatras.

Of the internal condition of the Athenian Duchy at this period we can glean but little. From the fact, however, that Duke John was able to lend money for the pay of the Angevin troops in the Morea, we may assume that his finances were satisfactory, and a Venetian document of 1278

[1] Τὸ ὄρος τοῦ Δρόγγου. Miklosich und Müller, iv., 331-6, 345-9; v., 260.
[2] Buchon, *Atlas*, plate xli., 20.

mentions subjects of the republic who were settled as merchants at *Satines*, as Athens now began to be called in the vernacular from an amalgamation of the preposition with the accusative (εἰς τὰς Ἀθήνας).[1] From a notice two years earlier we learn that at that time the beautiful abbey of Daphni was the sole surviving possession of the Cistercians on Greek soil. The ecclesiastical establishment of Athens had, indeed, become a comfortable home for those members of the ducal family who had entered the Church. We hear of two De la Roche who were canons of Athens at this period; one of them, Nicholas, has left his name as "founder" of some mediæval building on one of the pillars of the Stoa of Hadrian; the other, William, was made "procurator of the Athenian Church"; but, despite the prayers of the chapter, Clement IV. declined to appoint as Archbishop of Athens one who had "a grave defect in the matter of literature."[2] Obviously the influential canon was not a reading man.

Great changes had occurred in the Ionian islands during the period covered by this chapter. While Leukas still remained united to the Despotat of Epiros, whose ruler was now the feeble Nikephóros I., Corfù had become a possession of the house of Anjou, and Cerigo had passed into the hands of the great Monemvasiote family of Daimonoyánnes, with whom it remained for forty years. Over the three central islands of Cephalonia, Zante, and Ithaka, there now ruled "the most high and mighty palatine count, Richard Orsini," like his father Matthew, a vassal of the Prince of Achaia, and consequently bound by the same feudal tie to King Charles of Naples. In the next chapter we shall have occasion to mention this remarkable man, who was destined to play a conspicuous part in the history of both Corfù and Achaia. During the present period we find him confirming, in 1264, the possessions of the Catholic bishopric of Cephalonia, which, as we saw, was united with that of Zante, in a voluminous document of much value for the contemporary geography of

[1] *Archivio Storico Italiano*, Ser. III., vol. xxii., 16, 19; IV., i., 9; *Font. Rer. Austr.*, xiv., 178, 186.

[2] *Les Registres d'Urbain IV.*, iii., 426; Δελτίον, ii., 28; *Les Registres de Clément IV.*, i., 214, 245; Martène et Durand, *Thesaurus*, iv., 1453.

the diocese. The numerous Italian names which it contains point to the existence of a large Italian colony, the descendants of Margaritone's men. It specially mentions the island of Ithaka as part of his dominions, and calls the ancient home of Odysseus by its classic name, which also occurs in a Venetian document of some years later, where it is mentioned as the scene of piracies. Horses and mules seem to have been as scarce in his islands as in the time of Homer, for he had to ask permission of King Charles to import those animals from the rolling plains of Apulia to his rocky domain.[1]

The three Venetian colonies now left in Greece proper—at the town of Negroponte and the two Messenian stations of Coron and Modon—had naturally been affected by the disturbed state of the Levant during the hostilities between the Franks and the Emperor Michael VIII. Since the loss of Constantinople, Negroponte had become far more important to the republic, the salary of the Venetian bailie had been raised, and money had been spent freely on the town, so much so, indeed, that the Venetian Sanudo comments on the great expenses incurred by his fellow-countrymen in the Near East, "and especially for the preservation of Negroponte."[2] An inscription of 1273 tells how the then bailie built a chapel of St Mark—a proof of piety, or more probably of the increase of the Venetian colony.[3] The occupation of the whole island outside the walls of the capital must have greatly damaged the traffic in corn, oil, and wine, wax and honey, raw and worked silk, which are mentioned as the products of Eubœa in the thirteenth century,[4] and the same was the case with the wine and oil trade of the two Messenian stations, to which, however, on other grounds, Venice naturally attached great value. Scarcely a man-of-war, scarcely a trading ship on her way to the Archipelago, the Black Sea, or the Sea of Azov, failed to be sighted by the Venetian watchmen at Coron and Modon, so appropriately called "the chief eyes of the republic," and there was money, too, to be made by

[1] Miklosich und Müller, v., 16-67; *Font. Rer. Austr.*, Abt. II., xiv., 215; Sanudo, 116; *Arch. Stor. Ital.*, Ser. IV., i., 13.

[2] P. 174.

[3] Spon, *Voyage*, ii., 247.

[4] *Fontes Rer. Austr.*, xiii., 93, 95, 176, 177, 179, 181, 183; xiv., 15.

the Jewish, and not less by the Christian, tradesmen of the two ports, out of the pilgrims, who put in there on their way to the Holy Sepulchre. Whenever, too, the Franks were besieging a castle, it was here that they went for the makers of siege-engines. Coron was the more important of the two: its cochineal was celebrated, and when, about this time, the number of the captains of these stations was increased from two to three, two of the trio resided there, while in critical times a bailie was sent as a consul.

In the other parts of the Morea, there was a trade done in raisins and figs, oil, honey, wax, and cochineal, sufficient to attract the merchants of Florence and Pisa, while silk and sugar, small in quantity and poor in quality, were also produced; but the famous vineyards of Monemvasia, whence our ancestors got their Malmsey, had passed into the hands of the Greeks. During the intermittent war with the latter, the principality constantly suffered from lack of corn, which had to be imported, like horses, from Apulia. In 1268 the prince asked his new suzerain for the loan of 2000 ounces of gold (£4800), in order "to repair the ravages made by war on his land," and at the same time his private affairs were so unsatisfactory that he was forced to pledge valuables to the amount of 127 ounces (or a little over £300) at the pawnshops of Barletta, in order to pay his way. But at the time of his death, he was able to charge the annuity of £1054, which he left to one of his executors, upon the customs-dues of Glarentza, the chief port of Achaia, and the seat of a bank which used to lend money to the Angevin bailies, while, two years later, the revenues of the principality were required to furnish an annual salary of £1200 to one of those officials. A shrewd man and a court favourite, like Leonardo of Veroli, the Chancellor of Achaia, was able to amass a large fortune, and left behind him houses and lands scattered over the principality from Corinth to Kalamata. What is still more interesting is the fact that he had collected a small library.[1] From the inventory of his books we gather that his taste

[1] Χ. τ. Μ., l. 8430; *L. d. C.*, 378, 383; Heyd, *Geschichte des Levantehandels*, i., 300; *Les Registres de Nicholas III.*, 24; *Arch. Stor. Ital.*, Ser. III., xxii., 238; IV., iv., 16, 178, 182. Minieri Riccio, *Alcuni fatti*, 35, 49, 82; Hopf *apud* Ersch und Gruber, lxxxv., 307, 316, 317, 319.

lay chiefly in the direction of novels and medicine, for the list contains fourteen romances and two medical works. But our curiosity is aroused when we hear that he also possessed "a Greek book and a 'chronicle,'" and that he had a work in which he was interested copied for him by two copyists in the royal library at Naples, and carefully corrected by a French priest and two Italians. Obviously then, Franks of position sometimes spent the long winter evenings in the Achaian castles with books of history and romance, and some of them were able to read the language of their subjects. One Archbishop even translated Aristotle.

There was, however, another industry more lucrative than law or agriculture, which was then thriving in most parts of the Levant. Piracy has, in almost every age, been the curse of the Greek seas, and it flourished luxuriantly at this period.[1] A document of the year 1278, which contains the detailed report of three Venetian judges, appointed to estimate the damages sustained by subjects of the republic in Greek waters during recent years, throws a lurid light on the state of public security in the realm of Romania. We read of corsairs of many nationalities—Genoese (whose depredations were so numerous as to merit a special list all to themselves), Venetians, Lombards, Pisans, Sicilians, Provençals, Catalans, Spaniards, Greeks, Slavs, and half-castes. But Genoa had the distinction of furnishing most of the captains, and Venice that of supplying most of the crews. Perhaps the most famous of these pirates was John de lo Cavo (or de Capite), a native, and subsequently lord, of the island of Anaphe, whose professional headquarters were at Anæa, on the coast of Asia Minor opposite Samos, whose favourite haunt was the sea round Eubœa, and who succeeded Licario as imperial admiral. Among the many sufferers from his depredations was the father of the historian Sanudo,[2] who lost valuable merchandise on two Venetian vessels which fell into this corsair's clutches, and for which £10,752, or one-third of the value, was afterwards paid as compensation by the emperor. Another pirate, whose name became a household word in Greece, was Andrea Gaffore, a Genoese, whom Sanudo knew

[1] *Fontes Rer. Austr.*, xiv., 159-281.

[2] *Ibid.*, 337, 351; Sanudo, 132, 134, 146.

personally, and who, after a long career of plunder, settled down with his pile as a peaceful citizen at Athens, where we find him in the early part of the next century. Scarcely less successful a sea-robber was Roland, knight of Salonika, whose operations extended as far west as Zante. The profession was so lucrative, and was considered so respectable, that it became hereditary. The son of John de lo Cavo assisted his father; Gaffore had a brother in the business; the knightly Roland took his son-in-law, Pardo, presumably a Spaniard, into partnership. Men of distinguished lineage, Greeks and Franks alike, became corsairs. The great archontic families of Monemvasia, the Daimonoyánnai and the Mamonádes, figure conspicuously in the report of the Venetian judges, and one of the former, Paul Monoyánnes (as his name was written for short) became the first Greek lord of Cerigo, after the expulsion of the Venier dynasty by Licario. Sanudo specially speaks of the piracies committed by the Lombard barons of Negroponte, who found the harvests of the sea far more fruitful than those of their great island. Every year they used to send a fleet of 100 sail to pillage the coast of Asia Minor, and on one occasion they took booty to the value of 50,000 *hyperperi* (£22,400) at Anæa.[1] It was therefore no wonder that old Guglielmo da Verona could afford to maintain 400 knights, that the island was famous for its fine cavalry, which greatly injured the Greeks on land, or that Negroponte could boast of a rich Venetian banking-house, that of Andrea Ferro, which was able to finance the Franks of the Morea in their war against Michael VIII.[2] The other island barons followed the example of the Dalle Carceri clan in Eubœa, plundering Greeks and anyone whom they met, not sparing even the pious pilgrim on his way to the Holy Sepulchre. Even the ducal family of De la Roche gave shelter to corsairs in the beautiful Gulf of Nauplia, and thus brought down upon themselves, according to the devout Sanudo (mindful of his father's stolen cargo) the special displeasure of Providence, which had similarly punished the Venieri of Cerigo and the Viari of Cerigotto. Besides Anæa and Nauplia, Monemvasia

[1] Sanudo, 120, 127.

[2] Hopf *apud* Ersch und Gruber, lxxxv., 293.

and the islands of Skopelos, Keos, and Samothrace, were favourite lairs of the pirates. On one occasion, the Monemvasiotes looked calmly on, while a flagrant act of piracy was being committed in their harbour, which, as the port of shipment for Malmsey wine, attracted corsairs who were also connoisseurs. After the capture of Skopelos and Lemnos by Licario, the inhabitants of those islands emigrated to Eubœa, and turned pirates, so that it became the principal rendezvous of the fraternity and a nest of sea-robbers. During a war against the Emperor Andrónikos II., 300 privateers were sent out from Negroponte alone, and Sanudo had the honour of knowing a Cretan pirate, who used to boast that with his one ship he had done 400,000 *hyperperi* worth of damage (£179,200) to the Greek Empire. These privateers had, indeed, a regular fixed tariff, which was recognised as a custom of the trade. The captain was entitled to three *denarii* of spoil for every two which he had spent on fitting out his vessel; but, if he attacked the lair of a fellow-pirate, his gains, in consideration of the extra risk, or perhaps by way of salve to his professional conscience, were assessed at twice the amount of his outlay. Within the realm of Romania the privateer captain had also one-fifth of the takings, and enjoyed besides certain perquisites as dragoman and pilot.[1] But great as were the gains of the pirates, they represented only a part of the damage done. The misery and desolation which they caused defy calculation, and were by no means confined to one race, or creed. Neutrals, no less than open enemies, were considered as fair game by these gentry, and the losses of which the Venetians complained had all been sustained during the period when Michael VIII., whose flag these privateers usually flaunted, was supposed to be cherishing a "pure and guileless truce" with the republic.

Private commerce was, under these circumstances, attended with enormous risks, especially among the Greek islands. Traffic between Andros and Eubœa was specially dangerous, for to the normal perils of that mill-race, the Doro channel, was added the probability that John de lo Cavo or Daimonoyánnes would be lurking behind the

[1] Sanudo, 146.

Eubœan headland of Cape Mantello, as it was then named. We hear of a Venetian merchant of Athens plundered as he was sailing past Marathon; and often a well-filled merchantman got no farther than "the Columns" of Sunium; a ship was seized even in the port of Chalkis under the eyes of the bailie. The passage from Eubœa across to Atalante was infested by pirate brigs, and cargoes of beans and other articles of food, intended for the consumption of the Marquis of Boudonitza and his men, were taken at the landing-place. A harmless trader might easily find himself stripped of all but his shirt, or even deprived of that garment, and carried off to work in the prisons of Rhodes. Wherever there was a good harbour—in the Pagasæan Gulf, in the island of Ios, in Suda bay, in the extinct crater of Santorin, in the noble bay of Navarino, "the port of rushes," as the Franks called it—there was also a good place for the pirate captain and his crew. Maina had a peculiarly bad name for piracy even then, and ships anchoring in Porto Quaglio or off Œtylos often did so at the risk of their cargoes. The Gulf of Corinth was another risky place, and far up the west coast of Greece, the narrow channel of Corfù was still a resort of corsairs, who carried off their prisoners to the classic Butrinto—the "tall city of Buthrotum" of the *Æneid*—which had been taken by the Greeks from its Angevin commander. The point of Ithaka was another dangerous spot, the bishop of Cephalonia was plundered by Dalmatian pirates, and "Ambracia's Gulf" with its narrow entrance seemed to have been specially constructed for the purpose of incercepting Corfiote vessels on their way to the *skála* of Arta.

But there were land-rats no less than water-rats which disturbed the path of the merchant and the priest. The more or less intermittent Franco-Greek war which had gone on in the Morea since the fatal cession of the three castles had completely changed the conditions of life there. The profound security which we found existing in the early days of Prince William's reign had disappeared. The Venetians of Coron and Modon, though those places were specially guaranteed against attack in the arrangements made by the republic with Michael VIII., found that their neutrality availed them nothing when they met a Greek captain—half officer, half bandit—outside the narrow boundaries of the two Messenian colonies. On one occasion, the archdeacon of Modon, while travelling in the company of his bishop to Glarentza, was stopped at Krestena, near Olympia, and dragged before the emperor's brother, Constantine, then commanding in the Byzantine province. In vain the archdeacon protested that he was "a Venetian citizen"; his nationality was disregarded, and he was murdered by the soldiery. It is interesting to note that the Venetian judges assessed the value of a colonial archdeacon at 450 *hyperperi* (£201, 12s). Nor was Constantine Palaiológos's army less scornful when the local authorities of Coron sent him in a bill of damages for the loss of a cargo of Cretan cheese and wine. Venetian subjects languished in the dungeons of Kalavryta since the Greeks had dispossessed Geoffroy de Tournay of that fine castle, where an imperial commandant now flew the double-headed eagle from the keep.

Three-quarters of a century of Frankish rule had endowed Greece with a strange, yet often picturesque, geographical nomenclature. There can be no doubt that the Franks, not being Englishmen, had by this time learnt at least sufficient Greek for all ordinary colloquial purposes, though later than this, French, and excellent French too, was spoken at the court of Thebes. We are expressly told that Prince William of Achaia and Duke John of Athens spoke in Greek to the Greek commanders, the latter even using, perhaps unconsciously, an epigrammatic phrase of Herodotos, while Ancelin de Toucy, the Constable Chauderon, and Geoffroy d'Aunoy all spoke Greek, and Leonardo of Veroli read it.[1] But, all the same, the Franks, assisted by ignorant natives, had corrupted Greek proper names in a way often unrecognisable to those who have not read the French and Italian documents of the period. We have already mentioned how "Athens" had become "Satines," "Lemnos" "Stalimene," "Neopatras" "La Patre," "Lacedæmonia" "La Crémonie," and "Euripos" "Negroponte." But all over the Franco-Greek world the same process had been going on.

[1] *L. d. C.*, 338.

The island of Samothrace meets us frequently as "Sanctus Mandrachi"[1] (a saint invented to account for the name); "Ios" and "Anaphe," by the usual process of adding the final letter of the accusative of the article to the following noun, now figure as "Nio" and "Nanfio"; "Zetounion" (the Byzantine name for "Lamia") is, in Frankish parlance, "Giton" or "Gipton"; and Thebes had become "Estives" or "Stivas"[2] as early as the beginning of the twelfth century; Salona is, in French, "La Sole," or in Italian, "La Sola," which is the official designation on the coins of its French lords. "Naupaktos," corrupted into "Nepantum" as early as 1210, has by 1278 assumed the more modern form of "Lepanto," though the other corruption long survived in popular and official use, for example, on the coins of Philip of Taranto. The former obviously arose out of the Greek accusative (*εἰς τὸν Ἔπακτον*), the latter from the favourite Frankish method of placing the French definite article before a Greek word[3] ("Le Pakto"). Of this practice "L'Arte" ("Arta"), and "La Prevasse" ("Preveza") are other examples. Conversely, "Larissa" becomes "L'Arse." "Monemvasia" is gallicised into "Malevasie," and Italianised into "Malvasia," from which the transition is easy to the English form "Malmsey." "Livadostro," the port of Athens on the Corinthian Gulf, meets us as "Rive d' Ostre," and "Sunium" is already described as "the pillars" ("Colonne"), from its noble temple, and is yet further concealed under the guise of "Pellestello"[4] ("many columns," *πολύστυλον*), while in the French version of the *Chronicle of the Morea*, "Kalavryta" is "La Grite." Several well-known classical names had now vanished: thus Ossa had already received its modern name of Kissavos, and Taygetos that of Pentedaktylon.[5] Ithaka, in common parlance, no less than in learned Byzantine writers, maintained

[1] *E.g.*, *Fontes Rer. Austr.*, xiv., 205, 207, 212, 222.

[2] Sæwulf calls it "Stivas" in 1102 (*Recueil de Voyages*, iv., 384).

[3] Sáthas, Τὸ Χρονικὸν τοῦ Γαλαξειδίου, 16. Both ὁ Ἔπακτος and ὁ Πάκτος occur in the *Chronicle of the Morea*, ll. 3489, 3627. The earliest instance of the form "Lepanto" seems to be that in a document of 1278 (*Fontes Rer. Austr.*, xiv., 175).

[4] *Ibid.*, 192.

[5] Documents of 1276 and 1293 *apud* Miklosich und Müller, iv., 427; v., 155-61.

the name which had descended from the days of Homer, though it was also called Val di Compare.

Thus, if the Franks by the end of two generations had acquired the language, and made their mark upon the map of Greece, the Greeks had re-asserted themselves, alike in the south-east and in the north. Already the Frankish territories had greatly contracted, already the heroic age of Frankish Hellas was over. A new period was about to begin, when the fortunes of the country, hitherto directed by vigorous resident princes, were to depend on the Eastern policy of an Italian court and its ambitious monarch.

CHAPTER VI

THE ANGEVINS IN GREECE (1278-1307)

WITH the death of Prince William of Achaia, the house of Anjou became the dominant factor in Greek politics. Charles I., King of Naples and Sicily, was now, by virtue of the marriage-contract made between his late son Philip and Isabelle de Villehardouin, Prince, as well as suzerain of Achaia, and soon the mint of Glarentza issued coins with his name, followed by the princely title which he now assumed, upon them. The treaty of Viterbo, which had given him the suzerainty over Achaia, had made no mention of Athens; but though there is no direct authority for assuming that Duke John of Athens acknowledged Charles as his overlord, the King of Naples addressed him as a feudatory of Achaia, and John's successor, Duke William, recognised the King of Naples as his suzerain, only begging to be excused from doing homage in person at Naples. Charles was suzerain, too, of "the most high and mighty Count Palatine," Richard of Cephalonia, and in Corfù his captain and vicar-general governed the islanders for the Neapolitan crown. Finally, in Epiros, he considered himself, in virtue of the treaty of Viterbo, the successor of Manfred and Chinardo, though he had as yet made small progress towards the realisation of his claims in that difficult country—the despair of regular armies. Thus, in almost every part of the Greek world the restless Angevin had a base for his long-projected attack upon Constantinople, which the armistice between Venice and the Greek Emperor, the cunning intrigues and diplomatic reconciliation of the latter with the papacy, and his own preoccupations in Italy, had hitherto prevented.

Charles lost no time in assuming the government of the

principality of Achaia, and sent thither, as his bailie and vicar-general, Galeran d'Ivry, Seneschal of Sicily, who remained in his new post for two years. His appointment was notified to all the great feudatories of Achaia—to John, Duke of Athens, and his brother, William of Livadia; to Count Richard of Cephalonia; to the triarchs of Eubœa; to Isabella, Marchioness of Boudonitza; to Chauderon, the Constable, and St Omer, the Marshal of Achaia; and to the Achaian barons, Guy de la Trémouille of Chalandritza, Geoffroy de Tournay, Guy de Charpigny of Vostitza, and Jacques de la Roche of Veligosti. The captains of Corinth, Chloumoûtsi, Beauvoir, and Kalamata were ordered to hand over those important castles to him, and he was authorised to receive the homage of all the barons, knights, and other feudatories, "both men and women, both Latin and Greek."[1] Accordingly, upon his arrival at Glarentza, he summoned the prelates, barons, and knights of the principality, to hear the commands of his master. The assembly listened to the royal message, which bade them do homage to the bailie as the king's representative, and then Archbishop Benedict of Patras, whom the other barons had put forward as their spokesman, rose to reply. The primate pointed out that such a demand was an infringement of the customs of the country, which had been drawn up in writing and sworn to by their forefathers, the conquerors of the Morea. The feudal constitution provided, he said, that a new prince should appear in person, and swear before God and the people with his hand upon the gospels, to rule them according to their customs, and to respect their franchises, and then all the lieges were bound to do him homage, sealing the compact of mutual loyalty with a kiss on the mouth. "We would rather die and lose our heritage," added the bold ecclesiastic, "than be ousted from our customs." The primate's speech was not likely to please the bailie, but the assembly was unanimous in support of its leader, and it was obvious that the proud barons, jealous of their rights, were not going to

[1] *Arch. Stor. Ital.*, Ser. IV., i., 433; ii., 203; iv., 11; Riccio, *Nuovi Studii*, 11; Schlumberger, *Numismatique*, 315; Buchon, *Atlas*, pl. xxiv., 5. There is one of the coins of Charles I. as "Prince of Achaia" in the Doge's Palace at Venice, and the title occurs in the treaty of Orvieto.

do homage to a stranger who belonged to their own class. But, in the true spirit of constitutional monarchy, they were ready to make some compromise, so that his majesty's government might be carried on. The question of homage was put aside, and the bailie and the assembled vassals swore on the gospels—he to respect their customs, they to be loyal to Charles I. and his heirs.

Galeran d'Ivry does not seem to have kept his oath, and his administration was unpopular. He began by removing all the officials whom he had found in authority, just like a modern Greek prime minister, and thus created a host of enemies.[1] He was unsuccessful in a campaign which he undertook against the Greeks, who routed his troops in the defiles of Skortá and took many prisoners. The barons complained that the Angevin soldiers, instead of defeating their foes, plundered friendly villages, and that the lands which had been taken from them, and the late prince had bestowed upon his Turkish auxiliaries, should be restored. In 1280, two of their number, Jean de Chauderon and Narjaud de Rémy, went as a deputation to Naples, to complain of the bailie's unconstitutional acts. Charles issued orders that the old usages of Achaia should be respected, recalled Galeran d'Ivry, and appointed in his place Filippo de Lagonessa, Marshal of Sicily and ex-Seneschal of Lombardy.[2] But the experiment of sending bailies from Italy proved to be unsuccessful; accordingly, two years later, the King of Naples adopted the plan of choosing his vicar-general from the ranks of the Achaian barons. His choice fell upon Guy de la Trémouille, lord of Chalandritza, and head of one of the two families which still remained in undisturbed possession of the original baronies. But the baron of Chalandritza, though his family had come over at the Conquest, was not a sufficiently important person to impose his will upon his peers. His

[1] X. τ. M., ll. 7819-939; *L. d. C.*, 256-60; Angevin documents at Naples, quoted by Buchon (*Nouvelles Recherches*, I., i., 230-1) and Hopf (*apud* Ersch und Gruber, lxxxv., 316-17). The Greek, French, and Italian *Chronicle of the Morea*, make Hugues de Sully, who was never in Achaia, the first bailie after 1278, but mention Galeran d'Ivry as bailie in William's later years.

[2] Buchon, *Nouvelles Recherches*, I., i., 223; II., i., 327-8; *Arch. Stor. Ital.*, Ser. IV., iii., 12, 164.

barony consisted of no more than four knights' fees, and the ruined castle of Tremoulâ, near Kalavryta, which still preserves his name, is but small. Although the chivalry of Achaia was still so famous, that three of the Moreot barons—Jean de Chauderon, Geoffroy de Tournay, and Jacques de la Roche of Veligosti and Damalâ—were included by King Charles among the hundred combatants whom he took with him to Bordeaux in 1283, when it was proposed to decide the fate of Sicily by a duel between the two sovereigns of Naples and Aragon, yet the bailie found it necessary to employ Turkish, and even Bulgarian, mercenaries against the Greeks.[1] Such was the disaffection in the principality, that he received orders not to allow a single inhabitant to serve on garrison duty.

It is no wonder that after three years of office, Guy de la Trémouille shared the fate of his two predecessors. Charles I. of Naples had died in 1285; and, as his son and successor, Charles II. was at the time a prisoner of the house of Aragon, the affairs of Naples and of Achaia were conducted by the late king's nephew, Count Robert of Artois, as regent. One of his first acts was to remove the bailie of Achaia, appointing in his place a much more important personage—William, Duke of Athens, at that time the leading man in Frankish Greece. Connected through his wife with the energetic Duke of Neopatras, lord of Lamia in the north, directly interested, as baron of Nauplia and Argos, in the welfare of the Morea, he was the best possible selection, for in him the barons recognised the first among their equals. The Duke of Athens, whose coins may still be seen in the Archæological Museum at Venice, was also possessed of ample means, which he spent liberally for the defence of Greece. Thus, in 1282, in spite of the annual attacks of Licario on his coast, he had fitted out nine ships in Eubœa to co-operate with the Angevin fleet against the imperial navy; and, when bailie of the Morea, he built the castle of Demátra,[2] in the ever-unruly Skortá, a fortress which had

[1] *Arch. Stor. Ital.*, Ser. IV., iv., 354; v., 182-3; X. τ. M., ll. 8100-4, putting him, however, in the wrong place, *after* Duke William of Athens; Sanudo, 152; *L. d. C.*, 289, 367.

[2] Riccio, *Della Dominazione Angioina*, 1; X. τ. M., ll. 7990-8016;

been destroyed by the Greeks, and the site of which was perhaps at Kastri, to the left of the road between Tripolitza and Sparta. With the Venetian republic, which had trade interests at Athens, he was on such good terms, that when, in 1284, it was negotiating an armistice with the Emperor Andrónikos II., it expressly stipulated that the Duke of Athens should be included in it—a stipulation not, however, insisted upon in the actual treaty of the following year.[1] William was, however, well able to defend his land, and great was the regret when his valiant career was cut short in 1287, after only two years' office in Achaia.

In the Athenian duchy, he was succeeded by his only son, Guy II., who was still a minor, and for whom his Greek mother, Helene, daughter of the Duke of Neopatras, acted as regent—the first Greek ruler of Athens for over eighty years. In the administration of the Morea, he was followed by the great Theban magnate, Nicholas II. de St Omer, whom we have already seen defending the claim of his sister-in-law to the barony of Akova. The lord of half Thebes, like his father before him, he had built out of the vast wealth of his first wife, Princess Marie of Antioch, the noble castle of St Omer on the Kadmeia, of which only one tower now remains, but which was "the finest baronial mansion in all Romania." It contained sufficient rooms for an emperor and his court, and the walls were decorated with frescoes, illustrating the conquest of the Holy Land by the Franks, in which the ancestors of the Theban baron had played a prominent part. As his second wife he had married the widowed Princess of Achaia, and had thus come into possession of the lands in the Morea which she received in lieu of her widow's portion of Clermont and Kalamata, while his brother Jean had already established himself and founded a family in the peninsula. Nicholas had won the esteem of Charles I., who had sent him on a mission to the Armenian court, and he was thus well known to the Angevins. Like his immediate predecessor, he spent money in fortifications,

L. d. C., 385; *C. d. M.*, 461; Pachyméres, i., 413; Buchon, *Atlas*, pl. xxv., 5; Schlumberger, *Numismatique*, 338; Paparregópoulos (v. 153), identifies it with Karytaina.

[1] Luna, fol. 100.

building a small fortress to protect his wife's village of Maniatochorion against attack from the two neighbouring Venetian colonies of Messenia, and the strong castle of Avarino on the promontory at the north end of the famous bay of Navarino, upon the site where once had stood the palace of Nestor, where in classic days the Athenians had entrenched themselves at the beginning of the Peloponnesian war. But Nicholas de St Omer was not attracted to the spot by reminiscences of Homer or Thucydides. He was anxious to erect a mansion for his nephew Nicholas, and he chose the classic Pylos, with the noble bay at its foot, as a commanding position. We often find the place mentioned in the thirteenth century. The Franks called it "port de Junch"—the "harbour of rushes"—or "Zonklon," by a corruption of that word; but the Greeks described it already as "Avarînos"—a name which occurs not only in the Greek *Chronicle of the Morea*,[1] but in the earlier golden bull of Andrónikos II., dated 1293. The theory, therefore, so confidently put forward by Hopf,[2] that the modern name of Navarino is derived from the Navarrese company which occupied Zonklon a century later, falls to the ground. In all probability, Avarînos is a reminiscence, as Fallmerayer[3] long ago suggested, of the barbarous tribe of Avars, who, according to a Byzantine historian of that period, "conquered all Greece" in 589, and who, if we may believe a correspondent of the Emperor Aléxios I., "held possession of the Peloponnesos for 218 years." Thus, the name "Navarino" would arise, in accordance with the usual Greek practice, of which we had several examples in the last chapter, out of the final letter of the accusative of the article, *εἰς τὸν Ἀβαρῖνον*, or else, the name of the new settlement there, "Neo-Avarino," so called to distinguish it from St Omer's castle of "Palaio-

[1] Χ. τ. Μ., ll. 8056-99, 8105-9; *L. d. C.*, 273-6; Buchon, *Recherches historiques*, ii., 498, 501; *Nouvelles Recherches*, I., i., 227; II., i. 331; *La Grèce Continentale*, 460.

[2] *Apud* Ersch und Gruber, lxxxv., 212, 321; lxxxvi., p. 24.

[3] *Geschichte der Halbinsel Morea*, i., 188; Evagrios, *Hist. Eccles.*, vi., 10; Leunclavius, *Jus Græco-Romanum*, i., 278; Leake, *Travels in the Morea*, I., 411; Andrónikos writes εἰς τὴν Πύλον, τὸν καλούμενον Ἀβαρῖνον. *Cf.* the author's article in the *English Hist. Review*, xx., 307; xxi., 106; and Prof. Bury in *Hermathena*, xiii., 430.

Avarino," would easily be contracted into the form which the great battle which secured the independence of modern Greece has made known to every lover of Hellas.

The administration of the great Theban baron was disturbed by another of those feudal claims, which had now become common since the almost complete disappearance of the families of the original conquerors. It will be remembered that on the death of Geoffroy de Bruyères, his barony of Skortá had been divided into two halves, one escheating to the crown, the other being left in the hands of the widow. We saw how a certain knight, named Pestel, had claimed the barony, and how Prince William had ignored his claim. A new claimant now appeared in the person of another Geoffroy de Bruyères, a cousin of the late baron, who arrived from Champagne with elaborate proofs of his relationship and a recommendation from the Regent of Naples to the bailie that the High Court should decide the question. The Court met at Glarentza, and the bishop of Olena gave judgment in its name against young Geoffroy, on the ground that Skortá would only have descended to him, if he had been a direct heir of its late lord, according to the decision of Prince William. Ashamed to return to France empty-handed, the claimant resorted to craft to obtain the coveted barony. He pretended to be suffering from colic, which could be best cured by drinking rain water, such as was to be found in the cistern of the small but strong castle of Bucelet, or Araklovon, which commanded the defile of Skortá, and which had been held at the time of the Conquest by the heroic Doxapatrês. He first sent a trusty esquire to beg water from the benevolent governor, and then obtained leave to occupy a room in the tower, so that he might be able to drink the astringent water at his convenience. Soon he seemed to grow worse, and the unsuspecting governor permitted him to call his esquires to his bedside, so that they might hear his last dying depositions. Geoffroy then confided to them his plan. They were to induce the bibulous governor and his men to drink deep with them at a favourite tavern outside the castle gate, and then, when their guests had well drunk, they should seize the keys from the porter and bar out the intoxicated governor and garrison. The plan succeeded, and Geoffroy, now master of Bucelet, released some Greeks who were in the castle dungeon and despatched two of them by night to the imperial commander, offering to sell him the castle, of whose strategic value Geoffroy was well aware. He knew that Bucelet was the key of Skortá, and he surmised that the bailie would give him Karytaina, rather than that Bucelet, and with it, the whole of Arkadia, should fall into the hands of the Greeks. This surmise proved to be not far wrong. The Greek commander, overjoyed at the offer, hastened towards Bucelet with all his troops. Before, however, he had time to reach the castle, it had been closely invested by the Frankish soldiers, hastily summoned by the governor from their garrison duty at Great Aráchova. Such was the alarm caused in the principality, that the bailie himself marched at the head of all his available forces to Bucelet. Ordering Simon de Vidoigne, the captain of Skortá, to prevent the Greek army from crossing the Alpheios by the ford at Isova, he sent envoys to Geoffroy, offering him a free pardon if he would surrender the castle to him as King Charles II.'s vicar-general, but, in the event of refusal, threatening to pull it down about his ears. "Indeed," the messengers added, "Venetian carpenters have already been summoned from Coron to construct the necessary engines of war." The prudent Geoffroy now saw that the time had come for a compromise; he offered to give up the castle to the bailie, if the latter would promise him some fief upon which he could settle; the bailie consented, and this audacious piece of feudal blackmail was rewarded by the hand of a wealthy widow, Marguerite de Cors, who brought him her father's fief of Lisarea near Chalandritza, and her husband's fief of Moraina in Skortá.[1] As for the castle of Bucelet, it was shortly afterwards bestowed upon Isabelle de Villehardouin by King Charles II.

That monarch had been released from prison in 1289, and one of his first acts was to appoint a fresh bailie of the Morea. His nominee was Guy de Charpigny, Lord of Vostitza, head of the sole surviving great baronial family of the Conquest—for Guy de la Trémouille had now died without male heirs—

[1] X. τ. M., ll. 8110-458; *L. d. C.*, 276-87; *L. d. F.*, 94-8 (with considerable variations in detail from the other versions); *C. d. M.*, 462-5.

and a man known personally to the Neapolitan court.[1] But the Moreot barons were tired of this system of government by deputies. They had had in eleven years, six bailies —two foreigners, two of their own order, and two great magnates from the duchy of Athens. The foreigners had trampled on their privileges, their fellow-barons were not sufficiently far above them to secure their respect, and the duchy of Athens was now itself in the hands of a child and his mother. Meanwhile, the war against the imperial commanders at Mistrâ had gone on more or less continually ever since the death of William, for the Morea had been involved in the general Angevin plan of campaign against the Byzantine Empire. These facts had convinced the barons that their country could only be saved by a prince who would reside among them. Two of their number, Jean de Chauderon, the late prince's nephew and grand constable of the principality, and Geoffroy de Tournay, formerly baron of Kalavryta, were frequent visitors at the Neapolitan court, where they enjoyed greater esteem than any other nobles of the Morea. They had both fought for Charles I. at Tagliacozzo, they had both been chosen to fight for him at Bordeaux; and Chauderon held the post of admiral of the kingdom of Naples. Their advice was, therefore, likely to be accepted by the king. During their visits to Naples they had made the acquaintance of a young noble from Flanders, Florent d'Avesnes, brother of the Count of Hainault, and scion of a family which had greatly distinguished itself in the stormy history of the near East. His great-grandfather had stood by the side of Cœur-de-Lion at the siege of Acre; his grandfather had married the daughter of the first Latin emperor of Constantinople; his great-uncle had been the Jacques d'Avesnes, who had conquered Eubœa and been wounded at the siege of Corinth. Florent's father had been noted for his reckless extravagance and his amorous adventures, and, as he left seven children, there was not much prospect for a younger son of the family in the old home. Energetic and ambitious, the young noble was not content to live on the small appanage of Braine-le-Comte and Hal, which his eldest brother had given him; so, about two

[1] Buchon, *Nouvelles Recherches*, I., i., 223.

years before this date, he had gone to seek his fortune at the Neapolitan court, where he had received the post of grand constable of the kingdom of Sicily, and the captaincy of Corfù. But he was not satisfied with these dignities; he had, no doubt, heard of the discontent in the Morea with the existing method of government, and he saw therein a means of furthering his own ambition. Accordingly, he approached the two Achaian barons on the subject, and suggested that they should ask the king to give him in marriage the hand of the widowed Isabelle de Villehardouin, who was still living in the Castel dell' Uovo, at Naples, like a prisoner of state, and to appoint him Prince of Achaia. At the same time, he pointed out, that if he became prince, they would remain the masters. The scheme met with their approval; they chose a favourable moment for addressing the lame monarch, and then frankly laid before him the dangers of the present situation. "Your bailie and your soldiers," they said, "tyrannise over the poor, wrong the rich, seek their own advantage and neglect the country. Unless you send a man," they added, "who will always stay there, and who, as heir of the Villehardouins, will make it his object to advance the country's interests, you will—mark our words—lose the principality altogether." They then reminded King Charles that his sister-in-law, the late Prince William's daughter, "the Lady of the Morea," as she was called, was living in widowhood, and prayed him to marry her to some great nobleman, who would govern Achaia to his Majesty's benefit. Charles II. listened to their advice, realising that hitherto Achaia had been a source of expense to the crown of Naples and was being rapidly ruined. He gave his consent to the marriage, but only on condition that, if Isabelle survived Florent, neither she nor her daughter nor any other female descendant of hers, should marry without the king's consent. If this condition were not observed, the possession of the principality was at once to revert to the crown of Naples. This stipulation, against which the author of *The Chronicle of the Morea* strongly protests, was, twelve years afterwards, enforced against Isabelle herself, and, a generation later, against her ill-fated daughter Matilda.

Meanwhile, all parties were delighted at the marriage.

The Lady of the Morea, still only twenty-five years old, must have rejoiced at the prospect of leaving her gilded cage and returning to her native land, which she had left as a child eighteen years before. The wedding ceremony was performed with much state by the Archbishop of Naples, in September 1289, and the king invested Isabelle and her husband with the principality of Achaia. Then the young couple set out for their principality; on their arrival at Glarentza, the bailie hastened to meet them, and summoned the prelates, barons, knights, esquires, and burgesses to hear the orders of the king. In the Minorite church there, the king's letters were read aloud, both in Latin and in the vulgar tongue, after which, the new prince took the customary oath to observe the customs of the country and the franchises of his vassals, and then he received their homage and the possession of the principality from the hands of the bailie.[1] In the following spring, Charles II. ordered the title of "Prince of Achaia," which he and his father had used from the death of Prince William down to 1289,[2] to be removed from the Great Seal of the kingdom of Naples; henceforth it figures in the documents of Isabelle and Florent, and on the coins which they struck at Glarentza to replace the Achaian currency of Charles II. and his father.[3]

While the war against the Greeks had been going on all these years in the Morea, the house of Anjou had also pressed its claims in Epiros. So long as the Despot Michael II. lived, Charles I. had, indeed, been unable to make progress in the Highland country beyond the Adriatic. He had merely sent Jean de Cléry to take possession of the Epirote possessions, which the treaty of Viterbo had conferred upon him, and his envoy had occupied the excellent harbour of Valona, upon which modern Italy casts longing glances.

[1] X. τ. M., ll. 8476-8652; *L. d. C.*, 288-97; Buchon, *Recherches historiques*, ii., 498-9; *Nouvelles Recherches*, II., i., pp. 338-42; *C. d. M.*, 465-6; it is not necessary to assume, with Buchon, that "the vulgar tongue" was Greek; for Charles II. wrote, as usual, in Latin; hence "the vulgar tongue" would be French.

[2] He is so described in a letter of that year *apud* Muratori, *op. cit.*, xiv., 955.

[3] Coins of Charles II., Isabelle and Florent in Buchon, *Atlas*, xxiv., 6, 7, 8; and in Schlumberger, *Numismatique*, 315.

But, not many months after the death of Michael II., the Albanian chiefs, by reason of their "devotion to the holy Roman Church," recognised Charles of Anjou, the champion of the papacy, as their king, did homage to his representatives, and received from him a renewal of the privileges granted to their forefathers by the Byzantine emperors. Chinardo's brother was then made Viceroy of Albania, Chinardo's children were put safely under lock and key in the prison of Trani, the treaty of Viterbo was ratified by Charles's son-in-law, Philip I. of Courtenay, now titular emperor, at Foggia in 1274, and the feeble Despot of Epiros, Nikephóros I., unable to protect himself against the emperor Michael VIII., recognised Charles as his suzerain, sent his son as a hostage to Glarentza, and handed over to the Angevins the castle of Butrinto, the classic Buthrotum, and other places once held by Chinardo. A vigorous attempt was now at last made to attack the emperor by land and sea. A force of 3000 men was sent over to Epiros, and placed under the command of Hugues de Sully, nicknamed Le Rousseau from his red hair, a native of Burgundy, who had accompanied Charles to Naples, and had been appointed in 1278 Captain-General and Vicar of Albania and Corfù. Ros Solumâs or Rosonsoulês, as the Byzantine historians call him, was a big, handsome man, but a most unfortunate commander, proud, headstrong, and passionate. His men, among whom were many Saracens, shared his over-confidence, and were already partitioning in their own minds the dominions of the emperor, as the Frank Crusaders had really done three-quarters of a century earlier. But the Angevin expedition, which was to have conquered the empire, got no farther than Berat, the picturesque Albanian stronghold defended by its river and its rocky fortress. The emperor despatched a force to relieve the place, the red-haired giant fell from his horse, and, lying helpless in his heavy armour, was captured by the Greeks, or their Turkish auxiliaries.[1] On the news of his capture, his men fled in

[1] Buchon, *Nouvelles Recherches*, I., i., 206, 231-2 ; II., i., 314, 316-19 ; *L. d. C.*, 257-8 ; Pachyméres, i., 508-19 ; Nikephóros Gregorâs, i., 146-8 ; Sanudo, 129-30 ; Ducange, *op. cit.*, ii., 324 ; *Arch. Stor. Ital.*, Ser. IV., ii., 199, 355 ; iv., 17.

panic, and the captives were led, like prisoners in a Roman triumph, through the streets of Constantinople, where Sully languished for years in the imperial dungeons. Such was the joy of the emperor, that he commissioned an artist to depict the victory of Berat upon the walls of his palace. The reacquisition of Durazzo completed the success of his arms, and the harbour of Valona and the castle of Butrinto alone remained to the Angevins in Epiros. At sea, the Angevin fleet, manned by Franks from the Morea and partly led by Marco II. Sanudo, Duke of Naxos, did more harm than good to the Latin cause in the Levant, as the duke's relative confesses, so that the double attack upon the empire had failed. Nor was the treaty for the recovery of the realm of Romania, which was concluded at Orvieto in 1281, thanks to the efforts of Leónardo of Veroli, the ever-useful chancellor of Achaia, between Charles, "Prince of Achaia," his son-in-law, Philip I. of Courtenay, titular emperor of Romania, and the Venetian republic, any more productive of results. The treaty seemed on paper to be a masterpiece of statecraft, for it brought Venice, so long neutral, into line against the Greeks. Charles and Philip were to provide some 8000 horses and sufficient men to ride them; Venice was to equip forty galleys or more, in order to secure the command of the sea; the year 1283 was fixed for the expedition, in which all the three high contracting parties were to take part in person; finally, there was to be neither peace nor truce with Michael VIII. or his heirs. But nothing practical ever came of the treaty of Orvieto. History can only say of it, that it was one more of the many diplomatic failures to solve the Eastern question. Charles did, indeed, collect another small fleet, of which nine vessels were provided by Duke William of Athens, and six by the bailie of the Morea, Lagonessa, and the Venetians began to make preparations. But the French squadron fell foul of the Venetians, and the Greek admiral, John de lo Cavo, the terrible ex-pirate, captured two rich Venetian merchantmen.[1] Then, suddenly the Angevin power in Sicily received a blow, which in a single night destroyed all the ambitious plans of

[1] *Fontes Rer. Austr.*, xiv., 287-308, 337, 351; Laurentius de Monacis, 151; Sanudo, 130, 132, 173.

Charles against the East. In 1282 took place the Sicilian vespers.

Greek diplomacy had not been altogether unconnected with that ghastly tragedy. Excommunicated by the new pope, Martin IV., a Frenchman and a creature of Charles, Michael VIII. saw that the farce of uniting the Eastern and Western churches was played out. He accordingly entered into negotiations with the deadly enemy of the house of Anjou, Peter III. of Aragon, employing as his intermediaries his brother-in-law, Benedetto Zaccaria, member of a rich Genoese family which had been entrusted by the emperor with the administration of the rich alum mines of Phokaia in Asia Minor; a Lombard, named Accardo, from Lodi; and the celebrated Giovanni di Procida, who visited Constantinople in the guise of a Franciscan monk. The emperor was to pay the King of Aragon an annual subsidy of £26,880 so long as the war against the Angevins lasted, and some portion of this sum was provided by the clan of Zaccaria.[1] Michael VIII. received full value for his money; for the fall of the Angevin power in Sicily not only freed him from a dangerous enemy, but also deprived the Frank states in Greece of valuable support. Not without reason has it been said that the Sicilian vespers sounded the knell of French rule in Hellas.[2] Their immediate result was to stop any attempt to carry out the programme laid down at Orvieto. In Epiros the Angevin commanders contented themselves with holding the pitiful remnant of the Neapolitan possessions—a task rendered less difficult owing to the feeble character of the Despot Nikephóros I., the attacks made upon him and upon the emperor by the ever-restless bastard of Neopatras, and by the death, in the very year of the Sicilian vespers, of the emperor himself. The last act of Michael VIII. was to let loose the Tartars against the crafty rival at

[1] Sanudo, 132, 147, 173; Ptolemæus Lucensis *apud* Muratori, *op. cit.*, xi., 1186; Hopf, *Les Giustiniani*, 9; *Conspiration de Jean Prochyta* (ed. Buchon), pp. 1-6, 17-18; Nikephóros Gregorâs (*loc. cit.*) evidently alludes to this when he says that Michael sent money to "Frederick (*sic*), King of Sicily," to stop Charles's fleet, confusing King Peter of Aragon with his son Frederick, who became King of Sicily fourteen years later.

[2] Pouqueville, *Voyage dans la Grèce*, iv., 90.

Neopatras, who had so often been a thorn in his side. The death of the titular emperor of Romania in the following year removed one of the signatories of the treaty of Orvieto; another, the great Charles of Anjou, died in 1285, leaving his successor a prisoner of the Aragonese, and in the same year, Venice, the third member of that Triple Alliance, concluded an armistice for ten years with the new Emperor Andrónikos II. Both parties were given a free hand in Negroponte; but the emperor promised to respect the Venetian colonies of Crete, Coron, and Modon, and to include the Duke of Naxos and the lord of Tenos in the treaty, provided that they swore not to give refuge to corsairs. A year earlier Andrónikos had gained recognition in the west, and practically extinguished the claims of the house of Montferrat to the phantom kingdom of Salonika by his second marriage with Irene, daughter of the Marquis William VII. and of Beatrice of Castile, who brought it to him as her dowry.[1] Thus collapsed the coalition for the restoration of the Latin Empire.

Freed from the danger of attack from the Franks, Andrónikos II. resolved to secure himself against the intrigues of his hereditary rival, the Duke of Neopatras. The restless bastard had not been sobered by advancing years, and his eldest son, Michael, had begun to display all the ambitious activity which had characterised his father in his prime. The emperor thought it wise to take measures in time against a repetition of those movements in Thessaly which had given so much trouble to his father. In order to be quite sure of success, he tried both force and craft, sending an army and a fleet of about eighty ships under Tarchaneiótes and Aléxios Raoul, an official of French descent, from whose family, according to some authorities, the great clan of Rálles derives its origin and name; at the same time, he entered into negotiations with his cousin Anna, the masculine wife of Nikephóros I., Despot of Epiros, for entrapping young Michael by some feminine stratagem. Anna's skill proved superior to that of the imperial commanders. While

[1] Pachyméres, i., 524-5, ii., 87; Nikephóros Gregorâs, i., 149, 167, 168; *Fontes Rer. Austr.*, xiv., 322-53; *Memoriale Potestatum Regiensium*, *apud* Muratori, *op. cit.*, viii., 1164-5.

they wasted time in restoring the fortifications of Demetrias, near the modern Volo, until pestilence slew Tarchaneiótes and dispersed his followers, the cunning Princess of Epiros obtained possession of her nephew under the pretext of marrying him to one of her daughters, and then sent him in chains to Constantinople, where he languished in prison for the rest of his life. Once, indeed, he managed to escape, thanks to the aid of Henry, an Englishman, presumably a member of the Varangian guard, who had been appointed his chief gaoler. Hiring a fishing-smack, they set sail in the night for Eubœa, hoping to make their way thence to Athens, where Michael's sister, Helene, was then duchess and regent.[1] But one of those sudden storms so common in the Levant arose in the Marmara; their vessel was driven ashore at Rodosto, and they were there recaptured by the imperial authorities. Many efforts were made to induce Andrónikos to release his prisoner, but in vain. Years rolled on, and at last Michael, grown desperate, resolved to kill the emperor, even if he perished himself. His prison was near the imperial apartments, and he therefore determined to set fire to his cell, in hope that the flames would reach the emperor's bedchamber. Unluckily for the success of his plan, Andrónikos was still awake when the fire broke out; orders were at once given to extinguish the conflagration, and Michael, fighting like a tiger, was felled at the door of his cell by one of the axes of the bodyguard. His father had avenged him upon the treacherous Anna by ravaging the Despotat of Epiros; and it was to save himself from these attacks that the unwarlike Nikephóros consented to become tributary to the King of Naples.[2]

The founder of a dynasty is always able, and his son almost as invariably feeble. So it was with Andrónikos II. Nature had intended him for a professor of theology, to which engrossing subject he devoted what time he could spare from the neglect of his civil and military duties. In order to obtain money for the Orthodox Church and the imperial court, he allowed the navy to rot in the Golden

[1] Pachyméres, by a confusion, makes her ruler of Eubœa.

[2] Pachyméres, ii., 67-77, 201.

Horn, after the fashion of the present sultan; his courtiers told him that there was nothing more to fear from the Latins after the death of Charles of Anjou, so that an efficient fleet was a sheer extravagance. He dismissed the half-breeds, who were his best sailors, allowing some of them to enter the service of the Franks, and thus permitted the pirates to scour the seas unchecked.[1] Meanwhile, the handwriting was on the wall; the Turks were advancing in Asia Minor, yet the pedant on the throne of the Cæsars seemed to regard their intrusion as of less moment to the empire than that of the *filioque* clause into the creed.

Under these circumstances, it was no wonder that Andrónikos was glad to suspend, by agreement with the new Prince of Achaia, the attempts which his father had made for the reconquest of the Morea. The first act of Florent was to replace all the existing civil and military authorities by his own men, and to redress the grievances of the principality, which he found utterly exhausted by the exactions of the Angevin officials and mercenaries. He endeavoured to make the foreign blood-suckers atone for their maladministration by compelling them to disgorge their ill-gotten gains, and such was his severity towards them that he received a significant hint from King Charles to temper justice with mercy. As for the future, he wisely adopted the advice of such experienced men as old Nicholas de St Omer, Geoffroy de Tournay, and Jean de Chauderon, who urged him, in accordance with the general opinion, to make a durable truce with the Greek Emperor as the only way of preventing the further decline of the principality. He accordingly sent two envoys to the Byzantine governor (or κεφαλή) at Mistrâ, suggesting that an armistice should be concluded. The governors of the Byzantine province were, however, at that period, appointed for no longer than a year, and the then governor's term of office had almost expired. He, however, at the advice of the local Greek magnates, referred the proposal to the emperor, who joyfully accepted it, all the more so because he was at the moment harassed by the Turks in Asia, by the Despot of Epiros,

[1] Pachyméres, ii., 69-71; Nikephóros Gregorâs, i., 174-6.

and by the Bulgarian Tsar.[1] Andrónikos sent to the Morea a great magnate, Philanthropenós, who belonged to one of the twelve ancient Byzantine families, and was apparently the same person as the Aléxios Philanthropenós who was grandson of the former Byzantine admiral, and a few years later rebelled and proclaimed himself emperor.[2] The new governor met Florent at Andravida, where the heads of a treaty were drawn up in writing between them. But the cautious Fleming was still not content with the signature of an annual official, of however high rank. He pointed out that, as he was a prince, the emperor's autograph should accompany his own. Philanthropenós agreed; two Greek *archons* and two Greek-speaking French barons, Jean de Chauderon and Geoffroy d'Aunoy, baron of Kyparissia, accompanied him to Constantinople, and Andrónikos, glad to be relieved of the expense caused by the warfare in the Morea, signed the treaty with the purple ink, and sealed it with the golden seal in their presence. For full seven years the principality enjoyed repose, which was welcome to both Greeks and Franks alike. The ravages of the Angevin officials and their mercenaries were repaired; "all grew rich," says the chronicler, "Franks and Greeks, and the land waxed so fat and plenteous in all things, that the people knew not the half of what they possessed."[3]

Unfortunately, by a custom of international law which then prevailed, a truce between two rulers was considered no bar to the offer of assistance by one of them to the enemy of the other. One of the reasons which had induced Andrónikos to make peace in the Morea was, as we saw, his difficult position in Epiros. The Despot Nikephóros, or rather his wife Anna, who really inspired his policy, was at this moment smarting under that *spretæ injúria formæ*, which had caused so many woes to the ancient Greek world. She had rendered a great service to the emperor by betraying

[1] "L'Empereur de Jaguora" (*L. d. C.*, 300). "Jaguora" is Zagora, not Angora, as Buchon supposes.

[2] Pachyméres, ii., 210-29; Kritóboulos, the historian of Mohammed II., seems to allude to his appointment (Müller, *Fragmenta historicorum Græcorum*, v., 104).

[3] X. τ. M., 8653-8781; *L. d. C.*, 297-300, 472.

Michael of Neopatras into his hands, and she claimed her reward, which was to consist of a marriage between her very beautiful daughter, Thamar, and the emperor's eldest son. She added as an inducement, that after her husband's death she would transfer the Despotat to the emperor, regardless of the claims of her son Thomas, a child of feeble character, whom she judged incapable of governing in troublous times. The offer was a good one, for it would have ended the long rivalry between Epiros and Constantinople and have reunited a large part of the Byzantine Empire. But the patriarch opposed a marriage between second cousins; as a theologian, Andrónikos agreed with the patriarch, as a politician of short views, he fancied that he had found a better match for his son in the person of Catherine of Courtenay, granddaughter of Baldwin II., whose claims as titular empress of Constantinople would be extinguished by her marriage with the real heir.[1] As a matter of fact, this alternative alliance came to nothing, while the rejection of the beauteous Thamar determined her father to wipe out this insult. The bastard of Neopatras also, if we may believe the much later *Chronicle of Galaxidi*,[2] seized this opportunity of avenging the emperor's treatment of his eldest son, who was at that time a prisoner in Constantinople; "with tears in his eyes," he appealed to the mountaineers of Loidoriki and the sailors of Galaxidi to come to his aid. Two hundred chosen men came from either place with the intention to do or die; but in a battle near Lamia, they were basely deserted by their comrades; the Galaxidiotes perished to a man, boldly fighting sword in hand; a quarter of the contingent from Loidoriki was left on the field; and the bastard, who had witnessed so many fights, only escaped capture by flight. Nikephóros was now exposed to the full force of the imperial army, which, 44,000 strong, crossed over from Thessaly by way of Metzovo to Joannina, the second most important city of the Despotat, which had been recovered from its former imperial garrison. Meanwhile, the emperor had chartered sixty Genoese galleys with orders to enter the Ambrakian Gulf.

Thus menaced by land and sea, Nikephóros sought the advice of his chief men, who recommended him to seek the aid

[1] Pachyméres, ii., 153, 200-2.

[2] Pp. 203-4.

of Florent, who had married his niece and whose Frankish chivalry was famous in the whole Greek world. Envoys were accordingly sent in 1292 to the Achaian capital of Andravida, where the matter was discussed in the church of the Divine Wisdom; the older men, who remembered the mishaps which had accrued to the Morea from the Epirote campaign of Prince William, thirty-three years before, were opposed to a repetition of that adventure; but dynastic reasons and the national love of glory prevailed, and it was agreed, that Florent should join his wife's uncle with 500 picked warriors, on condition that the Despot gave them their pay and sent his only surviving son Thomas as a hostage to the Morea. At the same time, and on the same terms, Nikephóros secured the aid of Count Richard of Cephalonia and 100 of his islanders, sending him, as a pledge of his good faith, his daughter Maria.

The three allies met at Arta, and resolved on a march upon Joannina; but, before they had reached that place, the imperial army had fled in panic, nor could their chivalrous appeals to the honour of the Greek commander, whose Turkish and Cuman auxiliaries would only obey their own chiefs, prevail upon him to give them battle. After a brief raid into the emperor's territory, they were hastily recalled by the news that the Genoese galleys had arrived at the mouth of the Ambrakian Gulf, that the sailors had landed at Preveza, and that they were marching straight for Arta.[1] The Despot feared for his capital, for the Genoese were noted for their skill in sieges, and 1000 horsemen were despatched in hot haste to stop them. But the flight of the imperial army, which was to have co-operated with them by land, had discouraged the Genoese; some of their comrades were cut off by the cavalry; and, when Florent arrived and pitched his camp at Salagora, where the galleys were lying at anchor, so as to prevent them from landing, they sailed away to Vonitza on the south of the gulf,[2] whence they ravaged the Despotat unchecked as far as the island of Santa Mavra, which then formed part of it. Then they returned to Constantinople; the allies of the Despot dispersed; and his

[1] Here ends the Italian version of the *Chronicle*.

[2] Here ends the Greek version.

son was released from his detention at Chloumoûtsi. Count Richard of Cephalonia did not, however, send back his hostage, but married her to his eldest son John, a fine, strapping man, for whom no lady of Romania was good enough. Great was the indignation of Nikephóros, who had looked higher than the heir of the county palatine; but Epiros had no navy, and the count, safe in his island domain, could smile at his late ally's impotent wrath,[1] which was increased by the count's refusal to carry out his promise of bestowing the famous "island of Ithaka, or the fort of Koronós," in Cephalonia, upon his son.[2] Nikephóros had acted more generously, for he had grown fond of his handsome son-in-law, to whom he seems to have given the island of Leukas, or Santa Mavra, as it now began to be called.[3] The history of Santa Mavra, and the origin of its name, are somewhat obscure; but it appears to have belonged to the despots of Epiros, in connection with whom we have more than once had occasion to allude to it, down to a little before the year 1300, when it is mentioned, under the names of "Luccate" and "Lettorna," in two Angevin documents, as belonging to John of Cephalonia. In one of these documents, Charles II. of Naples gives John permission to build a fort in "Lettorna," and from this fort, which is known to have been subsequently called "Santa Mavra," some scholars derive the common name of the island, while others think that it had the name even before the erection of the fort.[4] Santa Mavra is a popular saint, alike in Greece and Italy, so that her name

[1] X. τ. M., ll. 8782 to end; *L. d. C.*, 302-20; *L. d. F.*, 100-3; Continuator Caffari *apud* Pertz, *Monumenta German. Hist.*, xviii., 338; Buchon, *Recherches historiques*, ii., 482.

[2] Riccio, *Saggio di Codice Diplomatico*, Supp., part I., 87. The south-east corner of Cephalonia is still called Koronoí.

[3] This is an inference from the two facts that Leukas is not mentioned among the dominions of Richard in the above-mentioned inventory of the bishopric of Cephalonia in 1264, and that it is mentioned as belonging to his son John in 1300; Romanós, Γρατιανὸς Ζώρζης, 166, 297.

[4] The *Livre de la Conqueste*, probably composed between 1333 and 1341, mentions "Saincte Maure" (p. 317) in describing the events of 1292; the fort is so described in an Angevin document of 1343, in Walter of Brienne's will in 1347, and in a Venetian document of 1355, where the island is still called "Lucate"—an indication that the fort was called Santa Mavra before the island. Romanós, *op. cit.*, 301-2; Blantês,

would appeal alike to the Italian Orsini and to the native Greeks.

The Despot was able to console himself for this *mésalliance* by a splendid match for his other daughter, the beautiful Thamar, whose slighted charms had been the cause of the late war. In 1294 the Epirote damsel was married at Naples to Philip, second son of King Charles II., who was thus able to recover by a dynastic alliance the ground which his house had lost by the sword beyond the Adriatic. The King of Naples laid his plans with much cunning. Before the marriage took place, he conferred upon his son the principality of Taranto, as being nearest to the coveted land of Epiros; his next step was to make his niece, Catherine of Courtenay, titular empress of Constantinople, ratify the treaty of Viterbo, and pledge herself never to marry without the consent of the crown of Naples—a piece of diplomacy which he attempted to justify by the most sickening and transparent excuses. He thus had in his own hands all the claims to the Latin Empire of Romania, which still counted for something in diplomatic circles. He then transferred all these claims, and the suzerainty over the principality of Achaia, the duchy of Athens, the kingdom of Albania, and the province of Wallachia (or Thessaly) to his son, on whom he also bestowed the island of Corfù with the castle of Butrinto on the opposite coast of Epiros and its dependencies—the remnant, in fact, of the Angevin possessions on the Greek mainland. Thus, in 1294, Philip of Taranto became suzerain of all the Frankish states in Greece, which the King of Aragon, the great rival of the house of Anjou, promised to respect, and actual owner of the Angevin dominion in Corfù and on the Epirote litoral, over which his father retained the overlordship. A prince so richly endowed with dignities and estates was a desirable son-in-law; nor was the Despot moved to reject such a marriage for his daughter on the ground that the King of Naples was still keeping his nephews, the sons of Helene and Manfred, in the dungeons of Santa Maria del Monte, the fine castle which still stands near Andria. He promised to give Philip, in addition to

'Η Λευκὰς ὑπὸ τοὺς Φράγκους, p. 25. *Cf.* the author's note in the *English Historical Review*, xviii., 513.

Thamar's dowry of £44,800 a year, the four fortresses of Lepanto, Vonitza, Angelokastro and Vrachori (the modern Agrinion); if his son Thomas died, Philip was to become Despot of all Epiros; if he lived to attain his majority, he was to hold the heritage of his ancestors as Philip's vassal, and cede the latter another castle or a maritime province.[1] On the other hand, Philip pledged himself to respect the religion of his wife and his future subjects; the first of these pledges he violated; the confidence of the Greeks in the second must have been shaken by the creation of a Catholic archbishopric in "the royal castle" of Lepanto, whose Greek metropolitan, hitherto the chief ecclesiastic of the Despotat, transferred his see to Joannina, out of the reach of "the boastful, haughty, and rapacious Italians."[2] Philip of Taranto was now, by this extraordinary arrangement, master of the best positions in Ætolia, and had a prospect of obtaining the whole of Epiros. The other branch of the Angeli, which ruled in Thessaly, was, indeed, naturally alarmed at this extension of Angevin sway in Western Greece, and the two younger sons of the old Duke of Neopatras made an attack upon Arta and captured Lepanto. The King of Naples in alarm bade Florent of Achaia and Hugues de Brienne, who was now guardian of the young Duke of Athens, defend Epiros. But this was a merely temporary acquisition, almost immediately relinquished; in fact, the chief result of these feuds between the two branches of the Angeli was to weaken both and so benefit the Angevins. Moreover, the Serbs had now occupied the north of the Despotat, so that the Albanian Catholic population naturally preferred the rule of a prince of their own faith to that of a sovereign who was a member of the Orthodox Church. Philip himself was able to pay but little attention to his transmarine possessions, for, like his father before him, he was taken prisoner by the Aragonese, at the

[1] Ducange, *op. cit.*, ii., 326-32; Buchon, *Recherches historiques*, i., 320-4, 455; *Nouvelles Recherches*, II., i., 306-8, 315-16, 407-9; I., i., 198-9; Hopf *apud* Ersch und Gruber, lxxxv., 338; Buchon identifies "le Blecola" with Vrachori; Pachyméres, ii., 202; Minieri Riccio, *Della Dominazione Angioina*, 7, 8; *Saggio*, Supp., part i., 56.

[2] Miklosich und Müller, i., 94, 470, where the date is erroneously given as "about 1284." It should be 1307. *Cf. Regestum Clementis V.*, ii., 89.

battle of Falconaria in 1299, and was not released till the peace of Caltabellotta in 1302. But during his captivity his interests were well looked after, and his father spared no pains to conciliate the Epirotes. Two years later, Charles II. renewed the settlement of 1294, and his son was henceforth styled "Despot of Romania and Lord of the Kingdom of Albania"—the former of which titles may be read on the coins which he struck at his mint of "Nepant," or Lepanto.[1]

The seven years' peace which the Morea enjoyed during the reign of Florent was disturbed by several violent incidents. Soon after the return of the prince from Epiros he had to pay a visit to his suzerain, the King of Naples, and during his absence in 1292 a piratical squadron under the command of Roger de Lluria, the famous admiral of King James of Aragon, made its appearance in Greek waters. Lluria's brother-in-law, Berenguer d'Entença, had already ravaged Corfù and the coast of the Despotat of Epiros, but this fresh expedition was much more destructive. Lluria himself afterwards told Sanudo, that he had plundered the emperor's dominions, because the latter had failed to pay the subsidy promised to King Peter of Aragon by Michael VIII., and, as the truce of Gaeta, between the houses of Anjou and Aragon, had barely expired, he did not attack the Franks of Achaia till he was attacked by them; but he damaged both Latin and Greek islands with piratical impartiality. Chios, then a Byzantine possession, yielded him sufficient mastic to fill two galleys; the Latin duchy of Naxos afforded him further booty, and then he steered his course for Monemvasia. Since the re-establishment of Byzantine rule in the south of the Morea, thirty years before, Monemvasia had greatly increased in importance. Michael VIII. had granted its citizens valuable fiscal exemptions; his pious son had confirmed their privileges and possessions, and in 1293 gave the metropolitan the title of "Exarch of all the Peloponnesos," with jurisdiction over eight bishoprics, some, it is true, still *in partibus infidelium*, and confirmed all the rights and property of his diocese, which was raised to be the tenth of the empire and extended, at any rate on paper, right across

[1] Sáthas, Τὸ Χρονικὸν τοῦ Γαλαξειδίου, 16; Schlumberger, *Numismatique*, 388; Riccio, *Saggio*, Supp., part i., 96.

the peninsula to "Pylos, which is called Avarînos." The emperor lauds, in this interesting and beautifully illuminated document, still preserved in the National Library and (in a copy) in the Christian Archæological Museum at Athens, the convenience and safe situation of the town, the number of its inhabitants, their affluence and their technical skill, their seafaring qualities, and their devotion to his throne and person.[1] Lluria doubtless found abundant booty in such a place; and he was able to sack the lower town without slaughter, for the *archons* and the people took refuge in the impregnable citadel which has defied so many armies, leaving their property and their metropolitan in his power. By the device of hoisting the Venetian flag and pretending to be a Venetian merchant, he managed to decoy a number of Mainates down to his ships, whom he carried off as slaves. Hitherto, he had not molested the Frankish part of the Morea, knowing it to be under the suzerainty of Anjou; but while he was watering and reposing at Navarino, a body of Greeks and Frankish knights under Giorgio Ghisi, the captain of Kalamata, and Jean de Tournay, "the finest and bravest gentleman in all Morea," fell upon his men. A hand-to-hand fight ensued; Lluria and Jean de Tournay charged one another with such force that their lances were shivered to splinters, and the French knight fell with all his weight over the body of his adversary. Lluria's men would have slain him, had not their leader bade them spare so gallant a warrior, in whom he recognised the son of an old acquaintance and whom he would fain have had for his own son-in-law. Most of the Franks and Greeks were soon either dead or prisoners, and it only remained for Lluria to assess and collect the ransom. For this purpose it was necessary to sail to Glarentza, the chief commercial place in Achaia, where the Princess Isabelle was then residing. When the red galley of the Aragonese commander with Jean de Tournay on board hove in sight, the Achaian admiral saluted him in her name, and beneath the shade of a tower by the sea-shore, at a place called Kalopotami, "the fair river," Isabelle and her visitor met. The good burgesses of Glarentza were requested to advance the

[1] Miklosich und Müller, v., 154-61; Phrantzês, 399; Doróthеos of Monemvasia, 400; Δελτίον τῆς Χριστ. 'Αρχ. 'Εταιρ., vi., 111-19.

ransom of the captives—£3584 for Ghisi, whose father, the lord of Tenos, was a wealthy man, as Lluria knew full well, for he had lately visited his island, and half that sum for Tournay. The Aragonese admiral was loud in his praise of the man who had unhorsed him; he gave him a fine horse and a suit of mail, as a remembrance, and released all the other prisoners to please him. Then he set sail for Sicily, laden with treasure "enough to satisfy five armies," not forgetting to plunder Patras, Cephalonia, and Corfù on the way. From this expedition Muntaner dates the lack of good men able to defend the Morea.[1]

Not long after Lluria's expedition the Slavs of Gianitza, near Kalamata, surprised, in a period of profound peace, the ancestral castle of the Villehardouins, where Prince William had been born and died, and absolutely refused to give it up to Florent. The latter appealed to the Byzantine governor at Mistrâ, but his reply was that the Slavs had neither acted by his advice, nor recognised his authority; "they are people," he said, "who do as they like, and only obey their own chiefs," a fairly accurate definition of the manner in which the Melings of Taygetos had always lived. Failing to obtain satisfaction from the emperor's representative, Florent sent two envoys to the emperor, Jean de Chauderon, the grand constable, and Geoffroy d'Aunoy, baron of Arkadia, who had both learnt the Greek language and Greek ways at Constantinople, where they had already been on an embassy, while the latter had married a relative of the emperor. At first Andrónikos II. refused to see them, for he was by no means anxious to order the restoration of Kalamata. But they chanced to meet Pierre de Surie, whom Charles II. had sent as an emissary to Naples to discuss the proposed marriage of the titular empress Catherine of Courtenay with the son of Andrónikos. To him they disclosed their business, and he contrived that the emperor should not only grant them an audience, but give them a favourable response. The delighted envoys were, however, informed by the marshal of

[1] *Le Livre de la Conqueste*, pp. 359-77, which, however, confuses the dates; Muntaner, chs. cxvi., cxvii., clix.; *Libro de los Fechos*, pp. 107-10. Bartholomæus de Neocastro and Nicolaus Specialis *apud* Muratori, *op. cit.*, xiii., 1185; x., 959; Sanudo, p. 133.

the Byzantine province of Mistrâ, who was then in Constantinople, that the emperor had none the less given secret orders, of which he would probably be the bearer, that the castle should not be given up. This man, Sgouro-mailly by name, was a half-caste from Messenia, a descendant of the Greek family of Sgourós and the French family of Mailly, and, unlike most of the *Gasmoûloi*, had a marked predilection for the Franks, though well aware that the half-castes of the Morea had a factitious importance at Constantinople which led to valuable posts. He therefore suggested that the envoys should return with him on his swift galley, and should at once obtain in writing the imperial order for the surrender of Kalamata. They acted on his advice; the half-caste was as good as his word; the castle was occupied by his followers, and at once restored to the Franks, to the great joy of Florent. Sgouro-mailly, however, paid dearly for his Francophil feelings. When he returned to his post at Mistrâ, he found a secret order from the emperor, bidding him on no account surrender Kalamata. Regarded as a traitor by the Greeks, he had to flee to Tzakonia; his office was taken from him, and he died in a humble straw-loft, a fugitive and an outlaw. A century and a half later we find his family still mentioned among the Moreot *archons*, and the name exists in the Peloponnese to-day.[1]

Another incident served to disturb the relations between Franks and Greeks, and illustrates the insolence of the Flemings, who had followed their countryman into the Morea, and had there received baronial lands, often at the cost of the old Frankish nobility. Among these newcomers were two near relatives of Florent,[2] Engelbert and Walter de Liedekerke, of whom the former succeeded old Jean de Chauderon, as grand constable, while the latter was appointed governor of the castle of Corinth. Walter was an extravagant man, who found his emoluments quite inadequate to his expenditure, and resorted to extortion in order to maintain

[1] *L. d. C.*, 335-59; Miklosich und Müller, iii., 290; Adamantiou (in Δελτίον, vi., 596) considers the name simply means "curly locks."

[2] They are described in the French and Spanish *Chronicles* as his nephews; but we are not told in the genealogy of Florent (Buchon, *Recherches historiques*, i., 499) that he had any sisters.

his establishment. So profound was the peace between Greeks and Franks at this time, that many of the emperor's subjects from the Byzantine province had settled on the fertile lands near the Corinthian Gulf, which they shared in common with the Frankish vassals of the prince. Among these settlers was a certain Phótios, cousin of Jacques le Chasy, or Zásses,[1] "the most gallant soldier that the emperor had in all Morea," who at that time held the old domain of the Tournay family at Kalavryta, and whose clan, perhaps of Slavonic origin, ruled over a part of Tzakonia. The serfs, who cultivated these lands, disliked Phótios's presence there, and complained to Corinth that they could not support the burdens of two lords. Their complaint was carried to Walter, who at once ordered the arrest of Phótios, on the ground that neither Franks nor Greeks had the right of settling on the common lands. When he saw that his prisoner was a rich man, he resolved to make him pay a heavy blackmail. He thrust him into the castle keep, and told him that unless he paid the damages for his trespass, assessed at more than £4480, he would hang him. Phótios at first refused to pay, but the governor ordered two of his teeth to be extracted—a form of argument so convincing that he was glad to compound with his gaoler for a tenth of the original sum. As soon as he was free, he appealed to the commander of the Byzantine province for retribution, and the latter laid the matter before Florent, who, however, supported his relative, adding that Phótios had got less than his deserts.

Finding justice thus denied to him, Phótios resolved to take the law into his own hands. Accordingly he lay in wait for Liedekerke at the little harbour of St Nicholas of the Fig-tree (the modern Xylókastro), on the southern shore of the Corinthian Gulf, thinking that the governor would probably land there to take his mid-day meal by the edge of an abundant spring. Presently, sure enough, a Frankish galley hove in sight, and from it there stepped ashore a noble baron with fair complexion and blond hair, the very image of Walter. Phótios, certain of his man, waited till the baron was seated at his repast, and then struck

[1] The name Chások was that of the Byzantine official who was stoned by the Athenians in 915.

him again and again with his sword, crying aloud with revengeful joy, "There, my lord Walter, take your money!" The wounded man's attendants shouted aloud, "Ha! Phóti, Phóti, what are you doing? You are killing the baron of Vostitza, by mistake for the governor of Corinth!" Horror-stricken at his mistake, for Guy de Charpigny, the late bailie of the Morea, was beloved by all, Phótios threw away his sword, lifted the wounded man tenderly in his arms, and begged his forgiveness. But it was too late; his innocent victim died of his wounds, nor did Florent, who realised that the fault lay with his own relative, venture to seek reparation by force from the Byzantine governor.[1]

At last the seven years' peace, which had so greatly benefited the Morea, came to an end. At Vervaina, between Tripolitza and Sparta, there was a beautiful meadow, on which an annual fair was held in the middle of June; it was a central position, so that Greeks and Franks alike flocked thither to buy and sell; such festivals were common in Frankish times as in classic days, and one of the privileges which Andrónikos III. gave to the Monemvasiotes was his special protection at all the Peloponnesian fairs.[2] Now it chanced on this occasion, that a French knight, who lived hard by, came to words with a Greek silk-merchant, and from words the arrogant Frank proceeded to blows. The silk-merchant returned to his home muttering vengeance, and conceived the design of capturing the castle of St George, which, from its commanding situation in front of Skortá, would be a peculiarly acceptable prize to the emperor. Having gained two traitors within the castle walls, he confided his plan to a fellow-countryman from Skortá, who commanded a body of Turkish mercenaries in the imperial service; a moonlight night was chosen for the venture, the traitors did their work, and next morning the Byzantine double-eagle flew from the castle keep, and the Turkish garrison mounted guard on the ramparts. When Florent heard the news at his favourite residence of Andravida, he

[1] *L. d. C.*, 325-35, which, however, inverts the chronological order of the last two incidents. The second has been made the subject of a modern tragedy, Φώτιος Ζάσσης, ἤτοι τὰ Καλάβρυτα ἐπὶ Φραγκοκρατίας.

[2] Bull of 1332, Phrantzês, 400.

marched at once to besiege the stolen fortress. But, though he swore that he would stay there till he retook it, though he summoned an experienced Venetian engineer from Coron who did some harm to the tower, though he fortified one strong position after another and built another castle which he called Beaufort, perhaps identical with "the Fair Castle" (Oraiokastro) in the mountains behind Astros, to command the pass to Skortá, and though he sent for soldiers from Apulia and obtained archers and spearmen from a powerful Slav chieftain who ruled in Maina, the fine castle held out. At last, when winter came, Florent withdrew. Before the following spring of 1297, he was dead. The French chronicler mourns his loss, "for he was upright and wise, and knew well how to govern his land and his people."[1] If he had the faults of a foreigner, he was a brave man who was yet a lover of peace. Unfortunately, like Prince William before him, he left no son, only one daughter, Mahaut or Matilda, who was a child of three years of age at her father's death. It seemed as if the destinies of Achaia were ever to depend on women. Her mother, Isabelle, continued to reign as Princess of Achaia, whose coinage bore her name, but she soon retired to her favourite castle of Nesi or L'Ille, as the Franks translated it, situated in the delightful climate of her own Kalamata. The administration of the principality she entrusted to a bailie, Count Richard of Cephalonia, who not long after married her widowed sister, Marguerite, and was connected with all the leaders of the Frankish world.[2] A new chancellor was appointed in the person of Benjamin of Kalamata, and a Greek named Basilópoulos became

[1] *L. d. C.*, 377-86, 472; Buchon, Χ. τ. Μ. (ed. 1825), p. xlvi.; *La Grèce Continentale*, 399 *sqq*. The Aragonese version of the *Chronicle* (pp. 103-6) narrates these last events quite differently. It says that the Byzantine governor ordered the purchase of as many horses as possible from the Franks at the most liberal rates, that he then sought an excuse for hostilities, took Nikli and the castle of Chalandritza, entirely destroyed the former town, and built the castles of Palaio-Mouchli (near the present railway between Argos and Tripolitza) and Cepiana (the ancient Nestáne, a little to the north of Mouchli) to command the plain.

[2] *Les Registres de Boniface VIII.*, ii., 523. His first wife had been a sister of Thomas III. of Salona.

chamberlain—a sign of the prominent position now occupied by the natives.

Florent had left his people at war with the Byzantine province, and it was therefore the first care of his widow to protect her frontier. This she did by building a new castle, Chastel-neuf as it was called, in the vale of Kalamata, through which the present railway travels. By this means the people of western Messenia were freed from the necessity of paying dues to the governors of the two nearest Greek castles, Mistrâ and Gardiki—the fortress which the emperor had built in the pass of Makryplagi, above the cave where the Greek commanders had taken refuge after that memorable battle.[1] But the barons thought that a politic marriage would be an even better protection for their country than strong walls. There was some talk of a union between the widowed princess and John, the son of the emperor. Andrónikos had himself been suggested as a husband for Isabelle more than thirty years earlier, so that there would have been some disproportion between the mature charms of the Achaian princess and the extreme youth of his son. This alliance fell through; but it was agreed, on the proposal of Nicholas III. de St Omer, the Grand Marshal of Achaia, that a marriage should be arranged between the little princess Matilda and his young cousin, Guy II., Duke of Athens, who had now come of age, and was regarded as "the best match in all Romania."[2]

The seven years' minority of the young Duke had been an uneventful period in the history of Athens. His Greek mother, Helene Angela, had provided him with a powerful guardian by her second marriage with her late husband's brother-in-law, Hugues de Brienne, who was now a widower, and who brought her half the great barony of Karytaina, which figures on her coins—almost the sole instance of a baronial currency in the Morea.[3] A delicate feudal question,

[1] X. τ. M., l. 5429; *L. d. C.*, 387.

[2] *Ibid.*, 388-90; Pachyméres, II., p. 290.

[3] Schlumberger, *op. cit.*, 325. The only other instance is that of a baron of Damalâ. But Neroûtsos (Δελτίον, iv., 114, *n.* 2) takes the inscription on this coin to mean "Lady of Gravia," the place which was part of her dowry.

the same which had led to war between Athens and Achaia a generation earlier, alone disturbed the repose of the ducal court, and threatened to renew that fratricidal strife. The Duchess of Athens had done homage to the Neapolitan court, but both she and her husband Hugues flatly refused to recognise themselves as the vassals of Prince Florent of Achaia, on the ground that there was no feudal nexus between the two Frankish states. Both parties appealed to their common suzerain, Charles II. of Naples, who, after a futile attempt to settle the matter by arbitration, finally wrote, in 1294, that when he had conferred Achaia upon Florent he had intended the gift to include the overlordship of Athens. Accordingly, he expressly renewed that grant, and peremptorily ordered Guy II., who had by that time come of age, and his vassals, among whom Thomas III. of Salona, Othon of St Omer, and Francesco da Verona are specially mentioned, to do homage to the Prince of Achaia. At last, after two years' further delay, the Duke of Athens obeyed.[1]

The coming of age of the last De la Roche Duke of Athens has been described by the quaint Catalan chronicler, Ramón Muntaner.[2] The ceremony took place on St John Baptist's day, 1294, at Thebes, whither the young duke had invited all the great men of his duchy; he had let it be known, too, throughout the Greek Empire and the Despotat of Epiros and his mother's home of Thessaly, that whosoever came should receive gifts and favours from his hand—"for he was one of the noblest men in all Romania who was not a king, and eke one of the richest." When all the guests had assembled, mass was celebrated in the cathedral by Nicholas, Archbishop of Thebes, and then all eyes were fixed upon the duke, to see whom he would ask to confer upon him the order of knighthood—a duty which the King of France or the emperor himself would have thought it a pleasure and an honour to perform. What was the surprise of the brilliant throng when Guy, instead of calling upon one of his great nobles, Thomas III. of Salona or Othon of St Omer, fellow-owner with the duke himself of the barony of

[1] *L. d. C.*, 269-71; Χ. τ. Μ., 7979-81, 8018-46; Buchon, *Nouvelles Recherches*, I., i., 233-5; II., i., 334-8; Riccio, *Saggio*, Supp., pt. i., 90; Sáthas, Τὸ Χρονικὸν τοῦ Γαλαξειδίου, 238.

[2] Ch. ccxliv.

Thebes, summoned to his side a young knight of Eubœa, Bonifacio da Verona, grandson of that Guglielmo I. who had styled himself King of Salonika and had played so large a part in the events of his time. Bonifacio was, however, a poor man, the youngest of three brothers, whose sole possession was a single castle, which he had sold the better to equip himself and his retinue. Yet no one made a braver show than he at the Athenian court, whither he had gone to seek his fortune; he always wore the richest clothes, and on the day of the great ceremony none was more elegantly dressed than he and his company, though everyone equipped himself and the jongleurs in the fairest apparel. He had fully a hundred wax tapers ornamented with his arms, yet he had borrowed the money for all this outlay, trusting to the future to pay it back. This was the man whom the duke now bade approach. "Come here," quoth he, "Master Boniface, close to my lord archbishop, for our will is that thou shalt dub us a knight." "Ah, my lord," replied Boniface, "what sayest thou! thou dost surely mock me." "No, by our troth," quoth the duke, "so do we wish it to be." Then Boniface, seeing that the duke spake from his heart, came and stood near the archbishop at the altar, whereon lay the arms of the duke, and dubbed him a knight. Then the duke said aloud, before all the company, "Master Boniface, custom it is, that those who make men knights should make them presents too. Howsobeit, it is our will to do the contrary. Thou hast made us a knight, wherefore we give thee from this moment 50,000 *sols* of revenue for thee and thine for ever, in castles and in goodly places and in freehold, to do therewith as thou wilt. We give thee also to wife the daughter of a certain baron whose hand is ours to bestow, and who is lady of part of the island and city of Negroponte."[1] The duke was true to his word; he gave him his own mother's dowry of Gardiki in Thessaly with the classic island of Salamis,[2] thirteen castles in all on the mainland of

[1] Muntaner says "a third part"; but Agnes was not one of the *terzieri*.

[2] So Hopf (*apud* Ersch und Gruber, lxxxv., 377) interprets "Selizirij," which occurs in the Venetian list of Greek rulers, drawn up in 1311-13, where Boniface figures as *dominator Caristi et Gardichie, Selizirij et Egue* (Hopf, *Chroniques gréco-romanes*, 177); Muntaner (ch. ccxliii.) mentions the thirteen castles; *L. d. C.*, 408, 415.

the duchy, and the hand of his cousin, Agnes de Cicon, lady of Ægina and Karystos. It was true that the latter castle was still in the hands of the Greeks, but not long afterwards Boniface showed that he had deserved his good fortune by wresting it from them. The Catalan chronicler, who had stayed in Boniface's house at Negroponte and had there heard the story of his sudden rise, might well say that this was the noblest gift that any prince made in a single day for a long time. The episode gives us, indeed, some idea of the wealth and splendour of the Burgundian dukes of Athens.

Such was the man whom Nicholas de St Omer proposed as a husband for Princess Isabelle's little daughter. Guy, on his part, gladly accepted the idea of an alliance, which, if he could obtain the sanction of the King of Naples, might one day, in due course of nature, make him Prince of Achaia, and thus end for ever the vexatious question of homage. So, when the Achaian envoys arrived, he at once agreed to their suggestion that he should pay a visit to their mistress and his suzerain. He sent for Thomas III. of Salona, his chief vassal and the most honourable man in all Romania, and for his other barons and knights, and set out in 1299 with his accustomed splendour for Vlisiri (or La Glisière, as the Franks called it) in Elis, a land of goodly mansions, where there was ample accommodation for the princess and all her retinue. There the marriage was arranged; Kalamata, the family fief of the Villehardouins, became the dowry of the bride; the bishop of Olena performed the ceremony; and, after some twenty days of feasting and rejoicings, the duke departed for Thebes with his five-year-old wife. The King of Naples, who at first protested against a marriage with this mere child, contracted without his previous consent, subsequently gave his approval; the qualms of Pope Boniface VIII. at the union of rather distant cousins, were pacified by the gift of twenty silken garments from the manufactories of Thebes. Such dispensations were commonly granted to the Frankish lords of Greece at this period, for, as the pope said in a similar case, their numbers had been so reduced by war, that they could scarcely find wives of their own social rank who were not related to them.[1]

Isabelle herself did not long remain a widow after her daughter's marriage. In 1300, Boniface VIII. held the first jubilee, or *anno santo*, of the Roman Church, and among the thousands who flocked to Rome on that great occasion was the Princess of Achaia. Before she sailed from Glarentza, she appointed Nicholas de St Omer bailie during her absence, as it was considered that Count Richard of Cephalonia, who was now her brother-in-law—for he had recently married her sister Marguerite, the Lady of Akova—had grown too old to govern the country in time of war. Isabelle met in Rome, not by accident—for negotiations had been going on for some time about the matter—Philip of Savoy, son of the late Count Thomas III. A child at the time of his father's death, he had been superseded in Savoy by his uncle, Amedeo V., but had received Piedmont as his share, and had fixed his sub-Alpine capital at Pinerolo, where his remains still lie. Philip was a valiant knight, not much over twenty, who could help her to defend her land against the Greeks and might even recover what her father had lost; the pope was in favour of the union, and the protest of King Charles II. of Naples, who appealed to the conditions laid down at the time of Isabelle's second marriage, was induced, on the papal intervention, to give his consent. At the palace where he was then staying, near the Lateran, he invested Philip of Savoy with the principality of Achaia, in the name of his own imprisoned son, Philip of Taranto, to whom, as we saw, he had transferred the suzerainty seven years before, and one of the witnesses of the deed was that same Roger de Lluria, now in the Angevin service, who had met Isabelle at Glarentza under such very different circumstances. The marriage, which took place in Rome in 1301, was a grand affair; the bill for the wedding breakfast—a very extensive one—has been preserved, and the frugal Greeks would have been surprised at the quantity of food provided for their new prince and his guests. A few days before the wedding,

[1] *L. d. C.*, 390-3; Sanudo, 136; X. τ. M., ll. 7982-4; *Les Registres de Boniface VIII.*, i., 485; ii., 465; Lámpros, Ἔγγραφα, 44; Grazie (1298-1304), fol. 16.

Isabelle bestowed the castle and town of Corinth upon her future husband, who, in his turn, promised to bring a certain number of soldiers with him to Greece for the defence of the land and the prosecution of the war. The honeymoon was spent in Piedmont, where the prince had to put his affairs in order. Indeed, it was not till the end of 1302 that the princess returned with him and a body of Savoyards and Piedmontese to her native land.[1]

Philip of Savoy swore, like his predecessor, to observe the usages of the land, and was greeted, in the name of the assembled vassals, by the Archbishop of Patras, who had played the most prominent part, alike when Charles I. had sent his first bailie and when Florent had been appointed prince. But the new prince soon tried to disregard the customs of the country. He knew that the King of Naples really disliked his marriage, and the knowledge that Charles II. might at any time depose him, and would probably do so in the event of his surviving Isabelle, increased his natural desire to make up for his heavy expenditure in coming, and to lay by for a rainy day. "He had learned money-making at home from the tyrants of Lombardy," it was whispered, when he began to practise a system of regular extortion. As soon as he had put his Piedmontese and Savoyard officers and soldiers into the castles of the Morea, he summoned his chief confidant, Guillaume de Monbel, whom he had brought with him from Italy, and took counsel how he could best fill his coffers. In this enterprise he received assistance from one of his predecessor's advisers, Vincent de Marays, a sly old knight from Picardy and a *protégé* of Count Richard of Cephalonia, who had a grudge against the chancellor, Benjamin of Kalamata, for having secured his patron's dismissal from the post of bailie. Benjamin was a rich man, who was a larger landowner than even Leonardo of Veroli had been, and therefore well able to pay blackmail. An excuse for extortion was found in the chancellor's omission

[1] *L. d. C.*, 393-8, 404, 434, 472; Χ. τ. Μ., ll. 8588-90; Guichenon, *Histoire généalogique de . . . Savoye*, II., *Preuves*, pp. 102-4; Buchon, *Recherches historiques*, ii., 379; *Nouvelles Recherches*, II., i., 339-43; Datta, *Storia dei Principi di Savoia*, i., pp. xv., 33-5; Hopf, *Chroniques gréco-romanes*, 231-5.

to send in his accounts of public monies received by him during several years; and he was forthwith arrested on a charge of malversation. Benjamin appealed in his trouble to his powerful friend, Nicholas III. de St Omer, whose appointment as bailie he had obtained, and who was at once the most beloved and the most dreaded man in Achaia. The haughty marshal marched straight into the chamber where the prince was sitting with the princess and his Piedmontese friends, and asked him point-blank, why he had ordered the chancellor's arrest. When Philip replied, that Benjamin owed him an account of the revenues which had passed through his hands, St Omer rejoined that the imprisonment of a liege for debt was against the customs of the country. "Hah! cousin," quoth the prince, "where did you find these customs of yours?" At that the marshal drew a huge knife, and, holding it straight before him, cried: "Behold our customs! by this sword our forefathers conquered this land, and by this sword we will defend our franchises and usages against those who would break or restrict them." The princess, fearing for her husband's life, exclaimed aloud; but St Omer reassured her by saying that it was not the prince but his evil counsellors whom he accused. The irate marshal was finally appeased by a soft answer; the chancellor procured his release from prison by a payment of 20,000 *hyperperi* of Glarentza (£8960) to the prince. From that moment the wily Benjamin ingratiated himself with his avaricious master, whose passion for money he well knew how to gratify at the same time as his own desire for revenge. At his suggestion, his enemy Count Richard of Cephalonia was compelled to lend Philip 20,000 *hyperperi*, for which he received almost nothing in return. But this was not all that the prince managed to squeeze out of the wealthy family of the Cephalonian Orsini. When, a little later, old Count Richard was killed by one of his own knights, whom he had struck on the head with a stick while sitting on the Bench at Glarentza, his son John I. had to purchase his investiture with his islands from his suzerain, the Prince of Achaia, by a large present of money. Not long afterwards he gave Philip a heavy bribe to decide in his favour an action brought against him in the High

Court of Achaïa by his stepmother, the Lady of Akova, for restitution of her late husband's personal property, valued at £44,800. The proud Nicholas de St Omer, however, espoused the cause of the lady, more from contempt and dislike for the venal prince than from a desire to punish the violence of his brother-in-law, the new Count of Cephalonia. Again, Philip had to suppress his indignation at the insolence of the greatest baron in the land, who boasted that he had royal blood in his veins, who was cousin of the Duke of Athens, and connected by feudal ties with the leading Achaian nobles; a compromise was made, by which the Lady of Akova was to receive one-fifth of the amount claimed. From other quarters, too, the Piedmontese prince extorted various sums. Basilópoulos, the Greek who had been appointed chamberlain, made him a compulsory present of £1344; the people of Karytaina contributed £1792; the citizens of Andravida, his favourite residence, £224; the burgesses of Glarentza, £268, 16s.; while the tolls of that port were charged with an annuity of £134, 8s. to one of his Piedmontese favourites. These transactions give us some idea of the wealth of Greece at this period.

Yet, in spite of all these "benevolences," the prince had to raise a loan from the Glarentza branch of the Florentine banking-house of Peruzzi, which financed our own sovereigns. At last his exactions led to a serious rising. The people of Skortá had always been the most turbulent element of the population, and their mountainous country—the Switzerland of the Morea—the most jealously guarded by the Franks. Yet, in spite of the well-known characteristics of these Arkadian mountaineers, and of the natural fortress which they inhabited, Philip, instigated by his evil genius, the old knight from Picardy, must needs impose an extraordinary tax upon the Arkadian *archons*. He was told that they were rich, and the large sum which he had already received from the Arkadian town of Karytaina doubtless made him think that they could well afford to pay more. But the natives of Gortys, from the Frankish times to those of M. Delyánnes, have been sticklers for their constitutional rights, guaranteed to them at the time of the Conquest. Their chief men met in the house of the two brothers Mikronâs, at the foot of the mountain, on which stand the lonely ruins of the noble temple of Bassæ, and swore, in a spirit worthy of the ancient Greeks, that they would rather die than pay a single farthing of the tax. The only man who might have prevented their rising was Nicholas de St Omer; but they knew that he was going to Thessaly; and, the moment that he had gone, they sent two spokesmen to Mistrâ to invite the Byzantine governor's aid and offer their land to the emperor. Their mission aroused no suspicion, for it was a common thing for pilgrims to visit the shrine of St Nikon at Lacedæmonia—the Armenian monk, who, after converting the Cretan apostates back to Christianity, had established himself in the latter part of the tenth century at Sparta, where his memory is still green. The governor received their offer with gladness; he assembled his troops on the famous plain of Nikli, whence the traitors guided them by a sure road into Skortá. Soon two Frankish castles, St Helena and Crève-Cœur, on either side of Andritsaina, were smoking ruins. But the Greeks, as the chronicler remarks, were better at a first assault than at a prolonged siege. Florent's newly-built castle of Beaufort resisted their attack, and when Philip approached, they speedily fled in disorder. The prince wisely abstained from carrying the war into the Byzantine province. He bade the terrified serfs, who had fled from Greeks and Franks alike, return to their homes; enquired from them the cause of the rebellion; and, when he was told that it was the work of a family party of *archons*, contented himself with confiscating the lands and goods of the latter.[1]

We saw that the rising would not have happened but for the absence of the marshal Nicholas de St Omer in Thessaly, and it is now necessary to describe the important events which had necessitated his presence there. In 1296, both Nikephóros, Despot of Epiros, and the bastard John I., Duke of Neopatras, had died; and, seven years later, the latter's son and successor, Constantine, had followed his father to the grave, leaving an only son, John II., who was still a

[1] *L. d. C.*, 398-405, 306, 413, 422-54, 472; *L. d. F.*, 111-13; Ducange, *op. cit.*, ii., 341-2; Gerland, *Neue Quellen*, 245; Riccio, *Studii Storici*, 30; Hopf *apud* Ersch und Gruber, lxxxv., 352; Datta, *op. cit.*, ii., 30-1.

minor at the time of his death. In his last will and testament Constantine had appointed his nephew Guy II., Duke of Athens, guardian of the child and regent of his dominions, not only because Guy was his nearest surviving male relative, but because the Athenian duchy, then the strongest of all the Frankish states, could alone protect Thessaly against the designs of the Emperor Andrónikos II. on the one side, and of the able and ambitious Lady Anna, of Epiros, who was regent in the name of the young Despot Thomas, on the other. Guy, who had already interests on the Thessalian frontier, joyfully accepted the honourable office, which flattered his ambition. He summoned Thomas of Salona, his chief vassal, Boniface of Verona, his favourite, and others from Eubœa, and at Zetouni, the modern Lamia, which his mother had brought as part of her dowry to the duchy of Athens, received the homage of the Thessalian baronage. There he arranged for the future government of his ward's estates. The Greek nobles were to guard the Thessalian castles, while he was to have the revenues, and provide out of them for the administration, of the country; as marshal of Thessaly, Guy appointed a nobleman who was viscount, or president of the Court of the Burgesses at Athens; as his bailie and representative in the government of the land the duke chose Antoine le Flamenc, a Fleming who had become lord of Karditza, on the margin of the Copaic lake, where a Greek inscription on the church of St George still commemorates him as its "most pious" founder, and who is described by the chronicler as "the wisest man in all the duchy." Feudalism, as we saw, had already permeated Thessaly under the rule of the Angeli; it was further strengthened by the Frankish regency; the Greek nobles learnt the French language, and coins with Latin inscriptions were issued in the name of the young Despot from the mint of Neopatras.[1]

The fears of the late Despot were speedily fulfilled. Scarcely had Guy returned to his favourite residence of

[1] Buchon, *Atlas*, plate xxxix., 5, who ascribes this coin erroneously to Aimone of Savoy. The inscription "Angelus Sab.' C. (=Sebastocrator, or Sebastocrator Comnenos) Della Patra," refers to John II. of Neopatras; Schlumberger, *op. cit.*, 382.

Thebes, when the ambitious Lady Anna of Epiros seized his ward's Thessalian Castle of Phanari—a place which still rises like a "watch-tower" above the great plain. The Duke of Athens, furious at this audacious act of a mere woman, summoned his vassals and friends, among them his cousin Nicholas de St Omer, to join him in the campaign against the Epirotes. Philip of Savoy, though on good terms with the Duke of Athens, who had done him personal homage for the duchy, the baronies of Argos and Nauplia and his wife's dowry of Kalamata, refused to give St Omer permission to leave the Morea. But the marshal departed, without his prince's consent, at the head of 89 horsemen, of whom no less than 13 were belted knights, and joined the duke not far from the field of Domokó, so memorable in the history of modern Greece. When he saw the assembled host, of which the duke begged him to assume the command, he was bound to confess that never in all Romania had he seen a braver show. There were more than 900 Frankish horsemen, all picked men; more than 6000 Thessalian and Bulgarian cavalry, commanded by 18 Greek barons, and fully 30,000 foot-soldiers. Against such a force the Lady Anna felt that she could do nothing; so, before it had advanced far beyond Kalabaka, on the way to Joannina, she offered to restore the stolen castle, and pay a war indemnity of £4480. Her offer was accepted; but, as it seemed desirable to find work for so fine an army, an excuse was made for an attack upon the Greek Empire, with which Athens was then at peace. The troops were already well on the way to Salonika, when the Empress Irene, who was living there separated from her husband, appealed to the chivalry of the Franks not to make war against a weak woman. Guy and his barons were moved by this appeal; they returned to Thessaly, and disbanded their forces.[1]

The crafty Lady of Epiros had succeeded in disarming one enemy; but she soon found herself attacked by another. Philip of Taranto had now been liberated from prison, so that his father thought that the moment had come to demand the performance of those exorbitant conditions, to which the late Despot of Epiros had consented at the time

[1] *L. d. C.*, 405-22; Nikephóros Gregorâs, i., 233 *sqq.*

of his daughter's marriage with the Angevin prince. Philip had not kept his part of the bond; for he had made the beautiful Thamar change her religion and her name; but his father, none the less, expected the precise fulfilment of the marriage-contract by the other side. He now requested the Lady Anna to hand over Epiros to Philip, or else to make her son Thomas do homage to the Prince of Taranto, on which condition he might hold the Despotat as the latter's vassal. Anna was a woman of spirit and resource; she never forgot that she belonged by birth to the imperial house, and, as a patriotic Greek, she preferred that her son's dominions, as it seemed difficult to maintain their independence, should belong to the Palaiológoi rather than to the Angevins. She accordingly made overtures to Andrónikos II. for the marriage of her son with his granddaughter, and replied to the King of Naples that Thomas was the vassal of the emperor alone. She added that the late Despot had no power to violate the laws of nature by disinheriting his son in favour of one of his daughters; she must therefore decline, so long as her son lived, to surrender to Philip anything beyond what he already held. Charles II. thought that it would be easy to conquer a woman and a boy; so, on receipt of this answer, he summoned his son's vassals, Philip of Savoy and Count John I. of Cephalonia, to his aid against the Despoina. But the strong walls of Arta, and the natural difficulties of the country, proved too much for the invaders, who soon abandoned their inglorious campaign. Anna prevented the co-operation of Philip of Savoy in a second attack upon her by a judicious bribe of £2688, while Philip, in order to have a plausible excuse for declining his suzerain's summons, issued invitations to all the vassals of Achaia to attend a general parliament on the isthmus of Corinth in the following spring of 1305.

On that famous neck of land where in classic days the Isthmian games had been held, the mediæval chivalry of Greece now assembled for a splendid tournament. All the noblest men in the land came in answer to the summons of the Prince of Achaia. There were Guy II. of Athens with a brave body of knights, the Marquis of Boudonitza, and the three barons of Eubœa, the Duke of the Archipelago and the

Count Palatine John I. of Cephalonia—the last anxious for judgment of his peers betwixt his jealous sister and her irascible husband, the Marshal Nicholas de St Omer, who summoned his Theban vassals to his side. Messengers were sent throughout the highlands and islands of Frankish Greece to proclaim to all and sundry how seven champions had come from beyond the seas and did challenge the chivalry of Romania to joust with them. Never had the fair land of Hellas seen a braver sight than that presented by the lists at Corinth in the lovely month of May, when the sky and the twin seas are at their fairest. More than a thousand knights and barons took part in the tournament, which lasted for twenty days, while all the fair ladies of Achaia "rained influence" on the combatants. There were the seven champions, clad in their armour of green taffetas covered with scales of gold; there was the Prince of Achaia, who acquitted himself right nobly in the lists, with all his household. Most impetuous of all was the young Duke of Athens, eager to match his skill in horsemanship and with the lance against Master William Bouchart, justly accounted one of the best jousters of the West. The chivalrous Bouchart would fain have spared his less experienced antagonist. But the duke, who had cunningly padded himself beneath his plate armour, was determined to meet him front to front; their horses collided with such force that the iron spike of Bouchart's charger pierced Guy's steed between the shoulders, so that horse and rider rolled in the dust. St Omer would have given much to meet Count John in the lists; but the latter, fearing the marshal's doughty arm, pretended that his horse could not bear him into the ring, nor could he be shamed into the combat even when Bouchart rode round and round the lists on the animal, crying aloud as he rode, "This is the horse which could not go to the jousts!"[1] So they kept high revel on the isthmus; alas! it was the last great display of the chivalry of "New France"; six years later many a knight who had ridden proudly past the fair dames of the Morea lay a mangled corpse on the swampy plain of Bœotia.

The tournament at Corinth was Philip's final appearance on the stage of Greek public life. Charles II. had consented

[1] *L. d. C.*, 454-62, 464-70, 472; Pachymères, II., 450.

with reluctance to his marriage; he was now resolved that the house of Anjou should have the real possession, as well as the shadowy suzerainty, of Achaia. Although Philip had responded to his previous summons to aid him in Epiros, towards the end of 1304 he had renewed his original declaration that Isabelle, by marrying without his consent, had forfeited the principality of Achaia, in accordance with the terms laid down at the time of her former marriage with Florent. Philip's refusal to assist his suzerain in a second Epirote campaign gave the King of Naples a further excuse for deposing the princess and her husband; such a refusal constituted a gross breach of the feudal code, which justified Charles in releasing the Achaian barons from their allegiance to their prince. The latter did not await that final blow; before it was delivered, he had quitted the Morea for his Italian dominions, against which the house of Anjou was also plotting, leaving his old enemy, Nicholas de St Omer, as bailie. If we may believe the Aragonese *Chronicle of the Morea*,[1] Isabelle's elder daughter, Matilda of Athens, claimed Achaia as her heritage from the bailie, who refused to hand it to her without orders from Naples. Her husband retaliated by seizing St Omer's half of Thebes, including the castle which bore his name. Charles II., however, bestowed the forfeited principality of Achaia upon his favourite son, Philip of Taranto, who soon afterwards arrived there on his way to attack the Lady of Epiros, and received the homage of the Achaian barons. Thus, both the actual possession and the suzerainty of the principality were once more in the hands of the same person. Any claims that Philip of Savoy and Isabelle might still entertain were bought by the King of Naples and his son, who, in exchange for their Greek dominions, promised to give them, upon the death of the existing countess, the county of Alba, on the shores of the Fucine lake, worth 600 gold ounces (£1440) a year, and to pay them, during the remainder of her life, an annuity of that amount. To the one child of their marriage, little Marguerite of Savoy, Charles II. promised sufficient land near Alba to yield a dowry of 200 gold ounces, or £480 a year, on condition that she ceded the two castles of

[1] Pp. 113, 114, where the chronology is obviously confused.

Karytaina and Bucelet, which her parents had bestowed upon her. By way of enhancing the importance of his gift, the king raised Alba to the rank of a principality; but he neither put Philip of Savoy into actual possession of it, nor paid him the promised annuity. Isabelle did not long survive the loss of her inheritance. In 1311, disregarding these arrangements with the King of Naples, she made a will, leaving her elder daughter, Matilda, heiress of all Achaia, with the exception of the three castles of Karytaina, Beauvoir (above Katakolo), and Beauregard (also in Elis), which were to form the dowry of her younger daughter, Marguerite. In the same year, Isabelle died in Holland—the country of her second husband. Philip of Savoy almost immediately remarried; and though his and Isabelle's daughter, Marguerite, renounced all her claims to Greece on her marriage in 1324, his descendants by his second marriage continued to style themselves "Princes of Achaia" till the extinction of their line a century later, and, like their ancestor, issued coins with that title engraved upon them. One of these Piedmontese princes even endeavoured to make good his pretensions, and down to the last century illegitimate descendants of Philip of Savoy usurped the name of Achaia.[1]

Princess Isabelle of Achaia is one of the most striking figures in the portrait-gallery of the ladies of the Latin Orient. Affianced when a mere child to a foreign prince whom she had never seen; torn from her home and sent to live in an Italian castle, which was to be almost a prison; widowed at an age when most women are not yet wed; separated for long years from her fatherland, till at last she was allowed to return as the wife of a gallant Flemish adventurer; widowed again, and then re-married, midst the pomp and ceremony of the papal court, to a third husband, only to die, after all these vicissitudes, still in middle age, an exile in a distant northern land—she was throughout her life

[1] X. τ. M., ll. 8588-90; *L. d. C.*, 473 (which gives the wrong date, however), 474; Buchon, *Nouvelles Recherches*, II., i., 339-43; I., i., 237; *Atlas*, xxiv., 9, 12-15; Guichenon, *Histoire généalogique*, I., 318; II., *Preuves*, pp. 104, 110, 111; Datta, *op. cit.*, i., 49-50, 56, 67, 89; ii., 45-50, 114; Ptolemæus Lucensis *apud* Muratori, *op. cit.*, xi., 1227, 1232; Muntaner, ch. cclxii; St Genois, *Droits primitifs*, i., 338.

the victim of dynastic politics. A brave woman, every inch a Villehardouin, she did not flinch from meeting the boldest corsair of that age on the sea shore; deeply imbued with piety, she founded the monastery of Sta. Chiara, near Olena. We can see her still, as she rode through the streets of Naples on her "sombre brown pillion of Douai cloth," which the careful Angevin provided for his prisoner of state—a cheap price to pay for keeping in his clutches the "Lady of the Morea."[1]

Philip of Taranto did not remain long in his Peloponnesian principality. As soon as he had received the homage of the barons, who were not sorry to be rid of his extortionate namesake, he set out for Epiros, to substantiate his claims there. But, woman as she was, the Lady Anna was too much for the Neapolitan prince; an epidemic came to her aid, and he returned unsuccessful to Naples. As his bailie in Achaia he appointed Guy II., Duke of Athens, the most important of all the contemporary Frankish rulers of Greece, whose wife, Matilda, as the elder daughter of Isabelle, would naturally represent in the eyes of the Moreot barons the princely house of Villehardouin.[2] In this way, perhaps, he hoped to satisfy her claims. Two years earlier, when still only twelve, she had attained her majority, and the festival had been celebrated at Thebes with all the customary splendour of the Athenian court, in the presence of her widowed aunt, the Lady of Akova, Nicholas de St Omer, the two archbishops of Athens and Thebes, and other high ecclesiastical and civic dignitaries.

It was, indeed, a time of great prosperity for the Athenian duchy, whose ruler was at once Duke of Athens, regent of Thessaly, and bailie of Achaia. We have already seen how great were the riches and position of the duke, who delighted in splendid apparel, and whose frescoed Theban castle rang with the songs of minstrels. Nor was this prosperity merely superficial. Now, for the first time, we find Attica supplying Venice with corn, which usually had to be imported into the duchy from the south of Italy; while the gift of silken

[1] *Arch. Stor. Ital.*, Ser. IV., iv., 176; *Les Registres de Boniface VIII.*, ii., 845; *Regestum Clementis V.*, i., 283.

[2] *L. d. F.*, 117.

garments to Boniface VIII. is a proof of the continued manufacture of silk at Thebes. No less than three series of coins were required for the commercial needs of the duchy in his reign. Athens, too, was a religious centre. We find Pope Nicholas IV.[1] granting indulgences to all who visited "Santa Maria di Atene" on the festivals of the Virgin, of St James the Apostle, and St Eligius, and on the anniversary of its dedication as a Christian church. It was now, too, that the canon Nicholas de la Roche founded an ecclesiastical building, perhaps the belfry of the ancient church of Great St Mary's, which stood till a few years ago, in the Stoa of Hadrian, while the great Byzantine monastery of Hósios Loukâs, near Delphi, received fresh lustre from the presence of the dowager duchess within its walls. Not far away, on an islet in the Gulf of Corinth, the persecuted Eremites from Italy begged Thomas of Salona to give them a refuge, only to find that even there the long arm of the mundane pope could reach them. Prosperous, indeed, must have been the region round Parnassos, for "the hero" Thomas had his private mint, which his jealous lord, the duke, tried to prohibit.[2] But the days of the ducal family were drawing to a close. The splendid magnificence of the duke could not conceal the incurable malady which was undermining his health; he had no heirs of his body; and, to the north, there lay that company of wandering Catalan warriors, which was already a menace to his dominions.

A hundred years had passed away since the Conquest, and Greece, in this first decade of the fourteenth century, was practically divided between the Duke of Athens, the Angevins, the Orsini, the Greeks, and the Venetians. The house of Anjou had obtained possession of Achaia from the family of the conqueror, had established itself in the finest of the Ionian islands, and had gained a footing here and there on the coast of Epiros. The Orsini had tightened their hold over their county palatine in the Ionian Sea, but neither Angevins nor Orsini had absorbed the Greeks, who

[1] *Registres*, 610; Schlumberger, *Numismatique*, 339; *Mélanges historiques*, iii., 27; St Genois, i., 336; Capricornus, fol. 337.

[2] Wadding, *Annales Minorum*, v., 324; vi., 1, 11; Sáthas, Τὸ Χρονικὸν τοῦ Γαλαξειδίου, 239.

were their neighbours. If Frankish influence, personified by the Duke of Athens and his viceroy, was predominant in Thessaly, an able and unscrupulous woman still held Epiros for the national cause, while the pope plaintively wrote that "much of Achaia was in Greek hands," and in vain ordered a tithe to be levied and paid to its prince for the recovery of what had been lost.[1] Venice, however, had maintained and strengthened her three colonies of Modon, Coron, and Negroponte. Lluria had spared the two Messenian stations on his cruise round the Morea, because their Venetian masters were at peace with the house of Aragon; but the republic, none the less, constructed an arsenal at Coron, and restored the walls of Modon. Their trade naturally suffered when the dominions of the republic were laid under an interdict by the pope, and after the great earthquake of 1304; but such was their prosperity in 1291, that it was ordered that 2000 ounces should be sent to Venice every year out of their surplus revenues, and a little later the salaries of their officials were raised. Finding that the wives of the governors interfered in the colonial administration, and that their sons engaged in commerce, the Home Government made a rule, that they must leave their female belongings and their grown-up sons behind them in Venice. Stringent regulations were also issued for the protection of the peasants' property, and it was the policy of the republican authorities to keep on good terms with both their Greek and Frankish neighbours; to the latter, however, they did not hesitate to lend the services of the famous engineers of Coron whenever there was a castle to besiege.[2]

We last saw the island of Eubœa almost entirely in the hands of the Greeks, thanks to the energy of Licario; but before the close of the century, the imperial garrisons had all been driven out of the island. The first step was the recovery of the two castles of La Clisura and Argalia, by treachery; as the island was specially excepted from the truce of 1285 between Venice and Andrónikos II., the process of reconquest could go on more or less uninter-

[1] *Regestum Clementis V.*, ii., 17, 19; iii., 84.

[2] *L. d. C.*, 472; Sanudo, *Vite de' Duchi*, *apud* Muratori, xxii., 580; Pachyméres, ii., 393; Pilosus, fol. 466.

ruptedly; till, finally, the quarrels between the Venetians and their Genoese rivals at Constantinople led, in 1296, to the renewal of hostilities between the former and the Greek Empire, and so afforded an excellent opportunity for recapturing the last remaining Byzantine fortresses of Karystos, Larmena, and Metropyle. The credit for this final blow belonged to Bonifacio da Verona, who thus obtained possession of the noble castle of southern Eubœa, which had been part of his wife's dowry; henceforth, in fact, as well as in name, the prime favourite of Duke Guy of Athens was baron of Karystos, and the most important of all the Lombard lords in the island. But the real influence over Eubœa was gradually passing into the hands of the Venetians. Not only did the latter buy more land round about Chalkis, but by the usual ill-luck which attended Frankish marriages in the Levant, the three great baronies of Negroponte were at this time almost entirely in the possession of women, so that the Venetian bailie acquired a predominant position, which was further enhanced by the popularity of several of those officials. The elder Sanudo,[1] however, a Venetian himself, noticed that the Greek peasants preferred the Genoese to the Venetians, hastening down to the shore with provisions as soon as a Genoese galley hove in sight, but by no means displaying the like alacrity when they descried the Venetian flag. And, as the same author shrewdly observed, "in Candia, Negroponte, and other islands, and in the principality of the Morea, although those places are subject to the Frankish sway and obedient to the Roman Church, yet almost all the inhabitants are Greeks, and inclined to that sect, and their hearts are turned towards things Greek; and, if they had a chance of displaying their preference freely, they would do so." A bigoted French bishop, like Gautier de Ray of Negroponte, cousin of the Duke of Athens, could still further estrange the "schismatic" Greeks from the Catholic fold. One other section of the community in that city—the Jews—had no special reason for loving the Venetian administration, for it was upon them that the burden of taxation was more especially laid. Thus, when the salaries

[1] *Istoria del Regno*, 125, 130, 131, 134, 143; and *Secreta Fidelium Crucis*, 299-300.

of the two Venetian councillors were increased, as compensation for their exclusion from trade, the difference was ordered to be defrayed by the Jews, who had also, in 1304, to pay the cost of fortifying with strong walls and gates the hitherto open Venetian quarter of the city of Negroponte. This precaution, followed by an order that henceforth the bailie and one of the two councillors must always reside within the walls, was due to an attempt by the Lombards to levy taxes on a Venetian citizen; it was then that Chalkis assumed the picturesque appearance of a walled city, which, in spite of modern acts of Vandalism, it still preserves. Occasionally, however, a Jewish family was specially exempted from taxation, as a reward for its loyalty to the republic. Thus, at the beginning of the fourteenth century, Eubœa possessed for Venice an importance second to that of Crete alone. It became the station of a Venetian fleet, and during the maritime war against Andrónikos II., which was concluded by the ten years' truce of 1303, it was a convenient basis whence privateers and *armatores* could swoop down upon those islands of the Archipelago which Licario had wrested from their Latin lords.[1]

Such was the condition of Greece, when a new race of conquerors from the West suddenly appeared there, and destroyed in a single day the most magnificent fabric which the Franks had raised in "New France."

[1] Predelli, *Commemoriali*, i., 4, 10, 35; *Les Registres de Boniface VIII.*, i., 408, 763; *Archivio Veneto*, xx., 81.

CHAPTER VII

THE CATALAN GRAND COMPANY (1302-1311)

THE history of Greece in the last quarter of the thirteenth century was more influênced by the long duel between the rival houses of Anjou and Aragon for the beautiful island of Sicily than by any other cause. It was the Sicilian vespers and their consequences which paralysed the schemes of the Angevins for the reconquest of the Latin Empire of the East; it was the restoration of peace in Sicily, after a twenty years' struggle, by the peace of Caltabellotta in 1302, which let loose upon the Greeks and the Frankish rulers of the Levant the terrible Catalan auxiliaries of the Aragonese party, and thus vitally affected for nearly a hundred years the fortunes of Hellas. What the Fourth Crusade was to the thirteenth century, the Catalan expedition was to the fourteenth, only that the rough mercenaries from Barcelona showed less regard for the Greeks than the motley band of younger sons and noble adventurers and astute Venetians, who had divided among themselves the fragments of the Byzantine Empire a hundred years before. The Catalans, like the Crusaders, have been very differently judged by Eastern and Western writers. Of the four contemporaries, who have left us accounts of their doings, the three Greeks —Pachyméres, Nikephóros Gregorâs, and the rhetorician Theódoulos—depict them as savages, whose sole idea was plunder; while their comrade and compatriot, Ramón Muntaner, is rather proud than otherwise of their exploits, and heaps upon the Greeks the same terms of opprobrium which we find applied to them a century earlier by the apologists of the Fourth Crusade. Modern writers have taken sides, according to their nationalities. To Stamatiádes the Catalans are the oppressors of the Greeks, to Moncada and Rubió y Lluch they are heroes worthy to be descendants of the Crusaders. If their career has been very variously judged, it has, at least, inspired two masterpieces of literature —the delightful *Chronicle* of Muntaner and the majestic prose of Moncada, a work justly esteemed worthy of a place in the library of Spanish classics.[1]

During the long struggle against the Angevins in Sicily, King Frederick II., who now ruled that debatable island, had thankfully availed himself of the stout hearts and stalwart arms of the Catalans. Their principal chief was one Roger de Flor, whose father, a German, had been falconer of the Emperor Frederick II., and whose mother was daughter of a prominent citizen of Brindisi, where Roger, like Margaritone a century earlier, was born. His father lost both life and property, fighting against Charles of Anjou at the battle of Tagliacozzo, so that the lad was early thrown on his own resources. But Brindisi was, in that age, one of the most important ports in the Mediterranean, whence there was constant communication with Greece and Syria—just the place, in fact, where an adventurous boy would find an opening for a career. One winter, when Roger was eight years old, the vessel of a Knight Templar lay in the harbour, close to his mother's abode; the nimble youth was soon free of the ship, running about the deck as if he had been bred to the sea. The captain took a fancy to him, offered to make a man of him, and when the ship at last sailed, Roger sailed with it. He soon became an experienced seaman, and, in due course was admitted a brother of the Temple, being ultimately entrusted with the command of the largest vessel belonging to the Order. He was present with this ship at

[1] The contemporary authorities for the Catalan expedition are Pachyméres, ii., 393-400, 415-42, 480-518, 521-58, 562 *sqq.*; Nikephóros Gregorâs, i., 218-33, 244-54; Theódoulos, Πρεσβευτικὸς πρὸς τὸν βασιλέα 'Ανδρόνικον and Περὶ τῶν ἐν τῇ 'Ιταλῶν καὶ Περσῶν ἐφόδῳ γεγενημένων *apud* Boissonade, *Anecdota Græca*, ii., 188-228; Muntaner, ch. cxciv. *sqq.*, and Nicolaus Specialis *apud* Muratori, x., 1050. Of the moderns the best are Moncada (died 1635), *Expedicion de los Catalanes;* Rubió y Lluch, *La expedicion y dominacion de los Catalanes en Oriente;* Stamatiádes, Οἱ Καταλάνοι ἐν τῇ 'Ανατολῇ; and Schlumberger, *Expedition des "Almugavares" ou routiers Catalans en Orient.*

the capture of Acre by the Egyptians, and was the means of conveying many of the fugitives and much treasure to a place of safety. But his large profits by this voyage aroused envy and suspicion; the Grand Master of the Order laid hands upon what property of Roger's he could find, and tried to arrest him; but the latter managed to escape to Genoa, where he equipped a galley of his own. Renouncing his allegiance to the Temple, he now offered his services to the Angevins, and, when his offer was coldly received, to King Frederick II., who graciously accepted them. Honours and wealth were bestowed upon him; he became Vice-Admiral of Sicily, and the most terrible corsair of the age.

The peace of Caltabellotta closed the active career of Roger and his band of Catalans in Sicily. Their present employer could no longer support them from the revenues of an island exhausted by twenty years of civil war; they could not return to Spain, because they had espoused the cause of King Frederick of Sicily against his brother, King James II. of Aragon, nor had these homeless wanderers any strong ties to bind them to their native land; moreover, the pope either had demanded, or seemed likely to demand, the surrender of their chief, the scourge of the Angevins, the renegade brother of the Temple. Frederick II. was, on his part, naturally desirous, like governments in our own time, to rid himself of such dangerous allies, now that he had no further use for their services. He had already offered them to Charles of Valois, husband of Catherine of Courtenay, titular Empress of Constantinople, whose claims to the Byzantine throne he had pledged himself to support.[1] As this venture against Andrónikos II. was not carried out, Roger bethought himself of offering his band of followers to the same emperor whom he had been expected to attack. Andrónikos, then hard pressed by the growing power of the Turks, welcomed Roger's proposal as a godsend. He accepted the latter's terms, which had been drawn up by Muntaner himself; Roger was to obtain the title of "Grand Duke," which was equivalent to Lord High Admiral in the Byzantine hierarchy, with the hand of the emperor's niece, Maria; his men were to receive pay at double the usual

[1] Ducange, *op. cit.*, ii., 335-6; Sanudo, 173.

rate, and four months were to be paid in advance, the first instalment being paid at Monemvasia. On these conditions, Roger sailed for Constantinople with thirty-six ships and 6500 men.[1] Of these, 4000 were the so-called *almugavari*, or "skirmishers," the most formidable infantry of the time, whose exploits led the terrified Pachyméres, by a false, but pardonable etymology, to connect them with the barbarous Avars. "Would that Constantinople," cried the historian, "had never beheld the Latin Roger!"

The name and fame of the Catalans were already known in the harbours of the Levant. As early as 1268, King James I. of Aragon, of whose dominions Cataluña formed a part, had allowed the merchants of Barcelona to establish consuls in the Byzantine Empire; and, about 1290, one of those officials is mentioned in a golden bull of Andrónikos II., which granted special privileges to merchants from Spain. Catalan trade had naturally followed the Byzantine flag at a time when the Greek emperors were instigating the house of Aragon against the hated Angevins in Sicily, and the East had had a taste of the Catalans' quality as fighting men. Michael VIII. had on one occasion employed a Catalan vessel to tackle a Genoese corsair, and we saw Catalan mercenaries assisting Licario against the Lombards of Eubœa and ravaging the Morea under Roger de Lluria. Thus the new Roger represented a force whose value the emperor was well able to estimate.

On their way to Constantinople, the Catalans plundered Corfù, then a possession of the Angevins, and put into Monemvasia, where the imperial authorities received them well. When they reached the capital, the emperor was as good as his word: the soldiers were given four months' pay in advance, and Roger received the hand of the fair Maria. When, somewhat later, another Catalan leader, Berenguer de Entença, Lluria's brother-in-law and "one of the noblest men of Spain," arrived with a fresh contingent, Roger relinquished to him the title of Grand Duke, and was yet further honoured by that of "Cæsar," one of the great Byzantine dignities, whose latest holders had been Aléxios Strategó-

[1] Muntaner, the best authority, gives 6500; Pachyméres, 8000; Nikephóros, 2000.

poulos, the conqueror of Constantinople from the Latins, and John and Constantine Palaiólogos, the uncles of the emperor. The Catalan commander was the last person who ever bore the title.

The newcomers soon proved to be a curse to the empire which they had been summoned to defend. If they defeated the Turks in Asia, they quarrelled with the Genoese in the capital and plundered the Greeks everywhere. When they had desolated Asia, they crossed over into Europe, and encamped at Gallipoli on the Dardanelles, where Alfonso Fadrique, a natural son of King Frederick of Sicily, joined them. Roger was now killed at Adrianople by orders of Michael, the emperor's son and colleague; but the deed only made the Catalans more desperate, and therefore more dangerous. Under Entença, Roger's successor, they entrenched themselves at Gallipoli, and defied the emperor; when Entença was captured by a Genoese fleet, they made Berenguer de Rocafort, a resolute soldier of humble origin, their leader, routed the imperial troops and wounded the emperor's son. Twelve councillors were appointed to assist Rocafort; a great seal was made bearing the image of St George and the proud superscription "the army of the Franks who reign over the kingdom of Macedonia," and was entrusted to the charge of Muntaner; three banners, those of Aragon, of Sicily, and of St George, accompanied the host to battle; a fourth, that of St Peter, waved on the topmost tower of Gallipoli. Their victories soon attracted a body of loyal and valuable allies—3800 Turks and Turkish renegades; ere long there was scarcely a town in Thrace and Macedonia which they had not sacked. But dissensions broke out among the Catalan leaders. Entença, who had secured his release, was murdered on his return by Rocafort's relatives, and that crafty chief persuaded his men to refuse to recognise the authority of King Frederick of Sicily, who was desirous to exploit for his own ends the triumphs of his former mercenaries, and had accordingly sent his cousin, the Infant Ferdinand, son of King James I. of Majorca, to take command of the company in his name.[1] Unable to assert his powers as King Frederick's delegate, the Infant resolved to

[1] Buchon, *Nouvelles Recherches*, II., i., 385-90.

return to Sicily; with him went the faithful Muntaner, while the main body, under Rocafort, having exhausted Thrace and plundered the monasteries of Mount Athos, moved to Kassandreia, the ancient Potidaia, a deserted city on the narrow isthmus which connects the peninsula of Kassandra with the rest of Macedonia.

It is at this point that the Catalan expedition begins to affect the history of Frankish Greece. On their way home, the Infant and Muntaner put into the Thessalian port of Halmyros, at that time under the regency of the Duke of Athens, and set fire to all that they could find, in revenge for the disappearance of some of their men and stores. After ravaging the island of Skopelos, still a Greek possession, they steered for Negroponte, where the Infant had been hospitably treated on his outward voyage. But at this moment there chanced to be in the harbour eleven Venetian vessels with Thibaut de Cepoy on board—a French nobleman, agent of Charles of Valois, who, in 1306, had renewed between his master and Venice the old arrangement made twenty-five years before at Orvieto for the recovery of the Latin Empire,[1] and who was now manœuvring to win over Rocafort and his Catalans to the service of the titular empress and her husband. Cepoy feared that Ferdinand, as the representative of the King of Sicily, might thwart his plan; his Venetian escort had heard that Muntaner's galley contained a goodly quantity of spoil; accordingly, they attacked the little flotilla, seized the chronicler's property and arrested the Infant, in spite of the safe conduct, which the barons of Negroponte had given him. Ferdinand and his faithful retainer were lodged in the house of Bonifacio da Verona, whence the Infant was handed over to Jean de Maisy, a well-connected Frenchman, who had recently become, by marriage with one of the Lombard heiresses, the next most important baron of the island. He was then escorted to Thebes, where Duke Guy of Athens, annoyed at the destruction of Halmyros, and already won over by Cepoy, shut him up in the castle of St Omer. Muntaner was sent back to Rocafort at Kassandreia, where he received an enthusiastic reception, and whence he shortly returned to

[1] Thomas, *Diplomatarium Veneto-Levantinum*, I., 48-53.

Negroponte, in quest of his stolen property. All efforts to recover it failed; but half a century later Venice paid back to the chronicler's granddaughter a tenth part of what he had lost at Negroponte.[1] A poorer and a wiser man—for he had learnt that it was dangerous to travel with young princes—Muntaner proceeded to Thebes, where Guy II., then already a prey to the malady which carried him off a year later, received him with courtesy. He was not the first Catalan whom the duke had met; for, three years earlier, Ferdinand Ximenes, the most respectable of all the Catalan leaders, had left Roger de Flor in disgust at his cruelty, and had spent some time at the Theban court, where he had been entertained with those honours which the lavish duke knew so well how to bestow. Muntaner, in response to Guy's polite attentions, asked for one favour only—that the Infant might be well treated and that he might be permitted to see him. The request was granted; the warm-hearted Catalan passed two days in the society of his young master, and when he departed, almost broken-hearted, for Sicily, he left behind him part of his scanty funds for the Infant's use, and made the cook swear on the gospels that he would not put poison into the royal prisoner's food. The Infant was subsequently released and sent to the King of Naples, at the request of Charles of Valois; after more than a year's honourable imprisonment at Naples, he was allowed to return to Majorca. We shall find him later on intervening, with fatal results to himself, in the affairs of Greece.

Meanwhile, the main body of the Catalans, in their camp at Kassandreia, were treating Macedonia as they had treated Thrace. Rocafort, hopelessly compromised with both the King of Sicily and the house of Aragon by his refusal to accept the authority of the Infant Ferdinand, had thought it prudent to take an oath of fealty to Thibaut de Cepoy as the representative of Charles of Valois, but, in spite of Cepoy's nominal leadership, he continued to be the guiding spirit of the Company. His ambition aimed at nothing less than a royal crown, and he dreamed of reviving for himself that kingdom of Salonika which Boniface of Montferrat had founded a century before, and which still lingered on as a

[1] Predelli, *Commemoriali*, i., 87; ii., 186, 190, 250.

titular dignity of the ducal house of Burgundy.[1] He had a seal executed, bearing the figure of St Demetrios and a golden crown, while he excited his men by promising them the plunder of Salonika, a rich and populous city, at that moment a particularly splendid prize, because its walls contained the two empresses, Irene, wife of Andrónikos II., and Maria, consort of his son and colleague, Michael. Just as Boniface's conquests had included Attica, so Rocafort, too, was plotting the ultimate dominion of the Athenian duchy. With this object he sought the hand of Jeannette de Brienne, half-sister of the childless Guy II., which the Empress Irene had already asked for her son Theodore. Guy had been too honest to accept her offer, which had been coupled with the proposal that he and she should simultaneously attack his ward, young John II. of Thessaly and Neopatras, and that the latter's dominions should be given to her son.[2] Negotiations went on, however, for some time between him and Rocafort; two of his minstrels were sent as his envoys to Kassandreia,[3] and he seems to have entertained the idea of using the Catalans to conquer the Morea in the name of his wife, the natural heiress of the Villehardouins,[4] who, as we saw, had in vain demanded it as her birthright from Nicholas de St Omer, when he had been left as bailie after the departure of Philip of Savoy. But Venice, alarmed for her colony at Negroponte, worked against a plan which would have exposed that station to a Catalan attack, and Rocafort, whose arbitrary acts had made him unpopular with his men, was arrested by the council of the Catalan Company, and handed over to Cepoy. The latter was by this time weary of his life with the wild Catalans, while his mission had no further object since the death of Catherine of Courtenay, the titular empress of Constantinople, at the beginning of 1308, and the consequent transference of her claims to her daughter, Catherine of Valois. He therefore determined to quit the Catalan camp with his prisoner. One night, without saying

[1] Buchon, *Recherches et Matériaux*, i., 68.

[2] Nikephóros Gregorâs, i., 237 (who, however, calls her, by a confusion, the duke's "daughter"); Lettere di Collegio, fol. 6.

[3] As we see from Cepoy's accounts; Ducange, *op. cit.*, ii., 355.

[4] Χ. τ. Μ., ll. 7275-81; *C. d. M.*, 456.

good-bye to a single soul, he embarked on some galleys which his son had brought from Venice, and next morning when the Company awoke, he was well out at sea, on the way to Naples. There he surrendered Rocafort to the tender mercies of that amiable sovereign, King Robert, who paid off an old grudge which he had against the bold Catalan by throwing him into the dungeons of Aversa, where he died of hunger.[1] Meanwhile, the Catalans, furious at the departure of their leader, repented of what they had done. In their rage they slew fourteen captains who had been the ringleaders in the revolt against Rocafort—a proceeding which still further diminished the number of prominent men among them. Until they could find a new chief, they elected a committee of four, chosen in equal numbers from the cavalry and infantry, besides the original Council of Twelve.

Such was the situation of the Catalan Company, when the last of the De la Roche dukes of Athens lay a-dying. Muntaner, as we saw, had found him very ill, when he visited Thebes, nor could the medical skill of the patriarch of Alexandria, who chanced to be in Eubœa and prescribed for the ailing duke, avail to save him. On 5th October 1308, "the good duke," Guy II., died. On the following day, he was laid to rest in "the mausoleum of his ancestors" at the famous Cistercian Abbey of Daphni on the Sacred Way, where a sarcophagus with a cross, two snakes, and two lilies carved upon it, which was perhaps his tomb, may still be seen lying outside in the courtyard. A certificate of his death and burial was drawn up by Archbishop Henry of Athens, the Abbot of Daphni, the ex-pirate Gaffore, now a peaceful Athenian citizen, and others, who implored, in the name of the widowed duchess, now left alone in the world

[1] Hopf and Gregorovius rejected the statement of Muntaner (ch. ccxxxix.), that Cepoy fled with Rocafort on the ground that the last section of his financial accounts, which have been preserved and published by Ducange (*op. cit.*, ii., 352-6), begins with 9th September 1309, which they therefore assumed, without evidence, to be the date of his departure from Greece. But Cepoy was always accustomed to divide his accounts at that date, because it completed the period of twelve months from the time of his departure from Paris in 1306. The mention of that date therefore merely means that the fourth year of his mission began then. According to Lettere di Collegio, f. 63, he was in Thessaly in 1309.

at the age of fifteen, the protection of her cousin, Count William of Hainault. Her husband had not, however, been dead four months, when she was affianced in the Theban minster, the scene of so many gorgeous ceremonies, to the eldest son of Philip of Taranto. Thither, for the last time, gathered the noble chivalry of Athens, to witness this latest sacrifice to the insatiable ambition of the Angevins.[1]

Guy II. had left no children, but fortunately the succession to his delectable duchy, of which he had appointed his bosom friend, Bonifacio da Verona, as temporary administrator, was not seriously disputed. Neither the French nor the Argive branch of the De la Roche family (the barons of Veligosti and Damalâ) made any claim to his inheritance; the husband of his aunt Catherine, Carlo de Lagonessa, seneschal of Sicily and son of the former bailie of Achaia, who had regarded himself a few years before as his heir, and Lagonessa's son, Giovanni, had both predeceased him,[2] so that there only remained his two first cousins, Eschive, Lady of Beyrout, daughter of his aunt Alice, and Walter, son of his aunt Isabelle and Hugues de Brienne, his stepfather. Hugues de Brienne had left Greece for Apulia after his stepson had come of age, and had been killed in battle in 1296. His son, Walter, Count of Lecce, accordingly came forward as Guy's successor. Dame Eschive of Beyrout asserted, however, that she had a prior claim, because her mother was the elder sister of Walter's mother. As the duchy of Athens was in the Angevin times a vassal state of the principality of Achaia, King Robert of Naples, the head of the Angevins, and Philip of Taranto, as Prince of Achaia and suzerain of Athens, referred the question in the middle of 1309 to the Achaian High Court, of which Philip's new bailie, Bertino Visconte, was the president. The High Court decided in favour of Walter, on the ground that he

[1] Pachyméres, II., 450, 595; Sanudo, 136; Muntaner, chs. ccxxxvii., ccxl., ccxliv.; X. τ. M., ll. 7263-9, 8046-55; Predelli, *Commemoriali*, I., 89; St Genois, i., 215, 338; Buchon, *Recherches historiques*, i., 473; *La Grèce Continentale*, 131-3. M. Millet, however, in his monograph on Daphni (p. 39), doubts whether the sarcophagus is the tomb of Guy, as the arms upon it were not those of his family.

[2] Riccio, *Studii storici sopra* 84 *Registri*, 54.

was a powerful and gallant man, while the Lady of Beyrout was not only a woman but a widow. When Eschive heard the sentence of the Court, she knelt down at the altar of the church of St Francis at Glarentza, where the barons had met, and prayed the Virgin that if her judges and her opponent had wrought injustice, they might die without heirs of their bodies. Then she departed to her own home, and Walter of Brienne entered into the peaceable possession of his cousin's duchy, which Bonifacio da Verona, who had acted as bailie during the interregnum, handed over to him.[1]

The new Duke of Athens was a true scion of the adventurous house of Brienne, who in his thirty years of life had seen much of the world. As a boy he must have spent some time at the Theban court, when his father was guardian of Guy II. When barely of age, he had been one of the "knights of death," who had gone to Sicily to support the cause of Anjou, and he had fought like the lion on his banner at Gagliano, when he and his comrades were treacherously led into an ambuscade. Like his suzerain, Philip of Taranto, he had been the prisoner of the Aragonese, but prison had not made him cautious, nor had defeat taught him the folly of despising the infantry of Spain. Thus the succession of this brave but headstrong soldier destroyed, instead of preserving, "the pleasaunce of the Latins" in Frankish Athens. Yet it is impossible not to admire the reckless courage of this most unstatesmanlike ruler. Those who have seen the knightly figure of the last French Duke of Athens step on to the stage in M. Rhangabês's gorgeously mounted play, "The Duchess of Athens"—a drama which, in spite of some glaring anachronisms, has given us a living picture of the brilliant French court of Thebes on the eve of the catastrophe—can feel all the pathos and all the pity of so promising a career so wantonly sacrificed.

Meanwhile, the Catalans were drawing nearer to the Athenian frontier. The position of the Company in the camp at Kassandreia had grown more and more precarious. In Macedonia they were threatened with starvation and the combined attack of all the neighbouring peoples. The emperor had cut off their retreat into Thrace by building a

[1] *L. d. F.*, 118-19.

long wall across the pass of Christopolis; while in the imperial general Chandrenós, if we may believe the eulogy of his relative, the rhetorician Theódoulos, they had found a foeman worthy of their steel, who pressed them hard in their station on the peninsula. Accordingly, they resolved to make a bold dash for Thessaly, "a land of plenty," or find an abiding settlement in one of the Greek countries to the south of it. The company now numbered not less than 8000 men, of whom some 5000 were Catalans, and the rest Turks, 1100 of the latter being converts to Christianity. On the borders of Thessaly, a portion of the Turks left them,[1] and the rest of the company, after wintering at the foot of Olympos, traversed the lovely vale of Tempe, the route of so many an army, and in the spring of 1309 debouched into the great Thessalian plain. The granary of Greece lay at their mercy, for John II. of Neopatras, its ruler, who had been emancipated from his Athenian guardian by the death of Guy II., was young in years and weak in health; fearing a usurpation on the part of one of the feudal barons of Thessaly, he had recently married, or at least betrothed himself to, Irene, natural daughter of the Emperor Andrónikos II.[2] But, as he had no heir, either annexation or anarchy seemed likely to follow the demise of the moribund duke, the last of his race.

The rest of the year was spent by the Catalans in ravaging Thessaly, till the inhabitants invoked the aid of the emperor, who not only ordered the redoubtable Chandrenós to pursue the Catalans, but summoned the people of Loidoriki and Galaxidi, districts which were included, as we saw, in the Wallachian principality of the Angeli, to join his standard against "the men of Aragon." Dissensions hindered the success of the Greeks till the arrival of Chandrenós gave unity of direction to their forces, and in two battles, in which the stalwart men of Galaxidi took a notable part, the Catalans

[1] Nikephóros (i., 248) makes *all* the Turks leave them; but Muntaner, the Aragonese *Chronicle*, and Théodoulos (ii., 201) state that the Turks were present at the battle of the Kephissós.

[2] Nikephóros in one place says that in 1309 he had been "lately married"; in another, that when he died in 1318, he had been "married three years" (i., 249, 278).

were defeated with much loss.[1] The Company was glad to make peace with the Thessalians; Chandrenós, having done his work, returned into Macedonia; and the Catalan leaders accepted the bribes and offers of the leading men of Thessaly to give them guides, who would conduct them into Bœotia and Achaia, "a luxurious and fertile land, endued with many graces, and of all lands the best to dwell in." Accordingly, in the spring of 1310, they crossed the Phourka Pass, suffering not a little from the nomad Wallachs who frequented that difficult country, and descended to Lamia.

An energetic soldier like the new Duke of Athens, whose name was famous in the kingdoms of the West, could scarcely be expected to acquiesce in the practical establishment of a Byzantine protectorate over the dominions of his predecessor's ward, John II. of Neopatras. From the brief account of Muntaner, it would appear that at this moment a species of triple alliance between the Greek rulers of Constantinople, Neopatras, and Arta, had been formed for the purpose of preventing the moribund principality of the Angeli from being annexed by the duchy of Athens. Against the allies Duke Walter bethought him of employing the venal arms of the wandering Catalans. The late Duke of Athens had already negotiated with them when they were still at Kassandreia; his successor was, moreover, personally popular with them; he had gained their respect fighting against them in the Sicilian war, and he spoke their language, which he had learnt when a child during his imprisonment as hostage for his father in the Castle of Augusta, near Syracuse. By means of the good services of Roger Deslaur, a knight of Roussillon, who was in his employ, he engaged them for six months at the high rate of 4 ounces (£9, 12s.) for every heavily-armed horseman, 2 ounces (£4, 16s.) for every light-armed horseman, and 1 ounce (£2, 8s.) for every foot-soldier—the same high scale of pay for which Roger de Flor had stipulated with Andrónikos II. eight years earlier. As soon as he met them—probably

[1] I see no reason to doubt the accuracy of the *Chronicle of Galaxidi* (p. 205) here, because it is exactly confirmed by the contemporary account of Theódoulos. As Sáthas points out (p. 225), the "Andréas" or "Andríkos" of the *Chronicle* is Chandrenós.

at Lamia[1]—he gave them two months' pay in advance. The Catalans lost no time in giving him value for his money. Turning back by the way they had come, they took Domokó. At the end of a six months' campaign they had captured more than thirty castles for their employer, and had once more ravaged the fertile plain of Thessaly so effectually, that its exports of corn and other products diminished after this raid. His three adversaries were glad to make peace with him on his own terms, and the news of his triumph penetrated to the papal court at Avignon, whence Clement V. wrote ordering the Athenian revenues of the suppressed Order of the Templars to be lent to so "faithful a champion" of the true Church against the "schismatic Greeks."[2]

Having used the Company to serve his purpose, the duke now desired, like all its previous employers, to get rid of it. He picked out 200 of the best horsemen and 300 foot soldiers from its ranks, gave them their pay and lands, on which to settle, and then abruptly told the others to be gone, first giving up to him the castles which they had captured in his name and the booty which they had taken. They declined to obey his orders, reminded him that he owed them four months' pay, but offered to do him homage for the conquered castles, if he would allow them to remain, as they had nowhere else to go.[3] Walter haughtily replied that he would drive them out by force, and made preparations during the autumn and winter to carry out his threat. His messengers went forth to all parts of the Frankish world in quest of aid against the common enemy. All the great feudatories of Greece rallied to his call. There came Alberto Pallavicini, Marquis of Boudonitza, and by his marriage with an heiress of the Dalle Carceri, hexarch of Eubœa; Thomas III. of Salona, that trusty vassal of the dukes of

[1] We know from a document quoted by Lunzi (*Della Condizione politica delle Isole Ionie*, 125) that Walter was before "la Gyrona" (=Gytona, the Frankish form for Zetouni, or Lamia) on June 6, 1310, and that is by far the most likely place for the meeting, being at the end of the pass from Thessaly.

[2] Sanudo, *Secreta Fidelium Crucis*, *apud* Bongars, ii., 68; *Regestum Clementis V.*, v., 235.

[3] X. τ. M., ll. 7282-92; *L. d. F.*, 117 (where Walter is confused with Guy II.), 119, 120.

Athens, who had lately become marshal of Achaia; Boniface of Verona, the powerful Eubœan baron, who owed everything to the favour of Walter's predecessor; and two other Eubœan lords, George Ghisi, owner of one of the three baronies of that island and master of Tenos and Mykonos, who had been captured by Roger de Lluria nearly twenty years before, and Jean de Maisy, who had received the custody of the Infant Ferdinand. The friendly Angevins, for whose cause Walter had fought in Sicily, willingly allowed their vassals in the Morea and their subjects in the kingdom of Naples to hasten to the Athenian banner, while the Duke of Naxos seems to have sent an island contingent.[1] Never had such a brave host marched under the leadership of a Duke of Athens. According to a Byzantine estimate, Walter's army numbered 6400 horsemen and more than 8000 foot soldiers; according to the Catalan Muntaner, it consisted of 700 Frankish knights and of 24,000 Greek infantry from his own duchy; while the Aragonese version of the *Chronicle of the Morea* assesses the numbers of the assembled force at more than 2000 horse and 4000 foot. With such an army, the contemptuous duke hoped not only to annihilate the Catalans at one blow, but to extend his frontiers to the gates of Constantinople.

The situation of the Catalan Company, now composed of 3500 horsemen and 4000 foot soldiers, including many of their prisoners, enlisted because of their skill as archers, was now desperate. Retreat would have exposed them to a fresh attack by the victorious Chandrenós; allies they had none, for Venice had returned an evasive answer to their pacific overtures to her bailie at Chalkis, and had just renewed for twelve years her truce with the emperor, which contained a special stipulation, that no Venetian subject, under pain of losing all his goods, should visit any place where the Catalan Company chanced to be.[2] Nothing therefore lay before them but the alternative of a glorious death, or a still more glorious victory. Like seasoned warriors, they chose their battlefield well. When spring came, they crossed the Bœotian Kephissós, and encamped

[1] *L. d. F.*, 120, confirming Sauger, *Histoire nouvelle*, p. 130.
[2] Thomas, *Diplomatarium Veneto-Levantinum*, i., 82-5.

not far from the right bank of that sluggish stream, which ambles under the willows, like the Avon at Rugby. They then proceeded to prepare the ground, which was to be the scene of their final struggle for existence. Nature seems to have intended the great plain of Bœotia for a battlefield. A few miles from where the Catalans had taken their stand, Philip of Macedon, more than sixteen centuries before, had won "that dishonest victory at Chaironeia, fatal to liberty," which destroyed the freedom of classic Greece; in the time of Sulla, the plain had thrice witnessed the clash of arms between the Roman masters of Greece and the Pontic troops of Mithridates. Now, after the lapse of 1400 years, it was to be the spot where the fate of Athens was to be decided. But the crafty Catalans did not put their trust in those arts by which the soldiers of Macedon and Rome had routed Greeks and Asiatics. They knew that they would have to face the most renowned chivalry of that day, knights who had made the names of Athens and Achaia famous all over the Eastern world, descendants of those tall horsemen, before whose coats of mail Sgourós had fled from Thermopylæ a century before. The marshy soil of the Copaic basin was an excellent defence against a cavalry charge, and the Catalans made this natural advantage more efficacious still by ploughing up the ground in front of them, digging a trench round it, and then irrigating the whole area by means of canals from the river. The moisture aided the germs of vegetation, and by the middle of March, when the Frankish army faced the Catalans, the quagmire was concealed by an ample covering of green grass.

On Wednesday, 10th March 1311, the Duke of Athens had assembled his forces at Lamia, where, as if by a foreboding of his approaching death, he solemnly made his last will and testament. The document, witnessed by Gilles de la Planche, bailie of Achaia, and by the two great Eubœan barons, Jean de Maisy, the duke's kinsman, and Bonifacio da Verona, provided for all the outstanding claims of his predecessor's widow on his estate, bequeathed the sum of 200 *hyperperi* (£89, 12s.) each to the cathedrals of Our Lady of Athens, Our Lady of Thebes, and Our Lady of Negroponte, to the great churches at Argos and Corinth, and to the church at Daulia, a similar sum to the Athenian and Theban Minorites, and to the Theban Frères Prêcheurs, and half that amount to the church of St George at Livadia, and to the church at Boudonitza. The duke appointed his wife, Jeanne de Châtillon, guardian of his two children, Walter and Isabelle, charged her to build a church to St Leonard in his Italian county of Lecce for the repose of his own and his parents' souls, but expressed the desire to be buried by the side of the last Duke of Athens in the abbey of Daphni, to which he left 100 *hyperperi* in land, or 1000 in cash, for celebrating his anniversary. His wife, the bishop of Daulia, and others, were to carry out these dispositions. Having thus made his will, Walter set out to attack his enemies.[1]

Following the present route from Lamia to Livadia by way of Dadí, Walter halted, after passing Chaironeia, near the spot where the present road to Skripou, the ancient Orchomenós, turns off. On the hill called the Thourion, which is still surmounted by a mediæval tower, he probably took up his stand on that fatal 15th of March to survey the field. But, before the battle began, the 500 favoured Catalans, whom he had picked out from the rest, came to him and told him that they would rather die with their brothers than fight against them. The duke told them that they had his permission to die with the others, so they departed and added a welcome and experienced contingent to the enemies' forces. When they had gone, Walter, impatient for the fray, placed himself at the head of 200 French knights with golden spurs and many other knights of the country and the infantry, and charged, with a shout, across the plain towards the grassy expanse, behind which the Catalans lay. Seldom had even Frankish Greece seen a braver sight than that of the martial duke and his mailed warriors, the flower of Western chivalry, with the lion banner of Brienne waving above them. But before the horses had reached the centre of the plain, they plunged all unsuspecting into the morass. Their heavy burdens and the impetus of their charge made their feet sink deeper into the yielding quagmire ; the shouts of "Aragon ! Aragon !" from the Catalans added to their alarm.

[1] D'Arbois de Jubainville, *Voyage paléographique dans le département de l'Aube*, 332-340.

Some rolled over with their armoured riders in the mud; others, stuck fast in the stiff bog, stood still, like equestrian statues, powerless to move. The Catalans plied the helpless horsemen with showers of missiles; the Turks, who had hitherto held aloof from the combat, for fear lest the Catalans and the French should join in attacking them, seeing that the battle was no mere feint, rushed forward and completed the deadly work. Still, despite their desperate situation, the French fought bravely, and the struggle was keen to the last. So great was the slaughter, that, if we may believe the Catalan chronicler, more than 20,000 foot-soldiers and all the 700 Frankish knights save two perished that day. Those two survivors were Bonifacio da Verona, who had always been a good friend of the Company, and Roger Deslaur, who had been the intermediary between it and the Duke of Athens. We know, however, from other sources, that at least two other knights, Jean de Maisy of Eubœa and the eldest son of the Duke of Naxos, who was wounded there, both survived, while the latter lived to marry Walter's half-sister Jeannette and to fight the Catalans again.[1] Two other great nobles, Nicholas III. of St Omer and Antoine le Flamenc, lord of Karditza, are known to have been alive after the battle, at which the former was apparently not present, while we may perhaps assume that the church of St George, which the Flemish knight erected in this very year at his Copaic village, was in pursuance of a vow made to the saint before he went into action.[2] But the fatal day of the Kephissós destroyed at one blow the noble chivalry of Frankish Greece. Almost all the leaders of the land, almost all the representatives of the old conquering families, were left dead in the Bœotian swamp. The Duke of Athens fell, and his head, severed from his body by a Catalan knife, was borne, many years afterwards, on a funereal galley to Brindisi, and thence escorted to Lecce, where it was buried beneath a marble monument, in the church of Sta. Croce, which his ill-fated son erected in

[1] Thomas, *Diplomatarium*, i., 111; Predelli, *Commemoriali*, i., 133, 134, 198, 204.

[2] Mr D. Steel, manager of the Lake Copais Company, has kindly had a fresh copy of this inscription made for me by his Greek draughtsman. The date is "6819, ninth indiction," *i.e.*, 1311, a very significant one.

his Italian residence, but which was destroyed, and with it the monument, when Lecce was fortified in the time of Charles V.[1] There fell, too, the Marquis of Boudonitza and the lord of Salona, those twin guardians of the Greek marches, whose dignities dated from the Conquest; and brave George Ghisi, and many another noble gentleman. It was scarcely a rhetorical exaggeration, when Theódoulos the rhetorician wrote, that not so much as an army chaplain [2] was left to tell the tale. To him and to the Greeks it seemed a glorious victory, which rid them of the masters who had ruled Greece for three generations, and whose pride had been the cause of their fall; even the Francophil *Chronicle of the Morea* admits that Walter's death was his own fault.[3]

After the battle, the victors occupied the French camp, and then marched to the neighbouring town of Livadia, one

[1] Galateus, *De Situ Iapygiæ*, 92; Della Monaca, *Memoria historica della Città di Brindisi*, 470; Summonte, *Storia della Città e del Regno di Napoli*, ii., 248.

[2] Μηδὲ πυρφόρον, a classical tag, "the priest who carried the sacrificial fire."

[3] There are two difficulties about the battle—its date and place. The Greek *Chronicle* (ll. 7295-300) gives "Monday, March 15, A.M., 6817, Indict. vii." (or viii., another MS.) = A.D., 1309; the French version gives the same day and month of 1310 (p. 240), but alters the year to 1307 elsewhere (p. 474). But in 1311 the 15th March was a Monday, and that date is absolutely fixed by Walter's will and by the "Necrologium Monasterii S. Nicolai et Cataldi" of Lecce, which I have examined at Naples, and which says "15 Martii obiit Gualterius, dux Athenarum, Brennæ et Lisii Comes, 1311, Ind. viiii." The four versions of the *Chronicle* and Sanudo all say that the place was Halmyros; but the well-known Thessalian town cannot be meant, as Neroûtsos (Δελτίον, iv., 130) and Giannópoulos (παρνασσός, viii., 76) believed, because nothing but the Bœotian plain suits the precise descriptions of Muntaner and Nikephóros. Halmyros ("the salt place") is, however, a common name in Greece, and there may well have been a spot so called in the Copaic district.

The contemporary authorities for the battle are:—Nikephóros Gregorâs, i., 251-4; Muntaner, ch. ccxl.; Theódoulos, ii., 200-1. To it refer X. τ. M., ll. 7272-300, 8010; *L. d. C.*, 239-40, 268, 474; *C. d. M.*, 456; *L. d. F.*, 120; Boccaccio, *De Casibus Virorum Illustrium*, p. 265; Villani *apud* Muratori, xiii., 379-80; Sanudo, *Istoria del Regno*, 125; Chalkokondýles, 19. A poem by Pucci, published in *Arch. Stor. Ital.*, Ser. III., xvi., 52, alludes to the fact of Walter's head being "cut off by the Company." A contemporary table of the rulers of Greece (Hopf, *Chroniques*, 177-8) marks the names of those who died.

17

of the strongest positions in the duchy, which had been a special appanage of the ducal family. But the Greek inhabitants opened the gates to "the Fortunate Company of the Catalans," receiving as their reward the full rights and privileges of Franks under the Great Seal of St George.[1] When the news of the French defeat reached Thebes, the citizens fled with all that they could carry to Negroponte—the general refuge of the Latin inhabitants of the duchy, where a Venetian fleet was at that moment watching events. But the abandoned city, the richest in all the duchy, was ruthlessly plundered by the rough soldiers of fortune, who then hastened to Athens. We would fain believe the story of the Aragonese *Chronicle*, that the heroic widow of the fallen duke, a daughter of a constable of France, defended the Akropolis, in which she had taken refuge with her little son, until she saw that there was no hope of succour, and then fled with young Walter to Naples, and thence to her old home in France.[2] But Nikephóros expressly says that the invaders surprised Athens and took it most easily, together with the possessions, wives, and children of the vanquished; a very late authority of more than doubtful value[3] adds that they burnt the grove of the nymphs at Kolonós, thus giving to the home of Sophoklês the desolate appearance which it still preserves. As no French leaders were left to lead a resistance against them, and the Greeks remained spectators of this change of masters, they were able to parcel out among themselves all the towns and castles of the duchy, except its Argive appurtenances beyond the isthmus, which the faithful family of Foucherolles still held for the exiled dynasty.[4] The widows of the slain became the wives of the slayers; each soldier received a consort according to his services, and thus many a rough warrior found himself the husband of some noble dame, in whose veins flowed the bluest blood of France, and "whose wash-hand basin," in the phrase of Muntaner, "he was not worthy

[1] Lámpros, Ἔγγραφα, 337.

[2] P. 121.

[3] The Chronicle of Anthimos (now ascribed to J. Benizélos), quoted by Fallmerayer, *Geschichte der Halbinsel Morea*, ii., 182.

[4] These are doubtless the places to which Clement V. alludes as still holding out in 1314. (*Regestum*, viii., 14; ix., 46.)

to bear." No wonder that these vagabonds decided to end their nine years' wandering and settle in this delectable duchy, which a kindly providence had bestowed upon them. Their Turkish allies, however, pined to return to their homes in Asia, although the Catalans offered to give them three or four places in the duchy in which to settle, and begged them to stay. They received as their share the horses, arms,[1] and military equipment of the fallen Franks, and departed on the best of terms with their Catalan comrades. Both parties promised to assist one another in case of need; but, before the Catalans had had time to perform their promise, their Turkish friends had succumbed to the craft of the emperor and his Genoese allies at the Dardanelles. Those who escaped the Byzantine sword, ended their days in the Genoese galleys.

The battle of the Kephissós, assuredly one of the strangest in history, had left both victors and vanquished without leaders. The Catalans had lost all their chiefs long before the fight, the French chivalry lay in the Bœotian swamp. But the Company felt that in its new situation it must have a commander of acknowledged rank and position. As they had no such man among them, the Catalans offered the command of the Company to one of their two noble prisoners, Bonifacio da Verona. The famous Eubœan baron was the most important Frank in the whole of Northern Greece; he was of high lineage, wealthy, able, and popular with the Catalans; Muntaner, as we saw, had lodged in his house at Chalkis, and describes him in enthusiastic terms as "the wisest and most courteous nobleman that was ever born." Wisdom and nobility alike disposed him to decline an offer which would have embroiled him with Venice and have rendered him an object of loathing to the whole Frankish world. He accordingly absolutely refused. The Catalans then turned to his fellow-captive, Roger Deslaur, the knight of Roussillon, who had neither

[1] Theódoulos (ii., 201), thus disposing of Buchon's ingenious theory that the armour, found at Chalkis in 1840 and now in the collection of the Historical and Ethnological Society at Athens, belonged to the fallen of the Kephissós and had been transported by Bonifacio to Chalkis. (*La Grèce Continentale*, 134 *sqq.*).

the territorial position, the family ties, nor the scruples of Bonifacio. He accepted; the Catalans made him their leader, and gave him the splendid castle of Salona, together with the widow of its fallen lord, Thomas III., the last De Stromoncourt.

Thus, after a duration of over a hundred years, fell at a single blow the French duchy of Athens. An artificial creation, imposed upon a foreign soil, it collapsed as suddenly as it had arisen, and it left few traces behind it. We have seen that under the dominion of the dukes of the house of De la Roche, trade prospered, manufactures flourished, and the splendours of the Theban court impressed foreigners accustomed to the pomps and pageants of much greater states. Never before, and never again, did the ancient city of the seven gates witness such a brilliant throng as that which made the frescoed walls of the great castle of St Omer ring with song and revelry; never before, and never again, did the violet crown of Athens encircle so romantic a scene, as when armoured knights and fair Burgundian damsels rode up to attend mass in St Mary's minster on the Akropolis. But the French society, which had made Attica the cynosure of the Levant, never took firm root in the land. The Greeks and the Franks seem to have amalgamated even less in Burgundian Athens than elsewhere; the French were, after three generations, still a foreign garrison, nor did they, as was the case in Norman England, form a powerful blend with the conquered race. Fascinating as is the spectacle of chivalry enthroned in the home of classical literature, it was an unnatural union, and, as such, doomed from the outset. But in the long history of Athens, not the least gorgeous page is that written by the dukes from beyond the sea.

If it made small mark on the character of the people, the French dynasty has, at least, bequeathed to us some visible memorials of its rule. All these rulers, except Othon and John, have left coins, which may be found in the doge's palace and elsewhere; while, by way of compensation, as we saw, a pious donation to the abbey of Bellevaux has preserved the seal of the first French ruler of Athens. If there be one building more than another where we should expect to discover traces of French influence, it is the famous monastery of Daphni, which Othon had granted to the Cistercians, and where his successors chose their graves. But, if we except the so-called tomb of Guy II., two rows of Gothic arcades alone recall this, the most brilliant period in the life of the abbey. Under the auspices of the dukes from Franche-Comté, the abbots of Daphni had played a considerable part in the ecclesiastical history of Greece. Popes had used them as intermediaries, and their quinquennial visits to the mother-abbey of Cîteaux must have helped to maintain the connection between France and Athens. But after the fall of the French duchy, the monastery declined; it is but little mentioned in the two succeeding centuries; it ceased to be the ducal burial-place, and was eclipsed by the greater glories of St Mary's minster, on one of whose columns the last known of its abbots has obtained such immortality as a meagre Latin inscription can confer.[1] Another inscription on the Stoa of Hadrian commemorates, as we saw, an Athenian canon of the ducal family; while Walter of Ray, who was bishop of Negroponte at the time of the catastrophe, found a sumptuous monument in the French abbey of Bèze.[2] To this period, too, has been ascribed the "Frankish monastery," the remains of which long stood at the foot of Pentelikon, and which was probably the Minorite establishment mentioned in the will of the last duke.[3] A much more striking foundation—the Gorgoepékoos church—was attributed by the enthusiastic Buchon to the French; but the general opinion is that it is a Byzantine structure. An imaginative Greek, going one step further, maintained that this beautiful little building was the chapel of the ducal palace, which he supposed to have stood on the site of the present cathedral.[4] But the residence of the French dynasty was at Thebes, and the commander of the Akropolis, who represented it at Athens, doubtless lived within the castle. Accordingly, it is in Bœotia rather than

[1] Millet, *Le Monastère de Daphni*, 40, 42, 57; Martène et Durand, *Thesaurus*, iv., 1320, 1422.

[2] *Académie de Besançon* (1880), 149-53, pl. v.

[3] Δελτίον, iv., 82, 136.

[4] Sourmelês, Κατάστασις συνοπτική, 36, *n.*

in Attica that we should expect to find buildings of this first Frankish epoch. The stumpy Santameri tower at Thebes still preserves the name of its founder; a bridge, formerly of five, but now of three, arches, which crosses the Melas some two miles below the village of Topolia, testifies to the activity of the French in that same Copaic district which witnessed their fall—a disaster perhaps commemorated by the little church at Karditza. Frankish coats of arms may be seen on the walls of the older church at Hósios Loukâs, one of which, two snakes supporting two crosses, bears some resemblance to the device on the tomb at Daphni. It is, indeed, not surprising that a monastery which was the abode of the prior and chapter of the Holy Sepulchre, and later on the residence of the dowager duchess of Athens, should contain Frankish memorials.[1]

Like the French dukes, their most important vassals, the lords of Salona, have perpetuated their names by a separate coinage, of which specimens minted by Thomas II. and Thomas III. from their own mint have been preserved.[2] But the splendid castle of Salona, which Honorius III. had helped to fortify, is the best memorial of that once powerful French family, although it is not easy to determine how much of the present structure is due to them, and how much to their successors. On the other hand, neither the Pallavicini of Boudonitza nor the branch of the ducal race which was established at Damalâ in Argolis seem to have left memories that can be identified save the ancient castle of the marquises. Both now lingered on in the female line alone—the usual lot of the Frankish nobles in Greece. Such was the end of that strange venture which had made Attica and Bœotia a "new France"; a few coins, a few arches, a casual inscription, are all that they have retained of their brilliant Burgundian dukes.

[1] Buchon, *La Grèce Continentale*, 246; *Atlas*, pl. xli., 7, 8, 16; Schultz and Barnsley, *The Monastery of St Luke*, pl. 14, D.

[2] Schlumberger, *Numismatique*, 349; Sáthas, Τὸ Χρονικὸν τοῦ Γαλαξειδίου, 239.

CHAPTER VIII

THE CATALANS AND THEIR NEIGHBOURS (1311-1333)

THE meteoric career of the Catalan Grand Company had placed it in the possession of the Athenian duchy, but had at the same time won for it a host of suspicious or vindictive enemies. The house of Anjou, as represented by Philip of Taranto, Prince of Achaia and suzerain of the Frankish states of Greece, naturally resented the capture of Athens by the enemies of his dynasty; the Venetians of Negroponte were justly alarmed for the safety of that important colony; the widow of the fallen duke was seeking to recover the duchy for her son; the two Greek states of Neopatras and Arta were ill-disposed to the appearance of these fresh intruders; the Emperor though not sorry that the Franks had received such a fatal blow, had not forgotten the destruction wrought by the Catalans upon his armies and his lands. Well aware of their critical position in a foreign land, surrounded by enemies, the victors of the Kephissós reluctantly came to the conclusion, that, if they wished to maintain their acquisitions, they must place themselves under the protection of some powerful sovereign. Their choice naturally fell upon King Frederick II. of Sicily, the master whom they had served before they left that island for the East ten years before, and who, by sending the Infant of Majorca to command them in his name while they were still in the Greek Empire, had shown that he had not relinquished the idea of profiting by their successes. Accordingly, in 1312, they invited the King of Sicily to send them one of his children, to whom they promised to take the oath of fealty as their lord and to hand over the command over all their forces. Frederick II. was only too pleased to accept an offer, which would add fresh lustre to his house. He told the Catalan envoys, that he would give them as their duke his second son Manfred; but, as the latter was at present too young to take personal charge of the duchy, he would send them a trusty knight, who would receive their homage and govern them in Manfred's name. For this important post he selected Berenguer Estañol, a knight of Ampurias, who set out with five galleys to take possession of his command. The Catalans received him well, Deslaur retired from his provisional leadership to his lordship of Salona on the arrival of the ducal governor, and we hear of him no more.[1]

The archives of Palermo unfortunately contain no documents relating to the early administration of Attica under the Catalan rule. But from the fairly frequent allusions to Athens in the last two decades of the Sicilian suzerainty we can form a tolerably complete idea of the system of government—a system which, with some modifications, may be assumed to have existed from the commencement. The two chief officials were the vicar-general and the marshal, both appointed by the duke, the former of whom exercised supreme political power as his deputy, while the latter was the military head of the state. The vicar-general was appointed during good pleasure, and took the oath of fidelity on the gospels to the duke or his representative, repeating it before the assembled *sindici*—a sort of parliament—of all the towns and cities of the duchy. From his residence at Thebes, the capital of the Catalan state, he could issue pardons in the duke's name to those accused of felony or treason; it was he who exercised judicial authority, administered the finances, provided for the defence of the land, inspected the fortresses, and often appointed their commanders. The position of vicar-general was one of considerable splendour; a major-domo presided over his household; a *procureur général* was attached to his

[1] Muntaner, ch. ccxlii.; *Libro de los Fechos*, 121; Sanudo, *Epistolæ*, *apud* Bongars, *Gesta Dei per Francos*, II., 305.

court. Later on, under the Aragonese supremacy, his powers were practically those of the duke himself.[1]

The marshal was always chosen from the ranks of the Company, and the dignity became hereditary in the family of De Novelles till a little before the year 1363, when the hereditary marshal had apparently been deprived of his dignity for rebellion against his sovereign. Roger de Lluria succeeded him as marshal, and, three years later, combined the two great offices in his own person, holding them both till his death, after which we hear of no more marshals. The probable explanation of this is not far to seek. There had probably been, as we shall see, a conflict between the vicar and the marshal, which proved that there was no room in the narrow court of Thebes for two such exalted officials; and, as Lluria, when he became vicar-general, was already marshal, such a combination may have seemed a happy solution of the difficulty.[2]

Greece has ever been the land of local government, and under the Sicilian domination each city and district had its own local governor, called *veguer*, *castellano*, or *capitán*—designations sometimes applied to the same person, sometimes distinct, as it was considered to be an abuse when more than one of these offices were concentrated in the same hands. We are expressly told that the "capitulations" agreed upon between the Catalans and their duke limited the duration of a *veguer's* office to three years, and on one occasion a "*capitán*, *veguer*, and *castellano*" of Athens was removed because his three years' term was up.[3] But there are examples of the appointment of these officials for life or during good pleasure.[4] They were sometimes nominated by the vicar-general, sometimes by the duke, and sometimes by the local representatives, for example, by the community of Athens, from among the citizens, subject to confirmation by the duke, and they had power to appoint a substitute

[1] Lámpros, Ἔγγραφα, 247, 286; *Mélanges historiques*, III., 53, 54; Rosario Gregorio, *Considerazioni*, II., 574.

[2] Lámpros, Ἔγγραφα, 240, 279, 282, 330, 350; Rubió y Lluch, *Los Navarros en Grecia*, 476; Rosario Gregorio, *Considerazioni*, II., 572, 575. *Cf.* the author's article in the *English Hist. Review*, xxii., 520.

[3] Lámpros, Ἔγγραφα, 249, 318.

[4] *Ibid.*, 276, 278, 280, 309.

in case of absence on public business. They were required, before entering upon their duties, to take an oath on the gospels before the vicar-general and the local community. These duties included the military command of the town and the hearing of criminal causes,[1] but a final appeal from their decisions, as from the civil and criminal jurisdiction of the vicar-general, lay to the ducal tribunal in Sicily, just as our Colonial and Indian Appeals go to the Privy Council in London. On one occasion, however, we find a lord justice appointed during good pleasure to try appeals on the spot—a system which must have saved much time and expense to the appellants.[2] We hear also of notaries, not infrequently Greeks, appointed by the duke for life, or even as hereditary officials, of a constable of the city of Thebes, and of a bailie of the city of Athens, apparently a municipal officer.[3]

The Catalan state enjoyed a considerable measure of representative institutions, such as the Catalans had for some time obtained in their native land. The principal towns and villages were represented by *sindici*, and possessed municipalities with councils and officials of their own. These municipalities occasionally combined to petition the duke for the redress of their grievances; their petitions were then sealed by the "Chancellor of the Society of Franks" with the seal of St George, which had been that of the Company in its wandering days. On one occasion the communities elected the vicar-general, and the dukes frequently wrote to them about affairs of state. They did not hesitate to send envoys requesting the recall of an obnoxious vicar-general, they spoke perfectly plainly to their sovereign, who on one occasion complained of their "morose answers," and their petitions usually, for obvious reasons, received a favourable reply. Later on, one of their principal demands was that official posts should be bestowed on residents, not on Sicilians. Attica for the Catalans was, in fact, their watchword. They were stubborn folk, perfectly contented to maintain the Sicilian connection, so long as they could manage their own affairs in their own way; in that, as in much else, they resembled our own self-governing colonies.

[1] Lámpros, Ἔγγραφα, 266, 277, 309.
[2] *Ibid.*, 239, 247, 295.
[3] *Ibid.*, 270, 312.

The feudal system continued, but with far less brilliancy than in the time of the French. The Catalan conquerors were of common origin; when they had been settled some years, we find very few knights among them, and even after seventy years of residence, the roll of noble families in the whole state contained only some sixteen names. The Company particularly objected to the feudal practice of bestowing important places, such as Livadia, upon private individuals, preferring that they should be administered by the government officials. As a code of justice, the "Customs of Barcelona" supplanted the "Assizes of Romania," and Catalan became the official, as well as the ordinary language. The dukes wrote in the language of Muntaner, not merely to their Catalan, but also to their Greek subjects, and we are specially told that the employment of "the vulgar Catalan dialect" was "according to the custom and usage of the city of Athens."

The ecclesiastical organisation remained much the same as in the Burgundian times. After the annexation of Neopatras, the two duchies contained three archbishoprics—Athens, Thebes, and Neopatras—the first of which had thirteen suffragan bishoprics, and the last one, that of Lamia or Zetouni. Thus Athens had gained two, and Thebes had lost two, suffragans since the early Frankish days; but of the Athenian bishoprics only four—Megara, Daulia, Salona, and Boudonitza—were actually within the confines of the duchy.

The church of St Mary at Athens, as the Parthenon was called, had twelve canons, appointed by the duke, whom we find confirming a Catalan as dean of the Athenian chapter, nominating the Theban archbishop, and bestowing vacant livings upon priests. Although in the last years of Catalan rule the clergy acquired great influence, and were selected as envoys to the ducal court, the law strictly forbade them to hold fiefs—a very necessary provision in a land won, and held, by the sword.[1] The Knights of St John, however, had property in the Catalan state, and the castle of Sykaminon, near Oropos, was theirs.[2]

[1] Rubió y Lluch, 472, 481; Çurita, *Anales*, II., 377; Lámpros, Ἔγγραφα, 271, 285, 306-7.

[2] *Ibid.*, 233; Δελτίον, v., 827; *Revue de l'Orient latin*, iii., 653.

Like the Franks, the Catalans treated the Greeks as an inferior race. They excluded them, as a general rule, from all civic rights—the exclusive privilege of the *Conquistadors*, as the Catalans styled themselves—and thus an unhappy Hellene was legally debarred from acquiring, selling, or disposing of his property as he chose. Even after his death, someone else might step in and take his possessions from his son, and we hear of slavery existing at Athens. As a general rule, too, intermarriage of the two races was forbidden, but to these enactments there were not a few exceptions. Greeks, who had deserved well of the Company in times of difficulty, like the people of Livadia, received the full franchise, and might even hold serfs, besides being permitted to marry their children to members of the dominant race. In the later Catalan period, we find Greeks occupying posts of importance, such as that of *castellano* of Salona, chancellor of Athens, and notary of Livadia. Once, at the very close of Catalan rule, Greeks are mentioned as sitting on the municipal council of Neopatras. Persons of such standing as a count of Salona and a marshal of the duchies married Greek ladies, and it was provided in such cases that the Greek might keep the orthodox faith; only, if the wife became a Catholic and then reverted, she paid for her double apostacy by the loss of her property. A similar penalty awaited any Catalan who was converted to the orthodox faith.[1] As for the Greek Church, it continued to occupy the inferior position which it had filled under the Franks. Of the former Frankish nobility we naturally hear nothing, as it had been annihilated at the battle of the Kephissós. The Burgundian burgesses are never mentioned. On the other hand, we find Armenians residing at Thebes and proving a source of revenue to the ducal exchequer.

The duke would naturally assume the crown lands of his French predecessors, and this ducal domain included lands and house property at Athens and Thebes. These houses at the capital were let, and the rent was paid in wax every year; occasionally, the crown was pleased to grant an annuity out of the proceeds of the "Theban wax tax" to

[1] Lámpros, *op. cit.*, 238, 272, 331, 337-8, 342; Rubió, *Catalunya a Grecia*, 46.

some deserving Catalan. We hear, too, of a land-tax (*jus terragii*) payable to the ducal court, to which also escheated the real and personal property of converts to the Greek faith.[1] But, as in the case of the British Empire and its colonies, the Sicilian Dukes of Athens did not estimate the value of the connection by the methods of an accountant. Upon them it conferred the prestige which has in all ages attached to the great name of Athens, while it also gave them an excuse for intervention in Eastern politics. To the Catalans, on the other hand, the protection of the Sicilian crown was of great practical value. Having no diplomatic service of their own, they looked to the ducal diplomatists to explain away any more than usually outrageous act of piracy which they had committed upon some Venetian subject; to say soft things on their behalf at the Vatican; to give them, in short, a status in the community of nations. They had all the advantages of independence, without its drawbacks; they lost nothing by having acknowledged the sovereignty of Sicily; and both they and their Sicilian dukes seem thoroughly to have understood their mutual relations.

For four years, till his death in 1316, Estañol governed the Catalan duchy wisely and well. Under his guidance, the Company maintained its martial spirit, which was the very essence of its existence, by expeditions in all directions—against the imperial fortresses on the borders of Thessaly, against the Angeli of Neopatras and of Arta, against the island of Eubœa, and in support of the claims of their old comrade, the Infant Ferdinand of Majorca, to the principality of Achaia. We may judge of the devastation wrought on these forays from the fact that Archbishop Bartholomew of Corinth was at this time allowed by Clement V. to defer payment of his predecessor's debts for three years, because his diocese "had been desolated and the city of Corinth destroyed by the Catalan Company," while the Archbishop of Thebes and Walter of Ray, Bishop of Negroponte, could not reach their sees. But Estañol was a diplomatist as well as a soldier. He managed to attack his enemies one at a time; and, as soon as his soldiers had exhausted the resources of

[1] Lámpros, *op. cit.* 234, 272, 291, 292, 299, 313, 350; Rubió y Lluch, *Los Navarros*, 465.

the country which they had invaded, they moved on, like locusts, to another. In vain the pope ordered the Latin patriarch of Constantinople to argue with the Catalan leaders on the error of their ways, and to excommunicate these spoilers of churches and slayers of churchmen in case of their continued disobedience to his voice; in vain he bade the Grand Master of the Knights of St John, but recently established in the island of Rhodes, to send four galleys to the aid of Walter of Foucherolles, who held the Argive fortresses with the title of "Captain of the Duchy" for the little duke's grandfather and guardian, the Constable of France; in vain he appealed to King James II. of Aragon to drive the Catalans out of Attica, and depicted the cruelties, robberies, and murders which they had perpetrated on the faithful children of the Church in those parts. The Catalans heeded not the patriarchal admonitions; the grand-master was occupied with the affairs of his new domain; while the politic sovereign, who had no desire to intervene in the affairs of his brother's duchy, replied that that "true athlete of Christ and faithful boxer of the Church," as the pope had called the late Duke Walter, had met with his deserts, and that the Catalans, if they were cruel, were still Catholics, who would prove a valuable bulwark of Romanism against the schismatic Greeks of Byzantium.[1]

Upon Estañol's death, the Company elected one of its own members, a knight, William Thomas, a man of higher rank than his fellows, as its temporary captain, until King Frederick had had time to send someone else to rule over them.[2] The king appointed his own natural son, Don Alfonso Fadrique, or Frederick, a man of much energy and force of character, whom we saw ravaging the coasts and islands of Greece some twelve years earlier. The "President of the fortunate army of Franks in the duchy of Athens," as the new vicar-general officially described himself, retained the leadership of the company for thirteen years—a position

[1] Muntaner, ch. ccxlii.; Çurita, *Anales*, bk. vi., ch. xii.; Raynaldus, *op. cit.*, v., 22-3; *Regestum Clementis V.*, vii., 72-3, 125, 238; viii., 14, 131-2; ix., 44-7.

[2] Buchon, *Nouvelles Recherches*, II., i., 394-6; Lámpros, Ἔγγραφα, 354-6.

of practical independence, as the nominal duke, Manfred, died in the year of Fadrique's appointment, and was succeeded in the title by his younger brother, William, likewise a minor. Moreover, he strengthened his hold upon Attica, and at the same time obtained a pretext for intervening in the affairs of Eubœa by his marriage with Marulla, the daughter and heiress of Bonifacio da Verona, "one of the fairest Christians in the world, the best woman and the wisest that ever was in that land," as Muntaner, who had seen her as a child in her father's house at Negroponte, enthusiastically describes her. Although the fair Lombard had a brother, the thirteen castles in the Athenian duchy and the other places which Guy II. of Athens had once bestowed upon her father, fell to her share.[1]

The Venetians had been alarmed for the safety of Eubœa from the moment when the Catalans had arrived in Greece. After the battle of the Kephissós, they increased the salaries of their officials in the island, and organised a fleet for its defence. To this fleet the Lombard lords were invited to contribute, and, with the exception of Bonifacio, they agreed to do so. That powerful and ambitious baron, who was on the best terms with the Catalans, refused, intending, no doubt with their aid, to make himself master of the island. The marriage of his daughter with their chief seemed to favour this plan.

Hitherto, the Catalans had contented themselves with preventing the Catholic bishop of Negroponte from returning to his see—which can scarcely surprise us, as he was a cousin of the French dukes of Athens—and with frequent plundering raids across the narrow sound, which separated them from the great island. A more serious campaign began, however, when Fadrique and more than 2000 men—among them Turkish mercenaries—marched across "the black bridge." In Negroponte these seasoned soldiers of fortune found little opposition. The baronage of the island, like the Frankish aristocracy in other parts of Greece, had suffered severely at the battle of the Kephissós, where two of the Eubœan lords, George Ghisi and Alberto Pallavicini, had fallen. Pallavicini's successor, Andrea Cornaro, a member of that

[1] Muntaner, ch. ccxliii., his last notice of the Catalans in Attica.

famous Venetian family, hastened to make his peace with the invaders, who entered Chalkis and forced the Venetian bailie to do likewise. Thus abandoned by their allies, the other triarchs appealed to Matilda of Hainault, at that time Princess of Achaia, as their suzerain; but she was alone and powerless to help; she had already contemplated ceding her phantom suzerainty over the island to Venice; and she now contented herself with pointing out to the doge the extreme danger which the island ran of falling into the hands of the Catalans. At this moment, Bonifacio da Verona died—the last survivor of the *ancien régime* of Frankish Greece—whereupon his son-in-law at once occupied the two important castles of Karystos and Larmena as part of Marulla's dowry. But the successes of the Company had so greatly alarmed Europe that a coalition of the European powers seemed likely to be formed against it; the pope complained bitterly that the Catalans, "the offscourings of humanity," employed infidel Turks against Christians, and urged Venice to drive them out; the exiled family of Brienne was plotting to regain its heritage; the Angevins protested against Fadrique's intervention in Eubœa. Under these circumstances, King Frederick of Sicily thought it prudent to order his daring son to desist from further conquests in that island, and Fadrique obediently retired from Eubœa, retaining, however, the two castles of Karystos and Larmena. But the Catalans had no real reason for fearing the active hostility of Venice, their nearest and most serious rival. The republic was informed by her agents that the very subjects of the young Duke Walter at Argos and Nauplia were in league with the Company—a proof that the Catalan usurpation was not unpopular in Greece. Her statesmen, always cautious, were, therefore, still less inclined to provide the money and the vessels for the restoration of the Brienne dynasty, even though the Duchess of Athens, after the fashion of kings in exile, made liberal promises of commercial concessions which it was not in her power to bestow. On the other hand, negotiations began between King Frederick and Venice, which ended in 1319 in a formal truce, renewed two years later, in which the triarchs were included. This remarkable agreement provided, under a penalty of £2240, that the

Company should fit out no fresh ships in the Saronic Gulf ("the sea of Athens") or in Eubœan waters; a plank was to be taken out of the hull of each of the vessels then lying in those stations, and their tackle was to be carried up to the Akropolis ("the castle of Athens") and there deposited. The Catalan ships in the Corinthian Gulf ("the sea of Rivadostria," or Livadostro) might, however, remain as they were. These stringent provisions were intended to check the growth of a Catalan navy, which had already become a menace to Venetian interests in the Levant. It is significant of the revived importance of the Piræus, that in a Genoese map of this period that harbour, usually called by the Venetians "the port of Sithines" (or Athens), figures for the first time by the name of "Lion," the later Porto Leone, derived from the colossal lion, now in front of the Arsenal at Venice, which then stood there. It was from there that Fadrique had been able to send two galleys to his Turkish allies; it was from there that his corsairs had preyed on Venetian commerce, and had wreaked their vengeance on the island of Melos, which belonged to the duchy of Naxos, for the part which the duke's son Nicholas had taken against the Catalans in the marshes of the Kephissós and in the plain of Elis. Even as far as Chios the Catalan galleys had penetrated, and had carried off from that fertile island the son of Martino Zaccaria, its Genoese lord, whose name had long been a terror to Latin pirates.

Venice profited by the war in Eubœa to extend her influence in that island. When she had got rid of the Catalan danger, she informed the triarchs of her intention of occupying the towns and fortresses as a reward for her trouble and expense. She was, indeed, the only power which could defend Negroponte from the ever-increasing Turkish peril, which menaced all the islands and coasts of Greece. Since 1314 the titular dignity of Latin Patriarch of Constantinople had been united with the see of Negroponte; but the patriarchal admonitions had no effect upon the adventurous infidels. The Archbishop of Thebes, who went on a mission to Venice to seek aid against the Turks, wrote to Sanudo that they had thrice invaded Eubœa in one year; the Venetian bailie feared that, if help were not forthcoming, that island would be ruined; one of his successors was compelled to pay blackmail to these marauders. There was always a danger of the Catalans and Turks uniting against Eubœa, for the former retained a fellow-feeling for their old comrades, and when Fadrique, a few years later, again intervened in the affairs of the island on behalf of his wife, who had latterly allowed her brother to enjoy the castle of Larmena, but claimed it again on his demise, the Turks were very active there. It is no wonder, therefore, that when the two former truces between Venice and the Company were renewed at Thebes in 1331, the Catalans had to promise to receive no Turks into their land or service, and to make no fresh treaties with those common enemies of the Latin race. A recent Turkish raid into Attica, in the course of which many of its inhabitants had been killed and others sold into slavery in Turkey, may have predisposed the Catalans to accept these terms. Alfonso pledged himself to allow no castles to be built within his territory of Karystos which he declined to sell to the republic, and from that time he molested the Venetians of Eubœa no more.[1]

Meanwhile, Fadrique had found leisure, while he was at peace with Venice, to extend the Company's authority over a large part of Northern Greece, where the dynasty of the Angeli had now become extinct. After the death of the last French Duke of Athens in the battle of the Kephissós, the feeble ruler of Thessaly had adopted the style of "Lord of the lands of Athens and Neopatras" (*Signore de le terre de Thenes e Patras*), in virtue of his kinship with the house of De la Roche. But John II., the last of the Thessalian Angeli, had none of the energy of his predecessors. His health had never been robust, and in 1318 he died without issue, leaving his rich dominions to be dismembered. So great was the confusion which at once ensued, that the metropolitan of Larissa could no longer exercise his sacred functions in that city. Feudalism, as we saw, had been

[1] *Regestum Clementis V.*, ix., 82; Raynaldi, *loc. cit.*; *Mélanges historiques*, III., 32-54; Thomas, *Diplomatarium*, i., 110-17, 120-2, 214-19; Predelli, *Commemoriali*, I., 163, 176, 189, 191, 195; II., 13; Sanudo, *Epistolæ*, *apud* Bongars, II., 298, 313-15; *Giornale Ligustico* (1888), p. 236; *Atti della Società Ligure di Storia Patria*, V., *Tavole*, iv., vi., vii.

readily developed on the congenial soil of Thessaly, where the Greek *archons* had copied, and copied for the worse, as is always the case when the East borrows the manners of the West, the institutions of the Franks. One petty tyrant now established himself at Trikkala; another, a member of the great family of the Melissenoí, held sway over the ruins of Delphi, then already known by its modern name of Kastrí, keeping on good terms with his Catalan neighbours at Salona by means of a matrimonial alliance between his sister and the marshal of the Company. Several towns were annexed by the emperor, who had long coveted the lands of his son-in-law, and the Holy Synod threatened fearful pains and penalties upon the heads of those Thessalians, who declined to submit to the rule of Byzantium. Venice obtained a share of the spoil in the shape of the port of Pteleon at the entrance of the Pagasæan Gulf, which the emperor voluntarily allowed her to take, rather than it should fall into the hands of the Catalans, who subsequently agreed not to molest it. A Venetian from Eubœa was appointed rector of this station—the sole point, except Modon and Coron, which the republic possessed on the mainland of Greece—and it remained in the occupation of Venice down to the capture of Eubœa by the Turks. But the best part of the country fell to the share of the Catalan Company. Sanudo tells us how Fadrique made himself master of one place after another, of Loidoriki and Siderokastro, of Gardiki and Lamia, of Domokó and Pharsala —names so well known in the annals of modern Greece. At Neopatras, the seat of the extinct dynasty, he made his second capital, styling himself Vicar-General of the duchies of Athens and Neopatras. Henceforth the Sicilian dukes of Athens assumed the double title, which may be seen on their coins and in their documents, and, long after the Catalan duchy had passed away, the kings of Aragon continued to bear it. Besides these various competitors for the heritage of the Angeli, there now appeared for the first time in the plain of Thessaly great masses of Albanian immigrants, who formed a new and vigorous element in the population. They ravaged all the open country; and, as they brought their wives with them, their numbers soon increased, and they began to take the place of the Wallachs, who had hitherto formed the bulk of the Thessalian population, and had given the country its name of Great Wallachia. The Venetians thought that this Albanian immigration had the great advantage of keeping the Catalans employed, so that they had less leisure to attack their neighbours. It was from these Albanians that the gaps in the population of Attica and the Morea were subsequently replenished.[1]

Thessaly was now in great part Catalan; Salona was the fief of the Company's former chief, Roger Deslaur; so that these soldiers of fortune were masters of practically all continental Greece, except the historic marquisate of Boudonitza and the Despotat of Epiros. After the death of the last of the Pallavicini marquises in the swamps of the Kephissós, his widow had married that same Andrea Cornaro, baron of Eubœa, whom we have seen contending in vain against the claims of Fadrique in that island. Fadrique punished him by ravaging the marquisate, without, however, annexing it to Athens. Indeed, on Cornaro's death, it passed, by the marriage of his stepdaughter, into the hands of a bitter enemy and former prisoner of the Catalans, the son of Martino Zaccaria, the Genoese lord of Chios. At his demise, his widow married in 1335 one of the noble Venetian family of Giorgi, or Zorzi, as it was called in the soft dialect of the lagoons, with which the marquisate remained till the Turkish Conquest. The marquises had long been peers and vassals of the principality of Achaia, and as such they continued to be reckoned during the whole of the fourteenth century. No proof exists that they ever depended upon the French duchy of Athens; but though their sympathies were now with Venice, they paid an annual tribute of four horses to the Catalan vicar-general.[2]

The same year which witnessed the extinction of the Angeli in Thessaly saw, too, the close of their dynasty in

[1] Nikephóros Gregorâs, i., 279, 318; Predelli, *Commemoriali*, I., 177; Sanudo, *Epistolæ*, *apud* Bongars, II., 293; Miklosich und Müller, I., 79; Çurita, bk. vi., ch. xii.; Schlumberger, *Numismatique de l'Orient latin*, 346; *Archivio Veneto*, xx., 84-5.

[2] Canciani, III., 507; Rubió y Lluch, 482; Çurita, bk. x., ch. xxx.; Hopf, *Chroniques*, 125, 230, and *apud* Ersch und Gruber, lxxxv., 425, 436.

Epiros. In 1318, the feeble Despot Thomas, the last of his race, was murdered by his nephew, Count Nicholas of Cephalonia, who married his widow, Anna Palaiologina, a granddaughter of the Emperor Andrónikos II. Thus connected with the imperial house, the Italian count sought to establish his authority over the Despotat of Epiros by drawing closer to the Greeks, whose religion he adopted, and in whose language his seal was engraved. By this means he hoped to checkmate the plans of Philip of Taranto, who was still meditating the conquest of the mainland, and to whom he boldly refused the homage due for his island domain. But the people of Joannina, at that time a populous and wealthy city, where Jews could make money, and where Hellenic sentiments were fostered by the fact that it was the seat of the metropolitan, preferred the rule of the Greek Emperor, frôm whom their Church received repeated favours, to that of the Latin apostate. For a time the latter thought it worth while to purchase the friendship of Byzantium and the title of Despot by keeping his oaths not to molest the Greeks of that city. But the death of his wife and the growing weakness of the empire convinced him that he had nothing to hope or fear from that quarter. The "Count Palatine, by the grace of God Despot of Romania," as he styled himself, accordingly invited Venice to assist him in driving the imperial troops out of Epiros, offering in return to hoist the lion banner on all his castles, to do homage to the republic for all his dominions, and to cede to it either the valuable fisheries in the lake of Butrinto opposite Corfù, or the sugar plantations of Parga—the town which, five centuries later, was destined to obtain such romantic notoriety, and of which this is perhaps the earliest mention. But the cautious Venetians were anxious not to endanger their commercial interests in the Greek Empire, with which they continued to be at peace, and they calmly reminded the count that there was no great novelty in his offer to become "their man," seeing that his ancestor Maio had more than a century earlier recognised their suzerainty over the three islands of Cephalonia, Zante, and Val di Compare (or Ithaka). Nothing daunted by this politic answer, and encouraged by the utter confusion at Constantinople caused by the quarrels of the elder and the younger Andrónikos, he openly attacked the strong city of Joannina. But at this point, in 1323, his career of crime was cut short by the hand of his brother, Count John II., who assassinated the assassin and received, in his turn, the title of Despot from Constantinople, on condition that he swore to govern Epiros, "not as its sovereign, but as the servant of the emperor." None the less, from his "castle of Arta," he issued coins, still preserved, modelled on those of the princes of Achaia, to facilitate trade with Latin countries. Even in the motley history of Frankish Greece we are struck by the incongruity of an Italian adventurer minting French pieces on "Ambracia's Gulf." But this vigorous scion of the Roman Orsini embodied in his person the strangest anomalies. Like his brother, the new Despot married another Anna Palaiologina and embraced the orthodox faith, while he sought, after the usual manner of usurpers, to connect himself with the native dynasty by assuming the three great names of Angelos, Comnenos, and Doúkas. As a proof of his ostentatious piety, he restored the famous church of Our Lady of Consolation at Arta, where an inscription preserving his name and that of Anna may still be seen. He was also one of the few examples in the history of Frankish Greece of a Latin ruler who patronised Greek literature. By his command, Constantine Hermoniakós composed a paraphrase of Homer in octosyllabic verse. The poem, if such we can call it, has no literary merit, but is an incontestable sign of an interest in culture even at the court of wild Epiros. Indeed, the courtly poet would have us believe that his master was "a hero and a scholar," and that the Lady Anna "excelled all women that ever lived in beauty, wisdom, and learning."[1]

South of the isthmus of Corinth, French influence was still predominant despite Catalan raids and intrigues. The

[1] Nikephóros Gregorâs, I., 283, 536, 544; Cantacuzene, I., 13; *L. d. F.*, 138; Raynaldus, v., 95; Miklosich und Müller, I., 171; v., 77-84, 86; Thomas, *Diplomatarium*, 146, 161, 168-70, *Archivio Veneto*, xx., 93; *Lettres secrètes de Jean XXII.*, i., 670; Romanós, *op. cit.*, 232-4; Schlumberger, *Numismatique*, 374, *Les Principautés franques*, 80; Δελτίον τῆς Χριστ. Ἀρχ. Ἑταιρείας, iii., 76.

faithful family of Foucherolles,[1] whom the last Duke of Athens had invested with lands at Nauplia and Argos, still held that sole surviving fragment of the French duchy for the exiled house of Brienne, while the principality of Achaia, though sorely tried, remained, amid many vicissitudes, under the authority of the Angevins. At the time of the Catalan Conquest of Athens, as we saw, it was in the hands of Philip of Taranto, who had left it to be administered by means of bailies. But two years after the fatal battle of the Kephissós, the possession of it was transferred to another by means of one of those diplomatic family compacts, so dear to the intriguing house of Anjou. At that moment, one of the most eligible heiresses of the Frankish world was the titular Empress of Constantinople, Catherine of Valois, a child barely twelve years old, and to obtain her hand was now the main object of Philip of Taranto's policy. On his side, there was no obstacle to the match, for his first wife, Thamar of Epiros, with whom his relations had become more and more strained after his unsuccessful expedition against that country, had been accused of adultery a few years earlier and was now dead. The young empress had, however, been betrothed already to Hugues V., Duke of Burgundy and titular King of Salonika, and it was therefore necessary to break off this engagement before Philip's plan could be realised. The French king, uncle of the girl, had no difficulty in making the French pope, Clement V., the subservient tool of his designs, for the papacy was now established at Avignon, and, as a preliminary move, the child-empress was made to express doubts as to the capacity of her almost equally childish *fiancé* to recover her lost empire. In order to compensate the house of Burgundy for the breach of the engagement, it was next arranged that Matilda, the young widow of Duke Guy II. of Athens, should marry the Duke of Burgundy's younger brother Louis. Matilda had already been betrothed, soon after her first husband's death, to the eldest son of Philip of Taranto; but, of course, that engagement was not allowed to stand in the way of the new family

[1] Raynaldus, v., 116; Hopf, *Chroniques*, 241; *L. d. F.*, 31 (which, by a characteristic anachronism, places them there in the time of Geoffrey I.).

compact. Philip of Taranto then conveyed to Matilda all his rights to the possession of Achaia, on condition that she should transfer them before her marriage to her future husband Louis; it was further provided, that, if he died without heirs, she should have nothing more than the life-ownership of the principality, which, after her death was to revert to the house of Burgundy in any event. At the same time, Louis received from his brother the barren title of King of Salonika, did homage to the Prince of Taranto for Achaia, of which the latter expressly retained the suzerainty, and promised to assist him in any attempt to recover the Latin Empire. The two marriages then took place, in 1313; Philip thus became titular Emperor of Constantinople, Louis of Burgundy Prince of Achaia and titular King of Salonika, and a coin and a magnificent seal still preserve the memory of his Achaian dignity.[1] The person who bore the loss of the whole transaction was the unhappy Matilda, who thus became merely life-owner of a principality, which she, as the eldest grandchild of Guillaume de Villehardouin, had not unnaturally considered as her birthright, and which her mother had bequeathed to her, all arrangements with the Angevins notwithstanding.

Unfortunately, Louis of Burgundy delayed his departure for Greece, and in his prolonged absence a claimant arose to dispute his title. Hitherto, amid all its trials under the government of women, foreigners, and absentees, Achaia had been spared the horrors of a contested succession; but that misfortune was now added to the other miseries of the land. Guillaume de Villehardouin's second daughter, Marguerite, Lady of Akova and widow of Count Richard of Cephalonia, was still alive, and, on the death of her elder sister in 1311, had laid claim to the principality on the ground of an alleged will made by her father. According to the provisions of this document, mentioned only by those authorities who have a natural bias for the Spanish side, the last Villehardouin prince had bequeathed Achaia to his elder daughter, with the provision that, if she died without children, it would pass to

[1] Buchon, *Recherches et Matériaux*, i., 54-5, 238-48; *Atlas*, xxiv., 10, 11; xxvi., 2; Ptolemæus Lucensis *apud* Muratori, xi., 1232; *L. d. C.*, 29, 474; *L. d. F.*, 124-7.

her younger sister. According to the marriage-contract of Isabelle in 1271 it was not in the power of her father to make any such disposition; and, even if he had, his younger daughter would still have had no claim, because her elder sister's daughter, Matilda, would have been the rightful princess. It was no wonder, then, that both the court of Naples and the leading Moreot barons—the small remnant of the Achaian chivalry which remained after the battle of the Kephissós—both rejected this unsubstantial pretext. So long, however, as her chivalrous protector, Nicholas III. de St Omer, lived, Marguerite was, at any rate, safe in the possession of her own barony. But, after his death in 1313, she found herself surrounded by personal enemies, such as her stepson, Count John I. of Cephalonia, and by Burgundian partisans, like Nicholas Mavro, or Le Noir, baron of St Sauveur, who had been appointed by the new prince as his bailie, and who was supported by the bishop of Olena. In this dilemma, she hit upon the idea of seeking an alliance with those Catalans whose exploits had amazed the whole Greek world. Before her marriage to the late Count of Cephalonia, she had been the wife of Isnard de Sabran, son of the Count of Ariano, in Apulia, by whom she had a daughter, Isabelle. This daughter she now married to the Infant Ferdinand of Majorca, who had played such an adventurous part in the history of the Catalan Company, whose name was well known in Greece, and who was now at the Sicilian court. The marriage was one of affection as well as of convenience. The susceptible Ferdinand fell in love at first sight of a damsel who, in the words of his faithful henchman Muntaner, was "the most beautiful creature of fourteen that one could see, the fairest, the rosiest, the best, and the wisest, too, for her age." Nor was the King of Sicily averse from a proposal which would make the house of Aragon supreme in the Morea as well as at Athens. Accordingly, the wedding was hurried on; by way of dowry for her daughter, Marguerite ceded to Ferdinand the barony of Akova and all her claims to Achaia, now more modestly assessed at "the fifth part of the principality," and the ceremony took place with great rejoicings at Messina. It was not, however, to be expected that the Burgundian party in the Morea would acquiesce in this arrangement. No sooner had Marguerite returned, leaving the newly married couple at Catania, than Nicholas Mavro and his confederates threw her into the castle of Chloumoûtsi. "Thou hast given thy daughter to the Catalans," they scornfully told her; "ill fortune shall attend thee, for thou shalt lose all thine own." Robbed of her baronial lands, the last child of the great Villehardouin died not long afterwards, in 1315, the prisoner of the unruly nobles. Two months later, her daughter followed her to the grave.[1]

Before her death, however, Ferdinand's young wife had given birth to a son, the future James II., last King of Majorca, and to this child she bequeathed her claims to Achaia. Assigning to his old comrade Muntaner the delicate task of conveying the baby to his mother, the Queen-Dowager of Majorca, at Perpignan, Ferdinand started with a body of soldiers to endeavour to make good these claims. Landing near Glarentza in the summer of 1315, he routed the small force which had sallied out to attack him, entered the town, and received the homage of the frightened citizens. He followed up this success by capturing the castle of Beauvoir, or Pontikokastro, the ruins of which still command the peninsula above Katakolo, and which Muntaner calls, not without reason, "one of the most beautiful sites in the world." All the plain of Elis was his, and his rapid triumph induced the three leaders of the Burgundian party—Mavro, Count John, and the bishop of Olena, to recognise his authority, which he endeavoured to justify by the publication of the testaments of Prince William, the Lady of Akova, and his own wife, as well as by that of his marriage-contract. He now styled himself "Lord of the Morea," and sought to consolidate his position by a second marriage with Isabelle d'Ibelin, cousin of the King of Cyprus. He even found time to mint money with his name at Glarentza.

But Ferdinand's usurpation was of brief duration. Louis of Burgundy and his wife now at last appeared to take possession of their principality. The Princess Matilda would

[1] Muntaner, chs. cclxi.-lxv.; Buchon, *Recherches historiques*, i., 439-42, 452, 475; *L. d. F.*, 121-2.

seem to have arrived first with a force of Burgundians, at the harbour of Navarino,[1] where Mavro hastened to meet her and assure her of his devotion to her cause. Adherents rapidly joined the French side; the Archbishop of Patras successfully held that city for her; a contingent was sent by her vassal, the Duke of Naxos, to assist her. But the Catalan soldiers of Ferdinand inflicted a severe defeat upon the Franks and their Burgundian comrades near the site of the ancient city of Elis, and the princess was obliged to send in hot haste to summon her husband. Almost immediately, Louis landed with his Burgundian troops from his Venetian ships with the Count of Cephalonia by his side, and soon the fortune of war turned. In vain the usurper sent to the Catalans of Athens and to his brother the King of Majorca for reinforcements; before they had had time to arrive, his cause was lost. On the advice of the Archbishop of Patras, Louis entered into negotiations with the Greek governor of Mistrâ; and, with a large contingent of Greek troops which made his forces three times more numerous than those of his rival, set out to attack him. On 5th July 1316, the two armies met at Manolada, the beautiful estate in the plain of Elis, which now belongs to the Greek crown prince. Ferdinand took up his position in a forest of pines, but his enemy set fire to the resinous trees, which nowhere burn so easily as in Greece, and thus drove the Infant out into the open. The impetuous Spaniard made straight for the division commanded by his mortal foe, Count John of Cephalonia, and broke through his line; the son of the Duke of Naxos was actually taken prisoner; but the Burgundians came to the Count's rescue; in the *mêlée*, the Infant's standard-bearer fell, whereupon his followers, all save some seven, fled, leaving their master almost alone. His few remaining companions urged him in vain to flee to Chloumoûtsi; while they were arguing with him, the Burgundians fell upon the little band, the Infant was surrounded, and, in spite of the orders of Prince Louis that his life should be spared, was decapitated on the field. His head, gashed with many

[1] *L. d. F.*, 128-32, which seems to me a trustworthy account, except for a few errors in the proper names; Schlumberger, *Numismatique*, 318.

wounds, was handed over to his implacable enemy, Count John, who next day caused it to be displayed before the gate of Glarentza. Still the sturdy infantry of Cataluña were for holding out; but their captain pretended that he had neither provisions nor pay to give them, and counselled surrender. A commission of twelve was elected to arrange affairs; bribery was freely employed; the Archbishop of Lepanto, naturally a warm partisan of the French party, disseminated the false news that the kings of Majorca, Aragon, and Sicily were dead; and when the long-expected reinforcements arrived from Majorca, they were told that peace had been already made. An honest Catalan, however, shouted out to them not to believe the traitors, but to land and avenge the Infant's death. At this, they disembarked and hastened up to Glarentza, where their comrades insisted on the gates being opened to admit them. Then the commander of the place called in the Count of Cephalonia, whose threats of starvation gradually cooled the enthusiasm of the garrison. The severed remains of the ill-fated Ferdinand were transported back on the Catalan galleys, and laid to rest at Perpignan. His best epitaph is that which his faithful old follower Muntaner has enshrined in his delightful *Chronicle*:—"He was the best knight and the bravest among all the king's sons of that day, and the most upright, and the wisest in all his acts." Thus ended one of the most romantic careers that even the mediæval romance of Greece can show.

Louis of Burgundy had nothing more to fear from his open enemies. The Catalans of Athens had turned back when they learnt at Vostitza, on the Gulf of Corinth, the news of the Infant's defeat and death; all the castles held for his rival had been handed over to him, except Glarentza, which was still occupied by the Catalans pending the settlement of their affairs. But the victor did not long survive the fall of his opponent. Barely a month after the battle of Manolada, before Glarentza had been evacuated, Prince Louis died, poisoned, as it was suspected, by the Count of Cephalonia, one of the darkest characters of that age. The Burgundians talked of avenging his murder with the aid of some of the Infant's followers; but a natural death a few months later removed the arch-criminal from the scene of his crimes.[1]

Matilda, barely twenty-three years old, yet already twice a widow, was now left alone to govern a country just recovering from civil war, where each unruly baron was minded to do what was right in his own eyes, and where anarchy was only tempered by Angevin intrigues. King Robert of Naples, whom historians have called "the wise," was an unscrupulous diplomatist, who saw in this state of things an opportunity for once more securing the possession of Achaia for a member of his house. Besides Philip of Taranto, he had another brother, John, Count of Gravina, in Apulia, and he accordingly resolved that the young widow should marry this man. Matilda, who had inherited the spirit of her race, refused to take the king's brother as her husband, whereupon Robert sent a trusty emissary, one of the Spinola of Genoa, to the Morea, to bring her to Naples by force. There she was compelled, in 1318, to go through the form of marriage with John of Gravina, who at once took the coveted title of Prince of Achaia. Even the king could not, however, compel her to recognise his brother as her husband, though he induced her to sign away her birthright in case she refused to do so. She appealed to Venice for aid, while her brother-in-law, Eudes IV., Duke of Burgundy, who had inherited claims on the principality under his brother's will, also protested against this arbitrary interference with his rights. But Venice did nothing on her behalf; and Eudes was effectually silenced by the purchase of his claims by Philip of Taranto. Matilda, now absolutely helpless but still defiant, was dragged before Pope John XXII. at Avignon, and ordered to obey. She replied that she was already another's, having secretly married Hugues de la Palisse,[2] a Burgundian knight to whom she was much attached. This confession was her ruin, for it gave the King of Naples an excuse for depriving her of her inherit-

[1] Buchon, *Recherches historiques*, i., 442-50, 475-6, ii., 455-9; Muntaner, chs. cclxvii.-lxx., cclxxx.; *L. d. F.*, 122-4, 127-37; Thomas, *Diplomatarium*, i., 112.

[2] Buchon thinks that he had long been settled in Greece. Perhaps La Palessien (*L. d. C.*, 466), in Cephalonia, was his family estate.

ance. He appealed to the clause in her mother's marriage contract, made thirty-three years before, which provided that if a daughter of Isabelle married without her suzerain's consent, the possession of Achaia should revert to the crown of Naples. Not content with this, Robert got up a story that Palisse had conspired against his life, and arrested the unhappy princess as his accomplice. For nine long years, in spite of appeals on her behalf by her cousin, the Count of Hainault, backed up by pecuniary arguments, she languished as a prisoner of state in the island fortress of Castel dell' Uovo at Naples, where, in happier days, her mother Isabelle had spent the early years of her married life. Her royal gaoler allowed her the sum of three ounces a month (£7, 4s.) for her maintenance, and when, at last, in 1331, death released her from his clutches, he paid her funeral expenses, and gave her, the lost scion of a noble line, royal burial in his family vault in the cathedral. No traces now remain of the marble monument which he erected over his unhappy victim, the last human sacrifice to Angevin intrigues. Thus closed the career of the Villehardouin family in the Morea; thus was the deceit of Geoffrey I. visited upon the head of his unfortunate descendant in the third generation.[1]

The Princess of Achaia had left neither children nor testament; but when her end was near, she declared verbally, before a number of witnesses, that she bequeathed all she had to her cousin, King James II. of Majorca, the son of her old rival Ferdinand, and the child whom Muntaner had prayed that he might live to serve in his old age. Meanwhile, however, her hated consort, John of Gravina, governed his principality by means of bailies, who held office for a year or two at the most, and were therefore unable to restore order and prosperity to the land.

The emperor, on the other hand, had recently adopted the sensible plan of appointing the imperial governor of Mistrâ, the "captain of the land and castles in the

[1] Buchon, *Recherches historiques*, i., 450-1; Ducange, *op. cit.*, ii., 380-2; *L. d. F.*, 137-9; Villani *apud* Muratori, xiii., 489, 523; Riccio, *Studii storici sopra* 84 *Registri Angioini*, 3, 29, 30; Predelli, *Commemoriali*, i., 189; Sir R. Rodd, *The Princes of Achaia*, ii., 282-7; *Lettres secrètes de Jean XXII.*, i., 862, 898; *Arch. Veneto*, xx., 93-4; St Genois, i., 360.

Peloponnese," as he was officially styled,[1] for an indefinite period, so that that official was able to gain a real acquaintance with local conditions and requirements. Thus, Cantacuzene, son of the man who was killed in the war of 1264, and father of the future emperor, governed the Byzantine province for eight years, till he was killed in 1316, and his successor, a very able general, Andrónikos Palaiológos Asan, nephew of the emperor and son of the Bulgarian tsar, remained in office for full six more. In his time the feeble Frankish principality, which had lost its ancient defenders, was still further curtailed by the loss of most of Arkadia, the strongest strategic position in the peninsula. The treacherous and venal commanders of the famous castles of St George, Akova, and Karytaina, sold them to Asan, who routed the bailie by means of an ambuscade, and captured the bishop of Olena and the grand constable, Bartolomeo Ghisi, who was at this time the leading man in Achaia. The result of this campaign was not only the loss of two more out of the twelve original baronies, of which only four—Patras, Veligosti, Vostitza, and Chalandritza—now remained in the hands of the Franks, but the conversion of the Franks of Arkadia to the Church of their conquerors—an inevitable movement, which the pope in vain urged the Archbishop of Patras to check. We can trace the growing importance of the Byzantine province and of the Greek Church in the inscriptions of Mistrâ, which begin at this period. In the early years of the fourteenth century the builders were hard at work there, restoring the church of the Forty Martyrs, and making a well; in 1312 the metropolitan church of St Demetrios was founded; it was then, too, that the interesting *Afentikó* church was built, while it was in these years that the emperor showered privileges and immunities from taxation upon the monastery of Our Lady of Brontochion, whose widely-scattered possessions, ranging from Karytaina to Passavâ, form a measure of Byzantine influence. Even in the still remaining "Latin part" of Arkadia the abbey was promised lands, whenever

[1] Golden bull of Andrónikos II., published by M. Millet in *Bulletin de Correspondance hellénique*, xxiii., 115. *Cf.* X. τ. M., 8694, 8708, 8716.

Providence should be pleased to restore that region to its lawful lord, the emperor.

Thus reduced in numbers and crippled in resources, menaced by the imperial troops in the interior, and harassed by Catalan and Turkish corsairs on the coast, the leading men of the principality decided between the painful alternatives of offering their country to Venice, or to the Catalans of Attica, the former for preference, so that at least they might find a protection which their absentee prince could not give them. They communicated their decision to the Venetian government, which was too cautious, however, to accept their offer, and continued to content itself with the two colonies in Messenia. At last, however, in 1324, John of Gravina set out for the Morea, and after stopping at Cephalonia and Zante, restoring his authority as suzerain over those rebellious islands, and deposing the Orsini dynasty, received the homage of the Achaian barons in the customary manner at Glarentza. But his sojourn in his principality was short and useless. An attempt, which he and his vassal, Duke Nicholas I. of Naxos, made to recover Karytaina failed, and the Greeks continued to make progress, in spite of a defeat inflicted on them by the duke in the plain of Elis below the castle of St Omer. The only lasting result of his expedition was the establishment in Greece of the great Florentine banking family of the Acciajuoli, which was destined to wear the ducal coronet of Athens. From them John of Gravina had borrowed considerable funds for his expenses in the Morea, and from him they received in return the fiefs of La Mandria and La Lichina, which we may identify with Lechaina, near Andravida. Numerous Neapolitans, who had followed him, also expected to be rewarded with lands which had fallen vacant owing to the almost complete disappearance of the old Frankish nobility, and thus there arose a new race of barons, who were ignorant of the language and customs of the people, while they lacked also the energy and courage of the original conquerors.[1] It is significant of this new order of things,

[1] *L. d. C.*, lxxviii., 476-7; *L. d. F.*, 140-7; Millet in *op. cit.*, xix., 269; xxiii., 113-18, 122; Bœckh, *Corp. Inscrip.*, 8762-4; Raynaldus, v., 200-1; Predelli, *Commemoriali*, i., 231; *Mélanges historiques*, iii., 54-7; Canta-

that one of the bailies of this period, Nicholas de Joinville, a noble and upright man, who did his best for the land entrusted to his charge, thought it necessary to add eight fresh articles, regulating the pay of soldiers, questions of succession, and the system of legal procedure, to the *Book of the Customs of the Empire of Romania*.[1]

John of Gravina soon grew tired of his Greek principality. In 1326 we find him in Florence, four years later he was senator of Rome, while a distinguished Roman, Guglielmo Frangipani, for many years Archbishop of Patras, acted as his bailie in Achaia—a post never before entrusted to a churchman, and a sure sign of the increasing power of the Achaian primates. Occupied exclusively with furthering Angevin interests in Italy, John never set foot in Greece again, and in 1333 severed all connection with it. Two years earlier, his brother and suzerain, Philip of Taranto, had died, and he refused to do homage to his nephew Robert. Thanks, however, to the mediation of Niccolò Acciajuoli, the representative of the great Florentine Bank at Naples, and chamberlain, some say lover, of the widowed Empress Catherine of Valois, the dispute between the uncle and the nephew was arranged. John of Gravina transferred to the empress, for her son Robert, the principality of Achaia, with its dependencies, in exchange for the Angevin possessions in Epiros, the kingdom of Albania, and the duchy of Durazzo, as well as the sum of 5000 ounces (£12,500) in cash, advanced by the serviceable Acciajuoli. Thus, once again, the suzerainty and the actual possession of Achaia were concentrated in the same hands, those of the claimant to the long defunct Latin Empire.[2]

Meanwhile, young Walter of Brienne, heir of the last

cuzene, i., 85; Nikephóros Gregorâs, i., 362; Buchon, *Nouvelles Recherches*, II., i., 33. That the Orsini dynasty was deposed in the Ionian islands by John of Gravina in 1324 is expressly stated by both Villani and the Aragonese *Chronicle*, and an Angevin bailie figures there in 1337 and 1356.

[1] Canciani, *op. cit.*, iii., 530; *Itinerarium Symonis Simeonis*, 15.

[2] Ducange, *op. cit.*, II., 214-15, 376; Buchon, *Nouvelles Recherches*, I., i., 54; Riccio, *Studii storici*, 17, 28. The tombs of the two princes of Achaia—Philip of Taranto and his brother John of Gravina—may still be seen in the church of S. Domenico at Naples.

Duke of Athens, had grown up to manhood, and thought that the time had come to attempt the recovery of his heritage from the Catalans. As a French noble, as Count of Lecce, and as son-in-law of Philip of Taranto, the titular emperor of Constantinople, he had every reason to expect the warm support of the house of Anjou in its interest, as well as his own. Philip saw that Walter's plans might be made to coincide with his own schemes for the reconquest of the Latin Empire, which he had never abandoned, and conferred upon him the title of his Vicar-General in Romania. Pope John XXII., like his predecessor, Clement V., was an ardent worker in his cause, writing to Venice on his behalf and bidding the Archbishop of Patras and Corinth preach a crusade against the "schismatics, sons of perdition, and pupils of iniquity," who had occupied the ancient patrimony of the lawful Duke of Athens and afflicted with heavy oppression the ecclesiastics and faithful inhabitants of Attica. But the Venetians, who could have contributed more to the success of the expedition than all the ecclesiastical thunders of Rome, just at this moment renewed their truce with the Catalans at Thebes. From that instant the attempt was bound to fail.

Walter was, like his father, a rash general, though he had already won the reputation of a wise administrator during a brief term of office as Angevin vicar at Florence. When he started for Epiros in 1331, a brilliant company of 800 French knights, 500 picked Tuscan men-at-arms, and a body of soldiers from his domain at Lecce accompanied him. At first success smiled upon his plans. He captured the island of Santa Mavra, which had belonged to the counts of Cephalonia since about the year 1300, and which had consequently formed part of the Despotat of Epiros since their usurpation of that state. On the mainland, the fortress of Vonitza, one portion of the quadrilateral which the unhappy Thamar had brought as her dowry to Philip of Taranto, but which had relapsed from the Angevin rule, and the city of Arta, fell into his hands. But when he proceeded to attack the Catalans, he found that he had to deal with cautious strategists, who never gave his fine cavalry a chance of displaying its mettle in a pitched battle. Their plan of campaign was to remain in their fortresses, allowing his impetuous followers to expend their energies on the open country. His father and mother had incurred heavy debts on behalf of their Greek dominions, and Walter had sold his property and pawned his wife's dowry to raise funds for the recovery of his duchy; but he had not calculated the cost of a protracted expedition, so that, ere long, he found it impossible to support the expense of so large a body of men, especially as the French contingent expected high pay and generous rations. A smaller force, particularly if aided by the Greeks, would have had more chance of success; but the native Athenians and Bœotians showed as little desire to fight for their lawful duke as they had shown to avenge his father's death. A correspondent of the contemporary historian, Nikephóros Gregorâs, wrote, indeed, that they were "suffering extreme slavery," and had "exchanged their ancient happiness for boorish ways." But either their sufferings were not sufficient to make them desire a change of masters, or their boorishness was such that they did not appreciate the advantages of French culture; in any case, they looked on impassively, while Walter's hopes daily dwindled away. Early in 1332, he retired to the Morea, whence, after a futile attempt to coerce the Catalans by the comminations of the great Archbishop Frangipani of Patras, he took ship for Italy never to return.[1] One irreparable loss, indeed, was inflicted upon Greece in consequence of his expedition. In order to prevent the castle of St Omer at Thebes from falling into his hands, and thus becoming a valuable base for the recovery of the duchy, the Catalans destroyed that noble monument of Frankish rule. Three years after their conquest of Athens, they had bestowed this splendid residence, together with the phantom kingdom of Salonika, upon Guy de la Tour, a noble French adventurer from Dauphiné, who had placed his sword at their disposal. More recently, Fadrique had granted the castle to Bartolomeo II. Ghisi, one of the chief magnates of Greece, who was at once triarch of Eubœa, great constable of Achaia, and lord of the islands of Tenos and Mykonos, and whose son had

[1] Buchon, *Nouvelles Recherches*, I., i., 30-3; Raynaldus, v., 495, 517; Villani *apud* Muratori, xiii., 717; Nikephóros Gregorâs, i., p. xciv.; Lámpros, Ἔγγραφα, 55.

married the daughter of the Catalan captain. Ghisi seems to have been a man of some literary and historic tastes, for the original of which the French version of the *Chronicle of the Morea* is an abridgment was found in his Theban castle. The abridgment has fortunately been preserved; but the castle with its historic frescoes and its memories of gorgeous ceremonies, when the song of the minstrel resounded through its vast halls and all the chivalry of Frankish Greece was gathered there, has perished, all save one short square tower, which still bears the once great name of St Omer.[1]

The only other results of Walter's expedition were the recognition of the shadowy Angevin suzerainty over Epiros by the despot John II., who, however, retained the substance of power, and struck coins at Arta bearing his name; and the retention of Vonitza and the island of Sta. Mavra by the titular duke of Athens. Later on, in 1355, the latter conferred Vonitza, "our castle of Sta. Mavra and our island of Lucate" upon Graziano Zorzi, an old comrade-in-arms, and a member of the great Venetian family which we have already seen established in the marquisate of Boudonitza.[2] Walter himself still occasionally dreamed of his restoration to Athens, but soon found a sphere for his activity in Italy. Summoned by the Florentines to command their forces, he became tyrant of their city, whence he was expelled amidst universal rejoicings in 1343, and where the traveller may now see his arms restored by the modern Italian authorities in the audience chamber of the Bargello. Thence he returned to his county of Lecce, and fell, thirteen years later, fighting as constable of France against the English at the battle of Poitiers. Before he left Lecce, he made his will, in which he mentioned all his possessions in Greece—his city of Argos, with its noble castle, the Larissa; the castles of Nauplia, Kiveri and Thermisi, Vonitza, and Sta. Mavra, with their constables and men-at-arms. Something was left to the religious orders of Patras and Glarentza, and to the churches

[1] Χ. τ. Μ., ll. 8086-92; *L. d. C.*, 1, 274; *Histoire de Dauphiné*, II., 151; *Bibliothèque de l'École des Chartes*, xxxiii., 183; *Mélanges historiques*, III., 27.

[2] Lunzi, *Della Condizione politica*, 121; Lámpros, Ἔγγραφα, 67; Romanós, *op. cit.*, 302.

and chapels of Nauplia and Argos, while part of the customs dues of this last city was set aside to endow a perpetual chaplaincy, whose holder was to say a daily mass for the soul of the pious founder. As Walter left no children, his sister Isabelle, wife of Gautier d'Enghien, succeeded to his estates and claims, and of her sons, one styled himself Duke of Athens, and another was lord of Argos and Nauplia. More fortunate in one respect than his predecessors who had reigned in Greece, Walter has left us a portrait of himself. Every visitor to the lower church of St Francis at Assisi—a church traditionally associated with the family of Brienne, who were *terciers* of the Order—has seen in the foreground of Lorenzetti's "Crucifixion" the knightly figure of the titular duke of Athens.[1]

Thus, during the twenty years which followed its conquest of Athens, the Catalan Company had strengthened its position and extended its possessions. To Attica and Bœotia it had annexed the duchy of Neopatras, including part of Thessaly, while Catalan lords held the castles of Salona and Karystos, and the island of Ægina. It had made terms with Venice, and so could afford to despise the schemes of the dethroned dynasty of Brienne and the ecclesiastical weapons of the papacy. In the bastard son of Frederick II. of Sicily it had found a leader, resolute in action, and skilful in taking advantage of his opportunities. All the more remarkable is the sudden and premature retirement of this successful chief from the leadership of the Company. At the time of Walter of Brienne's invasion, he was no longer vicar-general —a post occupied by Nicholas Lancia—and in the treaty of Thebes between the Company and Venice, he figures as merely "Count of Malta and Gozzo." Probably, had he been at the head of affairs at that moment, he would have saved his kinsman's castle of St Omer from destruction. We are not told the reason of his retirement; but, from the fact that he paid a visit to Sicily in the following year, we may perhaps infer that his too successful career in Greece had gained him

[1] D'Arbois de Jubainville, *Voyage paléographique*, 341-2; *Arch. Stor. Ital.*, Ser. III., xvi., 48; Galateus, *De Situ Iapygiæ*, 92; Hopf, *Chroniques*, xxix.-xxx., who rightly identifies "Chamires" with Kiveri opposite Nauplia and "Le Trémis" with Thermisi.

enemies at the Sicilian court, who may have accused him of aiming at independent sovereignty, and whose charges he may have thought it desirable to answer in person. Though he did not resume the leadership of the Company, he passed the rest of his life in Greece, where we hear of him among the principal Catalans in 1335, and where he died in 1338, leaving a numerous progeny. His eldest son, Don Pedro, was already lord of Loidoriki and Count of Salona, which had come into the hands of his father, presumably on the death of Roger Deslaur without heirs. His second son, Don Jaime, succeeded his elder brother in his estates, held for a time the island of Ægina, and became, later on, vicar-general of the Company; yet another son, Bonifacio, inherited Karystos and Lamia, and received from Don Jaime, with certain reservations, the island of Ægina, thereby reuniting the old possessions of his namesake and grandfather, Bonifacio da Verona. One interesting part of them, however, the sister-island of Salamis, seems to have been subdued by the Greeks, for we hear of it as paying taxes to the Byzantine governor of Monemvasia.[1] Thus, the fortunes of the family continued to be interwoven with those of the Catalan duchy till its fall.

All over Greece, these twenty years had wrought great changes. Alike in Thessaly and Epiros, the Greek dynasty of the Angeli had come to an end; and, while Byzantine officials, local magnates, Albanian colonists, and the Catalan Company had divided the former country between them, the latter was occupied by the palatine counts of Cephalonia, who had now been driven by the Angevins from their islands. The Angevins were, therefore, now both possessors and suzerains of most of the Ionian islands and of the principality of Achaia, much reduced, however, by the encroachments of the Greek governors, and still held the strong fortress of Lepanto, on the opposite shore of the Corinthian Gulf. The island of Sta. Mavra, the castle of Vonitza, on the Gulf of Arta, and the towns of Nauplia and Argos, owned the sway of Walter of Brienne, who appointed

[1] Thomas, *Diplomatarium*, i., 127, 214; Bozzo, *Notizie Storiche Siciliane del Secolo XIV.*, 607; Ducange, *op. cit.*, II., 204; Rosario Gregorio, II., 582-3; Rubió y Lluch, *Los Navarros*, 477; Hopf, *Karystos*, 588.

a "bailie and captain-general," assisted by a council. Venice, by her usual statecraft, had increased her hold upon Eubœa, had gained a footing at Pteleon in Thessaly, and had preserved her original colonies of Modon and Coron, in spite of inroads by the Greeks of Mistrâ, and troubles with those haughty neighbours, the Teutonic Knights of Mostenitsa. The republic felt strong enough, however, to allow a Greek bishop to reside there, although those patriotic and intriguing ecclesiastics were apt to foster the national instincts of their fellow-countrymen.[1] The lot of the latter was at this time lighter in the Frankish principality than under the Venetian flag; for, in spite of the strict orders issued to the colonial governors to treat the Greeks well, they emigrated in large numbers to Achaia, where taxation was less oppressive. Piracy was still, however, the great curse of the dwellers on the coasts of the Morea and in the Greek islands. On one raid the corsairs carried off, and sold as slaves, no less than 500 persons from the island of Culuris, or Salamis, while the Turks were an annual, and a growing menace. Yet these depredations had not yet destroyed the Greek forests. Those who know how bare most of Greece is to-day, will learn with surprise that Sanudo[2] thought that the timber required for his cherished crusade against the infidels could be obtained from Attica, the Morea, and the island of Eubœa.

Nor was trade lacking. Monemvasia, whence our ancestors got their Malmsey wine, under Byzantine rule, continued to be a flourishing port, whose merchants enjoyed special privileges and exemptions, confirmed by Andrónikos II. and III., and including protection at all the fairs and festivals of the peninsula. Glarentza, the seat of a Venetian consul, and Patras, that of a Venetian *podestà*,[3] under the enlightened administration of its great archbishop, Guglielmo Frangipani, were the chief commercial centres of the Frankish principality. The former was a very important mart for silk, raisins, and

[1] *Archivio Veneto*, xix., 115-16; Thomas, *op. cit.*, i., 105-7.

[2] *Secreta Fidelium Crucis*, 68; Predelli, *Commemoriali*, ii., 26.

[3] Phrantzês, 400; Gerland, *op. cit.*, 150; Pegalotti, *Della Decima*, III., 51, 60, 106-9, 145, 202; Schlumberger, *Numismatique*, 471, 476; *Archivio Veneto*, xiii., 152.

valonia, which had commercial relations with Apulia, Ancona, Florence, and Venice, as well as with Durazzo, Acre, and Alexandria; which, like Thebes, Corinth, and Negroponte, had its own weights and measures, and still possessed its own mint, whose masters were paid salaries of 300 *hyperperi* a year. But it had been already remarked at Venice, that the Achaian currency had depreciated by nearly a third since the days of Prince William, so that the Venetians had talked of establishing a mint at Coron and Modon. They never, however, carried out that project, and the mint at Glarentza continued to produce coins till about the year 1364, after which we have no more Achaian currency. In its place, the Venetians began to issue from the mint at Venice, about the middle of the fourteenth century, the so-called *tornesi piccioli* or *torneselli*, which henceforth served as the currency of their Greek colonies. and which were modelled on the old *tornesi* of the Achaian mint. In fact, classic Hellas was at this period a place where money was to be made, an undeveloped territory to be exploited by shrewd men of affairs. In that golden age of Italian banking, such men were not lacking. Now, for the first time, a new influence, that of high finance, had made its appearance in Frankish Greece in the person of Niccolò Acciajuoli, whose house was destined in another half century to put an end to Catalan rule in Athens and assume the ducal coronet on the Akropolis.

CHAPTER IX

THE RISE OF THE ACCIAJUOLI (1333-1373)

THE arrangement between John of Gravina and the titular empress, Catherine of Valois, had had the advantage of uniting all the Angevin dominions in Greece—the principality of Achaia, the county of Cephalonia, the castle of Lepanto, and the island of Corfù—in a single hand, and henceforth the jurisdiction of the Angevin bailie and the other chief functionaries of the Morea extended to the adjacent island of Cephalonia and to the "royal fortress" on the opposite coast of the Corinthian Gulf. Fortunately, too, although Robert, the young Prince of Achaia, for whom the empress had purchased the principality, was still a minor, his mother, who exercised supreme authority in his name, and even occasionally used the style of Princess,[1] was endowed with very masculine qualities, which she soon began to display in the management of this substantial fragment of her shadowy empire. A strong ruler was, indeed, much needed in the Morea, where the lax control of the late prince and the confusion of the last twenty years had increased the spirit of independence among the great barons, never at any time very tolerant of dictation.

Among these feudal lords, the most important were the Archbishop of Patras and the Genoese family of Zaccaria, whom we have already seen ruling the island of Chios, and who had lately acquired a footing in the Morea, to which they were destined, later on, to give its last Frankish prince. Both of these great personages considered themselves practically independent. Martino Zaccaria had succeeded

[1] Buchon, *Nouvelles Recherches*, I., i., 62 ; II., i., 103, 108.

the extinct family of De la Roche as baron of Damalâ in Argolis, where he actually dared to issue coins of his own. He had succeeded, too, the house of Trémouille at Chalandritza, and though the Greek Emperor had lately captured both him and his rich island, his son Centurione was in possession of both his Peloponnesian baronies. The Empress Catherine was specially warned of the designs which this crafty Levantine nourished against her authority by Niccolò di Bojano, a Neapolitan treasury official who drew up a report upon the state of her son's principality. Centurione, he told her, must be put in his proper place, or else neither she nor her son would ever obtain theirs in the Morea.[1] Patras, too, under its great archbishop, Guglielmo Frangipani, was practically autonomous, and Bertrand de Baux, the bailie whom the empress sent to govern Achaia, took the opportunity of his death to occupy the town and to besiege the castle. Pope Benedict XII.[2] entered a vigorous protest against this proceeding, claiming that Patras was under the direct jurisdiction of the archbishop, as the representative of the Holy See to which it belonged. He therefore ordered the bishops of Olena and Coron to lay the peninsula under an interdict. These difficulties convinced the empress that her presence was needed in the Morea; so, in 1338, she set out for Patras, accompanied by her trusted adviser, Niccolò Acciajuoli.

We have already had occasion to mention this remarkable man, whose house was destined, in characteristically modern fashion, to supplant the noble chivalry of Frankish Greece. The history of the Acciajuoli bears a striking resemblance to that of the great financiers of our own time. After they had become famous, courtly biographers provided them with a pedigree stretching back as far as the sixth century, accord-

[1] Schlumberger, *Numismatique*, 326; Ducange, ii., 265. This undated report refers to Catherine, not, as Ducange imagined, to Marie de Bourbon, because Bojano was dead in 1342. (Buchon, *Nouvelles Recherches*, II., i., 111). The allusions to "the Count of Cephalonia" and his war with "the Despot," which Hopf found it hard to explain, are easily explicable. The "Count" is John II. of Epiros, the "Despot" is Stephen Gabrielópoulos, a Thessalian magnate, to whom Cantacuzene (i., 473) expressly applies that title; the date must be 1333.

[2] *Lettres Communes*, i., 479; Raynaldus, vi., 115-16.

ing to which the founder of the family was Angelo, brother of the Emperor Justin II., and one of its members was created a baron of the holy Roman Empire by Frederick Barbarossa.[1] As a matter of fact, the Acciajuoli owed their origin to an enterprising citizen of Brescia, the Sheffield of Italy, who moved to Florence about 1160 and there established a steel-manufactory, which gave them their name. The "steel-workers" made money, lent it out at interest, and in due course became bankers, who played their part in the municipal life of their adopted city. They were also politicians of a practical sort, whose devotion to the Guelph cause brought them into relation with the Neapolitan Angevins, when the Florentines solicited the protection of King Robert of Naples against their Ghibelline enemies. That sagacious monarch rewarded one of the firm for his skill in transacting the royal business with the dignity of chamberlain and privy councillor, and the latter naturally thought that in the management of the Naples branch his son would find an excellent opening. In 1331, when barely of age, young Niccolò Acciajuoli arrived there accompanied by a single servant. But his skill in business, combined with an agreeable presence and chivalrous manners, won him the favour, perhaps the affection, of the titular empress, Catherine of Valois, who was left a widow in that year with three sons to bring up. He assisted her with their education, and it was he who arranged, as we saw, the exchange of the duchy of Durazzo for the principality of Achaia. The bank, of which he was the representative, was already interested in Greece, which the Italian financiers of that age regarded much as their modern representatives in London regard the colonies. Having succeeded in making his pupil Robert Prince of Achaia, the astute Niccolò resolved to acquire lands in the principality on his own account. He accordingly persuaded the bank to transfer to him the two estates, which it had received from John of Gravina, rounded them off by purchasing adjacent land, and further increased his holding by other properties at Andravida, Prinitza, Kalamata, and in the island of Cephalonia, which the empress bestowed upon him as the reward of his services. He thus became a vassal of the

[1] Fanelli, *Atene Attica*, 290.

principality, taking care, however, to obtain from his patroness the reduction of the feudal burdens attaching to his lands and the permission to dispose of them to any person capable of rendering the requisite military service. Before his departure for Greece, he provided that, in the event of his death, the revenues of these estates should be devoted to building that splendid Certosa near Florence, which is still his chief monument.[1]

The empress and her astute adviser must soon have seen for themselves the dangers to which Achaia was exposed. The Catalans of Attica were awkward neighbours, who required all the vigilance of the Knights of the Teutonic order; the Greeks had encroached on the principality from without, while within they now held many important offices; worst of all, the Turks, who had made enormous progress in Asia, now ravaged the Greek coast-line. The soundest and best managed portion of the principality was Patras, and the empress, who resided there, accordingly came to the conclusion that her wisest course, especially as she needed papal aid against the Turks, was to disavow her too officious bailie, and recognise the authority of the Holy See over that temporal barony. Henceforth, the archbishop could truly say that he held the town direct from the pope.[2]

Catherine remained two years in Greece, during which time Acciajuoli spared neither his purse nor his personal comfort in the cause of the principality. At his own expense he built a fort to defend the once fair vale of Kalamata, the garden of Greece, which was then lying a desolate waste, and his services were further rewarded by the gift of that barony, the fortress of Piada, near Epidauros, and other lands. Thus, as a large Peloponnesian landowner and the representative of his firm at the Glarentza branch, which then ranked in their books as of equal importance with their London office, the Florentine banker had a stake in the country which gave him a direct interest in its preservation, and induced him, even after the departure of his mistress, to act for a time as her bailie in Greece. He calculated, indeed, that, from first to

[1] Buchon, *Nouvelles Recherches*, II., i., 31-114, 117; G. Villani, M. Villani, and Palmerius, *De vitâ et gestis N. Acciajoli*, *apud* Muratori, xiii., 958, 1205-6; xiv., 166-7.

[2] Gerland, *op. cit.*, 159.

last, his bank had sunk 40,000 ounces (£96.000) in the Morea. When he returned to Italy in 1341, Boccaccio, afterwards his bitter enemy, addressed him an enthusiastic letter of welcome, in which he compared him to a second Ulysses.[1]

During her stay at Patras, the empress had also endeavoured to restore her influence in the Despotat of Epiros, where Lepanto alone remained of the former Angevin possessions. In 1335, the Italian Despot, John II., had met with the reward of his crimes at the hand of his "wise and learned" wife, who had poisoned him from fear of suffering a similar fate herself. She then assumed the regency for her youthful son, Nikephóros II., with the acquiescence of some; at least, of her unruly subjects. But the Emperor Andrónikos III. thought that the moment had now come for reuniting Epiros with the Byzantine Empire, especially as he had lately been forced to expel the Epirote garrisons from Kalabaka, Trikkala, and other places in Thessaly, which they had occupied on the death of Gabrieló-poulos, the local magnate who had ruled there. At the news of his approach, the regent herself advised submission, as resistance seemed hopeless, so that Andrónikos was able to accomplish without bloodshed what his predecessors had in vain struggled to obtain. No Greek emperor had visited Epiros since the time of Manuel I., nearly two centuries earlier; but the tour which Andrónikos made through the cities of the Despotat was not so much due to curiosity as to the desire to let his new subjects see that he wished to understand their requirements. Judicious grants of titles and annuities to leading men were intended to console the Epirotes for the loss of their independence, while the regent was prudently ordered to leave the country. But the love of freedom had become ingrained in the breasts of others of the natives by the experience of more than a century; with their connivance and the aid of his Frankish tutor, young Nikephóros, a boy with ambitions far above his years, fled across to the Empress Catherine at Patras, and asked her to restore him to his throne. The empress saw that he might be made the tool of Angevin interests in Epiros, and ordered one of her Neapolitan suite to conduct

[1] Buchon, *op. cit.*, I., i., 46; II., i., 114.

the lad back to his faithful subjects, who had meanwhile expelled the Byzantine viceroy and were clamouring for him. Andrónikos, accompanied by the future emperor, John Cantacuzene, now returned to Akarnania, where the latter's diplomacy was more successful than the former's strategy. The most obstinate resistance was offered by "Thomas's Castle," whither Nikephóros had fled, a strong fortress on the Adriatic, christened after the last Greek Despot, which could be easily provisioned from the sea. But, although the Empress Catherine sent a small fleet and troops from the Morea to assist her *protégé*, the arguments of Cantacuzene at last induced the garrison to surrender. He told them that the Angevins, in spite of their frequent efforts to conquer their country, had never succeeded in holding more than a few isolated positions, like Lepanto, Vonitza, and Butrinto, and those only with the consent of the Despot. Allies so weak, he said, would be of no avail against the imperial forces; while, even if they were, they would conquer Epiros for themselves and not for the Epirotes, in which case the natives would be the slaves of the Latins. "If you surrender," he concluded, "I will give my own daughter to Nikephóros, and will treat him as a son; my master will load him with honours, of which you too shall have your share." At this, the garrison opened the gates; the whole country once more recognised the authority of the emperor, and Nikephóros, scarcely compensated by a high-sounding Byzantine title, was led away to Salonika.

The specious arguments of Cantacuzene at Thomokastron had had their effect upon the Moreot troops, whom the empress had sent to aid in defending that castle. When they returned home, and found Catherine and her skilful minister gone, and the Turks ravaging their coasts unchecked, they reflected that in the Morea, too, the Angevins were powerless to aid. Impressed with the tact of Cantacuzene, whose father had been governor of Mistrâ, and who had himself been offered that post twenty years earlier, they entered into negotiations with him in 1341 for the cession of the principality of Achaia. Their envoys, the Bishop of Coron, and a half-caste, near Siderós, told the great man that he had won their hearts by his conduct in Epiros, and begged him to come in person and take over their country. All they asked was to keep their fiefs, and to pay the same taxes to the emperor as they now paid to their prince; on these terms they were ready to do homage and receive an imperial viceroy. Cantacuzene was naturally flattered by this request, not, as he told them, the first of the kind; he promised to visit the Morea in the following spring, sending meanwhile a confidential agent to win over dissentients and to show that he was in earnest. But the grandiose scheme which he had formed of thus reuniting the Byzantine Empire from Tainaron to Constantinople was never accomplished. The great Servian tsar, Stephen Dushan, had now begun his meteoric career of conquest at the expense of the Greek Empire, while the latter was soon distracted by the intrigues of the rival emperors, John Cantacuzene and John Palaiológos.[1]

Besides the party of Cantacuzene, there was still a section of the Franks which regarded King James II. of Majorca, the grandson of the Lady of Akova, as the lawful Prince of Achaia. The King of Majorca, whom we last saw carried in Muntaner's arms as a baby of a few weeks, had now grown up to manhood, and accordingly the cause for which his father, Ferdinand of Majorca, had fallen more than twenty years before was revived, though the old Catalan chronicler was no longer there to fight for it. A formal memoir was drawn up and sent to him, setting forth his rights, based upon the alleged will of his great-grandfather, Guillaume de Villehardouin, to the effect that if one of his two daughters died childless, the principality should go to the other or her heirs. Even so, James II. would have had no claim, for Isabelle de Villehardouin's daughter by her third marriage, Marguerite of Savoy, was still living; but the barons did not consider her existence as an obstacle to their plans. Their memorial informed the King of Majorca that the island of Negroponte with its two great barons, Pietro dalle Carceri and Bartolomeo Ghisi, who then held all the three divisions of the island between them; the duchy of Naxos, then

[1] Nikephóros Gregorâs, i., 536, 538-9, 544-6, 550-4, ii., 596; Cantacuzene, i., 77, 85-6, 473, 495, 499-504, 509-34, ii., 74-7, 80, 82, 83; Miklosich und Müller, i., 172-4; *Arch. Stor. per le Prov. Napol.*, viii., 225.

governed by Nicholas Sanudo; and the duchy of Athens, were all vassal states of the principality, though in the case of the last the feudal tie was ignored by the Catalans, "our bitterest foes." The whole peninsula, they told him, was divided between Prince Robert of Taranto, a minor and an absentee, for whom Bertrand de Baux, now restored to favour, was again acting as vicar; the titular duke of Athens, Walter of Brienne, who held Argos and Nauplia from Robert; the Venetians, independent masters of Modon and Coron; and the Greek Emperor. The whole principality contained more than 1000 baronies and knights' fees, each worth on an average 300 pounds of Barcelona a year; after deducting all expenses for garrisoning the castles, this would leave the prince with a nett revenue of 100,000 florins. This document, which gives a clear account of the Morea as it was in 1344, was signed by Roger, Archbishop of Patras; Philippe de Joinville, baron of Vostitza; Érard le Noir of St Sauveur, grandson of the man who had deserted the Infant of Majorca; Alibert de Luc, perhaps a descendant of one of the original barons of the Conquest, and many others. James II. adopted the title of "Prince of Achaia"—a style assumed with about equal reason by another James, son of Philip of Savoy by his second marriage, and by Omarbeg of Aidin, who had at least plundered his "principality." But his only act in that capacity was to confer upon Érard le Noir the hereditary dignity of Marshal of Achaia—an honour which was perhaps deserved, if we may believe the high praise bestowed by the anonymous chronicler of the Morea upon the benevolence of that baron, "a true friend to the poor man and the orphan." In 1349 James II. fell, like his father, in battle, fighting against the Aragonese, who had dispossessed him of his kingdom.[1]

Meanwhile, the growing Turkish peril had convinced the popes that it was wise to recognise the Catalan occupation of Athens as an accomplished fact. Three years after Walter of Brienne's unsuccessful expedition, Benedict XII. had ordered the Archbishop of Patras to excommunicate once more the leaders of the Company—William, Duke of

[1] Buchon, *Recherches historiques*, i., 452-3; Ducange, *op. cit.*, ii., 224-6; Datta, *op. cit.*, ii., 166; X. τ. M., ll. 8468-73.

Athens; Nicholas Lancia, his vicar-general; Alfonso Fadrique and his two sons, Peter of Salona and James; and many more. But Archbishop Isnard of Thebes, who was better acquainted with the local needs than the pope, and who saw the growing tendency of his flock to join the Orthodox Church, not only annulled this sentence of excommunication on his own authority, but also celebrated mass before the Company in the Theban minster; and, though Benedict at first disapproved of this arbitrary act and ordered the renewal of the excommunication, he came to see that the Catalans might be useful as a buffer state between the Turks and the West, and disregarded the ineffectual protest of the exiled Duke of Athens. The Latin Patriarch of Constantinople acted as intermediary; on his way to his residence at Negroponte, he stopped in Attica, where he found the Catalans willing to return to the bosom of the Church. He communicated their prayer to Benedict, who replied that he would hear it, if they would send envoys to Rome. His successor, Clement VI., anxious to form a coalition against the Turks, charged the patriarch with the task of making peace between the Catalans and Walter of Brienne, gave them absolution for three years, and invited Prince Robert of Achaia and his mother, the Empress Catherine, to contribute galleys to the allied fleet. The crusade had small results, but the reconciliation between the Catalans and the papacy was complete. Henceforth, those "sons of perdition" were regarded as respectable members of Christendom. Unfortunately, soon after they became respectable, they ceased to be formidable. Occasionally, the old Adam broke out, as when Peter Fadrique of Salona is found plying the trade of a pirate with the aid of the unspeakable Turk. But their Thessalian conquests were slipping away from the luxurious and drunken progeny of the hardy warriors who had smitten the Franks at the Kephissós, while the Venetians of Negroponte had no longer cause to fear their once dreaded neighbours. When the bailie wanted money for public purposes he borrowed it from a Catalan knight of Athens; when a Catholic Bishop of Andros had to be consecrated, the Athenian Archbishop came to perform the ceremony of laying hands on his suffragan in the church of the Eubœan capital—an arrangement which shows that the ecclesiastical organisation of Athens had not been disturbed by the Catalan conquest.[1] And in the war against Genoa, the Catalans rendered yeoman's service to the Venetians at Oreos.

Meanwhile, in distant Sicily, the shadowy Dukes of Athens and Neopatras came and went without ever seeing their Greek duchies. Duke William died in 1338, and his successors in the title, John and Frederick of Randazzo, the picturesque town built on the lava of Etna, both succumbed to the plague ten and seventeen years later—mere names in the history of Athens, where almost their only known acts are in connexion with the castle of Athens and the church of St Michael at Livadia. Soon, however, after the death of the latter, in 1355, his namesake and successor became also King of Sicily under the title of Frederick III. Thus, the two Greek duchies, which had hitherto been the appanage of younger members of the royal family, were now united with the Sicilian crown. For a moment, indeed, in 1357, the new King of Sicily, hard pressed by enemies in his own island, actually proposed to purchase the aid of Pedro IV. of Aragon by bestowing Athens and Neopatras upon that sovereign's consort and his own sister, Eleonora. But as no help was forthcoming from his brother-in-law, the proposal fell through.[2]

The new duke found himself at once called upon to answer two petitions from his distant subjects. Shortly before the death of his namesake and predecessor, a deputation had arrived from Athens and Neopatras, begging for the removal of Ramón Bernardi, the then vicar-general of the duchies, which were declared by the petitioners to be in danger, owing to the lack of proper authority. They suggested as suitable candidates for the post, Orlando de Aragona, a bastard of the house of Sicily, or one of Alfonso

[1] Ducange, ii., 204-5, 221 ; Raynaldus, vi., 286, 311 ; M. Villani *apud* Muratori, xiv., 371 ; Hopf, *Die Insel Andros*, 51 ; Lámpros, Ἔγγραφα, 55-82 ; *Lettres Closes de Benoît XII.*, 515 ; *de Clément VI.*, i., 162, 204.

[2] Çurita, II., 17, 129, 287 ; *Archiv. Stor. Siciliano*, vii., 196 ; John and Frederick of Randazzo are mentioned as dukes in two documents ; Lámpros, Ἔγγραφα, 255, 304.

Fadrique's sons, James and John. Frederick III. granted the prayer of the petitioners, and appointed James Fadrique vicar-general; a second petition prayed the duke to reward his strenuous labours in defence of the duchies. What those labours were the document does not specify; but we learn from another source that one of his services to his sovereign was to crush a revolt of Ermengol de Novelles, the hereditary marshal. We may surmise that the dualism between that powerful noble and the vicar-general had now developed into open rebellion; we know that the marshal lost his strong fortress of Siderokastron, which James Fadrique added to his own lands, and which his royal master confirmed to him; and we may assume that the De Novelles family was further punished by the loss of the marshal's *bâton*, which is known to have been held by Roger de Lluria during the rest of Ermengol's lifetime. On the present occasion the petitioners begged that the loyal James might have assigned to him as his reward the castles of Salona and Loidoriki with their appurtenances, which were his by law. They had belonged to his father, and had descended from him to his eldest son Peter, on whose demise without children, they should have come to James as next-of-kin. Owing, however, as it would appear, to the disturbed state of the duchy, those great possessions had been withheld from him.[1] All these facts point to the mutual jealousy of the great Catalan feudatories of each other, a jealousy which was sure to break out in civil war, whenever the vicar-general was weak. Naturally, an hereditary office-holder like the marshal, with a large stake in the country and a powerful Greek connection, would be a dangerous rival to a foreigner from Sicily, the creature of a distant sovereign.

James Fadrique did not long retain the office which the envoys of the duchies had begged the King of Sicily to bestow upon him. Possibly, like his father, he had enemies at court, who represented to his suspicious master that he was too powerful and too independent; at any rate, in 1359, Gonsalvo Ximenes de Arenos had succeeded him as vicar-

[1] This disproves Hopf's theory that Salona came into the Fadrique family by the marriage of Peter with an imaginary daughter of Roger Deslaur. Rosario Gregorio, II., 570-1, 582-3; Rubió, *Los Navarros*, 476.

general.[1] In that year, however, the post was conferred upon a great Sicilian noble, Matteo Moncada, or Montecateno, whose family had come from Cataluña to Sicily after the Vespers. Frederick added to his vicar's dignity by conferring upon him the lordships of Argos and Corinth and the marquisate of Boudonitza—dignities which were not his to bestow. For Argos still belonged to Guy d'Enghien; Corinth had lately been bestowed upon Niccolò Acciajuoli; while Boudonitza, though threatened by the Catalan Company, was in the possession of the Zorzi—an outpost against attacks from the north, where a new power was now established.[2]

The five years' civil war between John Cantacuzene and John Palaiológos and the Napoleonic career of Stephen Dushan, the great Servian tsar, who for a few years made the Serbs the dominant race of the Balkan peninsula, had profoundly affected Northern Greece. Cantacuzene's popularity was not confined to the Morea; from Thessaly, where the Byzantine Empire had latterly recovered much lost ground, but where the Albanians had seized the moment of the late emperor's death to plunder the towns, and from Akarnania, where his recent exploits were remembered, and whither the widow of the late Despot had escaped, came invitations to assume the government of those provinces. Cantacuzene was unable to go there in person at so critical a moment in his career; but he appointed as life governor of Thessaly his nephew John Angelos, an experienced soldier and a man of affairs, who assisted him with the famed Thessalian cavalry, completed the downfall of Catalan rule in that region, and made himself master of Ætolia and Akarnania, taking the ambitious Anna prisoner. He died, however, in 1349, and the great Servian tsar, who had already extended his sway as far as Joannina, then annexed the rest of north-west Greece and Thessaly to his vast empire, which extended from Belgrade to Arta. Besides styling himself "Tsar and Autocrat of the Serbs and Greeks, the Bulgarians and Albanians," Dushan now assumed the

[1] Lámpros, Ἔγγραφα, 239, 332, 334.

[2] Predelli, *Commemoriali*, II., 308; Hopf, *apud* Ersch und Gruber, lxxxv., 438-9.

titles of "Despot of Arta and Count of Wallachia." He assigned Akarnania and Ætolia to his brother, Simeon Urosh, who endeavoured to conciliate native sympathies by marrying Thomais, the sister of the deposed Despot Nikephóros II., while a Serb magnate, named Preliub, received Joannina and Thessaly, with the title of Cæsar, and made even the Venetians tremble in their settlement at Pteleon.[1]

While Thessaly and north-west Greece had thus passed in the middle of the fourteenth century under Servian rule, there had been, by way of compensation, a Greek revival in the Morea. In 1348, the Emperor John Cantacuzene, remembering the long connection of his family with a country in which both his father and grandfather had died, and of which he had been himself offered the governorship, sent his second son Manuel as governor to Mistrâ, not merely for a term of years, but for life. Manuel remained Despot of the Byzantine province till his death in 1380, and his long rule of thirty-two years contributed greatly to the prosperity of the Greek portion of the peninsula. Henceforth, Mistrâ assumed more and more importance as the seat of a younger member of the imperial family; and, as the Turks drew closer to Constantinople, more and more value was set on the strongly fortified hill near Sparta, whose fine Byzantine buildings still testify to the piety and the splendour of the Despots, and still bear their quaint monograms. The early years of the century, as we saw, had witnessed great ecclesiastical activity at Mistrâ. Manuel continued in the footsteps of Andrónikos II.; he erected a church of the Saviour; and a poem addressed by him to his father long adorned the church of the Divine Wisdom.[2] As is usual where there are Greeks, there was a desire for books at the new Sparta, and we are therefore not surprised to find men engaged in copying manuscripts there. Later on, when the Emperor John Cantacuzene had abandoned the throne for the garb of a monk, he spent a year with his son at Mistrâ, and

[1] Cantacuzene, i., 495; ii., 15, 239, 309-22, 355; iii., 147, 150, 155, 314; Nikephóros Gregorâs, ii., 596, 644, 656-8, 663; *Epirotica*, 210-11. Predelli, *op. cit.*, II., 181.

[2] *Bulletin de Corr. hellénique*, xxiii., 144; Miklosich und Müller, i., 472-4.

there, in 1383, he died and was buried.[1] He has given us in his history a graphic picture of the state of the peninsula at the moment of his son's appointment. Turkish raids, the rule of the Franks, and, worst of all, the constant internecine quarrels of the Greeks had brought the country to the verge of ruin. The towns had been divided by the party strife of their citizens, the villages had been devastated by foreign foes; agriculture was neglected, so that the Morea was "worse than the proverbial Scythian desert." The imperial historian, no mean judge of men, gives the Moreot *archons* much the same character as Nikétas Choniátes had given them more than a century and a half earlier: "Neither good nor evil fortune, nor time, that universal solvent, can dissolve their mutual enmity, which not only endures during their lifetime, but descends as a heritage to their children. These modern Spartans neglect all the laws of Lycurgus, but obey one of Solon—that which punishes those citizens who remain neutral in party strife!" Men of this kind, like the Albanians of to-day, had no appreciation for firm government, which interfered with their time-honoured custom of cutting one another's throats in some faction fight. They soon found a leader in a certain Lampoúdios, the cleverest scoundrel of them all, who had already rebelled against the Despot, but had been pardoned and provided with opportunities of rehabilitating his ruined fortunes. One of Manuel's wise measures was the creation of a navy for coast defence against the small bands of Turks from Asia Minor, which constantly molested the Peloponnesian coasts. For this purpose, he proposed to levy ship-money on the inhabitants, and the crafty Lampoúdios begged, and obtained, permission to collect it. He went all over the country, like a born demagogue, reproaching the people with being "voluntary slaves" of the Despot, creatures unworthy of their ancestors, the heroes who had fought—against each other—while the Franks were conquering Greece. The taunt and the threatened tax had their effect; the people rose at a given signal, seized the chief officials of the towns and villages, and

[1] So Hopf and Krumbacher, rejecting the version of Doúkas, that he died on Mt. Athos, and following the *Chronicle* published by Müller in *Sitzungsberichte der Wiener Akademie*, ix., 393.

marched on Mistrâ. But the news that the Despot was preparing to attack them with the 300 men of his Byzantine bodyguard, and a few Albanian mercenaries, who now for the first time appear in the history of the Morea, sufficed to cause a general panic. Manuel with his usual clemency pardoned the rebels, who for a long time kept the peace. But that their behaviour was due to fear rather than gratitude was demonstrated when his father fell and the Emperor John Palaiológos sent Michael and Andrew Asan as governors to the Morea. The whole province, with the exception of one faithful city, went over to the newcomers, but Manuel stood firm, drove out the Asans and secured his recognition by the imperial government. Henceforth, the Greeks acquiesced in his mild but firm rule; the local magnates abandoned politics for the less exciting pursuit of agriculture, and it became the fashion to acquire large estates and to develop the country. Those who know the Greek distaste for rural life will realise how marvellous the influence of Manuel must have been. The Cantacuzenes wisely based their national policy upon the support of the national Church; thus the emperor in 1348 confirmed by a golden bull the possessions of the great monastery of Megaspelaion, a direct dependency, or *stavropégion*, of the Patriarchate, which his predecessors had favoured, and the monks continued to dispose of their serfs as they chose; six years later, the monastery was assigned by the patriarch as residence for life to the Greek metropolitan of Patras, "Exarch of all Achaia," who since the Latin Conquest had been, of course, unable to occupy his titular see. All these things testified to the great Greek revival in the Morea. With his Frankish neighbours, however, Manuel was usually on excellent terms; they, too, learnt to respect his truthfulness, for his word was as good as his oath, and he never broke his engagements with them. Having been defeated by him at the outset, they became his allies, and agreed to assist him both within and without the peninsula at their own expense. This alliance proved most successful in repelling the Turks, who were now a serious danger to Franks and Greeks alike.

The Ottomans have always made and retained their conquests in the Near East, thanks to the quarrels of the

Christians, and it was the internal disputes of the Catalan state which now introduced them into Greece. In 1361, Moncada had been succeeded as vicar-general of the duchies by Roger de Lluria, a relative and namesake of the great Aragonese admiral, who had ravaged the Morea seventy years earlier. The Lluria family had gained influence at Thebes, of which city Roger's brother had recently been governor, while Roger himself had received grants from John and Frederick of Randazzo, and held the great office of marshal. There was, however, a party at the capital opposed to this now predominant family, while the new vicar found himself simultaneously involved in a quarrel with the Venetians of Eubœa arising out of a number of petty grievances on both sides. Thus pressed, Lluria resorted to the traditional policy of the Catalan Company and called in the Turks to his aid. They had not far to come, for Murâd I. had now transferred the Turkish capital from Brûsa to Adrianople, and they were already casting longing eyes on Greece. They readily responded to his summons, and in 1363 Thebes, the capital of the Catalan duchy, was occupied by these dangerous allies. The archbishop and an influential deputation from various communities in the duchies hastened to Sicily to lay their grievances before their duke. Frederick III. listened to the tale of their sufferings, re-appointed Moncada vicar-general, and ordered Lluria to obey the latter's orders. Pope Urban V., too, appealed to the religious sentiments of Lluria and his brother, and urged the Lombards and Venetians of Eubœa and the primate of Achaia to prevent the "profane multitude of infidel Turks" from entering the Morea, as was their intention. The common danger, even more than the papal admonitions, aroused all those interested in the peninsula to combine in its defence. The united efforts of Gautier de Lor, the bailie of Achaia, the Frankish barons, the Despot Manuel, the Knights of St John, and a Venetian fleet succeeded in burning thirty-five Turkish galleys which were lying off Megara. At this the Turks perforce abandoned their projected invasion, and retreated to their ally's capital of Thebes. The loyal union of Greeks and Latins had saved the Morea. This alone would entitle Manuel Cantacuzene to the eulogies which his father and his father's devoted friend, the littérateur Demétrios Kydónes, bestowed upon his wise administration.[1]

The distracted Frankish principality, nominally subject to an alien and absent prince, offered a sad contrast to the Byzantine province under a resident native governor. Prince Robert, who assumed the title of Emperor of Constantinople on the death of the Empress Catherine in 1346, from that moment never set foot in Achaia; indeed, he was for several years a prisoner in Hungary; and his main interest in his Greek dominions was that they enabled him to present large estates to his wife. He had married in 1347 Marie de Bourbon, widow of Hugues IV., King of Cyprus, and to her he assigned lands in Corfù and Cephalonia, the old Villehardouin family fief of Kalamata, and other places in Achaia, to which she added by purchase the baronies of Vostitza and Nivelet. The frequent changes of the Angevin bailies, which are recorded in the Aragonese *Chronicle of the Morea* at this period, naturally weakened still further the authority of the absent prince, while real power fell more and more into the hands of the Archbishop of Patras and the family of the Acciajuoli, who at last became identical. After his departure from Greece, Niccolò Acciajuoli had not forgotten to look after his great interests in that country. We may dismiss the story of a much later Neapolitan historian, that he was sent by Queen Joanna I. of Naples to receive the homage of the Athenians, whom the writer imagines to have been brought under her authority by two enterprising men from Lecce[2]—an obvious mistake, due to the subsequent rule of his family there. But he added to his already large possessions in Achaia the fortress of Vourkano, at the foot of classic Ithome, the picturesque site of the present monastery, and in 1358 received from Prince Robert the town and castle of Corinth, which was part of the

[1] Cantacuzene, iii., 85-90, 358-60; Nikephóros Gregorâs, iii., 248, *Chronicon Breve*, 515; Kydónes *apud* Boissonade, *Anecdota Nova*, 294; Miklosich und Müller, i., 326-30; v., 191-3; Raynaldus, vii., 108; *Lettres secrètes d'Urbain V.*, 163; *L. d. F.*, 151; Rosario Gregorio, II., 572-5; Predelli, *Commemoriali*, II., 304.

[2] Summonte, *Hist. di Napoli*, II., 601.

princely domain; two years afterwards, one of his family became through his influence Archbishop of Patras, a dignity subsequently held by two others of this clan, and estimated to be worth more than 16,000 florins a year.

The bestowal of the great fortress of Corinth upon the shrewd Florentine banker was a marked tribute to his ability. The dwellers on the shores of the gulf were now a prey to the Turkish corsairs, against whom Robert in vain asked the pope and the Venetians for aid. The pope was, indeed, fully alive to the Turkish peril, and suggested to the Knights of St John the acquisition of the defenceless principality; when this project failed, he begged Niccolò Acciajuoli to impress upon Robert the necessity of doing something to save Achaia from the infidels. The citizens of Corinth united their petitions to these admonitions of the pope; they told Robert that he had left them to the tender mercies of the Turks, who daily afflicted them, that their fortresses had lost many of their defenders by captivity and famine, that their land was a desert, and that unless he could provide some remedy, they must either go into exile or pay tribute to the enemy. Robert accordingly bestowed the town and castle, with all their appurtenances, including eight smaller castles, upon Niccolò Acciajuoli, who had meanwhile been created grand seneschal of Sicily and Count of Malta, as the most likely man to defend them. Niccolò spent large sums in repairing the fortifications of Akrocorinth, and obtained for his vassals from Robert the remission of all arrears due to the princely treasury, an order compelling all his serfs who had emigrated owing to the unsettled state of the district to return, and permission to render all the feudal service, for which he was liable on account of his other Peloponnesian possessions, exclusively in the frontier district of Corinth, more exposed than the rest of the peninsula to attacks from Catalans and Turks. Unable to return to Greece himself, he appointed his cousin Donato his representative at Corinth and in the rest of his Achaian fiefs, charging him to further the welfare of his dependants, to administer even-handed justice, to protect the Church—an injunction sometimes neglected—and to pay special regard to the fortifications. A swarm of Greeks—"Greeklings," the scornful Boccaccio calls them—crowded the almost regal audiences which he gave in his Italian palaces, and his will reads like an inventory of a large part of the Morea. He died in 1365, and lies in the noble Certosa which he had built near Florence to be his mausoleum.[1] Few who visit it reflect that it was erected out of the spoils of Greece.

Upon the death of the titular emperor Robert in 1364, the principality of Achaia was for the second time exposed to the evils of a disputed succession. Robert had left no children; but his stepson, Hugues de Lusignan, Prince of Galilee, who by the law of primogeniture should have been King of Cyprus, finding himself deprived of the Cypriote throne by his uncle, conceived the idea of seeking compensation in Achaia, which was claimed by the late prince's brother Philip, now titular emperor of Constantinople, who accordingly styled himself also "Prince of Achaia." Robert's widow, Marie de Bourbon, favoured her son's enterprise, and her territorial influence in the country, owing to purchase and her late husband's gifts, was greater even than that of Niccolò Acciajuoli himself. We learn from a list of the Achaian baronies in 1364, preserved by a lucky accident, that no less than sixteen castles were her property, including such strongholds as the great fortress of Chloumoûtsi, the old family castle of the Villehardouins at Kalamata, the two fortresses which the famous house of St Omer had built on the bay of Navarino and in the Santameri mountains above the plain of Elis, and Beauvoir, or "Mouse Castle," whose ruins still command the harbour of Katakolo. But the barons had appointed the lord of Chalandritza, Centurione Zaccaria, bailie of the principality on the death of Robert, and had sent him to receive Philip's oath as their new prince at Taranto. Thus, when Marie de Bourbon and her son arrived in Greece in 1366 with more than 12,000 troops from Cyprus and Provence, they found that Philip's bailie held all the fortresses for his master, except that of Navarino, while Angelo Acciajuoli, Archbishop of Patras and an adopted

[1] Ducange, ii., 233, 263-4; *L. d. F.*, 149-52; Buchon, *Nouvelles Rechcrehes*, I., i., 90, 98-100, 113; II., i., 143-204; M. Villani *apud* Muratori, xiv., 608; Raynaldus, vi., 515; *Lettres secrètes d'Urbain V.*, 55, 76; Lámpros, Ἔγγραφα, 106-7, 120-8.

son of the great Niccolò, had declared for Philip as lawful Prince of Achaia. Confident in their superior numbers, Marie and the Prince of Galilee besieged the castle of Patras. But the archbishop, though he had only 700 horsemen, possessed among the canons of his cathedral one of the greatest commanders of that age. Some years before, a young Venetian, Carlo Zeno, had received, as a mere boy, a canon's stall at Patras, then already regarded as the property of the Holy See. It was part of the canons' duty to guard the castle, or *donjon*, as it was called, of Patras, and this uncanonical work exactly suited Zeno. The lad cared more for fighting than for theology, and the almost constant warfare with Turkish pirates at the mouth of the Corinthian Gulf gave him ample outlet for his energies. Wounded in one of these skirmishes, the young canon had only recently returned to his stall, whence the archbishop summoned him to assume the command of the garrison. Zeno had learnt all the devices of Greek warfare; he waited till the besiegers were scattered about the country, plundering the rich environs of Patras, fell upon them with signal success, and not only defended Patras for six months, but carried the war to the walls of Navarino, where Marie and her son had taken refuge, and where the Emperor Philip's bailie lay a prisoner. The commander of Navarino now summoned the Despot of Mistrâ and Guy d'Enghien, the lord of Argos, to his aid, the civil war spread, and the Byzantine and Argive forces ravaged the plain of Elis. Fortunately, at this moment, a peacemaker appeared upon the scene, in the person of the chivalrous *Conte Verde*, Amadeo VI. of Savoy, who chanced to put in at Coron on his expedition to the East. He there received news of the siege of Navarino, and hastened to the aid of Marie de Bourbon, who was his wife's cousin; at the sight of his galleys, the archbishop's troops withdrew from the attack, whereon Amadeo offered his services as an arbitrator to the two parties. Both Marie and the archbishop accepted his offer; they met on neutral ground at Modon; Marie relinquished all claims to Patras, and recognised the independence of the archbishop, who, in return, agreed to make her a money payment. The collection of this money was entrusted to the ever-useful Zeno, who adopted the usual plan of inviting the citizens of Glarentza to subscribe it. Glarentza was then not only "the chief city of Achaia," but an important trade centre, though its mint had now ceased to issue the familiar Achaian coinage, the last specimens of which, bearing Robert's name, may still be seen in the Museo Correr at Naples. Boccaccio, who laid a scene of his novel *Alatiel* there, represents Genoese merchants as trading with Glarentza, and we know that it levied a duty of from two to three per cent. on all merchandise. It could therefore have well afforded to pay the indemnity. But a certain knight of Glarentza denounced Zeno as a traitor for having made peace on what he considered such unfavourable terms; Zeno challenged his accuser to a duel, was deprived of his canonry in consequence, and resigned the other ecclesiastical benefices which he held in Greece. The point of honour was referred to Queen Joanna I. of Naples, who decided in Zeno's favour; the latter, as the reward for his services, received from the Emperor Philip the post of bailie of Achaia, where for the next three years he remained to assist his old patron, the archbishop, and his successor, "with both hand and counsel." No further hostilities took place between the see of Patras and the Prince of Galilee, who continued to occupy the south-west of the peninsula, whence his followers were a menace to the neighbouring Venetian colonies. But the murder of his uncle, the King of Cyprus, in 1369, led him to leave Greece in order to push his pretensions to the throne of that island; and, in the following year, he and his mother signed an agreement with the Emperor Philip, by which they relinquished Achaia, except her widow's portion of Kalamata, in return for an annuity of 6,000 gulden. From that time till his death, nine years later, the Prince of Galilee troubled Greece no more; but we shall hear of his mother again in the tangled history of the principality, while an Isabelle de Lusignan, probably his daughter, married one of the Despots of Mistrâ, where her monogram has lately been found. The Emperor Philip, for his part, did not long enjoy the undisputed right to bear the title of "Prince of Achaia." He died in 1373, without having visited his Greek dominions; but in that short time, his bailie, a Genoese, had so harassed the Archbishop of Patras, that the latter, a Venetian citizen, actually offered his town and its territory to the republic of St Mark. The offer was not accepted then, but there was talk of removing all the Venetian trade from Glarentza to Patras, and thirty-five years later the administration of the town passed into the hands of Venice.[1]

While the Acciajuoli family had played so important a part in asserting the independence of the archbishopric of Patras, its members had continued to extend their territorial influence in other parts of the peninsula. By his will, Niccolò Acciajuoli had divided his Greek possessions between his eldest living son, Angelo, and his cousin and adopted son, also called Angelo, and afterwards Archbishop of Patras, whom we have just seen at war. To the former he had bequeathed "the most noble city of Corinth," with all the nine castles dependent upon it, as well as all the other lands and castles of which he was possessed in Greece, except those which he left to the latter. His adopted son's share was the castle of Vourkano in Messenia, and all his farms, rights, and vassals in the barony of Kalamata. The two Angelos were to share the expense of endowing a Benedictine monastery in the tenement of Pethone in the said barony Anxious for the further welfare of his house in Greece, the astute testator left still more property—"the lands which had formerly belonged to Niccolò Ghisi, the great constable of the principality of Achaia"—to his adopted son, on condition that the latter married Fiorenza Sanudo, the much-sought heiress of the duchy of the Archipelago. After the death of Niccolò, the Emperor Philip, as Prince of Achaia, duly conferred the castle and town of Corinth afresh upon his son Angelo, and a little later, as a reward for his trouble and expense in accompanying him to Hungary, raised him to the dignity of a palatine. But this Angelo was too much occupied with affairs in Italy, where he had inherited large

[1] Hopf, *Chroniques*, 227; *L. d. F.*, 152-5; Iac. Zeno, *Vita Caroli Zeni*, *apud* Muratori, xix., 212-14; Datta, *Spedizione in Oriente di Amadeo VI.*, 89-93, 186-9, 205-6; Guichenon, *op. cit.*, I., 416; Servion, *Gestez et Chroniques de la Mayson de Savoye*, II., 130-2; Boccaccio, *Decamerone*, Novel 7, Day II.; Pegalotti, *Della Decima*, III., 107; Gerland, *Neue Quellen*, 41-2; Millet in *Bulletin de Corr. hellénique* (1906), 453-9.

possessions from his father; he had received from Philip express permission to nominate a deputy-captain of Corinth in his place, and as such he selected Rainerio, or Nerio, Acciajuoli, another cousin and adopted son of Niccolò.

Young Nerio Acciajuoli, who was destined to make himself master of Athens and rule over the most famous city in the world, had already begun his extraordinary career in Greece. He, too, sought the hand of the fair Fiorenza Sanudo—the Penelope of Frankish Greece—who was now Duchess of the Archipelago, and his brother John, then Archbishop of Patras, aided him in this plan for bringing that delectable duchy into the family. But Venice was resolved that so great a prize should fall to the lot of none but a Venetian nominee, and she succeeded in frustrating Nerio's intended marriage. Baffled in the Ægean, he next turned his attention to the Peloponnese, where he purchased from Marie de Bourbon the baronies of Vostitza and Nivelet. Thus, when he became deputy-captain of Corinth with its dependency of Basilicata, the ancient Sikyon, his authority stretched along a large part of the southern shore of the Corinthian Gulf, as well as over the isthmus. Soon he became real owner of the Corinthian group of castles, which Angelo was glad to pawn to him for a sum of money paid down. The loan was never repaid; so, while Angelo and his offspring kept the empty title of Palatine of Corinth, Nerio remained in possession of this valuable position, which served him as a base for attacking the Catalans of Attica. Naturally, numbers of relatives and hangers-on of the Acciajuoli followed their fortunate kinsmen to Greece, so that a Florentine colonisation somewhat replenished the diminished ranks of the French settlers and the Neapolitan adventurers. The baronage of Achaia was, indeed, by this time a mixture of races; of those who figure in the feudal roll of 1364, the Acciajuoli hailed from Florence, the Zaccaria from Genoa, Marchesano from Nice; Janni Misito was apparently a Greek; in fact, Érard le Noir was almost the only Frenchman left among the great barons, and even his ancestors had not come over at the Conquest.[1] The old conquering families were extinct.

[1] Buchon, *Nouvelles Recherches*, II., i., 164, 175, 189-90, 204-14; Palmerius *apud* Muratori, xiii., 1228, 1230; Gerland, *Neue Quellen*, 141-5.

The Acciajuoli were not the only new Italian family which at this period laid the foundations of a dynasty in Greece. Among the favourites of the Angevins were the Tocchi, who had originally come from Benevento, and who were leading personages at the Neapolitan court. Flattering genealogists derived their name and lineage from the Gothic tribe of Tauci, which had followed Totila into Italy; but the first historic member of the clan was Ugolino, the grand seneschal. A Guglielmo Tocco had held the post of governor of Corfù for Philip I. of Taranto and his son, and became connected with one of the reigning families of Greece by marrying the sister of John II. of Epiros. His son Leonardo continued to enjoy the favour of Robert; he was one of the witnesses of his marriage-contract, he worked hard to secure his liberation from imprisonment in Hungary, and, by marrying the niece of Niccolò Acciajuoli, secured the influence of that powerful statesman. Accordingly, in 1357, Prince Robert bestowed upon him the county of Cephalonia, to which Leonardo might perhaps lay some claim as first-cousin of the last of the Orsini. To the islands of Cephalonia, Zante, and Ithaka, he added in 1362 that of Santa Mavra and the fort of Vonitza, whose inhabitants had grown tired of the Zorzi family, and summoned him to their aid—an episode which forms the subject of an unfinished drama by the modern poet Valaorites. If we may believe another modern writer, he promised to give them a share in the local administration, to respect their property, and to tolerate their religion. We know, however, from a contemporary document, that he showed his toleration by driving out the orthodox archbishop from the island. He thus reunited the old dominions of the Orsini, and he and his heirs, under the style of "Duke of Leucadia, Count of Cephalonia, and Lord of Vonitza," not only held their possessions for over a century, but, almost alone of the Frankish rulers of Greece, left representatives down to the present generation.[1]

[1] Buchon, *Nouvelles Recherches*, I., i., 307, 410; *L. d. F.*, 151; Remondini, *De Zacynthi Antiquitatibus*, 139, 142-3; Hopf, *Chroniques*, 182; Ducange, *op. cit.*, ii., 264, and Predelli, *Commemoriali*, ii., 263, give the date 1357 and his title; Mazella, *Descrittione del Regno di Napoli*, 643-5; Petritzópoulos, *Saggio*, 45; Miklosich und Müller, i., 493.

It is only in our own time that the family has become extinct.

It was not to be wondered that the Angevins should desire to see the Ionian islands in the hands of a strong man whom they could trust, at a moment when the adjacent continent, where they still held Lepanto, was in flames. On the death of the great Servian tsar, Dushan, in 1355, anarchy broke out in his rapidly formed empire, and every petty Servian satrap declared his independence. At the same moment, the death of Preliub, the Servian ruler of Thessaly, and the fall of John Cantacuzene from the Byzantine throne, completed the confusion. Such an opportunity seemed to the dethroned Despot of Epiros, Nikephóros II., favourable for the recovery of his inheritance. Since his surrender, he had been living as governor of the Thracian cities on the Dardanelles in the enjoyment of his imperial father-in-law's favour and confidence. He now marched into Thessaly, whose inhabitants received him gladly, and then crossed Pindos into Akarnania, whence he drove out the Servian prince, Simeon Urosh, thus reviving in his own person the ancient glories of the Greek Despotat of Epiros. But, from a desire to conciliate Servian sympathies, he was so foolish as to desert his devoted wife, in order to contract a marriage with the sister-in-law of the late Servian tsar. This act both offended and alarmed his Albanian subjects, particularly devoted to the Cantacuzene family, and then, as now, suspicious of Servian influence. The injured wife took refuge with her brother Manuel at Mistrâ, while the Albanians rose against her husband. Nikephóros summoned to his aid a body of Turkish mercenaries, who were ravaging Thessaly, and confidently attacked his rebellious subjects. Rashness had always been his chief characteristic, and in the battle which ensued, near the town of Acheloos in 1358, it cost him his life. Thus ended the Despotat of Epiros, and the lands which had owned the sway of the Greek Angeli and the Roman Orsini, now fell into Servian and Albanian hands. Simeon Urosh, who now styled himself "Emperor of the Greeks and Serbs," established his court, with all the high-sounding titles of Byzantium, at Trikkala, where an inscription still preserves his name, and obtained recognition of his authority, at least in name, over Epiros, as well as Thessaly. Henceforth, however, he devoted his personal attention exclusively to the latter, assigning Joannina to his son-in-law, Thomas Preliubovich, in 1367, and Ætolia and Akarnania to two Albanian chiefs, belonging to the clans of Boua and Liosa—a name still to be found in the plain of Attica. Thus, about 1362, all north-west Greece was Albanian, except where the Angevin flag still floated over the triple walls of Lepanto, and that of the Tocchi over Vonitza.[1]

The brief Servian domination over Thessaly was destined soon to yield before the advance of the all-conquering Turks. But the reigns of Simeon Urosh and his son John, who sought to live as men of peace in their Thessalian capital of Trikkala, have bequeathed to modern Greece the strangest of all her mediæval monuments. No one who has visited the famous monasteries "in air," the weirdly fantastic Metéora, which crown the needle-like crags of the grim valley of Kalabaka, has satisfactorily answered the question, how the first monk ever ascended the sheer rocks on which they are built, rocks to which the traveller must scale by swinging ladders, unless he prefers to be hauled up, fish-like, in a net. According to the late Abbot of Metéoron, who published a history of the twenty-four monasteries,[2] the origin of this aërial monastic community may be traced to the end of the tenth century, when a monk Andrónikos, or Athanásios, established himself there at the time when the great Bulgarian tsar Samuel was ravaging Thessaly. The same authority ascribes the foundation of the most accessible of the five still inhabited monasteries, that of St Stephen, to the beginning of the fourteenth century, and the monks there related to the present author how the pious emperor, Andrónikos the elder, when forced to abdicate, had come and settled for a little time there, under the name of Antónios, giving at his departure a considerable sum for the extension of the buildings. According, however, to a fifteenth century manuscript, preserved in a late copy at

[1] Cantacuzene, iii., 211, 310, 315-19; *Epirotica*, 211-16; Nikephóros Gregorâs, III., 249, 557; Παρνασσός, v., 191.

[2] Τὰ Μετέωρα.

Meteóra,[1] and to a monkish biography recently published by Professor Lámpros, it was the Abbot Neîlos of Doupiane, near the picturesque village of Kastráki, who, in 1367, first built four churches in the caverns, which we see in the rocks of that wild and savage valley of isolated crags, while the Athanásios who "first mounted to the flat top" of Metéoron was a contemporary of Simeon Urosh, who had been taken prisoner by the Catalans when a lad at Neopatras. In any case, the monasteries attained their zenith under the Servian rulers of Thessaly. John Urosh, who had been on Mount Athos as a youth, retired from the world to the pinnacle of Metéoron, as the largest of the monasteries is pre-eminently called, leaving two deputies to govern his dominions. The humble fathers received him with gladness; we can easily imagine the delight with which they listened to his tales of the career of politics which he had left, just as their modern successors love no talk so much as that of the stranger newly arrived from a ministerial crisis at Athens. By his energy and influence he was able to increase the importance of the monastery; in 1388, he founded the present church of the Transfiguration, as an inscription still preserved there states; while his genius for organisation was displayed in a larger sphere on behalf of his sister, the widowed Lady of Joannina, and in the less exalted task of managing the lands which she bestowed on the monastery, which still reverences his portrait with that of Athanásios, its pious founder. After presiding for seventeen years over the community as "father of Metéoron," he finally became Abbot—a title hitherto borne by no head of the Metéora monasteries, which had remained under the jurisdiction of the Abbot of Doupiane—and was consecrated a bishop by the metropolitan of Larissa, when, in 1393, the Turkish Conquest of Thessaly put an end to his temporal power. The Abbot of Metéoron became

[1] Translated in *Revue Archéologique* (1864), 157 *sqq.*, Νέος Ἑλληνομνήμων, ii., 61 *sqq.* There is no authority for the legend that a much greater man, the emperor John Cantacuzene, was "King Joseph," and arrived at Metéora in 1368. Not only the MS. but the *Epirotica* mention John Urosh by that title. Col. Leake (*Travels in Northern Greece*, iv., 539) heard the same tradition from the monks, and the note to Codinus, p. 286, cannot refer to Cantacuzene, who died long before 1411, but to him. A MS. now in the National Library at Athens bears his autograph.

the president of a monastic federation, of which the other monasteries were members, retaining the management of their internal affairs—a form of government which has now ceased. But his admirers still called him "King Joseph"—the monastic name which he had assumed—from the remembrance of his former dignity, and he died in 1411 in his lonely cell far above the intrigues and controversies of his time. Such was the euthanasia of the last Christian ruler of Thessaly.

Meanwhile, the Catalan duchy of Athens, like the principality of Achaia, had experienced the evils of a weak and absent sovereign, and of the consequent anarchy which ensued. We saw that, in 1363, in response to the Theban envoys, Frederick III. of Sicily had re-appointed Moncada as vicar-general for life, and had sent letters to the community of Thebes and to Roger de Lluria, bidding them obey this tried representative of the duke. But, although entrusted by his sovereign with very wide powers, Moncada does not seem to have occupied himself very much with the affairs of the duchy, nor even to have revisited it. At any rate, early in 1365, he was still only preparing to sail for Greece, where one great Catalan magnate after another acted as his deputy. First it seems to have been James Fadrique, Count of Salona, the former vicar-general, who governed in his stead; then, after Fadrique's death in 1365, we find Roger de Lluria once more rehabilitated and negotiating as "marshal and vicar-general" with the Venetians for the renewal of the treaty of peace between them and the Company. It is characteristic of Venetian policy towards the Latin states of Greece, that the republic emphatically rejected Lluria's request that the Company might be allowed to fit out a fleet at its own expense against its enemies. He was reminded that the old clause prohibiting the growth of an Athenian navy was still in force; thus did Venice crush the efforts of this mediæval Themistoklês, as in our own time the Powers have sealed up the Russian fleet in the Black Sea.

A letter of the governor of Livadia to Frederick III. depicts in dark colours the condition of the duchies at this period. Menaced from without by the Venetians of Eubœa and the Turkish peril, the Catalans were divided among themselves by party strife, which paralysed the central authority, and caused a general feeling of insecurity. One party wished to place the duchies under the ægis of Genoa, the natural enemy of Venice, while a rival to Lluria had arisen in the person of Pedro de Pou (the Catalan equivalent of *de Puteo*), who held the strong castle of Lamia. This man had long exercised the chief judicial authority in the duchies, and acted at this time as their vicar during the absence of Moncada. We may infer that the absent vicar-general had not forgotten Lluria's treasonable alliance with the Turks, which his master had not dared to punish, and may have found Pou a more loyal, or, at any rate, a more supple representative. Pou was, however, a grasping and ambitious official, as well as an unjust judge. While he allowed cases to be protracted for years, while he seized a Greek serf, the property of another Catalan, and sold him as a slave to Majorca, his advice to Moncada was most injurious to Lluria and his friends, whose castles he seized during an Albanian raid and then retained. The discontent culminated in a rising against the tyrant in the summer of 1366. Pou, his wife, and his chief followers were slain; Moncada's men who came to avenge them were killed; and Lluria once more acted as vicar-general. The victors sent an envoy to Sicily to justify their conduct to their duke, who wisely granted them an amnesty, which he had no power to refuse, and ordered all confiscated property to be restored. The experiment of allowing the vicar-general, as well as the duke, to remain in Sicily, while the duchies were administered by the vicar-general's vicars, had proved to be a failure; as a strong man on the spot, Lluria, now the enemy of the Turks, was the best selection; after some hesitation, due to the difficulty of solving the delicate situation created by Moncada's absence in Sicily, the natural desire not to offend that powerful noble, and an equally natural distrust of Lluria, King Frederick came to a decision, which was perhaps inevitable under the circumstances. Moncada was removed, and in May 1367, Lluria was formally re-appointed vicar-general during his sovereign's good pleasure, in consideration of his "strenuous defence of the duchies against the Parthians (or Turks)," when he had "shirked neither danger to his person nor expense to his pocket." The Thebans must have smiled when this diplomatic phrase of the ducal chancery was read to them; but it was the age and country of rapid changes of policy, and Roger de Lluria now found it worth while to be loyal. Honours were heaped upon him by his grateful, or nervous, master, the privileges granted to him by the last two Dukes of Athens were confirmed, and thenceforth to his death he combined the double qualities of marshal and vicar-general of the duchies.[1]

The declining power of the Catalan duchies inspired the heirs of Walter of Brienne with the idea of renewing the attempt which he had made so unsuccessfully nearly forty years before. His nephew, Sohier d'Enghien, who had borne the title of Duke of Athens, had perished on the scaffold at the hands of the regent of Hainault in 1366; but his brothers, Guy of Argos, and the Counts of Lecce and Conversano, asked the Venetian republic, of which they were honorary citizens, to aid them in the recovery of Athens by permitting them to use Negroponte as their base. The republic coldly replied that she was at peace with the Catalans, and must therefore decline. If we may trust a notice in the Aragonese *Chronicle*,[2] the Count of Conversano, at that time bailie of Achaia, none the less attacked Athens with an army from Achaia, and temporarily occupied the whole city except the Akropolis. But, in any case, through the good offices of the bailie of Negroponte, a treaty was made between the vicar-general and the lord of Argos, by which the latter's only daughter was to marry Lluria's son John, and Venice was to receive Megara as a pledge of good faith. The marriage did not take place, and ten years later we find John de Lluria a prisoner of the Count of Conversano.[3]

From some mysterious documents preserved in the

[1] Rosario Gregorio, II., 57-78; Guardione, *Sul Dominio dei Ducati di Atene e Neopatria* 22-4; Lámpros, Ἔγγραφα, 234-8, 254-61, 283, 302, 328, 343 (whence it is clear that Pou was slain before August 3, 1366, when Lluria first re-appears as acting vicar-general). *Cf.* the author's article in the *Eng. Hist. Review*, xxii., 519.

[2] P. 155.

[3] Rubió y Lluch, *Los Navarros*, 437, 440; Predelli, *Commemoriali*, III., 96; St Genois, i., 41.

Vatican archives, it would appear that another and much more elaborate matrimonial alliance was being projected at this time for the purpose of reconciling the claims of the house of Enghien to Athens with the ducal dominion exercised over it by the King of Sicily. The idea was to marry Gautier d'Enghien, now titular Duke of Athens, to Constance, daughter of John of Randazzo and first cousin of King Frederick. This intrigue occupied a number of celestial minds, but without result. It proves, at least, the tenacity of the claims put forward even at this late date by the heirs of the last French Duke of Athens.[1]

The domestic quarrels of the Catalans broke out again on the death of Roger de Lluria in 1370, and the mutual jealousies of the leading men were increased by the practice of sending strangers from Sicily to fill the most important posts in the duchies for life, or during good pleasure. Thus at this time, both the vicar-general and the captain of "the castle of Athens," belonged to the great Sicilian family of Peralta, connected by marriage with the royal house, but newcomers to Greece.[2] The Catalans had now been established for two generations at Athens, and they felt, like most colonies after that period, that the mother country should intervene as little as possible in their affairs, and that the best places should be held by the colonists. Being not only a colony, but a military commonwealth, they preferred that tenure of office should be short, so that those places should go round. Frederick III., docile as usual, granted both their requests; the captain of the Akropolis was removed because he had been three years—the old constitutional period—in office; henceforth the community of Athens was to elect its own captain from among the body of Athenian citizens, merely subject to the duke's confirmation. A similar arrangement was made at Livadia, whose governor had received and held all the three offices of *castellano*, *veguer*, and captain, as the reward for his services as a peacemaker during the barons' war, which had begun after Lluria's demise. These offices were now separated, as the Catalans

[1] Lámpros, Ἔγγραφα, 82-8, and *Eng. Hist. Review*, *loc. cit.*

[2] Matteo de Peralta was appointed March 31, 1370 (Lámpros, Ἔγγραφα, 314. *Cf. Ibid.*, 273, 317).

desired; but so morose was the reply of the people of Livadia, when asked to submit the names of their new officials, that the king took the matter into his own hands.[1]

A few lines about the Venetian colonies will complete this sketch of Greece in the second half of the fourteenth century. The importance which the republic attached to Modon and Coron may be inferred from the minute regulations for their government, the so-called "Statutes and Capitulations," which begin with this period. The two Messenian stations suffered, like the rest of the world, from the Black Death, so that it was necessary to send a fresh batch of colonists from home, and the franchise was extended to all the inhabitants, except the Jews. A curious regulation forbade the Venetian garrison to wear beards, so as to distinguish them from the Greeks. We still hear complaints of the maltreatment of the Greek peasants there, and their consequent emigration into the Frankish territory; but they now had influential spokesmen in the Greek bishops, who were permitted to reside in their ancient sees by the side of their Catholic colleagues. One of the latter, however, St Peter Thomas, effected many conversions, and even in that age, when the ecclesiastics wielded the greatest influence in Frankish Greece, his authority with the great nobles of Achaia was exceptional. Though usually more peaceful than the neighbouring states, the Venetian colonies were affected by the war between the republic and Genoa, which lasted from 1350 to 1355. In 1347 the Genoese had recovered from the Byzantines the rich mastic island of Chios, and entrusted its administration to a chartered company, or *maona*, which continued to manage it for more than 200 years. This step, and the exclusion of their commerce from the Black Sea, irritated the Venetians, who sent a fleet to the Levant, which made Negroponte the base of its operations. The large harbour between the classic bay of Aulis, where the Greek fleet had assembled before sailing for Troy, and the *Skála* of Oropos, was the scene of a Genoese defeat; but the vanquished retaliated by burning the Venetian and Jewish quarters of Negroponte and hanging up the keys of the town before the gates of Chios. The Venetians now induced both

[1] Lámpros, Ἔγγραφα, 249-52, 319-21.

John Cantacuzene and Pedro IV. of Aragon, whose rule over Sardinia had been undermined by Genoese intrigues, to join them in crushing the common enemy. The King of Aragon's action naturally predisposed the Catalans of Attica to take the same side as their fellow-countrymen; but Pedro declined to assist until Venice had paid to Muntaner's heirs the compensation due for the loss sustained by the Catalan chronicler at Negroponte half a century earlier. The aid of a Catalan force from Athens and Thebes enabled the Venetians to repel a Genoese attack on the fortress of Oreos, then a strong place, though now a mere ruin; but Pteleon, the importance of which had much increased of late, was exposed to the forays of the invaders, who also landed in the famous harbour of Navarino, and plundered the Venetians. Now that the Genoese family of Zaccaria had become barons in the Morea, it was inevitable that a war between the two rival republics should involve hostilities between it and the garrisons of the two Messenian colonies.[1] So risky had official posts in Greece become, that Venice found it necessary to raise the salaries of her governors of Modon and Coron, and of her councillors at Negroponte, in order to attract good men.

The damage done to Negroponte was soon repaired, and the war served to strengthen the growing power of Venice over the island. Indeed, Nikephóros Gregorâs, who himself visited the island during the war, remarks that "Eubœa has now been subject to the Venetians for many years." The population had been increased by many fugitives from Thessaly after the Catalan conquest of Athens, and there, too, all the natives of the city, except the Jews, now received the Venetian franchise after ten years' residence. Even the Jews, who had had to pay for fortifying the town of Negroponte more securely against the Turks, preferred to

[1] Miklosich und Müller, i., 333; Nikephóros Gregorâs, ii., 878; iii., 42-4, 46-51; Cantacuzene, iii., 209; Cortusii and M. Villani, *apud* Muratori, xii., 935-6; xiv., 82; Predelli, *Commemoriali*, ii., 204, 206, 215, 231, 248; Sáthas, Μνημεῖα, iv., 6. Nikephóros Gregorâs in the first passage quoted gives "Oreos" as the scene of the naval battle instead of "Oropos," which appears in the second. But "Oropos" is obviously correct, as "Oreos" is far too much to the north.

be under the direct authority of the bailie, to whom they now paid nearly £90, in taxes, instead of remaining "Jews of the Lombards," to whom they had paid only half that sum. The triarchs, now reduced to two — one a Ghisi, the other a Dalle Carceri—no longer opposed the republic, though they occasionally complained that the bailie interfered with them and even quashed the decisions of their judge; but feudal disputes were referred by common consent to the Latin patriarch of Constantinople, who, as we saw, now, *ex-officio*, held the see of Negroponte, and must, by that fact, have conferred dignity upon the island. Upon the triarchs was shifted the cost of fitting out the Eubœan galleys —a burden subsequently shared between them and Venice— while the bailie appointed the collectors of customs. Two of the chief fortresses of the island passed, too, into Venetian hands—Larmena and the "red castle" of Karystos. Venice had long striven to obtain the latter coveted position, even to-day a noble ruin, and then so strong that it could be defended by some thirty men-at-arms; at last, in 1365, after many attempts, she bought the whole barony, serfs and all, from Bonifacio Fadrique, for 6000 ducats.[1]

Thus, the chief results of the forty years which have been described in this chapter, were the revival of Greek influence in the Peloponnese, thanks to the statesmanship of the Cantacuzenes; and the rise of the Acciajuoli as a force in Greece, thanks to the shrewdness of a Florentine banker. At Athens, the ultimate goal of the latter's family, the Catalans have grown feeble and disunited; in Epiros and Thessaly, Serb and Albanian have displaced alike Frank and Hellene; while the Turk is waiting his time to supplant all four Christian races. In the Ionian islands a new and virile Italian dynasty has been founded; while Venice has tightened her hold on her Greek colonies. Such is the picture which Greece presents to us in 1373.

[1] Hopf, *Karystos*, 602-6; *Arch. Veneto*, xx., 90.

CHAPTER X

THE NAVARRESE COMPANY (1373-1388)

THE fast approaching Turkish danger ought to have aroused all the Latins of the Levant to present a united front against the common foe, whom concerted action might have kept at a distance. But the motley population of the Balkan peninsula had then, as now, no common bond which would prevent them from sacrificing the general welfare to some temporary advantage. Thus the Byzantine emperor, John V. Palaiológos, instead of joining the Serbs and Bulgarians in a league against Murâd I., had contracted a selfish alliance with the Sultan, which had not even the merit of saving him from the ignominy of sacrificing his honour in Venice and the religion of his ancestors in Rome for the vain hope of aid from the West. The new pope, Gregory XI., was, however, so much moved by "the tearful exposition" of the Archbishop of Neopatras, who told him how the Turks had subdued and held enslaved the Greek Christians almost up to the frontiers of the principality of Achaia and the duchy of Athens, and threatened the very existence of those states, that he summoned the Christian rulers of the East to a congress to be held at Thebes on 1st October 1373. The papal invitation was addressed to the real emperor, John V., and to the titular emperor, Philip III.; to the republics of Venice and Genoa; to the Knights of St John; to the kings of Cyprus, Hungary, and Sicily; to the last named's vicar-general of the duchies of Athens and Neopatras; Niccolò III. dalle Carceri, Duke of the Archipelago; Leonardo Tocco, Duke of Leucadia; Nerio Acciajuoli, "Prince of Corinth;" Francesco Giorgio, Marquis of Boudonitza; Francesco Gattalusio, "Prince of Mytilene"; and Ermolao Minotto, lord of little Seriphos. We can well imagine how the ancient city of Thebes was enlivened by the arrival of these more or less eminent persons, or their plenipotentiaries, how union against the infidel was preached by the Archbishops of Neopatras and Naxos, how their excellent advice was loudly applauded, and how personal jealousies conspired to render abortive the resolutions of the congress, just as they have marred those of every subsequent congress on the Eastern question. Scarcely had the delegates separated, when Nerio Acciajuoli, the boldest and astutest of them all, disregarding the pope's appeal to him as a champion of Christendom, seized the excuse afforded by the Company's refusal to hand over some of his fugitive vassals, to attack Megara and to make himself master of that important position on the way to Athens. It is remarkable as a proof that Catalan rule was not altogether unpopular in Greece, that one of its warmest defenders was a Greek notary, Demétrios Rendi, who a few years before had received the Catalan franchise and a grant of lands from Frederick III., and afterwards rose to wealth and importance at Athens. But, in all countries governed by foreigners, there are always natives bound by ties of interest to the governing class. Nerio returned with some distinquished captives to Corinth; Megara remained in his power, and its bishop was glad to find a living as priest of the chapel of St Bartholomew, which was in the governor's palace on the Akropolis. So weak was the once famous Company that it could not protect its own territory from the upstart Florentine. Disturbances, which broke out on the death of Matteo de Peralta, the vicar-general, in the following year, prevented reprisals; in his place, the various communities of the duchies, without waiting for orders from Sicily, unanimously elected Louis Fadrique, Count of Salona and grandson of the famous Alfonso, an excellent appointment—for Fadrique was now the most important member of the old colonial families—which Frederick III. did not fail to ratify.[1] He was wise to waive the irregularity of the

[1] Raynaldus, vii., 224; Buchon, *Nouvelles Recherches*, II., i., 218-20; Jauna, *Histoire générale des royaumes de Chypre, etc.*, ii., 882; Rubió y Lluch, *Los Navarros*, 464, 465, 474; Lámpros Ἔγγραφα, 286, 289-90, 298, 300, 323, 342.

election, for Fadrique had restored order to his Greek states.

The death of that weak monarch, in 1377, led to a complete change in the ducal dynasty. Frederick III., dying without legitimate sons, bequeathed the duchies to his young daughter Maria; but the succession was disputed by his brother-in-law, King Pedro IV of Aragon, who appealed to the principal of the Salic law as laid down by Frederick II. The prospect of having a girl at their head was naturally displeasing to the Catalans of Athens at a moment when the Turkish danger was imminent. It was no wonder, then, that all the three archbishops—Ballester of Athens, Simon of Thebes, and Matthew of Neopatras—and the principal barons and knights at once declared for Pedro IV. Among them were, first and foremost, the vicar-general, Louis Fadrique, Count of Salona and lord of Lamia, with his cousin, Don John of Aragon; the Count of Mitre, or Demetrias, on the Gulf of Volo, who kept 1500 Albanian horsemen in his pay, and enjoyed the privilege of bearing the royal standard; the governors of the four important military positions of Athens, Livadia, Salona, and Neopatras; the two brothers Puigpardines, lords of Karditza and Atalante; Pedro de Ballester, who held the sordid village of Kapraina, which has grown up on the site of Chaironeia; and Melissenó Novelles, half-Greek, half-Catalan, whose castle bore the name of Estañol. There was, however, a minority in favour of Maria of Sicily, the leader of which was Francesco Giorgio, Marquis of Boudonitza, who was naturally eager to shake off his vassalage to the vicar-general, and who, as a Venetian, had no sympathy with the Catalans. With him were Don Pedro Fadrique, lord of Ægina, whose rebellion caused him to forfeit his island to his cousin, the vicar-general; and Thomas de Pou, a son-in-law of Roger de Lluria. The burgesses, anxious for security, supported the King of Aragon.[1]

[1] Çurita, *Anales*, II., 377; *Indices*, 350-1; Rubió y Lluch, *Los Navarros*, 265, 266, 436, 440-2, 447-9, 477, 482. The latter shows from the Aragonese documents, that "Don Louis de Aragon, Count of Malta," whom Çurita quotes as a separate person, is none other than Don Louis Fadrique.

The Aragonese party, represented by the vicar-general and the governor of Athens, sent two envoys to Pedro IV.'s court, informing him that the people of the duchies awaited his commands, and craving him to appoint someone as his representative there. The king replied, thanking the vicar-general and the governor for their faithful services, and requesting them to remain in office until the arrival of the new vicar-general. For that post he selected, in 1379, Philip Dalmau, Viscount of Rocaberti, whose appointment he notified to the authorities and communities of Thebes, Athens, Livadia, Neopatras, and Siderokastron. At the same time, he sent Berenguer Ballester of Thebes, one of the envoys, back to the duchies, requesting that he might return, together with some other suitable person, authorised to offer their homage to the new "Duke of Athens and Neopatras."[1]

At this moment, however, another competitor appeared in the Catalan duchies. The origin of the Navarrese Company, which now attempted to repeat the exploits of the Catalan Company seventy years earlier, is still obscure. But it seems probable that it resembled that of its more famous predecessor. Employed by King Charles II. of Navarre in his struggle with Charles V. of France, the Navarrese Company found no further occupation at home when the two enemies made peace in 1366, just as the Catalans were no longer able to practise their profession in Sicily after the peace between the houses of Anjou and Aragon in 1302. But Don Louis, the adventurous brother of the King of Navarre, had just married the Duchess of Durazzo, who had inherited the claims of her grandfather, John of Gravina, to Albania, and when, in 1368, the Albanians captured Durazzo, and with it the last vestige of Angevin rule over their country, the chivalrous Louis naturally set about making preparations to recover his wife's lost dominions. A body of 800 Navarrese and Gascons, mostly men of good family, had accompanied him to Naples, where his wife resided; more followed, and a further force of 400 was furnished him by the King of Navarre, by the latter's chamberlain, Mahiot de Coquerel, whom we shall later on find as bailie of Achaia,

[1] Rubió y Lluch, *Los Navarros*, 444-51.

and others. But the death of Don Louis in 1376 put an end to his plans for the reconquest of Durazzo,[1] and we hear no more of the Navarrese Company till 1380. In that year, Jacques de Baux, titular emperor of Constantinople and Prince of Achaia, thought that the moment had come to occupy the Greek dominions, which should have been his, and that the Navarrese Company would be the best instrument for his purpose.

Philip III. had died, like his brother, without children, in 1373, so that his title of Emperor of Constantinople and his principality of Achaia should have passed to his nephew, Jacques de Baux, son of his sister, the widow of King Edward Baliol of Scotland, who had subsequently married François de Baux, Duke of Andria, in Apulia, a member of a distinguished Provençal family, which had followed the fortunes of Charles I. of Anjou to Naples, and had attained to high dignities under the Angevin rule. The Baux were already connected with Achaia, where Jacques's grandfather had been twice bailie for the Empress Catherine of Valois, and at first the barons recognised his mother as their lawful princess. Indeed, during the civil war between the Baux and Queen Joanna I. of Naples, who twice drove Jacques's rebellious father from her kingdom, the son found a temporary refuge, and perhaps recognition, in Greece. But as one of her numerous husbands had been the son of King James II. of Majorca, and therefore a direct descendant of the Villehardouins, Joanna might advance some sort of claim to the principality, to which he had already been a pretender. It seems probable that there had always been a party favourable to his pretensions, for it is remarkable that among the envoys whom the barons sent in 1374 to offer the princely dignity to Queen Joanna, was the same Érard le Noir, who had signed the similar document to the King of Majorca thirty years earlier. The embassy, which was very representative—for it included Leonardo Tocco, Count of Cephalonia, and, as such, one of the peers of the principality, and the two great barons, Centurione Zaccaria and Janni Misito—informed the queen that they would accept her as their princess on condition that she promised to maintain

[1] Rubió y Lluch, *Los Navarros*, 251, 254, 428, 430-5; Çurita, II., 377.

their old constitution, or, in other words, leave them alone. The queen naturally agreed to such easy terms, took the oath and the title of princess, and sent a bailie to govern in her name. This official was, however, a restless man, who not only broke the long peace between the principality and the Despot Manuel of Mistrâ, by besieging the oft-mentioned castle of Gardiki in the pass of Makryplagi, but also irritated the Venetians by raising a question as to the boundaries of their Messenian colonies. The queen was willing to refer this dispute to a joint commission, and told her bailie to treat the Venetians properly; but she had already grown tired of what had turned out to be a troublesome possession; so, when she had taken a fourth husband, Otto of Brunswick, in 1376, she conferred the principality upon him, and, in the following year, they pawned it to the Knights of the Hospital of St John of Jerusalem for five years, in consideration of an annual payment of 4000 ducats.[1]

The Knights of St John were no strangers in the Morea. Like the Templars and the Teutonic Knights, they had received four fiefs there at the time of the Conquest, and the possessions of the Templars had passed to them on the dissolution of that order in 1312. On the roll of 1364, we find two castles belonging to them; a little earlier, Innocent VI. had suggested that they should move from Rhodes, which had been their headquarters since 1309, to the Peloponnese, and defend it against the Turks. Their grand-master at this time was Juan Fernandez de Heredia, a noble and adventurous Spaniard, who had won the favour of Innocent VI., had become "the right arm of the Avignon papacy," had fought against the Black Prince at Poitiers, and had lately escorted Gregory XI. to Rome, when that pontiff, in obedience to St Catherine of Siena, ended the "Babylonish captivity" and returned to the widowed city. The barons, notably the Venetian Archbishop of Patras, welcomed the advent of so distinguished a soldier, who seemed a heaven-sent defender of their threatened land. A new and vigorous race of invaders had now appeared to contest the country with the remnant of the Franks. Since

[1] Ducange, II., 292-4; *L. d. F.*, 155-9 (which ends here); Predelli, *Commemoriali*, III., 129-31; Costanzo, *Storia del Regno di Napoli*, II., 21.

the collapse of the Despotat of Epiros, and the establishment of two Albanian chieftains on its ruins, the north of Achaia had been menaced by an Albanian immigration, as well as by Turkish raids. The very year after the Knights had acquired the principality, one of those chieftains, Ghin (or John) Boua Spata, who had already seized the possessions of the rival clan of Liosa at Arta upon the death of its chief by the plague, and had thus united Ætolia and Akarnania in his own person, captured Lepanto, and thus destroyed the last vestige of Angevin rule on the continent of Greece. For over eighty years the French lilies had waved over the triple fortifications of that celebrated castle; it had been part of the dowry which Philip of Taranto had received in 1294 with the unhappy Thamar; now it had gone, and an Albanian chieftain held one of the keys of the Corinthian Gulf. Heredia judged that this insult must be avenged; he crossed the gulf, and recaptured Lepanto. But his imprisonment by the Black Prince after the battle of Poitiers had not taught him prudence; he marched rashly into the heart of the enemy's country, intending to take Arta, was defeated by the Albanians, and brought as a prisoner to Spata. The chieftain was "a man of thought and action, in all things distinguished, and of striking beauty"; but, with all these qualities, he lacked generosity, and, without hesitation, he sold his noble captive to the Turks. In spite of the efforts of the Knights, assisted by the money of the Archbishop of Patras, to retain the important position of Lepanto, it fell again into the possession of the redoubtable Spata.[1] Heredia, after languishing for two years in prison, was ransomed in 1381, and returned to the Morea.

Meanwhile, the lawful heir of that principality thought

[1] *Epirotica*, 221, 223; Gerland, *Neue Quellen*, 43; Miklosich und *Müller*, ii., 11; Bosio (*Dell' Istoria della Sacra Religione . . . di S. Gio. Gierosolno.*, II., 126-9) gives a very picturesque, but mostly inaccurate, account of Heredia's campaign in Greece, making him scale the walls of Patras and slay the Turkish (!) commander with his own hand. Heredia then proceeds against Corinth, but is captured by the Turks, who obtain back Patras as part of his ransom. It need scarcely be said, that in 1378 Patras was not Turkish, nor had the Turks "lately taken the Morea." Bosio tells us, however, on the authority of the documents of the Order, of Heredia's captivity in Albania, and of his release in 1381.

that his hour of triumph had come. His rival, Queen Joanna of Naples, had recently been deposed by Pope Urban VI., and in Greece circumstances seemed peculiarly favourable to the claimant's plans; in Achaia, the Knights of St John were growing tired of their lease; in Attica there was a disputed succession. As instruments of his policy, Jacques de Baux naturally chose the men of the disoccupied Navarrese Company, who probably regarded him with favour as the husband of their late leader's sister-in-law. For him, they took Corfù from Queen Joanna's officials; and then directed their steps, early in 1380, towards Attica. There were special reasons for attacking the Catalan duchy. The Navarrese had an old grudge against Pedro IV., who had imprisoned their late beloved leader; Baux, as the uncle of Maria of Sicily, regarded Pedro as an usurper; while he was also connected with the family of Enghien, who were claimants to the duchy; moreover, as Prince of Achaia, he might claim suzerainty over Attica, as some of his predecessors had done, while, as titular emperor, he could cast the shadow of his authority over the whole Latin Orient.

The Navarrese Company was under the command of Mahiot de Coquerel and Pedro de S. Superan, surnamed Bordo, either because he had received the freedom of Bordeaux from our Black Prince, or, as is more probable, because he was a "bastard" (*bort*), like so many other famous commanders of the Middle Ages.[1] These experienced personages found valuable auxiliaries in the leaders of the Sicilian party. The Marquis of Boudonitza, whose castle commanded the defile of Thermopylæ, allowed them to pass beneath his walls and assisted their enterprise; Niccolò III. dalle Carceri, Duke of the Archipelago and lord of two out of the three great baronies of Eubœa, was their ally, hoping by means of their swords to make himself master of the city of Negroponte. From the Morea, the Knights of St John came to pillage the distracted duchy of Athens, where they possessed a stronghold in the castle of Sykaminon; and it seems probable that the Count of Conversano had made a second attack upon the lawful heritage of his house, for at the time of the Navarrese invasion, John de Lluria of Thebes

[1] Ducange's note to Cinnamus 392; Rubió, *ob. cit.*, 309, *n.* 2.

had been already two years his prisoner. Added to these misfortunes were the mutual jealousies of that city and Athens, which had recently aimed at some form of autonomy, and had chafed at being regarded as inferior to the capital in Bœotia. Finally, among the Greeks not a few were disaffected to the Catalan rule. It is no wonder, then, that one place after another fell rapidly into the hands of these fresh adventurers from the West, fresh in both senses of the word, if we contrast them with the degenerate grandsons of the Catalans who had conquered Attica. The fine castle, which still stands on the hill above Livadia, a noble monument of Catalan rule in Greece, was, indeed, bravely defended by its veteran governor William de Almenara and James Ferrer, a Catalan from Salona. The citizens were mostly loyal, for the Greeks of Livadia had received special privileges at the Catalan Conquest, and their town had attained great prominence under Catalan rule. But the treachery of a Greek from Durazzo opened the gates to the enemy, and Almenara lost his life in the vain effort to save the betrayed citadel. On the other hand, two Greeks, Dimitre and Mitro, gallantly defended Thebes, in the absence of John de Lluria, and of the three traitors who surrendered it to the Navarrese, two bore Spanish names. Rather than remain under these new masters, many of the terrified inhabitants of both these cities, Greeks as well as Catalans, fled for safety to the Venetian colony of Negroponte, where they remained for months, wandering about the island with their flocks and herds. Dimitre and Mitro were rewarded for their fidelity with the governorship of Salona, and that castle, as well as Lamia and Siderokastron, defied the assaults of the Navarrese, thanks to the efforts of the vicar-general on behalf of his own possessions, and the invaluable aid of the Count of Demetrias and his Albanians—not by any means the last service rendered by that sturdy race to Greece. Like Salona, the Akropolis of Athens offered a resolute resistance to the enemy. Galcerán de Peralta, the governor of the city, was unfortunately taken prisoner in a sortie, together with many others; but Romeo de Bellarbe, the commander of the castle, assisted by the faithful Greek notary, Demétrios Rendi, whom we saw fighting manfully at Megara six years earlier, baffled the machinations of a little knot of traitors and defied the soldiers of Navarre. The garrison had good reason to remember with gratitude the wise policy of their late duke, who had ordered that the revenues of certain lands, originally intended for the defence of the castle, but bestowed by his predecessors on a Catalan favourite, should again be devoted to that object. By the 20th May the Athenians could meet in security under the presidency of Romeo de Bellarbe for the purpose of drawing up a petition to King Pedro embodying their requests. As a similar assembly was held at Salona on the last day of the month, the invaders had by that time withdrawn to Bœotia, which was still in their power.[1]

These capitulations, drawn up in the Catalan language and still preserved in the archives of Barcelona, throw a flood of light upon the condition of the duchy in this, the last decade of its existence. They show us, too, that the leaders of the Aragonese party, scarcely emerged from a desperate struggle for the existence of the country, were fully conscious of the value of their services, and desired to have them amply rewarded. As is the case with most practical as distinct from philosophical politicians, the Athenian Parliament of 1380 mainly occupied itself with personal questions. The community of Athens prayed King Pedro to send them a vicar-general who would restore the country from the power of the invaders, or, failing that, to appoint Romeo de Bellarbe their governor for life, on the ground of his intimate personal acquaintance with their affairs and the poverty and distress of the people. They begged him to bestow upon Romeo all the Athenian property of three of his majesty's enemies, and to grant to his mistress, a Greek slave from Megara, the full rights and franchises of a Catalan. Large favours were asked for another Greek, the notary Demétrios Rendi, who had already received lands at Athens and the franchise from Frederick III., and whose loyalty to Pedro IV. had caused him pecuniary damage. The petitioners craved for him, for

[1] Rubió, *op. cit.*, 436-40, 443, 455, 463-8, 473, 474, 483, 485; Çurita, *loc. cit.;* Stefano Magni *apud* Hopf, *Chroniques*, 183; Lámpros, Ἔγγραφα, 267-8.

his relative, Joánnes Rendi, and for their descendants, all the rights and privileges enjoyed by the *Conquistadors* of the duchies, and that their property might be free from every kind of tax; furthermore, they asked his majesty to bestow upon him and his heirs for ever the office of Chancellor of the city of Athens, with an annual stipend of 40 gold dinars, payable out of the customs and dues thereof. They requested that Guerau de Rodonella, one of their envoys, Francisco Pons, and Berenguer Oroniola, might be rewarded with grants of traitors' or criminals' lands and possessions; that his majesty would be pleased to provide for the liberation from captivity of his loyal subject Galcerán de Peralta, for whom the Navarrese demanded a higher ransom than the Athenians could raise; and that he would confer upon Pedro Valter, who had been captured with Galcerán, all the notarial offices of both duchies for life. The king granted all these petitions, except the last, remarking that one clerkship would suffice to keep the worthy Valter in decent affluence; later on, he showered yet further benefits—lands, goods, and serfs, in both Athens and Thebes—upon the ever-useful Demétrios Rendi. From the time of the Frankish Conquest of Attica no Greek had ever risen to such distinction as this serviceable notary, whose good fortune was not even yet exhausted.

Of the sixteen clauses which compose the Athenian petition, four alone deal with questions of general policy. The first of these reflects that municipal jealousy, or spirit of local patriotism—the terms are synonymous—which has in all ages been characteristic of Greece. It consisted of a prayer that Athens might retain under the new *régime* that measure of autonomy which she had recently obtained from the central authorities at Thebes. This King Pedro absolutely refused, asserting his intention of treating the two duchies as an indivisible whole, governed by his vicar-general, without regard for any special aspirations for home rule which Athens might cherish. The second clause met with an equally decisive negative. The king declined to grant the request of the pious Athenians, prompted no doubt by the powerful ecclesiastics who had supported the Aragonese cause, that they might henceforth be permitted to bequeath their property and serfs to the Catholic Church for the good of their souls, and to emancipate their villains whenever they chose. According to the existing constitution of the duchies, this had been strongly forbidden, and a special proviso had nullified any such bequest, and ordered that all goods or serfs bequeathed to the Church should be forfeited to the use of the castle of Athens. The king, as a practical statesman, pointed out that the Catalans were only a small garrison in Greece, and that if Holy Church became possessed of their property, there would be no one left to defend the country, for the clergy were neither liable to bear arms nor dependent upon the royal jurisdiction. Besides, the existing law of Athens was also that of his kingdoms of Majorca and Valencia. Finally, the petitioners begged that they might continue to be governed by the customs of Barcelona, and that they might be joined for ever to the crown of Aragon—requests which his majesty naturally granted. These capitulations, laid before him at Lérida by the two Athenian envoys, Boyl, Bishop of Megara, and Rodonella, were solemnly signed by the king on 1st September, whereupon the envoys did homage to him as their lawful duke.

On the same day, Pedro IV. confirmed the capitulations drawn up at Salona, and laid before him by Bernard Ballester, who also represented the two important communities of Thebes and Livadia, which were still in the hands of the Navarrese. The petition of Salona is even more personal and egotistical than that of Athens, for it relates entirely to Don Louis Fadrique. It begged the king to bestow upon him and his heirs the dignity of Counts of Malta, to confirm to him the castle of Siderokastron, captured by his father from the rebellious Marshal Ermengol de Novelles, the island of Ægina, and any castles which he might be able to recover from the Navarrese and their allies before the arrival of the new vicar-general. The king, conscious of the Count of Salona's services, granted all these requests, and received the envoy's homage. Then he again notified his faithful subjects of his intention to send Rocaberti to govern them; ordered the new governor to allow the clergy of the duchies and their Latin and Greek dependants the privileges enjoyed by the Church in Aragon and Cataluña, and to see that their stolen property was restored; and granted the bishop of Megara twelve men-at-arms, with four months' pay, for the defence of "the Castle of Athens." Of that noble rock the poetic monarch—himself a troubadour and a chronicler—wrote to his treasurer in eloquent language as "the most precious jewel that exists in the world, and such that all the kings of Christendom together could in vain imitate." Thus, from the pen of a King of Aragon, we have the first allusion in the whole range of the history of Frankish Athens to the classic beauties of the Akropolis. The king had doubtless heard from the lips of the bishop, who was chaplain in the governor's palace, an enthusiastic description of the ancient buildings, then almost uninjured, which the latter knew so well. While Pedro IV. waxed enthusiastic over the classical glories of the Parthenon, his pious queen, Sybilla, was keen to possess the relics of the Virgin and other saints, which it then contained, and begged the archbishop to send them to her. Yet this rare "jewel," so dear at once to the man of taste and the devotee, could be defended in that age by a mere handful of men.[1] When, more than four centuries later, the Akropolis sustained its last siege, its garrison consisted of a thousand.

Their mission satisfactorily accomplished, the envoys departed, laden with marks of royal esteem; the Bishop of Megara was specially favoured, for the king not only granted him the goods of one of the Theban traitors, and ordered the payment to him of an annual stipend on account of "the Chapel of St Bartholomew in the palace of the Castle of Athens," but begged the pope to appoint him Archbishop of Thebes. Rocaberti, however, in consequence of important political events in Cataluña and Sicily, delayed his departure, so that he did not arrive in the Piræus, with his fleet of four galleys till the autumn of 1381, whereupon Louis Fadrique and Galcerán de Peralta, who had escaped from captivity, handed over their offices to him. His instructions were to establish friendly relations with all the neighbouring potentates, to grant a general amnesty in his master's name to all the inhabitants of the duchies, and to reward those who

[1] Rubió, *op. cit.*, 451-7, 461-71, 474, 476-9, 490; Δελτίον, v., 824-7.

had been conspicuous for their loyalty to the king. Royal letters had already been sent to "the Emperor" Matthew Cantacuzene, who, in 1380, had succeeded his brother Manuel as Despot of Mistrâ, commending the king's Athenian subjects to his good offices; the Venetian bailie of Negroponte had been requested to render aid against the Navarrese Company, and to prevent the Duke of the Archipelago and the Marquis of Boudonitza from molesting the king's Greek dominions; and similar appeals were made to Nerio Acciajuoli, the lord of Corinth; to Maddalena Buondelmonti, widow of the Count of Cephalonia and regent for her infant son; to the powerful Archbishop of Patras; and to the Grand-master Heredia, now liberated from his captivity, whose Knights had hitherto joined in pillaging the duchies. All these persons regarded the Navarrese as their common foe; of Heredia we are specially told that he and his Knights were Rocaberti's most valuable support, while Queen Sybilla of Aragon did not hesitate to ask him to bestow the Athenian castle of Sykaminon upon one of her *protégés*. The Navarrese Company, faced by this coalition, withdrew from Bœotia to the Morea, leaving, however, garrisons behind them in Livadia and Thebes, the former of which soon fell, while the latter was still in their possession two years later, and never appears again in the Aragonese archives. As a reward for what the good people of Livadia had undergone, they received from the king a formal confirmation of all the privileges conferred upon them by his predecessors, including the right to be governed by the usages of Barcelona. At their own request, he established in their town, where the head of St George was preserved, a branch of the order of that saint, the insignia of which he conferred upon the late vicar-general and other prominent men. But he privately ordered Rocaberti to bring with him, when he returned to Spain, the relic of the popular Greek saint[1]—an order, however, never executed. He also requested the vicar-general to restore to the rebel branch of the Fadrique clan all the castles and goods which they had forfeited. Among these was the classic island of Ægina, which thus came into the hands of

[1] Rubió, *op. cit.*, 330, 436, 453, 459, 472, 473, 482, 486-90, and *Catalunya a Grecia*, 57; Çurita, *Anales*, II., 378; *Indices*, 355.

Boniface's second son, John.[1] Finally, in order to fill up the gaps in the population of the duchy, caused by the Navarrese invasion, Pedro told his vicar-general to grant exemption from taxes for two years to all Greeks and Albanians who would come and settle there. This was the beginning of that Albanian colonisation of Attica and Bœotia, of which so many traces remain, both in the population and in the geographical nomenclature, to the present day.[2] Numbers of villages round Athens are still inhabited by Albanians, who speak Albanian as well as Greek, and such names as Spata, Liosia, and Liopesi are of Albanian origin.

While the Catalans were thus replenishing their Athenian duchy, their rivals and imitators, the Navarrese, had carved out for themselves a state in the Morea. Marching in 1381 along the south shore of the Corinthian Gulf, they found no one to contest their claims, for the Knights of St John, weary of their profitless lease of the principality, were ready to make terms with the new arrivals, and soon afterwards abandoned the country altogether. Their five years were not yet up; but, though the land tax of Achaia yielded them 9000 ducats, their expenses had been so heavy that they asked the Queen of Naples to relieve them of their bargain. But as she was murdered, and her husband captured by Charles of Durazzo in the following year, the Navarrese remained masters of the principality. Their commander Mahiot de Coquerel condescended, indeed, to call himself bailie for the titular emperor and Prince of Achaia, Jacques de Baux, so long as the latter lived. But when, in 1383, the last Latin Emperor of Constantinople died at Taranto without children, the Navarrese became absolutely independent. They and not he—as the pompous inscription on his tomb in the church of St Cataldo states—had "subjected by war the cities of Greece,"[3] and they remained the real masters of Achaia, although his heir, Louis of Anjou, the still living empress and former princess, Marie de Bourbon, and Charles of Durazzo, the new King of Naples, might each claim to be the rightful sovereign. The first two thought it worth while to transmit their unreal rights to their heirs—Louis of Anjou to

[1] In spite of the capitulations of Salona in the previous year.

[2] Rubió, *Los Navarros*, 460.

[3] Ducange, *op. cit.*, ii., 296.

his widow, Marie of Brittany; the empress to her nephew, Louis de Bourbon; and a further pretender arose in the person of Amadeo, grandson of Philip of Savoy, the former prince. Amid these conflicting claims, Mahiot de Coquerel was willing to keep up the fiction that he was the representative of Charles III. of Naples, the strongest and nearest of the claimants; but both he and Pedro, the famous bastard of S. Superan, who succeeded him as vicar in 1386, were, to all practical purposes, independent of foreign suzerainty. The Navarrese treated the country as a conquered land, just as the French had done, dividing the old fiefs, including most of the Acciajuoli estates, among themselves, except in one or two cases, where the barons came to terms with them. The Greek *archons* of Mistrâ, where Theodore Palaiológos, son of the Emperor John V., was now Despot, sided with them, and seized the opportunity to rebel against the imperial representative.[1] As for the Venetian governors of Modon and Coron, they were glad to make peace with these uncomfortable neighbours, who drew nearer and nearer to their two valued Messenian colonies. When the Navarrese occupied Navarino —a place already long known by that name—and the then important town of Androusa, which became their headquarters, it was felt that an arrangement must be made. The republic was particularly nervous about the fine bay of Navarino, which she feared might be purchased by her hated rival Genoa; she accordingly offered to buy it from the Navarrese. Her offer was declined, but she obtained the right of preemption to the place. Thus, this company of adventurers from Navarre had established itself as a recognised power in the Peloponnese by the side of the Greeks of Mistrâ and the two ancient colonies of Venice.

All efforts to oust the interlopers failed. Heredia, who had never abandoned the idea, which appealed to his romantic mind, of regaining the principality for the Knights of St John, did, indeed, succeed in purchasing Marie of Brittany's claim. But the rival claimant, Amadeo of Savoy, protested against this sale, and induced the anti-pope Clement VII. to annul it. Even then Heredia was not discouraged; as late as 1389 we find him endeavouring to

[1] Müller, *Byzantinische Analekten*, ix., 393; Chalkokondýles, 52.

organise an expedition to his beloved Morea. But that was his last effort; he spent the rest of his life at Avignon, surrounded by men of letters, and devouring in his library the romantic biographies of the great conquerors of olden times. To the last he kept up his interest in Greece; and it was by his command that in 1393 was compiled the Aragonese version of the *Chronicle of the Morea*, which, in spite of some glaring anachronisms, contains much valuable information about the later period of Latin rule. Louis de Bourbon seemed at one time a more formidable competitor; he entered into negotiations with discontented survivors of the old feudal nobility, like Érard le Noir, the baron of Arkadia, and we have it on the authority of his secretary, that "the Moreots were only waiting to receive him as their lord." But they waited in vain, for the Bourbon claimant never came, but remained till his death merely titular prince of Achaia—the last of that historic race which ever set up its title to rule over Greece. As for Amadeo of Savoy, he corresponded with the cautious Despot Theodore, and endeavoured to win over Venice to his side. Finally, as if there were not claimants enough, Pope Urban VI., "in the interests of peace and justice," appointed the Archbishop of Patras, whose see was now independent, as vicar-general of the principality.[1]

Besides the Navarrese, the Greeks, and the Venetian colonies, there were two other important factors in the politics of the Peloponnese—Nerio Acciajuoli, who held Corinth and its appurtenances; and the last fragment of the old Athenian duchy, the castles of Nauplia and Argos. There a woman, Marie d'Enghien, the last of her race, held nominal sway. But, on her father's death, Venice had convinced the two leading *archons* of Nauplia, Kamaterós and Kaloethés, by judicious bribery, that it was for the good of the place that she should marry a Cornaro. Thus, the republic was already practically mistress of those coveted fortresses.[2]

By this time, in Eubœa, too, Venice had become absolute mistress, except in name. In 1383, the assassination of the

[1] Buchon, *Recherches et Matériaux*, i., 258; Miklosich und Müller, iii., 249; Gerland, 133.

[2] Predelli, *Commemoriali*, iii., 157; Dorótheos of Monemvasia, 471.

powerful triarch, Nicolò III. dalle Carceri, who not only held two-thirds of the island but was also Duke of Naxos, removed her last rival—for he left no legitimate heirs. Seven years later, the holder of the other third, Giorgio Ghisi, bequeathed his share to the republic, which could thus have easily annexed the whole island, had she pleased. But, with its usual shrewdness, the Venetian Government saw that it would be more advantageous to retain the substance of power, while allowing petty lords to have the empty honour and large expense of maintaining the castles of the island. The example of Karystos had served as a warning; that coveted barony yielded to the Venetians less than one-third of what Bonifacio had obtained from it; many of the inhabitants had emigrated to Attica, and an attempt to colonise it with people from Tenedos failed. Accordingly, it was decided to let it to three Venetians, the brothers Giustiniani, at a very low rent.[1] The Greeks were among the first to benefit by this complete supremacy of Venice, for the Government, never unduly tender to the Catholic Church, abolished the tax which the Orthodox clergy had been accustomed to pay to the titular patriarch of Constantinople, who resided in Eubœa.

Freed from the horrors of civil war and foreign invasion, the Catalans of Attica had no reason to suspect that their doom was impending, and that in a few years their dominion would for ever pass away from Greek lands. Their absent sovereign with his rhapsodies over the Akropolis, and his vicar-general at Athens, both acted as if they regarded the duchies as now firmly assured to the crown of Aragon. To Rocaberti the connection seemed so durable that he was anxious to establish his family in Greece, and to secure for his son the famous fief of Salona. Louis Fadrique, the last count, died in 1382, after affiancing his sole heiress, Maria, to young Rocaberti, and the King of Aragon wrote urging her mother to hasten on the marriage, of which the castle of Siderokastron, granted to her father for his life, should be the reward. It was naturally to his interest that Salona, and Lamia, which went with it, should be in strong hands. The county had a large population of both Franks and

[1] Hopf, *Karystos* (tr. Sardagna), 90.

Greeks, and its geographical position made it a valuable bulwark against the Turks, now only a single day's journey from Neopatras. But before the wedding had been celebrated, Rocaberti had left Greece. In the late summer of 1382 we find him in Sicily, occupied in obtaining possession of the young Queen Maria, who, as the heiress of Frederick III., should have been Duchess of Athens, and whom Pedro IV. was anxious to have in his clutches. As his deputy at Athens, Rocaberti left behind him Ramón de Vilanova, a man of great valour and prudence, who governed the duchies well. During his time the last of the Navarrese must have left Bœotia, and the relations between the King of Aragon and his old enemies, now established in the Morea, became so good, that they assisted in repelling the frequent attacks made by the Greeks and Turks upon the duchy of Athens. We are told that Vilanova was preparing to recover what was in the power of these enemies, when the domestic quarrels between Pedro and his son John compelled him, too, to return to Spain, leaving the military command in the hands of Roger and Antonio de Lluria, sons of the former vicar-general, and entrusting the command of the castle and city of Athens and the other places in the duchies to a gallant soldier, Don Pedro de Pau. Rocaberti, who had espoused the cause of the king's son, consequently fell into disfavour with Pedro, who insisted upon his releasing his lieutenant Vilanova from the oath of fealty which the latter had taken to him, dismissed him from his post as vicar-general, and prevented the projected marriage between Rocaberti's son and the Countess of Salona. After a long delay, caused by important affairs of state at home, the king appointed, in June 1386, Bernardo de Cornellà as his vicar-general. The appointment was notified to all the friendly potentates of Greece, among whom the leaders of the Navarrese Company were now reckoned. The King of Aragon told them that his representative would co-operate with them, and would leave for Greece with a large force in the following spring. But before that date the ceremonious sovereign was dead, and most of the Athenian duchy no longer owned the sway of Aragon.[1]

[1] Rubió, *Los Navarros*, 460, 479-80; *Catalunya a Grecia*, 44-7; Çurita, *Anales*, ii., 387; *Indices*, 360.

Nerio Acciajuoli had long been watching attentively from the rock of Corinth, and from the twin hills of Megara, the rapid dissolution of the Catalan rule. He saw a land weakened by civil war and foreign invasion; he knew that the titular duke was an absentee, engrossed with more important affairs; he found the ducal viceroys summoned away to Spain or Sicily, while the old families of the duchy were almost extinct. He was a man of action, and he saw that the moment had come to strike. Like the clever diplomatist that he was, he had prepared the ground well, and had established friendly relations with most of his neighbours, Greeks and Latins alike. He had married his elder daughter, the beautiful Bartolomea, said to be the fairest woman of her time, to Theodore I. Palaiológos, the Despot of Mistrâ, to whom he promised as her dowry the future possession of Corinth, and this alliance secured for his schemes the approval of both the Despot and his brother Manuel, at that time Imperial Viceroy at Salonika. Through his trusty agent, the Bishop of Argos, he had gained the acquiescence of Pietro Cornaro, the Venetian consort of the Lady of Argos, and had conveyed some inkling of his schemes to his relatives in Italy. His own marriage with a Saraceno of Eubœa had connected him with one of the most influential families of that important island. The disturbed state of the Morea, where the Navarrese were threatening his son-in-law, the Despot, provided him with an excellent excuse for collecting an army, nominally for the aid of Theodore, really for the conquest of Athens. A letter of the Bishop of Argos, written early in 1385, informs us that Nerio was "gathering men-at-arms from every possible quarter," and that he could put into the field "full 70 lances, 800 Albanian horsemen, and a very large number of foot soldiers."[1] It only remained to provide for an attack by sea as well as by land. This was a more difficult matter, for it was against the policy of Venice to allow the Latin lords of the Levant to maintain navies. But Nerio had hired a galley from the Venetian arsenal at Candia, under the plausible pretext of keeping the twin seas on either side of

[1] Gregorovius, *Briefe aus der "Corrispondenza Acciajoli,"* 298-9; Chalkokondýles, 208.

the isthmus free from Turkish corsairs, whereas, as a matter of fact, he was giving them shelter at Megara. When all was ready, he easily found a *casus belli*.

The pride of a noble dame was the occasion of the fall of Catalan Athens, just as, two generations later, the passion of a beautiful woman led to the Turkish Conquest. Again and again the fair sex had played a leading part in the fortunes of Frankish Greece, owing to the absence of that Salic law which might have saved the country many disasters, but which would have robbed mediæval Greek history of half its romance. The county of Salona was the most important fief of the Catalan duchy, and at this time there dwelt in the old castle of the Stromoncourts and the Fadriques, the widowed Countess Helene and her only daughter Maria, to whom Rocaberti's son had been in vain affianced. Nerio now made an offer for the hand of the young countess, the greatest heiress of Catalan Athens, on behalf of his brother-in-law, Pietro Saraceno of Eubœa. The dowager countess, in whose veins was the blood of the Cantacuzenes—she was a direct descendant of the famous emperor and a cousin of the Despot of Mistrâ—scornfully rejected the proposal of the Florentine tradesman, and affianced her daughter to Stephen Doúkas, a Servian princeling of Thessaly. This alliance with a Slav naturally aroused the indignation of both Greeks and Franks at Salona. At this critical moment, Nerio's horsemen invaded Salona and the rest of the Catalan duchy, while his galley made straight for the Piræus. The details and precise date of this Florentine Conquest are unknown, but in July 1385 Nerio was already able to style himself "Lord of Corinth and the duchy,"[1] and in January 1387 he was signing a patent in that capacity in the city of Athens.[2] We now know, however, that the Akropolis held out for sixteen months longer. That noblest of all fortresses was commanded by Don Pedro de Pau, the gallant officer whom Vilanova had left behind him, and whose name deserves to be included in the long roll of heroes associated with the sacred rock. Down to almost the close of 1387 he managed

[1] *Dominator Choranti et Ducaminis*; Misti, xxxix., fol. 110, v.

[2] Buchon, *Nouvelles Recherches*, II., i., 221.

to keep up communications with the Home Government. In March of that year, his envoy, Rodonella, the same man who had laid the Athenian capitulations before Pedro IV. seven years before, appeared before Pedro's son and successor, John I., at Barcelona, to hear his majesty's pleasure concerning the duchies, and to do him homage. The new duke had already reappointed his friend Rocaberti vicar-general, and announced his intention of sending him with a fleet to "confound his enemies." This announcement was made to the Captain of the Navarrese Company, to the Archbishop of Neopatras, and to the Dowager Countess of Salona. From the phraseology of the royal letter to the archbishop, it is clear that much of that duchy was no longer in the possession of the Catalans, though the castle had not been taken; from the document addressed to the countess, we see that Salona was still hers, and that the king was anxious to secure the hand of her much-wooed daughter for the son of his favourite Rocaberti, although that damsel, the Helen of mediæval Greece, was already affianced to another. At the same time, his majesty assured the *sindici* of Athens that he would never "forget so famous a portion of our realm," which he hoped by God's grace to visit in person. Affairs of State at home prevented, however, this projected journey, while Rocaberti's promised fleet seems never to have arrived at the Piræus. On the contrary, in November 1387 we find him still lingering in Spain. Such was the practical sympathy shown by the effusive kings of Aragon for their distant dominions.

Meanwhile, abandoned by his Government at home, Don Pedro de Pau still held out—a lonely and pathetic figure on the Akropolis. Circumstances in Greece favoured his defence, for the attention of the besiegers had been distracted by a raid of Turkish pirates, which they joined the Venetian bailie of Negroponte in repulsing. On 5th November 1387, a rumour of the brave commander's death reached Cataluña, and a successor was appointed in the person of P. de Vilalba, who was to hold the two still unconquered castles of Athens and Neopatras. Eleven days later, however, a second messenger arrived with the news that Don Pedro was alive, and Vilalba's warrant was cancelled. From that moment the

Aragonese archives are silent as to the fate of Athens.[1] But a letter, preserved in the Laurenziana library at Florence, laconically informs us that on 2nd May 1388, "Messer Neri had the castle of Setines." The victor was unable at once to establish himself on the Akropolis, for plague had broken out at Athens, many had died, and among the victims had been his own valet. Nerio and all his family accordingly withdrew to Thebes to reflect in safety over his new position. His triumph was, indeed, complete; not only was he master of Athens, but a fortnight before the Akropolis fell he had yet further strengthened his position in Greece by bestowing the hand of his second and favourite daughter, Francesca, upon Carlo Tocco, the young Duke of Leucadia and Palatine Count of Cephalonia, the most powerful Latin ruler of the Levant.[2]

The Catalan rule over the duchies had thus ended for ever. The sovereigns of Aragon and Sicily might continue to style themselves Dukes of Athens and Neopatras—a title also borne by Queen Maria of Sicily and her husband,[3] and which was included among the dignities of the Spanish crown down to the end of the seventeenth century. Courtly Spanish poets might enumerate "thy great Athens, thy Neopatria," among the "good lands" of a dead Aragonese monarch, and the rulers of Sicily might gratify their vanity by appointing a titular vicar-general with a pompous patent to rid the land of the "tyrants" who had occupied it.[4] Alfonso V. even went so far as to create one of his subjects Duke of Athens, and in 1444 actually demanded the restitution of his two duchies.[5] But, since that memorable 2nd May 1388, the flag of Aragon has never waved again from the castle of Athens.

The Catalan Grand Company disappeared from the face of Attica as rapidly as rain from its light soil. Like their

[1] Rubió, *Catalunya a Grecia*, 42-53, 91, *n.*; *Los Navarros*, 491; Çurita, *Anales*, ii., 391; *Indices*, 360, 363, 367; Chalkokondýles, 69, 213; Hopf, *Chroniques*, 183; Misti, xxxviii., fol. 10; xl., fol. 17.

[2] Lámpros, Ἔγγραφα, 119.

[3] La Lumia, *Storie Siciliane*, III., 339, *n.* 1.

[4] Lámpros, Ἔγγραφα, 324-7.

[5] *Arch. Stor. per le Prov. Napoletane*, xxvii., 430.

Burgundian predecessors, these soldiers of fortune came, conquered, and disappeared, without taking root in the land. Only two generations had elapsed since the battle of the Kephissós, and already one family after another had died out, while now and again an old Catalan had returned to spend the evening of his life in his old home, so that King Pedro could point to the smallness of the Catalan garrison in Greece. After the fall of Athens, some, like the brothers Lluria, took ship for Sicily; others, like Ballester, the last Catalan Archbishop of Athens, returned to Barcelona, while others again lingered on for a time, among them the two branches of the Fadrique family, the former represented by the Countess of Salona and her daughter, the latter by John, the baron of Ægina. The masterful countess, either by her courageous defence or her patrician airs, sure to impress the Florentine upstart whom she had affronted, held her own for nearly six years longer. In 1390 we find King John of Aragon again asking the hand of her much-disputed daughter for a noble scion of the Moncada family.[1] The final disappearance of the county of Salona we shall see in the next chapter. The famous island of Ægina remained still longer in Catalan hands. From John Fadrique it passed, presumably by the marriage of his daughter, to the family of Caopena, then settled at Nauplia, whose name undoubtedly points to a Catalan origin, though Venetian genealogists make them come from the Dalmatian island of Lesina—a name easily confused with "Legena," the Venetian form of Ægina—and others suppose Cyprus to have been their home.[2] At Ægina the Caopena held sway till 1451, and this explains the boast of a much later Catalan writer, that his countrymen maintained their "ancient splendour" in Greece till the middle of the fifteenth century. It seems probable that, soon after the Florentine Conquest, the Catalan lord of Ægina conveyed thither the head of St George, which King Pedro had wished to have removed from Livadia to Spain, but which was still preserved there in 1393,

[1] Rubió, *Catalunya a Grecia*, 54, 61, 63-5; *Monumenta Ord. Frat. Prædicatorum*, vii., 71.

[2] Hopf, *Karystos* (tr. Sardagna), 67, 73. The name of Cao-Pinna is still common in Sardinia, where there are many Catalan families.

for the Venetians found it at Ægina when they became possessed of the island, and transported it thence to Venice in 1462.[1] We hear of a Catalan living at Modon in 1418, and of a Catalan corsair at Monemvasia in 1460, and in 1609 a Catalan was Bishop of Cerigo. There is still a noble family in Zante called Kataliános, and persons of the same name have been found at Patras, Kalamata, and Aigion within recent years. The island of Santorin possesses three families of Spanish origin—those of Da Corogna[2], De Cigalla, and Delenda, the latter a name common in Sardinia in the form Deledda. Thus, it happens that the present Roman Catholic Archbishop of Athens, Mgr. Delenda, is a descendant of its Catalan conquerors.

Memorials of the Catalan domination may still be seen in Greece. The fine castles of Salona, Livadia, and Lamia—all important places at that epoch, contain Catalan work, and the three ruined churches still to be seen within the precincts of the first of those fortresses were certainly used, if not built, by the devout soldiers of Spain who resided there. We know, too, that in their time there were churches of St George, St Mary, and St Michael at Livadia, but we are not told that they were of Catalan origin. Probably the row of towers between Thebes and Livadia dates from this period, as it was naturally most important to keep up communication between the capital and the chief fortress of the duchies. We are expressly told that they fortified the Akropolis, and that the governor had his residence and a chapel dedicated to St Bartholomew there. But of this nothing now remains. The Christian Archæological Museum at Athens contains, however, one very curious memorial of Catalan rule—a fresco of the Virgin and Child, with two armorial shields hanging from trees, and some mysterious letters in Gothic character, which came from the church of the Prophet Elias, near the gate of the Agorá.[3] The Gothic inscription on the west front of the Parthenon does not,

[1] Hopf, *Chroniques*, 202.

[2] Hopf (tr. Sardagna). in *Archivio Veneto*, xxxi., 163, says, on the strength of a genealogical tree at Santorin, that they came from Coruña. But they are heard of in the Archipelago in 1307, before the Catalan conquest of Athens.

[3] Δελτίον τῆς Χριστιανικῆς Ἀρχαιολογικῆς Ἑταιρείας, i., 65.

however, appear to be Catalan. It is no wonder that the Catalans left few great buildings behind them, when it is remembered that they lacked the stimulus of a ducal court, such as had existed in the time of the Burgundians, and that they were not, for the most part, the younger sons of noble houses, but a band of soldiers of fortune, who, by the strangest of accidents, had become the heirs of Periklês and Phidias. Being merely the representatives of the absent dukes, the Catalan vicars-general coined no money, but the kings of Sicily and Aragon bore the title of "Duke of Athens and Neopatras" on their coins.[1]

Such a society as this was not likely to encourage culture, and it is significant that the Catalan dialect has left no mark on the Greek language; yet even in Catalan Athens we find an Athenian priest copying medical works, while we know that the Catholic bishops of Salona and Megara had libraries.[2] But professional men seem to have been scarce in the country, if we may judge from the fact that on one occasion a doctor had to be sent from Sicily to Thebes.[3] Trade, on the other hand, naturally flourished between Barcelona and her Greek colony. The Venetian archives contain several allusions to the commercial relations between Thebes and both Barcelona and Majorca; Thebes, "the head, as it were, and mistress" of the cities of the duchies, had its own measures, and levied an octroi of 2 per cent. on all merchandise that went in or out of its gates; the contemporary geographer Abulfeda, mentions its gold and silver embroideries, but a Catalan traveller tells us that it suffered severely from earthquakes. Although Venice bound down the Company to keep no galleys in the Piræus, and prohibited the Catalans of Ægina from all traffic by sea, the "port of Athens" had recovered some of its importance, for we hear of a harbourmaster being appointed, and of ships from Spain being anchored there.[4] From the beginning of the fourteenth century

[1] Schlumberger, *Numismatique de l'Orient latin*, 345.

[2] Montfaucon, *Pal. Græca*, 70; Rubió, *Los Navarros*, 458, 475.

[3] Lámpros, Ἔγγραφα, 303.

[4] Predelli, *Commemoriali*, II., 22, 139, 141, 310, 325, 331; III., 69; Pegalotti, *Della Decima*, III., 51, 108, 109; Friar Jordanus, *Mirabilia Descripta* (tr. Yule), 2, 3.

it had borne the name of Lion, or Porto Leone, by which it was known down to late Turkish times, from the great stone lion which then stood there, and which was removed by Morosini to Venice, where it still guards the entrance to the arsenal, waiting for the day when all her stolen treasures shall be restored to free Greece. Athens, on the other hand, had sunk into insignificance, as compared with Thebes. The Westphalian priest, Ludolph, who travelled in Greece between 1336 and 1341, describes it as "almost deserted," and he adds the curious remark, which perhaps must not be taken too literally, that "there is not a marble column nor any good work of cut stone in the city of Genoa which has not been brought thither from Athens, so that the city has been wholly built out of Athens."[1] Forty years later the Catalans of Athens lamented to Pedro IV. their "poverty and distress." Livadia under the Catalans obtained an importance, which it retained in Turkish times; the county of Salona was the largest fief in the country; and the fortress of Siderokastron is described as "the key of the duchy of Athens."[2] Boudonitza, whose Venetian marquis was a Catalan vassal; Demetrias, "the boundary of Hellas," the last fragment of the Catalan possessions in Thessaly; Lamia, under its name of Citon; the Bœotian Karditza; Atalante, or La Calandri; Kapraina, the ancient Chaironeia; Stiris, or Estir, near the monastery of the Blessed Luke; and Vitrinitza, or La Veterniça, on the Gulf of Corinth, all figure in the history of the Catalan duchies; while their second capital, Neopatras, or La Patria, by furnishing one half of the ducal title, became a household word all over the Spanish world, and a Spanish poet commemorated it long after the last Catalan governor had left its walls.

The Greeks long remembered with terror the Catalan domination; a Greek girl in a mediæval song, prayed that her seducer might "fall into a Catalan's hands," and even a generation ago in Attica, in Eubœa, in Akarnania, Messenia, Lakonia, and at Tripolitza, the name of "Catalan" was used as a term of reproach; but the present author's enquiries in Greece have not succeeded in tracing this curious survival to

[1] *De Itinere Terræ Sanctæ*, 23; Rubió, *Catalunya*, 98.
[2] Guardione, *op. cit.*, 22.

the present day.. Professor Polítes, the leading authority on Greek folklore, states, however, that in Mane a child is sometimes christened "Catalan," as an omen of his future strength and courage, and that there the name is held in high esteem.[1] The distinguished Greek historian, Professor Lámpros, in his juvenile drama, "The last Count of Salona," and Koutoubáles in "John the Catalan, Archon of Olympos," have embodied in literature the Greek conception of the Catalans as monsters, but there is more of rhetoric than of history in those productions. That the Catalans were harder masters than the French is very probable; yet it is remarkable that the Greeks did not stir a finger to assist in a French restoration, when they had the chance. The probability is, that the Catalans have obtained their bad name from their cruelties before they settled down in Attica, and that they became staider and more tolerant as they became respectable; towards the close, as we have seen, King Pedro was not only liberal towards the Greeks, but waxed as enthusiastic as any philhellene over the splendours of the Parthenon. If, in spite of his liberality, they assisted Nerio, as has been plausibly argued, to conquer Athens, that merely proves that they recognised in him a strong man on the spot, connected by marriage with the chief representative of Hellenism in Greece, who would perhaps give them that peace which their absent duke could not ensure.

But if the modern Greeks do not view the Catalans with favour, the modern Catalans look back with justifiable pride on the connection between their countrymen and Athens. Catalan divines have truly boasted that their tongue was once spoken in the precincts of the Parthenon; Catalan poets and dramatists have chosen the Catalan Grand Company for their theme; to the labours of a brilliant Catalan scholar we owe the documents which have thrown so much light on this period; and in the history of Athens, where nothing can lack interest, these rough soldiers from the West are also entitled to a place.

About the same time that Nerio Acciajuoli obtained

[1] Stamatiádes, Οἱ Καταλάνοι, 223; Polítes, quoted by Rubió, *La Espedición*, 15-17; Legrand, *Recueil de Chansons populaires grecques*, p. xx.

possession of Attica, a relative of his completed the phenomenal good fortune of the family by becoming Despot of Epiros. We last saw all Akarnania and Ætolia in the possession of an Albanian chieftain, Ghin (or John) Boua Spata, while a Serb, Thomas Preliubovich, ruled at Joannina. "At first," says the *Chronicle of Epiros*, "he wore a fox's skin; but he soon threw it off, and put on that of a lion." Every class and race suffered from the persecutions of this petty tyrant; he first attacked the Greek Church, expelling the metropolitan, and distributing the ecclesiastical property among his Servian followers; then it was the turn of the native magnates, whom he either banished, or imprisoned, then that of the common people, whose food he taxed and whose savings he extorted. Wine, corn, meat, and cheese, the fish of the lake, the fruit of the orchards, all became monopolies of the tyrant, who compelled the peasants to work for him without pay. The Albanians do not usually turn the left cheek to the smiter; they called in the aid of their countryman, Boua Spata, who more than once besieged Joannina, but in vain. The Archangel Michael—so ran the story—saved the threatened city, and its tyrant, imitating Basil "the Bulgar-Slayer," was able to style himself with pride Thomas "the slayer of the Albanians," from the number of his victims. "All wickedness is small compared with the wickedness of Thomas"— such is the constant refrain of the tearful chronicler. Even his Serbs fled from before his face; and thus, having forfeited the sympathies of all, he completed his enormities by calling in the Turks. In 1385, for the first time, a Turkish force marched on Arta, under the command of Timourtash, carrying away a number of prisoners. Boua Spata, at this crisis, in vain proposed to Preliubovich an alliance against the common enemy; but vengeance was at hand, and before the year was out, the tyrant fell by the hands of his own bodyguard. The people of Joannina joyfully proclaimed his widow, who called her brother, the famous Abbot of Metéora, "King Joseph," to her councils, and, on his advice and that of the leading magnates, resolved to marry a strong man who could help her to reorganise her distracted country and protect it from the renewed attacks of the ambitious Spata. Such a consort was found in the person of Esau Buondelmonti, a Florentine of noble family, connected with the Acciajuoli and brother of the Duchess of Leucadia, in whose island dominions he was then residing. The elegant and quiet Florentine pleased the Servian widow all the more by contrast with her first husband's barbarous ways; indeed, according to one account, Esau had already been her paramour, having been captured in battle by Preliubovich, pardoned at the instance of his wife, and then having helped her to get rid of the tyrant. The people received him with intense relief; he restored their confiscated property, recalled the banished metropolitan, re-endowed the Church, opened the doors of the prisons, summoned back the exiled magnates, and abolished the hateful *corvées*. Like his predecessor, he strove to legitimise his rule with the Greeks by accepting the title of Despot from the imperial court at Constantinople; but he needed more efficient aid against Spata and his Albanians, and had to ask the Sultan Murâd I. in person for his protection—to such a state of weakness were the Christian states of the East now reduced. A Turkish force appeared at Joannina; Spata, who was besieging the town by both land and water, was forced to withdraw, and sorely-tried Epiros enjoyed for a few years the blessings of peace.[1]

Thus, in the year 1388, by an extraordinary coincidence, Florentines held sway alike at Athens, at Corinth, in Epiros, and in the island county of Cephalonia, where Esau's sister, the Duchess Maddalena, widow of Leonardo Tocco, was regent for her son Carlo,[2] himself affianced to an Acciajuoli. Another daughter of that dominant house charmed with her beauty the ceremonious Byzantine court of Mistrâ. If Florence was thus the leading Latin power in Greece, Venice came near her; for she was firmly settled in Crete, and was practically mistress of Eubœa and of Argolis, where a noble French dame still maintained the appearance of power in the last fragment of the old French duchy of Athens. Venice held, too, her Messenian colonies; the possession of

[1] *Epirotica*, 216-35; Chalkokondýles, 211-12; Gregorovius, *Briefe*, 304; Verino, *De Illustratione Urbis Florentiæ*, i., 120; ii., 22.

[2] Leonardo I. had died between 1374 and 1377; Buchon, *Nouvelles Recherches*, I., i., 309; Hopf, *Chroniques*, 183.

Pteleon gave her a post of observation in Thessaly; she had just acquired the island of Corfù, the key of the Adriatic; and in the Cyclades the new Italian dynasty was more susceptible to her influence than the previous dukes of the Archipelago had been. The Navarrese in the principality of Achaia, and the Catalans at Salona, completed the Latin element. While the Albanian chieftains still held Arta and Lepanto, and the Servian dominion was fast waning in Thessaly, the Turk was surely approaching. Already his aid is invoked in Greek affairs; already his shadow is over the vale of Tempe and the great Thessalian plain. Too late the Greek people, so long inarticulate, was growing conscious of its nationality and of its power. The last period of Latin rule at Athens witnessed, on the eve of the Turkish Conquest, the revival of the Greek Church and the national aristocracy.

CHAPTER XI

FLORENTINE AND VENETIAN ATHENS (1388-1415)

THE history of mediæval Athens is full of surprises. A Burgundian nobleman founding a dynasty in the ancient home of heroes and philosophers; a roving band of mercenaries from the westernmost peninsula of Europe destroying in a single day the brilliant French civilisation of a century; a Florentine upstart, armed with the modern weapons of finance, receiving the keys of the Akropolis from a gallant and chivalrous soldier of Spain—such are the tableaux which inaugurate the three epochs of her Frankish annals. But the merchant prince, whom a successful policy of enlightened selfishness had made the founder of the third and last Latin dynasty of Athens, was in a much more difficult position than either of his predecessors. It was true that his dominions, on paper at any rate, were almost as extended as ever had been those of the Burgundians and Catalans in their palmiest days. If, unlike the former, he did not own the Argolid, he held the stately castle of Corinth, the key of the Morea, with its ring of dependent fortresses. Chalkokondýles tells us that he possessed most of Phokis, the outlying parts, no doubt, of the Catalan county of Salona, and that his northern frontier marched with the confines of Thessaly. The three most prosperous cities of ancient Hellas—Athens, Thebes, Corinth—were all his. But the handwriting was on the wall: the Turk was hovering on the Macedonian border. Under these circumstances the keynote of the new ruler's policy was naturally conciliation of the Greeks. Now, for the first time since the day when Michael Akominátos had fled from his cathedral on the Akropolis before the Burgundian conquerors, a Greek metropolitan was allowed to reside at Athens.[1] He did not, indeed, recover the time-honoured church of Our Lady on that sacred rock—for the Parthenon continued, as before, to be the Catholic minster of the city—but conducted his services in what is now the military bakery, but which was in Turkish times "the mosque of the conqueror." This venerable edifice, now put to such base uses, was the metropolitan church of Athens during the rest of the Frankish period. Opinions differ as to the residence of the metropolitan; one archæologist thought that he had discovered fragments of the building in the Stoa of Attalos; the more probable view is that it was near the church of Dionysios the Areopagite under the shadow of the Areopagos, where travellers visited the metropolitan in the seventeenth century, until a fragment of the rock, loosened by an earthquake, fell and destroyed his abode.[2] Great was the surprise of the Holy Synod at Constantinople when the news arrived that, after nearly two centuries, an Athenian metropolitan could live in his see, instead of remaining, as most of his predecessors had done, merely a titular dignitary, who found occupation in attending the meetings of that august body. In the ecclesiastical documents[3] of the Catalan period we find frequent allusions to the metropolitans of Athens as members of the Holy Synod; and one of the exiled hierarchs died in Crete a martyr for his Church; but the local business had always been carried on in their absence by deputies, whose title was the more modest one of "first priest" (πρωτοπαπᾶς)[4] or "Exarch."[5] The degradation of the Athenian see to a lower place in the ecclesiastical hierarchy by Andrónikos II. was therefore justified.

Throughout the Frankish period the Greek ecclesiastical organisation had subsisted, with a few changes; but its existence had been merely on paper, so far as most of the

[1] Miklosich und Müller, ii., 165.

[2] Kampoúroglos, Ἱστορία τῶν Ἀθηναίων, ii., 37, 170, 304; Spon, *Voyage*, ii., 200; Philadelpheús, Ἱστορία τῶν Ἀθηνῶν, i., 178, 273, 278, 279, 312; ii., 91.

[3] Miklosich und Müller, i., 453, 456, 459, 467, 471, 476, 477, 488, 498, 558, 564.

[4] *Ibid.*, ii., 259.

[5] Lámpros, Παρνασσός, vi., 172.

Latin states of the Levant were concerned. The twelve metropolitan sees, which we found at the time of the Latin Conquest, had been increased to fifteen or sixteen in the time of Andrónikos II.; but it is significant that he awarded all the sees of Greece a lower place in the hierarchical scale, with the notable exception of Monemvasia—a natural tribute to the great importance of that city to the empire after its recovery in 1262. The Venetians, always more indifferent to religious fervour than other Catholics, had allowed the Greek bishops to reside in their colonies of Coron and Modon. But there was no room found for a Catholic archbishop and a Greek metropolitan in the same town. Hence the custom had arisen at the œcumenical patriarchate of tacking suffragan bishoprics, which had from time immemorial belonged to the "enslaved" metropolitan sees, on to other sees which had been so fortunate as to escape from the clutches of the Franks. It had become the practice, too, for the bishop of a "free" diocese to lay hands on those persons of an "enslaved" diocese who desired to enter the ministry.[1] But, as the Greeks had gradually recovered a large part of the Morea, two out of its five metropolitans—those of Monemvasia and Lacedæmonia—had been able to reside in their respective sees; while a third, his grace of Patras, though, of course, excluded from what was pre-eminently the Catholic city of the peninsula, had latterly resided, after a long homeless existence, in the splendid monastery of "the Great Cave," still the richest institution of the kind in Greece, which was a special dependency (or (σταυροπήγιον) of the patriarchate. North of the isthmus the occupation of Thessaly by the orthodox Serbs, after a temporary attempt to form a separate Servian church, had naturally involved the return of the metropolitan of Larissa, "Exarch of Second Thessaly and all Hellas," to that ancient city, and the capture of Lepanto from the Angevins by the Albanians had restored the metropolitan of Naupaktos, "Exarch of all Ætolia," to his old see in 1380, after long exile at Arta.[2] At Salona, thanks, no doubt, to the

[1] Miklosich und Müller, ii., 139.

[2] Dorótheos of Monemvasia, *op. cit.*, 397; Miklosich und Müller, i., 413, 493, 514, 587; ii., 11, 23, 270.

influence of its Greek countess, we now hear for the first time of a Greek bishop, whose example, like those of the restored metropolitans of Athens, inspires doubts as to the wisdom of this tolerant policy, from the Frankish point of view. The conquerors had now, however, to face this dilemma: either they must continue to exclude the higher Greek clergy, in which case they would lose the sympathies of their numerous and more and more indispensable Greek subjects, or they must permit them to return, in which case the patriotic aspirations of the orthodox hierarchy, combined with its intensely political character, would certainly lead to conspiracies against the temporal authorities, who were at once aliens and—worse still—schismatics. This was exactly what happened. The Greek bishop at Athens or Salona, became a political agent of Hellenism, a leader, or at least a representative, of the national party, just as he is to-day in Macedonia; unable to secure the triumph of Greek independence, he was ready, as is his fellow in Macedonia, to seek the aid of the Turk, as a preferable alternative to the rule of a Christian of another Church. Thus, the restoration of the Greek metropolitan see of Athens was an event of the first importance to Hellenism, and the Holy Synod was able to report with pride that under the tactful administration of Dorótheos, "Exarch of All Hellas, and president of Thebes and Neopatras," the Athenian Church, which had preserved the orthodox faith even without its hierarch, "seemed to have recovered its ancient happiness, such as it had enjoyed before the barbarian conquest."[1] As for the Catholic hierarchy, it continued as before, only that, instead of a Catalan, a Tuscan was archbishop at both Athens and Corinth.

But it was not the Greek Church alone which profited by the change of dynasty. Nerio's philhellenic policy—and it was policy, not sentiment, which made this hard-headed Florentine favour the Greeks—was also extended to the laity. Greek for the first time became the official language of the Government at Athens; thirty years before, it had been employed by the bailie of the titular duke at Nauplia. Nerio and his accomplished daughter, the Countess of

[1] Miklosich und Müller, ii., 165.

Cephalonia, used it in their public documents; the countess, the most masterful woman of the Latin Orient, proudly signed herself, in the cinnabar ink of Byzantium, "Empress of the Romans." This practice naturally necessitated the engagement of Greeks as secretaries and clerks. Nerio's secretary was a certain Phiomáchos, the ever-useful Demétrios Rendi continued to be notary of the city, and as his colleague we find another Greek, Nikólaos Makri. There is some evidence that Greek "elders" were allowed a share in the municipal government, as was the case under the Turks.[1] Even Florentines settled at Athens assumed the Greek translations of their surnames. A member of the famous Medici family had emigrated to Athens in the Catalan days; possibly he was one of the Tuscan men-at-arms who took part in Walter of Brienne's futile expedition; at any rate, a certain Pierre de Medicis "of Athens" held the office of bailie and captain-general of Argos and Nauplia for Walter, when the latter was tyrant of Florence, and we may conjecture that the titular duke was glad to employ as his deputy a Florentine and an old follower who had remained in Greece. This man's son had now settled in Athens, doubtless attracted by the success of his eminent fellow-Florentine. The Medici had intermarried with Greeks, and had now become so Hellenised as to call themselves Iatrós, instead of Medici. A century and a half later, their descendants still flourished at Athens and at Nauplia, and the family of Iatrópoulos claims them as its ancestors.[2]

Hitherto the career of Nerio Acciajuoli had been one of unbroken success. His star had guided him from Florence to Akrocorinth, and from Akrocorinth to the Akropolis; his two daughters, one famed as the most beautiful, the other as the most talented woman of her time, were married to the chief Greek and to the leading Latin potentate of Greece. These two alliances seemed to afford him protection against the only serious foe whom he had to fear, the vigorous and

[1] If, with Philadelpheús (i., 135), we accept the Θρῆνος, or "Lament for the Capture of Athens," as referring to this period.

[2] *Ibid.*, III., 248, 253; Buchon, *Nouvelles Recherches*, I., i., 131; II., i., 220; Gregorovius, *op. cit.*, ii., 227; Lámpros, Ἔγγραφα, 407; Sáthas, Μνημεῖα, viii., 370, 451.

unscrupulous leader of the Navarrese Company. The King of Aragon, in his palace at Barcelona, was far away; but the Navarrese were near at hand. They had never shown much love for Nerio, even when he was only lord of Corinth; they had seized many of his family estates; they would be only too glad, as his confidant, the worldly Bishop of Argos, had complained, "to do him some great harm." They had not forgotten their temporary occupation of the Athenian duchy, and they were now on excellent terms with the new King of Aragon, who still regarded himself as its lawful duke, and might at any moment employ their swords and their local knowledge against the usurper.[1] The most elementary common-sense suggested that he should not place himself in the power of these astute enemies. But success had apparently blinded the wily Florentine to the obvious dictates of prudence. He was now destined, thanks to his ambition and his rashness, to experience one of those sudden turns of fortune so peculiarly characteristic of Frankish Greece.

Nerio was naturally desirous of rounding off his dominions by the acquisition of the castles of Nauplia and Argos, which had been appendages of the French duchy of Athens, but which, during the Catalan period, had remained loyal to the family of Brienne and to its heirs, the house of Enghien. It chanced that in the very same year, 1388, which witnessed the fall of the Akropolis, Marie d'Enghien, the Lady of Argos, lost her Venetian husband, Pietro Cornaro. Thus left a young and helpless widow, and fearing an attack upon her possessions by her two ambitious neighbours, Nerio and his son-in-law, the Despot Theodore of Mistrâ, whose dominions came up as far as Astros, on the Gulf of Nauplia, the Lady of Argos transferred her Argive estates to Venice, in return for a perpetual annuity of 500 gold ducats to herself and her heirs, and a further life annuity to herself of 200 ducats. In the event of her death without heirs, she was allowed to bequeath the sum of 2000 ducats, payable out of the Venetian treasury, to whomsoever she pleased. She was, however, to forfeit all claim to the above annuities, if she married anyone except a Venetian noble. The ancient Larissa of Argos, the twin castles of Nauplia, "the Frank"

[1] Rubió, *Los Navarros*, 480, 492.

and "the Greek," as they were still called, and the noble gulf whose waves then washed their base, were cheap at the price.[1] Thus, Venice acquired the sole remaining dependency of the old French duchy of Athens, which remained in her hands for over one hundred and fifty years. Thus, the most shrewdly practical and least romantic of mediæval republics began her long domination over the ancient kingdom of Agamemnon. Thus, in the selfsame year, a Florentine banker became the heir of Theseus, a Venetian magistrate the heir of Atrides.

Before, however, the Venetian commissioner, Malipiero, had had time to take over the Argolid, the Despot Theodore, instigated by his father-in-law, Nerio, had seized Argos by a *coup de main.* Nerio regarded himself, and not Venice, as the successor of the De la Roche and the Brienne in places which had once been theirs, and in which he himself had property. His plan was, however, only half successful, for Malipiero persuaded the people of Nauplia to admit him as the representative of the most serene republic. Already incensed with Nerio, whom she accused of still harbouring Turkish corsairs at Megara to the detriment of her colonies, Venice retorted by breaking off all commercial relations between them and the subjects of Nerio and his son-in-law. The Athenians were no longer allowed to export their figs and raisins to Negroponte, nor to import their iron and ploughshares from Modon and Coron. At the same time, Venetian diplomacy made use of the Navarrese Company to punish the chief culprit. San Superan was on good terms with Venice; he had promised to compensate her subjects for the damage done by his men at the time of their invasion, to favour her commerce, and to dispose of no portion of the principality to her foes. He now willingly offered his services; the Venetian Archbishop of Patras did the same. The shrewd Florentine showed on this occasion a childlike simplicity, remarkable in one who had lived so many years in the Levant. He accepted the invitation of the Navarrese commander to a personal interview on the

[1] Thomas and Predelli, *Diplomatarium*, ii., 211-15; Caresinus, Sanudo, and Navagero *apud* Muratori, xii., 482; xxii., 760, 777; xxiii. 1072; Gerland, 159; *Chronicon Breve*, 516.

question of Argos, relying on a safe-conduct which he had received. To the men of Navarre the law of nations was mere waste-paper; the opportunity of securing their enemy was too good to be lost. San Superan bade Asan Zaccaria, the great constable of the Morea, arrest him, and on 10th September 1389, the order was executed.[1] At once the whole Acciajuoli clan set to work to obtain the release of their distinguished relative. His wife offered Theodore a large sum to surrender Argos. One of his brothers, Angelo, Cardinal Archbishop of Florence, sent a trusty emissary to the Despot, and implored the intervention of the pope; another, Donato, a Florentine Gonfaloniere, to whom Nerio's wife specially appealed for aid, persuaded his Government to despatch envoys to Venice, offering the most liberal terms, if the republic would secure Nerio's release. Donato was ready to place the cities of Athens and Thebes and part of the barony of Corinth in the hands of a Venetian commissioner as a pledge of his brother's sincerity, together with Nerio's merchandise in the city of Corinth to the value of from 12,000 to 15,000 ducats, so as to defray any expenses incurred by the republic in obtaining his release. He offered to go in person to Greece and see that Argos was handed over to Venice before his brother was set free, and appealed for mercy to one who was an honorary citizen of the republic. On the same ground, he applied for aid to Genoa, which had lately conferred the freedom of the city upon Nerio's daughter, the Countess of Cephalonia, and invoked the assistance of Amadeo of Savoy. The fear of Genoese intervention, and the news that the Despot was preparing to release his father-in-law by force, decided Venice to give way. After nearly a year's imprisonment near Vostitza and in the inland castle of Listrina (near Patras), Nerio obtained his release in the latter half of 1390 by sending his favourite daughter, the Countess of Cephalonia, as a hostage to Negroponte, and by consigning the city and castle of Megara and the value of his merchandise at Corinth to the Venetians, until they had obtained possession of Argos, which he promised to assist in securing for them, by force if necessary. If the Navarrese had hoped to annex his

[1] Gregorovius, *Briefe aus der "Corrispondenza Acciajoli,"* 305-6.

dominions during his captivity, they were mistaken, for his wife could point with pride to the loyalty of both his old subjects at Corinth and his new subjects at Athens to their imprisoned lord—a fact which shows that his philhellenic policy had borne fruit. But the men of Navarre, as was well known, were fond of money, and they, too, were determined to make their captive pay dearly for his liberty. In order to raise the money for his ransom, he stripped the silver plates off the doors of the Parthenon, seized the gold, silver, and precious stones which the piety of many generations had given to the ancient minster and to the cathedral of Corinth, and acquired, by lease or other means, various churches, including the Parthenon. The Despot was, however, in no hurry to surrender Argos. It was not till 1394 that Venice at last obtained possession of that coveted city, together with the castles of Thermisi and Kiveri. Then, at last, internal dissensions in his own dominions, where one of the hereditary *archons* of Monemvasia, a descendant of the Mamonâs who had parleyed with William de Villehardouin one hundred and fifty years before, aimed at practical independence with Turkish aid or under Venetian suzerainty, forced him to yield. Venice thereupon restored Megara to Nerio, together with a large sum of his money which she had still in hand. The administration of the Argolid was then settled; in the days of the titular dukes of Athens, Nauplia and Argos had been governed by a bailie or captain-general, assisted by a council; each of the two cities now received a *podestà*, or "captain," with a couple of governors under him, but the two administrations were to work in common, as at Modon and Coron; a deputation of Argives presented the capitulations of the towns at Venice, and received the ratification of their fiscal and feudal privileges. One of the first acts of the Venetian authorities was to erect a third fortress at Nauplia, on the north-west slope of Itsh-Kaleh, to which they gave the name of the Torrione. As at that time the site of the present lower town was covered by the sea, the place was extremely strong.

[1] Predelli, *Commemoriali*, III., 206, 208, 223, 231; Buchon, *Nouvelles Recherches*, II., i., 238-53, 254-6; Lámpros, Ἔγγραφα, 114; *Chronicon Breve*, 516; Dorótheos of Monemvasia, 472.

Nerio was not the man to forgive the Navarrese the trick which they had played upon him, especially as they had seized most of his family estates in the Morea and insisted in maintaining the old fiction, that the duchy of Athens was a fief of Achaia, and its master merely "lord of Corinth." He accordingly entered into relations with the pretender Amadeo of Savoy, who had been greatly moved at the news of his imprisonment, and was at this moment extremely active. Venice thought that the Savoyard might assist in capturing Argos for her, and undertook to transport him and his men to the Morea, and to make terms between him and the Navarrese when he arrived there. The Navarrese, on their part, alarmed by the approaching Turkish peril, offered to recognise his claims, provided that he would confirm them in the possession of the fiefs which they had won by their swords, with full right of sale if any of them wished to return to Navarre, would permit them to make certain gifts or bequests to the famous Minorite church at Glarentza, and would pay 20,000 gold ducats to San Superan. For Amadeo's guidance, they sent him a list of the fiefs which existed in the Morea in 1391. From this list we see that the twelve peers now consisted of the three dukes of Athens, the Archipelago, and Leucadia; the Marquis of Boudonitza, the Count of Cephalonia, and the Countess of Salona; the three triarchs of Negroponte; the barons of Arkadia and Chalandritza; and the Archbishop of Patras. Three other ecclesiastical barons are enumerated—the bishops of Olena, Modon, and Coron; and the two military orders of the Teutonic Knights and those of Rhodes.[1] Great, indeed, had been the changes since the Achaian peerage was founded nearly two centuries before. Arkadia, Chalandritza, and Patras were the only original baronies left, and they had all passed away from their original holders, for the two former now both belonged to the Genoese Asan Zaccaria, great constable of the principality, while Patras was practically an independent fief, held by the archbishop, who acknowledged no overlord but the pope. Moreover, nine of the peers resided out of the peninsula, whereas, even in the list preserved in the *Book*

[1] Predelli, *Commemoriali*, iii., 203, 209; Gregorovius, *Briefe*, 306; Buchon, *Recherches et Matériaux*, i., 288-99; Hopf, *Chroniques*, 229-30.

of the Customs of the Empire of Romania and composed somewhat earlier in this same century, there were only seven absentees. It is especially noticeable that the Ionian islands furnish two baronies, though Carlo I. Tocco was both Count of Cephalonia and Duke of Leucadia; but this is doubtless to be explained by the fact that on paper Amadeo had recently bestowed the former island, together with little Ithaka, upon a Greek supporter, one Láskaris Kalophéros, who had thus succeeded in theory to the realm of Odysseus.[1] We notice, too, that the vicar-general had managed to secure for himself the best of both the domanial and the baronial lands. Thus he held such celebrated places as Vostitza, captured from the Acciajuoli; Glarentza; Belveder, above Katakolo; the castle of St Omer, whose name is still preserved by the Santameri mountains; Androusa, or "Druse," in Messenia, now the capital of the principality; Kalamata, the old fief of the Villehardouins, and many smaller castles—comprising altogether about 2770 hearths out of more than 4050. Next to him in importance came Asan Zaccaria; but most of the old castles were now in the hands of soldiers of the Company; the strong position of Navarino, "Port Jonc" as it is still called in the document, was entrusted to two of those adventurers. Another personage, who figures largely in the transactions of this period, was Rudolph Schoppe, great preceptor of the Teutonic Knights, who resided at Mostenitsa. A century later, "the German house" at Modon was the usual stopping-place of German pilgrims to the Holy Land.[2]

These negotiations with the Navarrese did not prevent Amadeo from adopting a policy dear to diplomatists in our own day—that of insuring his position by making terms with the adversary of his allies. He sent envoys to Athens, and there "in the chapel of the palace" on the Akropolis, now the residence of "the lord of Corinth, of the duchy of Athens and of Neopatras," as Nerio styled himself, the latter pledged himself to aid Amadeo in taking the Morea from the Navarrese, and to induce his son-in-law, the Despot, to join

[1] Hopf *apud* Ersch und Gruber, lxxxvi., 48.

[2] Faber, *Evagatorium*, i., 39, 165; iii., 331; *Archives de l'Orient latin*, II., documents, 254.

in the attack upon them. As his reward, he claimed the restitution of his family property.[1] Thus, insured against all competitors, Amadeo might have been expected to act. But the death of his relative, the Count of Savoy, made his presence necessary at home; he wisely preferred to preserve what he possessed in Italy rather than make fresh acquisitions in Greece, and neither he, nor his brother and heir, Louis, did more than call themselves by the barren title of "Prince of Achaia," which appears on their coins.[2] With the death of Louis in 1418, the legitimate race of the Savoyard pretenders ceased, but as late as the last century a bastard of Savoy still styled himself "of the Morea."

While the Latin rulers of Greece were thus intriguing against each other, the Turks were threatening the existence of them all. The overthrow of the Servian empire on the fatal field of Kossovo in 1389 had removed the last barrier between Hellas and her future masters, and then, as now, the dissensions of Greeks and Slavs had made them unable to combine against the Moslem. In 1387 and the following year Turkish bands had appeared in the Morea, and in 1391 the redoubtable Evrenosbeg, "Brenézes," as the Byzantine historians call him, had been invited by the Navarrese into the Morea, to assist them in attacking the Despot of Mistrâ, and had occupied his capital, the new Greek town of Leondari, and the old Frankish castle of Akova.[3] Next year it was the turn of Thessaly, Bœotia, and Attica. Nerio thought that he had found a traitor in the newly restored Greek metropolitan, Dorótheos, whose theological rancour against the Latin Church was a sufficient reason to make him welcome the Turkish commander. The accused fled, for his life was in danger, protesting his innocence and maintaining an active correspondence with his flock. Nerio thereupon complained of his conduct to the œcumenical patriarch, alleging that he had repaired to the Turkish camp, and had promised the infidels, in return for their aid against the Latins, the treasures of the Athenian Church. The Holy Synod, however, pronounced the metropolitan to be innocent, on the excellent canonical ground, that the statements of

[1] Lámpros, Ἔγγραφα, 405-7. [2] Buchon, *Atlas*, xxiv., 14, 15.

[3] Hopf, *Chroniques*, 185; Doúkas, 47, 50; *Chronicon Breve*, 516.

heretics and schismatics were not evidence against bishops of the true Church, and allowed him to retain his three dioceses of Athens, Thebes, and Neopatras. But a century later, when the Latins no longer ruled over Athens, we find another œcumenical patriarch accusing the worthy Doróthcos of corruption for having divided in two the hitherto united sees of Daulia and Atalante. Nerio, however, cared nothing for the decision of the Synod; he refused to permit Doróthcos to return to Athens, and strongly expressed his preference—on the principle of *divide et impera*—for having two Greek metropolitans instead of one—namely, one for Athens, and the other for Thebes and Neopatras.[1]

The Bœotian raid of Evrenosbeg led to nothing more serious than the temporary loss of Livadia, which was recovered early in 1393 by Bertranet Mota, who is described as "one of the chief captains of the duchy of Athens,"[2] and who played an important part in the politics of those years—now acting as Nerio's gaoler in the castle of Listrina, now fighting for him against the Turks in Bœotia. But in 1393 Bajazet I., "the Thunderbolt," resolved to annex permanently a large part of northern Greece. He was now arbiter of its fate, and to his camp came trembling magnates to hear his decisions. With the contemptible Despot Theodore in his train, he took Pharsala and Domokó, whence the Servian governor, Stephen Doúkas Chlapen, viceroy for "King Joseph" of Metéora, fled to Nauplia, and then proceeded southward to Lamia. The Greek bishop betrayed that strong fortress, Neopatras fell, and many other castles surrendered on terms. Ecclesiastical treachery and corruption sealed the fate of Salona amid tragic surroundings, which a modern Greek drama has endeavoured to depict.[3] The dowager-countess had allowed her paramour, a priest, to govern in her name, and this petty tyrant had abused his power to wring money from the shepherds of Parnassos and to debauch the damsels of Delphi by his demoniacal incantations

[1] Miklosich und Müller, II., 165; Kampoúroglos, II., 135-6.

[2] Arch. Cor. Arag., Reg. 1964, fol. 72, v., 2243, fol. 123 (kindly communicated to me by D. Antonio Rubió y Lluch); Chalkokondýles, 145, 213; *Epirotica*, 242.

[3] Lámpros, Ὁ τελευταῖος κόμης τῶν Σαλώνων.

in the classic home of the supernatural. At last he cast his eyes on the fair daughter and full money-bags of the Greek bishop Serapheim; deprived of his child and fearing for his gold, the bishop roused his flock against the monster, and begged the sultan to occupy a land so well adapted for his majesty's favourite pastimes of hunting and riding as is the plain at the foot of Parnassos. The Turks accepted the invitation; the priest shut himself up in the noble castle, slew the bishop's daughter, and prepared to fight. But there was treachery among the garrison; a man of Salona murdered the tyrant and offered his head to the sultan; and the dowager-countess and her daughter in vain endeavoured to appease the conqueror with gifts. Bajazet sent the young countess to his harem; her mother he handed over to the insults of his soldiery; her land he assigned to one of his lieutenants, Murâd Beg. When the latter showed signs of independence, he was deposed and beheaded by his autocratic sovereign. Ere long, another act of blood completed the grim tragedy. The story reached the people of Salona that the sultan had murdered their fair young countess, considering a descendant of Aragon and Byzantium unworthy of his embraces. Such was the end of the famous fief of the Stromoncourts, the Deslaurs, and the Fadriques. Thus, in the early weeks of 1394 a Turkish governor was, for the first time, established on the northern shore of the Corinthian Gulf.[1]

[1] Nerio's letter of 20th February 1394 (Gregorovius, *Briefe*, 307) fixes the capture of Salona before that date. Thus the much criticised chronology of Chalkokondýles (67-9) is quite correct. N. de Martoni (*Revue de l'Orient latin*, III., 660) also alludes to it. *Cf.* also Χρονικὸν τοῦ Γαλαξειδίου, 206; Manuel Palaiológos, *Oratio Funebris*, *apud* Migne, *Patrologia*, clvi., 223, 228, 232; Phrantzês, 57; Miklosich und Müller, II., 270; Lámpros, Ἔγγραφα, 89. The name of the governor of Domokó, Ἐπικέρνεως, has puzzled readers of Chalkokondýles. Some have thought it a corruption of πιγκέρνα, but a Greek historian would not corrupt a well-known Byzantine title; Neroûtsos asserted that his family came from Cernagora (Montenegro); others have imagined a French family of Charny, whereas the Franks had long been extinct in Thessaly. I believe it to be a corruption of Chlapen, as we know that Stephen Doúkas Chlapen (Orbini, *Regno degli Slavi*, 271) was one of John Urosh's viceroys. It was he who was engaged to the Countess of Salona. The *Chronicon Breve* (517) mentions him at Nauplia.

The blow had fallen very near Athens, and Nerio wrote to his brother on the fall of Salona, that the Great Turk was expected to advance, and that war was imminent. The Turkish troops, however, once more evacuated his dominions; Thessaly became a *timar*, or hereditary fief of the redoubtable Evrenosbeg, but the hour of Athens was not yet come. The statesmanlike Florentine now reaped the reward of his politic treatment of the Greeks. When he had heard that the Turks were advancing, he had seized a number of women and children as hostages for the loyalty of the leading men in the small places, and had sent these hostages to Bœotia. When, none the less, the Greeks of those villages welcomed the Turks, he abstained from visiting their disloyalty upon the hostages. He felt sure that when the Turks retired, the Greeks, if not driven to desperation, would return to their allegiance, and his surmise proved correct. Again he had found that humanity was the best policy.[1]

Nerio had escaped for the moment by consenting to pay tribute to the sultan; but he hastened to implore the aid of the pope and of King Ladislaus of Naples against the infidels, who killed and tortured the Christians of Achaia and Attica. At the same time, like all usurpers, he desired to legitimise his position at Athens by obtaining formal recognition from an established authority. His family's fortunes had originated at the Neapolitan court; the king still pretended that he was the overlord of Achaia, of which, according to the old legal fiction, Athens was a dependency, and he had already given Nerio a mark of his favour by creating him bailie of Achaia. He now rewarded the services of the faithful Florentine in having recovered the duchy of Athens "from certain of the king's rivals," by conferring upon him and his posterity in January 1394 the title of duke, so long borne by its former rulers. As Nerio had no legitimate sons, the king consented that the title should descend to his brother Donato and the latter's heirs. Another of his brothers, Cardinal Angelo Acciajuoli, was entrusted with the duty of investing the new Duke of Athens with a golden ring, and was appointed in his stead bailie of

[1] Lámpros, Ἔγγραφα, 114; Raspe, v., fol. 16.

Achaia. But it was expressly stated that the duke should have no other overlord than the King of Naples. Thus, the old theory that Athens was a vassal state of Achaia received its deathblow. The pope completed the fortunes of the Acciajuoli by nominating the Cardinal Archbishop of Patras. The news that one of their clan had obtained the glorious title of Duke of Athens filled the Acciajuoli with pride, such was the fascination which the name of that city exercised in Italy.[1] Boccaccio, half a century before, had familiarised his countrymen with a title, which Walter of Brienne, the tyrant of Florence, had borne as of right, and which, as applied to Nerio Acciajuoli, was no empty flourish of the heralds' college.

The first Florentine Duke of Athens did not, however, long survive the realisation of his ambition. On 25th September of the same year he died, laden with honours, the ideal of a successful statesman. But, as he lay on his sick-bed at Corinth, the dying man seems to have perceived that he had founded his fortunes on the sand. Pope and king might give him honours and promises; they could not render effective aid against the Turks. The first Florentine Duke of Athens was also her first ruler who paid tribute to the sultan. It was under the fear of this coming danger that Nerio drew up his remarkable will.[2]

In making his final dispositions, the dying duke's first care was for the Parthenon, "St Mary of Athens," in which he directed that his body should be laid to rest. He ordered that its doors should once more be plated with silver; that all the treasures of the cathedral, which he had seized in his hour of need, should be bought up and restored to it; that besides the canons, who, as we saw, were twelve, there should always be twenty priests serving in the great minster day and night, and saying masses for the repose of his soul. For the maintenance of these priests and of the fabric of the church, he bequeathed to it the city of Athens with all its dependencies, and all the brood-mares of his valuable stud—

[1] Raynaldus, vii., 585; Gerland, 134; Fanelli, *Atene Attica*, 290-1; Gregorovius, *Briefe*, 309-10; Buchon, *Nouvelles Recherches*, II., i., 223-36.

[2] *Ibid.*, 254-62; Chalkokondyles, 213; Gregorovius, *Briefe*, 308.

for the Acciajuoli were good judges of horse-flesh.[1] Seldom has a church received such a remarkable endowment; the cathedral of Monaco, built out of the earnings of a gaming-table, is perhaps the closest parallel to the Parthenon, maintained by the profits of a stud-farm. He also restored two sums of money owing to it, ordered the restitution of the treasures which he had taken from the church of Corinth, bequeathed a splendid cross to the cathedral of Argos and a sum of money for a weekly mass there, and directed that all cathedrals and other churches which had come into his hands by lease or other means should return to their prelates and patrons at the end of the lease. He bequeathed his Argive property to build a hospital for the poor at Nauplia, which, restored by Capo d'Istria, is still in use, and placed both that and the nunnery which he had built there under the administration of his faithful councillor, the Bishop of Argos.[2] Nerio had treated the Latin Church with scant respect in his lifetime; he had seized its treasures, and had reinstated its hated rival; but he certainly made ample reparation on his deathbed.

Nerio's wife had died only three months before, so that he had not to provide for her; but made his favourite daughter, the Duchess of Leucadia, his principal heiress. While he left his other child nothing more than 9,700 ducats owed him by her husband the Despot, he bequeathed to her sister the castles of Megara and Sikyon (or Basilicata), all his other lands not specially left to others, and a large sum of money. She was to have Corinth also, despite the fact that it was to have belonged to the Despot after Nerio's death, so long as the children of Angelo Acciajuoli, who were its legal owners, did not repay the sum which their father had borrowed from Nerio. Besides these two daughters, Nerio had an illegitimate son, Antonio, by Maria Rendi, daughter of the ever-handy Greek notary. To this son he bequeathed the government of Thebes, the castle of Livadia, and all that lay beyond it, for Livadia, as we saw, though it had been annexed by the Sultan Bajazet, had been recovered by the Gascon

[1] Sáthas, Μνημεῖα, i., 178.
[2] Lamprinídes, Ἡ Ναυπλία, 109.

free-lance Bertranet for the duchy in 1393. As for his mistress, Nerio directed that she should have her freedom and retain all her property, including perhaps the spot between Athens and the Piræus which still preserves the name of her family—a provision all the more curious because Pedro IV. had, as we saw, conferred the full franchises and privileges of the conquerors upon her father and his family. To his brother Donato, who should have succeeded him in the title, the duke left his Florentine property and 250 ducats; he gave small legacies to his servants, and ordered that his cattle should be sold and the proceeds invested in Florence for religious and charitable purposes. As his executors he appointed the Duchess of Leucadia, his sister Gismonda (so long as she was in Greece), the Bishop of Argos, the governor of the Akropolis, and three other persons, two of them members of the Acciajuoli clan. Finally, he recommended his land to the care of the Venetian republic, to which his executors were to have recourse in any difficulty. He specially begged the republic to protect his heiress, the Duchess Francesca, and to see that his dispositions concerning the cathedral of Athens were carried out.

Donato Acciajuoli, Gonfalionere of Florence and Senator of Rome, made no claim to succeed his brother in the duchy of Athens, in spite of the natural desire of the family that one of their name should continue to take his title from that celebrated city. He had already had some experience of Greece, where he had acted as Niccolò's representative thirty years before, and he preferred his safe and dignified positions in Italy to the glamour of a ducal coronet in the East. But it was obvious that a conflict would arise between the sons-in-law of the late duke, for Nerio had practically disinherited his elder daughter in favour of her younger but abler sister. Theodore Palaiológos, who contended that Corinth had always been intended to be his after Nerio's death, besieged it with a large force, and took all the smaller castles of the Corinthian barony. Nerio's bastard, Antonio, and Bertranet Mota, the victor of Livadia, who had also profited under Nerio's will, threw their powerful aid on Theodore's side. On the other hand, Carlo Tocco, Duke of Leucadia, demanded from the executors the places bequeathed to his wife, and invited the Turks to assist him. Some 40,000 of those fatal auxiliaries obeyed his call; a sudden night attack upon the Despot's camp proved completely successful; 3000 of Theodore's cavalry were captured, and Theodore himself only just escaped. Carlo then signed a document, promising, on receipt of Corinth, to carry out all the testamentary dispositions of his late father-in-law. The executors, who had no option in the matter, thereupon handed over the great fortress to him. Leaving his brother Leonardo in charge of Corinth, and another official in command of Megara, he inveigled two of the Florentine executors into visiting him in his island of Cephalonia on their way home. As soon as he had them safe in the castle of St George, he told them that they should never leave the island alive, unless they restored him the compromising document. They replied that they had already sent it to Donato, whereupon he compelled them to sign another, stating that he had carried out the terms of Nerio's will. Against this act of violence they protested at both Florence and Venice, whose citizenship and protection against his obligations to Genoa he had recently asked. Well might that tried friend of the Acciajuoli family, the Bishop of Argos, urge the Archbishop of Patras to mediate between the rival kinsmen. For some months longer the civil war between them rendered the isthmus unsafe to travellers. An Italian notary has left us a graphic picture of the perils of a journey at this critical time from Athens to Corinth, how the Turks infested the Sacred Way, how all admission to the town of Megara was refused, for fear of the Despot's men, and how Nerio's elder daughter lay in wait to intercept her younger sister on her way to take ship at the port of Corinth for Cephalonia. The man of law was not sorry to find himself in the castle of Corinth under Carlo Tocco's protection, though the houses in that city were few and mean, and the total population did not exceed fifty families, or thirty fewer than that of Megara. The place did not boast a single inn, there was no bread to be had for love or money, but the excellent figs of the place and the hospitality of the Archbishop of Athens, an Italian, like himself, consoled the notary for his hardships. Such was life in the duchy of Athens in 1395.[1]

Not long afterwards the two sons-in-law of Nerio, frightened perhaps at the increasing audacity of the Turks, came to terms, and Tocco handed over the great fortress of Akrocorinth to the Despot Theodore. Its walls had struck the Italian notary as poor, and the donjon as insignificant; but the natural position of the citadel made it almost impregnable, and its acquisition by a Byzantine prince was regarded as a national triumph, commemorated by the erection of his statue over the gate.[2] Theodore hastened to ask the co-operation of Venice in repairing the Hexamilion, or six-mile rampart of Justinian across the isthmus, a part of which was still standing, while the rest was in ruins. Thus, after the lapse of nearly two centuries, the isthmus once more acknowledged the Greek sway The metropolitan of Corinth, so long an exile, at once returned to his see; one of his first acts was to demand, and obtain, the restitution by his brother of Monemvasia of the two suffragan bishoprics of Maina and Zemenó, which had been given to the latter's predecessor after the Latin Conquest of Corinth.[3] Such ire was common in celestial minds at this critical period, when all Greeks should have been united. Unhappily, the ecclesiastical literature of the fourteenth century shows us metropolitan arrayed against metropolitan, bishops persecuted by their superiors, and the Despot of Mistrâ, who should have been the recognised leader of Hellenism, thwarted by the Greek hierarchy.[4]

While Nerio's children had thus been quarrelling over Corinth, the Greeks of Athens had not been idle. It was not to be expected that the race, which had latterly recovered its national consciousness, and which had ever remained deeply attached to its religion, would quietly acquiesce in the extraordinary arrangement by which the city of Athens was to be the property of the Catholic cathedral. Sanudo, an

[1] Buchon, *Nouvelles Recherches*, II., i., 262-69; Gregorovius, *Briefe*, 309-10; N. de Martoni in *Revue de l'Orient latin*, III., 652-3, 656-9; Predelli, *Commemoriali*, III., 218, 236, 238.

[2] Νέος Ἑλληνομνήμων, II., 443-4. [3] Miklosich und Müller, ii., 287-91.

[4] *Ibid.*, i., 216-21; ii., 9-11, 23-5, 135-7, 249-55.

excellent judge of Eastern politics, had truly said that no power on earth could make the Orthodox Greeks love the Roman Church, and at Athens the professional jealousy of two great ecclesiastics embittered the natives against the alien establishment. Despite the warning which he had received from the treachery of Dorótheos, Nerio had felt obliged to permit another Greek metropolitan, Makários, to reside at Athens. This divine, thinking that the rule of a Mussulman pasha would be preferable to that of a Catholic archbishop, summoned Timourtash, the redoubtable Turkish commander, to rid Athens of the *filioque* clause, and his strange ally occupied the lower town. The Akropolis, however, held out under its brave governor, Matteo de Montona, one of the late duke's executors, who sent a messenger to the Venetian bailie of Negroponte asking for his aid, and offering to hand over Athens to the republic, if the bailie would promise that she would respect the ancient franchises, privileges, and customs of the Athenians. The bailie gave the required promise, subject to the approval of his Government; he sent a force which dispersed the Turks, and before the end of 1394, for the first but not the last time in history, the lion-banner of the Evangelist waved from the ancient castle of Athens.

The republic decided, after mature consideration, to accept the offer of the Athenian commander. No sentimental argument, no classical memories, weighed with the sternly practical statesmen of the lagoons. The romantic King of Aragon had waxed enthusiastic over the past glories of the Akropolis, and sixty years hence the greatest of Turkish sultans contemplated his conquest with admiration. But the sole reason which decided the Venetian Government to annex Athens was its proximity to the Venetian colonies and the consequent danger which might ensue to them if it fell into Turkish or other hands.[1] Thus, Venice took over the Akropolis in 1395, not because it was a priceless monu-

[1] Navagero *apud* Muratori, xxiii., 1075; Predelli, *Commemoriali*, III., 238. The text of the Venetian decision is printed in the *Sitzungsberichte der K. Bayerischen Akademie*, 1888, i., 152-8; Niccolò de Martoni, who visited Athens on 24th February 1395, says that the Venetians had "lately taken it,"—*Revue de l'Orient latin*, iii., 647.

ment, but because it was a strong fortress; she saved the Athenians, not, as Cæsar had done, for the sake of their ancestors, but for that of her own colonies, "the pupil of her eye." From the financial standpoint, indeed, Athens could not have been a valuable asset. A city which had complained of its poverty to the King of Aragon, and whose revenues Nerio had assigned to support the cathedral chapter, could not have been great or rich, nor can we well believe the statement of a much later Venetian historian that in his short reign he had found time to build "sumptuous edifices" and "spacious streets."[1] The Venetians confessed that they did not know what its revenues and expenses were; on this point their governor was to send them information as soon as possible; meanwhile, as the times were risky and the city would consequently require additional protection, involving extra expenditure, whereas some of Nerio's famous brood mares had been stolen and the available revenues consequently diminished, it was directed that only eight priests should for the present serve "in the church of St Mary of Athens." Upon such accidents did the maintenance of the Parthenon depend in the Middle Ages! The Government informed Montona's envoy, Leonardo of Bologna, that its officials would be instructed to preserve all the ancient rights, liberties, and customs of "our faithful Athenians," whose capitulations he had presented, as they had been presented fifteen years before to Pedro IV. Montona was to have 400 *hyperperi* a year, and his envoy 200, out of the city revenues, as their reward, but five years later we find the former complaining that this annuity had not been paid.[2] That official Greeks were favourable to Venice is shown by the fact that the city notary, Makri, was also awarded a sum of money.

The Venetian Government next arranged for the future administration of its new colony. The governor was styled *podestà* and captain, and was appointed for two years at an annual salary of £70, out of which he had to keep a notary, a Venetian assistant, four servants, two grooms, and four horses. Four months elapsed before a noble was found, in the person of Albano Contarini, ambitious of residing in

[1] Fanelli, 293. [2] Sáthas, Μνημεῖα, II., 6.

Athens on these terms. Two artillery officers, or *castellani*, were appointed at 6 ducats a month each to guard the castle, where one was always to be in the daytime and both were to sleep at night. Twenty men were to be engaged at 12 *hyperperi* a month each, for the garrison; if more men or money were wanted, Contarini was to ask the bailie of Negroponte or the *castellani* of the two Messenian colonies. Together with two ecclesiastical commissioners, he was to receive the revenues of the Church, so that the republic might not be out of pocket; later on he also had the appointment of the *castellani*.[1]

We are fortunately in a better position than was the Venetian Government to judge of the contemporary state of Athens. At the very time when its fate was under discussion, an Italian notary, Niccolò de Martoni, spent two days in that city, and his diary is the first account which any traveller has left us from personal observation of its condition during the Frankish period.[2] "The city," he says, "which nestles at the foot of the castle hill, contains about a thousand hearths," but not a single inn, so that, like the archæologist in some country towns of modern Greece, he had to seek the hospitality of the clergy. He describes "the great hall" of the castle (the Propylæa), with its thirteen columns, and tells how the churchwardens personally conducted him over "the church of St Mary," which had sixty columns without and eighty within. On one of the latter he was shown the cross, made by Dionysios the Areopagite at the moment of the earthquake which attended our Lord's passion; four others, which surrounded the high altar, were of jasper, and supported a dome, while the doors came—so he was told—from Troy. The pious Capuan was then taken to see the relics of the Athenian cathedral—the figure of the Virgin, painted by St Luke, the head of St Maccarius, a bone of St Denys of France, an arm of St Justin, and a copy of the Gospels, written by the hand of St Elena—relics which Queen Sybilla of Aragon had in vain begged the last Catalan archbishop to send her fifteen years before.

[1] Sáthas, Μνημεῖα, II., 3.

[2] The earlier fourteenth century traveller, Ludolf von Suchem, who mentions Athens, did not actually visit it.

He saw, too, in a cleft of the wall, the light which never fails, and outside, beyond the castle ramparts, the two pillars of the choragic monument of Thrasyllos, between which there used to be "a certain idol" in an iron-bound niche, gifted with the strange power of drowning hostile ships as soon as they appeared on the horizon—an allusion to the story of the Gorgon's head, mentioned by Pausanias, which we find in later mediæval accounts of Athens. In the city below he noticed numbers of fallen columns and fragments of marble; he alludes to the Stadion; and he visited the "house of Hadrian," as the temple of Olympian Zeus was popularly called, from the many inscriptions in honour of that emperor which were to be seen there. Twenty of its columns were then standing. He completed his round by a pilgrimage to the so-called "Study of Aristotle, whence scholars drank to obtain wisdom"—the aqueduct, whose marble beams, commemorating the completion of Hadrian's work by Antoninus Pius, were then to be seen at the foot of Lykabettos, and, after serving in Turkish times as the lintel of the Bouboun-istra gate, now lie, half buried by vegetation, in the palace garden. But the fear of the prowling Turks was a serious obstacle to the researches of this amateur archæologist. At Port Raphti, where he landed, he had been able, indeed, to admire the two marble statues, male and female, one of which still remains and has given the place its name of "the tailor's harbour." The more picturesque mediæval legend was that the woman, hotly pursued by the man, had prayed that they might be both turned into stone. At Eleusis, already called Levsina, he could see in the gloaming the marble columns and the arches of the aqueduct. But he tells us that both these places were infested by Turks, so that it was necessary to travel by night. On his way to Negroponte, he was only saved from falling into their hands by the characteristic unpunctuality of his muleteers—not a horse was to be had in Athens, and mules then, as now, were the sole means of conveyance in the country districts. Even so, he narrowly escaped being attacked by the Knights of St John, who held the castle of Sykaminon and who saw a Turk in every traveller, while the Albanians of Oropos were even worse marauders than the Turks. Yet our traveller notes that these gentry had spared the fair olive-grove of Athens.[1]

Such was the state of affairs which confronted the first Venetian governor of Athens. He had, indeed, no easy task before him. He found Turkish pirates infesting the coast of Attica, and the land so poor that he had to ask his Government for a loan of 3000 ducats. The Metropolitan Makários, a born intriguer, who had been plotting against the Despot in the Morea, as well as the Latins at Athens, was now in prison at Venice, but found means to continue his schemes in favour of the Turks.[2] The Athenian duchy was now terribly exposed to their attacks. By the fall of Salona she had lost her western bulwark: the warden of her northern marches, the Marquis of Boudonitza, had managed to retain his castle at Thermopylæ by payment of a tribute and by virtue of his Venetian citizenship.[3] But, in 1395, his marquisate and the Venetian station of Pteleon, in Thessaly, were the sole remaining Christian states of north-eastern Greece. All else was Turkish, as far south as Thebes, as far west as Lepanto. Even the Northern Sporades temporarily succumbed.

The Ottoman advance was fortunately, however, checked for a moment by the news that Sigismund, King of Hungary, had responded to the appeal of the Emperor Manuel II., and was marching on the Danube with the chivalry of the West to save the Byzantine Empire. Bajazet hastily retired from Greece to meet this new foe, whom he utterly routed in the great battle of Nikopolis. The defeat of this fresh crusade left Greece at the mercy of the conqueror. Marching himself against Constantinople, he despatched two trusty lieutenants, Jakûb Pasha and Evrenosbeg, with an army of 50,000 men to continue his interrupted Greek campaign. On crossing the isthmus, the forces divided: Jakûb marched upon Argos, Venice's recent acquisition, which surrendered, in 1397, without a blow, burnt the castle, and carried off 14,000 (some say, even more than 30,000) Argives into slavery—a number considerably superior to the present population of the town—

[1] *Revue de l'Orient latin*, III., 647-56.

[2] Miklosich und Müller, ii., 250, 256, 259; Predelli, *Commemoriali*, III., 238.

[3] Thomas and Predelli, *Diplomatarium*, ii., 292.

while Evrenos harassed the Venetian colonies in Messenia. After an attack on Leondari, the Turks recrossed the isthmus,[1] and would appear to have made themselves masters of the lower city of Athens. Neither Venetian documents nor Byzantine historians tell us of this capture of "the city of the sages" in 1397, of which Turkish writers boast.[2] But the Turkish account receives confirmation from a document of 1405, discovered at Zante and recently published,[3] which describes how Athenian families fled to that island before the Turks, and from a passage in the *Chronicle of Epiros*, which states that Bajazet subdued Athens. It is possible, too, that the above mentioned "Lament for the taking and captivity of Athens"[4]—a prosaic poem in sixty-nine verses of the "political" metre—also refers to this capture, though some critics have supposed the "captivity" to be that which the city suffered from Omar in 1456, or that the allusion is to the visit of Mohammed II. two years later. The writer, a priest, tells us how "the Persians," as he calls them, "first enslaved the region of Ligourió"—between Epidauros and Nauplia—"the feet of Athens"[5]—an allusion to the days when Argolis was a dependency of the duchy—and then came to Athens and "slew the priests, the elders, the wise, and all their council." Above all, he makes Athens mourn the enslavement of the husbandmen of the suburb of Sepolia, who will no longer be able to till the fields of Patesia.

Another enemy was ever on the watch for an opportunity to make himself master of Athens. The bastard Antonio Acciajuoli was not content with the cities of Thebes and Livadia, which his father had left him, but soon began to harry Attica with his horsemen, and to hound on the Turks, who readily responded to his exhortations. Successive Venetian governors depicted the pitiful state of the country

[1] Chalkokondýles, 97; *Chronicon Breve*, 516; Phrantzês, 62, 83; *Revue de l'Orient latin*, viii., 79.

[2] Hammer, *Geschichte des Osmanischen Reichs*, i., 252, 613.

[3] By Philadelpheús, i., 139, and Kampoúroglos, Μνημεῖα, ii., 153. *Cf. Epirotica*, 242.

[4] *Ibid.*, Ἱστορία, i., 117-24; Philadelpheús, i., 134-9.

[5] Professor Lámpros (Νέος Ἑλληνομνήμων, ii., 236) now suggests that Ἐλαιουργεῖα ("olive-yards") should be read.

and asked for reinforcements; the Home Government responded by raising the garrison to fifty-six men and the cavalry to fifty-five, and by authorising Vitturi, who was *podestà* in 1401, to spend 200 *hyperperi* on restoring the walls of the Akropolis. In order to pacify those Athenians who were discontented with the Venetian rule, he was ordered to issue a proclamation bidding them lay their complaints before the commissioners at Negroponte or Nauplia. But these measures were inadequate to save Athens. In the middle of 1402, the bad news reached Venice that the lower city, thanks to the treachery of its inhabitants, naturally favourable to one who was half a Greek, was in the hands of the bastard, but that the Akropolis still held out. The Senate ordered the bailie of Negroponte to proclaim Antonio an "enemy of the Christian faith," and to offer a reward of 8000 *hyperperi* to whosoever should deliver him up alive, or of 5000 to whosoever could prove that he had killed him. It also commanded him to relieve the Akropolis, and, if possible, lay Thebes, the lair of the enemy, in ashes. At the head of 6000 men, the bailie set out to perform the second of these injunctions. The bastard had only a tenth of that number at his disposal, but he placed them in ambush, we may assume in the Pass of Anephorites, which the Venetians were bound to traverse, took the enemy at the same moment in front and rear, and made the bailie his prisoner. Having nothing more to fear from Venice, he returned to the siege of the Akropolis.[1]

The republic received the news of his victory with alarm, not so much at what might befall Athens, as at the possible loss of her far more important colony of Negroponte. Commissioners were hastily despatched to make peace with Antonio; but the bastard, sure of being undisturbed by the Turks, calmly continued the siege of the small Venetian garrison of the Akropolis. Vitturi and Montona held out for seventeen months altogether, until they had eaten the last horse and had been reduced to devour the plants which grew on the castle rock. Then they surrendered and were allowed to retire penniless to Negroponte, which the Venetian councillors had put into a state of defence.

[1] Sáthas, Μνημεῖα, II., 7, 45, 60, 75, 91, 92; Chalkokondýles, 213-14.

Antonio was master of Athens; the half-caste adventurer had beaten the proud republic.[1]

Venice attempted to recover by diplomacy what she had lost by arms. She possessed in the person of Pietro Zeno, lord of Andros, a diplomatist of unrivalled experience in the tortuous politics of the Levant. Zeno's skill had contributed to the cession of Argos; it was now hoped that he might be equally successful with Athens. In spite of the capture of Bajazet by Timur at the battle of Angora in 1402, and the divided state of the Turkish Empire, both he and Antonio knew that the fate of Athens depended upon Suleyman, the new ruler of Turkey in Europe, and to his court they both repaired, armed with those pecuniary arguments which are usually found most convincing in all dealings with Turkish ministers. The diplomatic duel was lengthy; Antonio was already favourably known as a suppliant of the late sultan, while Zeno worked upon the Turkish fears of the Mongol peril, and pointed out that the Christian league, which had been formed by the two republics of Venice and Genoa, the Greek Emperor, the Knights of St John, and the Duke of Naxos, was not to be despised. He also spent his employers' money to good purpose, and finally gained one of those paper victories, so dear to ambassadors and so worthless to men of action. The sultan promised to Venice the restitution of Athens and the grant of a strip of territory five miles wide on the coast opposite the whole length of the island of Eubœa; he ceded the Northern Sporades to the emperor, ratified the recent transfer of Salona by Theodore Palaiológos to the Knights of St John, and consented not to increase the tribute paid by the Marquis of Boudonitza, although the latter had been caught conspiring against his Thessalian governor.[2] But Suleyman took no steps to make Antonio carry out his

[1] Sáthas, *op. cit.*, I., 4, 5; II., 95-103; Jorga, "Notes et Extraits," in *Revue de l'Orient latin*, iv., 303.

[2] Jorga, iv., 259-62; Thomas and Predelli, *Diplomatarium*, II., 290-3; Lámpros, Ἔγγραφα, 392. This treaty bears no date; it must have been not earlier than 1404, the date of Theodore's grant of Salona to the Knights of St John. According to Chalkokondýles (174) and Doúkas (79) the sultan also ceded Thessaly as far as Zetouni. *Cf.* Bessarion (Migne, clxi., 618).

part of the treaty, while the latter had powerful friends in Italy—Pope Innocent VII., Ladislaus of Naples, and Cardinal Angelo Acciajuoli—working on his behalf. Accordingly, Venice, nothing if not practical, reconciled herself to the loss of a place which it would have been expensive to recover. To save appearances, Antonio, in 1405, was persuaded to become her vassal, holding "the land, castle, and place of Athens, in modern times called Sythines," on condition that he sent every year a silk *pallium* worth 100 ducats to the church of St Mark. He was to make peace or war at the bidding of his suzerain, to give no shelter to her foes, to join in repelling attacks on adjacent Venetian colonies. He undertook to compensate Venetian subjects for their possessions seized during the war, to pay the value of the munitions which he found in the Akropolis, and to restore the goods of the late governor of Athens to his heirs. He was also to banish for ever the mischievous Greek metropolitan Makários, who had apparently escaped from his Venetian dungeon. On these terms the republic agreed to pardon the erring Antonio for all the harm which he had done her, and to receive him under her protection. He was, however, in no hurry to carry out his promises. He had to be sharply reminded that he had not sent the *pallia*, and had not evacuated the strip of territory opposite Eubœa, which the sultan had ceded to Venice, "the continent," or "Staria" (Στερεά), as the Venetians called it. Unless he mended his ways, the republic warned him that she would retract her promise to let him retain Athens. A compromise was made, by which he was allowed to keep the fortresses in the coveted piece of land, such as Sykaminon and Oropos, provided that he built no more. Nine years later, he was still trying in vain to obtain further concessions from the Venetians.[1]

The latter consoled themselves for the loss of Athens by two fresh acquisitions in Greece. The fortress of Lepanto—one of the most famous names in the history of Christendom—was still in the possession of the Albanian family of Boua

[1] Predelli, *Commemoriali*, III., 309; Sáthas, *op. cit.*, I., 52; II., 135, 184, 183; Jorga, iv., 284. The "Staria" was *not* five miles of territory, as h s been supposed, but *tantum infra terram quantum capiunt miliaria v., tantum quantum est longa insula* (Jorga, *loc. cit.*).

Spata, but seemed likely to fall ere long into the hands of the Turks, with whom its lord was in agreement. Ever since the Turkish Conquest of Salona with its admirable harbour of Galaxidi, corsairs had preyed upon Venetian commerce in the Gulf of Corinth, and it was feared that the Venetian island of Corfù would be damaged, if the Turks were able to convert Lepanto into what it became in the seventeenth century—a "little Algiers." Rather than that this should happen, Venice resolved to acquire the place. As far back as 1390, a daring Venetian captain had hoisted the lion-banner on its walls; but he had not been supported by the Venetian admiral, and had paid for his premature act by the loss of his eyes. Four years later, the inhabitants, alarmed by the Turks, had offered their town to the republic, but the offer was cautiously declined. At last, in 1407, Venice made up her mind that the psychological moment had arrived. Two versions exist of the way in which she attained her object. According to the official story, the then lord of Lepanto, Paul Boua Spata, sold it for the sum of 1500 ducats; but a more probable account informs us that a Venetian detachment suddenly landed, and that its commander inveigled the ingenuous Albanian under promise of a safe-conduct to his camp, and then threatened to cut off his head, unless he gave up the town. A *capitano* or *rettore* was appointed, who was dependent on the governor of Corfù, except during the temporary occupation of the much nearer town of Patras. The cost of keeping up the fortifications, which are still one of the most picturesque sights of the beautiful gulf, was defrayed out of the valuable fisheries of Anatolikó. For ninety-two years Lepanto remained in Venetian hands, and its "triple tiara" of walls was called by a Venetian historian "the strongest bulwark of the Christian peoples."[1] But Venice was wise enough to supplement this defence by an annual tribute of 100 ducats to successive sultans.[2]

A year later, in 1408, the republic rented Patras for five

[1] Sáthas, *op. cit.*, I., 1, 2; II., 64, 70, 172, 180, 187-9, 231; III., 75; *Nuovo Archivio Veneto*, xv., 284-5; Sanudo, *apud* Muratori, xxii., 837; Jorga, iv., 295.

[2] Thomas and Predelli, *Diplomatarium*, II., 303, 318, 345, 368.

years from its archbishop, Stephen Zaccaria, at an annual rent of 1000 ducats. The archbishop was harassed by the Turks, and wanted to spend three years in study at Padua, while the Venetians were glad to acquire a place where they had so much trade. He retained his spiritual jurisdiction, while they appointed their own *podestà*, who decided all temporal matters in the archbishop's name, and was assisted, according to the custom of the place, by a certain number of citizens. The Venetians took over the serfs, received the revenues of the Archbishopric—the duties on wine, corn, oil, silk, and cotton, which, though much diminished, still amounted to some 15,000 ducats, and raised the tribute of 500 ducats, which the city had already been compelled to pay to the Turks, and which was remitted to the sultan by the Prince of Achaia together with his own contribution. Both Patras and Venice benefited by these arrangements. The latter now held the two keys of the gulf in her hands; the former experienced the good effects of a practical administration, which spent the balance of the revenues on the defences, repaired the walls and the palace, whose noble hall was adorned with frescoes of the destruction of Troy, and stationed an "admiral" at the mouth of the gulf to keep off corsairs. The numerous Venetian mercantile colony naturally felt safer under the flag of the republic than under the crozier of a spiritual prince. Unfortunately, the archbishop desired to return, and at the end of the five years' lease, he received back his dominions. But the fear of a new foe, the Greeks of Mistrâ, soon drove him to place Patras, with the seven fortresses dependent on it, once more in the power of the republic, and in 1417 a Venetian governor again took up his abode in the old castle of the Franks. The pope, however, objected to this alienation of ecclesiastical property; Venice had to restore it two years later to the feeble rule of the archbishop, with the natural result that, a few years afterwards, the Roman Church lost Patras for ever. By clutching at the shadow, she had lost the substance.[1]

[1] Gerland, 162-71; Predelli, *Commemoriali*, iii., 335; *Diplomatarium*, II., 303; Sáthas, *op. cit.*, I., 2, 15, 21-30, 34, 41, 51, 68, 76-89, 91-6, 101, 106; II., 216, 260; Sanudo *apud* Muratori, xxii., 839, 917; N. de Martoni, *op. cit.*, III., 661.

Further Venetian attempts at territorial expansion in the Morea were not successful, the offer of Megara had no attractions, as the place was too remote, but in Epiros the famous rock of Parga had, in 1401, become a dependency of Corfù,[1] with which it remained connected till the memorable cession by the British in 1819; while in 1390 the two islands of Mykonos and Tenos had been bequeathed to the republic. The islanders petitioned the Venetian Government not to dispose of them, "seeing that no lordship under Heaven is so just and good as that of Venice," whereupon the latter farmed them out, after a public auction, to a Venetian citizen, who agreed to pay an annual rent of 1500 *hyperperi* out of the 1800 which represented the insular revenues, and who was dependent on the bailie of Negroponte. With them went the classic island of Delos, "le Sdiles," then a favourite lair of Turkish pirates, who drew their water from the sacred lake, of which Callimachus had sung.[2] Of all the Venetian acquisitions in the Ægean, this was the most durable.

Thus, in the first decade of the fifteenth century, the Venetian dominions in the Levant were increasingly important—a fact fully recognised by the Home Government. The documents of the period are full of provisions for the colonies, inspired by the Turkish peril, and of concessions to the natives. Commissioners are sent to enquire into their condition, with power to examine Greeks as well as Latins; in Negroponte, all the inhabitants, except the Jews, whose taxes are doubled, are to have privileges, the oppressive hearth-tax is temporarily removed, and the barons are ordered to arm their serfs with bows and arrows, and see that they practice them. The Home Government grants a humble petition of the islanders, praying that their good old customs may be observed, pluralities prevented, local offices made annual, and limited to those who have lived five years in the island, and the serfs exempted from the duty of acting as beaters at the bailie's hunting-parties. Still, the island was not prosperous; there was a large deficit in the annual budget of the colony; the vassals complained of their poverty, their ineptitude for trade, and their struggle to live on their rents.

[1] Sáthas, II., 29, 35, 46.

[2] Predelli, *Commemoriali*, iii., 278, 354; Sáthas, II., 163, 168, 178.

About this time the total population consisted of 14,000 families, and the city of Negroponte, though much smaller than it once had been, could boast of a fine church, a rich Franciscan monastery, and a nunnery. But what most struck travellers was the picturesque castle—now alas! no more—in mid-stream, approached by a wooden draw-bridge on either side. The local legend made it the abode of fairies, the enchanted fortress where the Lady of the Lake had held Gauvain captive. The beauty of the Lombard and Venetian damsels of Negroponte, who dressed in Italian fashion, seemed to be due to their descent from these fairy mothers.

In order to prevent the growing danger of the acquisition of landed property in the island by the Jews, the latter were forbidden to purchase real estate beyond the Ghetto, and the Cretan system of letting land on long leases of twenty-nine years was introduced so as to give the tenants more interest in the soil; finally, any "Albanians or other equestrian people," who would emigrate to Eubœa, were given full freedom and grants of uncultivated land, provided that they brought, and kept, horses for the defence of the island. Albanians, too, were induced to settle at Argos, Astros on the Gulf of Nauplia was occupied, and the fortifications of Nauplia were ordered to be repaired. So greatly did that colony prosper under its new rulers, that soon a considerable annual surplus was remitted out of its revenues to the Cretan administration. In view of the increasing peril of invasion, the cautious republic was ready to give favourable consideration to the Despot Theodore's plan of rebuilding the "six-mile" rampart across the isthmus, while by treaties with successive sultans in 1406 and 1411 she secured that her Greek colonies should not be molested.[1]

During the brief Venetian occupation of Athens, the Peloponnese had been a prey to those jealousies which had distracted it at the time of the Frankish Conquest. The Despot, though he was the brother of the reigning Emperor Manuel II., had never succeeded in imposing his authority

[1] Sáthas, II., 27, 30, 56-9, 60-2, 79, 83, 122-4, 224; III., 1, 2, 74, 95; Jorga, iv., 291, 296; N. de Martoni, *loc. cit.*; Thomas and Predelli, *Diplomatarium*, ii., 299, 303.

upon the proud and stubborn *archons*, whose ancestry was as ancient as his own. If we may believe the iambic poem inscribed on the door of the former church at Parori, near Mistrâ, during the first five years of his reign they had thwarted him in every way, striving either to drive him out of the country or to murder him, the veritable "gift of God." One of these local magnates, a Mamonâs of Monemvasia, a descendant of the man who had handed over that great fortress to Villehardouin, held the office of "Grand Duke," or Lord High Admiral, and comported himself as an independent princelet. When Theodore had asserted himself and expelled him, Mamonâs had not hesitated to submit his hereditary right to tyrannise over his native city to the arbitrament of the sultan, who ordered his restoration. Whenever the Despot tried to make his authority respected, his rebellious Greek subjects found allies in the Navarrese, and Theodore was thus forced in self-defence to look elsewhere for support. At this time some 10,000 Albanians had emigrated from their homes in Thessaly and Akarnania before the invading Turks, and had encamped with their wives and children on the isthmus. Thence they sent spokesmen to the Despot, asking permission to settle in his dominions. Most of his advisers opposed the idea, on the ground that the manners and customs of these strangers were not those of the Greeks. Theodore saw, however, as his predecessor Manuel Cantacuzene had done, that these highlanders should furnish him with splendid fighting material, with which he might keep his *archons* in order. He admitted the Albanians to the peninsula; they occupied uninhabited spots, planted trees in places whence brigandage had driven the pacific natives; while, when it came to fighting against the rebels and their Navarrese allies, they and their leader, Demetrios Ral, or Raoul, an ancestor of the great family of Rálles, undaunted by San Superan's mail-clad horsemen, succeeded in capturing that proud warrior and his brother-in-law, the Constable Zaccaria, the former captor of Nerio. Nothing but the fear of the Turks and the good offices of Venice secured their release.[1] Imitating

[1] Manuel Palaiológos, *op. cit.*, 211-15, 228-9; *Chronicon Breve*, 516; Phrantzês, 57; *Bulletin de Corr. hellén.*, xxiii., 151-4.

the example of Nerio, San Superan obtained in 1396 from Ladislaus of Naples the title of hereditary Prince of Achaia, to which Pope Boniface IX., without encroaching on the rights of the Neapolitan king, added that of "standard-bearer" of the Church.[1] Soon afterwards, in 1402, he died, the type of a successful adventurer, who had never scrupled to use the Turks when it suited his purpose. His widow Maria succeeded him as Princess of Achaia and regent for his eldest child; but the real power was vested in her nephew, Centurione Zaccaria, the ambitious baron of Kyparissia.[2]

The Despot Theodore had soon convinced himself that the Albanians alone would not suffice to save his land from the Turks. He could not appeal for aid to his brother, the Emperor Manuel II., for the latter had gone to London to crave the help of Henry IV., leaving his wife and children in charge of the Venetians at Modon. Indeed, it seemed as if Theodore himself might have to seek a refuge in some Venetian colony.[3] In this dilemma, he bethought him of the Knights of St John, who had previously held Achaia, and were known to be bold and experienced soldiers. He accordingly went to Rhodes in 1400 and sold Mistrâ, Kalavryta, and Corinth, to the Knights. When the news reached Greece, great was the indignation of the natives; even the laboured funeral oration, which the Emperor Manuel subsequently delivered over his brother, fails to justify this craven act. The panegyrist strove, indeed, to show that his brother had conferred a greater benefit upon Hellenism by ceding Akrocorinth than by regaining it five years before; in vain, he quoted Solomon in proof of his brother's wisdom, and pronounced the admirable maxim—utterly disregarded by the Greeks in practice—that, after all, it was better to give Corinth to one's fellow-Christians than to let it fall into the hands of the infidels. This was not the opinion of the people. The Knights, indeed, occupied Corinth, where the Greek party had not had time to take firm root, and where they strove to make their rule popular by all manner of con-

[1] Predelli, *Commemoriali*, III., 240; Raynaldi, viii., 72; Riccio, *Notizie Storiche*, 67.

[2] Buchon, *Nouvelles Recherches*, II., i., 273.

[3] Jorga, iv., 228.

cessions; but at Mistrâ, the capital and the seat of the metropolitan of Lacedæmonia, the Greeks rushed with sticks and stones to slay the envoys of the Order. The metropolitan intervened to save their lives, and gave them three days to quit the district, whereupon the fanatical people entrusted him with the supreme temporal power, and refused to receive back the Despot, until he had repaid the purchase-money to the Knights and vowed never to dream of such a monstrous transaction again. He saw that what he had regarded as a masterpiece of diplomacy had well-nigh cost him his dominions. Moreover, the defeat and capture of the dreaded Sultan Bajazet removed for a time the prospects of a fresh Turkish invasion. Theodore thought that the Knights, having served their turn, were no longer needed; and successfully applied his diplomatic talents to the task of ejecting them with the least possible amount of friction. A money payment, and the cession of the old county of Salona, with the barony of Lamia, which Theodore, as the representative of the last countess, had occupied on the news of the Turkish defeat at Angora, but which he was too weak to hold, settled the claims of the Knights, and both parties separated on the best of terms. In 1404, Theodore re-entered Corinth, and the Knights crossed the gulf to take possession of Salona. But there, too, they found the Greeks fanatically opposed to "the French priests." When they tried to bribe the mountain folk to rise against the Turks, who had re-occupied the country, the crafty Greeks took their money and then laughed at them, and the monkish chronicler naïvely justifies his countrymen's conduct towards the Frankish "Antichrists," who got no more than they deserved. All that they accomplished was the building of a church at Galaxidi, the ruins of which still disguise, in a corrupted form, the name of St John of Jerusalem. Even the formal acquiescence of the new sultan in their occupation of Salona availed them nothing in the face of this Greek opposition, and the old Frankish barony was soon all Turkish again.[1]

[1] Phrantzês, 63; Chalkokondýles, 97, 206; Manuel Palaiológos, *op. cit.*, 244-72; *Chronicon Breve*, 517; Χρονικὸν τοῦ Γαλαξειδίου, 207-9; Bosio, II., 117; Thomas, *Diplomatarium*, II., 290-3.

Theodore did not long survive his diplomatic triumph. In 1407 he died, and, as he left no heirs, the Emperor Manuel II. appointed his own second son, Theodore II., who was still a minor, as his brother's successor. Over the remains of the late Despot the emperor delivered, a few years later, a pompous funeral oration, still preserved, in which he lauded his brother to the skies in faultless Greek and with great wealth of classical allusion, attributed to his wise policy in calling in the Knights the revival of prosperity in the peninsula, and exclaimed that the Peloponnese was his brother's monument—"a monument, too, not dead, but alive!"

The Despot's last act before his death had been to attempt what his predecessors had been compassing for a century and a half—the conquest of the Frankish principality, now in the hands of a new and energetic ruler. Centurione Zaccaria, son of the former constable and nephew of the last prince, was not the man to be content with governing in the name of his aunt and her infant children. He had the effrontery to ask Venice, to whose care San Superan had committed his heirs, for assistance in his ambitious design of setting them aside, just as, two centuries before, the first Villehardouin, with Venetian aid, had deprived Champlitte's successor of his heritage. Then he applied to King Ladislaus of Naples, who still posed as overlord of Achaia, and obtained from him, in 1404, the coveted title of Prince of Achaia. The Neapolitan monarch salved his conscience for thus depriving San Superan's children of their birthright by pretending that they had not notified their father's death within the time prescribed by the feudal law. Thus, the great Genoese family from which Centurione sprang had reached the summit of its ambitions by a quibble similar to that by which the first Villehardouin had won Achaia. But the handwriting was on the wall. He was the last of the long series of Frankish Princes of Achaia; weakened by internal dissensions, the diminished state was destined to succumb ere long to the brief revival of Hellenism at Mistrâ. Meanwhile, Centurione's most pressing foes were those of his own race. One of his most important peers, Carlo Tocco, Count of Cephalonia, at once obtained from the King of Naples the abolition of the feudal tie, which had united his island county to Achaia for 170 years — an event commemorated on the only coin of his dynasty, now in the British Museum. Not content with that, he and his brother, Leonardo of Zante, seized Glarentza, from which they were finally dislodged by the united efforts of the Zaccaria clan and the Albanian troops of the prince. The latter, feeling himself insecure, begged his ancestral city of Genoa to look upon him as her son and citizen.[1]

The Tocchi were at this time among the most ambitious and able of the Latin dynasties in the Levant. We have seen how Carlo I., Duke of Leucadia and Palatine Count of Cephalonia and Zante, had married the favourite daughter of Nerio Acciajuoli, and had played an active, if devious, part in the execution of his father-in-law's will. His wife, the Duchess Francesca, one of the ablest and most masterful women of the Latin Levant, in which her sex had played so prominent a part, was the ruling spirit in his councils. To her influence was due the restoration of the Greek archbishopric of Leukas; she was sufficiently Greek and sufficiently proud to sign her letters in Greek, and with the cinnabar ink of Byzantium : " Empress of the Romans " ; and she possessed all her father's brains, and inherited his political ideas. In her castle of Santa Mavra—the irregular, hexagonal building which is still preserved—and in her court at the castle of St George in Cephalonia, which served as barracks during the British occupation, but which now remains a deserted landmark of foreign rule, she presided over a bevy of fair ladies. Old Froissart tells us, how the Comte de Nevers and the other French nobles, whom the sultan had taken prisoners at the battle of Nikopolis, were received there by her with splendid hospitality on their way home. The ladies were exceeding glad, he says, to have such noble society, for Venetian and Genoese merchants were, as a rule, the only strangers who came to their delightful island. He describes Cephalonia as ruled by women, who scorned not, however, to make silken coverings so fine that there were none like them. Fairies and nymphs inhabited this ancient realm of

[1] Sáthas, *op. cit.*, II., 30, 109, 155, 165, 168, 194; Schlumberger, *Numismatique*, 391 ; Riccio, *Notizie Storiche*, 67.

Odysseus, where a mediæval Penelope governed in the absence of her lord. Events were soon to extend his rule over the neighbouring continent, where we last saw his uncle, Esau Buondelmonti, holding sway.[1]

The Florentine ruler of Joannina was anxious to secure immunity for his people from the attacks of the great Albanian clan of Spata, which had its capital at Arta. Accordingly, on the death of his beloved wife, he had contracted a second marriage with a daughter of old Ghin (or John) Boua Spata, its chieftain. But this act of policy had the very opposite effect of what had been expected, for it brought Evrenosbeg and a Turkish army upon Epiros, and made the Albanians more jealous than ever of the Italian interloper. Buondelmonti proved a match for the Turks in that difficult country; but in his new brother-in-law, Ghin Zenevisi, Lord of Argyrokastron, he found a more dangerous antagonist. During an expedition to punish this treacherous chieftain, he was taken prisoner, and only released, thanks to the good offices of his influential Florentine relatives, and of the Venetian governor of Corfù, on payment of a large ransom. We last hear of him in 1408, when he died without offspring, and, in the ordinary course, his nephew, Carlo Tocco, should have succeeded him.[2] But, no sooner was Esau dead, than another Albanian chief, Maurice Boua Sgourós, who had seized the succession of his brother Ghin at Arta, made himself also master of Joannina, whence Tocco was unable to dislodge him. Both parties appealed for aid to Venice, which, after her acquisition of Lepanto, was not at all desirous to see a vigorous Italian princelet establish himself on the mainland. Sgourós, when hard pressed, called in the Turks, which had the effect of frightening all parties into peace. But, though Tocco temporarily relinquished the places which he had taken on the mainland, he did not abandon his claim to the old Despotat of Epiros. The

[1] Miklosich und Müller, II., 139; III., 253; Buchon, *Nouvelles Recherches*, II., i., 254, 283, 286; Froissart (ed. Buchon), xiv., 57, 58; Meliarákes, Γεωγραφία τοῦ Νομοῦ Κεφαλληνίας, 34; Blantês, Ἡ Λευκάς, 58.

[2] A golden bull of his, dated 1408, and published by Romanós (Περὶ τοῦ Δεσποτάτου, 168), disproves the statement of the *Epirotica*, that he died in 1400.

various races of Epiros seem to have grown weary of the Albanian ascendancy; already another rival had endeavoured to obtain as many diverse racial sympathies as possible by describing himself as a "Serbo-Albano-Boulgaro-Wallach"—a name worthy of Aristophanes himself. Tocco and his consort were doubtless popular with the Greek element; supported by them and with his own right arm, he would appear to have at last vanquished his enemy in a battle, which was fatal to the latter; early in 1417, he had already made himself master of "the land of Arta," and in 1418 he was able to style himself "Despot of the Romans." His dominions embraced, besides his islands, Epiros, Ætolia, and Akarnania; he resided now at Arta, now at Joannina, and now in his insular castles, while the relatives of his fallen rival emigrated to the Morea, where they and their descendants, later on, played a prominent part. Thus he and his masterful wife had established in North-west Greece, a compact dominion, broken only by the Venetian castle of Lepanto. That, too, he offered to buy; but he received the haughty answer, that the republic had "never been accustomed to sell her fortresses, and is quite capable, even if they were not remunerative, of supporting their cost."[1]

The ten years' fratricidal struggle between the four sons of Bajazet I. had given Greece as a whole a welcome respite from Turkish invasions, and a Byzantine governor actually ruled, for the first time for generations, in Lamia. But the two surviving fragments of Latin rule in North-east Greece—the Venetian marquisate of Boudonitza and the Venetian station of Pteleon—were, from their isolated position, peculiarly exposed to attack. Suleyman, as we saw, had guaranteed the independence of the Marquis Giacomo on continued payment of a tribute, which was also claimed from Pteleon; but the Turks none the less became so threatening that he removed his vassals and cattle to the safer castle of Karystos in Eubœa, which his brother now held from the Venetians. The danger increased when Suleyman's brother, Musa, seized the Turkish throne in 1410. The new sultan's

[1] *Epirotica*, 235-8; Sáthas, i., 34; ii., 114, 234; iii., 64, 174; Hopf, *Chroniques*, 195, 301, 342, 368; Lami, *Deliciæ Eruditorum*, v., p. cxx.; Jorga, iv., 581.

26

victorious troops marched straight, like a new army of Xerxes, against the historic fortress which, for two centuries, had guarded the Pass of Thermopylæ. The marquis defended it, like a second Leonidas, but he was assassinated by a traitor within the walls. Even then, his sons, aided by their uncle, the baron of Karystos, held the castle for some months longer, in the hope that Venice would send aid to her children in distress. Aid was, indeed, ordered to be sent; but, before it arrived, Boudonitza had fallen—surrendered at last by its gallant defenders on condition that their lives and property were spared. The Turks violated their promise, robbed their prisoners of all that they possessed, and incorporated the marquisate with the Pashalik of Thessaly. Young Niccolò Zorzi, the late marquis's heir, and his uncle, Niccolò of Karystos, were dragged off as captives to the sultan's court at Adrianople, where Venice did not forget them. In the treaty of 1411, between Musa and the republic, the sultan promised to release the young marquis, for love of Venice, seeing that he was a Venetian, to vex him no more, if he paid the tribute agreed upon, and to allow his ships and merchandise to enter the Turkish Empire on payment of a fixed duty. But young Niccolò, after what had occurred, felt insecure in his ancestral castle at the northern gates of Greece. In 1412 we find him sending the Bishop of Thermopylæ to ask for archers from Negroponte and the protection of the Venetian admiral, in case the Turks, or their vassal, Antonio of Athens, should attack him.[1] His request was granted; but his marquisate was doomed.

Mohammed I. had indeed promised on his accession in 1413, to be a son to the Greek Emperor Manuel, who had helped him to the throne; and he had told the envoys of the Despot Theodore, the Prince of Achaia, and the Despot of Joannina, that he wished to be at peace with their masters.[2] But he did not spare the Venetian Lord of Boudonitza. His fleet sailed to Eubœa, and, after ravaging the island, crossed over to the mainland. On 20th June 1414 the castle fell,

[1] Hopf, *Karystos* (tr. Sardagna), 55-8, 90; Thomas and Predelli, *Diplomatarium*, ii., 203; Sáthas, II., 155, 210, 270; Jorga, vi., 119.

[2] Doúkas, 97.

its fortifications were destroyed, numbers of the marquis's subjects were dragged off as slaves, and the historic marquisate which had lasted over two hundred years, disappeared from the face of Greece. Young Niccolò fled to Venice, which afforded him shelter and endeavoured to recover for him his lost dominions. When the republic, after a brilliant victory over the Turkish fleet, forced upon Mohammed the treaty of 1416, one of the conditions was that the marquis should be restored, if he did homage and paid tribute to the sultan. But his castle was now in ruins, and he was glad to cede the vain honour of bearing the title to his uncle, the baron of Karystos, receiving for himself the rectorship of Pteleon, as the reward of the services of his father, "killed by the Turks in the cause of Venice." From that time we hear of him no more; but his uncle, Niccolò of Karystos, was prominent in the diplomatic negotiations of the period. He went as Venetian ambassador to both the Emperor Sigismund and Pope Martin V., and it was on an embassy to Murâd II. at Adrianople that he died, it was said, of poison administered by the sultan's orders. The title of Marquis of Boudonitza and the barony of Karystos lingered on for two generations in his family, and at the present day his descendants, the Zorzi of S. Giustina still exist in Venice. Such was the tragic end of the marquisate, which Boniface of Montferrat had conferred upon the Pallavicini, and which had passed from them to the family of Zorzi.[1] A picturesque ruin still marks the spot where the Italian marquises held their court.

With the fall of Boudonitza, the brief restoration of Byzantine rule in Lamia passed away, and the whole of continental Greece, from Olympos to Bœotia, was Turkish, except where the Eubœan governor of Pteleon kept the Venetian flag still flying. Despite the late sultan's promise not to molest the Venetian colonies, every year the Turks

[1] Sanudo *apud* Muratori, xxii., 890, 911, 1043; Navagero, *ibid.*, xxiii., 1080-1; *Cronaca di Amadeo Valier*, fol. 259 (Cod. Cicogna, No. 297) in Museo Correr; Sáthas, iii., 429-31; Jorga, iv., 561; v., 196. Much confusion has been caused by the fact that both uncle and nephew had the same name. I have followed the account given by Hopf in his *Karystos* (tr. Sardagna), rather than that in his history (lxxxvi., 73-6), because we know (Jorga, iv., 546) that the uncle was five years in prison.

descended in smaller or larger numbers upon Eubœa, and on one of these raids some 1500 of the islanders were carried off into captivity, and the town of Lepso, the modern Ædepsos, where the Greeks go to take the hot baths, was destroyed. So wretched was existence in the island at this time, that the inhabitants petitioned Venice for permission to become tributaries of the Turks. This request the proud republic refused; but it was obvious, as the petitioners pointed out, that Negroponte was now, like Lepanto, "on the frontier of all her Levantine possessions," and had therefore to bear the brunt of every Turkish invasion. Attica was still more exposed to these dreaded enemies, and in 1415 Antonio Acciajuoli applied to Venice for munitions from Negroponte and leave to deposit his animals and property there in case of attack. A year later the Turks ravaged his duchy and forced him to pay tribute. Happily the great Venetian naval victory over the Turks in 1416 checked for a time the Ottoman advance, and the subsequent treaty, which the sultan made with the victors three years later, procured a breathing space for the Latins of the Levant. Mohammed I. even went so far as to threaten with condign punishment, Antonio Acciajuoli, who had maltreated some Venetian subjects, or anyone else who should dare to lay a finger on any Venetian colony.[1] Thus, Greece enjoyed a welcome respite from the Turkish peril. Had her rulers been wise, they would have availed themselves of it to consolidate their forces against the common enemy, who was so soon to destroy their dominions. But when have the Eastern Christians been united against the Crescent? Yet few moments were more favourable than this, when the Turkish ruler was pacific, when his Empire was just emerging from a long civil war, and when, by a curious irony of fate, Hellenism was displaying a consciousness of its past and a concern for its future such as it had not shown since the Frankish Conquest. It was, alas! the last flicker of light before the long centuries of Turkish darkness.

[1] Sanudo *apud* Muratori, xxii., 896; Sáthas, III., 100-2, 125-7, 129-31, 190; Thomas and Predelli, *Diplomatarium*, ii., 318-20.

CHAPTER XII

THE GREEK RECONQUEST OF ACHAIA (1415-1441)

EARLY in the year 1415, the Emperor Manuel II. paid a memorable visit to the Peloponnese. His object was to establish his son Theodore, now of age, in the governorship of Mistrâ, to do what was practicable for the defence of a province which had attracted greater attention at the Byzantine court since the rest of the empire had been so woefully curtailed by the Turkish Conquests, and to pronounce a funeral oration over his late brother. The Venetians gave him a state reception when he stopped at Negroponte on his way. But they were so much alarmed at the arrival of a ruler, who naturally personified the reviving idea of Hellenism, that they at once dismissed the Greek mercenaries of their Peloponnesian colonies. From Eubœa the emperor sailed to Kenchreai, the port of Corinth, where he received the homage of the Prince of Achaia, and where he assembled the people of the peninsula. He then set them to work to rebuild the great rampart across the isthmus which his brother had proposed. Under the imperial eye the workmen laboured so fast, that in twenty-five days a wall 42 stades in length, strengthened by 153 towers and a ditch, and terminated by a castle at either end, stretched from sea to sea. The emperor built on the site of the rampart which the Peloponnesians had raised on the approach of Xerxes, which Valerian had restored when he fortified Greece against the Goths, which Justinian had again constructed when Greece was threatened by the Huns and Slavs. An inscription in honour of Justinian came to light in the course of the work, and it was hoped that the wall of Manuel would prove as durable as his. Remains of the Hexamilion may still be seen between the modern town of Corinth and the Canal, while its name is preserved by a hamlet on the line to Argos. But the restoration of the wall availed little against the bravery of the Turks; for, as Thucydides had observed centuries before, it is men and not walls that make a city. If we may believe a Byzantine satirist—and his statement is in keeping with their character—the Peloponnesian *archons* showed so little patriotism and so much jealousy of the emperor, that they rose and threatened to destroy the rampart when it was barely finished. Such was their insubordination, that, when he returned to Constantinople, Manuel thought it prudent to take them with him. Before he left, he announced the completion of the work to the doge, who sent his congratulations, and authorised the governors of the Venetian colonies in the Morea to assist in its defence. But, when asked to contribute to the cost of maintaining it, the Venetians excused themselves, on the plea that they were incurring heavy expenses for defending other parts of Greece against the Turks. So unpopular was the tax imposed upon the Greeks for the support of the Hexamilion, that many serfs fled into the Venetian colonies to escape it, and a few years later the Despot Theodore II. actually offered to transfer the custody of the great wall to the republic. But the selfish Venetians would only consent to this, if they also received a mile or two of land inside it, and if Theodore would pay half the cost of defence. Such was the attitude of the two powers most vitally interested in the preservation of the peninsula at a time when union alone could have saved it from the Turks.[1]

There was at least one man then living in the Peloponnese who was well aware that more than ramparts of stone was needed to secure the independence of the peninsula. The Platonic philosopher, George Gemistós, or Pléthon, as he afterwards called himself, had been engaged for the last twenty years in teaching the doctrines of his master in the

[1] Phrantzês, 96, 107, 108; Chalkokondýles, 183, 216; Doúkas, 102; Mázaris *apud* Boissonade, *Anecdota Græca*, III., 177; *Chronicon Breve*, 517; Sáthas, i., 115; iii., 110, 113, 116, 126, 177, 179; Jorga, iv., 547, 554-5, 558, Νέος Ἑλληνομνήμων, ii., 451-4, 461-6.

picturesque Byzantine capital of Mistrâ. Even to-day, when the Mistrâ of the Palaiológoi is a deserted town, the traveller, wandering among the ruins of the palace, visiting the beautiful Byzantine churches, and climbing up to the castle hill, may form some idea of the civilisation of the mediæval Sparta. Mistrâ was at this time more than 150 years old; and, as the Byzantine empire had shrunk to a few islands and a small tract of land near Constantinople, the Greek province of the Peloponnese and its capital had assumed an importance which they had not before possessed. The second son of the emperor now regularly resided there, and already there lay buried at Mistrâ the ex-Emperor John Cantacuzene, his sons Matthew and Manuel, and the Despot Theodore I. To this beautiful spot, within sight of the ancient Sparta but in a far finer situation, Gemistós had moved from the Turkish capital of Adrianople. If we may assume that "the philosopher George," to whom the *littérateur* Demétrios Kydónes addresses three or four playful letters, is none other than he, his choice of abode seems to have surprised the elegant Byzantine world, which, like modern French novelists, could conceive of no life as worth living except that of the metropolis. "You thought," writes Kydónes, "that this mere shadow of the Peloponnese was the Islands of the Blessed; to your wild philhellenism it seemed as if the soil of Sparta were enough to show you Lycurgus, and that you would be his companion."[1] There was not a little truth in the remark, for the economic schemes of Gemistós were better fitted for Plato's *Republic* than for the Moreot society of the fifteenth century. But, in point of culture, Mistrâ could have compared favourably with some modern seats of learning. No less famous a man than Bessarion came from distant Trebizond to hear this disciple of Plato expound the master's teaching, while in Hierónymos Charitónomos, whose funeral oration over Pléthon has been preserved, Mistrâ produced one of the earliest teachers of Greek in the University of Paris.[2]

[1] Boissonade, *Anecdota Nova*, 303. There is no anachronism in the assumption, for Kydónes is known to have been alive as late as 1397, about the time of Gemistós's removal to the Morea. The plague alluded to in the letters may have been that of 1399.

[2] Platina, *Paneg. in laudem Bessarionis*, 2.

Gemistós was doubtless emboldened to address his scheme for the regeneration of the Peloponnese to the emperor by the favourable reception accorded to a previous letter, in which he had urged Manuel to pay a personal visit to the peninsula, if he cared anything for its safety.[1] In that letter and in an appeal to the Despot Theodore, he foreshadowed the proposals which he embodied in a memorial to the patient emperor, handed to him while he was still at the isthmus. He began by proclaiming the Hellenism of Greece, and, overlooking the existence of various other races in the Peloponnese, he pointed to the speech and education of the people as proofs of their Greek origin. But all was not well in this citadel of the race, which neither its strong natural defences nor the Isthmian wall could protect without drastic reforms. According to the philosopher of Mistrâ, the radical defect in the existing system of military service was that the taxpayers were summoned away from their agricultural pursuits to bear arms. So long as campaigns were short this did not greatly matter; but the continual and lengthy calls upon the people in consequence of the frequent domestic wars and Turkish invasions had made them less and less inclined to respond. Hence few put in an appearance when war was proclaimed; and even those few were badly armed and anxious to quit the camp for their domestic duties. As a consequence, it had been found necessary to hire foreign mercenaries for the defence of the country—a plan which increased the taxes, corrupted the natives, and was quite inadequate in an emergency. To remedy this, Gemistós suggested that justice demanded a division of the products of the country into three equal shares between the three classes of producers, capitalists, and officials, the last of which included the soldiers, the *archons*, and the court. The first class, which was by far the most numerous, would keep one-third of what it produced, would pay one-third to the capitalists, and one-third in the form of a tax to the State for the maintenance of the soldiers and officials. A peasant proprietor who owned his own cattle and instruments of labour, would, of course, retain two-thirds of his produce. In districts

[1] Πρὸς τὸν Βασιλέα, *apud* Müller in *Sitzungsberichte der Wiener Akademie* (1852), ix., 400-2.

where most of the peasants were fit for military service, they should be grouped in pairs, each pair having property and capital in common, so that one man would cultivate the soil while the other was performing military service, and *vice versâ*. The official class should be excluded from trade (as was the case in the Venetian colonies), and exempt from payment of taxes in consideration of its public services. The peasants, who would thus be the sole taxpayers, and whom Gemistós calls in truly Spartan phraseology "Helots," should no longer be expected to undertake forced labour or to pay a number of small taxes at frequent intervals to an army of tax-collectors. In place of those irksome imposts, the new Lycurgus advocated, centuries before Henry George, a single tax, payable, not in cash, but in kind, and amounting to one-third of all crops and young animals. The "Helots," no longer liable to military service, would thus be able to support themselves and their families, remunerate the capitalist, and also provide for the maintenance of the official, non-producing class. Gemistós would have assigned one "Helot" for the support of each foot-soldier, and two for that of each horseman, while he left it to the discretion of the sovereign to select as many "Helots" as he thought adequate for that of the officers and of the reigning house, suggesting, however, three for the former. One section of the unproductive class—the clergy—received scant favour from this unorthodox philosopher, who drew his inspiration from Plato rather than from the Fathers of the Church. He was willing to concede three "Helots" apiece to the bishops, as state officials, but to the monks, "who, under the pretence of philosophic enquiry, claim the largest share of the public revenues," he refused even the smallest aid from the funds of the State. They were, he said, "a swarm of drones," who deserved no other privilege than that of enjoying their possessions free of taxation. Or, at least, let them hold public offices without salary, as the "ransom" which they paid for the retention of their property. It is not surprising that this attack on their order gained for Gemistós the bitter hatred of the clergy; even after his death they refused him burial in consecrated ground, and it is not at Mistrâ, but in the cathedral of Rimini that we must seek his remains. Not content with having thus excited one powerful interest against him, the dauntless visionary attacked another—the landed interest—by boldly proposing the nationalisation of the land—a measure which, so he believed, would make the Peloponnese blossom like the rose.

By these reforms Gemistós confidently hoped to support in the least irksome manner a force of some 6000 native soldiers. But his reforming zeal was not confined to the question of national defence. A strong patriot, he wished to erect a high fiscal barrier, a tariff Hexamilion, against the foreigner. A land such as ours, he told his distinguished correspondents, is essentially agricultural; that is our principal occupation; we can produce in the Peloponnese all that we want, except iron and arms, and we should be much better without foreign clothes, seeing that the peninsula yields wool, flax, hemp, and cotton. Why then import wool from the Atlantic Ocean, and have it woven into garments beyond the Ionian Sea? Accordingly, he advocated a high export duty of fifty per cent. on the fruits of the earth and on other useful products of the country, unless they were exchanged for iron or arms, in which case they should be exported free of charge. Taxes and salaries being paid in kind, and the export of cotton being sufficient, in his opinion, to pay for the imports of iron and arms, Gemistós saw no further need for money. The Peloponnese was, at this time, flooded with bad foreign coins—for the Despots of Mistrâ, so far as is known, never issued any currency of their own, though Theodore I. pledged himself in 1394 not to imitate the Venetian coinage, while he received permission to copy other currencies, which looks as if he had contemplated the establishment of a mint.[1] This evil the philosopher accordingly desired to remove. Lastly, he turned his attention to the reform of the penal code. Capital punishment, formerly usual, had fallen into abeyance; while, in its place, the judges inflicted the barbarous penalty of amputation, or in too many cases let the criminals off scot-free. Gemistós deplored both this excessive cruelty and this excessive leniency; he thought it far better to chain the criminals in gangs and set them to work at the repair of the Isthmian wall.

[1] Predelli, *Commemoriali*, III., 223; Schlumberger, *Numismatique*, 322.

He concluded his scheme of reforms, by modestly offering his own services to carry them out. The offer was declined; the Emperor Manuel was a practical man, who knew that he was living, not in Plato's republic, but in the dregs of Lycurgus.[1] The philosopher continued, however, to enjoy the favour of the imperial family. When the Emperor John VI. visited the Morea in 1428, he consulted him on the Union of the Eastern and Western Churches, and confirmed the grant of two manors, Phanarion and Vrysis, made to Gemistós and his two sons by the Despot Theodore II. It is interesting to note that one of the conditions was the payment by the lord of the manor of the *floriatikón*, or tax for the maintenance of the Isthmian wall. Gemistós showed his gratitude by a florid funeral oration, still preserved, over the Despot's Italian wife, Cleopa Malatesta.[2]

About the same time that Gemistós drew up his scheme for the regeneration of the Morea, a Byzantine satirist composed, in the manner of Lucian's *Dialogues of the Dead*, a bitter pamphlet, in which he gives us his impressions of the Peloponnese. The satire may be overdrawn, but it is nearer to life than the idealism of the Platonist. In place of the "purely hellenic" population of Gemistós, Mázaris tells us that there are in the peninsula seven races, "Lacedæmonians, Italians, Peloponnesians, Slavonians, Illyrians, Egyptians, and Jews, and among them are not a few half-castes." These are precisely the races which we should have expected to find there. The "Lacedæmonians," as Mázaris himself explains, are the Tzákones, who had "become barbarians" in their language, of which he gives some specimens. The "Italians" are the Franks of all kinds—French, Italians, and Navarrese; the "Peloponnesians" are the native Greeks; the "Slavonians" are the tribes of Ezerits and Melings about Taygetos; the "Illyrians" are the Albanians whom Theodore I. had admitted to the peninsula; the "Egyptians" are the gypsies, whose name, like that of the Jews, is still preserved in the

[1] *Περὶ τῶν ἐν Πελοποννήσῳ πραγμάτων. Λόγοι, ά καὶ β'*, *apud* Migne, *Patrologia Græca*, clx., 821-64. *Cf.* Tozer in *Journal of Hellenic Studies*, vii., 353.

[2] Miklosich und Müller, iii., 173-6; Sgurópoulos, *Vera Historia Unionis*, § 6, ch. x.

various "Gyphtókastra" and "Ebraiókastra" of Greece. Mázaris goes on to make the shrewd remark, true to-day of all Eastern countries where the Oriental assumes a veneer of Western civilisation, that "each race imitates the worst features of the others," the Greeks assimilating the turbulence of the Franks, and the Franks the cunning of the Greeks. So insecure were life and property, that arms were worn night and day—a practice obsolete in the time of Thucydides. Of the Moreot *archons* he gives much the same account as the Emperor Cantacuzene; they are "men who ever delight in battles and disturbances, who are for ever breathing murder, who are full of deceit and craft, barbarous and pig-headed, unstable and perjured, faithless to both emperor and Despots."[1] Such men were not likely to sink their private differences and rally round their sovereign's representative in a firm and united stand against the Turk.

Manuel's sojourn in the Peloponnese seems, at least, to have had some effect in reducing to order and civilising the lawless and savage population of Maina. Like the Bavarian rulers of Greece in the nineteenth century, the Byzantine sovereign destroyed numbers of the towers, which were the refuge of the wild Mainate chieftains. It was he, too, as two Greek panegyrists inform us, who stamped out their brutal but very ancient custom, mentioned by the Greek tragedians, of cutting off their enemies' fingers or toes, and dipping these ghastly trophies in the festive bumper, with which they drank to the health of their friends. In a land where stones were so plentiful and imperial officials so rare, the towers soon rose again, but this grim practice (*μασχαλισμός*, as it was called by the ancients) is never mentioned again.[2]

After the departure of the emperor, the Morea enjoyed relative repose, broken only by occasional conflicts between the Greeks and Centurione, the Prince of Achaia, in the course of which the Venetian colonies suffered from the uncontrollable Albanians of the Despot, while the old Frankish principality steadily dwindled away almost to nothing before

[1] Ἐπιδημία Μάζαρι ἐν Ἅιδου, *apud* Boissonade, *Anecdota Græca*, iii., 164, 168, 174, 177-8.

[2] Isidore of Monemvasia and Argyrópoulos in Νέος Ἑλληνομνήμων, ii., 181-4.

the Greek attack. The imperial family continued to display a strong personal interest in the peninsula; John, the heir and associate of Manuel II., spent a year there, during which he captured Androusa, the capital of the principality; and, when he returned home, his youngest brother, Thomas, was sent there, attended by the historian Phrantzês, a native of Monemvasia, who was destined to play an active part in the last act of Greek freedom, and to describe the events of his time for the edification of posterity. Nor were the Greeks the only enemies of Centurione; an Italian adventurer, named Oliverio, seized the important port of Glarentza, forced the Prince of Achaia to bestow it upon him with the hand of his daughter, and then sold it to Carlo Tocco, who had long desired that foothold in the Morea. Feeling his position daily more insecure, Centurione tried to dispose of the principality. He first offered it to his ancestral city of Genoa, much to the alarm of her rival, Venice, and then to the Knights of St John, who declined, owing to the Turkish danger in Asia Minor, to interfere again in its administration; he was even quite willing to make a bargain with the republic of St Mark. The latter was desirous of extending her possessions in the peninsula, or of even acquiring the whole of it, not from ambitious motives, as she truly said, but from fear lest it should fall into the hands of an enemy who might injure her trade and colonies. Indeed, the lack of settled government, and of any proper police, practically ruined her traffic in the Malmsey wine, which it then produced. In 1417 she had garrisoned Navarino, just in time to prevent its occupation by the Genoese; in 1423 she legalised her position there by purchase, and she rounded off her Messenian colonies by the acquisition of several other important castles. These greatly strengthened her position in the south of Messenia; communication by land between Modon and Coron was now secured by the fortress of Grisi, which was of great value when the sea was beset by Turkish ships. New regulations were drawn up for this enlarged strip of Venetian territory. In 1439, we are told, it included seven castles, three of which, including Navarino, were placed under the jurisdiction of Modon, and the other four under that of Coron; in each of these seven strongholds a Latin governor, chosen from among the Venetians of the two colonial capitals, held office for two years, and at the end of his term, a councillor of the colony went and heard any charges which the people might have against him.

Not satisfied with these piecemeal acquisitions, the republic, in 1422, sent a commissioner to examine thoroughly and report upon the defences, the revenues and expenditure of the Morea, and to sound the Despot Theodore, the Prince of Achaia, and Carlo Tocco, with a view to obtaining all, or most, of the Greek Despotat; the whole of the principality of Achaia, either at once, or on the death of Centurione; and the valuable mart of Glarentza. The commissioner presented a thorough and satisfactory report to his Government; the Morea, he wrote, yields more than Crete; it comprises more than 150 castles, its circumference is 700 miles; its soil contains deposits of gold, silver, and lead, and it exports silk, honey, wax, grain, poultry, and raisins. It is curious to compare this statement with that of Gemistós. The philosopher had made no mention of the silk industry, which still flourished, while the commissioner omitted the cotton, which figured so largely in the schemes of Pléthon, and to which there is frequent allusion in the Venetian documents. The large amount of merchandise which Nerio Acciajuoli had stored at Corinth, the great value of the Venetian wares which we find at Patras, and the existence of a considerable Jewish colony there, confirm the commercial importance of the country. Even in the midst of war's alarms, a wealthy Venetian merchant, settled at Patras, had customers on both sides of the Corinthian Gulf, and that city was the home of several well-to-do families, whose standard of living would have incurred the censure of the philosopher. In spite, then, of all it had undergone, the constant civil wars, the Turkish depredations, the eight plagues of the last two generations, and at least one great earthquake, the Peloponnese would seem to have been well worth acquiring. Had Venice annexed it, she might perhaps have saved it, or at least postponed its fall. But the negotiations came to nothing, and the republic contented herself with urging united action against the Turks.[1]

The warning was indeed needed. The warlike Murâd II. was now Sultan, and in 1423, when the negotiations were barely over, the great Turkish commander, Turakhan, invaded the Morea with an army of 25,000 men. Accompanied by the sultan's frightened vassal, Antonio Acciajuoli of Athens, Turakhan made short work of the vaunted Hexamilion, whose defenders fled as soon as they saw him approach, and marched upon Mistrâ, Gardiki, in the pass of Makryplągi, and the town of Leondari. In one difficult defile the Greeks fell upon him, defeated him with much loss, and recovered most of the rich booty which he had taken. But this check proved to be only temporary. Tocco's representatives at Glarentza purchased their own safety by betraying to the Turks the pass of Kissamo, which exposed the Venetian colonies to attack. A string of 1260 Venetian subjects and some 6000 Greeks followed the homeward march of the Turkish commander. But the Albanian colonists were resolved that he should not leave the Morea without feeling the weight of their arms. They gathered at Davia, near Tripolitza, under a general of their own race, and prepared to attack. They paid dearly for their daring, many were slain, about 800 were captured and massacred, and towers of Albanian skulls, such as that which still stands near Nish, marked the site of the battle. The emperor was obliged to purchase peace by promising that the Morea should pay an annual tribute of 100,000 *hyperperi*, and that the walls of the Hexamilion should be left in ruins. Even this sharp lesson did not teach the princelings of the Morea wisdom; scarcely had the Turks withdrawn, than Theodore attacked Centurione and made him his prisoner.[2]

A more attractive and more energetic figure now appeared

[1] Phrantzês, 109, 110, 138; Chalkokondýles, 241; Sanudo, in *op. cit.*, xxii., 916, 943; Sáthas, i., 52-60, 64, 65, 68-70, 74, 75, 92, 104, 106-8, 115-19; iii., 185, 207, 449-50; Jorga, iv., 582, *n.* 3, 607, 615; Gerland, 171, 211-16; *Chronicon Breve*, 518; *Journal of Hellen. Studies*, xxvii., 300-1.

[2] Chalkokondýles, 238-9; *Chronicon Breve*, 518; Phrantzês, 117; Sanudo, in *op. cit.*, xxii., 970, 975, 978; Buchon, *Nouvelles Recherches*, II., i., 272; Sáthas, iii., 268; Jorga, v., 136, 145.

among the Greeks of the Morea—that of the man who was destined to die on the walls of Constantinople, the last Emperor Constantine. The Despot Theodore was subject to fits of depression; he did not get on with his Italian wife; and then the intrigues of Mistrâ seemed to him vanity, and the life of a monk preferable to that of a ruler. In one of these moods, he announced his intention of entering a monastery, and of handing over the government to his active brother, Constantine. The Emperor John VI., who now sat on the throne, agreed to this plan, and, in 1427, set out for the Morea with his brother Constantine and the faithful Phrantzês, in order to install the new Despot. But, when the imperial party arrived, they found that Theodore, like several other sovereigns in love with the charms of private life in theory, but in practice wedded to the delights of power, had changed his mind. The local magnates, he told them, would not permit the abdication of their beloved Despot. It therefore became necessary to provide Constantine, who had hitherto been content with some towns on the Black Sea, with an appanage somewhere else, and this led to the reconquest of the Frankish Morea.

The plan of campaign was skilfully laid. First, an attack was made upon Glarentza and the other possessions of Carlo Tocco in the peninsula. Some of these surrendered, and a politic marriage between Constantine and Carlo's niece Theodora (daughter of Leonardo of Zante) brought him Glarentza as her dowry. The historian Phrantzês took over the town on his behalf, and Constantine fixed his residence in the historic castle of Chloumoûtsi, which Geoffroy II. de Villehardouin had built two centuries before. Patras was his next objective, and the papacy now realised too late its folly in compelling the Venetians to restore it to the much weaker government of the Church. On the death of the late archbishop, Venice had in vain appealed to Martin V. to appoint one of her citizens to the vacant see; but the pope thought that he would better secure the town against Greek attacks by sending as archbishop, Pandulph Malatesta of Pesaro, whose sister Cleopa was wife of the Despot Theodore. But this connection failed to save the place. The first attack of the three brothers was, indeed, only partially successful, for their quarrels prevented united action, and the citizens were thus able to purchase a brief respite by an annual tribute of 500 pieces of gold to Constantine. In 1429, however, Constantine and the faithful Phrantzês made a second attempt to obtain possession of Patras. The offer of some of the local priests and leading citizens to hand over the town was considered unpractical, so, on Palm Sunday, the Greek forces, with myrtle boughs in their hands, began the attack. On the Saturday before Easter, a sudden sortie was made from the Jews' gate ; it was repulsed, but as Phrantzês and his master ventured too near the walls, Constantine's horse was shot under him by a well-aimed arrow. The future emperor fell to the ground, and would have been killed by the enemy, had it not been for the devotion of his companion, who kept them at bay until Constantine had had time to disentangle himself from his charger and escape on foot. Phrantzês and his favourite steed were both wounded, and the historian was taken prisoner and chained in a disused granary, where for forty days he had ample leisure for meditating, amidst ants, weevils, and mice, on the rewards of loyalty. When his name-day arrived, the pious Phrantzês prayed to his patron saint St George to deliver him ; his prayer was heard, his chains were removed, and he was able to correspond with Constantine. At his suggestion, a conference was held between the besiegers and the besieged, at which the latter consented, on condition that Constantine would retire to Glarentza, to surrender the town, if their archbishop, who had gone to seek aid of the pope, did not return from Italy by the end of May. Phrantzês was released more dead than alive, but his master's expressions of gratitude and a present of fine clothes and money consoled him for his forty days' imprisonment. Constantine had, however, almost immediate occasion to demand from him a further proof of devotion. Scarcely had he reached Glarentza than he received a haughty message from the sultan, forbidding him to besiege Patras, as it paid tribute to the Turks. Constantine was a man of action, and he at once resolved to take the town first and then make diplomatic excuses afterwards. Accordingly, as soon as the time agreed upon had expired and there was no sign of the archbishop, he returned to Patras, and there in the church of its patron saint, St Andrew, received the keys of the town. His entry was a veritable holiday; flowers rained on him from the windows; it was roses, roses all the way, when, for the first time for 225 years a Greek conqueror trod the streets of the archiepiscopal city. Only the old feudal castle and the archbishop's palace near it held out, in the hope that Pandulph would return. Next day the citizens swore fealty to the Despot in the church of St Nicholas, an historic building unhappily destroyed by an explosion less than a century ago;[1] and, at their request, Phrantzês, their late prisoner, was appointed their governor.

Before, however, he took up his duties, he was sent to explain away as best he could to the sultan the annexation of Patras. At Lepanto, on the way, he fell in with two Turkish envoys and the Archbishop of Patras, who had heard of the loss of his see, and had put in with one of the Catalan galleys furnished him by the pope, at the Venetian station on the north coast of the gulf. Phrantzês and the archbishop tried hard to pump one another without success; but in the evening the artful historian, at the imminent risk of getting drunk himself, as he sadly confesses, made the Turks intoxicated and then opened their letters. Arrived at the sultan's court, he received peremptory orders to bid his master restore Patras to its rightful lord; but Phrantzês knew his Turks; he made friends with the sultan's Prime Minister, pacified Turakhan on his way back, and was able to assure his sovereign that the Turks would not molest him. Pandulph in despair offered Patras to Venice; but, as it was no longer his to offer, the cautious republic declined. Still the fine old castle held out, till, in May 1430, hunger forced the garrison to yield. The Catalan galleys of the pope proved useless to Pandulph, for, though they captured Glarentza, their captain at once sold it back to Constantine. The latter ordered the destruction of that famous town, from fear lest it should be occupied again by an enemy. The churches and monasteries, where once the High Court of Achaia had met, were dismantled, the monks, the *archons*, and the poor became homeless exiles, and from the ruin of Glarentza a Greek poet traced the beginning of the future

[1] Gerland, 117, *n.* 1.

emperor's ill-fortune. Meanwhile, however, the goddess smiled on him. The last Latin Archbishop of Patras, baffled in his hopes, retired to his native Pesaro, where his remains lie; his name is, however, still preserved in two inscriptions, which now serve as doorposts of the inner entrance of the castle which his men had so manfully defended. But to the Greeks the capture of Patras will be ever associated with the name of the last Emperor of Constantinople, whose exploits in the Morea well deserved the encomium composed by a Byzantine rhetorician of that day.[1]

Nearly all the Peloponnese was now in the hands of the three brothers, Theodore, Constantine, and Thomas. Besides Glarentza and Patras, which he had won for himself, Constantine had received from Theodore the old barony of Vostitza, which adjoined that of Patras, and in the far south of the peninsula, on the west of Taygetos, the strong castle of Leuktron, the creation of the last Villehardouin prince, together with a large strip of Maina. Theodore had also transferred to him the administration of the great possessions of the Melissenós family during the minority of the present representative, and these included the richest part of Messenia, with such places as Androusa, Kalamata, Nesi, Ithome, and the Lakonian Mantineia, the ancient Abia, where another brother, Andrónikos, had taken up his abode after he had sold Salonika to the Venetians. Meanwhile, Thomas had not been idle. He had obtained Kalavryta from his brother Theodore, and at the time of the surrender of Patras was besieging Centurione in the castle of Chalandritza. In September 1429, the Prince of Achaia was reduced to make terms with his assailant; he gave his elder daughter Catarina in marriage to Thomas; and, passing over his bastard son, conferred upon her the remains of the Frankish principality as her dowry, reserving for himself nothing except the family barony of Kyparissia and the title of prince. The wedding took place at Mistrâ in January 1430, and Thomas received

[1] Bœck, *Corpus Inscriptionum Græcarum*, No. 8776; Δελτίον, i., 523; Phrantzês, 122-39, 144-58; Θρῆνος τῆς Κωνσταντινουπόλεως, ll. 52-62; Chalkokondýles, 206, 239-42; Sáthas, i., 160-2, 191; *Chronicon Ariminense*, *apud* Muratori, xv., 939; Dokianós *apud* Hopf, *Chroniques*, 251.

from his imperial brother the title of Despot. Two years later the last Prince of Achaia died, when Thomas, fearing the intrigues of his widow, kept her in prison for the rest of her life. Centurione's son, Giovanni Asan, seems to have sought refuge in Venetian territory, where we shall find him a quarter of a century later. At the same time, the Greeks annexed the ancient fiefs of the Teutonic Knights at Mostenitsa; and to complete the symmetry of the peninsula, an exchange was effected between Thomas and Constantine, the former, as the heir of Centurione, taking Glarentza, and the latter Kalavryta. Thus, in 1432, after the lapse of two hundred and twenty-seven years, the whole peninsula was Greek, save where the Venetian flag waved over the colonies of Modon and Coron, with their seven dependent castles, and the territory of Nauplia and Argos. Never since the old Byzantine days had there been such uniformity.

The rule of the Franks in Achaia had latterly been simply an element of discord; but in its earliest stage it had wrought no little good to the land and people. A fair-minded modern Greek historian has contended that his countrymen owe the warlike spirit, which they showed after the Turkish Conquest down to the time when they at last regained their freedom, to the example of the splendid Frankish chivalry, which had taught Greek fingers to war and Greek hands to fight. Certainly, there is a great contrast between the feeble resistance offered by the Peloponnesians to the Franks in the thirteenth century and their constant insurrections against the Turks. Only, we must not forget in this comparison the fact that the Albanians—that nation of fighters—were not represented in the Morea at the time when the Franks arrived. But there can be no doubt that during a large portion of the reigns of the Villehardouin princes, the peninsula experienced all the advantages of strong and vigorous personal rule. Trade flourished, the alien Church was kept in its place, the Greeks had at least as much liberty as their own emperors and their own local tyrants had allowed them. We may, indeed, distinguish three periods in the history of Frankish Achaia. The golden age terminated with the cession of the four castles in 1262, which led to the reintroduction of Byzantine influence and the consequent duel between Hellenism and the Franks, of which the Morea was the theatre for the next one hundred and seventy years. The second period lasted down to the year 1311, the fatal date of the battle of the Kephissós, which profoundly affected the fortunes of all Frankish Greece. During this half century there were short periods of peace and plenty, as in the reign of Florent of Hainault, but the country had become depopulated by the long wars of its soldierly Prince William, and after his death without a male heir, the Angevin connection, with its evils of absenteeism and dynastic intrigue, sorely tried this fairest portion of "new France." The barons, always the peers of the prince, aimed at being the masters of the Angevin bailies, and would tolerate no interference with their right to liberty, which was often merely a euphemism for liberty to riot. Meanwhile, foreigners—Flemings, Neapolitans, and Savoyards—ignorant of the manners and language of the country, took the place of the old French families, which by some inscrutable law of population had become extinct, or else survived in the female line alone after two or three generations. During the third period these evils were aggravated, and others were added. The disputed succession to the throne more than once afflicted the land with the curse of civil war, while the Byzantine governor first ceased to be a merely annual official, and then became an important member of the imperial family. Mistrâ waxed as Constantinople waned, until at last, two centuries too late, the Morea once again became a Greek state. We have compared the Frankish Conquest of Achaia with the Norman Conquest of England; but the similarity unfortunately ceased with the conquest. The Morea had her Wars of the Roses before the two races, the conquerors and the conquered, had been thoroughly amalgamated; she lacked the long line of able sovereigns, and above all, the sturdy burghers, who contributed so much to the stability of our national institutions, while in Greece the Roman Church, except in Corfù and the Cyclades, remained to the last that of a small minority, whereas in England it was that of the people even before the conquest. Where the two nationalities were united in marriage, the half-castes who were the offspring of these unions, usually sided with the Greeks, manned the imperial ships, fought in the imperial armies, and held office in the imperial administration. Now and again self-interest led a *Gasmule* to identify himself with the Franks; but in most cases the legal maxim held good—*partus sequitur matrem.*

For us, however, after the lapse of nearly five centuries, the brilliant French chivalry of Achaia still lingers on in many a ruined keep, in many a mouldering castle, in the Norman arch of Andravida, in the great fortresses of Karytaina and Chloumoûtsi, in the splendid isolation of Passavâ. Elis still preserves in the names of her prosperous little towns, and in the trappings of her horses, the memory of the bright days when gentle knights pricked over the plain that leads to Olympia or rested for shelter from the noon-day sun beneath the oaks of Manolada; when many a pleasaunce studded the smiling country round Vlisiri; when monks from far-off Assisi chanted their vespers in the Minorite church of rich Glarentza.

At the same time when the Frankish rule in Achaia ended, the Turks made further conquests in Northern Greece. In 1423, Andrónikos Palaiológos, who governed Salonika, afflicted by elephantiasis and harassed by the Turks, had sold that great city, the second of the empire, to Venice, which was also anxious to accept the offer of the Greek captain of Lamia to transfer the port of Stylida and the village of Avlaki, half-way between Stylida and Lamia, to the strongest of the Christian powers interested in the Levant, as the best means of saving the latter place, temporarily regained from the sultan.[1] The republic thought sufficiently highly of her new purchase to bestow the title of duke upon the chief official whom she sent there, and to pay an annual tribute for it to Murâd II. But her occupation of Salonika was very short and by no means beneficial either to Venice or to her colony in Eubœa. Lamia and its territory soon fell again into Turkish hands, and the unhappy Eubœans complained that they were more harried than ever by those invaders, who carried off so many captives that the island was in

[1] Sáthas, i., 140, 149; iii., 250, where "Zeffali Zitoni" is a corruption of κεφαλὴ Ζητουνίου.

danger of becoming depopulated. This so greatly alarmed the Home Government, that the bailie received instructions to inspect and repair, by means of the forced labour of the serfs, all the fortresses of Eubœa, and to restrict the sale of wine to those strongholds so as to induce people to inhabit them. In consideration of the pressing danger, his salary was increased, but all other expenses in the island were reduced, and the Duke of the Archipelago was reminded that it had always been the custom of his predecessors to light signal fires, warning the colonists of Eubœa when a Turkish fleet was approaching. In 1430, Salonika fell finally before the Ottoman arms, and then the Venetians of Eubœa feared that their turn would come. More than 5000 of the islanders were in captivity, and stores and 200 men were sorely needed to defend the eleven castles of the island. Venice hastened to save her colony by concluding peace with Murâd II.[1]

On the opposite side of Greece, however, the Latins were not so fortunate as to escape. In 1429, Carlo I. Tocco had ended in his capital of Joannina his long and successful reign. "In military and administrative ability he was," as Chalkokondýles says, "inferior to none of his contemporaries," and under him the dynasty of the palatine Counts of Cephalonia had reached its zenith. Having no legitimate heirs, he left the island of Sta. Mavra and the strong fort of Vonitza on the Ambrakian Gulf to his widow, the able and masculine Duchess Francesca, divided Akarnania among his five bastards, and bequeathed the rest of his continental and insular dominions to his nephew, Carlo II. Such an arrangement was sure to lead to civil war; the Albanians hated the Italian rule, which had weighed heavily upon them; the bastards, after the fashion of this degraded period, appealed with their approval to the sultan, and Memnon, the ablest and most unscrupulous of the five, was particularly importunate in imploring Murâd II. to restore him to his heritage. Carlo II. in vain invoked the good offices of his brother-in-law, Constantine, and the latter despatched his handy man, Phrantzês, whose decision all the parties swore to accept.

[1] Sáthas, iii., 306, 349, 372, 388-91; Thomas and Predelli, *Diplomatarium*, ii., 345.

Phrantzês met, however, with his usual ill-fortune. Off the small islands near Sta. Mavra, once the abode of the Homeric Taphians, "lovers of the oar," a Catalan galley, in the pay of the Duchess Francesca, captured the historian and sold him and his suite at Glarentza for a ransom such as no archæologist would now fetch. Meanwhile, the fall of Salonika had left the sultan free to respond to the bastard's appeal. Two previous attempts to enter Epiros had been checked by the natives in the difficult passes of Pindos. But a Turkish army under Sinan Pasha now appeared under the walls of Joannina, preceded by a letter from the sultan, calling upon the inhabitants to surrender, promising not to deprive them of their city, and bidding them decide ere it was too late for repentance. Sinan Pasha reiterated the orders and promises of his master, who had sent him, he told them, "to take the duke's lands and castles," and threatened to treat any place which resisted as he had treated Salonika. "The Franks," he pointed out to the Greeks and Albanians, "are merely seeking to ruin you, as they ruined the Thessalonians; whereas I will allow the metropolitan to have all his ecclesiastical rights, and the *archons* to keep all their fiefs." These arguments convinced the inhabitants that further resistance was useless; Carlo II. was allowed to retain the rest of Epiros, Akarnania, and his islands, on payment of an annual tribute; the *archons* purchased the continuance of their privileges by the usual capitation-tax. On 9th October 1430, Joannina surrendered, and has ever since belonged to the Turkish Empire. A small Turkish colony settled there, and soon a new version of the Rape of the Sabine women provided them with Christian wives. Carlo did not feel secure against the invasion of his reduced dominions, especially as his cousin, Memnon, continued to haunt the sultan's court and grovel before his patron "like a respectful servant." We accordingly find him asking Venice for protection, as otherwise he "will be forced to come to some arrangement with the Genoese, the Catalans, or the Turks." A similar appeal was made by the dowager duchess, from whose island the Turks carried off 500 souls. The Venetians were anxious that the Ionian islands, which carried on a large trade with their possessions, should not be lost; they therefore urged the duchess to defend her own, as "so masculine a lady" well could, and told Carlo that they would treat him as a Venetian citizen, and elect him a noble of the Grand Council. This did not, however, prevent Memnon and his brother Ercole from conspiring with his continental subjects against him, until he purchased peace by allowing them to retain what they had occupied. The "Despot," or "Lord of Arta," as he styled himself, thenceforward remained for many years on good terms with both them and the sultan.[1]

Meanwhile, under the statesmanlike rule of Antonio Acciajuoli, the duchy of Athens had been spared the vicissitudes of the other Latin states in the Levant. While all around him principalities and powers were shaken to their foundations; while that ancient warden of the northern march of Athens, the marquisate of Boudonitza, was swept away for ever; while Turkish armies invaded the Morea, and annexed the Albanian capital to the sultan's empire; while the principality of Achaia disappeared from the map in the throes of a tardy Greek revival; the statesmanlike ruler of Athens skilfully guided the policy of his duchy. At times even his experienced diplomacy failed to avert the horrors of a Turkish raid; we saw how the Turks had ravaged his land in 1416, how Mohammed I. had threatened to chastise him for injuring some Venetian subjects, how, in 1423, Turakhan had forced him, as a vassal of the sultan, to join in the invasion of the Morea. The historian Doúkas[2] even represents him as helping the Turks against Salonika. But, as a rule, the dreaded Mussulmans spared this half-Oriental, who was a past-master in the art of managing the sultan's ministers. From the former rulers of Athens, the Catalans and the Venetians, he had nothing to fear. Once, indeed, he received news that Alfonso V. of Aragon and Sicily, who never forgot to sign himself "Duke of Athens

[1] Chalkokondýles, 236-8; Phrantzês, 154, 155, 157; Spandugino (ed. 1551), 25-8; *Epirotica*, 242-6, 254; Jorga, vi., 75, 82; Miklosich und Müller, i., 191; iii., 282; Sáthas, iii., 416; Buchon, *Nouvelles Recherches*, II., i., 350-2; Brocquière, *Voyage d'outremer* in *Mémoires de l'Institut*, v., 587.

[2] P. 197, where he is called ἀρχηγὸς Θηβῶν. He styles himself either "Duca" (Buchon, *Nouvelles Recherches*, II., i., 273) or more usually αὐθέντης Ἀθηνῶν Θηβῶν καὶ τῶν ἑξῆς (*ibid.*, 289, 290, 296).

and Neopatras," had invested a Catalan named Thomas Beraldo with the Athenian duchy, and intended to put him in possession of it. So great was Antonio's alarm that he asked the Venetian Government to order its bailie in Negroponte to protect him. But Venice reassured him with the shrewd remark that the Catalans usually made much ado about nothing,[1] and nothing further was heard about the matter. On her part the republic was friendly to the man who had supplanted her, when once she had come to an understanding with him. She twice gave Antonio permission, in case of danger, to send the valuable Acciajuoli stud—for, like his father, he was a good judge of horse-flesh—to the island of Eubœa; and she ordered her bailie to "observe the ancient commercial treaties between the duchy and the island, which he would find in writing in the chancery of Negroponte." When he complained that a number of Albanian families had emigrated from his duchy to Eubœa, they were sent back with all the more readiness because they were useless. At his request the Eubœan peasants were at last allowed to cultivate the five-mile territory which the Venetians still held as a strategic position on the mainland opposite the island. But when he asked permission to construct two galleys, he received a flat negative, even though he offered to join the republic against the Turks. Nor was he more fortunate in his protest against the arrangement by which Venice secured to herself the future possession of Ægina. That classic island had passed, as we saw, about the end of the fourteenth century, from the family of Fadrique to that of Caopena. But, in 1425, Alioto Caopena, at that time its ruler, placed himself under the protection of the republic in order to escape the danger of a Turkish raid. The island must then have been fruitful, for one of the conditions under which Venice accorded him her protection was that he should supply corn for her colonies. While he retained his independence, he agreed to hoist the banner of the Evangelist, whenever desired, and it was stipulated that, if his family became extinct, Ægina should become Venetian. Against this treaty Antonio of Athens, one of whose adopted daughters had married the future lord of Ægina, Antonello

[1] Jorge, v., 122.

Caopena, in vain protested. To the Florentine Duke of Athens, Ægina, as a Venetian colony, might well seem, as it had seemed to Aristotle, the "eyesore of the Piræus." But a quarter of a century later, a Venetian colony it was.[1]

With another Italian commonwealth, his family's old home of Florence, Antonio maintained the closest relations. In 1422, a Florentine ambassador arrived in Athens with instructions to confer the freedom of his city upon the Athenian ruler, and to inform him that Florence, having now become a maritime power (by the destruction of Pisa and the purchase of Leghorn), intended to embark in the Levant trade, and asked from him as favourable treatment as the Venetians and Genoese merchants received in his dominions. The ambassador was directed to make a similar request of Carlo I. Tocco, on the ground that his mother, Maddalena Buondelmonti, was a Florentine. Antonio gladly made all Florentine ships free of his harbours, and halved the usual customs dues in favour of all Florentine merchants throughout his dominions. Any rights which he might thereafter grant to Venetians, Catalans, or Genoese, were to be theirs also.[2]

Visitors from Tuscany, when they landed at Riva d'Ostia on the Gulf of Corinth, must, indeed, have felt themselves in the land of a friendly prince, though the court on the Akropolis presented a curious mixture of the Greek and the Florentine elements. Half a Greek himself, Antonio chose both his wives from that race—the first the beautiful daughter of a Greek priest, to whom he had lost his heart in the mazes of a wedding-dance at Thebes, and whom, though she had a husband already, he made his mistress, and subsequently his wife; the second was Maria Melissené, a daughter of the great Messenian family, who brought him Astros, Leonidi, and other places in Kynouria, the land of the Tzákones, as her dowry. As he had no children, he adopted the two daughters of Protimo, a nobleman of Eubœa, whom he married to Niccolò Giorgio, the titular marquis

[1] Sáthas, i., 178, 179; iii., 6, 225, 281, 287, 319, 420; Chalkokondýles, 215-16. The best account of the mediæval history of Ægina is in Baron Sardagna's version of Hopf's *Karystos*, pp. 66-72.

[2] Buchon, *Nouvelles Recherches*, II., i., 287-90.

of Boudonitza and baron of Karystos, and to Antonello Caopena of Ægina. The latter was a great favourite at the Athenian court, as he was useful to his father-in-law.[1] The succession to the duchy being thus open, members of the Acciajuoli clan, sons of Antonio's uncle Donato, whom King Ladislaus of Naples had appointed Nerio's heir in 1394, and who was now dead, came to Athens to pay their respects to their prosperous relative. Of these cousins, Franco settled in Greece at the castle of Sykaminon, near Oropos, which had belonged to the Knights of St John, and acted as Antonio's ambassador during negotiations with Venice; Nerio twice visited the Athenian court, and was long the guest of his cousin, the Duchess of Leucadia; Antonio was made bishop of her other island of Cephalonia, and Giovanni archbishop of Thebes, where another Acciajuoli had been his predecessor. Towards the close of Antonio's long reign a second generation of this family had grown up to manhood in Greece. Foremost among these younger cousins were Franco's sons, Nerio and Antonio, both destined to be dukes of Athens; their sister, Laudamia, Lady of Sykaminon, and her husband, a member of the great Florentine family of Pitti; two other grandchildren of Donato, Niccolò Machiavelli and Angelo Acciajuoli, both spent some time in Greece, where the latter, a devoted adherent of Cosimo de' Medici, was banished when his chief was exiled by Albizzi from Florence. A branch of the Medici, as we saw, was already established at Athens. Thus, with such names as Acciajuoli, Medici, Pitti, and Machiavelli at the Athenian court, Attica had, indeed, become a Florentine colony.[2]

Antonio and his Florentine relatives must have led a merry life in their delectable duchy. In the family correspondence we find allusions to hawking and partridge shooting, and the ducal stable provided good mounts for the young Italians, who scoured the plains of Attica and Bœotia in quest of game. The cultured Florentines were delighted with Athens and the Akropolis. "You have never seen," wrote Niccolò Machiavelli to one of his cousins, "a

[1] Chalkokondýles, *loc. cit.*; Phrantzês, 159.

[2] Buchon, *op. cit.*, 269-86, 294; Predelli, *Commemoriali*, iii., 309; Mai, *Spicilegium Romanum*, i., 460; Sáthas, III., 100.

fairer land nor yet a fairer fortress than this"—a sentiment which recalls the rhapsody of Pedro IV. over the castle of Athens. It was there, in the venerable Propylæa, that Antonio fixed his ducal residence. In the closing years of the Catalan rule there had been, as we saw, a palace and an adjoining chapel of St Bartholomew on the Akropolis; but under both the Burgundians and the Catalans, Thebes had been the usual residence of the head of the state. The Acciajuoli, however, made Athens their capital and the Propylæa their home. No great alterations were required to convert the classic work of Mnesiklês into a Florentine palace. All that the Acciajuoli seem to have done was to cut the two vestibules in two, so as to make four rooms, to fill up the spaces between the pillars by walls (which were seen by Dodwell, Leake, and other travellers of the early part of the last century, and which were only removed in 1835), and to add a second story, of which the joist-sockets are still visible, to both that building and to the Pinakothéke, which either then, or in Turkish times, was crowned with battlements.[1] It has been conjectured from a passage in an anonymous account of the antiquities of Athens,[2] composed probably in 1458, that the ducal chancery, whence the Acciajuoli issued their Greek documents, was in this latter edifice. Here, too, was the chapel of St Bartholomew, to which Pedro IV. alluded, and in which Nerio I. signed a treaty with the envoys of Amadeo of Savoy. The vaulted arches of this chapel and the central column which supported them were still to be seen in 1837. To the Florentine dukes, too, is usually ascribed the construction of the square "Frankish tower," which was pulled down in 1874 by an act of vandalism unworthy of any people imbued with a sense of the continuity of history. This tower, 85 feet high, 28½ feet long by 25½ feet broad, and 5¾ feet thick at the base, was built of large stones from the quarries of Pentelikon

[1] Burnouf, *La ville et l'Acropole d'Athènes*, 80. *Cf.* his plan of the Akropolis under the Franks, pl. vi.; Stuart and Revett, *Antiquities of Athens*, II., ch. v., pl. 1.

[2] Τὰ *θέατρα καὶ διδασκαλεῖα τῶν* 'Αθηνῶν, *apud* Laborde, *Athènes aux xv., xvi., et xvii. Siècles*, i., 20; Wachsmuth, *Die Stadt Athen*, i., 738. But Professor Lámpros, in a note to his translation of Gregorovius (ii., 359, *n.* 2), thinks that καγκελλαρία means a portico.

and the Piræus, all taken by the mediæval architects from the classical buildings of the Akropolis. High up, on the north side of the tower, was a little square turret projecting from the wall, and on the top beacon-fires could be kindled which would be visible from Akrocorinth. Placed opposite the graceful temple of Nike Apteros, it commanded the sea-coast and the plain and mountains of Attica, save where the cathedral of Our Lady shut out a part of Hymettos. A wooden staircase, fastened into the walls, such as one sees in some of the Venetian *campanili*, enabled the Florentine watchman to ascend to the top, and sweep land and sea for Turkish horsemen or rakish-looking galleys. Such towers may still be seen near Moulki in Bœotia and in the island of Eubœa. In addition to these erections on the Akropolis, some archæologists have regarded the Acciajuoli as the authors of the marble steps which lead up to the Propylæa, more usually ascribed to the Romans,[1] and others have believed that it was they who first surrounded the famous Klepsydra with bastions, so as to provide the Akropolis with water;[2] in that case, Odysseus was merely following their example when he fortified the well in 1822.

Nor did they limit their activity as builders to the castle rock alone. To the Florentine, if not to the Burgundian period, is now assigned the so-called wall of Valerian,[3] of which the remains are still visible in an Athenian backyard, with sheds and hutches under it. The anonymous writer above mentioned alludes to "the splendid abode of the polemarch"—a name supposed to be his way of expressing the title of the Frankish governor of the town—in the Stoa of Hadrian, where frescoes, still quite fresh, are even now visible. The same author says that the dukes possessed a beautiful villa at the spring of Kallirrhoe, where they used to bathe, and that close by they were wont to pray in a church

[1] Burnouf, 75, 76, 85, 87; Leake, *Topography of Athens*, i., 73; Finlay, iv., 170 (who thought the tower earlier than the Acciajuoli); Buchon, *La Grèce Continentale*, 67, 127 (who considered it to have been the ducal prison).

[2] Pittakys, *L'Ancienne Athènes*, 155; Curtius in *Archäologische Zeitung* for 1854, p. 203.

[3] Wachsmuth, I., 724. Both Cyriacus of Ancona and the anonymous visitor of 1466 speak of the "new walls" of Athens.

which had in pagan times been "a temple of Hera," or, more correctly, of Triptolemos. In this church, called St Mary's on the Rock, the Marquis de Nointel had mass recited when he visited Athens in 1674. His companion, Cornelio Magni, also alludes in his "Description of Athens," to a church on the bridge over the Ilissos, then "all in ruins but still displaying the traces of the Acciajuoli arms," while he found the lion rampant of Brescia, the emblem of the ducal family, which visitors to the famous Certosa know so well, still guarding—*auspicium melioris ævi*—the entrance of the Turkish bazaar.[1] A few years later, a chapel called Hágios Fránkos is mentioned by the Venetian writer, Coronelli,[2] as "having been built by the Acciajuoli"; on the other hand, the statement of the Florentine biographer, Ubaldini,[3] that Antonio erected the lion of the Piræus, which gave the harbour its mediæval name of Porto Leone, is incorrect, for we saw that it was already so called a century earlier. But enough has been said to justify both his remark and that of the Athenian historian, Chalkokondýles, that Antonio's long pacific and economic administration enabled him to beautify the city.

Of literary culture there are some few traces in Florentine Athens. It was in Antonio's reign that Athens gave birth to her last historian, Laónikos Chalkokondýles, the Herodotos of mediæval Greece, who told the story of the new Persian invasion, and to his brother Demétrios, who did so much to diffuse Greek learning in Italy. Another of Antonio's subjects, Antónios the Logothete, is known to scholars as a copyist of manuscripts at Siena; and it is obvious that the two Italian courts of Athens and Joannina were regarded as places where there was an opening for professional men, for we find a young Italian writing from Arezzo to Nerio, in order to obtain, through the latter's influence with Carlo I. Tocco and Antonio, a chair of jurisprudence, logic, natural or moral philosophy, or medicine, at either of their courts—he did not mind which.[4] Even a Greekling of Juvenal's time

[1] Laborde, i., 18, 19; Stuart (I., ch. ii., pl. 1) gives a picture of the Παναγία στὴν Πέτρα, which was destroyed by Hadji Ali in 1778; Magni, *Relazione*, 14, 49, and *Viaggi*, 466, 491; it is marked in his plan.

[2] *Tavola*, 36.

[3] *Origine della famiglia degli Acciajuoli*, 176.

[4] Montfaucon, *Palæographia Græca*, 76, 79, 94; Buchon, *Nouvelles Recherches*, II., i., 276.

could have scarcely offered to teach such a variety of subjects. Unfortunately, we are not told whether the versatile candidate's modest offer was accepted.

Thus, for a long period, the Athenian duchy enjoyed peace and prosperity, broken only by the pestilence which visited it in 1423, driving Antonio to seek safety at Megara.[1] Yet, if we may judge from the complaints which he made about the emigration of a few hundred Albanians from his dominions, it would seem that the land had become depopulated, and that there was a lack of men to till the soil. A similar phenomenon is observable in the Greece of to-day, where even the most fertile districts are being rapidly denuded of their male inhabitants. But the modern Greeks have not the twin institutions on which mediæval society rested—serfdom and slavery. Both continued to exist under the Acciajuoli. Antonio granted, and his successor confirmed, the Frankish privileges to a Greek, from which we learn that those who did not enjoy the franchise were still liable to furnish baskets, new wine, oil, and other articles; while the Duchess Francesca of Leucadia made a present of a young female slave to her cousin Nerio, with full power to sell or dispose of her as he pleased. Yet there continued to be a growth of Greek influence at Athens, as was natural under a dynasty which was now half hellenised. The notary and chancellor of the city continued to be a Greek; the public documents were drawn up in the Pinakothéke in that language; and a Greek *archon* was now destined to play a leading part in Athenian politics.[2]

When, in 1435, after a long reign of thirty-two years, the longest of any Athenian ruler till the time of King George, Antonio was one summer morning found dead in his bed, the victim of an apoplectic stroke, two parties, an Italian and a Greek, arose to dispute the succession. The Italian candidate, young Nerio, eldest son of Franco Acciajuoli, baron of Sykaminon, whom the late duke had adopted as his heir, occupied the city. But the Duchess Maria Melissené and her kinsman, Chalkokondýles, father of the historian and the leading man of Athens, held the castle. Well aware, how-

[1] Buchon, *Nouvelles Recherches*, II., i., 272, 279, 280.

[2] *Ibid.*, 285, 290, 296-7.

ever, that the sultan was the real master of the situation the Greek *archon* set out for the Turkish court with a large sum of money to obtain Murâd II.'s consent to this act of usurpation. The sultan scornfully rejected the 30,000 gold pieces which the Athenian *archon* offered him, cast him into prison, and demanded the surrender of the duchy, at the same time sending an army under the redoubtable Turakhan to occupy Thebes. Chalkokondýles managed to escape to Constantinople, whence he took ship for the Morea; but on the way, falling in with some vessels belonging to the Frankish party at Athens, he was seized and sent back as a prisoner to the sultan, who pardoned him. This futile attempt was not, however, the only effort of the Greeks to make themselves masters of Athens. Even before the death of the duke, Constantine Palaiológos had sent his trusty emissary Phrantzês on a mission to the Athenian court, and the duchess now requested him to return with a large force of soldiers and a formal document setting out the agreement made between her and his master. This arrangement was, that Constantine should take the duchy of Athens, and that she should receive in exchange lands in Lakonia near her own family possessions. This diplomatic scheme, which would have united nearly all Greece under the Palaiológoi, was frustrated, as the other had been. Turakhan had already invested, and soon took, Thebes, while the Frankish party at Athens, which included the other leading Greeks hostile to Chalkokondýles, had at once seized the opportunity of his absence to decoy the duchess out of the Akropolis, and to proclaim Nerio. Peace was secured by the marriage of the new duke with the dowager duchess, and by the banishment of the family of Chalkokondýles. Venice, which might have interposed as the late duke's suzerain, instructed her bailie at Negroponte, whither many Athenian serfs had fled, not to interfere with the occupation of Athens by either of the two parties, or even by the Turks. At the same time, he was to suggest diplomatically to Nerio that he should offer to recognise the Venetian suzerainty.[1] The only interest which

[1] Chalkokondýles, 320-2; Phrantzês, 158-60; Sáthas, i., 199; iii., 427 (which proves, by the phrase, *ex matrimonio secuto*, that Maria actually married Nerio).

the republic had in endeavouring to recover the city was to prevent its falling into dangerous hands. As for the Turks, although Phrantzês betook himself to Turakhan's headquarters at Thebes, and was assured that the Turkish commander would have granted his request, had he known a little earlier, they did not molest the new duke. The Turkish policy has always been to govern by dividing the Christian races of the Near East; and the Sultan was well content to allow a Florentine princeling to retain the phantom of power so long as he paid his tribute with regularity.

The weak and effeminate Nerio II. was exactly suited for the part of a Turkish puppet. But, like many feeble rulers, the "Lord of Athens and Thebes," as he officially styled himself, seems to have made himself unpopular by his arrogance, and a few years after his accession he was deprived of his throne by an intrigue of his brother, Antonio II. He then retired to Florence, the home of his family, where he had property, to play the part of a prince in exile, if exile it could be called. There he must have been living at the time of the famous council, an echo of whose decisions we hear in distant Athens, where a Greek priest, of rather more learning than most of his cloth, wrote to the œcumenical patriarch on the proper form of public prayer for the pope. A bailie—so we learn from one of his letters[1]—was then administering the duchy pending Nerio's return, for Antonio had died in 1441, his infant son, Franco, was absent at the Turkish court, and his subjects had recalled their former lord to the Akropolis, preferring the rule of a grown-up man, however feeble, to that of a child, who was enjoying so dubious an education. Presenting his Florentine property to Tommaso Pitti, his man of business, to whom he owed money, Nerio returned to his palace on the Akropolis, where we shall presently find him entertaining the first archæologist who had visited Athens for centuries.

[1] Chalkokondýles, 322; Buchon, *Nouvelles Recherches*, II., i., 298-302; Ubaldini, *op. cit.*, 177; Gaddi, *Elogiographus*, 90-4; and *Corollarium Poeticum*, 33; Νέος Ἑλληνομνήμων, i., 43-56.

CHAPTER XIII

THE TURKISH CONQUEST (1441-1460)

THE Frankish principality of Achaia being now extinct, it might have been expected that common-sense and the common danger from the Turks would have convinced the Greeks that union and disinterested endeavours were needed to consolidate and defend against the Turks what had been so slowly and laboriously won back from the Latins. But that *nota inter fratres inimicitia*, which Tacitus had remarked as a characteristic of human nature in his time, was intensified in the case of the four surviving brothers of the Emperor John VI.—Theodore, Constantine, Thomas and Demétrios. The Peloponnese, as we saw, was now divided amongst the three former, while the fourth had not yet obtained an appanage in the peninsula. Unhappily, the prospect of the imperial succession was an apple of discord among them, and the Byzantine court became a hot-bed of fraternal intrigues, which were naturally continued in the residences of the three Despots in the Morea. The emperor, who wished Constantine to succeed him, was desirous of keeping the trio in Greece; while Constantine and Thomas wanted to have the peninsula to themselves, and the former did not hesitate to seek the consent of the sultan to this scheme through the mediation of the ever-useful Phrantzês, his unfailing emissary in all dubious, or diplomatic, transactions. Civil war accordingly broke out between Theodore and his two brothers, which it required all the efforts of two imperial embassies to assuage. It was agreed that Constantine should go to live in Constantinople, leaving the Morea to Theodore and Thomas, and there he remained as regent for the emperor, while the latter, accompanied by

Demétrios and the œcumenical patriarch, set out to achieve the union of the Eastern and Western churches at the councils of Ferrara and Florence. On his journey to Italy, the emperor landed at Kenchreai, traversed Greece on horseback, preached the blessings of brotherly love to the two Despots, and ordered the philosopher Gemistós to accompany him to the council. Then he took ship at the Venetian harbour of Navarino. The insecurity of the Greek seas at that period may be judged from the fact that the emperor and his ship-load of learned theologians ran imminent risk of being captured by a Catalan corsair who was lurking behind the island of Gaidaronisi, near Sunium.[1] Their sufferings and labour were in vain; and on their return journey, wherever they stopped in Greece, at Corfù, Modon, and Chalkis, the Greek clergy indignantly remonstrated with them on the concessions which they had made. The Greeks of Corfù, who had no bishop of their own, bitterly remarked that the Latin archbishop would now press his claim to ordain their priests; those of Chalkis, where the returning theologians took part in a service in a Catholic church, declared that henceforth they could no longer exclude the Latin clergy from performing mass in the Greek churches.

During the six years between 1437 and 1443, during which Constantine was mainly absent at Constantinople, the Morea enjoyed the blessing of having practically no history. We find Thomas administering justice and confirming sales of property at Patras, and Theodore ratifying the ancient privileges of the inhabitants of Monemvasia. All the Despot's subjects, whether freemen or serfs, were permitted to enter or leave that important city without let or hindrance, except only the dangerous denizens of Tzakonia and Vatika, whose character had not altered in two hundred years. The citizens, their beasts, and their ships, were exempt from forced labour; and, at their special request, the Despot confirmed the local custom, by which all the property of a Monemvasiote who died without relatives was devoted to the repair of the castle; while, if he had only distant relatives, one-third of his estate was reserved for that purpose. This

[1] Phrantzês, 161-3; Doúkas, 214; Jorga, vi., 389, 393; Sguorópoulos, *Vera Historia Unionis*, § 4, chs. iv., vi.; § 11, chs. vi.-viii.

system of death-duties (τὸ ἀβιωτίκιον, as it was called) was continued by Theodore's successor, Demétrios, by whom Monemvasia was described as "one of the most useful cities under my rule." The prosperity of Patras, on the other hand, must have suffered by the transference of the Venetian trade to Lepanto, previously only a cattle-market, which, in consequence, began to pay its expenses.[1] To the eye, however, of a literary observer, the Humanist, Francescus Philelphus,[2] there was "nothing in the Peloponnese worthy of praise except George Gemistós," or Pléthon, as he now called himself, who had returned from Florence, and was holding a judicial post at Mistrâ. "The Palaiológoi princes themselves," added the critic, "are oppressed by poverty, and even their own subjects ridicule and plunder them. The language is depraved, the customs are more barbarous than the barbarians." Yet it is to these barbarians that we owe those beautiful Byzantine churches, the Pantanassa and the Peribleptos, at Mistrâ.

In 1443 a fresh distribution of the Moreot Governments took place. In view of the succession to the throne of all the Cæsars, both Constantine and Theodore were anxious to obtain the city of Selymbria, on the Sea of Marmara, which was close to the capital. Finally, an arrangement was made by which Theodore received Selymbria, where he died of the plague five years later, and ceded his province in the Morea to Constantine. An inscription in the chapel of Our Lady of Brontochion, at Mistrâ, still commemorates Theodore's temporary aspirations for the peace of the cloister, and a feeble monody has been preserved in remembrance of this feeble ruler.[3]

Thus, Constantine now held the larger portion of the peninsula, including Patras, Corinth, and Mistrâ, in each of which he was represented by a governor, in the case of Mistrâ the faithful Phrantzês, whose jurisdiction included not only the capital, but the village of Jewish Trype, at the mouth of the Langada Gorge, Sklavochorio (the ancient Amyklai), and several other villages in the neighbourhood. Phrantzês

[1] Miklosich und Müller, iii., 258; v., 170-4; Gerland, 218, 222; Sáthas, iii., 413, 458.

[2] *Epistolæ*, bk. v., fol. lvii.

[3] *Byz. Zeitschrift*, ix., 641.

received on his appointment strict injunctions to abolish a number of offices and to establish one-man rule at Mistrâ, while a single minister in attendance (called καθολικὸς μεσάζων) was attached to the person of the sovereign wherever he went. Constantine's first act after his arrival was to rebuild the Isthmian wall, which Turakhan had destroyed a second time during a raid into the Peloponnese in 1431; the next was to renew, this time by force of arms, the attempt which he had made by diplomacy nine years before, to recover the Athenian duchy for himself and the cause of Hellenism, which he personified. The moment seemed singularly favourable, for a weak man held sway at Athens, and the Turks, hard pressed by the Hungarians and Poles, whom Pope Eugenius IV. had marshalled against them, defied by Skanderbeg in Albania, defeated by John Hunyady at Nish, threatened by the appearance of a Venetian fleet in the Ægean, were unable to protect their Athenian vassal. He, therefore, cheerfully responded to the appeal of the papal envoys, marched into Bœotia early in 1444, occupied Thebes, ravaged the country to the gates of Livadia and as far north as Lamia and Agrapha, and compelled Nerio II. to pledge himself to pay tribute. The Wallachs of Pindos now descended upon the Turks of the great Thessalian plaïn, and received from the victorious Constantine a governor whose seat was at Phanari; one of the Albanian clans in Phthiotis, to which the sultan had granted autonomy, joined his standard; 300 Burgundian auxiliaries arrived to swell his forces, and he was so flushed with success that he did not scruple to arouse the wrath of Venice by seizing the port of Vitrinitza, on the Gulf of Corinth, which had been ceded by the Turks to the governor of Lepanto. Thus, for a moment, almost all the Morea and the greater part of continental Greece acknowledged the sway or the suzerainty of a Greek prince. Never, since the time of the Frankish Conquest, had the Hellenic cause been so successful. The news spread to Italy; Cardinal Bessarion hastened to congratulate Constantine on the fortification of the isthmus, and urged him to transfer his capital from Mistrâ to Corinth. At the same time, he bade him become the Lycurgus of the new Sparta—lightening taxation, checking extravagance in dress and servants by strict sumptuary laws, preventing the export of corn, building a navy from the wood of the Peloponnesian forests, and searching for iron in the folds of Taygetos. Above all, the cardinal advised him to send a few young Spartans to learn letters and arts in Italy and so qualify as literary and technical instructors of their fellow-countrymen. While the patriot churchman dreamed of a revival of ancient Hellas by the genius of Constantine, the court of Naples heard that he had actually occupied Athens; and Alfonso V. of Aragon, who had never forgotten that he was still titular duke of Athens and Neopatras, wrote at once demanding the restitution of the two duchies to himself, and sent the Marquis of Gerace to receive them from the conqueror's hands. But, before the letter was despatched, the fate of Greece had been decided on the shores of the Black Sea. The perjury of the Christians, who had broken their solemn oaths to keep peace with the sultan, had been punished by their crushing defeat at Varna in November 1444. Venice made peace to save her colonies; the rest of Greece lay at the mercy of the victor.[1]

Nerio II. was the first sufferer for his compulsory alliance with the Greek Despot. Omar, the son of Turakhan, governor of Thessaly, ravaged Bœotia and Attica, as a punishment for his weakness. Nerio now saw that his only hope lay in obsequiousness to the Turks, whose star was again in the ascendant, and sent an envoy to the sultan, expressing his willingness to pay the same tribute as before. On these conditions he purchased safety from the Turks, but at the same time called down upon himself the vengeance of Constantine, who marched against Athens, and endeavoured to take it. Nerio now called upon the sultan to protect him; his appeal was supported by Turakhan, whose Thessalian province had suffered from Constantine's recent successes; and Murâd, true to the traditional Turkish policy of support-

[1] Chalkokondýles, 283, 305, 306, 318, 319 (where for Φανδρίου I read Φαναρίου); Phrantzês, 157, 193-6, 200-1; *Chronicon Breve*, 518, 519; Doúkas, 223; Magno *apud* Hopf, *Chroniques*, 195; Sáthas, i., 208; Jorga, viii., 6; Alfonso V.'s letter in *Archivio Storico per le Prov. Napoletane*, xxvii., 430-1; Cyriacus of Ancona in Fabricius, *Biblioteca Latina mediæ et infimæ Ætatis*, vi., addenda, p. 12; Νέος Ἑλληνομνήμων, III., 15-27; iv., 23.

ing the weaker of two rival Christian nationalities, accordingly sent an ultimatum to Constantine, demanding the evacuation of the Turkish territory which he had occupied. As Constantine refused, the sultan resolved to chastise the bold Greek who dared to disobey him.

In 1446 all Murâd's preparations were made, and he set out from Macedonia to invade Greece, with a commissariat so splendidly organised as to call forth the enthusiastic praise of the Athenian historian. North of the isthmus he met with no opposition, for Constantine, with his brother Thomas and the whole force of the Peloponnese, amounting to 60,000 men, had retired behind the newly restored walls of the Hexamilion. At Thebes an Athenian contingent joined the sultan under Nerio, who had thus the petty satisfaction of assisting his present against his late master. After encamping for a few days at a place called Mingiai to prepare his cannon and fascines, Murâd drew up his forces in front of the Isthmian wall. A spy, who was despatched from the Greek headquarters, came back with an alarming report of the strength of the Turkish army, which stretched from sea to sea, and implored the Despot to send an embassy to the sultan with all speed, and so avert, if possible, the evils which his rashness had brought upon the Peloponnese. Constantine ordered the spy to be thrown into prison for his frankness, and rejected his advice. He had, indeed, sent Chalkokondýles, father of the historian, as an envoy to the sultan, but his instructions were to claim the isthmus and the Turkish possessions recently captured in continental Greece—a claim which, as the historian admits, was excessive, and so irritated Murâd that he threw the ambassador into prison. When, however, the sultan came to examine the imposing walls of the Hexamilion, he remonstrated with old Turakhan for having advised him to attack such apparently impregnable lines so late in the season—for it was now 27th November. But the veteran, who knew his Greeks and had already twice taken the Isthmian wall, maintained that its defenders would not resist an attack, but would flee at the news of his arrival at the isthmus. In this expectation the sultan waited several days before ordering the attack; but, as Constantine showed no sign of surrender, he ordered his cannon to open fire on the wall. On the evening of the fourth day, the fires in front of the Turkish tents, and the strains of the martial hymns which rose from the Turkish camp, warned the Greeks that, according to their custom, the besiegers would begin the assault on the next day but one. On the following evening the sutlers dragged the siege engines into position, and at dawn next day, 10th December, the band sounded the signal for the attack. While some endeavoured to undermine the wall, and others placed scaling ladders against it, the Turkish artillery prevented the defenders from exposing themselves over the battlements. The honours of the day rested with a young Servian janissary, who was the first to scale the wall right in the centre under the eyes of the sultan—a sad but characteristic example of the manner in which the Turks in all ages have used the Slavs against the Greeks and the Greeks against the Slavs. Others followed him, the Greeks were driven down from that point of the battlements, a panic seized them, and they fled in disorder, followed by the troops near them. The two Despots in vain endeavoured to rally their panic-stricken men; then, finding their efforts useless, and suspecting the Albanians of treachery, they fled also; while the Turkish soldiers poured over the fatal battlement, through a breach in the wall, and finally through the gates. Some fell upon the ample plunder which they found in the Greek camp, others slew or captured the fleeing Greeks; the whole isthmus, laments a Greek poet, was strewn "with gold-winged arrows, jewelled swords, and the heads and hands and bodies of men." The sultan stained his laurels by two hideous acts of cruelty. Three hundred Greeks, who had fled to Mount Oneion, above Kenchreai, he induced to surrender, and then butchered in cold blood; six hundred of his soldiers' captives he purchased, in order to sacrifice them as an acceptable offering to the Manes of his father.

The two Despots retreated into the far south of the peninsula, for they knew that the citadel of Akrocorinth had neither provisions nor munitions sufficient to resist a long siege; they had staked and lost their all at the isthmus, and they had to face a revolt headed by a Greek *archon*, who proclaimed Centurione's bastard son, Giovanni Asan, as legitimate Prince of Achaia. If hard pressed by the Turks, they were resolved to quit the country. Meanwhile, leaving old Turakhan, who knew the Peloponnese well, to pursue them, the sultan marched along the south shore of the Corinthian Gulf with such rapidity that, on the same day on which he captured the isthmus, he surprised Basilicata, the ancient Sikyon, whose entire male population had gone to defend the Hexamilion, with the exception of a few who had taken refuge with the women and children in the Akropolis. This small garrison soon surrendered; the sultan set fire to the town, and then continued his march to the wealthy city of Vostitza, which met with a like fate at his hands. When he reached Patras, he found that all the inhabitants, except some 4000 who had occupied the castle and the palace, had fled across the gulf to the Venetian colony of Lepanto, which had secured immunity by continuing to pay him tribute. The occupants of the palace surrendered, and were enslaved; but the people in the splendid old castle, even though a breach was made in the walls, hurled blazing resin and pitch on to the heads of the janissaries, and so maintained their position. The sultan had to content himself with burning and destroying the town, whose wealth had made it the "purse" of Constantine, and with ravaging the country as far as Glarentza. Meanwhile, Turakhan had returned from his raid; and, as the season was far advanced and the Despots were willing to make peace on his terms, and pay him a tribute, Murâd withdrew to Thebes, leaving the Hexamilion a heap of ruins, and taking more than 60,000 captives with him. On his approach, the terrified Thebans abandoned their homes, only to fall into the clutches of the Turkish army at the isthmus. The news of the fall of the Hexamilion had been at once followed by the submission of all Constantine's recent conquests in continental Greece; and the Bey of Salona swore on the Koran that no harm should befall the revolted people of Loidoriki and Galaxidi, if they would return to their allegiance.[1]

On the death of his brother, the Emperor John, in 1448,

[1] Chalkokondýles, 320, 322, 341-50, 408; Doúkas, 223; *Chronicon Breve*, 519, 520; Phrantzês, 202, 203; Magno and Ἄνθος *apud* Hopf, *Chroniques*, 194, 267; Θρῆνος τῆς Κωνσταντινουπόλεως, ll. 67-90; Χρονικὸν τοῦ

Constantine succeeded, in spite of the intrigues of his younger brother Demétrios, to the imperial title. It is a picturesque fact, which the Greeks should not forget when they raise their contemplated monument to him, that the last emperor of Constantinople was crowned at Mistrâ, where his first wife, Theodora Tocco, like Cleopa Malatesta, the wife of his brother Theodore, lay buried in the Zoodótou monastery. After the coronation on 6th January 1449, the new emperor sailed on board a Catalan ship for the imperial capital, where he met his two surviving brothers. Thomas he confirmed in the dignity of a Despot, upon Demétrios he bestowed his previous government, with the exception of Patras, which was added to that of Thomas. Before the two Despots left for the Morea, they solemnly swore, in the presence of their aged mother, their brother the emperor, and all the leading members of the Senate, to live in unity and brotherly love.[1]

Shortly after the accession of Constantine to the imperial throne, his great adversary, Murâd II., rounded off his Greek conquests by annexing practically all that remained of the former Despotat of Epiros. For many years Carlo II. Tocco had remained at peace with his cousins and with the Turks. When the antiquary, Cyriacus of Ancona, visited the "King of the Epirotes," as he styles him, in 1435 and 1436, the latter gave him a letter of introduction, which ensured him a warm welcome at a marriage festivity in the family of the Despot's cousin Turnus. In 1444, however, when the fortunes of the sultan seemed to be waning, and his brother-in-law, the Despot Constantine, made his brilliant but short-lived conquests in nothern Greece, Carlo also threw off the Turkish suzerainty. In this bold step he was advised and assisted by his father-in-law, Giovanni, the above-mentioned Marquis of Gerace, a member of the great Sicilian family of Ventimiglia. Landing with a small body of cavalry, the marquis routed with great loss a large army of Turks which was besieging his son-in-law. On his return home, however, shortly afterwards, Carlo was captured by treachery or a Turkish stratagem, and reduced to his former

Γαλαξειδίου, 209, 210; Jorga, viii., 33, 34; Thomas, *Diplomatarium*, ii., 368; Cyriacus of Ancona *apud* Tozzetti, *Relazioni di Alcuni Viaggi*, v., 442.

[1] Phrantzês, 204-6.

state of vassalage. Unfortunately, he died on 30th September 1448, before his eldest son, Leonardo III., had reached manhood, so that there was no one strong enough to protect his continental dominions. The four governors, whom the late Despot had appointed guardians of his children, thought that the only way to save their threatened heritage was to invoke the protection of Venice; Zante hoisted the banner of St Mark; the captain of Sta. Mavra offered his island to the republic; while others of the islanders sent to Alfonso V. of Naples, mindful of the connection between the ducal family and the Neapolitan crown. But while Venice was negotiating, the sultan acted. On 24th March 1449, the Turks took Arta, and annexed all the continental dominions of the house of Tocco, except the three points of Vonitza, Varnazza, and Angelokastro, which thenceforth, under the name of Karl-ili, or "Charles's country," formed a part of the Turkish Empire, still preserving in its Turkish name the memory of Carlo Tocco.

Venice was now more than ever anxious to prevent the loss of the island county of Cephalonia or its occupation by another Christian power, such as the King of Naples. She really wanted absolute possession of the central Ionian group, such as she had long enjoyed in Corfù, and she actually ordered Vettore Cappello, her admiral, afterwards famous as the captor of Athens, and whose effigy still adorns the portal of Sant' Aponal at Venice, to take steps for the annexation of Zante. Pensions, it was thought, would reconcile any of the chief inhabitants who now enjoyed offices—and such were numerous under the Tocchi—to the change of ruler. But it soon became evident that neither the "Despot of Arta," as Leonardo III. still styled himself, nor his brothers wished to surrender their heritage. Another proposal, that Venice should occupy the islands during his minority, was rejected, and ultimately the negotiations terminated by the republic, with the advice of "the Councils of Cephalonia and Zante," taking him, his brothers, and successors under her protection. Henceforth Leonardo III. was included in Venetian treaties, though the kings of Naples continued to regard him as their vassal.[1]

[1] Æneas Sylvius, *Europa*, 406; Magno *apud* Hopf, *Chroniques*, 196;

While the Italian rule in continental Greece was thus drawing to a close, an antiquary, for the first time since the Conquest, visited the country. This mediæval Pausanias, Cyriacus of Ancona, has left us, together with numerous ancient inscriptions and not a few sketches of classical monuments, some brief notes on the distinguished personages whom he met in the course of his extended travels. A merchant by profession, like Schliemann, whom in some respects he resembled, he taught himself Greek, and was consumed by a burning enthusiasm for the memorials of classic Hellas. As his notes often contain no indication of the year in which they were written, an exact chronology of his Greek journeyings is extremely difficult ; but he seems to have first visited the Levant in 1412, and we find him reading daily the Greek, Latin, and mediæval historians to Mohammed II. during, or immediately after, the siege of Constantinople,[1] that is to say, in 1452 or 1453. His preserved fragments refer, however, mainly to three Greek journeys, the first of which extended from the end of 1435 to about the middle of 1436, the second took place in 1437, and the third and longest lasted from 1443 to 1449, when the Genoese Government describes him, in a letter of recommendation, as "now returning west," after "having visited Epiros, Ætolia, Akarnania, the Morea, Achaia, Athens, Phokis, Bœotia, Crete, and the Cyclades."[2]

The worthy antiquary, on the first of these journeys, arrived in Greek waters towards the end of December 1435. The plague then raging at Corfù prevented him from touching at that island, where, during one of his previous voyages, he had acquired some Greek manuscripts.[3] He accordingly spent Christmas at the Corfiote dependency of Butrinto, on the opposite coast, and thence proceeded to Arta, where Carlo II. Tocco received him most hospitably. "The King of the Epirotes," as Cyriacus calls him, gave the traveller every

Navagero *apud* Muratori, xxiii., 1113 ; *Epirotica*, 254 ; Sansovino, *Dell' Origine dei Turchi*, 154 ; Jorga, vii., 424 ; viii., 45, 54, 55 ; Predelli, *Commemoriali*, v., 37, 204 ; *The Chronicles of Rabbi Joseph*, 283.

[1] Zorzi Dolfin, *Cronaca dell' Assedio di Constantinopoli*, *apud* De Rossi, *Inscriptiones Christianæ Urbis Romæ*, II., i., 374.

[2] Jorga, viii., 55.

[3] *Kyriaci Anconitani Itinerarium* (ed. Mehus), 29, 30.

facility for seeing the sights of his dominions. His majesty's secretary, Giorgio Ragnarolo of Pesaro, assisted his fellow-countryman; and, thus supported, the antiquary was able to visit Rogus, where he found "the head of the Virgin's mother, the body of St Luke, and the foot of St John Chrysostom"; the ruins of the old Roman colony of Nikopolis, founded to commemorate the victory of Actium; and the remains of Dodona. He then travelled southward through Akarnania and Ætolia, stopping at Vonitza, so important in the mediæval history of the country, gazing across at Ithaka from the coast of the mainland, and finally arriving at the ancient Kalydon, whence he set out for Patras. Before, however, he had left "the Royal city of Akarnania," he had prudently submitted, in a letter still preserved,[1] the manuscript account of his journey in Epiros to the "King of the Epirotes," in case any of his observations should fail to please the royal eye! From Patras he crossed over to the Venetian colony of Lepanto, and ere long we find him at Kirrha, the ancient port of Delphi, then called "Ancona" (from the "elbow" of land on which it stood), or "the Five Saints" (from some church of that name). At Salona he mentions the church of the Transfiguration, but he has little or no regard for what is post-classical. He scornfully remarks, in the narrow spirit of the archæologist for whom contemporary Greece has no interest, that Delphi "is called Castri by the foolish Greek populace, which is quite ignorant where it was"; but he inspected with keen interest the ruined walls, the remains of the round temple of Apollo, the amphitheatre, and the hippodrome, wandered among the broken statues which covered the ground, and admired the large and richly ornamented tombs. Thence he proceeded to Livadia by way of the noble Byzantine monastery of Hósios Loukâs, where the monks showed him a very ancient collection of sacred books. At Livadia he noted a large temple of Hera in the ruined city; and, after a digression to Orchomenos, arrived at Thebes, which, though no longer the capital of the duchy, was still the occasional residence of the Duke of Athens, for our traveller specially mentions the "royal court" there. A brief visit to Chalkis and Eretria concluded this part of his

[1] Published in *Studi e documenti di Storia e di Diritto*, xv., 337.

tour, and on 7th April 1436 he reached Athens, where he stayed for fifteen days, the guest of a certain Antonelli Balduini. On this occasion he does not seem to have been presented to Nerio II., nor does he tell us much about the contemporary state of the city at the beginning of the new reign. His days are entirely devoted to visiting the antiquities, to making sketches, and to copying the inscriptions which he finds on the monuments. Many of them relate to the Emperor Hadrian—the great philhellene, who, as the inscription on his arch reminded the traveller, founded a new Athens, which began where that of Theseus ended. He noted down the emperor's celebrated edict at the gate of Athena Archegetis regulating the oil-trade; he transcribed the inscription commemorating the completion by Antoninus Pius of Hadrian's aqueduct,[1] which, like the Capuan notary forty years earlier, he was informed by the local *ciceroni* to have been "Aristotle's Study"; he, too, alludes to the statue of the Gorgon on the south of the Akropolis; he, too, describes the temple of Olympian Zeus, of which he counted one more column than his predecessor had done, as the "house," or "palace of Hadrian." Similarly, he mistook the choragic monument of Lysikrates for the marble seats of a theatre. The perfect "temple of Mars," as he calls the Theseion, "with its thirty columns," and "the fifty-eight columns and noble sculptures on the pediments, frieze, and metopes of the Parthenon" naturally aroused his admiration. But, unlike the pious notary, he tells us nothing of its condition as the cathedral of Athens, beyond two casual allusions to the recent restoration of a pillar, and to an inscribed ancient marble urn inside, which may perhaps have served either as a font or for holy water. He alludes, however, to the church of St Dionysios under the Areopagos. His general impression of Athens is striking. "Everywhere," he writes, "I saw vast walls decayed with age, and inside and outside the city incredible marble buildings, houses, and temples, all kinds of sculptures executed with marvellous skill, and huge columns—but all these things a mass of great ruins."

[1] Tozzetti, *Relazioni di Alcuni Viaggi fatti in Toscana* (2nd ed.), v., 414-16.

Down at the Piræus the antiquary could trace the huge foundations of the ancient walls, part of two round towers was still standing, and the entrance of the harbour was guarded by the huge marble lion, now in front of the arsenal at Venice. Phaleron, or Porto Vecchio, he ignores.

Of contemporary Athens he gives us the barest glimpses. He tells us that it possessed a "north" and a "west gate," as well as "the gate of the new city," and that of the castle—the same number which the Jesuit Father Simon enumerates more than two centuries later; that it had "new walls"—a statement, corroborated by that of another traveller thirty years afterwards, which might indicate the so-called wall of Valerian as the work of the Acciajuoli; and that the Theseion lay outside the town. Of the inhabitants he says nothing; as living Greeks, they had for him no interest; was he not an archæologist?

After a day at Eleusis, where, like the Capuan, he noted the ruins of an aqueduct, Cyriacus journeyed by way of Megara to the isthmus, still strewn with the walls erected by Manuel II. and destroyed by the Turks five and thirteen years earlier. Rapidly visiting Corinth and the amphitheatre and brick baths of Sikyon, he made an excursion up to Kalavryta, where he met a kindred soul, one George Cantacuzene, a scholar learned in Greek literature who possessed a large library, from which he lent the wandering archæologist an Herodotos and several other books—an interesting proof of the existence of culture in the Morea at this period. On the way down the valley, the traveller stopped to see the image of the Virgin, attributed to St Luke and still preserved in the monastery of Megaspelaion, and thence returned by way of Patras, at the beginning of May, to the dominions of his friend, the "King of the Epirotes," who gave him the above-mentioned letter of introduction to his cousin Turnus. The Tocchi were interested in literary matters; Orlando, the brother of Turnus, is known to have employed a Greek priest to copy manuscripts of Origen and Chrysostom for him, and Turnus heartily welcomed Cyriacus at his daughter's wedding at Orionatium in the middle of May. Two days later his guest crossed over to Corfù, saw part of the old walls and the remains of the ancient city of Palaiopolis, and then returned with his sketches and a goodly collection of inscriptions to his native land.[1]

But the love of travel did not allow him much repose. In July of the following year he is sketching the walls of Kythera and admiring those of Epidauros Limera, near Monemvasia. In August he is at Zante, "the island of Epiros" as he calls it, in allusion to its union with the continental dominions of the Tocchi, and it was probably there that he received a letter of introduction to Carlo II.'s ambitious cousin, the bastard Memnon, who seems at this time to have been governor of Charpigny in the Morea, the old feudal castle of Hugues de Lille. He gives us a pretty picture of his meeting with Memnon "at the clear springs of the Alpheios," where the bastard was surrounded by his huntsmen, some bearing a straight-horned stag, others a huge she-bear, and others again a haul of fish fresh from the river. Memnon not only gave him a warm welcome, but presented him with the skin of the bear, and escorted him to Mistrâ, where he arrived a week later. There he visited Theodore II., then the reigning Despot, examined the statues, the columns, and the marble stage of the gymnasia on the site of classic Sparta, and speculated on the origin of the name of its mediæval successor, which he believes to have been due to the cheese-like shape of the hill of Mistrâ.[2] Of the beautiful Byzantine churches of the Moreot capital he is as silently disdainful as any classical archæologist of our own day. Yet this very period was the golden age of architecture at Mistrâ. The Florentine arcades (due, no doubt, to the influence of the Despots' Italian wives) and the Peribleptos church belong to the first half of the fifteenth century; only a few years before Cyriacus's visit, Joánnes Frangópoulos, the marshal of the Morea, had presented the charming Pantanassa as "a small thank-offering" to the Virgin.[3]

In 1443 Cyriacus returned once more to Greece with letters for the two Despots of the Morea, and, apparently in February 1444, he revisited Athens.[4] An extremely interesting letter,

[1] *Epigrammata reperta per Illyricum*, iii.-v., ix.-xix., xxviii., xxxi., xxxii., xxxv.; *Itinerarium*, 62, 64-70; Montfaucon, *Palæographia*, 79, 80.

[2] *Epigrammata*, xxxvii., xl.; *Itinerarium*, 72.

[3] *Bull. Corr. Hell.*, xxiii., 134-7.

[4] The year of this visit to Athens must have been 1444, and not 1447,

which he wrote from Chios on 29th March of that year, describes his second impressions of the place. After mentioning the Tower of the Winds, the "Temple of Æolus," as he calls it, he goes on to say how, accompanied by the duke's cousin and namesake, he went to pay his respects to "Nerio Acciajuoli of Florence, then Prince of Athens," whom he "found on the Akropolis, the lofty castle of the city." Again, however, the archæological overpowered the human interest; of the living ruler he tells us nothing; his attention, as he says, was rather attracted by the Propylæa, in which was the ducal residence. He describes in enthusiastic language the splendours of the architecture—the marvellous portico of four polished marble columns, with ten marble slabs above, and the court itself, where two rows of six huge columns three feet in diameter supported the marble ceiling, and where the walls on either side, composed of polished pieces of marble all of equal size, were approached by a single large and splendid entrance. After sketching the building, he hastened on with even greater eagerness to reinspect the Parthenon; again he enumerates its fifty-eight columns, twelve on each front and seventeen on each side; he alludes to the battle of the Centaurs and the Lapithæ sculptured on the metopes, to the sculptures of the pediments, and to the frieze of the cella, which he supposed to represent the victories of Athens in the time of Periklês. During the next five years he continued his journey in the Levant; he had an audience of Murâd II. at Adrianople before the disastrous battle of Varna, and describes a hunting party near Constantinople, at which the Emperor John VI. and the ex-Despot Theodore II., who had then left the Morea, were present. At the Dardanelles he spoke with some of the Greek captives, whom Murâd II. had carried off from the Peloponnese. In his repeated visits to the islands of the Archipelago, he received assistance from the Latin rulers, themselves in some cases men of culture, interested in the

as assumed by Gregorovius and others, because the letter from Chios is dated: *Kyriaceo die*, *iv. Kal. Ap.* Now, 29th March fell on a Sunday in 1444, and we know from another letter of Cyriacus to the Emperor John VI., written before June 1444, that he left Chalkis for Chios on *v. Kal. Mart.* of that year (Fabricius, *loc. cit.*), Mommsen is wrong in making *Kyriaceo die* mean Wednesday, which will not fit other dates.

classic treasures of their diminutive dominions. Thus, Crusino I. Sommaripa of Paros took a pride in showing him some marble statues, which he had had excavated, and allowed him to send a marble head and leg to his friend, Andriolo Giustiniani-Banca of Chios, a connoisseur of art and a writer of Italian verse, to whom many of his letters are addressed.[1] So deeply was Cyriacus moved by Crusino's culture and kindness, that he too burst out into an Italian poem, of which happily only one line has been published. Dorino I. Gattilusio of Lesbos aided him in his investigation of that island, nor was Francesco Nani, the Venetian governor of Tenos and Mykonos, any more backward in paying him attention, escorting him to Delos and back in his state galley with fourteen rowers.[2] In another Venetian island, that of Crete, Cyriacus attended a shooting match, held at Canea, in which the archers were dressed as heroes of different nations and the winner received a eulogy from the pen of the archæologist. Early in 1448, he revisited Mistrâ; on the road, the site of Sparta with its ruins inspired him with an Italian sonnet, in which he contrasted the classic city of heroes with the mediæval capital over which Constantine Palaiológos then ruled. At least, however, the Spartans of the fifteenth century had not lost their physique, for a tall youth of immense strength carried the worthy antiquary across a stream under his arm, and then broke an iron rod to show his power. The poem, too, though not flattering to Mistrâ, was translated into Greek, and this rendering, still extant, has been attributed[3] to Gemistós Pléthon. There is nothing improbable in this meeting of the archæologist and the philosopher, who may have already made one another's acquaintance at Florence, for in 1450, just before his death, the latter composed a complimentary letter to the Despot Demétrios on his reconciliation with his brother,[4] and wrote a funeral oration on the death of their mother, the dowager empress. While at Mistrâ, Cyriacus seems to have been the guest of Constantine, for we find him writing, on 4th

[1] Hopf, *Les Giustiniani*, 149.

[2] *Bulletino dell' Istituto* for 1861, pp. 183, 187.

[3] By Professor Lámpros, Παρνασσός, vii.

[4] Still in MS. *Cf.* Migne, *Patrologia Græca*, clx., 802.

February 1448, at the latter's court, an account of the Roman calendar in Greek, which he dedicated to the Despot.[1] From Mistrâ he made excursions to Coron, where the Venetian officials, aided by a Cretan scholar, one of the Calergi, showed him the antiquities, and to Vitylo, where Constantine's governor, John Palaiológos, entertained him and showed him the ancient materials, of which the castle was constructed. The last stage of this long journey was another visit to Epiros, in October 1448. Cyriacus found his old host, Carlo II., just dead, and Leonardo III. reigning in his stead. Here the antiquary revisited his old haunts of Dodona and Rogus, and composed three Italian sonnets for the repose of Carlo's soul.[2] The results of his long archæological investigations he embodied in three large volumes, of which only fragments have come down to us. His original drawing of the west front of the Parthenon[3] and those of other Athenian monuments have been preserved in a manuscript formerly belonging to the Duke of Hamilton, but now in the Berlin Museum, and are the earliest extant reproductions of those buildings. Sketches of the same front of the Parthenon, of the Tower of the Winds, of the Monument of Philópappos, showing the king in a four-horse chariot, of "a round temple of Apollo at Athens" (perhaps that of Augustus), and of the noble lion of "the port of Athens" facing the two round towers, may be seen in the Barberini manuscript of 1465, now at the Vatican,[4] which contains the diagrams of San Gallo. As that eminent architect took the explanatory text almost *verbatim* from Cyriacus, he has been assumed to have copied the latter's drawings, and this is all the more probable because the sketch of "the temple of Apollo" was drawn and given to

[1] Printed in *Revue des Études grecques* for 1896, p. 228. The year is fixed because it was written on Sunday, 4th February, and because we know that Bollani, whom Cyriacus mentions as Castellan of Coron, had been elected in April 1447.

[2] Colucci, *Delle Antichità Picene*, xv., 110; Tozzetti, v., 66-9, 422-3, 437, 439-42, 449, 460.

[3] Reproduced in *Jahrbuch der K. Preussischen Kunstsammlungen*, iv., 81.

[4] No. 4424, folios 28, 29, 32; Laborde (i., 32) has reproduced folio 28. *Cf.* De Rossi, *op. cit.*, II., i., 363.

its owner, as is expressly stated, by "a Greek in Ancona," the residence of the antiquary. Copies of the traveller's sketches of the Cyclades exist in a manuscript at Munich,[1] whereas we have not a trace of his contemporary, Francesco Squarcione of Padua, who is said to have "travelled all over Greece."[2]

The fall of Greek rule in the Morea was now fast approaching, hastened by the fraternal quarrels of the two Despots, Thomas and Demétrios. Neither their solemn oaths at Constantinople, nor the imminent Turkish peril prevailed over their mutual selfishness and ambition. The only point on which they were unanimous was their desire to extend their dominions at the cost of the Venetian colonies, especially Nauplia and Argos, which complained loudly to the mother-country for protection, and demanded a copy of the privileges granted it after its capture by the Turks in 1397.[3] Thomas managed to obtain a start of his brother, and, reaching the Morea first, seduced the subjects of Demétrios from their allegiance. The latter, destitute of national feeling, sent his brother-in-law, Matthew Asan, to call in the aid of the Turks, and thus compelled Thomas to come to terms and submit their dispute to the arbitration of their brother, the emperor. As the two Despots, however, still continued to quarrel, Mohammed II. ordered old Turakhan to assist Demétrios, and at the same time, in view of the future conquest of the peninsula, to destroy all that remained of the Hexamilion. Thomas then made peace with his brother, surrendering to him Kalamata in exchange for the Arkadian district of Skortá, which he had taken. So great was the joy of the old philosopher and patriot Pléthon, that he took up his pen for the last time to congratulate Demétrios on this reconciliation. Then he died, full of years, fortunate in escaping the disgrace of seeing the country a Turkish province. "Sparta," cried his friend Hierónymos Charitónymos in his funeral oration, "is no longer famous ; we lovers of learning shall soon be scattered to the ends of the world"—a prophecy only too true, and too soon fulfilled.[4]

[1] Cod. Lat., 716 ; *cf. Bulletino dell' Istituto*, *loc. cit.*

[2] Scardeonius, *De Antiquit. Urbis Patavii*, 370.

[3] Sáthas, Μνημεῖα, i., 212-13 ; Thomas and Predelli, *Diplomatarium*, ii., 381 ; Jorga, viii., 69, 70, 79, 95.

[4] Migne, *Patrologia Græca*, clx., 807.

In October 1452, when Mohammed II. was ready for the attack on Constantinople, he sent Turakhan back to the Morea to keep the two Despots busy there with their own defence, so that they might not send assistance to their imperial brother. Accompanied by his two sons, Achmet and Omar (the future conqueror of Athens), and at the head of the European army of the Turkish Empire, the old commander again arrived at the isthmus. The walls had been repaired, and the resistance offered by their defenders was such that the capture of the rampart cost many lives. When the Greeks fled, Turakhan marched through the centre of the peninsula by way of Tegea and Mantineia as far as Ithome and the Messenian Gulf, plundering and taking prisoners as he went. Neokastron, presumably the "Chastel-Neuf" mentioned in the feudal list of 1364, fell before him; but Siderokastron in Arkadia justified its name and defied all his efforts. Nor was that the only Turkish reverse. As Achmet was retiring through the Pass of Dervenaki, between Mycenæ and Corinth, that death-trap of Turkish armies, where 370 years later another Ottoman force met a similar fate, he was surprised by Matthew Asan, brother-in-law of Demétrios, defeated and taken as a captive to Mistrâ. The victory was the last ray of dawn before the darkness of centuries. King Alfonso of Naples, who had long been intriguing with Demétrios, sent his congratulations, and talked of invading Turkey; but the Turks had achieved their object, and the besieged of Constantinople applied in vain to the Despots for corn and soldiers.[1]

The news that the city was taken, and the emperor slain, fell like a thunderbolt upon his wretched brothers, who naturally expected that they would be the next victims. Their first impulse, and that of their leading *archons*, was to rush down to the nearest port and take ship for Italy—an act of cowardice which had the worst effect upon their already discontented Albanian subjects. But as, one after another, important Greeks arrived from Constantinople—men like Cardinal Isidore, who had played a prominent

[1] Chalkokondýles, 374, 375, 378, 381, 382; Phrantzês, 235, 236; Kritóboulos, i., 19; *Archivio Storico per le Prov. Napoletane*, xxvii., 612, 823.

part at the Council of Florence and had been taken prisoner by the Turks, and Phrantzês, whose loyalty to his master had exposed him to a similar fate—the two Despots plucked up sufficient courage to remain, and sent envoys to the sultan's court at Adrianople, in the hope that the conqueror would leave them the shadow of sovereignty so long as they paid the annual tribute of 10,000 or 12,000 ducats which he imposed upon them.[1] Some of the Greek nobles wished, indeed, to proclaim Demétrios emperor, but this was too much for the fraternal jealousy of Thomas, and the idea was dropped. Meanwhile, the smouldering discontent of the Albanians, ill-treated by the Greek officials and fired by the great exploits of their countryman, Skanderbeg, in Albania, had burst out into one of those rare efforts for independence which that strange race has occasionally shown. Some 30,000 of these nomads rose against the Despots, at the instigation of one of their native chieftains, Peter Boua, nicknamed "the lame," a member of the family which had once held Arta and Lepanto. Various dissatisfied Greek *archons* joined the movement, for the greedy Byzantine officials who held the chief posts at the petty courts of Patras and Mistrâ were extremely unpopular with the natives of the peninsula. Among these Greek rebels the most prominent was Manuel Cantacuzene, who was lord of all Braccio di Maina, and could not forget that his ancestors were of imperial lineage and had once ruled at Mistrâ. Thomas had in vain tried to arrest him, as a dangerous pretender; he was now proclaimed Despot by the Albanians, whose national vanity he flattered by taking the Albanian name of "Ghin," and calling his wife "Cuchia."

In the pitiable condition of Greece at that time it was obvious to both parties that they could only obtain, or retain, the government of the Morea by foreign aid. Accordingly, they both applied to the only two foreign Powers which were strong enough to assist them—Venice and the sultan. The republic was at first not disinclined to listen to the proposals

[1] Phrantzês, 309; Doúkas, 314 (who puts the tribute at 10,000 ducats); Chalkokondýles, 399, 400, 416 (who puts it at 12,000 gold pieces); Kritóboulos (I., 74; III., 1) estimates it at 6000 gold pieces; Cambini, Rabbi Joseph, and Æneas Sylvius (*cf. infra*) at 17,000.

of the Albanians to submit to Venetian rule. Venice had been constantly harassed by the Despots, and on one occasion had plainly told the Emperor Manuel II. that the members of his family were "worse neighbours than the Turks";[1] in this very year of the rebellion, Demétrios had been molesting the Venetian colonies. The first impulse of the Venetian Government was, therefore, to instruct its officials in the Morea to encourage the insurgents until it had had time to decide upon its policy. More cautious counsels, however, prevailed—for Venice did not want to embroil herself with the sultan—and it was proposed that Vettore Cappello should proceed to the Morea, to urge the desirability of unity on the contending parties, and to negotiate for the peaceful acquisition of such maritime places as Glarentza, Patras, Corinth, and Vostitza, but only in the event of a possible Genoese or Catalan occupation of the peninsula. He was to protest, and the protest was perfectly genuine, that the republic did not seek these territorial acquisitions from motives of ambition, but simply in order to save the country. The news that a Genoese fleet was hovering off the Morea and that the Albanians were negotiating with that rival republic, naturally alarmed the statesmen of the lagoons.[2]

The sultan acted, however, while the Venetians debated. He saw that a strong Albanian principality in the Morea would be less to his interest than the maintenance of the two weak Byzantine states of Patras and Mistrâ. He therefore resolved to aid the Despots in suppressing the revolt, without, however, utterly annihilating the revolted; he chose, in other words, that policy of making one Christian race balance another, so skilfully followed by his successor in Macedonia at the present day. Omar, son of old Turakhan, was despatched to carry out these instructions; he inflicted a slight defeat on the Albanians, and obtained from the grateful Demétrios the release of his brother Achmet as his reward. Another pretender, however, now appeared on the scene, in the person of Centurione's son, Giovanni Asan. The so-called "Prince of Achaia" had been imprisoned with his eldest son since his ineffectual rising in 1446 in the castle of

[1] Jorga, iv., 596.

[2] Sáthas, i., 215-27; Magno *apud* Hopf, *Chroniques*, 199.

Chloumoûtsi, and it had been rumoured that Thomas had allowed these dangerous representatives of the old dynasty to die of hunger. They were, however, still alive, and had eagerly listened to the plans of a fellow-prisoner, a Greek agitator of obscure origin, named Loukánes, who had received preferment from Theodore II., but had strongly opposed the influence of Byzantine officialdom in his own, and his countrymen's interest. These prisoners of state now persuaded their gaoler to release them, whereupon they threw the weight, Centurione of his name, Loukánes of his ability, on the side of the insurgents. There must still have been many Franks who regarded the only son of the last Frankish ruler of Achaia as their legitimate sovereign, and even Venice and Alfonso of Naples thought it desirable to congratulate "Prince Centurione" on his release, and to give him and his wife their coveted title. Phrantzês, who knew Peloponnesian politics well, and who had just entered the service of the Despot Thomas, considered his escape so serious that he interrupted a mission to the Servian court as soon as he heard the news, and Matthew Asan, the brother-in-law of Demétrios, was despatched to the sultan to ask for further assistance. This time Mohammed II. sent old Turakhan himself to the aid of the Despots, whose two capitals of Mistrâ and Patras were besieged by the insurgents. Turakhan, with his two sons and a large force, arrived in October 1454, and told the two Despots, who had in the meanwhile compelled the enemy to raise the siege of those towns, that the presence of one or other of them with his troops was essential to the success of his plans. First, accompanied by Demétrios, he attacked the Albanians at a place called Borbotia, which they strongly fortified, but from which they fled by night, leaving about 10,000 men and women prisoners of the allies. Next it was the turn of Thomas, who took part with the Turkish commander in the capture of Ithome and Aëtos—a place which had recently hoisted the flag of Centurione, and which added another 1000 to the ranks of the captives. At this the rest of the Albanians submitted, on condition that they should keep the lands which they had taken and the cattle which they had plundered—an arrangement which well suited the sultan's policy of playing off the two races against one another. The pseudo-despot, Cantacuzene, disappeared, till four years later he returned as the decoy of the sultan, while Centurione found a refuge among the Venetians at Modon, where he remained for some two years. It was then thought desirable to confirm his devotion to Venice by the grant of a small pension, lest he should lend his name to some Turkish or other enterprise for the conquest of the Morea; especially as, early in 1456, we find him a pensioner of King Alfonso at Naples; accordingly, in 1457, the republic granted him an annuity, on condition that he continued to reside at Modon, or "wherever else he could be most useful" to her. Seven years later he settled, like his enemy Thomas, in Rome, and thenceforth drew a monthly pittance from Paul II. till 1469, when he died, the last of his famous race to claim the title of "Prince of Achaia."[1] As for the Albanian chief, Peter Boua, he was confirmed by the Turks in his privileges, and, nine years later, headed another rising of his countrymen. Having thus restored the authority of the two Despots, old Turakhan gave them, before he departed, the excellent advice to live as brothers, to reward their loyal subjects, and to repress at once the germs of sedition. Needless to say, his advice was not taken.[2]

The sultan was now the real master of the Morea. The two Despots were his tributaries, and the Greek *archons*, degenerate scions of old Moreot families such as those of Sophianós and Sgouromallaîos, hesitated as little as Albanian chiefs like Peter Boua or Manuel Raoul to acknowledge him as their sovereign on condition that he took none of their property and spared their children from the blood-tax. Two of them even offered to hand over to Venice Mouchli, between Argos and the modern Tripolitza, and the three castles of Damalâ, Ligourió, and Phanari in Argolis—an offer which the Venetian Government found very tempting, as the three Argive castles were near the sea-coast. Meanwhile both Thomas and Demétrios went on intriguing as before.

[1] Sáthas, i., 229; *Secreta*, xx., f. 133; *Liber Depositarii S. Cruciatæ*, ff. 123-48, 81-87.

[2] Chalkokondýles, 406-14; Phrantzês, 383-5; Cambini *apud* Sansovino, *op. cit.*, 152; Spandugino (ed. 1551), 41-2; Æneas Sylvius, *Europa*, 405; Ἄνθος *apud* Hopf, *Chroniques*, 267; *Archivio Storico per le Prov. Napoletane*, xxvii., 834-5; xxviii., 193, 203.

Both had tried to negotiate a matrimonial alliance between their children and the family of Alfonso V. of Aragon and Naples, who sent an envoy to examine the Isthmian wall, and report on the defences of the country, while Thomas invoked the aid of Venice to prevent his brother from thus re-introducing Spanish influence into the Morea to the detriment of both the republic and himself. While Demétrios appointed the scholar Argyrópoulos as his envoy, and told him to seek the aid of the pope and of Charles VII. of France, Thomas sent the serviceable Phrantzês to smooth over his disputes with the Venetians, and obtained a safe conduct for himself and his family for the Venetian colonies and the loan of both a Venetian and a Neapolitan galley, on which he could flee in case of need. Nevertheless, the two brothers might, perhaps, have preserved the shadow of authority for the rest of their lives, had they abstained from any act which could offend their all-powerful suzerain, the sultan. But the old intriguer Loukánes could not rest from attempting to stir up Byzantine officials and native Peloponnesians alike to revolt; and, in spite of the wise refusal of Matthew Asan, the governor of Corinth, who knew his Turks only too well, to join in these schemes, the tribute to the sultan was allowed to fall into arrears. So long as there was any danger from the Albanians, the Despots had been willing enough to pay what their deliverer asked as the price of his assistance. But after the revolt had been suppressed, they omitted to remit their annual ransom. Their excuse was that neither their Albanian nor Greek subjects would pay their respective quota unless the land of the peninsula were divided in equal portions. The Turkish view, however, was that the Despots received the amount regularly, but spent it on themselves.[1]

The sultan sent frequent embassies to demand payment, and at the same time to report on the state of the country He was afraid that the constant quarrels of the Despots would end in a Venetian or Aragonese occupation of the Morea, which he thought would make a good base for his projected

[1] Miklosich und Müller, III., 290; Sáthas, i., 230-32; Phrantzês, 385; Chalkokondýles, 413-14; Kritóboulos, III., 1; *Archivio Storico per le Prov. Napoletane*, xxviii., 200.

attack upon Italy and which he had no wish to see in the hands of a strong Western power. When, therefore, some three years' tribute was in arrears, he despatched an ultimatum to the Despots, giving them the alternative of peace with payment, or the loss of their dominions. Emboldened by the appearance of the fleet sent out by Pope Calixtus III. to the Ægean, Thomas, the more energetic of the two brothers, refused to pay; this refusal led to his own and his brother's ruin.

In the spring of 1458, at the head of an army of 80,000 cavalry and a large body of infantry, Mohammed II. arrived in Thessaly, where he halted to rest his men and to give the Despots a last chance of payment. It was currently reported at the time, that had they done so, the sultan, who had other pressing business on hand, would have abandoned his expedition at that eleventh hour. But when no envoy arrived from the Morea, he ordered his army to advance through Thermopylæ into Bœotia, and encamped on the classic field of Platæa at the river Asopos, till his scouts had examined the mountain passes leading to the isthmus. While he was there, messengers arrived from Thomas, begging for peace and bringing a part of the tribute, 4500 gold pieces. But it was too late; the sultan took the money, and told the trembling emissaries that he would make peace when he was in the Peloponnese. Then, as his scouts reported the passes to be unoccupied, he proceeded to the isthmus, where he arrived on 15th May. He met with no resistance at the Hexamilion; but a short experience of the natural and artificial fortifications of Akrocorinth convinced him that it could only be taken by surrender or starvation. There is only one approach to the citadel, and the steepness of the ground would not permit him to plant his batteries near enough to the walls to have any effect upon them; while, even if he could have succeeded in battering down the triple line of walls, an assault would have been most difficult. Accordingly, he left half his forces under the command of Mahmoud Pasha, a Greek renegade and the first Christian who ever occupied the post of Grand Vizier, to invest the place, and proceeded to reduce the neighbouring fortresses by force or threats. He then marched into the interior of the peninsula, devastating and destroying as he went. At Nemea he turned westward, and besieged Tarsos, a place to the north of Lake Pheneos, which surrendered and furnished some 300 youths to the janissaries. But Doxies, the Albanian chieftain of the district, occupied a very strong position on a high hill with a band of Greeks and Albanians, and prepared to defy the great sultan. Unfortunately the besiegers cut off the water supply, and thus compelled the heroic defenders, who had been constrained to bake their bread with the blood of their slaughtered cattle, to sue for peace. Mohammed treacherously seized this unguarded moment to attack the place, which thus fell into his hands. The ancient feudal castle of Akova was taken by storm; the fortress of Roupele, in which a number of Albanians and Greeks had taken refuge with their families, after two days' desperate fighting, during which the Turkish losses were such that the sultan ordered a retreat, surrendered just as he was departing. Mohammed sent the inhabitants to colonise Constantinople, with the exception of some twenty Albanians who had surrendered at Tarsos and had broken their parole not to fight against him again. As an awful example he ordered their ankles and wrists to be broken—an act of cruelty commemorated by the Turkish name for the place—"Tokmak Hissari," or "the castle of ankles." Thence he marched into the territory of Mantineia, accompanied by Ghin Cantacuzene, the leader of the Albanian insurrection of 1453, whom he had summoned to join him, thinking that his influence with the Albanians would be useful. The ex-Despot was sent to try his persuasive powers on the people of Pazanike; but his mission only made them more obstinate; his Turkish companions accused him of treachery, and he was driven from the sultan's camp. Alarmed for his safety, he fled to Hungary, where he died.

Finding that the enemy had occupied a strongly fortified position, Mohammed encamped near Tegea, and held a council of war. The two Despots had meanwhile fled to the sea-coast—Thomas with his family to the Lakonian Mantineia, Demétrios to Monemvasia. The sultan's ardent desire was to see and capture that famous fortress, "the strongest of all cities that we know," as Chalkokondýles justly called it. But his advisers represented to him the difficult nature of the country which he would have to traverse, so he prudently decided instead to attack Demétrios Asan in Palaio-Mouchli, then one of the most important places in the peninsula. Here again, the sultan cut off the water supply, and after three days, Asan surrendered on favourable terms, receiving the town of Loidoriki as a fief for his son. The sultan now marched across country by a difficult route to Patras, the abandoned capital of Thomas, whose citizens he found fled to Lepanto and other Venetian colonies, except the garrison of the castle. The latter made no resistance, their lives were spared, and the conqueror was so struck with the fertility and situation of the town at the mouth of the Corinthian Gulf, that he offered freedom, immunity from taxation for several years, and the restitution of their property to all the inhabitants who would come back. After garrisoning the castle, he despatched a portion of his forces to overrun Elis and Messenia, and then returned along the coast of the gulf to Corinth, occupying Vostitza on the way.

Although it was now July, he found Akrocorinth still untaken, for Matthew Asan, who had been absent at Nauplia, had succeeded in entering the fortress by night with seventy men and partially revictualling it. As Asan boldly refused to surrender, and there was no longer provender for the beasts of burden in the Turkish camp, Mohammed resolved to bombard the entrance with stone balls made from the ruins of the ancient city of Corinth. At last a breach was made in the outermost of the three walls; but when, after a hand-to-hand fight, the Turks assailed the second rampart, they were greeted with such volleys of large stones that they had to retire with heavy loss. So powerful, however, for that period was the Turkish artillery, that a stone ball weighing nearly 900 lbs. and fired at a range of about a mile and a half destroyed the bakery of the citadel and the arsenal. At this juncture, the Turkish detachment which had been sent to plunder Elis and Messenia arrived at Corinth with some 15,000 head of cattle, so that the besiegers had ample supplies for a long blockade, while the small stock of provisions which Asan had brought with him was now all but exhausted. The Greeks complained to their metropolitan, who treacherously informed Mohammed of the state of affairs. The sultan then again called upon Asan to surrender, and the latter, seeing that the majority was opposed to further resistance, went forth under a flag of truce, together with Loukánes, who had been in command during his absence, and made terms with the sultan. On 6th August, Corinth, "the star castle," as the Turks called it, surrendered; the inhabitants were left unmolested, but ordered to pay tribute; while the conqueror demanded from the Despots an annual tribute of 3000 gold pieces and the cession of the city and district of Patras, Vostitza, Kalavryta, and all the country which he had traversed with his army—about one-third of the whole peninsula—and threatened a renewal of hostilities in case of refusal. Asan proceeded to Trype at the mouth of the Langada Gorge where the two Despots were waiting, and laid these hard terms before them. But, hard as they were, there seemed to be no option but to accept them. True, the patriotic Phrantzês sneered at the men who had surrendered the key of the Morea and complained that Thomas had given away valuable cities "as if they were of no more account than the vegetables in his garden." Mohammed left a garrison of 400 picked men of his own bodyguard in Corinth, thoroughly provisioned all the fortresses which seemed to be in good condition, destroyed the others and sent their inhabitants to Constantinople, where he settled the skilled workmen in the city and the peasants in the surburban villages. Then, appointing Omar, son of Turakhan, governor of the new Turkish province in the Morea, he set out in the beginning of the autumn of 1458 for Athens, the city which that warrior had captured.[1]

The end of the Italian rule at Athens had been marked by a domestic tragedy which might have attracted the dramatic genius of her great classic writers. In 1451—the same year that had witnessed the death of Murâd II.—died Nerio II. We catch a last characteristic glimpse of him in the middle of that year, when the Venetian envoy to the

[1] Kritóboulos, III., 1-9; Doúkas, 339-40; *Historia Politica*, 31; *Chronicon Breve*, 520; Chalkokondýles, 442-52; Phrantzês, 387-8; Ἄνθος *apud* Hopf, *Chroniques*, 267-8; Cambini, 152; Æneas Sylvius, *Europa*, 405; Magno *apud* Hopf, *op. cit.*, 200. The amount of the tribute given by Kritóboulos seems more probable than the 500 pieces of Chalkokondýles.

new sultan was directed to ask that potentate to urge upon his vassal, "the lord of Sithines and Stives," the necessity of settling the pecuniary claims of two Venetians.[1] After the death of his first wife, Maria Melissené, Nerio, like his brother Antonio, had married one of the daughters of Niccolò Zorzi or Giorgio of Karystos, titular marquis of Boudonitza. The Duchess Chiara—such was the name of this passionate Venetian beauty—bore him a son, Francesco, who was unfortunately still a minor at the time of his father's death. The child's mother possessed herself of the regency and persuaded the Porte, by the usual methods, to sanction her usurpation. Soon afterwards, however, there visited Athens on some commercial errand a young Venetian noble, Bartolomeo Contarini, whose father had been governor of the Venetian colony of Nauplia. The duchess fell in love with her charming visitor, and bade him aspire to her hand and land. Contarini replied that, alas! he had left a wife behind him in his palace on the lagoons. To the Lady of the Akropolis, a figure who might have stepped from a play of Æschylus, the Venetian wife was no obstacle. It was the age of great crimes. Contarini realised that Athens was worth a murder, poisoned his spouse, and returned to enjoy the embraces and the authority of the duchess.

But the Athenians soon grew tired of this Venetian domination. They complained to Mohammed II.; the great sultan demanded explanations; and Contarini was forced to appear with his stepson, whose guardian he pretended to be, at the Turkish court. There he found a dangerous rival in the person of Franco Acciajuoli, only son of the late Duke Antonio II. and cousin of Francesco, a special favourite of Mohammed and a willing candidate for the Athenian throne, who had only been awaiting a favourable moment to return. When the sultan heard the tragic story of Chiara's passion, he ordered the deposition of both herself and her husband, and bade the willing Athenians accept Franco as their lord. Young Francesco was never heard of again; but the tragedy was not yet over. Franco had no sooner assumed the government of Athens, than he ordered the arrest of his aunt Chiara, threw her into the

[1] Jorga, viii., 78.

dungeons of Megara, and there had her mysteriously murdered. A picturesque legend,[1] current three centuries later at Athens, makes Franco throttle her with his own hands, in a still more romantic spot—the monastery of Daphni, the mausoleum of the French dukes—as she knelt invoking the aid of the Virgin, whereupon he cut off her head with his sword. So deep was the impression which her fate made upon the popular imagination.

The legend goes on to tell how her husband, "the Admiral," had come with many ships to the Piræus to rescue her, but arrived too late. Unable to save, he resolved to avenge her, and laid the grim facts before the sultan. Mohammed II., indignant at the conduct of his *protégé*, but not sorry, perhaps, of a pretext for destroying the remnants of Frankish rule at Athens, ordered Omar, son of Turakhan, the governor of Thessaly, to march against the city. The lower town offered no resistance, for its modern walls had but a narrow circumference, and its population and resources were scanty. Nature herself seemed to fight against the Athenians. On 29th May, the third anniversary of the capture of Constantinople, a comet appeared in the sky; a dire famine followed, so that the people were reduced to eat roots and grass. On 4th June 1456, the town fell into the hands of the Turks.[2] But the Akropolis, which was reputed impregnable, long held out. In vain the constable of Athens and some of the citizens offered the castle to Venice through one of the Zorzi family; the republic ordered the bailie of Negroponte to keep the offer open, but took no steps to save the most famous fortress of Christendom; in vain he summoned one Latin prince after another to his aid. From the presence of an Athenian ambassador at the Neapolitan court,[3] we may infer that Alfonso V. of Aragon, the titular "Duke of Athens," was among their

[1] Kampoúroglos, Μνημεῖα, III., 141.

[2] A contemporary note in MS., No. 103 of the Liturgical Section of the National Library at Athens, quoted by Kampoúroglos, Μνημεῖα, II., 153, fixes the date at "*May* 4, 1456, Friday," but in that year *June* 4, not May 4, was a Friday, which agrees with the date of June 1456 given by Phrantzês, the *Chronicon Breve*, the *Historia Patriarchica*, and in Nerozzo Pitti's petition of 1458 in the Florentine Archives (*Balie*, xxix., f. 67.)

[3] *Archivio Storico per le Provincie Napoletane*, xxviii., 203.

number. Demétrios Asan, lord of Palaio-Mouchli, who was Franco's father-in-law, was also endeavouring to dispose of his city to Venice at this time, so that he could not help his kinsman; and the papal fleet, which was despatched to the Ægean, did not even put into the Piræus. Meanwhile, Omar, after a vain attempt to seduce the garrison from its allegiance, reminded Franco that sooner or later he must restore Athens to the sultan who gave it. "Now, therefore," added the Turkish commander, "if thou wilt surrender the Akropolis, His Majesty offers thee the land of Bœotia, with the city of Thebes, and will allow thee to take away the wealth of the Akropolis and thine own property." Franco only waited till Mohammed had confirmed the offer of his subordinate, and then quitted the castle of Athens, with his wife and his three sons, for ever. At the same time, his uncle, Nerozzo Pitti, was deprived by the Turks of his Athenian property, his castle of Sykaminon, and his island of Panaia, or Canaia, the ancient Pyrrha, opposite the mouth of the Maliac Gulf, and retired penniless to a Theban castle, with his wife and eleven children. As compensation for these losses, the Florentine Government allowed him to sell his house in Florence, which was all that he had left; many others, like him, were ruined and exiled. The last Latin Archbishop of Athens, Niccolò Protimo of Eubœa, quitted the Akropolis with the duke; he was assigned the possessions of the Latin Patriarchate in his native island; in 1461 he was consoled for the loss of his see by the archbishopric of Lepanto, which he held to his death in 1483, and even then the popes continued to confer the phantom title of Archbishop of Athens on absentees.[1] It was not till 1875 that a Catholic archbishop again resided at Athens.

Such was the state of affairs when Mohammed II., having punished the Despots of the Morea, arrived at Athens in the early autumn of 1458. His biographer, the Greek Kritóboulos, who became governor of his native island of Imbros under the Turkish dispensation, tells us that this cultured sultan,

[1] Chalkokondýles, 453-5; Phrantzês, 385; *The Chronicles of Rabbi Joseph*, 281; *Historia Politica*, 25; *Historia Patriarchica*, 97, 124; *Chronicon Breve*, 520; Sáthas, i., 230; v., 6; vi., 165; Sansovino, 153; Æneas Sylvius, *Europa*, 405; Baphius, *De Felicitate Urbis Florentiæ*, 38; Pagnini, *Della Decima*, ii., 251; Ubaldini, 177-8; Reg. Vat. 491, f. 304; Eubel, ii., 40.

who knew Greek, and whom he audaciously describes as "a philhellene," was filled with desire to behold "the mother of the philosophers," as a Turkish historian calls Athens. Mohammed had heard and read much about the wisdom and marvellous works of the ancient Athenians; we may surmise that Cyriacus of Ancona had told him of the Athenian monuments when he was employed as a reader to His Majesty at the siege of Constantinople. He longed to visit the places where the heroes and sages of classic Athens had walked and talked, and at the same time to examine with a statesman's eye the position of the city and the condition of its harbours. When he arrived at the gates, if we may believe a much later tradition, the abbot of Kaisariané handed to him the keys of the city—in return for which he ordered that the famous Byzantine monastery at the foot of Hymettos, which had enjoyed complete fiscal exemption under the Latins, should never pay more than one *sequin* to the Turkish governor.[1] There is nothing improbable in the tradition, for the abbot was probably the most important Greek ecclesiastic left at Athens, the Metropolitan Isidore, a friend of Phrantzês, having fled to the Venetian island of Tenos, where his tomb was discovered near the foundations of the famous Evangelistria church some sixty years ago.[2] The sultan spent four days in admiring the monuments and in visiting the harbours of this new possession, "of all the cities in his Empire the dearest to him," as the Athenian Chalkokondýles proudly says. But of all that he saw, he admired most the Akropolis, whose ancient and recent buildings he examined "with the eyes of a scholar, a philhellene, and a great sovereign." Like Pedro IV. of Aragon before him, he was proud to possess such a jewel, and in his enthusiasm he exclaimed: "How much, indeed, do We not owe to Omar, the son of Turakhan!"

The conquered Athenians once again were saved by their ancestors. Like his Roman prototype, Mohammed II. treated them humanely, though he carried off many of their women and children to his seraglio, he granted all their petitions, and gave them many and various privileges. The contemporary historians do not tell us of what these privileges

[1] Spon, *Voyage*, ii., 155, 172. *Cf.* Kampoúroglos, 'Ιστορια, II., 21-3.
[2] *Idem.*, Μνημεῖα, II., 18; Phrantzês, 203.

consisted; but there were Athenians in the seventeenth century who could show patents of fiscal exemption, granted to their ancestors by the conqueror. It is not improbable that the local Greek authorities, the so-called δημογέροντες, or "elders of the people," of whom we found a trace under the rule of the Acciajuoli, and who are often mentioned in the seventeenth and eighteenth centuries, were recognised by Mohammed. It is probable, too, that the same statesmanlike sovereign, who converted the œcumenical patriarch into a useful instrument of his far-sighted policy, favoured the re-establishment of the Orthodox Church in the position of the leading Christian denomination at Athens. At any rate, while the Uniate Archbishop shared the fate of his Catholic colleague, we find a metropolitan of Athens resident there a generation after the Turkish Conquest, and another is mentioned[1] as taking part in ecclesiastical business at Constantinople in 1465. But, if the last Latin Archbishop of Athens was turned out of his noble cathedral as soon as the Turks became masters of the Akropolis, the Parthenon was not for long restored to the Greek Church. It has, indeed, been assumed from the practice of the Turks at Constantinople and elsewhere, that the most important church of Athens was immediately devoted to the worship of Allah. But two writers subsequent to the capture of Athens, the anonymous author of 1458 and the anonymous author of 1466, both distinctly allude to the Parthenon as still a church.[2] Possibly it may have been part of the wise policy of Mohammed to conciliate the Greeks and further estrange them from the Latins by allowing them to resume, for a time at least, the use of their noble cathedral. However that may be, ere long it was converted into a mosque, called in the early part of the seventeenth century, the *Ismaïdi*, or "house of prayer," and soon from the tapering minaret, which rose above it, the muezzin summoned the faithful to worship. A like fate befell the church which had served as the orthodox cathedral during the Frankish domination. This church, now the

[1] Kampoúroglos, Μνημεῖα, i., 358; ii., 226; Ἱστορία, ii., 147-8; Reg. Vat., 469, f. 392; 479, f. 14.

[2] "È nel detto castello una chiessia che già fu tempio"; *Mitteilungen des k. deutsch. Arch. Instituts (Athen)*, xxiv., 73.

military bakery, received in honour of the sultan's visit, the name of *Fethijeh Jamisi*, or "mosque of the conqueror," and still preserves the traces of the purpose to which it was put. In its place the orthodox adopted as their "Katholikón," or metropolitan church, that of St Panteleémon, which stood in the square where the public auctions are now held.[1] It was a tradition in the seventeenth century that Mohammed II. had also ordered, as a mark of his special favour for Athens, that the city should not be made the capital of a *sandjak*, or province, so as to spare it the usual exactions of the provincial governor's retinue.[2] But in 1462 there is mention of a *subassì* of Athens,[3] and it has therefore been assumed by modern Greek historians, that from the time of the Conquest down to about 1610 or 1621, the city was governed by that official, who, after the capture of Negroponte in 1470, was the subordinate of the pasha of that province. His *konak* was at the Stoa of Hadrian, while the *disdar-aga*, or commander of the garrison, occupied a part of the palace of the Acciajuoli in the Propylæa, and the Erechtheion served as his harem.

The anonymous treatise on "The Theatres and Schools of Athens," which was probably composed by some Greek at this moment, perhaps to serve as a *vade mecum* for the sultan, whose eager enquiries about the meaning and history of the monuments it may have endeavoured to satisfy, gives us an interesting, if unscientific, idea of Athens as she was after two and a half centuries of Frankish rule.[4] The visitor could glean from this curious guide-book, apparently the work of a local antiquary, the popular names bestowed by the natives upon the classical monuments. Thus, the choragic monument of Lysikrates was then, as in the time of Michael Akominátos, "the lantern of Demosthenes," a name still current in 1672; the Tower of the Winds was

[1] Kampoúroglos, Ἱστορία, ii., 37, 275, 304; Philadelpheús, i., 178, 273, 312.

[2] La Guilletière, *Athènes Ancienne et Nouvelle*, 157, 160.

[3] Sanudo *apud* Muratori, xxii., 1172; Malipiero, *Annali* in *Archivio Storico Italiano*, vii., 12; A σούμπασης is also mentioned in 1506; Kampoúroglos (ii., 77-83), however, thinks that down to 1470 Athens was the seat of a pasha, but he adduces no other authorities than modern historians, such as Hammer and Daru. *Cf.* Philadelpheús, i., 287-8.

[4] The date of 1458 or 1460 exactly fits the allusion to "the duke" in the past tense, and to the Parthenon as a Christian church.

supposed to be "the school of Sokrates," just as the caverns at the foot of the hill of Philópappos are still known as the philosopher's prison; the gate of Athena Archegetis was transformed in common parlance into "the palace of Themistoklês"; the Odeion of Periklês, restored in Roman times, was shown to visitors as "the school of Aristophanes," and that of Herodes Atticus as "the palaces of Kleonides and Miltiades." Near "the lantern of Demosthenes" the natives pointed out to the curious stranger the spots where once had stood the houses of Thucydides, Solon, and Alkmaion. "The school of Aristotle" was placed among the ruins of the theatre of Dionysios, and above it our author mentions the sun-dial and the two pillars of the choragic monument of Thrasyllos, and repeats the story that a Gorgon's head was formerly to be seen in an ironbound niche between them—all of which statements are confirmed by the similar "Description of Attica," probably composed about the year 1628.[1] Another "school," that of Sophoklês, was supposed to have occupied a site to the west of the Akropolis, while outside the city the anonymous author alludes to the Academy, which he supposes to have been at Basiliká, on the left as one goes down to Phaleron, and not at Kathemia, near Kolokynthou; to the Eleatic school at Ambelokepoi; to the Platonic at Patesia (or "Paradeisia"), and to those of a certain Polýzelos and Diódoros, on Hymettos, whose name the Italians had corrupted to "Monte Matto," or "the Mad Mountain." Wild as these statements are, they yet contain important topographical facts. They prove that the ancient deme of Alopeke had already received its modern designation of Ambelokepoi; that Patesia, whose name has been erroneously derived from the fact of the "Pâdishâh" having pitched his headquarters there, was still known by its picturesque name of "Paradeisia"; and that the old tradition that two of the monasteries on Hymettos—probably Kaisariané and Astéri—had once been schools of philosophers, which seems to have actually been the case at the close of the fourth century,[2] was still preserved. For the anonymous writer, as

[1] Περὶ τῆς Αττικῆς *apud* Philadelpheús, i., 189.

[2] Sourmelês, Κατάστασις συνοπτική, 43 *n.*, 46, 47 ; Synésios *apud* Migne, lxvi., 1523.

for Cyriacus, the Olympieion was the ruins of a palace, and, like the traveller from Ancona, he mentions three gates of the city. On the Akropolis he mistook the temple of Nike Apteros for "a small school of musicians, founded by Pythagoras"; he mentions the Propylæa as the ducal palace, with the former chancery adjoining it; and he elaborately describes the "Church of the Mother of God," the foundation of which he attributes to Apollós and Eulógios, both patriarchs of Alexandria in the sixth century. Allusion has already been made to his mention of the ducal villa of the Acciajuoli at the spring of Kallirrhoe, and to the neighbouring chapel, where they were wont to pray. This chapel had now been converted by "the pious" Greeks into an orthodox church of St Mary's on the Rock. Perhaps the most curious tradition preserved in this pamphlet is the incident taken from the apocryphal "Acts of St Philip." The apostle — such was the legend — had spent two years at Athens, whither the scribe of the Chief Priest[1] of Jerusalem followed him to controvert what he said. At last, the apostolic patience failed, and in the midst of the Athenian Agorá the saint caused the earth to open and swallow up his irreverent adversary. A church of St Philip was founded to commemorate the event, and this church, completely restored in our own generation, still preserves, together with the quarter to which it has given its name, the quaint mediæval legend of the apostle and the scribe. Thus, at the close of the Frankish domination, the *ciceroni* of Athens had identified their city with some of the most famous names, alike of pagan and of Christian story.

On the fifth day after his arrival, the heir of these great men left Athens for Bœotia, examining with his usual minute care all the places of interest, and obtaining information about them. From Thebes—the abode of his vassal Franco—he sent a message to the terrified bailie of Negroponte that he proposed to visit that city on the following day. When he reached the summit of the Pass of Anephorites, he paused for a quarter of an hour, as many a traveller has done since, to admire the magnificent situation of the great island spread

[1] Laborde, i., 17-20; Kampoúroglos, Ἱστορία ii., 299; Neroûtsos in Δελτίον, III., 75.

out like a map at his feet—the narrow channel of the Euripos, with its oft-changing tide, more like a river than an arm of the sea, the picturesque fortress, which then stood in mid-stream, and the bridge which connected the city of Negroponte with the continent. The islanders, alarmed at the force of a thousand cavalry which accompanied him, thought that their last hour had come; they picked up sufficient courage, however, to go out to meet him with rich gifts in their hands; the sultan received them affably, rode across the bridge, and spied out for himself the possibilities of capturing the place. The information which he then gleaned was put to good use when, twelve years later, he besieged the city. Then, the same day, 2nd September, he returned to Thebes, whence he departed on the morrow for Macedonia.[1] His trembling vassal must have heaved a sigh of relief when this terrible visitor was gone.

Scarcely, however, had he left Greece than disturbances again broke out in the Morea. In October, the sultan had sent one of his officials to complete the formalities of the recent peace, to receive the oaths of the two Despots, and to demand from Demétrios the hand of his only child, Helene, and from Thomas the cession of the castles which he had not yet transferred to the sultan's commissioner. Thomas complied with this demand; Demétrios sent Matthew Asan to ask Mohammed for the islands of Lemnos and Imbros in return for his daughter and his principality. According to another account, Asan was instructed to ask the sultan for aid against Thomas, who seemed to be constitutionally incapable of learning by experience, and who, early in 1459, committed the double mistake of attacking his brother and revolting against his suzerain.

The crafty and ambitious officials who infested the two petty courts of the Morea, among them the veteran intriguer, Loukánes, "the curse of the Peloponnesians," as Phrantzês calls him, fanned the smouldering embers of fraternal hatred; some of the Albanian chiefs, impatient of Turkish rule and anxious to imitate the deeds of their great countryman, Skanderbeg, joined with these Greek counsellors in inciting

[1] Kritóboulos, III., 9; Magno *apud* Hopf, *Chroniques*, 200; Chalkokondýles, 547.

Thomas to "eat his oaths, as if they were vegetables." The connivance of Omar, the Turkish governor, was suspected, and the sultan suspended him from both his Peloponnesian and Thessalian commands, and despatched Hamsa Zenevisi, "the carrier of falcons," a renegade Albanian, to succeed him in the Morea. Hamsa's first act was to arrest Omar and the latter's father-in-law Ahmed; his next to relieve the Turkish garrison of Patras, which was besieged by Thomas's men. The successes of the latter at the expense of the Turks were confined to the capture of Kalavryta, for Corinth and the other places which Loukánes had promised to win by treachery remained true to the sultan. Demétrios, however, lost one strong place after another—Karytaina and St George in Arkadia, Bordonia and Kastritza, near Sparta, Kalamata, Zarnata, Leuktron, and most of Maina; but the commanders of some of these castles, instead of taking the oath to his rival, simply proclaimed their own independence, thus yet further weakening the unhappy country, while the Albanians, bent on plunder, increased the confusion by changing sides "thrice a week," and deserting now Thomas, now Demétrios, as it suited their purpose. Thomas, however, continued to hold his own; he forestalled his less active brother in an attempt to capture the important town of Leondari, and the latter withdrew to his capital of Mistrâ. But the Turkish troops now arrived at Leondari from Patras, easily threw into confusion the forces of Thomas, who was more skilled at palace intrigues than at strategy, and blockaded the Despot in the town, where fever and famine soon made their appearance. Hampered, however, by the number of his captives, the Turkish commander raised the siege, and, leaving one of his lieutenants to support his ally Demétrios at Mistrâ, repaired to the sultan to ask for reinforcements. Thus, Thomas was free to resume the offensive against the Turkish garrisons. A gleam of common sense or a pang of conscience prompted him to desist, at least for a little, from attacking his brother; in the church at Kastritza he met Demétrios; the Metropolitan of Lacedæmonia, clad in his episcopal cope, the symbol of justice, celebrated the Holy Eucharist with all the impressive rites of the Orthodox Church; and when, in the noble language of the liturgy of St Chrysostom, he bade the people "draw nigh in the fear of God, and with faith and love," the two brothers approached together, and swore on the Holy Sacrament to keep the peace.

But even the most solemn oaths had long ceased to bind the consciences of the two Palaiológoi. They were soon engaged in a fresh fratricidal war, the one relying on Turkish aid, the other on a body of 300 Italian foot soldiers sent by Bianca Visconti, Duchess of Milan, and by Pius II., who wrote to the rulers of Europe that "almost all the Morea had risen against the Turks," and pointed out that the peninsula was the bulwark of Christendom against the infidels.[1] The sultan ordered Zagan Pasha, a Christian renegade of marked ability, whom he had promoted to be governor of the provinces of Thessaly and the Morea, to attack Thomas. Zagan entered the peninsula in March 1460, raised the siege of Achaia, near Patras, which the Despot was bombarding, and compelled him to retreat to the south of Messenia. Finding his military operations unsuccessful and his Italian mercenaries dispersed, Thomas now begged for peace, which Mohammed, anxious to chastise the Turkoman chief, Usun Hasân, in Asia, was willing to grant, on condition that the Despot restored any Turkish forts which he had taken, that he withdrew his troops from any which they were besieging, that he agreed to pay at once a tribute of 3000 gold pieces, and promised to appear in person before the Turkish envoy at Corinth within twenty days' time. Thomas was prepared to accept these terms, but, as his subjects declined to contribute the money, he was unable to pay. This final breach of his engagements so infuriated Mohammed, that he postponed his intended expedition into Asia, and set out in May 1460 to make short work with both Despots. He waited three days at Corinth for the arrival of Demétrios; but the latter, who had been blockaded with his family by his brother in Monemvasia, sent his brother-in-law, Matthew Asan, in his stead with valuable presents to pacify the sultan, to whom he had omitted to send his daughter Helene, as stipulated. Mohammed, however, was not to be pacified; he ordered Asan under arrest, and, instead of entering the territory of Thomas, his open enemy, he despatched Mahmoud Pasha

[1] Raynaldus, x., 198; *Pii. II. Commentarii* (ed. 1614), 61-2.

with all speed to Mistrâ, whither Demétrios had gone in consequence of the hostilities which his brother was carrying on from Kalamata. Demétrios, on finding his capital surrounded by the Turks, resolved to shut himself up in the fine old castle; but when he learnt that his brother-in-law was a prisoner, he agreed to obey the summons to surrender, if he received a written guarantee by the hand of the latter. Mahmoud at once released Asan and sent him, as desired, together with Hamsa Zenevisi, in whom the Despot had confidence, to accept his surrender. One Greek historian suggests that the whole affair was a comedy carefully arranged beforehand, and that Demétrios was not sorry of an excuse for getting rid of his irksome sovereignty in the Morea in return for compensation elsewhere. But, however that may be, Mohammed, who arrived on the morrow, received him with the honour due to a descendant of emperors, rose from his seat as the trembling Despot entered his tent, offered him his right hand, gave him a place at his side, and endeavoured to reassure his fears by splendid gifts and still more splendid promises. But none the less he treated him as a prisoner, he gave him clearly to understand that Greek rule at Mistrâ was now at an end, and appointed Hamsa Zenevisi governor of that famous city, which had for all but two hundred years been the capital of the Byzantine province. At the same time, the sultan reiterated his claim to the hand of the Despot's daughter, who, with her mother, was still sheltering at Monemvasia. Isâ, son of the Pasha of Uskub, and Matthew Asan, were accordingly sent to demand the surrender of the city and of the two princesses. The Monemvasiotes handed over the imperial ladies to the envoys of the sultan and the Despot; but, relying on their immense natural defences, animated by the sturdy spirit of independence which had so long distinguished them, and inspired by the example of their governor, Manuel Palaiológos, they bade them tell Mohammed not to lay sacrilegious hands on a city which God had meant to be invincible. The sultan is reported to have admired their courage and wisely refrained from attacking the impregnable fastness of mediæval Hellenism. On 30th May, he placed the daughter of Demétrios in his seraglio, and despatched her with her mother, under charge of an eunuch, to Bœotia, whither Demétrios himself was shortly sent to join them. Meanwhile he accompanied his captor. At this the governor of Monemvasia transferred his allegiance to Thomas; but the latter, himself a fugitive and soon an exile, was incapable of maintaining his sovereignty. A passing Catalan corsair, one Lope de Baldaja, was then invited to occupy the place; but the liberty-loving inhabitants soon drove out the petty tyrant whom they had summoned to their aid; and, with the consent of Thomas, placed their city under the protection of his patron, the pope. Pius II. gladly appointed both spiritual and temporal governors of the rock which had so long been the stronghold of orthodoxy.[1]

Having thus wiped the province of Demétrios from the map, the sultan turned his arms against Thomas. Bordonia was abandoned at his approach by its cowardly *archons;* but the strong fortress of Kastritza, built on a sheer rock, and approached by a single entrance, and that fortified by a triple wall, for a time defied the assault of the janissaries. Urged on by promises of plunder, they returned to the attack, drove the garrison back into the Akropolis, and forced them from sheer exhaustion and lack of water to surrender on terms. In flagrant violation of this solemn convention, Mohammed beheaded or impaled all the male survivors, to the number of 300, ordered the local chief, Proinokokkâs, to be flayed alive, enslaved the women and children, and levelled the castle with the ground. Leondari he found deserted by its inhabitants, who had taken refuge in the almost impregnable stronghold of Gardiki. After in vain offering them terms, he ordered his men to attack the place, which resisted for no more than a single day, for the heat was intense and the crowd of fugitives was so great that both water and provisions ran short. Here, again, Mohammed violated his oath to spare the lives of those who surrendered; he collected the men, women, and children together in a small plain to the number of 6000, bound them hand and foot, and then ordered them to be massacred in cold blood. The chief men of the place, who belonged to the family of Bocháles, escaped the general fate, thanks to the intercession of the Beglerbeg Mahmoud, who was connected with them

[1] *Pii. II. Commentarii*, 103-4; Raynaldus, x., 241-2; Magno, *op. cit.*, 203-4.

by marriage, and made their way to Naples. The surrender of Gardiki was promptly followed by that of the castle of St George, whose governor, Korkódeilos Kladâs, lived to head an insurrection against the Turks some years later. One place after another now opened its gates to the invaders—Kyparissia, till lately the residence of the Despot Thomas; Karytaina; Androusa and Ithome; from the first of these cities and its fertile neighbourhood, the garden of Greece, no less than 10,000 people were dragged off to Constantinople. Meanwhile, Thomas had made no attempt to defend his dominions. On the news of the sultan's advent at Mistrâ, he had shut himself up in the sea-coast town of Mantineia on the Messenian Gulf, whence he could easily escape in case of need. Seeing that all was lost, and that Venetian territory alone remained safe, he now set out for Navarino. But Mohammed began to inspect the Messenian colonies of Venice, as he had inspected Negroponte; as he drew nearer, the Venetian authorities urged Thomas not to involve them in diplomatic difficulties by remaining defiantly in their station of Navarino, and offered him two ships on which to make his escape. The terrified Despot thereupon fled to Marathos, and on the same day that the sultan came in sight of Navarino, set sail with his wife and family and with some of his nobles from the neighbouring harbour of Porto Longo for Corfù. There he arrived on 28th July, where, five days later, the faithful Phrantzês joined him. Neither ever saw the Morea again.

The Venetians had good cause to fear that the anger of the sultan would now fall upon their colony. They were, it is true, at peace with Mohammed, but he had just shown his disregard of international law by killing some of the people of Modon who had come out to him with a flag of truce, and by annexing some Venetian villages on the ground that they had belonged to the Greeks and were therefore his. The authorities of Navarino accordingly hastened to renew the treaty with the conqueror and endeavoured to mollify him by the offer of hospitality—an offer which did not restrain his horsemen from making an incursion into the town and slaying a number of Albanians from the surrounding districts. Then the sultan marched away to the North, accompanied by Matthew Asan, while Demétrios, for whom Mohammed had no further use, was sent to join his family in Bœotia. Meanwhile, Zagan Pasha had been busily occupied in the west of the peninsula. Chloumoûtsi fell; and Santameri, the famous castle of Nicholas III. de St Omer, which was held by some Albanians, and in which most of the neighbours had deposited all their valuables, surrendered on terms. Next day, however, the Illyrian apostate broke the convention, slew many of the inhabitants, and enslaved the rest—an act of treachery which was also a political blunder, for it inspired the other garrisons, which still held out, with the courage of despair. Zagan might plead that he was only imitating his master, for Mohammed had ordered the flaying of his old Albanian opponent Doxas, or Doxies, now captain of Kalavryta, who had played fast and loose with both Greeks and Turks. But the sultan saw his officer's mistake, and at once tried to undo it by depriving Zagan of his command, and by ordering the release of the captives of Santameri. This politic act had the desired result; most of the forts round Patras hastened to surrender; and when the sultan arrived there almost the only place which still held out was Salmenikon, a very strong mountain fortress between Patras and Vostitza defended by Graitzas Palaiológos, who if not a genuine son of the imperial race, proved himself far worthier of the name than the two miserable Despots. This courageous soldier paid no heed to the sultan's summons to capitulate; in vain the Turkish gunners bombarded the place, in vain the janissaries marched to the assault. After a seven days' siege, the enemy, however, cut off the water supply, and the lower town, crowded with Greek and Albanian fugitives, then surrendered; some 6000 captives swelled the train of the conqueror, who set aside the promising boys for his corps of janissaries, and distributed the others among his captains. Still Palaiológos held the Akropolis of the town, and declined to yield unless the sultan would move a stage away from it. Mohammed agreed, and marched down to Vostitza, leaving Hamsa Zenevisi, whom he had appointed in Zagan's room, to take over the place. But, after the lesson of Santameri, the Greek commander had little confidence in Turkish oaths; he therefore resolved to make a preliminary trial of Hamsa's sincerity, and sent out a detachment of the garrison laden with baggage, to see whether the Turks would allow them a free passage. The temptation to attack and plunder them proved too strong for the Pasha; he broke his sovereign's pledge, with the result that Palaiológos refused to surrender. The angry sultan now re-appointed Zagan governor of Thessaly and the Morea, but Salmenikon still held out. At last, in 1461, after a year's siege, the gallant commander capitulated, and made his way, with all the honours of war, into Venetian territory at Lepanto. Such was the admiration which he inspired in his opponents, that the Grand Vizier Mahmoud was heard to exclaim: "I found many slaves in the Morea, but this was the only man." The Venetian senate received with gladness so courageous a soldier, and appointed him commander of all the light horse of the republic. It is from him that the Athenian Palaiológoi, of whom we hear a century later, were perhaps descended.

From Vostitza the sultan set out to Corinth, by way of Lake Pheneos and Phlious. Treacherous to the last, he issued a proclamation granting a full pardon to all who would lay down their arms and provide his soldiers with provisions, and then seized those who trusted him. Phlious he thought it necessary to overrun, because the Albanians had collected all their belongings there, and had been followed by many kindred spirits, who were ready to revolt at a signal from them. Then, leaving Zagan behind him to make a tour of the conquered Morea and to re-organise a government, Mohammed recrossed the isthmus in the late summer of 1460. His campaign had been a complete success. He had finally destroyed the last vestiges of Greek rule in the peninsula, and had annexed the whole of it to the Turkish Empire, save where the Venetian banner still waved over the colonies of Nauplia, Argos, and Thermisi, Coron, Modon, and Navarino, and where Monemvasia acknowledged the sway of the pope. His Greek biographer tells us that nearly 250 forts had fallen before him, and he had carried off thousands of the inhabitants, including many of the men of wealth, to Constantinople—the adults to repopulate his capital, the boys to serve in the corps of janissaries. The rest of the leading men fled to the Venetian colonies, and thus the country, deprived of its natural leaders, lay at the feet of the conqueror.[1]

The fate of the Palaiológoi deserves the notice which mankind usually bestows upon sovereigns in exile. Demétrios received from Mohammed the islands of Imbros and Lemnos, which his friend, the historian Kritóboulos, had been the means of securing for the Turks, together with a portion of Thasos and Samothrace, and the valuable mart and salt-mines of Ænos. These possessions, which had belonged to the great Genoese family of Gattilusio, brought in 600,000 *aspers* a year, in addition to which Demétrios received an annuity of 300,000 more from the mint at Adrianople. He was thus able to spend his time in riotous living and hunting till he was so unfortunate as to incur the sultan's anger. If we may believe the story of Phrantzês, a bitter enemy of Matthew Asan, that individual, who had accompanied his brother-in-law to Ænos, was accused of embezzling money from the salt-works by the sultan, who not only threatened him with impalement, but suspected Demétrios of being his accomplice, and deprived him of all his allowance, except just sufficient to keep body and soul together. A later writer, however, considers Demétrios to have been the culprit, and says that he was only saved from execution by the intervention of Mahmoud Pasha. One day, however, when Mohammed was hunting, he met the poor exile on foot, and was so deeply moved at the sight that he gave him a sum of 50,000 *aspers* from the proceeds of the corn-tax, much less than what he had enjoyed, but still enough to live on. In 1470 the Despot ended his pitiable career as a monk, David by name, at Adrianople, and as his daughter never married Mohammed after all—for the sultan feared that she might poison him—this branch of the family became extinct.[2]

[1] Chalkokondýles, 455-9, 470-85; Phrantzês, 388-97, 405-9; Doúkas, 340; *Chronicon Breve*, 521; Kritóboulos, iii., 14, 15, 19-24; *Historia Politica*, 32-3; Magno, *op. cit.*, 201, 203, 204; Sansovino, *op. cit.*, 152, 156; Kritóboulos, the apologist of Mohammed, makes no mention of the sultan's acts of perfidy. For the Athenian Palaiológoi, *cf.* Kampoúroglos, Μνημεῖα, i., 89; iii., 251-6.

[2] Kritóboulos, iii., 14, 15, 24; Phrantzês, 413-14, 427-9, 447; Chalkokondýles, 469, 483, 494; Spandugino, 43-4; *Historia Politica*, 35-6.

The sultan was naturally anxious to get Thomas as well as Demétrios into his clutches, in order to prevent him intriguing with the Western Powers against the Turkish Empire. He therefore sent an agent to Corfù with a request that the Despot would depute one of his *archons* to treat of peace and to arrange for an appanage, on which Thomas could live. But when the Despot's emissary arrived at the sultan's headquarters with a proposal to exchange Monemvasia for another sea-coast place, the latter flung him into prison, and only released him in order that he might convey to his master Mohammed's command that either Thomas or one of his sons should appear in person. Meanwhile, Thomas had despatched George Raoul to seek the aid of Pope Pius II., and on 16th November, 1460, set out for Ancona, accompanied by most of his magnates, and bearing the head of St Andrew, which had so long been preserved at Patras. The relic was a valuable asset, for many princes offered large sums for it, and its possessor had no difficulty in disposing of it to the pope in return for an annuity. The precious relic was deposited for safety in the castle of Narni, while Thomas proceeded to Rome, where Pius II. bestowed on him the Golden Rose, the symbol of virtue, a lodging in the Santo Spirito Hospital, and an allowance of 300 gold pieces a month, to which the cardinals added 200 more—a sum which his followers considered barely enough for his maintenance, and certainly not enough for theirs. Venice, indeed, contributed a sum of 500 ducats to his treasury, and concluded a treaty with him against the Turks, but there were no practical results of this alliance. Meanwhile, on 12th April, 1462, the day after Palm Sunday, Pius II. received the head of St Andrew at the Ponte Milvio, on the spot where the little chapel of that Apostle with its commemorative inscription now stands. Cardinal Bessarion handed the case containing it to the pope, who bade the sacred skull welcome among its relatives, the Romans, "the nephews of St Peter"—a ceremony depicted on the tomb of the Pontiff in Sant' Andrea della Valle. Shortly afterwards, the Despot's wife, who had remained with her family at Corfù, died and was buried in the church of SS. Jason and Sosipater, whereupon Thomas summoned his two sons and his daughter Zoe to join him. But before they arrived, he died, on 12th May 1465, and was buried in the crypt of St Peter's; but so completely has this scion of an imperial race been forgotten that no one knows his grave; yet every visitor to Rome unconsciously gazes on his features, for on account of his tall and handsome appearance he served as a model for the statue of St Paul, which still stands at the steps of St Peter's.[1]

The family of Palaiológos was now represented by his two sons and his two daughters. The elder daughter, Helene, widow of the last Despot of Servia, resided at the court of her son-in-law, Leonardo III., at Sta. Mavra, and a local legend, devoid of historical accuracy, ascribes to her the erection of the church whence the town received its name, in gratitude for the deliverance of herself and her daughter from shipwreck on 3rd May, the day of Sta. Mavra.[2] There she died as the nun Hypomoné in 1474, leaving two other daughters, one of whom died childless, while the third married the son of the Albanian hero, Skanderbeg, in whose descendants, and in those of the Tocchi, there thus flowed the blood of the Palaiológoi. Thomas's younger daughter, Zoe, or Sophia, was married first to a Caracciolo, and then to the Grand Duke Ivan III. of Russia, to whom she brought a dowry of 6000 gold pieces, provided by Pope Sixtus IV.—an event commemorated by one of the paintings in the Santo Spirito Hospital. With her daughter, the wife of Alexander Jagellon of Poland, the female line came to an end. The two sons do not seem to have profited much by the strict injunctions which Bessarion had laid down for their education. The elder, Andrew, who bore the empty title of Despot, which we find on his seals,[3] and continued to draw his father's allowance from the pope, fell into dissolute habits, and married a woman, named Catherine, off the streets of Rome, by whom he had no children. In such company, and with scarcely a rag to clothe his limbs, he aroused the pity or contempt of the Romans. His annuity was reduced; he had to take a back place at papal

[1] Phrantzês, 409-13, 415; Chalkokondýles, 485; *Pii. II. Commentarii*, 130, 192 *sqq.*; Spandugino, 42-3; Eroli, *Miscellanea Storica Narnese*, i., 70; Ciacconius, *Vitæ Pontificum*, II., 1076; Fortini, *Solenne Ricevimento della Testa di S'. Andrea Apostolo.* [2] Petritzópoulos, *op. cit.*, 48.

[3] Νέος Ἑλληνομνήμων, I., 426; Gottlob, *Aus der Camera Apostolica*, 292.

ceremonies. Once he was seized with the idea of recovering the Morea with Neopolitan aid, and induced Sixtus IV. to give him 2000 gold pieces for the purpose; but in 1494 he ceded all his rights to Charles VIII. of France, and in his last will and testament in 1502, he left Ferdinand and Isabella of Castille his heirs. In that year he died in Rome in such great misery that his widow had to beg his funeral expenses from the pope.[1] His younger brother, Manuel, a man of more spirit, preferred the risk of death at the hands of the sultan to the prospect of starving at the papal court. But to his surprise Mohammed gave him an establishment and a daily sum for its maintenance.[2] He remained a Christian, as did his elder son, who died young; but his second son, Andrew, became a Mussulman and is last heard of as Mohammed Pasha in the reign of Suleyman the Magnificent. Though the family of the Despots of the Morea would thus appear to have been long extinct, a Cornish antiquary announced in 1815 that the church of Landulph contained a monument to one of Thomas's descendants. But this claim is genealogically unsound, for there is no historical proof of the existence of the supposed third son of the Despot, mentioned in the brass plate at Landulph.[3] But after all, the world has not lost much by the extinction of the race, which, if it vainly tried to save Constantinople by an act of heroism, foolishly lost the Morea by its dissensions.

The faithful retainers of the Palaiológoi, disgusted at the prospects offered them in Rome, scattered all over Europe. Many followed the Grand Duchess Sophia to Russia, where they became absorbed in the Muscovite nobility; some went to France; others to Venice or Palermo; others again, like Nicholas Melissenós, the *fiancé* of Phrantzês's daughter, to Crete. The historian had declined to accompany his master to Rome; he remained in Corfù, moving from one village to another, till he finally settled down in the monastery of SS. Jason and Sosipater. A visit to the Despot Andrew in Rome at the time of his sister's first engagement, and a summons from the widowed Princess of Servia to the court of Leonardo

[1] Phrantzês, 424-5, 450; J. Volaterranus, *Diarium Romanum*, *apud* Muratori, xxiii., 157; *Mémoires de l'Académie des Inscriptions*, xvii., 572; Çurita, *Anales*, v., 210.
[2] *Historia Politica*, 34; Spandugino, 43.
[3] *Archæologia*, xviii., 83 *sqq*.

Tocco at Sta. Mavra, broke the monotony of his life. At last, the busy diplomatist, his career closed, became a monk, under the name of Gregórios, and in his silent cell occupied himself with composing, at the request of some noble Corfiotes, the story of his troublous times,[1] till at last he was laid to rest by the side of his master's consort in the quiet church at Kastrádes. Phrantzês did not write without anger or bias; but he has given us a living picture of the leading actors in the tragic drama in which he too had played a part. And to-day, beside the tomb of mediæval Greece's last contemporary historian, the friend of the young Greek kingdom may meditate on the causes which for nearly four centuries placed the Greeks beneath the sway of the Turks.

The fall of the two Greek principalities in the Morea was closely followed by the destruction of the fragments that remained of the duchy of Athens. On his way back from the peninsula in 1460, Mohammed II. revisited Athens and reinspected the old city and the harbours. Unfortunately, the janissaries stationed on the Akropolis told him that some Athenians had conspired to restore Franco. The sultan not only arrested ten of the richest citizens and took them away to Constantinople, but resolved to rid himself of his former favourite. Franco, as the man of the Turk, was at the moment serving with his Bœotian cavalry in Mohammed's camp, and received orders from his suzerain to join in the attack which was about to be made on Leonardo III. Tocco in western Greece. The "Lord of Thebes" so strongly objected to being compelled to fight against his fellow-Christians, that, though he received as large revenues from Thebes and Livadia as he had ever had from Athens, he had written to Francesco Sforza of Milan offering his services as a *condottiere* for the sum of 10,000 ducats a year.[2] He was forced, however, to obey the sultan's orders, and, after defeating Tocco, repaired to the headquarters of Zagan, the governor of the Morea. Zagan had meanwhile been told by Mohammed to kill him. The Pasha invited him to his tent, and detained him in conversation till nightfall; then, as the unsuspecting Franco was on his way back to his own tent,

[1] Phrantzês, 411, 424, 425, 429, 430, 453.
[2] Νέος Ἑλληνομνήμων, i., 216-18.

the Pasha's guards strangled him. Such was the sorry ending of the last "Lord of Thebes." Thereupon, Mohammed annexed Thebes and all Bœotia, and thus obliterated the last trace of the Frankish duchy of Athens from the map. Franco's three sons, Matteo, Jacopo, and Gabriele, with their mother, were taken to Constantinople and enrolled in the corps of janissaries, where one of them afterwards showed military and administrative ability of so high an order as to win the favour of his sovereign. Their mother, a daughter of Demétrios Asan of Mouchli, and famed for her beauty, became the cause of a terrible tragedy, which convulsed alike court and church. George Amoiroútses, the former minister and betrayer of the last Emperor of Trebizond, fell desperately in love with the fair widow, to whom he addressed impassioned verses, and swore, though he had a wife still living, to marry her or die. The œcumenical patriarch forbade the bans, and lost his beard and his office rather than yield to the sultan. But swift retribution fell upon the bigamist, for he dropped down dead, a dice-box in his hand.[1]

Though the Acciajuoli dynasty had thus fallen for ever, members of that great family still remained in Greece. An Acciajuoli was made civil governor of the old Venetian colony of Coron, in Messenia, when the Spaniards captured it from the Turks in 1532. When they abandoned it, he accompanied them, but was captured by an Algerine pirate, who sold him as a slave to a Greek. Eventually he was re-sold to a Spaniard, only to die in poverty at Naples, where his race had first risen to eminence, and where it became extinct.[2] At the beginning of the last century the French traveller, Pouqueville,[3] was shown at Athens a donkey-driver named Neri, in whose veins flowed the blood of the Florentine dukes; and the modern historian of Christian Athens, Neroûtsos, used to contend that his family was descended from Nerozzo Pitti, lord of Sykaminon and uncle of the last duke of Athens.[4] In

[1] Chalkokondýles, 483-4; *Historia Patriarchica*, 97-100; Spandugino, 44; Ubaldini, 178-9, Δελτίον τῆς Ἐθνολογικῆς Ἑταιρίας, II., 281-2; *The Chronicles of Rabbi Joseph*, 281-2.

[2] Litta, viii., Tab. 4.

[2] *Voyage dans la Grèce*, iv., 90.

[4] Kampoúroglos, Μνημεῖα, i., 289-92; Ἱστορία, ii., 45.

Florence the family became extinct only so recently as 1834; and the Certosa and the Lung' Arno Acciajuoli still preserve its memory there. In the Florence gallery, too, are two coloured portraits of the dukes of Athens, which would seem to be those of Nerio I. and the bastard Antonio I. In that case, the Florentine dukes of Athens are the only Frankish rulers of Greece, except the palatine counts of Cephalonia, whose likeness has been preserved to posterity.

Thus ended the strange connection between Florence and Athens. A titular duke of Athens had become tyrant of the Florentines, a Florentine merchant had become Duke of Athens; but the age when French and Italian adventurers could find an El Dorado on the poetic soil of Greece was over.

The Turkish conquest of continental Greece was completed by the campaign against Leonardo III. Tocco, in which the unhappy Franco had been forced to take part. For several years, in spite of an occasional dispute with his Venetian protectors, the Duke of Leucadia had enjoyed peace in his islands, while the three points which he still held on the mainland remained unmolested by his Turkish neighbours. But he was so patriotic or so impolitic as to second Skanderbeg in his rising against the Turks, and this brought down upon him the vengeance of the sultan. According to one account, he was taken prisoner at Corinth, whence he escaped by the aid of a corsair to Sta. Mavra; but he lost the last of his continental possessions, except the strong fortress of Vonitza on the Ambrakian Gulf. When, three years later, he heard that Venice was preparing to recover the Morea from the Turks, he begged the aid of the republic, whose honorary citizen he was, in reconquering the old Despotat of Arta, where he still possessed many adherents. This scheme, however, came to nothing.[1]

To complete the picture of continental Greece as she was at the date of the Turkish Conquest, it remains to describe the condition of the Venetian colonies. North of the isthmus, Lepanto, for which the republic continued to pay an annual tribute of 100 gold ducats to the sultan, had increased

[1] Magno, 201; Predelli, *Commemoriali*, v., 131; Lunzi, *Della Condizione*, 178-81.

in population owing to the immigration of fugitives from the Despotat of Arta and from the Morea. These immigrants, mostly Albanians, had their own chief, and obtained exemption from obnoxious *corvées* on their boats and beasts of burden. But an earthquake and the cost of repairing the fortifications unfortunately made it necessary to reduce the garrison and thus diminished Venetian influence in Epiros.[1] Both Lepanto and Pteleon, the Venetian station at the entrance of the Gulf of Volo, were now surrounded by the Turkish empire, so that their position was naturally precarious. It had been decided that the garrison of Pteleon should be Italian, and that a citizen of Eubœa who knew Greek and was acquainted with Thessaly should be its rector, and, as we saw, the post was held for seven years by Niccolò Zorzi, son of the last Marquis of Boudonitza; but after his time, the old system of appointing a governor direct from Venice was adopted.[2] The five-mile frontage on the mainland opposite Eubœa is mentioned as still belonging to Venice in 1439, but its cultivation was of doubtful advantage to the islanders, because, though corn could now be exported in large quantities, their peasants were constantly surprised while at work by the Turks.

Of the great island itself the republic had been practically absolute mistress ever since the disappearance of the Dalle Carceri and Ghisi families towards the end of the last century. When the three great baronies then became vacant, the Venetian bailie disposed of them as seemed most to the interest of his Government, bestowing the third of the Ghisi upon a number of small holders, and the two-thirds of the Dalle Carceri upon Januli d'Anoe, whose family retained its share till the Turkish Conquest, and upon Maria Sanudo, whose share descended to the Sommaripa of Paros. But all these feudal lords, like the Zorzi of Karystos, were the creatures of the republic, and the real governor of the island was the Venetian bailie. All the fortresses in D'Anoe's barony, for example, were garrisoned by Venetian troops; it was to Venice that his vassals appealed for justice, and every four months the baron himself was bound to present

[1] Sáthas, i., 213; v., 2-5; Thomas and Predelli, *Diplomatarium*, ii., 345, 383.

[2] Sáthas, iii., 223, 430, 452, 455.

himself at Negroponte with two good horses and an esquire.[1] Next to the republic, the most important person in the colony was the titular patriarch of Constantinople—a dignity still connected with the see of Negroponte. In 1426, we are told that he owned a quarter of the island and that he had many serfs, but that he shirked his share of the public burdens.[2] After the peace of 1430 between Venice and the sultan, the island enjoyed a brief revival of prosperity, and the lamentations of the colonists were less loud. A protective measure to encourage the local wine trade proved most beneficial, and the famous plain of Lilanto, which a special official, the *potamarch*, was bound to keep irrigated, was then called "the life of this island, the eye and garden of Negroponte," as it still is.[3] Care, too, was taken to humour the Jews, who were the chief merchants and who bore the chief burden of taxation, and their ghetto at the capital was enlarged. Originally, they had lived outside the city; but they had entered the walls for greater security; in 1355 the ghetto had been assigned to them, and finally, in 1440, their numbers had so much increased that its boundaries were extended, with the proviso that if they dwelt beyond a certain tower they would forfeit their houses and be banished for ever. Orders, too, were given that the ghettos at Karystos and Oreos were to be repaired, that the law should be equal for them and the Christians, and that the public hangman should no longer be chosen from among them.[4] But there were signs that the island was declining. The harbours of Negroponte and Karystos became choked with sand; the walls needed repair; the plague made such havoc, that the vassals of Karystos were reduced to between two and three thousand; Catalan corsairs still infested the coasts; the Albanian immigrants were becoming restive; and the Turks, after a long interval, resumed their operations, so that the captain of the bridge was ordered to pass the night there. Then came the alarming news of the destruction of Christian rule in Constantinople and on the mainland, and the scare of Mohammed II.'s visit. Taxes were hastily remitted to pacify the islanders, and the Home Government

[1] Sáthas, i., 197-8; iii., 316-18.
[2] *Ibid.*, iii., 312.
[3] *Ibid.*, iii., 361, 452-7.
[4] *Ibid.*, iii., 279, 464.

became seriously alarmed about the island, "on the possession of which depends the maintenance of our sea-power," as they wrote to the bailie.

It is to the closing years of Venetian rule in Negroponte that we owe the copy of the *Book of the Customs of the Empire of Romania*, to which allusion was made in the third chapter. In 1421 a commission of twelve citizens was ordered to be elected for the purpose of drawing up in a single volume the laws and customs prevalent in the Latin Orient. The work was not finished till thirty years later, when the last Latin Archbishop of Athens, Niccolò Protimo, himself a native of the island, was entrusted with the collation of the completed copy sent from Negroponte with that preserved in the chancery at Venice. It was then found that the Eubœan code contained 147 more articles than the Venetian, and of these only 37 were approved. The code, as we have it, consists of 219 articles with 8 extra articles added by Nicholas de Joinville, bailie of Achaia more than a century earlier, and is written in the Venetian dialect.[1]

South of the isthmus, the two groups of Venetian colonies in Argolis and in Messenia had suffered considerably, as we saw, from the disturbed state of the peninsula, now from the Despots and now from the Turks. The population of Nauplia had been increased by a settlement of Albanians, and a band of gypsies had been encamped there as far back as the end of the fourteenth century under a chief, or *drungarius*, to whom special privileges were granted. But the local aristocracy claimed the exclusive right to hold the various offices, as of yore, and complained of the condition of the walls and the riotous behaviour of the light horsemen in the suite of the governor.[2] At Modon and Coron the treatment of the serfs was the most important question at this period; they complained that they had to provide straw and grass for the horses of the governor, and to lend their own animals for his hunting-parties; and they were subject to a *corvée*, or *parapiasmo*, as it was called, of two days a month; but they seem to have prospered under

[1] Sáthas, iii., 225; Magno, 198; Canciani, *Leges Barbarorum*, iii., 497.

[2] Sáthas, iii., 192, 443; iv., 187-91; Hopf, *Geschichte*, lxxxvi., 113.

Venetian rule, for there were rich peasants among them who were willing to pay a large sum for enfranchisement. The Greek bishop was now allowed to live in the town of Coron, instead of some miles outside, and twice a year the Greek priests and monks paid a tax to the republic. Emigration, however, was such an evil, that the taxes were lowered in order to encourage people to live in the colony.[1]

While, all around, principalities were falling, Venice had, at this eleventh hour, added to her Greek colonies. In 1451, the classic island of Ægina, which she had long coveted, became hers. It had been arranged, twenty-six years before, as we saw, that, when the Caopena family became extinct, the republic should take their inheritance. In 1451, Antonello Caopena, son-in-law of the Duke Antonio I. of Athens, died without heirs, after having bequeathed the island to Venice. The islanders welcomed Venetian rule; the claims of Antonello's uncle Arnà, who had lands in Argolis, where a mountain still bears his name, were satisfied by a pension, and a Venetian governor, or *rettore*, was appointed, who was dependent on the authorities of Nauplia. After Arnà's death, his son Alioto renewed his claim to the island, but was told that the republic was firmly resolved to keep it. He and his family were pensioned, and one of them loyally aided in the defence of Ægina against the Turks in 1537, was captured with his family, and died in a Turkish dungeon. Venice, however, ransomed his wife and children, who came and settled as poor and simple citizens on the lagoons. There they remained till, in 1648, the last of the race died, as priest of S. Giovanni in Bragora. Such was the end of the Catalan lords of Ægina.[2]

Two years after the annexation of Ægina, the Venetian admiral occupied the Northern Sporades—Skyros, Skiathos, and Skopelos—the original fief of the Ghisi, which had belonged to the Byzantine Empire for nearly two centuries. Now that that empire had fallen, the islanders were absolutely defenceless against the attacks of pirates. One

[1] Sáthas, iii., 343, 421, 459; iv., 29; v., 94; Jorga, vi., 379; viii., 95.

[2] Magno, 197; Mar, iv., f. 80, 83; Hopf, *Karystos* (tr. Sardagna), 71 *sqq*. The mountain peak of Arnâ is near Epidauros, where Arnà's lands lay (Meliarákes, Ἄργολις, 65).

party preferred the mild rule of the Gattilusii of Lesbos, another that of the *maona*, or Genoese Company, which ruled over Chios, but the majority favoured a Venetian protectorate, of which their neighbours in Eubœa had had so long an experience. Accordingly, they offered their island home to the Venetian admiral, on condition that he would confirm their ancient privileges and preserve their episcopal see. At first he hestitated, for three of the four castles of Skyros were now in ruins, and such an acquisition seemed therefore to be more of an expense than a profit to his Government. An embassy sent by the natives to the Genoese forced him, however, to consent, for he knew that Venice would not tolerate her great rival so near her most important colony. Two Venetian rectors, dependent on the bailie of Negroponte, were sent to govern the islands, the republic granted their privileges and heard their petitions, and they remained in her possession till 1538.[1]

Finally, as we saw, two of the Cyclades, Tenos and Mykonos, had been under Venetian authority since the extinction of the Ghisi family in 1390, and had been farmed out to a Venetian citizen, who was dependent on Negroponte. But the islands were so poor and so thinly inhabited, that the rent was reduced. Turkish depredations were frequent, and the islanders complained to the Senate, to which they were faithful even when misgoverned. In 1430 a governor was accordingly sent direct from Venice, the two islands were declared independent of Eubœa, and the privileges of the people were confirmed. Still, the most ample franchises could not keep off Catalan and Turkish corsairs.[2] Thus, in 1460, the dull uniformity of Turkish rule spread over the land, save where the dukes of the Archipelago and the Venetian colonies still remained the sole guardians of Western culture, the only rays of light in the once brilliant Latin Orient.

[1] Magno, 198-9; Navagero *apud* Muratori, xxiii., 1116; Chalkokondýles, 431; Sáthas, v., 45.

[2] Sáthas, iii., 144, 181, 414; iv., 236.

CHAPTER XIV

THE VENETIAN COLONIES (1462-1540)

AFTER the fall of the duchy of Athens and the principality of Achaia, the only Latin possessions left on the mainland of Greece were the papal city of Monemvasia, the fortress of Vonitza on the Ambrakian Gulf, and the Venetian colonies, composed of four distant and isolated groups—the Messenian stations of Coron and Modon with its dependency, Navarino; the castles of Argos and Nauplia, to which the island of Ægina was subordinate, and the frontier fortresses of Lepanto and Pteleon. It only remains, then, to complete the history of Frankish rule on the Greek continent by describing the fortunes of these lingering offshoots of Italy down to the capture of the last of them by the Turks in 1540. With them, for the sake of clearness, we may include the fate of the Venetian island of Negroponte and that of the insular domain of the Tocchi in the palatine county of Cephalonia.

However little the Venetians might desire it, a war between the republic and the sultan was clearly inevitable; they were convinced that the great conqueror intended to round off his Greek territories by the acquisition of their remaining colonies upon Greek soil, and they wisely availed themselves of the short breathing-space afforded by the sultan's attack upon the empire of Trebizond to put their fortifications in order. An inscription on the ruins of Coron still commemorates the repair of that outpost,[1] while Ægina obtained money for her defences by the unwilling sacrifice of her cherished relic, the head of St George, which had been carried thither from Livadia by the Catalans after their

[1] *Risposta di Jacopo Grandi*, 144; Buchon, *La Grèce Continentale*, 454 (the latter gives the date wrong); Sáthas, i., 237-8.

expulsion from the Athenian duchy. The kings of Aragon had not abandoned the hope of obtaining possession of the coveted head. Alfonso V. had sent an emissary to carry it off; but a great storm prevented his design, and the relic was restored to the church of St George, in the lofty town of what is now Palaiochora. In 1462, however, the Venetian Senate ordered the relic to be removed to S. Giorgio Maggiore at Venice, and this time, to the dismay of the Greeks, the saint wrought no miracle to prevent this act of sacrilege. On 12th November, it was transported from Ægina by Vettore Cappello, the famous Venetian commander, and placed in S. Giorgio, and the monastery and the Senate tried to soothe the feelings of the Æginetans by giving 100 ducats apiece towards fortifying the island.[1]

The Turks soon found an excuse for hostilities. An Albanian slave, the property of the governor of Athens, had run away with some of his master's property, and had sought refuge in the house of Valaresso, one of the councillors of Modon. The Venetian authorities of that colony refused to give him up, whereupon, in November 1462, Omar, son of Turakhan, the captor of Athens, marched upon Lepanto, and almost took that important fortress; while Isâ, who had succeeded Zagan in the governorship of the Morea, occupied Argos without a blow, owing to the treachery of a Greek priest, and Turkish bands ravaged the country round Modon. The war-party in Venice then persuaded the Government to fight, and in 1463 a war began, which lasted, more or less continuously, till 1479. Bertoldo d'Este was appointed commander-in-chief of the Venetian land forces, and ordered to proceed to Nauplia and co-operate with the fleet under Loredano; while the heroic Albanian leader, Skanderbeg, was provided with subsidies, in order that he might create a diversion among the mountains of his native land. D'Este recruited his forces by opening the Cretan gaols and converting the prisoners into soldiers. At the same time he issued a proclamation, calling upon the Greeks to rise and regain their freedom with his assistance. The long rule of the Franks had had the effect of making them far more warlike

[1] Magno, *apud* Hopf, *Chroniques*, 202; Cornelius, *Ecclesiæ Venetæ*, viii., 173-93, 270-1; Malipiero, *Annali*, in *Archivio Storico Italiano*, vii., 12.

than they had been at the time of the Latin Conquest; and, provided that they were sure of foreign aid, they were ready to rise against the Turks. The Spartans took up arms under the leadership of Michael Rálles, a primate belonging to a distinguished Lacedæmonian family of Norman or Albanian origin. The Arkadians found a chief in Peter Boua—the same Albanian who had headed a rising against the Greeks nine years earlier, and the Mainates, as ever, showed a spirit of independence. Monemvasia, weary, as was to be expected, of papal rule, begged the protection of a state which of all Catholic communities was notoriously the least bigoted; the pope was far off, the papal governor was helpless; and ere long a Venetian *podestà*, paid out of the treasury of the Venetian islands of Lemnos or Crete, was sent out to the great fortress.[1]

At first, fortune smiled on the Venetian arms. Argos was speedily retaken; its castle, the famous Larissa, soon hoisted the lion-banner of St Mark; another old Frankish town, that of Vostitza, drove out the Turks; and D'Este was able to send home a long list of fortresses which had joyfully opened their gates to his men. Among them it is interesting to notice such familiar Frankish names as Karytaina, Santameri, and Geraki, which now reappears after a long silence. Several strong positions, however, remained in Turkish hands, chief among them Akrocorinth, whose fate was certain to determine that of the rest. Accordingly, D'Este and Loredano set to work to besiege it. But first, in order to encourage the Greeks, they rebuilt the famous wall across the isthmus, which had been destroyed by Murâd II. The two commanders put the first stone in its place, and their example filled their men with such zeal that in fifteen days the restored Hexamilion, 12 feet high and flanked with 136 towers, stretched from sea to sea. A religious ceremony celebrated the completion of the work; an altar was erected in the middle of the wall; mass was performed; and the flag of the Evangelist was hoisted over the ramparts. Such an achievement was

[1] The acquisition of Monemvasia was, according to Phrantzês and Magno, in 1464; but Malatesta's secretary puts it in 1463. The Venetian document (Regina, fol. 52) appointing its *podestà* is dated 17th September 1464.

thought worthy of a picture on the ceiling of the Doge's Palace. Unfortunately the work had been too hastily done; the wall was too low, and the stones had no mortar to keep them together.

The success of the Venetians was now checked. D'Este, uncautiously removing his helmet in the heat of an attack on Akrocorinth, was struck by a stone, and died of the wound. The same day the news arrived that Mahmoud Pasha, the grand vizier, with the victorious army which had just ended for ever the ancient kingdom of Bosnia, was marching to the assault of the Isthmian wall. Its defenders, without a general, decimated by dysentery, and alarmed at the great numerical superiority of the enemy, abandoned the Hexamilion without striking a blow, and retreated to Nauplia. The Turks once more destroyed the rampart across the isthmus, reoccupied Argos, levelled that city with the ground, and sent its inhabitants to Constantinople, where they received lands and houses from the sultan at the Peribleptos monastery. A much worse fate was reserved for the loyal subjects of Venice in Messenia, many of whom were sawn asunder by the orders of Mohammed II. Finding that their Venetian allies were unable to defend them, the Spartans retired to the fastnesses of Taygetos, whence the Turks in vain endeavoured to lure them by promises of amnesty.[1]

Venice was not, however, discouraged by the failure of her arms. Sigismondo Malatesta, the husband of Isotta and the builder of the cathedral in his native town of Rimini, was appointed as D'Este's successor; but that most famous scion of his family gained little glory from his Peloponnesian campaign. He succeeded, indeed, in taking two of the three rings of walls which compose the old Byzantine capital of Mistrâ; but the splendid castle resisted his assaults, discord broke out in his camp, and he hurriedly returned home to defend his interests there against the pope, with no other prize than the bones of the philosopher Gemistòs Pléthon,

[1] Phrantzês, 414-15; Chalkokondýles, 545, 555-64; *Chronicon breve*, 521; Magno *apud* Hopf, *Chroniques*, 202-3; Ἄνθος, *ibid.*, 268; Sanudo and Navagero *apud* Muratori, xxii., 1172-3; xxiii., 1121-3; *Lettera d'un Segretario*, *apud* Sáthas, vi., 95-7; Daru, *Histoire de Venise*, ii., 443-6; Kritóboulos, bk. iv., ch. 16; v., 1, 2; Lámpros, Ἔγγραφα, 134-5; Regina, fol. 52, 56 (in *J. H. S.* xxvii., 241).

whose neo-Platonic doctrines he had embraced, and whose remains he laid in the cathedral at Rimini, where the tombs of the Spartan sage and the Italian lord may still be seen.[1]

Venice now sent one of her most distinguished sons to the front. Vettore Cappello had had a large experience of Greek affairs, and the news of his appointment to the command of the fleet in the Levant inspired the troops with fresh hopes. Nor did his first achievements belie their expectations. Directing his course to the north of the Ægean, he completed the conquest, begun by his predecessors, of the group of islands which had once belonged to the Gattilusii, and then cast anchor at the Piræus in the summer of 1466. For a brief moment Athens figured again in the pages of history. Cappello marched upon the city before dawn on 12th July, and captured the whole of the lower town. The sack yielded his men a large booty, but he spared the lives of the Greek inhabitants, and contented himself with firing the Turkish ships in the harbour. As the Akropolis was strongly fortified and well provisioned, he made no attempt to besiege it, and sailed away to Patras.

If this second Venetian capture of Athens had no practical results, it has at least afforded us a last glimpse of the city, for to this moment we may ascribe the anonymous description, written by a Venetian, which was published a few years ago.[2] The author tells us that almost all the rock on which the castle stood was then surrounded with houses; he alludes to the great strength of the Akropolis, and distinguishes between the "modern walls" of the city and the ancient circumvallation, which was "larger than that of Padua." The west portal of the Stoa of Hadrian then served as the gate of the town; the Tower of the Winds, later on a *tekkeh* of Dervishes, was then a Greek church; and near the Stadion there dwelt the *fraticelli della mala opinione*—an heretical sect, which, rooted out of Western Europe, had thus found a refuge under the tolerant rule of the Turks. Of the other ancient monuments, the cultured visitor describes the Temple of Olympian Zeus, which then had one column less than in

[1] Sanudo and Navagero in *op. cit.*, xxii., 1179-82; xxiii., 1123; Malipiero, 32-6; Sáthas, i., 242-57; vi., 87, 92-4, 98; Sansovino, f. 194.

[2] *Mitteilungen des k. deutschen Arch. Instituts* (*Athen*), xxiv., 72-88.

the time of his predecessor, Cyriacus; the arch and aqueduct of Hadrian, the latter still locally known as "Aristotle's Study"; the choragic monument of Lysikrates, the monument of Philópappos, the west wing of which had partially collapsed since the visit of the antiquary of Ancona; the Theseion, or "temple of the Gods"; the Roman market-place with the gate of Athena Archegetis and the pillar of Hadrian inscribed with the regulations for the oil trade. He also mentions a Roman tomb to the north of the Olympieion, which has escaped the notice of other travellers. As the Turks were in possession of the Akropolis, he was, as he says,[1] "unable to approach" sufficiently near to examine the monument of Thrasyllos, and could only descry the west front of the Parthenon, which was still a church. That, and the "ancient palace" of the Acciajuoli in the Propylæa, are the only buildings which he could see clearly from below, and which he therefore mentions as standing there. Down at the Piræus he admired the famous lion, from whose mouth—so he was told—water used to flow; and on the Sacred Way, he waxes enthusiastic over the marbles and mosaics of Daphni, "the most beautiful I have ever seen." From this time forth, Athens disappeared from the ken of Europe for more than a century. A German traveller who passed by it in 1483 speaks of "the faint and almost obliterated vestiges of Athens," which he did not deem worthy of a visit; and seven severe plagues and the tribute of Christian children decimated the scanty population.[2]

Disasters now again befell the Venetian arms. Barbarigo, the governor of the Morea, weary of a year of inaction, resolved, against the better advice of Rálles, to undertake the siege of Patras, and allowed himself to be enticed into an ambush by the Turks under the redoubtable Omar.

[1] *Mitteilungen des k. deutschen Arch. Instituts* (*Athen*), xxiv., 76. This passage fixes the date at 1466, for the Akropolis was then inaccessible. The only other historical indication in the narrative is the allusion to D'Este's death before Corinth in 1463. The omission of all mention of the Turks also points to a moment when the city was in Venetian hands.

[2] The authorities for the capture of Athens are:—Sabellico, Dec. III., Lib. 8; Secreta, xxii., fol. 186; Magno, 204; Phrantzês, 425; Sanudo and Navagero (xxii., 1183; xxiii., 1125); Malatesta's secretary (Sáthas, vi., 99); Malipiero, 37.

Both the Venetian and the Moreot chieftains were impaled by the brutal conqueror; Cappello's efforts to take Patras failed; the land forces retreated to Kalamata, where, beneath the old castle of William de Villehardouin, they sustained a fresh defeat; and the admiral withdrew to Negroponte, where he died of a broken heart. For five months he had never been seen to smile. His kneeling figure, the hat, —his coat-of-arms—and an inscription commemorating his deeds at sea and his death in Eubœa, adorn the portal of the church of S. Aponal in Venice.[1]

For the next three years a desultory struggle was waged in the Morea, with results unfavourable to the republic. The death of Pius II. at Ancona had prevented the crusade which his zeal and the tireless eloquence of Bessarion had organised; his successor, Paul II., though a Venetian, lacked enthusiasm; and the selfish policy, for which Venice was distinguished, had prevented the other Italian states from rallying to her aid against the Turks. Skanderbeg alone of her allies remained in arms, and with his death, in 1468, she would gladly have come to terms with the sultan on the basis of *uti possidetis*. Of the 122 castles of the Morea, only 26 were now in Venetian hands; more than 40 castles lay in ruins; over 50 flew the Turkish flag, among them the old Frankish stronghold of Geraki. Still Venice retained all her old colonies except Argos; her rectors held sway over Maina and Lemnos; her *podestà* governed the sheer rock of Monemvasia; the Greeks of Mitylene had gone to cultivate the waste lands of her cherished Negroponte.[2]

Mohammed II. had long coveted that splendid island, and the moment had now arrived for the realisation of his cherished plan. So well-informed a Government as that of Venice could not be in any doubt of what was intended, nor was it forgotten that the sultan had once already inspected Negroponte. From all sides, from Cyprus, Rhodes, and Cephalonia, from Naples and from Burgundy, the republic sought aid in the defence of her prized possession; but of all these allies, one alone, the Count of Cephalonia, sent a

[1] Foregoing authorities and Sansovino, f. 203; Sáthas, i., 258; vii., 7, 8, 15, 26, 48; Kritóboulos, v., 13: Chalkokondýles, 558.

[2] Magno, 205-6.

galley to join the Venetian fleet. "The princes of Christendom," it was said, "looked on as if in a theatre."

Early in June 1470, the Turkish fleet of 300 sail, with 60,000 or 70,000 men on board, issued from the Dardanelles; and, after taking Imbros, and making a futile attempt to capture the strong castles of Lemnos and Skyros, traversed the Doro channel at the south end of Eubœa, and proceeded up to Negroponte. On the way, the Turkish admiral occupied the castle of Styra and the great square tower, which still stands in the village of Basilikó, near Chalkis, and on 15th June cast anchor in the bay of Burchio, the modern Bourkos; there his men disembarked and planted their tents on the shore of Millemoza, as the inmost recess of that bay was called, within a short distance of the land walls of the city. The next two days were occupied in skirmishes, but on the 18th the ardour of the garrison was checked by the spectacle of a long line of Turkish troops descending through the pass of Anephorites along the road from Thebes,[1] headed by the great sultan himself. For two hours Mohammed II. stood at the head of the bridge over the Euripos and carefully examined the enchanted castle, which stood in the middle of the stream till a wanton and useless act of Vandalism in our own time removed it. Then, judging that mode of entry into the city impracticable—for the stream is a mill-race and the drawbridge was up—he moved to the Punta, or Bocca di S. Marco, as the narrow entrance of the small bay to the south of the Euripos was then called, and ordered a bridge of boats to be constructed across to the island. Over this, at the Ave Maria, a third of the army passed; next morning the sultan, his son, and the bulk of the army followed. Mohammed established his headquarters at Sta. Chiara, half a mile from the city, and his lines extended past the Nun's Mountain, as the eminence of Veli Baba behind Chalkis was then called from a convent of the Virgin which stood there, past the suburb of S. Francesco and as far as the fountain of Arethusa, on the road to Eretria. On the mainland of Bœotia, at the Forks, as the present fort of Kara Baba was then described, a battery

[1] "Struez" is no doubt meant for "Stives"—the natural way for the sultan to come.

was placed, so that the city was completely invested except on the north. On that side, however, the sultan constructed a second bridge of boats, which were dragged over land from the bay of Burchio to the Atalante channel.

The condition of the place, as its defenders well knew, was not satisfactory. The walls had been, indeed, repaired forty years before; and on every battlement of the sea-wall the lion of the Evangelist bade defiance to the infidels; a moat washed the walls on the land side, so that it was completely surrounded by water; but the republic had strangely omitted to fortify the two heights which commanded the town, that of the Forks and that of the Nun's Mountain, trusting to her fleet to save Negroponte in her hour of need. Unfortunately, the fleet was under the command of Niccolò da Canale, a better lawyer than seaman, who, instead of giving battle to the Turkish armada, had dallied off the island of Skiathos, and then sailed away to Candia, to the great surprise of the Cretan authorities.

At the time of the siege, the bailie was Paolo Erizzo, who had actually completed his two years' term of office, but who had remained on at his post in the hope that his presence might be of use. For a similar reason, Giovanni Bondumier, the *ex-provveditore*—for in view of the Turkish peril, a *provveditore* as well as a bailie had latterly been sent to Negroponte—was still in the city, though his successor, Alvise Calbo, had actually arrived. These men were the soul of the defence of Negroponte, and were bravely supported by the numerous Venetian colony. The city contained 2500 souls, besides fugitives, and the garrison had recently been strengthened by 700 men from Candia and a force of 500 foot soldiers under the leadership of a Dalmatian named Tommaso, who was in charge of all the engines of war. Against them was the vast host of the Turks, variously estimated at 120,000 and 300,000 men, exclusive of the naval forces.

On 25th June, when he had made all his preparations, the sultan, through an Italian interpreter, summoned the bailie to surrender, saying that he was resolved to have the city, but that, if the bailie would yield at once, he would exempt the inhabitants from all taxes for ten years, would give to every noble who had a house two, and would allow the bailie and the *provveditore* to live in comfort at Negroponte, or else would assign them a liberal allowance at Constantinople. To this the bailie ordered his aide-de-camp to reply, that Venice had made Negroponte her own, that ten or twelve days at the most would decide her fate, and that, with God's help, he would burn the sultan's fleet and root up his tents, so that he would not know where to hide his diminished head. At this bold reply all the men on the wall shouted aloud, and the interpreter was bidden go tell his master to eat swine's flesh, and then try to storm the moat. This insult was faithfully reported to Mohammed, who from that moment resolved that the garrison should have no mercy.

The same evening the bombardment began. The sultan had twenty-one (according to another account, forty-two), powerful pieces of artillery, which he had placed in commanding positions, both on the island and at Kara Baba, and which kept up a continuous fire day and night. None of the 120 huge stones which they fired failed to fall into the doomed city, and to this day they may be seen piled up in one of the squares of the town, a memento of the great siege. Meanwhile, a first assault was made upon the walls. The Turks threw fascines into the moat; but the defenders succeeded in setting fire to them, and the besiegers were forced to retreat with heavy loss. On 30th June a second assault was made with still more disastrous results, but the day witnessed two serious catastrophes for the Christians. The Turkish cavalry scoured the island as far north as Oreos, killing every one above the age of fifteen; the castle of La Cuppa was betrayed, and the 3000 Greeks, who had fled there for safety, were butchered in cold blood before the walls of Negroponte. The same fate overtook the crew of a vessel, laden with troops and munitions of war, which unwittingly fell into the midst of the Turkish fleet in the bay of Burchio.

There was a traitor, however, in the capital as well as at La Cuppa. A Dalmatian named Luca, from the island of Curzola, was found missing, and the story of an old Greek woman, who was intimate with the mistress of the Dalmatian captain, Tommaso, aroused the suspicion of the bailie. The missing man's brother was arrested, and, under threat of torture, confessed that Luca had been sent by Tommaso's orders. The latter's trumpeter, he added, could tell the reason. The trumpeter, confronted with the bailie, at once made a complete disclosure of the plot. "We are all foes of Christendom," he said, and then went on to accuse a certain Albanian, employed in the governor's palace, of having been in Turkish pay for the last seven years. This man's house was searched, and three arrows with compromising inscriptions were discovered there. The first, in Greek, ran as follows: "I am thy servant; what I have promised is ready"; the other two, in Turkish, came from the sultan's camp, and bade the traitor perform his promise, for the sultan had come at his words, and could tarry no longer. The news that the plot was out soon reached the arch-traitor, Tommaso. The Dalmatian resolved to brave it out; he mounted his horse, and, at the head of a hundred of his men, rode towards the piazza, vowing that he would cut off the nose of the fellow who had arrested his friends. But the bailie had meanwhile made his preparations; the square was lined with troops, and in the centre Erizzo himself was walking calmly up and down with a number of Venetian nobles, as if nothing had happened. On seeing the traitor, the bailie asked him why he had come with such a retinue, thus leaving the walls unguarded. Disarmed by Erizzo's innocent air, Tommaso dismissed his men, and followed the bailie into the latter's palace, to discuss some question of repairs to the ramparts. But scarcely had he crossed the threshold than Alvise Dolfin stabbed him in the neck. Fifty swords flashed through his body, as many of his company were put to death, and their captain with his secretary and trumpeter hung by one foot from the pillars of the bailie's palace. Their corpses were then taken down, quartered, and fired from the guns into the Turkish camp. So savage was the vengeance which the Venetians took upon the Dalmatian's men, that the bailie lamented the loss of so many marksmen.

The sultan, ignorant of the traitor's death, made a third assault on the land walls at the Burchio ravelin, which Tommaso had promised to surrender. To keep up the deception, the Venetians hoisted the Turkish flag—the signal agreed upon—over the tower of the Temple, and the

Turks, rushing on "like pigs," went to the slaughter, instead of to the sack of the city. Moreover, the able-bodied lads of the town now took the place of the executed marksmen on the walls, and they made such excellent practice that the sultan sent to ask who they might be. He was told that they were reinforcements from Nauplia, who had crossed the Euripos despite the vigilance of his guards at the bridge, a fable which cost those unhappy men their heads. For three more days and nights the sultan continued to bombard and demand the surrender of the city, and on the morning of 11th July prepared to make a more vigorous assault than ever on the damaged line of wall between the tower of the Temple and the Porta di Cristo, the chief land-gate, while his fleet directed its attack against the ruined ramparts of the ghetto. Suddenly, however, Canale's fleet of 71 sail was seen coming down the Atalante channel. In a moment, the situation was changed. The sultan expected the Venetian admiral to break the northern bridge of boats, fire the other and shut him up in the island. According to one account, he shed tears of rage; according to another, he actually mounted his horse to recross the bridge, and was only held back by his most trusted pasha. Modern expert opinion agrees with the sultan; had Canale done his duty, he could have saved Negroponte and ruined the great conqueror.

But the legal mind, and perhaps the paternal affection, of the Venetian admiral—for his son was on board—hesitated till it was too late. In vain two Cretan gentlemen begged permission to charge with their galley against the bridge of boats. The commander replied that he must wait till all his vessels had come up. Corruption was rife in the fleet; no one stirred; the tide in the Euripos turned; and, Canale quietly cast anchor in the bay of Politika, six miles up channel. Meanwhile, the great man of action who commanded the besiegers acted. He lined both the Bœotian and the Eubœan shore with soldiers to prevent Canale from landing; he posted marksmen on the northern bridge to repulse an attack, and offered the whole booty of the city to his men. Early on the morning of the next day, seeing that Canale was still inactive, he made his final assault upon the town. He had previously filled the moat with casks, dead bodies and fascines, so that the heap of material thrown into them overtopped the broken walls. Over this improvised road, which emitted a fearful stench, the Turks rushed to the attack. The garrison, weary and worn, raised black flags of distress as a signal to Canale, but in vain; still, though abandoned by the fleet, it gallantly held its ground till two hours after daybreak, when the besiegers carried the Burchio ravelin; a few moments later all the walls were in the possession of the enemy. Even then the fighting continued in the narrow streets, which were barricaded with beams, casks, and chains, while the women hurled boiling water, quick-lime, and pitchers on the heads of the Turks. Forcing their way, foot by foot, the invaders at last, at mid-day, gained the square. There Calbo, the *provveditore*, fell, sword in hand; his predecessor, Bondumier, was butchered in the house of Paolo Andreozzo, who himself survived to write the story of the siege. The bailie and a number of gentle ladies and children found refuge in the castle in the Euripos, and pulled up the drawbridge, hoping that the fleet would even now come to their rescue. Canale did, indeed, make a show of attacking the bridge of boats, but when he saw the Turkish flag waving over the city, he turned and left the poor wretches in the castle of the Euripos to their fate.

That fate was, indeed, terrible. Mohammed had vowed to avenge the insults levelled at him from the walls, and he kept his vow. But the castle was strong, and his emissaries, Mahmoud Pasha, the Turkish admiral, and the Italian interpreter, found it necessary to promise the lives, but not the liberty, of the inmates. The sultan was furious at being thus baulked of his prey. He issued instant orders that every living soul, down to the very children at the breast, should be cut in pieces on the bridge. For Erizzo he reserved an even worse fate. Sarcastically remarking that he had promised to spare the bailie's neck, but not his body, he ordered him to be placed on two planks and sawn asunder—a fiendish act commemorated by one of the paintings on the ceiling of the Doge's Palace.[1] According to one account, which has been eagerly accepted by a host

[1] So Cicogna and Litta; the present official view is that Alban d' Armer (*cf. infr.*) is the person represented.

of Venetian dramatists, but for which there is little historical evidence, Erizzo's only daughter, Anna, refusing to yield to the desires of her father's murderer, was killed before the sultan's eyes. In his thirst for blood, the conqueror rode through the streets to see if the cupidity of his janissaries had spared the lives of his victims, and massacred all he could find before the church of the Holy Apostles, on the shore of the bay of Burchio, at his own headquarters, and at San Giovanni Bocca d'Oro; to make assurance doubly sure, he ordered his galleys to be searched, and issued a proclamation that any of his men who was guilty of concealing a Frank should be beheaded. His special vengeance fell upon the lads who had made such excellent practice from the walls. One of the fairest cities in Greece was converted into a charnel-house; the heads of the slain were heaped up in the Piazza di S. Francesco, in front of the official residence of the Latin patriarch; the Euripos ran red with the blood of the corpses thrown into it. It was calculated that 77,000 (other estimates give 25,000 or 30,000) Turks and 6,000 Christians had perished in the siege. It was said that every male in Negroponte over the age of eight years was cut in pieces.

The rest of the great island now surrendered. Historic castles, like Karystos, the fief of the Zorzi; Ædepsos, the property of the Sommaripa of Paros; Oreos, the third of the three original baronies, then a Venetian stronghold, all yielded. Pteleon, with its dependency of Gardiki, succumbed three days after the fall of Negroponte, despite the heroic efforts of its rector to save the last outpost of Christendom in northern Greece. Its site was left desolate; its inhabitants were sent to swell the Christian population of Constantinople. Thither the sultan himself set out, after presenting the fallen city of Negroponte to his son and leaving a garrison behind him, while his fleet, laden with booty and captive women and children, set sail for the Dardanelles. Once again, the irresolute Canale allowed it to pursue its way unmolested, "courteously escorting it," as the Turkish admiral sarcastically said, "alike on its outward and its homeward voyage."

When the news of the fall of Negroponte reached Venice, great was the lamentation. Many nobles fell ill of grief and shame—grief at the death of their relatives and friends who had been engaged in trade there, shame at "the worst tidings ever received by the State." Their indignation demanded a scapegoat, and in the person of their incompetent admiral one was ready to hand. Pietro Mocenigo was appointed to take his place, with orders to send Canale home in irons. That pitiful officer, conscious of his approaching disgrace, made a half-hearted attempt to recover the lost city. With 94 sail he cast anchor in the bay of Aulis, where once the Greek fleet had waited on the way to Troy. A blunder in strategy cost him the lives of some of his most valuable men; and, before he had had time to repair it, Mocenigo arrived. Canale hastened to meet him and to yield him the honour of recapturing the city. Mocenigo sarcastically bade him keep for himself the credit of the undertaking; and, when Canale declined, ordered his arrest. Placed on his trial at Venice, the miserable man was banished to Porto Gruaro, where he died; his successor abandoned all hope of regaining Negroponte, and since 1470 the island has owned no master save the Turk and the Greek.[1]

The Lombard and Venetian families, so long settled there, have left no descendants in Eubœa. One doctor in the island still bears the name of Venezianós; but of the offspring of the three barons and of the Venetian merchants, who had once enlivened the shores of the Euripos with their festivities or enriched them with their trade, not a trace remains there. Hard, indeed, was the lot of most survivors of the siege. Many had lost all that they possessed, and

[1] The authorities for the siege of Negroponte, which I have used are:—Rizzardo, *La Presa di Negroponte*; Jacopo dalla Castellana, *Perdita di Negroponte* (both eye-witnesses); the two poems, *Il Pianto di Negroponte*, and *La Persa di Nigroponte* (the last three in *Archivio Storico Italiano*, *Appendice*, ix., 403-40); *Continuatio Chronici Bononiensis*, Sanudo, and Navagero (Muratori, xviii., 779-80; xxii., 1190-1; xxiii., 1128-9); Malipiero in *Archivio Storico Italiano*, vii., 48-55; the Latin treatise *De Nigroponti Captione* in the Basle (1556) ed. of Chalkokondýles (pp. 330-2), of which there is an Italian version in Sansovino (pp. 322-3); Magno, 207; Sabellico, Dec. III., Lib. 8; Phrantzês, 448; *Historia Politica*, 44; *Chronicon breve*, 521-2. The best modern account is Admiral Fincati's able article in *Archivio Veneto*, xxxii., 267-307.

noble ladies, who had lived as local magnates in Eubœa on estates which had belonged to their ancestors for centuries, were compelled to subsist on charity as pensioners of the Venetian Government in the convent of St Philip and St James. Twenty-seven of these ladies, "most unhappy of mortal women," appeared before the doge and begged for bread. Twenty years later they received the house of a pious lady, which became the monastery of the Holy Sepulchre, as their abode. One high-born dame of the great family of Sommaripa was carried off into slavery with her daughter, and recovered by the Venetians at Smyrna, when they took that city. The Government, indeed, ordered that Canale should be made to refund the amount of his salary during the time that he had been admiral, and that this sum should be devoted to ransoming the prisoners. One of them used his eyes to such good purpose during his imprisonment at the Dardanelles, that he set fire to the naval arsenal of the Turks at Gallipoli. Special grants were made to the children of Alvise Calbo and Bondumier, and the last baron of Karystos was appointed governor of Lepanto; but most of the refugees ended their days in poverty.[1] The Latin patriarch of Constantinople, who for more than a century and a half had held the see of Negroponte, and whose possessions in the island had been so great, had already ceased to reside there; but the Catholic bishoprics of Eubœa now ended their career. For the second time, Archbishop Protimo of Athens, who had been living in the island, found himself an exile, and wrote pitifully to the pope that he must either beg or starve.[2] Thus closed the long Lombard and Venetian history of Negroponte—a history which is still commemorated, despite modern Vandalism, by the winged lions on the walls, which Erizzo so bravely defended, and by the fine escutcheons in the little museum at Chalkis.

Despite the heavy blow which she had received, Venice manfully continued the struggle against the great sultan. Further losses were incurred in the Morea; Vostitza

[1] Cornelius, *Ecclesiæ Venetæ*, xi., 272-9, 293-6; Magno, 208; Navagero, xxiii., 1130, 1146; Malipiero, 67; Cippico, *P. Mocenigi Gesta* (ed. 1656), 350; Wadding, *Annales*, xxv., 195.

[2] Mas Latrie in *Revue de l'Orient latin*, III., 445; Reg. Lat., 722, f. 291t.

surrendered; Belveder, or Pontikokastro, above the harbour of Katakolo, followed its example, and the Turks set fire to its deserted walls, and left it the ruin which it still remains. The Venetians themselves burnt the old castle of Kalamata, the birthplace of William of Achaia, rather than that it should fall into Turkish hands; thousands of Greeks from the ancient episcopal see of Olena and two other places in Elis, upon which the republic had bestowed special privileges, emigrated to Zante, where the Tocchi were better able than the republic to protect them. Nauplia was almost driven to yield from lack of food, but was relieved in time. As the sea still washed the base of the rock, and at that time not a single house stood in what is now the lower town, it had nothing to fear from an assault.[1] The war dragged on for some nine years more, despite efforts to make peace, which were bound to fail, because the republic asked for the restitution of Negroponte. The operations were, however, for the most part outside of Greece. Pope Sixtus IV. succeeded in inducing the kings of Naples and Cyprus and the grand master of the Knights of Rhodes to join Venice in a holy league; the Shah of Persia was incited to attack the Turks in Asia and claim the fallen empire of Trebizond; the Grand Duke Ivan III. of Russia offered to invade Constantinople, as son-in-law of Thomas Palaiológos, and therefore heir of Byzantium. For a time the fortunes of war turned; Mocenigo bombarded Smyrna; Loredano saved Lepanto. The Turks were naturally eager to capture this last Venetian fortress of northern Greece, and its neglected walls and dwindling population seemed to favour the enterprise. But, though in 1477 a large army besieged it for three months, and the Turkish artillery battered down a large part of the ramparts, the bravery of Antonio Zorzi, its rector, and the prompt arrival of Loredano's fleet forced the Turks to retire with no other success than the capture of the outlying forts of the colony.[2] But the republic had had enough of fighting.

[1] Malipiero, 59, 65; Sanudo, xxii., 1192; Navagero, xxiii., 1129; Magno, 203; Sáthas, i., 269; v., 27-9; Dorótheos of Monemvasia, Βιβλίον Ἱστορικόν, 473.

[2] Malipiero, 106, 114; Sanudo, 1207; Navagero, 1146-7; Sabellico, Dec. III., bk. 10; Ἄνθος, 268; Sáthas, vii., 17.

The King of Naples, who had designs upon Cyprus which clashed with her own, had not only broken up the league against the sultan, but had even made an alliance with him—the first instance of those unnatural, but by no means uncommon, unions. The Turks were pressing hard the Venetian possessions in Albania, and Skutari was doomed. So, after sixteen years of warfare, peace was concluded in 1479. Venice restored to the sultan all the castles in the Morea taken during the war and the island of Lemnos, on condition that the garrisons were granted an amnesty and allowed to depart if they so desired. Thus, after the peace of 1479, Venice still retained the fortress and territory of Lepanto north of the Corinthian Gulf, and the colonies of Nauplia, Monemvasia, Coron, Modon, and Navarino in the Morea. A boundary commission was appointed to delimitate their frontiers; after much discussion, the "impregnable" fortress of Thermisi, on the coast opposite Hydra, with its valuable salt-pans, the adjacent Kastri, and the ruined fortress of Kiveri, opposite Nauplia, were included in the territory of the latter, and Monemvasia was allowed to retain Vatika. Ægina remained subject to the governor of Nauplia. The Ionian islands of Corfù, Paxo, and Cerigo, with their dependencies; the northern Sporades; two of the Cyclades—Tenos and Mykonos; and Crete, completed the diminished dominions of the republic in the Levant.[1]

While Venice had thus lost Negroponte and Argos by the war, the long struggle had been even more disastrous to the Greeks. The Venetians, whose navy was far superior to that of the Turks, gained most of their successes at the expense, not of the sultan but of his Greek subjects, just as, in the Greco-Turkish war of 1897, a bombardment of Smyrna or Salonika would have mainly injured the Hellenic population of those two great Turkish towns. The Turks, likewise, carried off numbers of Greeks from the places which they captured, and thus the unhappy natives were the chief sufferers from the victories of their friends or the successes of their enemies. Yet the war had shown that the Hellenic race

[1] Miklosich und Müller, *Acta et Diplomata*, III., 293-309; Predelli, *Commemoriali*, v., 228-30, 238-9; Sáthas, vi., 121, 126, 142, 214, 219-20; Navagero, 1166.

could produce splendid fighters, and the name of Maroúla, the heroine of Lemnos, might well rank with the ancient Spartans or the modern women of Souli. At a critical moment during the siege of that island, the girl seized the sword and shield of her dying father and charged the Turks at the head of the wavering garrison. As a reward for her services, she was allowed to choose a husband from among the noblest officers of the Venetian army, while the republic provided the marriage portion.[1] It was then, too, that the Venetians first employed the Greeks and Albanians of the Morea as light horsemen against the Turks. Thus arose the famous corps of *stradioti*, who in the sixteenth century demonstrated all over Europe even as far as Scotland, that Greek valour was not extinct. According to the learned Greek historian, whose researches have thrown a flood of light upon their organisation and exploits, their name is not derived from the Greek word στρατιῶται ("soldiers"), but from the Italian *strada*, because they were "always on the road," and had no fixed abodes. They were mainly recruited from Lakonia; but the most valiant were the men of Nauplia and Thermisi. Among their leaders we find many historic names, such as those of Boua and Palaiológos, whose bearers were descendants or relatives of the men who had fought the good fight for the liberty of the Peloponnese. But they had their weaknesses as well as their good qualities, and their inordinate vanity was the favourite theme of Venetian comedians, just as Plautus had satirised the boastfulness of the *Miles Gloriosus* for the amusement of the ancient Romans. A Venetian historian said that they were "fonder of booty than of battle," and Tasso has blamed their rapacity in the line:

"Il leggier Greco alle rapine intento;"

but other poets have sung of their triumphs. Indeed, there were bards in the ranks of the "wanderers" themselves, and a whole literature of their poems has been published, mostly written in a peculiar dialect resembling that now spoken in Calabria, where many Greek songs are still sung by the descendants of the numerous Epirote families settled there after the Turkish Conquest—the third time that Magna Græcia had received a large Greek population. One of their

[1] Sabellico, Dec. III., bk. 10.

number, Marullus, of whom it was said that he "first united Apollo to Mars," wrote Latin alcaics and sapphics, which, if not exactly Horatian, are, at any rate, as good as the ordinary product of the sixth-form intellect. Another, Theodore Spandounis, or Spandugino, more usefully employed his pen in the composition of a work on the *Origin of the Ottoman Emperors*, with the patriotic object of arousing the sympathy of sixteenth century statesmen for the deliverance of Greece. The *stradioti*, were, however, mightier with the javelin and the mace—their characteristic weapons—than with the pen. The long javelin, which they carried on horseback, was a particularly formidable weapon. Shod at both ends with a sharp iron point, it could be used either way with equally deadly effect; and if it failed, the agile horseman could seize the mace which hung at his saddle bow, and bring it down on the skull of an opponent.[1] Unfortunately, the blow was rarely struck for Greece, and the skull was usually that of a Christian, against whom the *stradioti* had no personal or national quarrel.

The base ingratitude of Venice sacrificed by the peace of 1479 one of the last independent Latin rulers of Greece. Leonardo III. Tocco had still preserved his islands of Cephalonia, Zante, Sta. Mavra, and Ithaka, with the solitary fortress of Vonitza on the Ambrakian Gulf. During the war he had acted as an intermediary between the two combatants, had sent a galley under his brother to the relief of Negroponte, and had been included in the alliance between the republic and the King of Naples against the Turks in 1471. During this sixteen years' struggle, his islands had been the refuge of many thousands from the mainland. No less than 15,000 had fled to Sta. Mavra, and 10,000 Greeks and Albanians had emigrated from the west of the Morea to Zante, where they made unfruitful lands blossom like the rose, and where they formed an almost independent community under a Venetian official, called by the name of consul, much as did the Albanian colonies of Sicily in later times.

[1] The *locus classicus* for all that concerns them are volumes vii., viii., and ix. of Sáthas's Μνημεῖα Ἑλληνικῆς Ἱστοριάς, which contain documents relating to them from 1464 to 1570, and some of their literary productions. *Cf. ibid.*, iv., pp. lix. and 417, and Cippico, *P. Mocenigi Gesta*, 343.

Thus, while the continent was being devastated with fire and sword, the islands flourished. When Phrantzês visited the court of Sta. Mavra, where the duke resided, he found all well there and Leonardo his own master—for he had put to death the four governors whom his predecessor had appointed over him. Çurita tells us that at the time of the Turkish Conquest Cephalonia was most fertile: in its two large harbours big vessels could lie; and it contained more than 6000 houses, with a population of 40,000 souls. Zante, at the same time, had 25,000 inhabitants, and the Spanish historian remarks that Leonardo's state brought him in more than 12,000 ducats a year, and was large enough to entitle it to the rank of a kingdom. The administration of the islands was well organised; in Zante and in Cephalonia there was a vice-regent, or captain, who represented the duke, and who exercised judicial powers, and we hear of financial officials of the ducal court named *μαστρομασσάροι*, of procurators, and of treasurers. The Catholics of Zante had their cathedral of the Redeemer in the castle, not far from the Franciscan monastery; in the Catholic monastery of the Prophet Elias were the tomb and escutcheon of Carlo I. It was at this period that the church of St Nicholas on Mount Skopos was founded, and that Leonardo made various grants to the Latin bishopric of Cephalonia and Zante, and directed the bishop to reside in the latter, and more Italian, island. But he did not limit his favours to the Catholics; he saw that the Greeks, if harshly treated, might "prefer the mufti's turban to the cardinal's hat," and he therefore revived in 1452, the ancient orthodox bishopric of Cephalonia, which had been a "widowed see" since the early days of the Orsini, and gave the bishop jurisdiction over both Zante and Ithaka. He was to be elected from each of the two larger islands in turn, and was to be, as of old, a suffragan of the Metropolitan of Corinth. With his sanction, too, a noble lady named Kleopa endowed the convent of St John Baptist in Zante.[1] But though he made these concessions, and though he was sufficiently Hellenised as to use Greek in his documents, he is said to have been regarded by the islanders as a tyrant. Their disaffection naturally facilitated the Turkish Conquest.

[1] Chiótes, Ἱστορικὰ Ἀπομνημονεύματα, ii., 532-3, 628.

Leonardo III. had married, in 1463, Militza, the granddaughter of Thomas Palaiológos; but, after her death, he sought to contract a politic alliance which would ensure him that protection which Venice seemed unable or unwilling to afford him. In 1477 he therefore wedded a Neapolitan lady of high degree, who was niece of King Ferdinand I. But the effect of this stroke of policy was the very opposite of what he had expected. Venice had no desire to see the old Neapolitan influence re-established in the Ionian islands, and had disregarded Ferdinand's protest that the Tocchi were his vassals. Accordingly, she revenged herself for this *rapprochement* with Naples by leaving Leonardo out of the treaty of peace. This act of omission cost him his sceptre.

Leonardo was bound by treaty, not only to pay an annual tribute of 4000 ducats to the sultan, but to make a present of 500 more every time that a Turkish *Sandjakbeg* or provincial governor came to Joannina or Arta. It chanced at this moment that one of these personages arrived, who was not yet sixteen years of age, and who had been degraded from the superior rank of pasha. The Duke of Leucadia treated this juvenile official, who chanced to be a relative of his own, with scant consideration, sending him a gift of fruit, instead of money. The young governor's pride was injured, and he lodged a complaint at Constantinople, that during the late war Leonardo had harboured Venetian light cavalry in Zante, at the same time recalling the fact that he had not been included in the recent peace. Mohammed was only too glad of an opportunity to round off his conquests by the annexation of almost the last Christian state in Greece, which would serve as a base for his intended attack on Italy. He therefore ordered Ahmed Pasha of Valona to attack Leonardo with twenty-nine ships. The duke did not await the Turkish invasion. He knew that the Venetians would not, and the Neapolitans could not, help him, and that his own subjects detested him. So, long before the pasha appeared, he collected all his portable valuables, hired a Venetian merchantman, and fled from Sta. Mavra to the strongest of his castles, Fort St George, in Cephalonia. But he did not trust the garrison; the Turks who were approaching got sight of his treasure-ship, so he hastily embarked on board another Venetian vessel that lay in the harbour with his wife, his son Carlo, and his two brothers for Taranto, whence he proceeded to Naples. Ahmed, saluted by the Venetian admiral as he sailed down the channel of Corfù, easily captured Vonitza, the last vestige of the old Despotat of Epiros, and the islands of Santa Mavra, Cephalonia, and Ithaka, cutting to pieces all the ducal officials, burning the castle of Cephalonia, and carrying off most of the peasants to Constantinople; there the sultan separated the husbands from their wives, and mated both sexes with Ethiopians, in order that they might produce a race of grey slaves. The pasha then proceeded to attack Zante, but here he was met by the Venetian admiral, who protested that the island was inhabited by a colony of Venetian subjects from the Morea—the recent immigrants—who had hoisted the lion-banner of St Mark, and who were protected by 500 light horse under the redoubtable Peter Boua. The matter was referred to Constantinople—and, meanwhile, the Albanian *condottiere* twice defeated the treacherous invaders—but with no other result than that those islanders who chose were allowed to leave—a permission of which some thousands availed themselves. Then the pasha ravaged "the flower of the Levant" with fire and sword, and destroyed most of its churches and all its habitations. Thus, in 1479, after an existence of well-nigh three centuries, the county palatine of Cephalonia, the picturesque realm of many a mediæval Odysseus, disappeared in the dull monotony of the Turkish Empire. In Zante, in Ithaka, and in Cephalonia, the Turkish sway was of very brief duration; nor was it unpopular with the Greeks, who seem to have preferred the Turkish officials to their own bishop; but in Sta. Mavra, with one scanty interval, it lasted for over two centuries. The Turks converted the church of the saint into a mosque; the island was governed by a bey, who, after the capture of Lepanto, in 1499, depended on the pasha of that place; and Ottoman families immigrated to take the place of those unhappy Leucadians, whom Ahmed Pasha had sold as slaves for no more than ten *soldi* apiece.[1]

[1] Miklosich und Müller, v., 69-72, 260; Lunzi, 180-98; Remondini, *op. cit.*, 146; Serra, *Storia di Zante*, and Magno *apud* Hopf, *Chroniques*, 344-5, 208; Sansovino, 197; Sáthas, i., 269-71; vi., 17, 21, 215, and in

Leonardo III. and his family had meanwhile met with a friendly reception from King Ferdinand I. of Naples, who bestowed on him an annuity of 500 florins and the lands of Briatico and Calimera in Calabria; in 1480 he arrived with his son and his brothers in Rome to beg an annuity from Sixtus IV., who gave him 1000 gold pieces and promised him 2000 a year—an event still commemorated by one of the paintings in the Santo Spirito Hospital. After a short stay in Rome, he returned to Naples and proceeded to plan the recapture of his dominions. The Tocchi were an enterprising family, not likely to abandon the idea of reigning in Greece at the first rebuff. The Roman diarist Volaterranus tells us that he once heard a bastard son of Leonardo, a daring young fellow of two-and-twenty, say: "Though we have lost our rings, we have still got our fingers entire," and this youth is mentioned as being at Zante in 1481. In the same year his father Leonardo and a Neapolitan fleet in vain summoned the Turkish *subassì* of Cephalonia and Zante to surrender;[1] but Leonardo's brother Antonio and a band of Catalan mercenaries about the same time easily recovered the two islands—for the garrison of the former was weak, and that of the latter had fled in alarm at his approach. But Antonio's success aroused the jealousy of Venice, which had no desire to see the islands in the possession of the King of Naples or his vassals. The governor of Modon in 1482 dislodged Antonio and his Catalans from Zante, but he managed to retain Cephalonia till the following year. His exactions, however, irritated the natives; his connivance with corsairs, who made the island their rendezvous, alarmed the Venetians; and, in 1483, after a futile attempt to buy him out, the republic, aided by many of the islanders, prepared to attack him. Thereupon, the garrison of the castle slew him, and opened their gates to the Venetian commander, who then without opposition made himself master of the whole island and appointed its first Venetian governor. But, while

Ἑστία of 1885, No. 506; Çurita, vol. v., bk. iv., ch. xxx.; Phrantzês, 429 (where the corrupt word μαστραϊδιαῶν refers to the μαστρομασσάροι, officials well known in the Ionian islands); Predelli, *Commemoriali*, v., 203, 212; Sabellico, *loc. cit.*; Feyerabend, *Reyssbuch*, ff. 351, 372.

[1] Sáthas, i., 279; vi., 228, 230; Faber, *Evagatorium*, iii., 345-6.

Leonardo III. asked for the restitution of the two islands from the sultan, the latter demanded them for himself. Venice in vain strove to retain Cephalonia, which in 1485 she had to cede to Bajazet II., till it finally passed into her hands in 1500. But she succeeded in keeping Zante, on condition of paying an annual tribute of 500 ducats, and the "flower of the Levant" thenceforth remained Venetian down to the fall of the republic.[1]

The Tocchi made no further efforts to recover their island domain, for the kings of Naples were now threatened by France, and had no wish to irritate the sultan into a second attack upon Otranto. Leonardo III., after going as Neapolitan ambassador to Spain, where he was welcomed with royal honours, received the Apulian town of Monopoli, the home of the first palatine count of Cephalonia, from Charles VIII. of France in 1495, when the latter invaded Naples, and perished beneath the ruins of his house in Rome, under the pontificate of Alexander VI. His eldest son, Carlo, whom Ferdinand I. had promised to treat as his own child, and who received both Neapolitan and papal pensions, after fighting in the armies of the Emperor Maximilian I., died at his house in the Via S. Marco, in Rome, under Leo X. Leonardo's two sons by his second marriage naturally received favours from the Spanish dynasty, alike at Naples and in Spain itself. One of them, Ferdinand, or Don Ferrante, obtained the Lombard castle of Refrancore from Maximilian I., acted as Spanish ambassador to the court of Henry VII. of England in 1506 in the affair of the Duke of Suffolk, and tried to keep the peace between François I. and the Emperor Charles V. in 1535—an event commemorated on his tomb in Madrid. Carlo's descendants claimed to be treated as princes of the blood, on the ground that they represented both the Byzantine and Servian dynasties. They continued to style themselves Despots of Arta until, in the seventeenth century, they substituted for this title that of Prince of Achaia,[2] perhaps on the ground that

[1] J. Volaterranus and Navagero *apud* Muratori, xxiii., 102-3 (=part III., 12-13, in new edition), 1180-1, 1189; Lunzi, 199-219; Sáthas, i., 315; vi., 334, 336; Predelli, *Commemoriali*, v., 248, 317; Miklosich und Müller, *Acta et Diplomata*, III., 332.

[2] Çurita, vol. iv., bk. xx., ch. lxxiii.; vol. v., bk. v., ch. xxvi; Serra

Thomas Palaiológos, whose representatives they were by the female line, had married the heiress of the last Frankish Prince of Achaia. At Naples they built a palace in the present Corso Vittorio Emanuele, now known as the Palazzo Troise, but formerly called by the people the Palazzo del Santo Piede, from the foot of St Anna, which Leonardo III. had brought with him from Greece, and which was there preserved. The family has only recently become extinct, but a room of the palace still contains a collection of the portraits of the former palatine counts of Cephalonia, while the family titles and the sacred foot have passed to Carlo Capece Galeotta, Duke of Regina, the head of the Neapolitan Legitimists.[2] But it has never been suggested that the Albanian question should be solved by the restoration of this estimable nobleman to the seat once occupied by the family at Joannina.

In their islands the Tocchi have left but few memorials behind them. Their arms, three blue waves on a silver shield, surmounted by a head of Pegasus, can no longer be seen on the castle walls and on the bells of the Panagia Anaphonetria church at Zante,[3] while one coin alone still commemorates their sovereignty in the Ionian Sea.

The twenty years' peace between Venice and the Turks, which followed the conclusion of this war, was by no means a period of repose for the Greeks. Scarcely had the late war ended than a national insurrection broke out in Maina under the auspices of a guerilla leader, Korkódeilos Kladâs, the prototype of the chieftains who played so great a part in the War of Independence more than three centuries later. Kladâs had been one of the last of the Peloponnesian warriors to submit to Mohammed II. at the time of the Conquest, and the conqueror had thought it politic to bestow upon him the rich plain of Helos, near Sparta, as a military fief.[4] Helos, according to one theory, had in old times given to the Helots their name; but Kladâs had more of

apud Hopf, *Chroniques*, 345; Mazzella, *Descrittione del Regno di Napoli*, 643-8; Sansovino, 197; Buchon, *Nouvelles Recherches*, I., i., 325-35; II., i., 354-6; Gottlob, *op. cit.*, 293. The tomb was destroyed two centuries ago.

[2] De la Ville, in *Napoli Nobilissima* for 1900, pp. 180-1.

[3] K. Mazarákes of Zante has kindly examined for me both the bells and the escutcheon on the castle. Both are Venetian, the latter that of Donato da Leze, governor 1504-6.

[4] Phrantzés, 407.

the Spartan than of the Helot in his composition. The Venetians, recognising his abilities during the war, had appointed him captain of the Greeks in their service, the so-called *stradioti*.[1] But the Venetian politicians soon found, as many governments have discovered since, that a dashing leader of irregulars, however useful in time of war, is apt to be an embarrassment in time of peace. Kladâs did not acquiesce in the cession of the region known as "the arm of Maina" (*Brazzo di Maina*) to the Turks. He escaped from Coron to Maina and raised the standard of revolt, round which several thousand outlaws and irregulars speedily gathered. The Venetian authorities, afraid lest Mohammed should suspect them of having instigated the movement, at once arrested the family of Kladâs, and bade the Mainates hand over the rebel chief to the Turkish governor of the Morea. In order to secure the performance of this command, they put a heavy price upon the head of their former captain. But the Mainates showed no desire to sell their leader, who signally routed a Turkish force which was despatched against him. Dissensions, however, broke out between him and another insurgent captain of *stradioti*, Theodore Boua, and a fresh Turkish army succeeded in penetrating into parts of Maina which no Mussulman foot had as yet ever trodden. But Kladâs, though at bay, was not taken. Some Neapolitan galleys chanced to be lying off the coast, and the outlawed chieftain, after a last gallant and successful attack upon the Turks, escaped on board and sailed to Naples, where he received a warm welcome from the king, who was anxiously expecting the descent of the Turkish fleet upon the Adriatic coast of his kingdom. Kladâs figures no more in the history of Greece; but we find him fighting by the side of Skanderbeg's son for the Neapolitan cause in Epiros, and King Ferdinand I. thought so highly of his services that he granted him, and bade his son continue, a yearly allowance out of the treasury.[2]

A fresh insurrection broke out in 1489; but a far more

[1] Sáthas, Μνημεῖα, vii., 20.

[2] *Ibid.*, i., 271, 273-9; vi., 147-50, 154-6, 158, 168, 171, 180, 200, 221, 222, 226-9; Ἑλληνικὰ Ἀνέκδοτα, I., ξη'-ξθ'; Τουρκοκρατουμένη Ἑλλάς, 36-45.

imposing movement now occupied the attention of Europe. Andrew Palaiológos, the elder son of the last Despot of the Morea, and nephew of the last Emperor of Constantinople, after endeavouring to persuade the Neapolitan court to aid him in the reconquest of his father's province, found a readier hearing from the ambitious King of France, Charles VIII. In 1494, a solemn meeting took place between him and the king's representative, Cardinal York, in the church of San Pietro in Montorio, at Rome, where the former transferred all his imperial rights and claims to the most Christian king, on consideration of an annual payment of 4300 gold ducats and a grant of lands yielding a further annual income of 5000 gold ducats, the cardinal also pledging King Charles to restore Palaiológos to the Despotat of the Morea, for which the Despot should yield "a fair, white steed" on St Louis' Day to the king, in token of homage.[1] In the same year Charles VIII. set out on his famous expedition to Naples, preceded by a grandiose proclamation, announcing his intentions against the Turks, and heralded by the verses of a courtly poet who foretold that he would "pass beyond the sea, then enter Greece, and by his prowess be acclaimed King of the Greeks." The news of his plans spread across the Adriatic, and Thessaly and Epiros awaited the advent of the conqueror of Naples. The Turks quitted the coasts in alarm, and the sultan prepared to retire bag and baggage into Asia.[2] In Monemvasia a plot was organised with the connivance of Andrew Palaiológos, whose name was still popular there, for delivering that strong Venetian fortress to his French ally.[3] But the triumphs of the French king had excited the jealousy of Europe; Venice arrested one of his principal agents, and forbade all ships to sail from the Venetian ports for Greece; and Charles retreated to France, leaving the unhappy Greeks to pay the penalty of their credulity with their lives. Such has been the usual result of foreign intervention in the affairs of Greece. *Quicquid delirant reges, plectuntur Achivi.*

[1] *Memoires de l'Academie des Inscriptions*, xvii., 539.

[2] "Pour se sauver delà en Asie avec tout son train"—the first use of Mr Gladstone's classic phrase. *Ibid.*, xvii., 567.

[3] Sanudo, *Diarii*, i., 703.

These recent services of Venice to the sultan did not for long retard his designs upon her possessions in the Levant. Excited by her Italian enemies, of whom Lodovico il Moro of Milan was the worst, he began a fresh Turco-Venetian war in 1499. Lepanto, her last scrap of territory in continental Greece, was the objective of both his land and his sea forces. The population of the Venetian colony on the Corinthian Gulf had considerably increased, owing to the immigration of people from Zante, when the Turks had taken that island; and, though many had doubtless returned, now that "the flower of the Levant" was in the hands of Venice, there were nearly 7000 persons in the town shortly before it fell. The Lepantines had, however, received little attention from the Home Government, though their envoys occasionally journeyed with petitions to the metropolis. For thirty years no Venetian commissioner had been sent to hold an enquiry into the administration of this outlandish place; and when, at the eleventh hour, in the very year of its capture, one of those officials at last arrived, he found that the poor had been much oppressed by the nobles and citizens, who formed a class apart from the people, and had established a council of thirty for the management of public affairs. The colony, as delimitated after the last war, contained, besides Lepanto itself, four other castles, all in bad repair, and so carelessly guarded that the garrison of one of them was represented by one old woman! Something had, however, been done for the fortifications of the town. The late rector had died of his exertions on the defences, and Sanudo has preserved a contemporary plan of the place, with its triple ring of walls and the castle at the summit, which gave it then, as now, the appearance of the papal tiara. Such was the condition of the city, which a Venetian historian has called "the strongest bulwark of the Christian peoples."[1]

The fate of Lepanto was decided, however, not by land, but by sea. The Venetian fleet, which should have prevented the Turkish admiral from entering the Gulf of Corinth, was commanded by Antonio Grimani, a man who

[1] Sáthas, Μνημεῖα, v., 7-12; vi., 218-19; Sanudo, *Diarii*, ii., 165, 292-4, 534, 790; Cappelletti, *Storia della R. di Venezia*, vi., 365; Lamansky, *Secrets de l'État de Venise*, 593.

owed his position to his wealth and his connections rather than to his skill as a seaman. He now repeated the timorous tactics which, twenty-nine years before, had cost the republic Negroponte. He allowed the Turkish fleet to creep up the west coast of the Morea beneath the walls of the Venetian castle of Navarino, or Zonchio, as the Venetians still called it. When the Turkish admiral moved thence to the islet of Prodano, a battle became inevitable. But in this conflict, which has taken its name from Zonchio, the Venetian commander, blinded by jealousy of his much abler colleague, Loredano, took the part of a spectator. In vain Loredano and Alban d'Armer, another Venetian captain, boarded the biggest of the Turkish vessels. The intrepid Turk set fire to his ship; the flames spread to theirs also; all three perished, and the island of Sapienza long preserved the name of Borrak Reis, the author of this heroic suicide. According to a less probable story, Armer escaped the fire, only to be sawn asunder by the Turks. At that time the French were the allies of Venice; but not even the arrival of a French fleet could stir the dilatory Venetian admiral into activity. After three futile engagements, the Turkish galleys entered the Gulf of Corinth, and the fate of Lepanto was sealed. The garrison had already repelled seven attacks, and when the vessels were first sighted, the bells were rung in a joyful peal, for they thought that it was Grimani, coming to their relief. The fatal truth turned their rejoicing to despair; next day, the Albanians in the town sent seven envoys to treat with the Turks. These emissaries returned, clad in cloth of gold, and laden with promises of fiscal exemption for ten years, and with the guarantee that the lives and property of all the inhabitants should be spared. Thereupon the city surrendered, and on the next day, 29th August, the castle hauled down the lion-banner, which for ninety-two years had floated over Lepanto. The Turkish soldiers were forbidden to sack the town; a careful inventory was made of everything that it contained; and the patriotic Archbishop Saracco, who had stayed to comfort the besieged, was allowed to go free and tell the sad tale at Venice.[1] Great was the

[1] Sanudo, *Diarii*, ii., 1235, 1290-4, 1323, 1339-40; iii., 11-14; Malipiero, *Annali*, 174-80; Haji Kalifeh, *The History of the Maritime Wars*,

indignation of the Venetians when the news arrived. Public opinion at once recognised that Grimani, and not Moro, the governor of Lepanto, was responsible for its loss. Street-boys went about singing doggerel verses against "Antonio Grimani, the ruin of the Christians"; the Government ordered his arrest; his enemies demanded his head. Meanwhile, the wretched man, after a feeble attempt to take Cephalonia, had retired to Corfù, whence he was brought as a prisoner to Venice and put upon his trial. Family influence was used to the utmost to procure his acquittal; the proceedings were protracted until public indignation had somewhat cooled; and in the end his punishment was banishment to the island of Cherso in the Quarnaro.[1] Twenty-one years later the man who had lost Lepanto became Doge of Venice. A smaller culprit, the commander of the castle, found to have taken a bribe, was hanged between the red columns of the Doge's Palace—a striking example of Juvenal's saying, that one scoundrel obtains the gallows, another the diadem.[2]

The sultan now held the key of the Corinthian Gulf, and he at once gave orders to secure the entrance by the erection of two forts on either shore, at Rhion and Antirrhion, where little more than a mile of sea, the so-called "little Dardanelles," separates Roumeli from the Morea. In three months' time these forts were finished, and, though damaged by the fortunes of war, have ever since remained—a picturesque memorial of Bajazet II.[3] But he was not satisfied with this conquest; when Venice sued for peace, he demanded nothing less than the cession of Nauplia and her two Messenian colonies; and when she refused, he resolved to take them by force. In the following year, 1500, he entered the Morea at the head of a large army, and ordered

19-21; *Chronicon Venetum, apud* Muratori, xxiv., 113-14, 117; Bembo, *Rerum Venetarum Historia* (ed. 1551), ff. 100-4; Sansovino, f. 200; *Historia Politica*, 56. The best modern account is Admiral Fincati's *La deplorabile Battaglia Navale del Zonchio* in the *Rivista Marittima* for 1883, pp. 185-213.

[1] Sanudo, *Diarii*, iii., 5, 66, 172-4; Malipiero, *Annali*, 182.

[2] Bembo, f. 153; Sanudo, *Diarii*, vi., 85.

[3] Sanudo, *Diarii*, iii., 30, 40, 54; *Chronicon Venetum*, xxiv., 128; Haji Kalifeh, *Cronologia historica*, 137.

an attack upon Nauplia. Though Palamidi was still unfortified, the place was defended by four castles—the two old "fortresses of the Franks and the Greeks," as they were still called, the Venetian Torrione, and the Castel dello Scoglio, on the islet of St Theodore, the modern Bourtzi;[1] the population of the colony had increased since the Turkish Conquest of the Morea, for seven years' residence conferred local citizenship; and the *stradioti*, if at times a source of anxiety to the governor and a cause of friction with the Turks of Argos, were first-class fighting men. Accordingly, the Turkish cavalry were defeated, nor was an attack on the strong castle of Navarino more successful. Bajazet therefore decided to concentrate his efforts on Modon, the Port Said of Frankish Greece, the important half-way house between Venice and the Holy Land, at which every traveller stopped on his way to the East. A pilgrim who visited it in 1484 was struck by its thick walls, its deep ditches, and its strong towers; ten years later it was being further fortified. The cathedral of St John, though a mean structure, contained the venerated remains of St Leo, and the head of St Athanasius; the "German House" of the Teutonic Knights is mentioned by every visitor. The Venetian Government found, indeed, that the budget of the colony always showed a deficit; but Modon was none the less a flourishing place, where a number of Jewish silk-workers found employment. It possessed a fine artificial harbour, and an enthusiastic traveller of this period exclaims that you can find vessels there "for every part of the world, for Modon is, as it were, half way to every land and sea." It boasted a busy market in the suburb, where a colony of gypsies had settled, and where the Turks of the country made their fortunes by selling pigs to the Giaours, whom it was worth their while, therefore, not to harass. No less than 5000 of these animals were exported to Venice, and much of the wine which passed for Malmsey in the West really came from Crete or Modon —for the Turks who now owned the vineyards round Monemvasia had ceased to plant vines. "The mere thought of the muscat of Modon delights me," writes worthy Father

[1] Sanudo, *Diarii*, iii., 838, 900; Dorótheos of Monemvasia, 472; Lamprinídes, Ἡ Ναυπλία, 131-2.

Faber, while as for oranges, they were dirt cheap. Such was the condition of the ancient Venetian colony on the eve of its capture.[1]

Cabriel, the governor, had made preparations for the Turkish siege. Immediately after the fall of Lepanto, he had written home for supplies, and the republic had at once ordered the despatch of men, munitions, and money for the defence of a place which was so very dear to her heart. Many small houses outside the town were burned, so as not to give cover to the enemy, and a dam was built across the mouth of the harbour, so that only a single ship could enter at a time. Most of the women were sent to Crete, and the garrison of 7000 men was in excellent spirits. For a month Bajazet in vain besieged the town by land and sea, while 500 cannon played upon its walls. The sultan was on the point of abandoning the siege, when an unfortunate act on the part of the garrison delivered the place into his hands. Four Venetian and Corfiote galleys suddenly appeared with supplies at the mouth of the harbour; the delighted inhabitants rushed down to the beach to greet their deliverers; the walls were temporarily deserted; and the janissaries seized this opportunity of entering at the tower of the governor's palace, where their continuous cannonade had destroyed the fortifications. The people rushed back to the defence of the town, but it was too late: in despair, they set fire to their own homes, and more than half the city was laid in ashes. The sultan showed no mercy to those who had so bravely withstood his armies for a month; the Catholic bishop was slain as he was addressing his flock; all the males of twelve years and upwards were beheaded; but the governor was spared to serve as a decoy-duck elsewhere. The rest of the women and children fled in panic to the Turkish fleet, and were sold as slaves to every quarter of the Mussulman world. Thus, on Sunday, 9th August 1500, Modon fell, after having belonged to Venice for nearly 300 years. Delighted with his prize, Bajazet promoted the janissary who had first mounted

[1] Faber, *Evagatorium*, i., 39, 165; iii., 314, 331, 333, 337, 338, 343; Feyerabend, *Reyssbuch*, ff. 37, 55, 125, 182-3, 351; Casola, *Viaggio*, 37-8; Sáthas, i., 295.

the walls to be a *sandjak*, or provincial governor, and on the first Friday after the capture, when the fire was at last spent, rode to the desecrated cathedral, there to offer up his thanksgivings to the God of battles, to whom, as he confessed when he gazed at the deep moat, he owed the conquest of this strong city. No time was lost in repairing the walls, and every village in the Morea was ordered to send five families to repopulate Modon.[1]

The fall of Modon brought with it the loss of Navarino and Coron. Contarini, the commander of Navarino, as soon as he was convinced that Modon had really been taken, surrendered that strong fortress—an act of cowardice which cost him his head. The punishment was not undeserved, for the place had provisions for three years, and 3000 men to defend it. The authorities of Coron wished to hold out; but they were overruled by the terrified inhabitants, who were promised favourable conditions if they yielded, and death if they resisted. Their lives were indeed spared, but they were driven into exile, and the revenues of both Coron and Modon were thenceforth dedicated to Mecca. At Coron, too, the sultan prayed in what had so long been the Catholic church to Allah, and then set out to besiege Nauplia, taking with him the governor of Modon as a proof that that colony had succumbed. Cabriel, however, escaped, and another Venetian from Coron, who had held office at Nauplia, fled on horseback into that city and urged the citizens, whom he had been sent to convince of the folly of resistance, to resist to the last. A brave messenger from Monemvasia, at the risk of impalement, which had befallen two of his comrades, stripped off his clothes and swam across the harbour with letters announcing the speedy arrival of the Venetian fleet. The mettle of the garrison and the strength of the fortifications caused Bajazet to desist from the difficult enterprise and retire, content with the capture of Vatika, to Adrianople.

The Venetian colony in the Argolid was saved, but great was the grief of the metropolis when the news of Modon's loss arrived. The Council of Ten burst into tears

[1] Sanudo, *Diarii*, iii., 574, 602, 620, 637, 688-94, 717-18, 733; Sáthas, i., 316-18; Sansovino, f. 201; Bembo, ff. 110-14; *Historia Politica*, 56-8; *Chronicon breve*, 522; Haji Kalifeh, *The Maritime Wars*, 21-3.

when the sad tidings were announced to them, and the whole city was overcome with sorrow. Nor was this remarkable; for Modon, as the republic informed the Princes of Europe, had been "the receptacle and special nest of all our galleys, ships, and vessels on their way to the Levant." Together with Coron, it had been the earliest acquisition of the republic on the mainland of Greece, and the Venetian archives contain a whole literature concerning the administration of these two Messenian colonies. The dependent castle of Navarino was, indeed, almost immediately recaptured by a clever ruse, but retaken by Kemal Reis in the following year; and both Modon and Coron, thirty years later, succumbed for an instant to Christian fleets. But the flag of the Evangelist never waved again from their towers till the day when Morosini, imitating Bajazet II., went in state to attend a thanksgiving service in the consecrated mosque of Modon. Zante took its place as a port of call, while the survivors found a home in the newly-won Venetian island of Cephalonia.[1]

The republic had several times attempted to recover that island, which she had been forced to surrender in 1485. Thanks to the efforts of Pope Alexander VI., King Ferdinand of Spain was induced to send his famous captain, Gonzalo de Córdoba, to her aid. The Spanish and Venetian fleets, the latter under Pesaro, were designed for the recovery of Modon; but, as timber was required for the necessary siege engines, they sailed to Cephalonia, an island now singularly barren but then covered with forests, which have given its name to the Black Mountain. To provide useful employment for the soldiers while the timber was being cut, the two commanders resolved to attack the fortress of St George, which had been the favourite residence of the Tocchi, and was still the capital of the island. The castle stands upon a steep and high mountain, and was defended by 300 men. But the besiegers erected a rampart high enough to enable them to command the position; a friendly Greek kept them supplied with provisions, and on 24th December 1500 the

[1] Sanudo, *Diarii*, iii., 688, 719, 771, 811, 833, 901-2; iv., 328; Bembo, ff. 115, 117, 123; Sansovino, f. 201; Sáthas, i., 318; vii., 67; Dorótheos of Monemvasia, *loc. cit.*

capital of Cephalonia fell. An inscription was immured over the main entrance to commemorate an event which placed the island for well-nigh three centuries under Venetian rule,[1] and the loyal Cephalonian and his descendants were rewarded with perpetual exemption from all dues.

Another of the Ionian islands, that of Sta. Mavra, now passed, but only temporarily, into the possession of the republic. The Spanish captain had sailed back to Sicily after the capture of Cephalonia, and Pesaro had contented himself for the moment with burning the Turkish arsenal at Preveza; but in the following summer, aided by a papal fleet under the command of his namesake, the Bishop of Paphos, he attacked the sole Ionian island which was still Turkish. Sta. Mavra had recently received a considerable number of Jewish refugees from Spain, who were always welcomed by the Turks,[2] and it was a lair of corsairs who preyed on the shipping of the Venetian islands. Leonardo Tocco had strengthened the old fortifications, which were defended by a considerable Turkish garrison. But the papal commander occupied the shallows which separated the town from the mainland, and the Venetian admiral bombarded the castle with such vigour that, after six days, the Turks considered the desirability of surrendering. While they were deliberating, the besiegers entered, and thus, on 30th August 1502, Sta. Mavra fell. At first sight it seemed to be a valuable prize; a large sum of money belonging to the sultan was found in the treasury, a number of captive Mussulmans became slaves, and strategically it was "a beam in the Turk's eye," "the key of Corfù, Cephalonia, and Zante." But its loss so infuriated Bajazet II. that he refused to make the peace which Venice was anxious to obtain, unless it were restored to him, and a party in the island was intriguing with the Turks, with whom the natives had intermarried. The republic reluctantly consented to surrender a place which she had begun to fortify, and a year and a day after its capture the first Venetian governor

[1] Sanudo, *Diarii*, iii., 1274, 1639 (who gives the date, which was wrongly copied by Hammer, ii., 611). *Cf.* Bembo, ff. 115-17; Sansovino, f. 201; Lunzi, *Della Condizione*, 222-7; Sáthas, v., 155-6.

[2] *Risposta di Jacopo Grandi*, 22.

handed over Sta. Mavra to the Turks. Nearly two centuries were to elapse before the lion-banner again flew from the old castle of the palatine counts.[1]

The results of the war had been disastrous to Venice; the tomb of her victorious admiral, in the church of the Frari still magniloquently records his Greek triumphs, and portrays the two captured Ionian castles; but her sole gain was Cephalonia; and the peace of 1502-3 left her nothing but Nauplia and Monemvasia, with their respective appurtenances, in the Morea. She failed to retain Maina, which the son of Kladâs had won for her;[2] and against the sack of Megara by the men of Nauplia she had to set the temporary capture of the castle of Ægina by the redoubtable Kemal Reïs and the carrying off of 2000 Æginetans—a foretaste of what that fair island was to suffer a generation later.[3]

For more than thirty years Greece ceased to be the battlefield between Venice and the sultans, for both parties were occupied elsewhere; the treaty of 1502-3 was renewed[4] in 1513 and 1521, and the Venetian colonies were thus able to enjoy a long period of repose before their final catastrophe. From the petitions of those communities and the reports of their governors we are able to form a clear idea of their condition during this last generation of Venetian rule. Peace did not bring them plenty, for both Nauplia and Monemvasia bitterly complained that the restriction of their respective territories after the last war had deprived them of the lands which they had been wont to sow. All their supplies of corn had now to be imported from the Turkish possessions, and it was thus in the power of the Turks to starve them out by simply closing the frontier, while corsairs rendered dangerous all traffic by sea, and many a fisherman of Nauplia was carried off and put up for ransom at the old Frankish castle of Damalâ, now included within the Turkish boundary.[5] The total population of the town of Nauplia was

[1] Sanudo, *Diarii*, iv., 313, 315, 394, 645, 667, 781; v. 46-7, 85; Bembo, f. 141; Sansovino, f. 202; Predelli, *Commemoriali*, vi., 65-6; Miklosich und Müller, iii., 344-54.

[2] *Ibid.*, iii., 17, 730; Sáthas, v., 152.

[3] *Ibid.*, iv., 83, 604; Bembo, f. 114.

[4] Miklosich und Müller, iii., 360; Predelli, *op. cit.*, vi., 131.

[5] Sáthas, iv., 197, 220, 230; vi., 247-8, 254; Sanudo, *Diarii*, xxix., 482.

nearly 10,000, while the whole colony, which comprised the castles of Thermisi and Kastri, contained 13,299 souls.[1] In 1519, its government was reformed; the system of having two rectors was found to lead to frequent quarrels; and the republic thenceforth sent out a single official styled "bailie and captain," assisted by two councillors, who performed the duties of *camerlengo* by turns. The bailie's authority extended over the rector of Ægina, whereas Kastri had been granted to two families, the Palaiológoi and the Alberti, whose administration was the cause of much discontent.[2] Early in the sixteenth century a democratic wave passed over the colony. Society at Nauplia was divided into three classes —nobles, citizens, and plebeians; and it had been the ancient usage that the nobles alone should hold the much-coveted local offices, such as that of judge of the inferior court and inspector of weights and measures. The populace now demanded its share of these good things, and the Home Government ordered that one at least of the three inspectors should be a man of the people. The democracy managed, too, to make its influence felt on the Municipal Council of Thirty, which met with closed doors, to the no slight scandal of the governor, who complained to Venice of such irregular proceedings. In order to spare the pockets of the community, it was ordered that appeals from his decision should lie to Crete, instead of Venice. Economically, the colony paid its way, though for twenty years the inhabitants were granted exemption from local dues as the reward of their fortitude in the late war; an octroi duty on all foreign animals, a tax on donkeys, and a duty on the salt-pans of Thermisi, were the chief imposts; but a serious drain on the budget was the *bakshîsh* paid to the Turkish governor of the Morea and to the *voivode* who was stationed at the frontier.[3] The fortifications, too, were allowed to fall into disrepair, and were inadequately guarded. The low sea-wall had never been completed; the hill of Palamidi was still unenclosed; the "castle of the Greeks" on Itsh Kaleh was unguarded and almost in ruins; and it was difficult to get men to garrison the

[1] Report of 1531, Sáthas, vi., 249.

[2] *Ibid.*, iv., 220; vi., 246, 254; Sanudo, *Diarii*, xxvii., 315, 338, 358.

[3] Sáthas, iv., 195, 198, 200, 203, 215, 219, 223; vi., 245-6, 252.

island fortress where the executioner now resides. The peasant-soldiers of Nauplia used sometimes to leave the "castle of the Franks" with only half a dozen men in it, while they went out to earn their living, for they were badly paid; and racial jealousies divided the *stradioti*, Greeks refusing to serve under Albanians, and Albanians under any chief who was not of their own clan. The fact that both races had their own "chief priest," or *protopapâs*, would not tend towards greater union, while the presence of a Catholic bishop—for Nauplia now figured as an episcopal see—must have increased the causes of discord. Worst of all, the Turks were always in and out of the town, and knew perfectly well all the weak points of a strategic position, which a high Venetian officer had declared to be "most important not only to Venice but to all Christendom."[1]

Ægina had always been exposed to the raids of corsairs, and was cursed with oppressive governors during these last thirty years of Venetian rule. The island was remote and lonely; Venetian nobles were as little anxious to go there as are modern Italian officials to go to Sardinia; and we may thus explain the high proportion of bad rulers at this period of its history. Three rectors of Ægina were severely punished for their acts of injustice, and we have a graphic account of the reception given by the suffering Æginetans to the captain of Nauplia, who came to hold an enquiry into the administration of one of these delinquents. We are told how all the people came out on to the square of Palaiochora with loud shouts of "Justice! Justice! Marco! Marco!"; how they had given a sack full of documents, setting forth their privileges, to the rector, and how he had returned the precious papers all mice-eaten and in pieces; how he had spurned their ancient right to elect an islander to keep one key of the money-chest; and how they threatened to leave the island in a body with the commissioner, unless he avenged their wrongs. A Latin inscription over the door of the Latin church of St George at Palaiochora, the arms of the visiting councillor of Nauplia, and a jug below, still record the last of these enquiries, in 1533. The inscription has a

[1] Sáthas, vi., 244-5, 250-1; Sanudo, *Diarii*, vii., 654; xi., 138; xxvi., 457, 476; xl., 338; Lamansky, 608.

pathetic interest, for it is the last memorial of mediæval Ægina. Four years later the mountain capital was a smoking mass of houses and ruined churches.[1]

Monemvasia had suffered a long blockade during the last war; she had lost her outlying castles of Rampano and Vatika, her famous vineyards and her cornfields were in Turkish hands. But she remained what she had been for centuries—an impregnable fortress, the Gibraltar of Greece. The Venetians renewed the system, which had prevailed under the Despots of the Morea, of devoting one of the local imposts to the repair of the walls; the Venetian *podestà* seems to have been a popular official; and the republic had wisely confirmed the special privileges granted by the Byzantine emperors to the church and community of this favoured city. Both a Greek metropolitan and a Latin archbishop continued to take their titles from Monemvasia, and the most famous of these prelates was the eminent scholar, Marcus Mousoûros. In 1524, however, despite the thunders of the œcumenical patriarch, the Greek and the Italian arranged between themselves that the former should retain the see of Monemvasia and that the latter should take a Cretan diocese.[2] The connection between the great island and this rocky peninsula was now close. The Greek priests of Crete, who had formerly gone to Modon or Coron for consecration, after the loss of those colonies came to Monemvasia; the Cretan exchequer contributed to the expenses of the latter, and judicial appeals from the *podestà* of Malmsey lay to the colonial authorities at Candia, instead of being remitted to Venice; for, as a Monemvasiote deputation once plaintively said, the expenses of the long journey had been defrayed by pawning the chalices of the churches. Even now Monemvasia is remote from the world; in those Venetian days she was

[1] Sáthas, v., 39-40; Sanudo, *Diarii*, vii., 258; xvi., 651, 655-7; xvii., 79-80; xviii., 98; xix., 343; xx., 150, 182; xxii., 468, 529; xxiv., 49; xxxii., 402; lviii., 556. The inscription has, I think, never been published. I copied it on the spot. "Tempore syndicatus clariss. domini Antonii Barbaro Dignissimi Consiliarii Nauplii Romanie Die Prima Aprilis MDXXXIII." The jug, not a Venetian emblem, was perhaps added by Barbarossa, the jug-maker's son.

[2] Νέος Ἑλληνομνήμων, III., 56; Sanudo, *Diarii*, vii., 714; xxiii., 536; xxiv., 669; xxv., 64; xxix., 402; xxxi., 227; xxxv., 363; xliv., 475; lv., 296.

seldom visited, not only because of her situation, but because of the fear which ships' captains had of her inhabitants.[1]

The long peace was interrupted in 1531 by a sudden descent upon Modon by the Knights of St John. Driven from Rhodes by the Turks eight years earlier, the Knights had not abandoned the idea of settling in the Levant, and the Venetian island of Cephalonia,[2] and the Turkish fortress of Modon were alternately suggested as suitable places of abode. Even when Malta had been granted to them by the Emperor Charles V., they continued to plan the capture of the former Venetian station in Messenia, which in their hands would have become an outpost of Christendom. Two Greeks, who had formerly been servants of the Order in Rhodes, but who now held posts at the harbour of Modon, entered into the plot; a flotilla was equipped under the command of Fra Bernardo Salviati, prior of Rome and nephew of Pope Clement VII.; and two schooners were laden with planks in such a manner as to conceal a number of armed men below. One of these innocent-looking vessels was entrusted to Yánni Skandáles, a Greek from Zante and son of the friendly customs' official at Modon; and its Greek crew was disguised as janissaries. While the rest of the squadron remained behind the island of Sapienza, the schooners went on in advance to Modon. The two confederates kept their word; the harmless merchants and the false janissaries were allowed to land, and the latter spent the night in the tower on the mole, of which Skandáles's father was governor, pledging the garrison in the excellent local vintage. To secure or slay the sleepy and drunken Mussulmans was easy; the tower was captured; the soldiers landed from the two schooners; and the town was soon entirely in their possession, except the former palace of the Venetian governor above the land gate, whither the rest of the garrison had hastened. The Knights were, however, slow in arriving from Sapienza to complete the capture; so that, before their cannon had made the least impression on the palace, a large Turkish force was reported to be approaching. Accordingly, after sacking the place, they

[1] Sanudo, *Diarii*, xi., 349; xxxiii., 366; Sáthas, iv., 224, 227, 229, 234; Lamansky, 059; Feyerabend, *Reyssbuch*, f. 112.

[2] Sáthas, vi., 278.

sailed away with 1600 captives. Their adventure, reported to the pope, it is interesting to note, by one of the Acciajuoli, was welcomed in Rome, but caused much annoyance to Venice, anxious not to provoke the anger of the sultan, who might hold her responsible for the acts of her Ionian subjects. Accordingly, as a measure of precaution, Skandáles was banished from Zante.[1]

In the following year the Greek coasts were exposed to a much more serious visitation. War broke out between Charles V. and the sultan, and the former, more anxious to damage the Turks than to benefit the Greeks, the exploits of whose ancestors left him cold, despatched the famous Genoese admiral, Andrea Doria, to the Levant. Doria gained a series of rapid successes. The allied imperial, papal, and Maltese squadron, with the aid of the Greek inhabitants, speedily captured Coron;[2] a *Te Deum* of triumph was sung in the reconsecrated cathedral, and at the moment of the elevation of the Host the standards of the three confederates were run up on the walls. Mendoza, a Spaniard and a Knight of Malta, was left behind with a garrison of his countrymen, Acciajuoli was appointed civil governor, and Doria sailed away to Patras, whose garrison capitulated and whose inhabitants he pillaged. He completed his cruise by an attack on the two castles which Bajazet II. had built on either side of the entrance to the Gulf of Corinth; the castle of the Morea surrendered; but the garrison of the other fired the powder-magazine and perished beneath the ruins of the fortress.

Nothing but harm accrued to the Greeks from Doria's expedition, and they had, indeed, good reason to pray for deliverance from their deliverers. Deluded by his promises and elated at his victories, they rose and slaughtered their Turkish masters, who retaliated upon them as soon as the Genoese admiral had set sail. Charles V. soon realised that he could not permanently keep an isolated station in

[1] Sanudo, *Diarii*, liv., 603-8; lv., 9-13, 25, 49, 85; Spandugino *apud* Sáthas, ix., 193-4; Bosio, III., 75-6, 103-7; *Codice Diplomatico Gerosolimitano*, II., 204.

[2] There is a curious painting of this event in the Archivio at Siena, on one of the covers of the old Treasury registers, or *tavolette*.

Messenia, far from his own dominions and exposed to continual Turkish attacks. So, after once relieving the beleaguered garrison, he endeavoured to transfer to Venice or to the Knights of Malta the responsibility of its defence. The former, with characteristic prudence, declined to accept her former colony, just as she had refused the offer of the castles formerly dependent upon Monemvasia. The latter knew that they could never maintain it without Venetian aid, and they knew, too, that the selfish republic would never tolerate the intrusion of another Christian power in the Morea, and had refused to co-operate in the capture or support of Coron. Meanwhile, the Turks were keeping up a continuous blockade, and hunger and plague were reducing the strength of the garrison. At last, in 1534, the emperor resolved to abandon it and remove its inhabitants to his own dominions. This compulsory emigration of the people, mostly Albanians—for the Greeks had been transferred to Cephalonia thirty years before—recalls the cession of Parga by Great Britain three centuries later. They sought refuge in the churches, and implored the Divine Providence to avert from them the miseries of exile; but they found that they must either submit to the Turk or obey the commands of the emperor. Many died of plague on the voyage to Sicily, while the survivors were attacked by the terrified population of Messina on landing, and driven into the lazzaretto like pariahs. So wretched was their condition, that the emperor granted to those of them who took up their abode in Naples a yearly allowance and valuable fiscal exemptions, as well as the possession of the Greek church of SS. Peter and Paul, which had been founded at Naples by one of the Palaiológoi more than twenty years earlier. In return, they entered his service as *stradioti*, and displayed in other lands a valour which might, under better auspices, have saved their beloved home from the Turk. Others settled in Calabria and the Basilicata, others again in Sicily, and an Albanian monk at the Greek monastery of Grotta Ferrata, near Rome, told the author that most of the Albanians from his part of Sicily were the descendants of these exiles from Coron. One Greek, who had specially distinguished himself in the siege and defence of the place, received from the emperor the barren honour of knighthood, and a grant of the villages of Leondari and St George of Skortá, "whensoever it should please God to drive out the Turks."[1]

In 1537, Suleyman the Magnificent declared war upon Venice, and the Turkish fleet, under Khaireddîn Barbarossa, after a vain attempt to take Corfù, and after ravaging the Ionian islands, in October fell upon Ægina, then well inhabited. No considerations of sentiment stayed the hands of the red-bearded pirate. His men scaled the high rock in the interior of the island, which resembles the Akropolis of Athens, and on which, from fear of corsairs, the mediæval capital was built. On the fourth day, Palaiochora fell; the town was destroyed; but the Latin church, which we saw mentioned four years earlier, was spared; the grown-up men were butchered, and the governor with one of the Caopena, who had come to the rescue of his ancestors' island, and more than 6000 women and children were carried off as slaves. So thoroughly did the Turks accomplish their hideous work, that when Baron de Blancard touched at Ægina with a French fleet soon afterwards, he found not a single soul on the island.[2] Few now set foot in the abandoned streets of this town of churches, where the scanty inhabitants of the scattered hamlets still worship, save when, once a year, the pious islanders assemble round the marvellous spring in the church of Our Lady to keep the festival in honour of the Virgin's birth. From below, the mountain side seems covered with buildings, and the castle stands out from the flat summit of the rock, just as if the Venetian sentinels were still on the watch for pirates in the Saronic Gulf below. Remains of

[1] Guazzo, *Historie*, ff. 124, 128-30; P. Jovius, *Historiæ sui temporis*, ii., ff. 116-18, 126-8; Bosio, III., 114-16, 125-7, 132; Sanudo, *Diarii*, lvii., 94-5, 182, 227, 668, 678; Paruta, *Historia Venetiana*, i., 328, 333, 339; Mustoxidi, Ἑλληνομνήμων, 147-9; Duplessis, *In Difesa dei Nazionali Greci per la Chiesa di rito Greco . . . di Napoli.* I could not find in the Greek Church at Naples the tombs mentioned by Mustoxidi; but there is one of a *stradioto*, who died in 1607.

[2] Paruta, i., 381; Maurocenus, *Historia Veneta*, 182; A. Cornaro, *Historia di Candia*, II., f. 92; Charrière, *Négociations de la France dans le Levant*, i., 372; Haji Kalifeh, *The Maritime Wars*, 58; Sáthas, ix., 199; Hopf, *Karystos* (tr. Sardagna), 72; Dorótheos of Monemvasia, 437. *Cf.* my article on Palaiochora in the *Morning Post* of 23rd December 1904.

frescoes still cover the crumbling walls of the old Venetian chapel within the castle walls, where the last Venetian governor, warned that Barbarossa's pennant had been sighted, flung himself down on his knees and prayed the preoccupied saints to save this outpost of the republic from the enemy. No site in Greece is more lovely, none more mediæval. Palaiochora belongs to a world very different from ours; it tells us of what life—and death—must have been like in the last years of Venetian rule in the small Greek islands.

Meanwhile, the Turks, acting under orders from Kassim Pasha, were striving to capture the last two Venetian colonies in the Morea. The operations before Nauplia began on 14th September, and it was soon obvious that the Greek and Albanian *stradioti* intended to make a desperate defence. Two successful sorties as far as Argos adorned the walls of Nauplia with many a Turkish head, and even when Kassim himself arrived, his men made little impression on the stout hearts of the garrison. At the two outlying fortresses of Kastri and Thermisi he was more successful; the defenders of Kastri preferred slavery to being burned alive inside the castle, and the four Palaiológoi, whose fief it was, were beheaded at Argos. Upon this Thermisi surrendered; but neither of these disasters diminished the heroic courage of the men of Nauplia. Fresh supplies were thrown into the town, but the lack of water began to be severely felt—for the cisterns were running dry—and a party which sallied forth to fetch water from the wells near Mount Elias, was surprised by the Turks, and Vettore Busichio, the bold captain of the light Albanian horse, was mortally wounded. Kassim now occupied the hill of Palamidi, which the Venetians had neglected to fortify, and which commanded the town, and moved his headquarters from Argos to Tiryns, and thence to the church of St Friday, only a thousand paces from Nauplia. But, in spite of the heavy missiles discharged from the heights of Palamidi, where the convict prison now stands, by a big Turkish gun, which the besieged nicknamed "bone-breaker" with a humour worthy of Ladysmith, the place held out, and further reinforcements arrived. Kassim next dug trenches close up to the edge of the moat; but the men whom he placed there fell victims to a bold night attack. At last, when the siege had lasted fourteen months, he retired with the bulk of his army to Argos, leaving a small garrison on Palamidi, which was speedily captured by the Venetians and its newly-erected bastions destroyed. Desultory skirmishes went on during the spring of 1539, but Nauplia, like Monemvasia, proved too strong for the Turks to take.[1]

Venice was no longer alone in her struggle against the sultan, for Pope Paul III. had at last succeeded in forming a league between the Emperor Charles V., the republic, and himself. The fleet of the three allies assembled at Corfù, and sailed to Preveza, where Barbarossa had taken up his position. There, at the mouth of the Ambrakian Gulf, where, sixteen centuries before, the fate of the Roman world had been decided, the hostile navies met. Unfortunately, the command of the imperial vessels had been entrusted to Andrea Doria, who showed, as was natural in a Genoese, little enthusiasm in the cause of Venice. Owing to his timorous tactics, the victory rested with Barbarossa, and the *rapprochement* between Charles V. and the French monarch broke up the league. Venice had no option but to make such terms with the sultan as she could obtain. Humiliating, indeed, was the peace of 1540; Venice ceded Nauplia and Monemvasia—her two last possessions in the Morea;[2] and Admiral Mocenigo was sent to break as best he could to her loyal subjects the sad news that the republic for whom they had fought so well and had endured so many privations had abandoned their homes to the Turk. The Venetian envoy, if we may believe the speech which Paruta puts into his mouth, repeated to the weeping people the ancient adage, *ubi bene, ibi patria*, and pointed out to them that they would be better off in a new abode less exposed than their native cities had been to the Turkish peril. In November a Venetian fleet arrived in the beautiful bay of Nauplia and off the sacred rock of Monemvasia, to remove the soldiers, the artillery, and all the inhabitants who wished to live under Venetian rule. Then the banner of the Evangelist

[1] Guazzo, ff. 205-8; Dorótheos of Monemvasia, 437-8; Paruta, i., 379-80, 391-2, 412, 439.

[2] Predelli, *Commemoriali*, vi., 236, 238.

was lowered, the keys of the two last Venetian fortresses in the Morea were handed to Kassim Pasha, and the receipts for their transfer were sent to Venice.[1]

The inhabitants of the two cities had been loyal to Venice—for not only had the *stradioti* fought like heroes, but no less heroic had been the conduct of the 7000 Nauplians who had died of hunger and enteric rather than surrender—and Venice was loyal to them. The first idea of transporting the Monemvasiotes to the rocky island of Cerigo was abandoned, in deference to the eloquent protests of the metropolitan, and lands were assigned to the exiles in the more fertile colonies of the republic. A commission of five nobles was appointed to consider the claims and provide for the settlement of the *stradioti* from Nauplia and Monemvasia, and this commission sat for several years, for the claimants were numerous, and not all genuine.[2] Some, like the ancient Monemvasiote family of Daimonoyánnes, former lords of Cerigo, received lands in Crete,[3] where the last "chief priest" of Nauplia and some of the Athenian De' Medici, who had so long been settled there, also found a home; one of the latter clan returned to the land of his ancestors, and was glad to accept a small post at Verona.[4] The Caopena, whose father, captured at Ægina, perished in a Turkish dungeon, settled at Venice, where a century later the family became extinct.[5] Others were removed to Corfù, where they formed an integral part of the Corfiote population, and where the name of the *stradioti* is still preserved in a locality of the island; while others again were transplanted to Cephalonia, Cyprus, or Dalmatia. Not a few of them were soon, however, smitten with homesickness; they sold their new lands, and returned to be Turkish subjects at Nauplia and Monemvasia.[6]

Thus fell the last Latin colonies in the Morea. For nearly a century and a half the Lion of St Mark did not own

[1] Paruta, i., 451-3.

[2] Lami, *Deliciæ Eruditorum*, xv., 203; Sáthas, viii., 310-13, 320-1, 335, 344, 377-8, 441-3.

[3] *Ibid.*, 342, 413, 450, 454; Sansovino, *Cronologia del Mondo*, f. 185.

[4] Sáthas, viii., 370, 451, 455.

[5] *Ibid.*, 434, 457.

[6] *Ibid.*, 396.

a single inch of soil on the mainland of Greece, where since the early years of the thirteenth century he had constantly retained a foothold. But the Venetian fortifications of Nauplia, with here and there a winged lion or a dated tablet, remained to remind the *rayah* of the Venetian days; and the pictures and churches of Monemvasia, the encircling walls, the quaint Italian chimneys, and the well-head up in the castle, which bears the date of 1514, the arms of the republic and of her last *podestà*, Antonio Garzoni, and the initials and escutcheon of Sebastiano Renier, who had also her representative, still speak to us of this first Venetian occupation.[1]

With the disappearance of the Venetian flag from the mainland, the Greeks lost the refuge which they had been accustomed to find since the Turkish Conquest in the Venetian settlements. Most of their leaders had, like Michael Rálles, found a shelter beneath the banner of St Mark, and it was there that the klephts, who afterwards played so great a part in the liberation of Hellas, first organised their raids. That the Greeks at that period, whatever might have been the case in the eighteenth century, preferred Venetian to Turkish rule, seems obvious from the alacrity with which they flew to arms at the bidding of their Latin allies. Up to 1540 the republic was always at hand to suggest, if not to urge, the possibilities of a successful rising, and the Venetian settlements maintained the Western standard of culture in the midst of the general stagnation which fell upon Turkish Greece. At the same time, the flight of the winged lion from the Morea meant for that sorely-tried land a respite from the almost constant turmoils, to which it had been exposed since the removal of Guillaume de Villehardouin's strong hand first plunged the peninsula into anarchy. Under the Turks there was at last a dull uniformity, which was not without the advantage that it consolidated the various elements of the nation.

[1] *J. H. S.*, xxvii., 240.

CHAPTER XV

CORFÙ (1214-1485)

WE have described in the previous chapters the rise and fall of the various states of continental Greece, whose history occupied the period between the Latin and the Turkish Conquests. We must now turn to the two principal island possessions of the Franks, omitting, for the sake of clearness, those minor places in the Ægean whose fortunes do not affect the main narrative. These two insular states are the duchy of Naxos, and the colony of Corfù. In the history of both, Venetian enterprise played a conspicuous part. Both survived, though for different periods of time, the establishment of Turkish rule on the mainland, and Corfù, the most important of the Ionian islands, was practically never subjected to the Mussulman yoke. But in other respects the careers of the two exhibit widely different results of Latin rule in the Levant.

The island of Corfù, the loveliest spot in all Greece, has had a history separate, down to very recent times, from the rest of the country. Even the other Ionian islands, except the little island of Paxo, lie far away from the ancient home of the Phæacians. For well-nigh three centuries its history was quite distinct from theirs, and it was not till after the Turkish Conquest of the mainland of Greece, that they were all united under the Venetian banner, which waved over them until the downfall of the republic in 1797.

We saw in the second and third chapters how, after two Venetian attempts to colonise Corfù, the island was captured by Michael I., Despot of Epiros, about the year 1214, with whose continental dominions it remained united for half-a-century. We saw, too, how one Despot after another ratified and extended the privileges of the Corfiote Church, which they wisely recognised as the bulwark of their rule over the islanders, and which furnished them, from the pen of the metropolitan, George Bardánes, with plausible arguments against the theologians of the Nicene Empire. Under the sway of the bastard Michael II., the island was specially favoured. An usurper, he was bound to conciliate his subjects, and we accordingly find him lavishing one privilege after another upon the fortunate Corfiotes. At the end of 1236, immediately after he had made himself master of the island, he not only confirmed their former rights, but made them and their villains practically exempt from taxation and customs duties;[1] ten years later, by two successive golden bulls, he freed the thirty-two priests of the town of Corfù, who formed a religious corporation, from all forced labour,[2] and bestowed similar privileges upon the thirty-three country popes, who were consequently described as the "freemen" (or Λευθεριῶται), forming a regular caste, into which none but members of their own families could enter.[3] From the scanty notices of the period when Corfù belonged to the Despotat of Epiros which have come down to us, it is clear that this was the zenith of the orthodox church in the island. Long after the times of the Despots, the Corfiote clergy were wont to produce their charters when they sought for redress from their Angevin or Venetian rulers, and the institution of the thirty-two town priests still existed in the middle of the fifteenth century,[4] when it was regarded as the mainstay of orthodoxy in the island. These privileged priests never forgot their benefactors, and the wise ecclesiastical policy of the Despots of Epiros saved the Greek Church through centuries of Roman Catholic predominance.

Of the civil administration of the Despots in the island we know scarcely anything, beyond the fact that in their time it was divided into ten "decarchies"[5]— possibly a continuation

[1] Barone, *Notizie Storiche di Re Carlo III. di Durazzo*, 61-4.
[2] *Ibid.*, 65-6; Sáthas, Μνημεῖα, I., 48-9.
[3] Romanós in Δελτίον τῆς Ἱστ. καὶ Ἐθν. Ἑταιρίας, II., 594-6.
[4] Phrantzês, 412; Lamansky, *Secrets de l'État de Venise*, 050.
[5] Δελτίον, II., 594.

of the Venetian system of colonisation by ten nobles, possibly a survival of the old Roman *decuriones*, or local landowners. It is interesting to notice that among the names of these "decarchies" which have come down to us, one at least, in the slightly corrupted form of "Bistoni," preserves that of the classic mountain of Istone, the modern Santi Deka, which figures in Thucydides' account of the Corcyræan sedition. The oldest historian of Corfù may be exaggerating when he says that the Despots of Epiros "adorned the city with most noble buildings";[1] but tradition and probability are with him when he ascribes to them the castle of Sant' Angelo on the west coast, whose ruins, in a superb situation above the blue Ionian sea, still preserve the name of that adventurous race.

Michael II., as we saw, considered it necessary to secure the alliance of King Manfred in his struggle for the leadership of the Greeks. Accordingly, in 1259, he married his beautiful daughter Helene to the sovereign of the Two Sicilies, to whom she brought as her dowry Corfù, the fortresses of Butrinto, Suboto, and Valona, and one or two other places on the mainland. It was not the first time that the island had been a Sicilian possession, for more than once in the course of the twelfth century the Normans of Sicily had temporarily occupied it. Unable, however, to govern it in person, Manfred entrusted the island, together with his possessions in Epiros, to his admiral, Filippo Chinardo, who, as a Frank from Cyprus, had had experience of managing Greeks, and who endeavoured to win over the Corfiotes by exempting them from the duty of repairing the Sicilian fleet. Even after Manfred had fallen at the battle of Benevento and his widow and children were prisoners of Charles of Anjou, Chinardo maintained his position in Corfù and the Epirote fortresses for a few more months. The crafty Despot of Epiros gave him the hand of his sister-in-law, and recognised him as lord of the island by regarding it as her dowry, now that his daughter, its rightful owner, was in prison. Chinardo felt himself secure enough to bestow Corfiote fiefs upon his lieutenants,[2] thus extending

[1] Marmora, *Della Historia di Corfù*, 210.

[2] Buchon, *Nouvelles Recherches*, II., i., 309-10; Del Giudice, *La famiglia di Re Manfredi*, 428.

the feudal system which had been founded under the Greeks and which so long prevailed in Corfù. But there was a Greek party in the island which was in communication with the Despot, and the latter had no difficulty in procuring his assassination. Michael II. did not, however, reap the profit of his crime. One of Chinardo's newly created barons, Garnier Aleman, a member of the Provençal family which we saw installed at Patras, had the strongest motives of personal interest to keep out the Greeks. He naturally turned for aid to his fellow-countryman and fellow-Catholic, Charles of Anjou, who regarded himself as the representative of the conquered Manfred in all the latter's possessions. On hearing of Chinardo's murder, Charles had, in January 1267, appointed the murdered man's son captain of Corfù. But Aleman's position and services called for this reward, and the office of captain and vicar-general was transferred to him by the cautious king.[1] The treaty of Viterbo, two months later, formally recognised Charles's rights over the lands "which had been held by Manfred and Filippo Chinardo." Thus, in 1267, began the Angevin domination over Corfù.

For the next few years, however, Charles of Anjou was too much occupied with Italian politics to devote his personal attention to that grand scheme for the conquest of the Eastern Empire, which had been conceived at Viterbo, and towards which he, like Bonaparte five centuries later, considered the occupation of Corfù to be the first step. He added indeed the style of "King of Corfù" to his other titles, and deputed Prince William of Achaia to make arrangements for its custody; but he thought it expedient to allow Aleman to remain in undisturbed and practically independent possession of the island and its castles, excusing him from rendering any account of his administration, and pardoning any offence which he might have committed against the king's orders. It is clear that the diplomatic monarch was anxious not to offend the proud Provençal baron, to whom he owed the island; it is clear, too, that he desired to conciliate the Greek party among the Corfiotes;

[1] Minieri Riccio, *Alcuni fatti*, 21, 24, 37; Del Giudice, *Codice Diplomatico*, I., 278, 298.

one of his first acts was to recall all the natives who had fled the island, except those implicated in Chinardo's assassination; another was to guarantee to all the citizens the security of their lives and the enjoyment of their property according to the usages and customs of the island.[1]

Just as the death of the Despot Michael II. gave Charles the opportunity of carrying out his long-deferred plans in Epiros, so that of Garnier Aleman in 1272 made him for the first time the real master of Corfù. Aleman's son was satisfied with a money payment and with confirmation of his family fiefs in the island, and Giordano di San Felice, the new vicar-general and captain of Corfù, took possession in Charles's name of the three fortresses of Castel Vecchio, Castel Nuovo (as the two summits of the present Fortezza Vecchia were then called), and Sant' Angelo. Under his jurisdiction were the castles of Suboto and Butrinto, "the key of Corfù," as the Venetians called the latter, which had once belonged to Manfred and Chinardo, which had been retaken by the Greeks, but which, in 1279, was restored to Manfred's conqueror by the feeble Despot Nikephóros I.[2]

The Angevin rule, as might have been anticipated from its origin, was especially intolerant of the orthodox faith. Charles owed his crown to the pope, and was anxious to repay the obligation by propagating Catholicism among his orthodox subjects. The Venetians, as we saw, had enjoined tolerance of the Greek Church during their brief period of domination; the Despots of Epiros had made it a privileged body; now for the first time the islanders learnt what religious persecution meant. The metropolitan of Corfù, whose dignity dated from the tenth century, and who had played so conspicuous a part in the disputes between Epiros and Nice, was deposed, and in his place a less dignified ecclesiastic, called "chief priest" (μέγας πρωτοπαπᾶς) was substituted. This personage was elected by the thirty-two

[1] Del Giudice, *La famiglia di Re Manfredi*, 403-4; *Codice Diplomatico*, i., 307; ii., 35; Mustoxidi, *Cose Corciresi*, pp. lvii., 442; Buchon, *op. cit.*, 406.

[2] *Ibid.*, 397, 405-7, 409-12, 414-16; Buchon, *op. cit.*, 309, 407; Riccio, *Il Regno di Carlo I.*, 58, 60, 87, 107; *Saggio di Codice Diplomatico*, i., 99, 175, 180; the history of Butrinto has been summarised by Romanós in the Δελτίον, III., 554 *et sqq.*

priests of "the sacred band" and by the same number of local nobles, while eight similar ecclesiastics were appointed for the benefit of the Greeks throughout the island. The title of "Archbishop of Corfù" was usurped by Antonio, a Latin priest, and the principal churches, including the cathedral, which was then in the fortress, were seized by the Catholic clergy; the residence of the metropolitan had already been pulled down by Chinardo. It was not till the Russians landed in Corfù a hundred years ago that the Greek Church recovered its high position in the island, though the successors of Charles showed their willingness to grant favours to the Greek clergy.[1]

Towards another religion, that of the Jews, the Angevins were sufficiently tolerant to induce that race to settle for the first time in any numbers in the island, where a ghetto and its vicar are mentioned in 1365; but the injunctions of successive sovereigns, bidding the Corfiotes treat them well, would seem to show that this protection was seldom efficacious against the prejudices of the natives, prejudices not quite extinct in our own day. That these Jews came from the Levant rather than from Italy seems proved by the curious fact that the Greek is the older of the two Corfiote synagogues, and that the earliest known example of vulgar Greek prose is a translation of the Book of Jonah for the use of the synagogue in Corfù.[2]

The military and civil administration was placed, as was natural, in the hands of Italians or Provençals. At the head of the government was the captain, or vicar-general, usually directly dependent upon the king, but at times specially placed under the supreme authority of the royal representative in Albania. A *magister massarius*, or treasurer (so called because one of his duties was to look after the material of war and other instruments of the *massa*, or public "estate") was the second Angevin official, and in the middle of the fourteenth century the two offices were united in the same person. A third official was styled

[1] Marmora, 216; Mustoxidi, 410; Del Giudice, *op. cit.*, 425, 434; *Les Registres de Grégoire X.*, 208.

[2] Romanós, Ἡ Ἑβραϊκὴ κοινότης τῆς Κερκύρας, 4, 5; Δελτίον τῆς Ἱστ. Ἑτ., ii., 605.

inquisitor.[1] The High Court of Justice, or *Curia Regis*, was composed of the captain, a legal assessor, and a notary, all foreigners and all appointed by the sovereign, together with two or three Corfiote judges, who from their tenure of office were styled *judices annuales.* This court, which sat to try all civil and criminal cases, met in the *loggia* adjoining, or in a palace "above the iron gate," an important entrance, the custody of which was entrusted to a special officer.[2] The official language of the court was Latin, but we find the captain signing his name in French, and there was a public notary for the Greek tongue, in which contracts between a Greek and a foreigner were drawn up.[3] One of the first acts of the Latin rulers was to introduce the feudal usages and customs of the Empire of Romania.[4]

The island, under the Angevins, was divided into four bailiwicks, each administered by a bailie, and called respectively the Circle, the Mountain, the Centre, and Levkimme after the White Cape at the South. The old decarchies, however, continued to exist, as in the days of the Despots. The land belonged partly to the royal domain, and partly to the barons, to whom it had been granted by the sovereign.[5] One of Charles's chief instructions was to draw up a complete list of the Corfiote fiefs, distinguishing those created by Manfred and Chinardo from those of Greek origin.[6] This list has been lost; but, if we may believe the historian Marmora,[7] there were twenty-four at the time of the Angevin occupation. These fiefs passed into the possession of Provençal or Italian families like that of Goth (or Hugot), which had accompanied Charles to Naples, or those of Altavilla, S. Ippolito, and Caracciolo. This great Neapolitan clan left its name long imprinted on the land which was once its property. Even the little group of

[1] Marmora, *loc. cit.*; Del Giudice, *op. cit.*, 423; Romanós, Δημοσία Πρᾶξις.

[2] Δελτίον, ii., 603, 606; Del Giudice, *Codice Diplomatico*, i., 308; Barone, 24, 26; Romanós, Δημοσία Πραξις, 7.

[3] Barone, 25; Romanós, Γρατιανὸς Ζώρζης, 311-13.

[4] Del Giudice, *La Famiglia di Re Manfredi*, 410.

[5] Barone, 22-4; Δελτίον, ii., 605.

[6] Del Giudice, *La Famiglia*, 428.

[7] P. 283.

the Othonian islands formed one of the fiefs in the gift of the sovereign of Corfù.[1]

The Latin barons formed a council which met in the arcades near "the iron gate," and which elected the above-mentioned "annual judges," four officials, named *sindici*, who were the representatives of the community, and two others, bearing the ancient Byzantine title of *catapan*, who looked after the food supplies. As time went on, baronies were conferred on Greeks who had rendered services to the sovereign, such as the family of Kavásilas from Epiros; and, towards the close of the Angevin period, we find the community, or at least the principal persons composing it, summoned by the sound of the bell for the discussion of public affairs. One prince after another, as the Corfiotes confessed, conferred privileges upon them.[2]

The island was, indeed, valuable to the Angevins for other reasons than its strategic position. Charles I. found it well suited for horse-breeding; it possessed valuable salt-pans; it produced plenty of wine; and its olive-trees, though not what they afterwards became in the Venetian times, are already mentioned in the fourteenth century. The fisheries of Butrinto were a source of revenue, and there was sufficient trade to attract a Venetian, as well as a Jewish colony, to the island.[3] Moreover, the Corfiotes, descendants of the sea-faring Phæacians, were bound to furnish crews for the Angevin fleet.

The Sicilian Vespers and the consequent struggle between the houses of Aragon and Anjou entailed the vengeance of the former party upon the unhappy Corfiotes, who had the misfortune to be subjects of the latter. Roger de Lluria twice ravaged the island, burning and destroying the castle; Berenguer d'Entença and Berenguer Villaraut both raided this beautiful spot; and, on its way to Constantinople, the Catalan Grand Company did not fail to plunder it.[4] Nor were the Aragonese fleets the only evils of which the

[1] Buchon, *Nouvelles Recherches*, II., i., 409; Barone, 20, 23, 25.

[2] Marmora, 221; Mustoxidi, lx., lxvii.; Buchon, *op. cit.*, I., i., 410.

[3] Barone, 25, 29; Predelli, *Commemoriali*, ii., 21.

[4] Muntaner, chs. cxvi., cxvii., clix.; N. Specialis *apud* Muratori, x., 960; Predelli, *Commemoriali*, i., 31.

islanders complained. The captains at this period were absentees—men of great name and lineage, like Hugh of Brienne, baron of Karytaina; Count Richard of Cephalonia; and Florent d'Avesnes, Prince of Achaia; who had more important interests elsewhere, and whose deputies oppressed the people. Charles II. of Naples, who was now their sovereign, showed, however, that he wished them well. In 1294, he confirmed[1] the golden bull which the Despot Michael II. had issued in 1236; in the same year he bestowed the island, together with the castle of Butrinto and its dependencies, upon his fourth son, Philip of Taranto, on the occasion of his marriage with the fair Thamar of Epiros, reserving to himself the overlordship as a matter of form. Thus the Prince of Taranto repeated the diplomatic marriage of Manfred under more favourable auspices. Holding Corfù, with its dependencies and the dowry of Thamar on the mainland, he seemed to occupy a stronger position than any previous Latin ruler of the island. So far as high-sounding titles went, there was soon no personage in the Latin Orient so magnificent as the new "Lord of Corfù," as he styled himself on his coins, who was also titular Emperor of Constantinople, Prince of Achaia, and Despot of Romania.[2]

His long reign of nearly forty years over the island was, if we may believe the indiscriminate panegyric of Marmora, a second golden age, during which a well-beloved prince governed a devoted people. He strengthened the Catholic element, and at the same time encouraged agriculture by conferring upon the archbishop the waste and uncultivated lands of the island for the support of the established church.[3] He issued orders for the protection of the Jews, whose Sabbath services were disturbed, whose possessions were liable to seizure, and whose services were enlisted as galley-slaves, or worse still, as public executioners, a duty all the more repugnant because the gallows were erected in the Jewish cemetery.[4]

[1] Barone, 60.

[2] Buchon, *Nouvelles Recherches*, II., i., 407; Riccio, *Saggio di Codice*, supp., part I., 79; Schlumberger, *Numismatique*, 389; *Supplément*, 22.

[3] M. Mustoxidi, Ἱστορικὰ Ἀνάλεκτα, 98.

[4] A. Mustoxidi, *Cose Corciresi*, 445; Ἑλληνομνήμων, 486 (more accurate than Buchon, *op. cit.*, I., i., 408).

But there are some dark shadows on the picture, which the courtly artist has omitted. So ardent a Catholic as the Prince of Taranto could scarcely be expected to tolerate the Greek Church, which represented a national as well as a religious force, especially as the Greek emperor had recently bestowed upon the new metropolitan of Joannina the offensive title of "Exarch of Corfù." There was, too, the alarm of Greek invasions from the mainland opposite. At one moment we find the Despot Thomas of Epiros scheming with the Greek emperor's admiral to make a descent from Valona on Corfù; at another it is Count John II. of Cephalonia who threatens the fortunate island; or, again, it is the imperial fleet which blockades the harbour. Philip's governors, too, oppressed even the Catholic Church; and the prince, always an absentee and for some years a prisoner, was not able to keep a tight hand upon them. Still, in the Venetian times, the Corfiote nobles looked back on the good Prince of Taranto as the founder of many of the privileges which they enjoyed, and he confirmed and strengthened the feudal system by grants of new baronies to his friends.[1] Among these was Guglielmo Tocco, who, as his governor in Corfù, laid the foundations of that remarkable family's fortunes in the Ionian islands.[2]

Philip's son, Robert, was a minor at the time of his father's death, and his mother, the titular Empress Catherine of Valois, exercised authority in her own and his name in Corfù, as well as in Achaia. Robert followed his father's policy of protecting the Corfiote Jews, and of rewarding his faithful adherents, both Greek and Italian, by the bestowal of feudal lands. He confirmed the local privileges, especially those of the thirty-three country priests, granted a century before by the Despot Michael II., and released them from the exactions of the *magister massarius* and from the obligation, which lay upon all the Corfiotes, of making a present to the prince whenever they appeared in his presence. The fertile island enabled him, too, to make provision for his wife, Marie de Bourbon, in the event of her widowhood, and during the struggle which arose between the widow and her

[1] Thomas, *Diplomatarium*, 135, 161.

[2] Buchon, *Nouvelles Recherches*, I., i., 410.

brother-in-law, Philip II. of Taranto, she had sufficient authority in Corfù to repeat her late husband's orders on behalf of the Hebrew colony.[1] But, from the death of his brother in 1364, Philip II. exercised the rights of sovereignty over the island. He, too, strove to protect the Jews, ratified the franchises so long enjoyed by the village popes, and ordered his officials not to interfere in the affairs of the Greek clergy, the punishment of whom he allowed the *protopapádes* of the city of Corfù to determine, as had been their immemorial custom. In this tolerant policy he was guided by Romanópoulos, the archbishop, who, though a Greek by race and a Catholic by religion, had neither the Chauvinism of a naturalised foreigner nor the bigotry of a convert.[2] According to some authorities, it was during this reign that the fief of the gypsies, of which we shall hear more in the Venetian period, was first created. At any rate, the gypsies, of whom we have seen traces in other parts of Greece, where the various Γυφτόκαστρα still preserve their name, seem to have crossed over to Corfù from the mainland during the Angevin domination. These may have been the oft-mentioned "men from Vagenetia" in Epiros, who first found refuge at the courts of the Corfiote barons in the reigns of Charles II. and of Philip I. of Taranto. Catherine of Valois and her son Robert made these serfs, whose name still lingers in Corfù, a source of revenue, by imposing a poll-tax upon them, to be paid by their feudal lord when they entered the island and his service; and Philip II.'s second wife, Elizabeth of Hungary, to whom he granted Corfù on his marriage in 1371, tried to seize them all and make them serfs of the princely domain. Against this high-handed act the barons successfully protested.[3]

Both Elizabeth[4] and her husband died in November 1373, and his young nephew, Jacques de Baux, became the

[1] Mustoxidi, *op. cit.*, 447-9, lxi.; Romanós in Δελτίον, ii., 601; and Ἑβραϊκὴ Κοινότης, 5.

[2] Δελτίον, 587; Marmora, 223; Miklosich und Müller, v., 67; Buchon, *op. cit.*, I., i., 413.

[3] Mustoxidi, *op. cit.*, 449; Hopf, *op. cit.*, lxxxvi., 33, 186; Barone, 25; Romanós, Δημοσία Κερκυραϊκὴ Πρᾶξις; Albánas, Περὶ τῶνύὲν Κερκρα τίτλων, 13, 29.

[4] Crassulto, *De Rebus Tarentinis* in *Raccolta di Varie Cronache*, v., 1.

heir of all his titles and dominions. The Corfiote barons, however, were as little inclined as their fellows in the Morea, to accept his sway. During the civil war, which raged between the Baux and Queen Joanna I. of Naples, Jacques found a temporary refuge in his Greek estates; but the Ionians, headed by Guglielmo and Riccardo d'Altavilla proclaimed the Queen of Naples as Lady of Corfù, the suzerainty over which had been preserved, as we saw, ninety years before, to the Neapolitan Crown. Joanna retained possession of the island for seven years; she pacified the Greeks by renewing the privileges of the thirty-two city priests, granted by the Despot Michael II., and confirmed by her predecessors; she guaranteed to the citizens their old customs and the franchises bestowed upon them by a long line of Angevin princes; she extended her protection to the Jews; she encouraged the immigration of the "men from Vagenetia"; and ordered her officials to see that the Venetian merchants, so long established there, enjoyed their time-honoured rights undisturbed.[1] But, in 1380, Jacques de Baux thought that the moment was favourable for the assertion of his claims in Greece. The Navarrese Company was despatched thither to do his work, and its first achievement on Greek soil was the capture of Corfù. The last titular emperor of Constantinople did his best to win adherents in the island. Almost his sole act was to purchase the support of the powerful baron, Adamo di Sant' Ippolito, by the grant of the island of Paxo, which had belonged to Filippo Malerba of Verona, a recent captain of Corfù—one of the few allusions to the smallest of the Seven Islands during the Angevin period.[2] But the distracted politics of the time made the baron of Paxo soon forget his benefactor. Charles III. of Durazzo descended upon Naples, and robbed Joanna of her crown and life. Corfù, too weak to stand alone, was divided into three factions—that of the usurper; that of Joanna's heir, Louis of Anjou, one of whose officials was pleased to style himself "Marquis of Corfù"; and that of Jacques de Baux, whose Navarrese garrisons must have

[1] Sáthas, *op. cit.*, i., 47; iii., 31; Barone, 22, 24, 26, 65; Lunzi, 79-82; Predelli, *Commemoriali*, iii., 130.

[2] [Archduke Salvator,] *Paxos und Antipaxos*, 9-13.

been detested alike by Greeks and Italians. Sant' Ippolito and Riccardo d'Altavilla saw that it was their interest to worship the rising sun. They succeeded, not without considerable labour and expense, in driving the Navarrese veterans out of the castles of Corfù and Butrinto; most of the barons joined them; and, in 1382, Charles III. was lord of the island. The usurper showed the usual "kindness of kings upon their coronation day"; he rewarded the services of the two most conspicuous traitors, graciously received a deputation of Italians and Greeks, renewed the ancient privileges of the city and its thirty-two Greek priests, endeavoured to repair the ravages which the recent struggle had made in its finances, assured the Jews of his royal protection, and confirmed important feudal lords, such as the Caracciolo, in their fiefs.[1] To those who remember Corfù in the days of the British protectorate, when the island of Vido in the harbour was defended by those strong fortifications which we subsequently blew up, it may be of interest to recall that it formed one of his feudal grants. It was then known as the island of Santo Stefano[2]—a name derived from the old church, which our engineers sacrificed in 1837. At the time of the siege of 1537 it was called Malipiero, but later in the sixteenth century it received from its then owner the name of Vido, changed by the French, during their brief occupation, into Île de la Paix.

There was, however, another Power, which had long coveted Corfù, and had been closely following the various revolutions in the ownership of the island. Venice had never forgotten that the key of the Adriatic had once been hers; during the Angevin period she had made successive attempts to obtain it—in 1314 and 1351 by purchase, in 1355 by a *coup de main.* More recently, negotiations had been opened with Jacques de Baux for the mortgage, lease, or purchase of the island; but these negotiations also fell through. Meanwhile, the Venetian consul, after the fashion of Levantine consuls in our own day, was busy preparing public opinion in Corfù for a Venetian occupation. There was a party among the Corfiotes, which could not help

[1] Mustoxidi, 452-3; Barone, 18, 20, 22, 23, 24-6, 29.
[2] Buchon, *Nouvelles Recherches*, II., i., 409-11.

contrasting the unbroken continuity of Venetian administration with the continual civil wars of Naples. Money was freely spent and promises as freely made to wavering nobles, who may have been frightened by the execution of one of their order for high treason, but who, when death had removed both Jacques de Baux and Charles III., found themselves without a sovereign lord. Their allegiance to the throne of Naples at this moment received a further shock from the discovery that the baron, who held the city and castle for the late king, was an impostor who had forged his patent. While the Neapolitan party advocated loyalty to Ladislaus, Charles's little son and successor, some thought of Genoa, others of Venice, and others again actually offered their country to Francesco da Carrara, Signor of Padua, who at once sent Scrovigno, a trustworthy servant of his own and of the late king, to occupy the place. That Corfù should fall into the hands of her bitterest foe was more than Venice could stand; a recent incident had made it unnecessary to spare the susceptibilities of the Neapolitan court any longer. Miani, the Captain of the Gulf, chanced to be in Corfiote waters at the time; he landed and explained to a meeting of the citizens that his government was both willing and able to protect them, that Genoa, the only other maritime power, would treat them like slaves, while Padua had no navy. These arguments proved effective; the town was peaceably surrendered; and Scrovigno shut himself up in one of the two forts of the sea-girt castle. But siege materials were despatched from Venice, the castle was besieged, and Scrovigno was glad to escape by night on a Genoese galley. Miani then summoned the garrison to surrender; once again, after the lapse of 170 years, the lion banner was hoisted over Corfù; thenceforth it floated there for more than four centuries. A few places, however, held out some time longer for the King of Naples—the second of the city forts, the lofty castle of Sant' Angelo on the west coast, the recently constructed castle of Cassopo at the north of the island, and that of Butrinto on the opposite main. These strongholds were, however, all surrendered or taken; that of Cassopo was destroyed for fear lest it should fall into the hands of the Genoese; strange legends grew up around its ruined ramparts; and a hundred years later, travellers were told that it had been deserted because a fiery dragon had poisoned the inhabitants with his breath.[1] As for Butrinto, its governor, Riccardo d'Altavilla, who had received his post from Charles III., capitulated as soon as he had secured his reward from the Venetian commander.[2] Malipiero arrived from Venice as rector and *provveditore* of Corfù.

On 28th May, 1386, a meeting of the commune or "of the larger and saner part of it," was summoned by the sound of the bell to elect a deputation which should do homage and present the petition of the commune to the Venetian government. All the three races of Corfù—Italians, Greeks, and Jews—were represented among the six Corfiote envoys, and the fact that the name of "David, son of Simon," figures beside that of the proud Altavilla, shows the influence of the Hebrew element in the island. The deputation was instructed to beg that the new masters of Corfù would observe all the privileges granted to the community by the Angevins; that the republic would never dispose of the island; that all fiefs should be confirmed, and that the barons and Holy Church might continue to exercise the right of dragging their recalcitrant serfs before the captain, who would keep them in prison till their lords should have obtained satisfaction; that the captain should administer justice, in civil and criminal matters alike, with the assistance of the "annual judges," according to the ancient custom; that, whereas the commune had resigned to the new rector the time-honoured Corfiote privilege of exemption from all taxes and tolls, in consideration of the prosperity of the town, an annual salary should be paid to a doctor, the walls should be repaired, and a *loggia* erected for the honour of the republic and the island; and that all the provisional arrangements made between Miani and the community should be ratified. A second meeting, held on 9th June, proclaimed the formal acceptance of Venetian rule, because the island was deprived of its lawful

[1] Feyerabend, *Reyssbuch*, 36, 54, 185; *Revue de l'Orient latin*, I., 231; III., 666.

[2] Lunzi, 85-105; Mustoxidi, 455, lviii., lxiv.; Marmora, 231; Sanudo and Navagero *apud* Muratori, xxii., 760-1; xxiii., 1070-1; Thomas and Predelli, *Diplomatarium*, ii., 185; *Arch. Veneto*, xvii., 252.

protector, "coveted by its jealous neighbours, and almost besieged by Arabs and Turks"; and conferred the post of captain and *magister massarius* upon Miani, as a token of gratitude for his peaceful occupation of the city.[1]

The six envoys met with a warm reception from the Venetian aristocracy and a handsomely furnished palace was placed at their disposal. On 8th January, 1387, they obtained an audience of the doge, whom one of their number addressed, so it is said, in the florid style of the Levant. He spoke of their past history—how Corcyra had been ruled by Roman and Greek emperors, by Despots and kings, and expressed the hope that the Venetian lion, the king of beasts, would scorn to tyrannise over his subjects, but would be content with their homage and leave them their ancient liberties. The doge was graciously pleased to accept the one and confirm the other, with a few alterations and additions. Thus, it was provided that justice should be administered by the Venetian governor and the "annual judges," according to the customs of Venice, to which an appeal would lie; but no Corfiote was to be tried outside the island, except on appeal. A Greek notary was to be elected, according to usage, to draw up citations on the Greeks, and two officers of the court were to be appointed to serve them. A clause was inserted, owing perhaps to the experience of Crete, ordering the island barons to perform their feudal service with good and sufficient war-horses; another prohibited the Venetian officials from forcing the Corfiotes to sell them food or to fish for them; while a third directed that the measure for the sale of new wine should be stamped by the authorities in October, or oftener, but that the customary fee should be only paid once a year. Finally, the offices of *catapan* and syndic were to be retained, and no one except the governor was to interfere with them.[2]

Great was the joy of the Corfiotes at the return of their envoys with the charter of the island; nor had they reason to

[1] Mustoxidi, lx.-lxiii.; Thomas and Predelli, *op. cit.*, ii., 199-204; Sanudo, *op. cit.*, xxii., 751.

[2] Marmora, 238; Mustoxidi, lxiv.-lxviii.; Thomas and Predelli, *op. cit.*, ii., 204-9.

repent their change of masters. The Venetian bailie, as the governor was called by the express desire of the islanders, reduced the chaos of the last few years to order. During the general confusion of the interregnum, various persons had appropriated public property, which they were now compelled to restore. Such was the popularity of the new government, that the municipality granted it the proceeds of the two per cent. customs duty, which had lately been imposed, in order to hasten the restoration of the walls.[1]

Venice was, however, anxious to legalise her position as mistress of the island. The Queen-regent of Naples complained of the annexation; Ladislaus, when he came of age, demanded, and attempted to exercise, his rights, but hinted that he did not mind coming to terms. The negotiations were protracted till 1402, when Ladislaus finally sold the island with all its dependencies to the republic for 30,000 gold ducats.[2] Thus ended the rule of the Neapolitan princes over the fairest of Greek islands, and with it their last connection with Greece. In its early days it was, on the whole, easy, though its ecclesiastical policy was unfair to the church of the majority. Later on, when it was weak at home it was ineffective at Corfù. Every revolution at Naples had an echo in the island, with the worst effect upon the morality of its public men. It became the highest form of statesmanship to go over to the winning side, in the certainty of obtaining a fief or an office as the reward of disloyalty. On the other hand, the insecure title of these successive rulers made them peculiarly ready to respect the ancient privileges of the islanders. Indeed, it is probable that, in the Angevin days, when the sovereign was always an absentee, Corfù was a paradise for the barons and an inferno for their serfs. The chief result of the Neapolitan domination was to strengthen the feudal system and so to confirm that spirit of aristocracy which still characterises the Ionian islands.

Modern Corfù contains scarcely a trace of its Angevin rulers. The church of Santo Stefano has vanished, Cassopo is a heap of ruins, and one coin alone preserves the name of

[1] Marmora, 249; Buchon, *Nouvelles Recherches*, II., i., 423.

[2] Mustoxidi, lxviii. to end; Lunzi, 117-18; Thomas and Predelli, *op. cit.*, ii., 263-89.

the princes of Taranto,[1] from which a recently extinct Corfiote family boasted its descent. The Angevin barony of De Martina, once held by the Tocchi, which till lately survived in the topography of the island, has now changed its name.[2] But the pilgrimage church on the summit of Pantokrátor dates from this period.

The administration of Corfù during the Venetian period was modelled on that which had long prevailed in the older colonies of the republic. For the first twenty-four years, the government was entrusted to a single Venetian official, styled "bailie and captain," who was elected by the Home Government and held office for two years. But, in 1410, it was decided that two councillors should be sent from Venice to assist him in the exercise of civil and criminal jurisdiction and to perform the duty of chamberlain. Each of the councillors was to receive 300 gold ducats a year, and two towers of the city were assigned as their abodes. They and the bailie were ordered to sit in court five days a week, and the "annual judges," whose numbers were now increased to three, one Latin and two Greeks, continued to act as their assessors. The peasants, however, soon found that the presence of the two councillors tended to protract litigation and led to their having to supply two more officials with fodder for their horses. They accordingly petitioned for a return to the former system of one-man rule, which is really more beneficial to the poor in southern countries than more democratic arrangements. Their prayers were, however, rejected, and the island continued to provide posts for the two councillors. We are specially told, that, though the Venetian officials were forbidden to engage in trade, these appointments were considered as the plums of the colonial service. So, in the British days, the pleasant island of the Phæacians was regarded as the best of our foreign stations.[3]

The power of the bailie was further limited by the institu-

[1] That which bears the inscription of *Johs Despotus Curfou Civis*, which Buchon ascribed to John of Gravina, who was never lord of Corfù, has been described by Schlumberger (*op. cit.*, 389) as a forgery. Could it refer to Count John II. of Cephalonia, who styled himself "Despot," and threatened Corfù?

[2] *Δελτίον*, II., 597, *n.* 2; Gerakáres, Κερκυραϊκαὶ Σελίδες, 53.

[3] Sáthas, *op. cit.*, ii., 249; iii., 88, 247; Marmora, 256.

tion of a third office, that of the *provveditore*, who was in command of the garrison and resided in the fortress, and who also decided those moot points of feudal law which were of frequent occurrence in a community such as Corfù. He was, moreover, judge in disputes between the citizens and the garrison, and his authority extended over the island barony of Paxo, which was treated by the Venetians as by their predecessors, as an integral part of its larger neighbour. It continued to belong to the great baronial family of Sant' Ippolito, which in 1423 fortified it against the Turkish corsairs, who were wont to carry off the defenceless serfs. When that clan became extinct, it passed to the other great Neapolitan house of Altavilla, and thence to the republic. In 1513, however, it was sold, together with the taxes which it paid, to the family of Avrámes, which treated the inhabitants so badly that many of them fled to Turkish territory. In consequence of this, it was restored to the jurisdiction of the *provveditore*, who was locally represented by a leading native. As time went on, that important official assumed also the title of "captain," which had originally been borne by the bailie, and his delegate in Paxo was accordingly styled "captain" also.[1]

In the sixteenth century the appointment of the great naval authority of *provveditore generale del Levante*, whose headquarters were Corfù, completely overshadowed that of all the other Venetian officials in the Ionian islands. His arrival for his three years' term of government was regulated by an elaborate code of etiquette, still preserved in a special volume in the Corfiote archives; the Jews had to provide the carpets for the streets, along which the great man would pass; the heads of both the Latin and the Greek Church greeted him with all the splendid rites of their respective establishments; a noble Corfiote pronounced a panegyric upon him in the church of St Spiridion, before whose remains his excellency would kneel in prayer ere returning to his palace, where obsequious Hebrews, laden with flowers, bent low as he crossed the threshold. Strict orders were issued to these officials that they should respect the rights of the natives, and spies, known as "inquisitors over the affairs of

[1] Sáthas, iii., 249, 422; v., 235; Lunzi, 252, 348; *Paxos und Antipaxos*, 13-14; Buondelmonti, 55.

the Levant," were sent from time to time to the islands for the purpose of checking the Venetian administration and of ascertaining the grievances of the governed, who had, as under the Angevins, the often-exercised privilege of sending special missions to lay their complaints before the Home Government. We can see from the Venetian archives what Ionian historians unanimously assert to have been the case, that redress was almost invariably granted, though the abuses of which the natives complained were apt to grow up again.[1]

A large share in the local administration was granted to the inhabitants, or rather to the aristocracy. At the time of the transfer of the island to Venice, the General Assembly consisted of the principal citizens, Greeks as well as Italians; but, as time went on, strange elements, Albanians and Cephalonians, crept into this body, so that, in 1440, it was ordered that the bailie, with the advice of the "good citizens," should choose some seventy prominent persons as a council for the term of one year; half a century later, this body was increased to 150—a total preserved till the last years of Venetian rule. There were henceforth two councils—the General Assembly and the Council of 150. The former became an oligarchy, composed exclusively of Greek and Italian nobles, together with a few foreigners who had resided ten years or married into a Corfiote family. But when the numbers of the nobility were much diminished by the first great Turkish siege in 1537, new families were added to the list from the burgher class, the qualification for noble strangers was subsequently reduced to five years, and Marmora gives the names of 112 noble families inscribed in the "Golden Book" of the Corfiote aristocracy when he wrote his history in 1672. The "Golden Book" was burned as the symbol of hated class distinction in the first enthusiasm for liberty, equality, and fraternity, after the French republicans took possession of Corfù. As all the nobles were debarred from engaging in trade, it may readily be imagined that a premium was put upon place-hunting. Very early in the Venetian period we hear of the number of Greek lawyers—then, as now, the plague of Greece. It only re-

[1] Lunzi, 253-65.

mained to discourage agriculture by compelling the nobles to reside in the city if they wished to take part in the Assembly, and the corruption of Corfiote society was complete. To these arrangements we may trace the neglect of country life and the consequent distress of the island in the present day.

The General Assembly met every year at the end of October to elect the Council of 150 from among its own members. At first it seems to have held its sitting in "the hall above the Chancery"; but, after that building was destroyed by the Turks at the time of the first siege, it was convened in a quaint house, decorated with pictures of Nausikaa welcoming Odysseus and of other scenes from the early history of Corcyra, and situated on the esplanade between the Fortezza Vecchia and the town. This interesting memorial of Venetian rule has long since been swept away.[1]

It was the policy of the Venetian Government to leave the Corfiotes all the minor offices, and it was the desire of the islanders that these offices should be annual, so that they might be enjoyed by as many people as possible. Thus, the Council of 150 elected the three "annual judges," who, besides sitting as assessors of the bailie and the two councillors in the High Court, formed a petty tribunal of their own for the trial of cases where the sum at issue was small. It elected the four syndics, two Greeks and two Latins during the period of which we are treating, who were required to be at least thirty-eight years of age and who were the representatives of all classes of the community, collectively and individually, bringing their grievances before the Venetian authorities, and also regulating prices in the market—a function which bordered on that of the still existent *catapans*. It chose, too, the clerk of the Court, two taxing masters, who regulated the scale of law costs; the *giustizieri*, or officials who stamped the weights and measures; and the person entrusted with the census, which was supposed to be made once during each bailie's term of office.[2] In 1470, it obtained the privilege of electing the captain of the war galleys fitted

[1] Lunzi, 274; Marmora, 312-13; Sáthas, ii., 159; iii., 467; v., 226, 249.
[2] Buchon, *Nouvelles Recherches*, II., i., 425.

out at Corfù, a wise concession of the Venetian Government, which found, on the great day of Lepanto, that its Corfiote captains were worthy descendants of the seafaring Phæacians. Venice was unwilling, however, to relinquish to the natives the posts of constable of the island, captain of "the iron gate," dragoman, and salt commissioner; but the command of the castle of Sant' Angelo, which included some petty judicial authority, passed in time into the hands of the Council. Later on, too, the Council elected a species of cabinet, called the *Conclave* and composed of the three "annual judges," the four syndics, and five other officials, whose number was fixed in the seventeenth century, and whose meetings were held with closed doors.[1]

The dependencies of the colony on the mainland likewise furnished posts, some of which were in the gift of the Council, and all were held by Corfiote nobles, usually for a year. Butrinto was the most important of these stations, both strategically and economically, for it was not only "the guardian and right eye" of Corfù, but yielded from its fisheries, once the property of Cicero's friend, Atticus, 1300 ducats a year.[2] More interesting, however, from Byron's noble lines and from its dramatic history in the early days of the British protectorate, when official ignorance of geography abandoned it to the Turks, was "Parga's shore"—an outpost boldly occupied on his own responsibility by the Venetian bailie of Corfù in 1401, and accepted, after some hesitation, by the republic. This hesitation was not unwarranted, for, despite its poetic name, the practical Venetians found that the place, whose sugar had proved so remunerative to Count Nicholas of Cephalonia a century before, now cost more than it was worth, and accordingly several times urged the inhabitants to emigrate over the narrow channel to the islet of Antipaxo, where they enjoyed the right of tilling the land, or even to Corfù, where uncultivated ground was always at their disposal. But then, as in 1819, the Pargians showed a touching, if inconvenient, attachment to their ancient home, which was well situated

[1] Sáthas, i., 112-14, 221; ii., 151, 213, 221; v., 224, 251; Lunzi, 279-87, 299-302; Marmora, 9, 270, 314.

[2] Sáthas, v., 250.

for purposes of piracy, and they combined devotion to Venice, from whom they had obtained excellent terms, with the lucrative traffic of selling the weapons sent for their defence to the neighbouring Turks. The governorship of Parga, at first bestowed on a Corfiote noble for life and then placed at the disposition of the Council, was, at the petition of the Pargians, in 1511, taken from that body and transferred to the Venetian authorities of Corfù: but it was ultimately restored to the Council. The post could not, however, have been either lucrative or easy; for out of his exiguous salary the governor had to provide each Pargian family with five measures of salt a year, and each priest and local magnate with a dinner on Christmas eve and at Epiphany, while a local council of thirty-two managed most of the affairs of this small community, and a *πρωτοπαπᾶς* looked after its spiritual welfare.[1] All the inhabitants were soldiers, and many of them pirates, and they were known to imprison a Venetian governor, just as the Albanians of to-day besiege a Turkish Vali, till they could get redress. At the same time as Parga, Corfù acquired the castles of Saiada and Phanari, which with La Bastia, Suboto, and Strovili made up the continental dependencies of the island in the fifteenth century. For a brief period Lepanto was placed under the jurisdiction of Corfù.[2] Under Venetian protection, too, were the monks who inhabited the ancient home of the harpies, the Strivali islands, where Theodore Láskaris and Irene had long ago established a Greek monastery of the Redeemer. Thither in the thirteenth century the Benedictines had gone, and on one occasion we find the pope appointing the prior of "Our Lady of Stropharia." When, however, the Greeks recovered Achaia, the Emperor John VI. restored the monastery of the Redeemer. Every passing ship reverently greeted and gave alms to the monks, whose exploits against the Turks who had dared to set foot on their wind-swept solitude

[1] Sáthas, ii., 45-6, 232; iii., 32, 466; v., 256, 328-30; Marmora, 253, 282, 285; Thomas, *Diplomatarium*, i., 170; Predelli, *Commemoriali*, i., 217; Jorga in *Revue de l'Orient latin*, vi., 378; P. A. S., Ἡ Πάργα, 75-7; U. Foscolo, *Prose Politiche*, 447-52.

[2] Sáthas, iii., 32; v., 246, 336.

enhanced the prestige of their sacred habit among pilgrims on their way to the Holy Land.[1]

The ecclesiastical policy of the Venetians was always less bigoted than that of other Catholic powers; and while, as Catholics, they continued to give precedence to their own Church, which in Corfù became a perquisite of the great Venetian families, they never forgot that the interests of the republic were of more importance than those of the papacy. Accordingly, they studiously prevented any encroachments on the part of either the œcumenical patriarch or the pope, fearing the political influence of the one and the theological fanaticism of the other. The externals of the Angevin ecclesiastical system were therefore retained as being well adapted to this cautious policy. The head of the Orthodox church was still called "chief priest" (*μέγας πρωτοπαπᾶς*), while the title of archbishop was reserved for the aristocratic Venetian who was the head of the Catholic clergy. The "chief priest" was elected by thirty chosen members of the General Assembly and by the "sacred band" of the thirty-two city priests, whose numbers, however, in the later Venetian period, were really only twenty. His term of office was five years, at the end of which time, if not re-elected, he sank into the ranks of the ordinary clergy, from whom he was then only distinguished by his crimson sash. Merit had, as a rule, less to do with his election than his relationship to a noble family and the amount of the pecuniary arguments which he applied to the pockets of the electors, and for which he recouped himself by his gains while in office. In each of the four bailiwicks into which Corfù was still divided, and in the island of Paxo, then, as now, a part of the Corfiote diocese, there was a *πρωτοπαπᾶς* under his jurisdiction, while he was dependent upon no other ecclesiastical authority than the œcumenical patriarch, with whom, however, he was only allowed to correspond through the medium of the Venetian bailie at Constantinople. He had his retinue of officials

[1] *Les Registres de Boniface VIII.*, ii., 540; *Revue de l'Orient latin*, i., 232; iv., 508, 563; Feyerabend, *Reyssbuch*, ff. 125, 233; Faber, *Evagatorium*, i., 164; Buochenbach, *Orientalische Reyss*, 34; Chiótes, Ἱστορικὰ Ἀπομνημονεύματα, ii., 535; *Purchas His Pilgrimes*, vii., 546.

with high-sounding Byzantine titles; he enjoyed considerable honours; and from his decision in ecclesiastical cases there was no appeal. Two liberal popes, Leo X. and Paul III., expressly forbade any interference with the religious services of the Greeks on the part of the Latin archbishop, and the doges more than once upheld the ancient charter of the city priests and the privileges of "the decarchy" of the thirty-three rural popes. At the same time, measures were taken to prevent the increase in the number of Greek priests, monks, and churches, which gave the Venetians cause for alarm, because they were well aware that to the Greeks politics and religion are inseparable. This was especially the case, when numbers of fugitive priests sought refuge in the island after the capture of Constantinople and the Morea. But, in spite of all regulations, the Orthodox church kept alive the national feeling in the island. Mixed marriages were allowed; and, as the children usually became Orthodox, it is not surprising to learn that twenty years before the close of the Venetian occupation there were only two noble Latin families which still adhered to the Catholic faith.

It was a natural result of the Venetian policy that there was less bitterness in Corfù than in most other places between the adherents of the two religions. The Catholics took part in the religious processions of the Orthodox; the college of thirty-two priests on the eve of Christmas and Epiphany delivered an eulogy of Venetian rule at the bailie's palace, whereupon two condemned prisoners were released to them, after the fashion of Barabbas. When the body of St Spiridion was carried round the town, the Venetian authorities and many of the garrison paid their respects to the sacred relics; twenty-one guns were fired from the Old Fortress, and the ships in the harbour saluted. The Orthodox clergy reciprocated these attentions by meeting the Catholics in the church of St Arsenios, the tenth century bishop who had been the first metropolitan of Corfù, where the discordant chanting of Greeks and Latins represented their theological concord, and by praying for the pope and the Latin archbishop at the annual banquet in the latter's palace. They were ready, also, to excommunicate refractory villages at the bidding of the Government, and this practice, which filled the superstitious peasants with terror, was one of the greatest social abuses of Corfù. It is not quite extinct in Greece even now.[1]

The position of the Corfiote Jews, though far less favourable than that of the Orthodox, was much better than that of the Hebrew colonies in other parts of the Venetian dominions. In the very first days of the Venetian occupation an order was issued to the officials of the republic, bidding them to behave well to the Jewish community and to put no heavier burdens upon them than upon the rest of the islanders. Many of the Venetian governors found it convenient to borrow not only money, but furniture, plate, and liveries from them. That they increased in numbers—owing to the Jewish immigration from Spain and Portugal in 1492 and from Naples, Apulia, and Calabria half a century later—may be inferred from Marmora's statement that in 1665 there were about 500 Jewish houses in Corfù; and the historian, who shared to the full the dislike of the Hebrew which has always characterised the Greeks and has been always cordially reciprocated, naïvely remarks that the Corfiote Jews would be rich if they were let alone.[2] They paid none of the usual taxes levied on Jewish banks at Venice; and when, by the decree of 1572, they were banished from Venetian territory, a special exemption was granted to the Jews of Corfù. They were allowed to practice there as advocates, with permission to defend Christians no less than members of their own race. They had their own council, and elected their own officials, representing the Greek and the "Apulian" or "Spanish" synagogues—for from 1540 there were two—who managed the internal affairs of the ghetto.[3] Outside its limits they were allowed to own real property worth no more than 4000 ducats between them—indeed, public opinion would have left them no land but their graves—and they were expressly forbidden to have serfs, or to take land or villas on lease, with the exception of one house for the personal use of the lessee. But the effect of this enactment was nullified by means of

[1] Sáthas, i., 46-51; ii., 143, 150, 193; iii., 33, 431; Lunzi, chs. xi. and xii.; Lamansky, 050; Misti, xii., f. 54; Marmora, 319-22.

[2] P. 430.

[3] Romanós, Ἑβραϊκὴ Κοινότης, 8.

mortgages; and if a Jew wanted to invest money in houses he had no difficulty in finding a Christian who would purchase or rent them with borrowed Jewish capital. Nor was it easy to confine the growing Jewish colony within its separate quarter. When the old ghetto, "the mount of the Jews,"[1] was pulled down in 1524 to make room for the fortifications, orders were given to choose a new site; but sixty years later we find a Venetian report complaining that they were living among the Christians and even in the castle. Later plans of the city show us, however, the ghetto marked in the same place and called by the same name as the still surviving *Hebraïká*.[2] At the same time, the Jews had to submit to some degrading restrictions of costume. They were compelled to wear a yellow mark on the breast, as a badge of servitude, and a Venetian ordinance naïvely remarks that this was "a substitute for the custom of stoning, which does so much injury to the houses." True, a money payment to the treasury secured a dispensation from the necessity of wearing these stigmas; but it is obvious from the complaints of their envoys that the Jews were badly treated by the natives, who refused them access to the principal well and harried them while they were doing their marketing. Absurd tales, too, were current about them. The old fable that Judas Iscariot was a native of the island, was still told to travellers, who were shown a lineal descendant of the arch-traitor. They were expected to offer a copy of the law of Moses to a new Latin archbishop, who sometimes delighted the other Corfiotes by lecturing them on their shortcomings. Finally, they were forbidden to indulge in public processions—an injunction perhaps quite as much in their own interest as in that of the public peace.[3]

The feudal system continued to form the basis of Corfiote society, and became the bulwark of Venetian rule. The new masters of the island confirmed the Angevin barons in their fiefs, but created few more, so that towards the end of the Venetian period the original twenty-four baronies had

[1] Sáthas, iii., 46; Romanós, *op. cit.*, 9; Marmora, 286.
[2] Marmora, 364-5.
[3] *Ibid.*, 255-6, 286, 370, 430, 437; Sáthas, ii., 150-3, 206; v., 261; Buochenbach, *Orientalische Reyss*, 27; Lunzi, 455-61.

dwindled to from twelve to fifteen, among them two still bearing the names of the extinct clans of Altavilla and Sant' Ippolito, one or two held by old Greek families, and the rest by Venetian aristocrats long settled in the island. For as the "Customs of Romania" continued to prevail, it followed that the Salic law did not obtain in Corfù; accordingly, there, as elsewhere, many baronies passed into the hands of women, who usually found husbands in the Venetian aristocracy. In theory each baron had to keep at least one good horse and a certain number of retainers for the defence of the island, and to present himself with them for review in the castle on the 1st of May. We have an account of the brave show made by the barons, then fourteen in number, in 1515; but in practice this chivalrous custom was usually allowed to lapse. A less picturesque but far more efficacious body was the armed band of the peasants, the so-called *cernide*, which guarded the coast and at times furnished the republic with some of her best seamen. In this body all between the ages of twenty and sixty-five were bound to serve. A clause in the charter of Parga specially stipulated that the natives of that rock-fortress should only be liable for service in defence of their own home.[1]

By far the most interesting of the fiefs was that of the Ἀθίγγανοι or gypsies, who were about a hundred in number and were subject to the exclusive jurisdiction of the baron upon whom their fief had been bestowed—"an office," as Marmora says, "of not a little gain and of very great honour." Their feudal lord could inflict on them any punishment short of death—a privilege denied to all his peers; they were his men and not those of the Government, which could not compel them to serve in the galleys or render the usual feudal services of the other peasants. They had their own military commander, similar to the *drungarius* of the gypsies at Nauplia, and every May-day they marched, under his leadership, to the sounds of drums and fifes, bearing aloft their baron's banner, and carrying a May-pole decked with flowers, to the square in front of the house where the great man lived. There they set up their pole and sang a curious song in honour of their lord, who provided them with refreshment and on the

[1] Sáthas, i., 267-9; Lunzi, 452-4, 467 *et sqq.*; Marmora, 259, 283-4.

morrow received from them their dues. Originally granted to the family of Abitabuli, whose name perhaps came from the *habitacula*, or encampments of these vagrants, and then held by the house of Goth, the fief of the gypsies was conferred in 1540, after the great siege of Corfù, upon Antónios Eparchos, a versatile genius, at once poet, Hellenist, and soldier, as compensation for his losses and as the reward of his talents. By a curious anomaly the jurisdiction of the gypsy baron extended over the peasants of the continental dependencies of Corfù. It is therefore possible that the serfs called *vaginiti*, whom we found under the Angevins, and who emigrated from the mainland, and paid a registration fee on their arrival, were gypsies.[1]

The Corfiote serfs were of three classes, those of the republic—for Venice had domain lands in the island, which were usually let to the highest bidder on a twenty-nine years' lease—those of the Latin Church, and those of the barons. The Corfiote peasants, though they sometimes amassed sufficient money to enfranchise themselves, and though Venice often lent a ready ear to their grievances, were worse off under the feudal system than their fellows on the mainland under Turkish rule. They had no political rights whatever; they were summed up in the capitulations at the time of the Venetian occupation, together with "the other movable and immovable goods" of their lords; and it is no wonder that they sometimes ran away to escape the tyranny of a hard master. The peasants on the domain lands had a lighter lot than the other two classes; though all except the priests were liable to forced labour, they could obtain exemption on payment of a very small sum. Their chief grievances were that they were compelled to labour on Government works in the town at times when they wanted to be sowing their corn or gathering their grapes; that they had to cut firewood for the bailie, and to provide oil even in years when the olives did not bear. Occasionally we hear of a peasants' insurrection against their oppressors, and Marmora remarks in his time that "the peasants are never contented; they rise against their lords on the smallest provocation." Yet, until the last century of her

[1] Lunzi, 464-6; Sáthas, iii., 31, 38-40; the words of the gypsy song are quoted in the Ὁδηγὸς τῆς Κερκύρας (ed. 1902).

rule, Venice had little trouble with the inhabitants. She kept the nobles in good humour by granting them political privileges, titles, and the entrance to her navy; and, so long as the Turk was a danger, she was compelled, from motives of prudence, to pay a due regard to their wishes. Moreover, by an almost complete neglect of education, the republic was able to prevent the growth of an intellectual proletariat, such as in the British times furnished an ample supply of political agitators.[1]

During the four centuries of her rule, Venice did practically nothing for the mental development of the Corfiotes. No public schools were founded; for, as Count Viaro Capodistrias informed the British Parliament much later, the Venetian Senate never allowed such institutions to be established in the Ionian islands.[2] When the Catholic archbishop wanted an excuse for remaining in Venice, he pleaded that he could not study theology at Corfù. The administration was content to pay a few teachers of Greek and Italian; and to grant the Ionian youths the special privilege of taking a degree at the University of Padua without examination. Moreover, the Corfiote student after his return soon forgot what he had learned, retaining only the varnish of culture. There were exceptions, however, to this low standard. When Cyriacus of Ancona visited Greece, he was able to purchase Greek manuscripts at Corfù. Others were copied by the exiles who fled there after the conquest of the Morea. In the sixteenth century there was quite a number of Corfiote writers—poets like Eparchos and Tribóles, the traveller Noúkios, the theologian Kartános; but they mostly wrote abroad. It was a Corfiote who founded at Venice, in 1621, the Greek school, called Flangineion, after the name of its founder, Flangínes, which did so much for the improvement of Greek education, and which still exists by the side of S. Giorgio dei Greci. But even in the latest Venetian period there were few facilities for obtaining knowledge in Corfù. No wonder that the Corfiotes were easier to manage in those days than in the more enlightened British times, when newspapers abounded and

[1] Sáthas, ii., 169; iii., 77, 85, 89, 290, 422.

[2] *Remarks respectfully committed to the Consideration of the British Parliament*, 64.

some of the best pens in Southern Europe were ready to lampoon the British Protectorate.[1]

The long Venetian domination exercised a natural influence on the language, especially in the town. At the time of the annexation, the islanders had stipulated, as we saw, that a Greek notary should be appointed, as under the Angevins, for serving writs in Greek on the Greeks, and a Greek interpreter formed part of the Venetian administration. From 1524 dates the appointment of the first Greek teacher. That Greek continued to be used in private documents, while Venetian or Latin was the official language, is clear from the will of one of the barons, which has been preserved, and which is drawn up in Greek, though the testator was of Frankish origin. But at the time of the battle of Lepanto, when Venice was particularly anxious to conciliate her Greek subjects, the bailie issued a Greek translation of his proclamations for the special benefit of the country folk.[2] It was among them, of course, that the language of Hellas held its firmest roots, and even to-day it is almost the only tongue understood in the country-districts of Corfù, while Italian is readily spoken in the town. In the Venetian times, the dialect of the rulers was the conversational medium of good society, and the young Corfiote, fresh from his easily won laurels at Padua, looked down with contempt upon the noblest and most enduring of all languages, which had become solely the speech of the despised peasants. Still, nature will out, and Greek idioms occasionally penetrated the Venetian dialect of Corfù. But it was only towards the close of the Venetian domination that Greek became fashionable. Two Corfiotes, Eugénios Boúlgaris and Nikephóros Theotókes were the pioneers of modern Greek, and in one of Goldoni's comedies we are told that the street-boys of Corfù sang ditties in that language.[3]

The Venetian flag naturally attracted a far larger amount of shipping to the island, which served as a half-way house

[1] Sáthas, ii., 245 ; v., 269 ; Marmora, 433 ; *Kyriaci Anconitani Itinerarium*, 29 ; Veloúdes, Ἡ ἐν Βενετίᾳ Ἑλληνικὴ ἀποικία (ed. 2), 116.

[2] Romanós, Γρατιανὸς Ζώρζης, 57, 59, 314-20. Gerakáres, *op. cit.*, κζ΄.

[3] Romanós, *op. cit.*, 29-30 ; Goldoni, *La famiglia dell' Antiquario*, Act II., Scene 10.

for galleys between Venice and Crete, and a traveller, who visited it in 1480, says that the harbour "was never empty." But these visits of the fleet led to many fatal brawls, while Ionian commerce was hampered by the selfish colonial policy then prevalent in Europe, which aimed at concentrating all colonial trade in the metropolis, through which Corfiote exports had to pass. This naturally led to a vast amount of smuggling, even now rampant in Greece. Among the exports we read of valonea, cotton, all sorts of fruit, and salt, which was sent to the other Venetian colonies in Dalmatia and Albania; a considerable amount of wine was produced; and the oil-trade, now the staple industry of Corfù, was so greatly fostered by a grant of twelve gold pieces for every plantation of 100 olive trees, that in the last half century of the Venetian rule there were nearly 2,000,000 of these trees in the island. Even the now bare islet of Vido, which the French made a solitude and called it Île de la Paix, was, in Marmora's time, so thickly planted with olives, that it "looked like a forest swimming in the waves." Yet Corfù then, as now, presented the paradox of great fertility combined with great poverty. When the corn raised on the mainland was exported abroad, instead of being kept for the consumption of the colony, the Corfiotes were in despair, for their island did not produce nearly enough grain for the whole year; hence its export was more than once forbidden by the paternal administration, and public granaries in which officials were ordered to deposit a part of their pay, were established to mitigate the severe famines. The taxes consisted of a tithe of the oil, the crops, and the agricultural produce; a money payment on the wine sold; a "chimney-tax" on each house; and export duties of 15 per cent. on oil, 9 per cent. on salt, and 4 per cent. on other articles. There were also import duties of 6 per cent. on Venetian, and of 8 per cent. on foreign, goods. The salt-pans of Levkimme formed a Government monopoly, and the importation of foreign salt was punished by banishment. The fisheries of Butrinto were let, as we saw, to a Corfiote, and yielded 1300 ducats a year.[1] Corfiote merchants received

[1] Sáthas, i., 112-14; ii., 126, 131, 140, 307; iii., 33, 90, 200, 302, 356, 359, 470; v., 224, 227, 228; Marmora, 10, 257, 258; Lunzi, ch. xv.;

the same treatment in Venice as those of Candia and the other Greek colonies, and the *bezzoni* and *tornesi* of the Venetian mint did duty in Corfù.[1]

It is to Venice that Corfù, almost more than any other place in Greece, owes its present appearance. The streets, the fortifications, the houses are all Venetian rather than Greek; indeed, in some respects, the traveller just landed there can scarcely fancy that he has set foot on Greek soil, for neither forty-three years of union with Greece, nor fifty years of British protection, nor yet the brief interregnum of French and Russian rule, have succeeded in removing the mark of Venice. The lion of St Mark still watches over the walls; from his mouth the water still flows at the fountain of Kardáki, where Venetian ships used to fill their tanks; the castles still retain their Venetian names, a Corfiote village on the slopes of Pantokrátor is still called Enetía. The whole fabric of modern Corfiote society, the conditions of land tenure, and the habits of the people are still largely based upon the Venetian polity. The titles, which the Ionians almost alone of Greeks still use, are relics of the days when the shrewd statesmen of the mercantile republic, like our modern Prime Ministers, closed the mouths of obstreperous subjects or rewarded loyal services by the bestowal of honorary distinctions. Many of the most ardently Greek opponents of the British Protectorate bore aggressively Italian names, and among the modern Corfiote Members of Parliament there are some whose Italian origin is scarcely concealed by the classical terminations of the Greek declensions.

If we would figure to ourselves what Corfù was like during the first 150 years of the Venetian domination, that is to say, up to the period of the first great Turkish siege, we must remember that the town, despite the resolutions of the Venetian Government, remained unwalled, and that its sole defences were, as in Angevin times, the two fortified peaks of what is now known as the Fortezza Vecchia, then distinguished as the "old" and "new castles" (the latter built by Charles I. of Anjou), whose commanders changed every

Jervis, *History of the Island of Corfù*, 125; Botta, *Storia Naturale dell' Isola di Corfù*, 61; Faber, *Evagatorium*, iii., 351.

[1] *Archivio Veneto*, xvii., 88; xviii., 114.

sixteen months. Familiar landmarks were the two towers, in which the councillors resided, the "tower of the iron gate," the church of St Nicholas, and that of the Holy Apostles.[1] In 1394, a Corfiote baron of Neapolitan origin, Pietro Capece, built the Catholic convent and church of the Annunziata, the oldest of all the extant Latin churches in the town, which he subsequently placed under the care of the bailie, and which contains many tombs and inscriptions, mostly relating to Corfiotes who fell in the Turkish wars. Another church, that of St Michael, attributed by some to the Despots of Epiros whose name it bore, is said by Marmora to have been perhaps founded on the day when the islanders resolved to accept the sway of Venice. But the most famous shrine in the island was that of Our Lady of Cassopo, to which homeward-bound mariners were wont to pay their respects, and which rose on the site of the altar of Zeus, before which Nero had inaugurated his artistic tour of the Greek provinces. Around it there had grown up a much-frequented market, which was free from all dues.[2] Owing to the number of poor and infirm pilgrims who passed through the island to and from the Holy Land, a hospice was provided for their accommodation; but towards the end of the fifteenth century their usual abode was the cloister of the Bare-footed Friars. Upon travellers from the north, the town did not at that time make a favourable impression. The streets were "narrow, dark, and smelly," the place swarmed with "abject persons," and the pious pilgrim was offended by the contrast between the meanness of the archiepiscopal residence and the numbers of the Jews.[3] Yet at the time of the siege we hear of the "beautiful and splendid houses" of the suburbs and of the splendid Avráme Palace by the sea-shore—a mansion adorned with fine marble statues, and standing in a lovely garden. It is interesting to note that visitors were shown the rock which Pliny the elder had long ago identified

[1] Sáthas, ii., 10, 81, 85, 87, 116, 117; iii., 46.

[2] Marmora, 232, 251; Sáthas, ii., 141; iii., 30, 85, 263, 460; Buondelmonti, 54, 55, and his plan of the island; Burney MS. 213, f. 23.

[3] Feyerabend, *Reyssbuch*, ff. 36, 351; Casola, *Viaggio*, 34-5; Sáthas, iii., 57; Jovius, *Historiæ sui temporis*, ii., f. 186; Guazzo, *Historie*, f. 203.

with "the ship of Ulysses."[1] Another spot associated with classical Corfù, the ancient Hyllæan harbour, now received its modern name of Chalikiópoulo from the family of that name to which it belonged.[2]

The Turkish peril had not become acute at the time of the Venetian occupation. The neighbours of the new Venetian colony were either Italian princelets, like the Tocchi, who ruled over the other Ionian islands, and like Esau Buondelmonti, the Despot of Joannina, or else Albanian chieftains who had established themselves at various points in Epiros after the break-up of the Greek Despotat. It was the policy of the republic to play off the Italians against the Arnauts and the Arnauts against the Italians. Thus, when Esau was captured by the Albanians, the bailie of Corfù intervened to obtain his release and entertained him in the castle; while, on his death, the Corfiotes assisted the Albanians to occupy Joannina, rather than that it should fall into the hands of his ambitious nephew, Carlo Tocco, who was a vassal of the King of Naples to boot. The latter's aggressive and successful policy in Ætolia and Akarnania led to occasional friction with Venice, but never endangered the safety of Corfù.

It was otherwise, however, with the Genoese. These commercial rivals of Venice did not abandon all hope of obtaining so desirable a possession until some time after the establishment of the Venetian protectorate. Twice, in 1403 and again in 1432, they attacked Corfù, but on both occasions without success. The first time, under the leadership of Marshal Boucicaut, they tried to capture the impregnable castle of Sant' Angelo, which was courageously defended by a Corfiote noble, and were routed by the island militia with great slaughter near the village of Doukades. The second attempt was more serious. The invaders effected a landing, and had already ravaged the fertile island and burned the borgo and suburbs of the capital, when on the seventh day a sudden sally of the townsfolk and the garrison checked their further advance. Many of the Genoese were taken prisoners, while those who succeeded

[1] Faber, *op. cit.*, iii., 347.

[2] Romanós, Γρατιανὸς Ζώρζης, 316; Sáthas, v., 318.

in escaping to their vessels were pursued and severely handled by the Venetian fleet. The further attempts of Genoese privateers to waylay merchantmen on their passage between Corfù and Venice were frustrated, and soon the islanders had nothing more to fear from these Christian enemies of their protectors. The raid had proved what Venetian statesmen had once doubted—the fidelity of the Greeks; but the loss of life and property which it had caused, and which was intensified by visitations of the plague, led the Government to grant five years' exemption from all services and dues to all who would settle in the island.[1]

Meanwhile, however, the Turks had been rapidly gaining ground on the mainland opposite. The first serious alarm arose when they captured the harbour of Valona, one of the keys of the Adriatic, from Regina Balsha, the lady of the place.[2] In 1430 Joannina fell, and in the following year the Turks made their first attack upon Corfù; but the repulse with which they met discouraged them from renewing the attempt for more than a century. Henceforth, however, especially after the disappearance of the Tocchi from the continent, the continental dependencies of Corfù were constantly exposed to the danger of Turkish or Albanian attack. The people of Parga, in particular, suffered terribly for their devotion to Venice; their homes were captured, their wives and children carried off, and it required a vigorous effort by the Corfiotes to recover the rocky fortress, which was now their outpost against the Turk.[3]

After the fall of Constantinople and the subsequent collapse of the Christian states of Greece, Corfù became the refuge of many distinguished exiles. From the imperial city came the famous family of the Theotókai, which has given so many leading men to the island of its adoption.[4] From the Morea fled the last Despot Thomas Palaiológos

[1] Marmora, 253-7; Chalkokondýles, 265; Sanudo *apud* Muratori, xxii., 1030; Sáthas, III., 433, 445, 466, 472; *Kyriaci Anconitani Itinerarium*, 29, 30.

[2] Sáthas, III., 159, 181.

[3] Kalligâs, Μελέται, 653; P. A. S., Ἡ Πάργα, 80-1; Marmora, 260-1; Sáthas, v., 328.

[4] Romanós, Γρατιανὸς Ζώρζης, 99.

with his wife and family, the historian Phrantzês, and the ancestor of the Corfiote historian Marmora. Phrantzês wrote the story of his troubled times at the instance of some noble Corfiotes in the repose of the Phæacian island, and his remains, with those of his master's consort, the Despoina Caterina, sleep in the church of SS. Jason and Sosipater. So great was the influx of Greek priests that Venice became seriously alarmed lest they should undermine the loyalty of her Corfiote subjects, and issued an order that the ancient "college of 32" should hold no more meetings, and that all popes settled in the island during the last ten years should leave it. But the need of humouring the Greeks in view of her own struggle with the Turks induced her to pursue her usual tolerant policy.[1]

The religious enthusiasm of the Greeks increased all the more, because at that time Corfù became the shrine of her famous saint, Spiridion, a Cypriote bishop who took a prominent part at the council of Nice, and whose remains had been transferred to Constantinople. A priest, named Kalochairétes, brought the holy man's body and that of St Theodora, the consort of the Iconoclast Emperor Theóphilos, to Corfù in 1456, and upon his death his two eldest sons became proprietors of the male saint's remains, and his youngest son received those of the female, which he bestowed on the community. The body of St Spiridion ultimately passed to the distinguished family of Boúlgaris, to which it still belongs, and is preserved in the church of the saint, just as that of St Theodora reposes in the cathedral. Four times a year the body of St Spiridion is carried in procession, in commemoration of his alleged services in having twice delivered the island from plague, once from famine, and once from the Turks. His name is the most wide-spread in Corfù, and the number of boys called "Spiro" is legion.[2]

During the operations against the Turks at this period the Corfiotes distinguished themselves by their active co-

[1] Lamansky, 047, 049, 050; Marmora, 267.

[2] Brokínes, *Περὶ τῶν ἐτησίως τελουμένων ἐν Κερκύρᾳ λιτανειῶν τοῦ θ. λειψάνου τοῦ Ἁγίου Σπυρίδωνος* (English tr. by Mrs Dawes); Marmora, 261-7, 287; Sáthas, v., 260.

operation with their protectors. We find them fighting twice at Parga and twice at Butrinto; during the long Turco-Venetian war, which broke out in 1463, we hear of their prowess at the isthmus of Corinth, beneath the walls of Patras, and behind the ramparts of Lepanto; it was a Corfiote who temporarily gained for the republic the castle of Strovili on the mainland, and even in her purely Italian wars the islanders assisted. The privilege of electing the captain of the Corfiote war-galleys was the reward of this loyalty. Meanwhile, headed by their archbishop, they worked on their own fortifications, and, regardless of archæology, found in their ancient city, Palaiopolis, a handy quarry. It seems, indeed, as if the words of Marmora[1] were then no mere servile phrase: "Corfù was ever studying the means of keeping herself a loyal subject of the Venetians."

[1] Sáthas, v., 222, 224, 246, 336-9; vi., 219; vii., 11; Marmora, 268-70, 324-5, 333; P. A. S., Ἡ Πάργα, 81-4; Malipiero, *Annali*, 89, 110.

CHAPTER XVI

THE IONIAN ISLANDS UNDER VENICE (1485-1540)

THE sequel of the long war which ended in 1479, fatal as it was to the ancient domination of the Italian counts of Cephalonia over the four Ionian islands which had so long formed a separate Latin state, enabled Venice to increase her possessions in the Ionian Sea. We saw in a previous chapter how in 1482 and the following year, she drove Antonio Tocco out of Zante, and Cephalonia, when he had recovered them from the Turks, and how she was forced to cede the latter of her conquests to Bajazet II., but managed to keep permanent possession of "the flower of the Levant," on payment of an annual tribute of 500 ducats, which continued from 1485 down to its abolition by the treaty of Carlovitz in 1699, and formed a heavy burden on the revenues of the island.

The first care of the Venetians was to repopulate their new possession, which had not recovered during the brief restoration of the Tocchi from the emigration and devastation caused by the Turkish Conquest. The authorities of the Venetian colonies on the mainland were ordered to offer lands to settlers in the island; especially to *stradioti* from Modon, Coron, Nauplia, and Lepanto, who would serve as a protection; numbers of those light horsemen accepted, on condition that they should be free from tithes and from all compulsory feudal service for four years; and thus the republic soon had at her disposal a seasoned body of men—at once colonists and cavalry—for they had to keep their own horses—under the command of Theodore Palaiológos, perhaps a son of the defender of Salmenikon, who had already acted as an agent of the republic in sounding the opinions of the people of Cephalonia. In comparatively few years' time, the *stradioti* of Zante numbered 1500 families; and, though they were liable to serve outside the island, they had a strong motive for settling there, in that they could bequeath their lands. The loss of Lepanto, Modon, and Coron naturally increased the tide of immigration to Zante; the Knights of Rhodes received lands there; in 1528, despite plague and earthquakes, the population had reached 17,255 souls, and among them were some of the most illustrious Greek families of Crete, Constantinople, and the Morea. The island replaced Modon as the port of call on the way to the East; a flourishing town grew up at the water's edge, where the modern capital stands; and successive governors noted with alarm the steady depopulation of the old mediæval city on the castle hill, where the civil and ecclesiastical authorities lived, and strove by fiscal privileges to prevent the human current from flowing downwards.[1]

The new colony was at first ordered to be governed by the laws of Lepanto, but the administration of Zante was later assimilated to that of Corfù. Down to 1545 it was entrusted to a single *provveditore*, who was at first a subordinate of the governor of Modon; but, in that year, at the request of the community, two councillors were appointed in Venice to accompany him, and to hold office for the term of two years, like himself. These councillors took it in turns to act as treasurer, a month at a time, and, together with the *provveditore*, they administered justice, an appeal lying from their decisions to Corfù. A secretary completed the resident Venetian official hierarchy.[2] There was, however, a much greater personage, the *provveditore generale del Levante*, an official first appointed in 1500, after the loss of Modon, whose commission included the supervision of all the Venetian colonies, but more especially Zante, in consequence of its increased importance. Every year it was

[1] Sáthas, v., 75-6, 81-3, 91, 96; vi., 253-63; vii., 43; Lunzi, 203-4; Remondini, *De Zachynthi Antiq.*, 147; *Chronicon breve*, 522; Mustoxidi, Ἑλληνομνήμων, 299-300; Bembo, f. 15; Chiótes, Ἱστορικὰ Ἀπομνημονεύματα, ii., 305-11, 633.

[2] Sáthas, v., 100, 103; vi., 269; vii., 45.

his duty to visit the various islands; on his arrival the powers of the local governor lapsed, and those who had grievances hastened to lay them before him. The day of his arrival was a public holiday; the Greek and Latin clergy walked in procession to his palace; the Catholic bishop and the Greek "chief priest" offered him respectively the cross and the Gospels to kiss; then they all proceeded in state to the Catholic cathedral, where the rival heads of the two churches sat side by side; the *protopapâs* wished the republic and her representative many years; the bishop celebrated mass; and a banquet to the magistrates and the nobles ended the day.[1]

In Zante, as in Corfù, there was a General Council, composed of all the nobles, which met once a year to elect a smaller council, whose numbers, limited to 100 down to 1545, were finally fixed at 150. The organisation of the latter was deliberately borrowed from the similar body at Corfù; and, like it, the Zantiote Council of 150 had the right of conferring the local offices, which were few, unimportant, and highly coveted. This body also elected the three annual judges, and the captains of any galleys that were fitted out at Zante. The community had the right of sending deputations for the redress of grievances at its own expense to Venice, or to the *provveditore generale*, whose headquarters were Corfù. Society in Zante was formed on aristocratic lines; the islanders were divided into three classes—the people, the burghers, and the nobles; and the feudal system, introduced by the Latin counts, had split up the island into twelve fiefs. The noble families were for long unlimited in number; in 1542, however, it was ordained that no newcomers, except those who had emigrated from Nauplia and Monemvasia (then recently lost), could form part of the General Council unless they had resided for five years; and the total was finally fixed at ninety-three, the place of an extinct family being filled by the ennoblement of a family of burghers. There was no distinction, as at Corfù, between Latin and Greek nobles; the population of Zante was a mixture of races—Italians, Greeks from many parts of the Morea, and Jews, who had a ghetto walled in and guarded—and it was to this truly Levantine characteristic that Venetian governors

[1] Sáthas, i., 319-20; Lunzi, 314-16.

attributed the difficulty of keeping order. Homicide was common, and the Mainate emigrants took the blood-feud with them to Zante.[1]

The Catholic Church required re-establishment, for the Turks had destroyed the Franciscan monastery and the old cathedral in the castle, and the only Catholic place of worship left in the early years of the sixteenth century was a small chapel, which served as a barn. Under these circumstances, it was not to be wondered at that the Catholics had become converts to the Greek Church. The island now, however, became again the seat of a Catholic bishop. From the time when Honorius III.[2] had added the see of Zante to that of Cephalonia, its holder had hitherto always styled himself "Bishop of Cephalonia and Zante," and had resided down to the time of Leonardo III. Tocco in the former and more important island. When, however, the last of the Palatine counts restored the Greek bishopric of Cephalonia and Zante, he ordered that the next Catholic bishop, Giovanni Ongaro, while retaining the double title, should reside in Zante, where the number of Italians was larger than in the more purely Greek island, and thither, after the Venetian Conquest, the exiled Latin prelate returned. When, in 1488, he was laid to rest in the *duomo*, his successor altered his title, styling himself as His Grace "of Zante and Cephalonia," the change in the order of the islands being doubtless due to the fact that Cephalonia was still in the power of the Turks. Even after it too became Venetian, Zante continued to be the residence of the Catholic bishop and to give him his first title, as is still the case. For long, however, the Catholic prelates were absentees; one of the Medici of Nauplia held the see for many years without visiting his flock; the number of Catholics naturally dwindled; and the Cephalonians complained that their children were left unconfirmed and the Latin churches allowed to fall into ruin. In Zante, however, the Venetians founded the still existent Catholic cathedral of S. Marco, which replaced the old minster of the Redeemer up in the

[1] Sáthas, v., 100, 112; vi., 257, 275; Hopf *apud* Ersch und Gruber, lxxxvi., 186; Lunzi, ch. viii.; Mercati, *Saggio Storico Statistico di Zante*, 33.

[2] *Regesta*, II., 50.

castle; the monastery of Santa Maria delle Grazie; and S. Antonio ai Lazzaretti, besides restoring the old cathedral in the time of Sixtus V., whose arms were placed in the church, and the ancient Franciscan monastery, afterwards converted into barracks.[1]

The Greek bishop of Cephalonia, whom Leonardo III. had appointed, was still living at a very advanced age when the Venetians occupied Zante, and his successors, like their Latin rivals, included both islands in their titles, and claimed to exercise authority over both. Hence disputes arose between them and the *protopapâs* of Zante, an official elected by the Council of 150 for the term of five years, who was the real head of the Greek Church in the latter island. These disputes were further accentuated by the attempt of the metropolitan of Corinth to interfere in the affairs of a see, which was held by one of his suffragans. This interference was stopped by the Venetians, who forbade Greek priests to go to the mainland for consecration. A further grievance of the Orthodox Zantiotes was that the Cephalonian clergy always elected a native of that island to the episcopal, or archiepiscopal throne, as it became in 1632, while they had no voice in the election; it was accordingly at last decided that a Zantiote must be chosen on every third vacancy.[2] The incident was typical of the jealousy between the islanders; and it is characteristic of Greek life, that when, in the sixteenth century, the Cephalonians claimed precedence over Zante, they quoted to the Venetians in support of their claim the fact that in the Homeric catalogue the people of Zakynthos are only cited as the subjects of Odysseus![3] Some of the Catholic bishops of Zante, like Medici, contravened the privileges of the Orthodox, ordering Catholic priests to perform services and baptisms in Greek churches.[4] But against this the republic, true to her principles of toleration, promptly protested. Venetian policy in these islands was to pay respect to the Orthodox hierarchy, and at the banquet in honour of the *provveditore generale* at

[1] Sáthas, v., 79-80, 95, 180-1; Lunzi, ch. xiii.; Chiótes, II., 298, 492, 497, 506, 515, 532-4; vi., 98-103; Mercati, 31.

[2] Sáthas, v., 80, 108, 109, 136, 140, 188; Chiótes, II., 520, 527; Miklosich und Müller, v., 74-6. [3] Sáthas, iv., p. iv. [4] *Ibid.*, v., 167.

Cephalonia, the Orthodox bishop sat at his right hand and ate from a plate of gold.

When, in 1500, Cephalonia also became a Venetian possession, it was treated in the same way as Zante. The island needed cultivation; for the Venetian Government during its previous brief occupation between 1483 and 1485 had ordered that it should be made to appear as desolate as possible, in order that the sultan might not think it worth while to insist upon its evacuation. The Turkish domination and the various attempts of the Venetians to recapture the island had naturally prevented its improvement, so that the first act of the latter, when they recovered it, was to plant there a military colony of *stradioti* from Modon and Navarino, with other survivors of those fallen towns, confiscating a part of five feudal baronies for the purpose. So greatly did Cephalonia increase in population, that, in 1548, despite the great Turkish raid of ten years earlier, it contained 15,304 souls, while the policy of fining all who left their lands untilled increased its fertility. But at this period there was only one fortified town in the island, the castle of St George, which the Venetians restored—for Assos was built later—and the inhabitants lived for the most part in scattered hamlets, which afforded a temptation to foreign and native thieves. Its government during the previous Venetian occupation had been modelled on that of Lepanto; it was now assimilated to that of Zante. But the character of the two islands, though separated by only a narrow channel, was widely different. Cephalonia, owing to its purer Hellenic population, was actuated by the democratic sentiments engrained in the Greek race, despite the existence of six baronies, a relic of the feudal system. The meetings of the Cephalonian Council were noted for their turbulence and irregularity, of which the Venetian governors often complained. The request for a "Council of primates" had been granted in 1506 on condition that every councillor should reside not more than a mile from the capital; but in 1548 we are told that "there was neither means nor place of meeting." Tumultuous gatherings, at which even peasants took part, were held in the street, and we hear of 800 or 900 persons electing the captains of the galleys, the three annual judges, and the other local officials. Hence, while Corfiote nobles temporarily resident in Zante and Zantiote nobles in Corfù were allowed to take part in the General Council of their hosts, both islands scornfully refused the privilege to Cephalonians. After half a century of Venetian rule, a governor sums up the condition of the island in a sentence: "The inhabitants are poor and idle; civilisation and municipal laws there are none." Yet the natives, like true Greeks, had even then a yearning for education. "There is not a single schoolmaster in all Cephalonia," they pathetically wrote to Venice, and they begged that a portion of the fines paid by criminals might be set aside to provide a teacher's salary. Their petition was granted, and at Zante the abbot of the Anaphonetria monastery was obliged to pay 150 ducats to the community every year as the pay of a schoolmaster. Otherwise a single Italian master in either island represented the most cautious republic's total contribution to public education.[1]

Under the jurisdiction of Cephalonia was the ancient home of Odysseus. After its devastation by Ahmed Pasha in 1479, Ithaka remained deserted and unclaimed till 1503, though it is mentioned several times during the previous war as a station of the Venetian fleet.[2] But in that year a party of Venetian subjects landed on the island with their oxen, and began to cultivate it. The governor of Cephalonia, afraid of remonstrances from the sultan, advised caution, and reported the matter home.[3] Thereupon, in 1504, an order was issued from Venice for repopulating "an island named Val di Compare situated opposite Cephalonia, at present uninhabited, but reported to have been formerly fertile and fruitful." Accordingly, lands were offered to settlers free from all taxes for five years, at the end of which time the colonists were to pay to the treasury of Cephalonia the same dues as the inhabitants of that island. The offer of the Senate seems to have been successful; among those who accepted it were the families of Boua Grívas, Petalâs, and Karavías, which last in modern times produced a local

[1] Sáthas, v., 150-5, 163, 175, 179, 186-7, 200; vi., 279, 281, 285; vii., 86, 120; Lunzi, 205, 216, 227-31, 318-23, 472; Chiótes, iii., 75.

[2] Sanudo, *Diarii*, iii., 444, 488, 498, 500.

[3] *Ibid.*, v., 883.

historian of Ithaka. In 1545, the tithe of Ithaka—82 bushels of wheat—figures in the budget of Cephalonia, and three years later the retiring governor of the latter island reported that "under the jurisdiction of Cephalonia there is another island named Thiachi, very mountainous and barren, in which there are different harbours and especially a harbour called Vathi or Val de Compare; in the which island are hamlets, in three places, inhabited by about sixty families, who are in great fear of corsairs, because they have no fortress in which to take refuge." These three hamlets are doubtless those of Palaiochora, Anoe, and Exoe, which are regarded as the oldest in the island. In 1563, Ithaka is described as "very well populated, for many Cephalonians go to live there," and we obtain a glimpse of its internal government. In 1504 a Venetian governor had been appointed, and a certain Pugliese had subsequently been made "captain" of Ithaka for life. On his death, in 1563, Venice allowed the Cephalonian council to elect one of its members every year to fill his place "without any cost to the republic," on condition that he recognised in all things the superior authority of the *provveditore*, who paid it an annual visit. Ithakan interests were represented by two "elders of the people" (δημογέροντες), who acted as assessors to the "captain," and the natives, after several complaints to Venice against his extortion and interference in their local affairs, at last secured the abolition of this office, so that thenceforth the two "elders" ruled alone. Every year the principal men of the island met to elect the local officials. Small as it is, Ithaka boasted of one feudal barony, held by the family of Galátes—the only Ithakan family which enjoyed the privileges of nobility in the Venetian period. It had first received exemptions from Leonardo III. Tocco, and it is still extant in the island.[1]

At first both Zante and Cephalonia were a drag on the Venetian exchequer, for both required development, and the former was saddled with the Turkish tribute. But the introduction of the currant in the first half of the sixteenth

[1] Sáthas, v., 157, 202; vi., 284, 285; Karavías, Ἱστορία τῆς νήσου Ἰθάκης, 69; Lunzi, 348-50 (Greek ed., pp. 83-5); Meliarákes, Γεωγραφία τοῦ νομοῦ Κεφαλληνίας, 150, 191; Chiótes, II., 228.

century [1] enormously increased the revenues of Zante. The wholesale conversion of corn-fields into currant plots caused, however, such alarm that the local authorities applied to Venice for leave to root up the currant bushes. The republic replied by allowing the currants to remain, but at the same time levied a duty (the "new tax," as it was called) upon them, the proceeds of which were devoted to the purchase and storage of bread stuffs.[2] The two islands were also useful to the fleet, which bought its wine at Zante, and obtained its masts and spars from the forest on the Black Mountain, which the republic reserved for her exclusive use.[3] She took over at the outset all the salt-pans, fisheries, mills, and other appurtenances of the Palatine counts,[4] and farmed out the taxes in the usual manner. They chiefly consisted of a tithe on the produce, from which the *stradioti* were exempt, and which was assessed by assessors named *scontri*, annually elected by the governor and Council; of a house-duty, or *livello;* of a duty on all wine sold; and of the so-called *preda*, a tax on flocks and herds. Out of the corn paid as tithe by the Zantiotes sufficient was ordered to be sent to Venice every year to defray the amount of the Turkish tribute on that island.[5] Thus, a century later, it came to be said that, if Corfù was useful to the republic as a strategic position, the other two islands were valuable from their revenues. Nor were the Cephalonians and Zantiotes, if we may believe the reports of their Venetian governors, otherwise than loyal to the republic. They knew that they had no alternative but Turkish government, and they saw, too, from their vicinity to the Morea, that their fellow-Greeks there were worse off than themselves. The peasants might not like the obligation to serve in the armed force or man the galleys of the islands, which the nobles were so proud to command. But they knew that the blood-tax, the παιδομάζωμα, of the Turks was harder than these milder forms of conscription. The

[1] It is spoken of as "recent" in 1541 (Sáthas, vi., 268); in 1552 Zantiote currants were sent to England (Feyerabend, *Reyssbuch*, f. 376).

[2] Lunzi, 433-4.

[3] Sáthas, v., 97, 170, 177; vi., 278.

[4] *Ibid.*, v., 156.

[5] *Ibid.*, v., 77, 88, 94, 161; vi., 266-7, 272, 284.

Zantiote peasants hated their own aristocracy; the Cephalonians often quarrelled among themselves; but neither island ever rose against the republic which secured them the almost uninterrupted blessings of peace.

The Turco-Venetian war of 1499-1502, which gave Cephalonia to Venice, scarcely affected the sister-islands. Zante was reassured by the coolness of a *stradioto* at the moment of a scare of invasion. Corfù, which Bajazet II. had threatened ten years earlier, prepared for an attack, and the houses of the suburb were sacrificed to the defences of the city.[1] But the colony sustained no loss save the temporary capture of Butrinto; while a Corfiote captain, one of the ancient family of Goth, greatly distinguished himself by running the blockade of Modon, receiving in return for his services the jurisdiction over the fief of the gypsies.[2] For a whole generation the Ionian islands enjoyed, like the other Venetian colonies, the long peace.

At last, however, after rather more than a century of almost complete freedom from attack, Corfù was destined to undergo the first of the two great Turkish sieges, which were the principal events in her annals during the Venetian occupation. In 1537 war broke out between the republic and Suleyman the Magnificent, at that time engaged in an attack upon the Neapolitan dominions of Charles V. During the transport of troops and material of war across the channel of Otranto, the Turkish and Venetian fleets came into hostile collision, and though Venice was ready to make amends for the mistakes of her officials, the sultan resolved to punish them for the insults to his flag. He was at Valona, on the coast of Epiros, at the time; and, removing his camp to Butrinto,[3] whose commander surrendered at his approach, he gave orders for the invasion of Corfù.

The island was not taken unawares. The presence of the

[1] Sáthas, vi., 237-9; vii., 66; Malipiero, 169; *Chronicon Venetum*, *apud* Muratori, xxiv., 150.

[2] Marmora, 277; but Lunzi says that the fief had been granted to his family a generation earlier.

[3] So Paruta and the Duke of Naxos; and the position of Butrinto makes this more probable than La Bastia or Paramythia, the alternative sites for his camp.

sultan in Epiros and the naval operations of Andrea Doria to the north and south of Corfù had put the authorities on their guard, and Admiral Girolamo Pesaro with a large fleet, which was joined by a contingent of five Ionian galleys, had been despatched to Corfiote waters. The town still relied for its protection upon the two fortified peaks of what is now called the Fortezza Vecchia, defended by a garrison of some 2000 Italians and the same number of Corfiotes, under the command of Naldo, an officer who had distinguished himself in the Italian wars, while four galleys, with their crews on board, lay behind the breakwater below the fortress. The place was well supplied with guns and ammunition; it contained provisions for three years; and its defences were strengthened by the destruction of 3,000 houses in the suburbs, which might have served as cover to the enemy.

The Turks, under the command of the redoubtable Khaireddîn Barbarossa, the most celebrated captain in the service of the sultan, landed at Govino, where the much later Venetian arsenal now stands, towards the end of August, destroyed the village of Potamó, and marched upon the capital. On the 29th another force of 25,000 men crossed over to join him, these operations being facilitated by the fact that Pesaro had sailed up the Adriatic without engaging the Turkish fleet. The mart, as it was called, which lay outside the city walls, was speedily taken, and its remaining inhabitants found the gates shut against them and were forced to crouch under the castle ramparts on the rocky promontory of S. Sidero or behind the breakwater. The Corfiote traveller, Noúkios, an eyewitness of the siege, has left a graphic account of the sufferings of these poor wretches, huddled together on a narrow ledge of rock, without food or shelter, and exposed to the stones of the garrison and to the full force of one of those terrific storms of rain not uncommon in Corfù at that season. Those who could afford to bribe the soldiers on the walls were pulled up by means of ropes, while the rest were left to die of cold or hunger. When it seemed that the siege was likely to last, the Venetian governor, in order to economise food and space, turned out of the fortress the old men, women, and children, who went to the Turkish lines to beg for bread. The Turkish commander, hoping to work on the feelings of the garrison, refused; so the miserable creatures, repudiated alike by the besieged and the besiegers, wandered about distractedly between the two armies, striving to regain admission to the fortress by showing their ancient wounds gained in the Venetian service; and, at last, when their efforts proved unavailing, lying down in the ditches to die. Meanwhile, for three days and nights the suburbs were blazing, and the Turks were ravaging the fair island with fire and sword. The castle of Sant' Angelo on the west coast alone resisted their attacks. More than 3000 refugees from the countryside had congregated within its walls, and four times did its brave Corfiote garrison repulse the enemy. Barbarossa, whose headquarters were at the Avráme Palace on the sea-shore, now began the bombardment of the fortified peninsula, which contained the mediæval city of Corfù. He planted a cannon on the islet of Vido, then called Malipiero, the pleasaunce of a nobleman, and noted for its abundance of game. But the gunners made such bad practice that in three days they only hit the mark five times, while the rest of their shots flew over the fortress into the sea on the other side. Nor was Barbarossa more fortunate in an attempt to bombard the city from his own galley; a well-aimed shot struck the vessel; and, when he retired in the direction of the fountain of Kardáki, where ships were accustomed to water, and began a cannonade of the place from that side where the walls were lower, the great distance caused most of his projectiles to fall short of the mark. At this, Ayas Pasha, the grand vizier, resolved to see for himself the prospects of taking the city; he therefore ventured out one dark and rainy night to inspect the moat and the walls. What he saw convinced him that Corfù could only be captured after a long siege, whereas the month of September had now begun and sickness had broken out among the half-starved Turks. He therefore advised the sultan to abandon the attempt. Suleyman first resolved to try the effect of persuasion upon the garrison; he therefore sent a Corfiote prisoner to frighten the Venetian authorities into surrender. The bailie, Simeone Leone, and the *provveditore*, Luigi da Riva, dismissed the sultan's envoy without a reply, and a brisk cannonade from the castle batteries proved an effective answer to fresh demonstrations of hostility. Suleyman accordingly made a virtue of necessity; the grand vizier sent for the Venetian representative at Constantinople, who was at the sultan's headquarters, and offered to raise the siege, if the republic would compensate his master for his losses; but, before any reply could arrive from Venice, the siege had been already raised. After firing all the houses that remained standing in the suburbs, the Turks were ordered to embark; their fleet made one more demonstration; but on 11th September, after a stay of only thirteen days in the island, they recrossed the channel to Epiros. But in that short time they had wrought enormous damage. The Corfiote traveller tells us that they had destroyed "all the works of men's hands" throughout the island, and that they slew or carried off all the animals they could find; sparing only the trees and vines owing to the suddenness of their departure. The Duke of Naxos wrote to the pope, that two large cities might have been built out of the houses and churches which they had destroyed; the privileges and letters-patent of the islanders had perished in the flames or had been used as ammunition, and a Corfiote petition states that they carried away more than 20,000 captives. The population was so greatly reduced by this wholesale deportation, that the nobles had to be recruited from the burgesses, and nearly forty years afterwards the whole island contained only some 17,500 inhabitants, or less than one-fifth of the estimated population in classical times. Among these captives was a young girl, Kalé Kartánou, whom (and not a Baffo of Paros) the Corfiote historians believe to have been the mother of Murâd III.[1]

Great was the joy in Venice at the news that the invaders had abandoned Corfù, and public thanksgivings were offered up for the preservation of the island, even in the desolate condition in which the Turks had left it. Planks were sent to rebuild the suburb; the Italian mercenaries who had maltreated the inhabitants during the siege were hanged; and a noble Venetian was beheaded. The Greeks had made

[1] Noúkios, Ἀποδημιῶν, 7-14; Paruta, I., 372-9; Maurocenus, 176-81; Marmora, 301-12, 327; Haji Kalifeh, *The History of the Maritime Wars*, 57-8; Guazzo, ff. 199, 201-4; Jovius, ii. ff. 186-8; Buchon, *Recherches*, ii., 466-7; M. Mustoxidi Ἱστορικὰ καὶ Φιλολογικὰ Ἀνάλεκτα, 83-97, 193.

immense sacrifices in their determination never to yield—they could not have fought better, it was said, had they been fighting for the national cause—and they had their reward. The new bailie, Tiepolo, contented everyone, we are told, by his wise provisions; he restored order out of chaos, and did his best to promote peace with the Turks; while the republic bestowed upon Eparchos, the distinguished Corfiote scholar and envoy, the vacant fief of the gypsies, as compensation for his losses and as the reward of his services. But the chief result of the siege was the tardy but systematic fortification of the town of Corfù, at the repeated request of the Corfiote Council, which sent several embassies to Venice on the subject. More than 2000 houses were pulled down in the suburb of San Rocco to make room for the walls, for which the old city of Palaiopolis once more provided materials, and Venice spent a large sum on the erection of new bastions. Some parts of the Fortezza Vecchia date from this period; what is now called the Fortezza Nuova was built between 1577 and 1588, when the new works were completed. The traveller Buochenbach, who visited the island in 1579, gives the inscriptions placed on two of the new bastions; we have two plans showing the fortifications of the citadel and of the town about this time; and visitors to Venice will remember the models of Corfù in the arsenal and on the outside of Sta. Maria Zobenigo.[1]

The other Ionian islands suffered in less degree at the hands of the Turks. They ravaged Paxo, carried off over 13,000 souls from Cephalonia, descended upon Zante, and burnt Parga, whose inhabitants long wandered homeless about the mountains of Epiros, until Venice at last restored their beloved abode.[2] They laid in ashes the monastery of the Redeemer on one of the Strivali islands, the Strophades of the ancients—a building already once before destroyed by the Turks—despite the prowess of those very muscular

[1] Sáthas, v., 269; Lamansky, 611; Guazzo, f. 208; Miklosich und Müller, iii., 364-6; M. Mustoxidi, *op. cit.*, 52, 193; Buochenbach, *Orientalische Reyss*, 24; Marmora (364-5) and Jervis (*History of the Island of Corfù*, 126) give the two plans.

[2] Paruta, i., 379; P. A. S. Ἡ Πάργα, 86; Sáthas, v., 98, 289; viii., 331; Guazzo, f. 242; Maurocenus, 181.

Christians, the monks, whose martyrdom was commemorated by a Zantiote poet.[1] Finally, the devastation of the Venetian islands was completed by a raid upon the southernmost of them all, Cerigo.

This seems the most appropriate place to describe the vicissitudes of Kythera, or Cerigo, which, though neither geographically nor any longer politically one of the Ionian group, was so reckoned during the British occupation and during the last eighty years of Venetian rule. The history of the fabled home of Venus was absolutely different from that of the other Greek islands, in some respects resembling that of the Cyclades, in others that of the Ionian islands, just as it is placed half-way between the two. At the time of the Conquest, in 1207, it was occupied, as we saw, by the Venetian family of Venier, self-styled descendants of the goddess of love, who took the title of Marquis of Cerigo, because they guarded the southern marches of Greece, while the same style was adopted by their fellows, the Viari, who held sway over the islet of Cerigotto, famous in our own time for the discovery of the bronze statue of "the youth of Antikythera."[2] When, however, the Greeks recovered Monemvasia, the position of the two marquises became dangerous. It would appear from a confused passage of the Italian memoir on the island, that the natives of Cerigo, impatient at the treatment which they received from their Latin lord, sent a deputation to invoke the aid of the Greek governor of the new Byzantine province.[3] At any rate, Licario's famous cruise among the Latin islands proved fatal to the rule of both the Venetian marquises. A governor was sent to Cerigo from Monemvasia; but ere long the island was conferred by Michael Palaiológos upon Paul Monoyánnes, one of the three great Monemvasiote *archons*, who is described in a Venetian document as being, in 1275, "the vassal of the Emperor and captain of Cerigo." Monoyánnes fortified the island, where his tomb was discovered during the British protectorate, and it remained in the possession of his family till 1309, when intermarriage

[1] Sáthas, Μνημεῖα, v., 78-9, 102; Τουροκρατουμένη Ἑλλάς, 122.

[2] Chilas, *Chronicon*, *apud* Hopf, *Chroniques*, 346.

[3] *Antique Memorie di Cerigo*, *apud* Sáthas, vi., 301.

between the children of its Greek and Latin lords restored Cerigo, with the approval of Venice, to the Venieri.[1]

The island now received a strict feudal organisation, which long continued to affect its topography and its land tenure. It was divided up into twenty-four *carati*, or shares, six of which were owned by each of the four brothers Venier, while the fertile plain and the castle of Kapsali were held in common. In order to increase the population, the brothers invited Cretans to settle there, granting them exemption from all services and dues for ever. The rest of the islanders were simple serfs, whom the brothers divided among them like so much live stock; these *pároikoi*, as they were called, ran with the land; they could not marry without the consent of their lords; they could not engage in any except the smallest trade; they could not quit the island without leaving a pledge of their return; in short, they were at the beck and call of their masters, or worse, of their masters' agents, for the marquises usually preferred residence in Crete to their ancestral castle of Kapsali, where one of the clan held the command for the others.[2]

Such was the state of Cerigo down to 1363, the year of the great Cretan rebellion. In that rising the Venier family took a very prominent part; Tito Venier was one of the ringleaders, and both he and two other members of his family paid for their disloyalty with their heads. A Venetian fleet arrived off Cerigo, and young Piero Venier, who held the castle, had no option but to surrender. The republic took possession of the island, and for thirty years it formed a Venetian colony, governed by a *castellano*, sent every two years from Crete.

The Venieri did not, however, abandon the hope of recovering their confiscated marquisate; they had influence at Venice; they had not all been disloyal to the mother country; and, accordingly, in 1393, a portion of the island was restored to them. Henceforth, eleven out of the twenty-four shares were held by Venice, and the remaining by the

[1] Sanudo, *Istoria del Regno*, *apud* Hopf, *Chroniques*, 127; *Fontes Rerum Austricarum*, xiv., 181; Hopf, *apud* Ersch und Gruber, lxxxv., 310; Sansovino, *Cronologia del Mondo*, 185; *Arch. Veneto*, xx., 92.

[2] Sáthas, vi., 302-3; Stai, *Raccolta di antiche autorità*, 45.

Venieri—an arrangement which we find in force two centuries later—but the republic continued to appoint the governor. In fact, the system adopted resembled the administration of Tenos in the sixteenth century. The Venieri were never disturbed again in the possession of their thirteen shares; down to the fall of the republic in 1797 they remained "partners," or *compartecipi*, of Venice; and their name is still borne by humble inhabitants of Cerigo.[1]

The organisation of this distant colony by the republic resembled that of Corfù. In 1502 the governor received the higher rank of *provveditore*, the first of whom was specially sent out to strengthen the fortifications of the castle, above whose gate may still be read the date of 1503, when the old fortress was enlarged.[2] This official, who exercised judicial, executive, and military powers, was dependent on the Government of Crete, so long as that great island remained Venetian; during the brief Venetian occupation of the Morea in the eighteenth century, he took his orders from there; and, finally, after the peace of Passarovitz, he became the subordinate of the *provveditore generale del Levante* at Corfù. Appeals lay from him to those officials, and from them to the Home Government. In 1573, on the petition of the principal inhabitants, a Council of thirty was established, whose members formed a close oligarchy, and a "Golden Book" was started, in which the names of the nobles and their sons were registered. This body, which existed down to 1797, had the exclusive right of electing the local authorities from its own ranks, including two councillors, who acted as assessors of the governor, and three judges of petty sessions, who had jurisdiction in small cases. The Council also had the privilege of electing envoys, or *sindaci*, who were commissioned to lay any complaints which the islanders had against the Venetian governor or his subordinates before the authorities at Venice. But the local historian informs us that Venice always upheld her own officials.[3] To her the island, from its geographical position, was of much importance after she lost her last stations in the Morea. Cerigo

[1] Sáthas, vi., 303-5; Chilas, 347, 350; *Relazioni degli Ambasciatori Veneti*, Ser. III., iii., 13; Stai, *Raccolta*, 46.
[2] Sáthas, vi., 306; Stai, 48.
[3] Stai, 50-1.

was then her only port of call between Zante and Crete; it was also an excellent post of observation where news could be easily obtained from the Morea and ships sighted at a huge distance. From March to October, the dangerous months, a guard was always mounted on Cape St George, beacon-fires were lighted at night, and the Cretan Government was kept advised of the approach of a Turkish fleet; in short, Cerigo was "an eye of Crete"; but, after the loss of that island, it too lost its importance, and after the peace of Passarovitz it was practically useless.[1]

To the inhabitants, however, the situation of the island was a doubtful advantage, for it exposed them to the attacks of corsairs and Turks. True, it was defended by three castles, in which Venice kept a small garrison, paid by the Cretan Government. But, in 1537, it suffered terribly from Barbarossa's raid. From the castle of San Dimitri, at that time the chief place of the island, 7000 souls were carried off without the least resistance, and the other towns were sacked and destroyed. This raid made a profound impression on the islanders, and "Barbarossa's sack of Palaiochora" was long spoken of as the blackest day in the annals of Cerigo. The survivors either fled to the thickets, or else escaped to the Morea, whence it was difficult to entice them back. Hence the land went out of cultivation; the population sank in 1545 to 1850, and the Venetian part of the island yielded less than a quarter of the corn which it produced before the war. Such was the distress that, in 1562, all the inhabitants desired to emigrate into Turkish territory. Their misery was, indeed, due to domestic tyranny, as well as to foreign invasion. The Venieri let their portion of Cerigo to local personages, who farmed the taxes, and their share of the island came to be called the *Commessaria* from being managed by these *commessi*, or agents, who ground down the peasants with every kind of exaction. It was impossible to induce their victims to bring their woes before the Venetian governor, because as the peasants shrewdly remarked, "our rectors come and go, while our tyrants live permanently here." In vain, both Venice and the Venieri tried to lure the peasants back by

[1] Sáthas, vi., 286, 289, 290; Lamansky, 660 *et sqq.*

exemptions for five years from the *terzarie*, or third of the produce, which was the chief revenue of the island. A Venetian governor declared that he had never heard of a single fugitive who had returned. Hence the Venetian commissioner who visited Cerigo in 1563 reported that all the revenues of the republic's portion, amounting to an average of 500 ducats, were eaten up by the officials' salaries and the costs of the swift vessels which carried news to Crete.[1]

The Venieri and the Venetians treated the Greek Church with leniency. The famous golden bull of Andrónikos II., issued in 1293 during the brief sway of the Greeks over the island, mentions the bishopric of Kythera as already existing, and names its bishop as first among the suffragans of the metropolitan of Monemvasia. We hear, indeed, of a *πρωτοπαπᾶς* instead of a bishop in the second half of the fourteenth century; but later on the chief ecclesiastic of the island had the episcopal title, and enjoyed the exclusive right of ordaining the Cretan priests. The best known of the series, Maximus Margoúnios, who was appointed towards the close of the sixteenth century, won fame as a Greek scholar, a theologian, a letter writer, and a lyric poet. It is only in our own time that the exigencies of local politics threatened for a moment this ancient see.[2] And down to our own day the Kytherians, whether at home or at Athens, celebrate every 7th October (n.s.) the festival of their patron saint, Our Lady of the myrtle bough, whose image borne by the waves to the island and found in a myrtle tree represents the Christian version of Aphrodite rising from the sea.

The peace of 1540, which restricted the possessions of Venice in the Levant to Crete and Cyprus—the latter soon to go—the solitary outpost of Tenos in the Ægean, and six out of the seven Ionian islands with their dependencies of Parga[3] and Butrinto on the mainland, greatly increased the

[1] Sáthas, v., 53-62; vi., 287, 288, 292, 306, 307; Stai, 54; Cornaro, MS. "Historia di Candia," II., fol. 92; Lamansky, *loc. cit.*

[2] Stai, 49-50; Chilas, 348; Lami, *Deliciæ Eruditorum*, ii., 292-318; ix., 1-61; Horatio F. Brown, *The Venetian Printing Press*, 135; Sáthas, v., 66-75; Δελτίον τῆς Χριστ. 'Αρχ. 'Ετ., vi., 115.

[3] Predelli, *Commemoriali*, vi., 236.

importance of this last group to the republic. We saw how the *stradioti* from her lost colonies in the Morea found a home in Corfù; and, were we to continue the story of the Ionians under Venetian rule, we should find that they came at last to represent all that was left of her once splendid colonial empire in Greece. But the history of the Ionian islands down to the fall of the republic in 1797 is beyond the scope of the present work.

CHAPTER XVII

THE DUCHY OF THE ARCHIPELAGO (1207-1463)

TO complete the history of Frankish Greece it only remains to describe the most romantic and also the most durable of all the creations of the Fourth Crusade—the island duchy of the Archipelago. Italian rule over the classic home of lyric poetry which the noble verses of Byron have immortalised, established by the swords of a handful of aristocratic freebooters, not only survived by more than a century the Latin states of the mainland, but continued to exist in isolated fragments down to the seventeenth and even to the eighteenth century.

We saw in the second chapter how, in 1207, the Venetian Marco Sanudo and his comrades made themselves masters of the isles of Greece, and how the bold adventurer fixed his residence at Naxos. The Byzantine capital had been in the south, where the ruins of the castle of Apaliri still mark the site. The conqueror founded the present city. There, on the hill above the sea, where the arches and tortuous lanes of the upper town still recall the picturesque rock-villages of the Italian Riviera, he built a strong castle, flanked with twelve large towers, and a great square donjon in the middle, a fragment of which stands to-day, a monument, like the tower at Paros, of Italian rule in the Archipelago. There, too, he erected a Catholic cathedral, on which, in spite of its restoration in the seventeenth century, his arms may still be seen; while below, the remains of a massive mole tell of his efforts to shelter the port which the little island of Palati protects on the other side. It was he, too, according to one authority, who made boat-houses for a small fleet of galleys,[1] so necessary to the lord of an insular realm.

[1] Lichtle, MS. ("Description de Naxie"), however, assigns them to the Knights of Rhodes. *Cf. Byz. Zeit.*, xi., 496-8.

Sanudo, though a Venetian citizen and descended, so flattering genealogists afterwards pretended, from the historian Livy, had no intention of acknowledging the suzerainty of the republic and of becoming a mere republican governor, although the deed of partition had assigned Andros and most of the other Cyclades to the Venetians. He did homage to the Latin Emperor Henry, the over-lord of the Frankish states in the Levant, who invested him with his islands "on a freer tenure than any baron who was then in all the empire of Romania,"[1] and erected them into a duchy, then known by its old Byzantine name of "the Dodekánesos" (or "the Twelve Islands"), but soon called the "duchy of Naxos," or, "of the Archipelago"—the form into which the Latins corrupted the Greek term "Aigaîon Pélagos." Duke Marco I. remained true to his sovereign; one account represents him as being at the emperor's side when he died at Salonika.[2] Towards his mother country, however, he was not so loyal. When, in 1212, the Cretans, under the leadership of the Hagiostephanitai, rose against Venice, Tiepolo, then Duke of Candia, summoned Marco Sanudo to his aid, stimulating his patriotism by the promise of 30 knights' fees in the colony. According to another account, Sanudo had already been promised broad lands in Crete as the reward of his services at the time of the sale of the island to Venice. At any rate, he came with a large body of men, speedily stamped out the rebellion, and claimed his reward. When Tiepolo delayed to carry out his part of the bargain, the Duke of Naxos listened willingly to the treacherous suggestion of a Cretan *archon*, named Skordili, that he should seize the island with the assistance of the Greeks. The idea appealed to his ambition, and his soldiers, discontented at the scarcity of bread in the market, were glad of an excuse for war; the Greeks fraternised with them; the town of Candia was soon theirs; the Venetian duke, disguised as a woman, was let down from the wall, and escaped to the neighbouring castle of Temenos, which the Byzantine conqueror Nikephóros Phokâs had founded 250 years before on the double hill

[1] *Pacta Ferrariæ*, published by Hopf, *Andros* (tr. Sardagna), 167; Zabarella, *Tito Livio Padovano*, 56, 78; Sauger, *Histoire nouvelle*, 13-14.

[2] *Ibid.*, 23, 27-8.

which is so prominent a landmark to the mariner. Marco, leaving his relative Stefano in charge of the town, then set out with his army of Greeks and Italians to conquer the other forts of the island. But his career of conquest was checked by the arrival of Venetian reinforcements at the port of Fair Havens, whereupon Tiepolo sallied forth from his stronghold, occupied and fortified a commanding position at Upper Sivriti, the modern Amari, while Marco was compelled to hide in a cave, waiting for help from his island duchy. Then Tiepolo by a brilliant *coup de main* recovered Candia without bloodshed, and put the commander in chains. Though the castle of Belvedere in the south and all the district from Mylopotamos as far west as cape Spada was still his, Marco saw that further resistance was useless; but he made, as might have been expected from so clever a diplomatist, most favourable terms for himself. On condition that he surrendered the seven castles which he held, he was to receive 2500 *hyperperi*, to take from the land which was still his 3000 bushels of corn and 2000 of oats, while twenty Greek *archons* who had been compromised in the rebellion were allowed to leave the island with all their property. Sanudo promised never to set foot in Crete again, unless the Duke of Candia summoned him to his aid, and in 1213 he returned to Naxos. But the failure of this attempt to make himself "King of Crete" did not in the least damp his ardour. He fitted out eight galleys, descended upon the coast of Asia Minor, and captured Smyrna; but the fleet of Theodore Láskaris, the Emperor of Nice, nearly four times larger than his own, defeated and captured him. He was forced to restore his conquests, but his valour and beauty appealed so strongly to the emperor, that he not only liberated his prisoner, but bestowed upon him the hand of his sister.[1]

Thus allied by marriage with an Orthodox sovereign, the first Duke of Naxos, who, as a Venetian, was not likely to be a bigot, naturally showed a wise spirit of tolerance for

[1] L. de Monacis, 154-5; A. Dandolo and Sanudo *apud* Muratori, xii., 338; xxii., 545; E. Dandolo, *Cronaca Veneta*, fol. 44-5; Cornelius, *Creta Sacra*, ii., 241-9; Tafel und Thomas, ii., 159-66. *Cf.* Gerola, *Monumenti Veneti nell' isola di Creta*, i., 105, 181, 191, 195, 219, 237, 265, 284, 285.

the religion of his Greek subjects. Provided tha
Church was not molested, they had little objection tc
governed by an Italian; so, when they saw that he
intention of banishing their metropolitan—a positio
offered to the exiled Michael Akominátos of Athens
patriarch of Nice[1]—or of taxing their monasteries, h
became popular in the *Borgo* and adjacent "Neochor.
new town, where the Greeks clustered at the foot c
castle hill. Many Catholics, however, doubtless flocked tc
Cyclades to make their fortunes in the delectable duchy w.
he had founded, and a Catholic archbishopric was there
established for their welfare at Naxos, with four suffraga
at Melos, Santorin, Tenos, and Suda, as Syra was called
the Middle Ages, while the bishop of Andros was placed, a
we saw, beneath the see of Athens.[2] Such was the beginning of the Latin Church in the Archipelago, which has proved the most durable of all the Frankish institutions in the Levant; for even to-day Catholics are numerous there and a Catholic archbishop still resides in the town of Naxos. About the year 1227 the creator of the new state closed his successful career, the career of a typical Venetian adventurer, brave, hard-headed, selfish, and unscrupulous; in short, just the sort of man to found a dynasty in an age when a weak empire had been dismembered and in a part of the world where cleverness counts for more than heroic simplicity of character.

His son and successor, Angelo, though the child of a Greek mother, rendered loyal service to the decaying Latin Empire, doing homage successively to Robert, John of Brienne, and Baldwin II., and distinguishing himself—it is said—by his vigour in the defence of Constantinople against the Greeks of Nice and their Bulgarian allies in 1236, when his large contingent of ships did great execution, and he led the vanguard with Geoffrey II. of Achaia.[3] This incident had a profound effect upon the external relations of the duchy; for, as we saw in a previous chapter, it was out of gratitude to the Prince of Achaia that the Emperor

[1] Lámpros, Μιχαὴλ Ακομινάτου, ii., 154-5.

[2] *Les Registres d'Innocent IV.*, iii., 196, 207, 239, 328; *Les Registres de Grégoire IX.*, i., 613; Sauger, 11-13.

[3] *Ibid.*, 40-4.

Baldwin II. conferred upon the latter the suzerainty over the Archipelago. Angelo received from the emperor a leaden bull setting forth this new feudal bond, by which the dukes of Naxos became vassals and peers of the principality of Achaia, and which, though occasionally disputed by Venice, was still in force at the close of the fourteenth century.[1] In virtue of this arrangement, Angelo and the other lords of the Cyclades were summoned by their suzerain, Prince William of Achaia, to assist him at the siege of Monemvasia in 1247, and to aid him in his ill-starred campaign, which ended with the battle of Pelagonia in 1259. Both Angelo and the Grand-Duke of Lemnos were invited by Venice to join in maintaining the crumbling fabric of the Latin Empire in 1260; and, in the following year, when the fugitive Emperor Baldwin II. landed at Negroponte and proceeded to Thebes, the Duchess of Naxos, a French dame of high degree who had been married in his palace at Constantinople in happier days, met him with grand presents. The penniless emperor had nothing substantial to give her in return; but he knighted her son Marco, the future duke, who had studied in the best school of chivalry, the court of William of Achaia, and bestowed upon her husband the empty title of "King."[2] By his assistance to the Latin Empire, Angelo had, however, incurred the wrath of Vatátzes, the Emperor of Nice, who had revenged himself by capturing from him the island of Amorgos and bestowing it upon Geremia Ghisi, chief of a Venetian family related to the Sanudi, which already held all or part of no less than eight islands, and was therefore second to the ducal dynasty alone. Sprung originally from Aquileia, the Ghisi were more loyal to Venice than their independent cousins, and every St Mark's day the offering of a large wax-candle in the great church signified that they remained true sons of the republic.[3] Angelo behaved towards the Venetians much as his father had done. When a fresh rebellion broke out against their rule in Crete in 1229, he obeyed the summons of the Duke of Candia, and

[1] Sanudo *apud* Hopf, *Chroniques*, 124.

[2] *Ibid.*, 100, 102, 115, 172; Χ. τ. Μ., ll. 2891-6; *L. d. C.*, 119, 145; *L. d. F.*, 52, 56, 61.

[3] Ersch und Gruber, lxvi., 336.

built, at his request, the castle of Suda. But when the Cretans implored the aid of Vatátzes, and a Nicene fleet of thirty-three sail arrived off the island, Angelo abandoned the Venetian cause and returned to his duchy, bribed, it was said, by the money of the Greek emperor.[1] He ended his long reign in 1262 "beloved by his people," if we may believe a late panegyrist, and "worthy," according to the same authority, "of the Empire of the East."

Nearly half a century had now elapsed since the foundation of the duchy, and the Latin rule seemed to be well-established. A Venetian document[2] of this period informs us that all the islands possessed fortresses, of which the picturesque ruins of the castle of Andros may be taken as a specimen. Situated on a rock at the mouth of the harbour, and approached by a stone bridge of a single span, which has defied the tremendous storms of seven centuries, and by three steps, it bore over the entrance a statue of Mercury.[3] The statue has disappeared; but the castle of green stone, the work of Marino Dandolo, its first Venetian lord, still remains, though the sea has eaten away its face till it is as jagged as the teeth of a saw, and a vaulted roof inside one of the blocks of masonry may have been the baronial chapel. Sometimes, as in the case of the tower at Paros, the petty lords of the islands built their residences out of the marble fragments of some classical monument, and thus destroyed what had hitherto escaped destruction. But though each island baron needed one or more castles for his own abode or for the protection of his subjects against corsairs, he did not always reside there himself. While the dukes habitually lived in their picturesque duchy, not a few of their vassals, who had property or official posts in Crete, Negroponte, or in some other Venetian colony, preferred the more brilliant and amusing society of those places to the solitary splendour of a grim baronial castle on some rock

[1] L. de Monacis, 156; A. Dandolo *apud* Muratori, xii., 346; Cornelius, *Creta Sacra*, ii., 263; who all ascribe this incident, by an anachronism, to Marco Sanudo.

[2] Hopf, *Chroniques*, 175-6.

[3] Bartolomeo dalli Sonetti, *Periplus*, 21; Hopf, *Andros* (tr. Sardagna), 161.

in the Ægean which the ancient Romans, whose descendants they boasted themselves to be, had regarded as a dismal exile for traitors rather than an agreeable pleasaunce. Thus, Marino Dandolo of Andros, one of the pleasantest and most fertile of the Cyclades, an island of streams and lemon-groves and ferns, usually governed it from his palace in Venice, and the Barozzi of Santorin spent less time in their castle of Skarós than on their Cretan estates. Besides, as time went on, the baronies of the Archipelago became a school for the governors and diplomatists whom the republic of St Mark required in the Levant, and it was thence that she often selected her bailies of Negroponte and her captains of Modon and Coron.

Already, in the mouths of Venetian colonists and sailors, the nomenclature of the Cyclades had been strangely distorted. Delos had become "Sdili"; Syra was "Lasudha"; Patmos is scarcely recognisable under "Sanctus Joannes de Palmasa"; "Serfentò" and "Sifantò" were the corruptions of "Seriphos" and Siphnos"; "Fermene" had taken the place of Thermia, or Kythnos. Already, too, in the above-mentioned Venetian document, the name[1] "Arcipelago" is used for the Ægean —*Egeopelagus*, as it figures in the Latin titles of the later dukes.

The rule of the Latins over the Cyclades received, however, a severe shock during the reign of Marco II., the third duke. The Greek cause was now everywhere in the ascendant, for not only had the Latin Empire fallen, but the Byzantine double-eagle now waved over the south-east of the Morea, whence Tzákones and half-castes flocked to man the navy of Michael VIII., whose admiral, Philanthropenós, was despatched against the Ægean islands. The native population of the Cyclades was naturally excited by these successes of its race, and the island of Melos, the nearest to the great Greek stronghold of Monemvasia and situated on the main route between that place and Constantinople, was specially affected by the national movement. A Greek monk placed himself at the head of the insurgents, who seized the castle and drove out the Latins. But Marco II.

[1] It also occurs in the treaty of 1268; (*Fontes Rerum Austriacarum*, part ii., xiv., 96).

possessed all the vigour of his family. He assembled a fleet of sixteen galleys, and, with the aid of some French adventurers from Constantinople, carried the fortress of Melos in less than a couple of hours, but wisely pardoned the rebels, with the exception of the ringleaders. The monk, however, he thought it necessary to punish, as an example to the others. He therefore had him bound hand and foot, and then thrown into the sea. This combination of clemency and cruelty had the desired effect.[1] But a far more dangerous antagonist now appeared in the Archipelago. We have already described the career of Licario—the Italian of Eubœa, who was driven by the aristocratic pride of the Lombard lords into the service of the Greek emperor, and who inflicted such immense damage upon his own countrymen. We saw how he took Skopelos, an island supposed to be impregnable, from the Ghisi; but this was only one of his exploits in the Archipelago. The rest of the Northern Sporades—Skyros, Skiathos, and Chiliodromia—were now all recovered for the Byzantine Empire; and Lemnos, the fief of the Navigajosi, shared their fate. The island was strongly fortified, and the principal castle was held by Paolo Navigajoso, who still bore the proud title of Grand Duke, or Lord High Admiral, of the fallen Latin Empire, with a garrison of 700 men. So desperate was his resistance, that the Greek emperor offered him 60,000 gold *hyperperi* for his castle—an offer disdainfully refused by that brave and wealthy noble. Even after Paolo's death, the Grand Duchess, a sister of Duke Marco II. of Naxos, still held out; till, when the siege had lasted three years, she departed with all the corn in the granaries, the lead off the palace roof, and the clothing and money in the castle. Thenceforth Lemnos, like the Northern Sporades, remained in Greek hands till the fall of Constantinople. Ten other islands were at the same time lost for twenty years or more, and their Latin lords were expelled. The Ghisi were driven from Amorgos, Seriphos, and Keos; the Barozzi fled from Santorin; the Duke of Naxos was deprived of Ios, Siphnos, Sikinos, and Polykandros; the Quirini, who vaunted that they were of even nobler origin than the Sanudi, belonging to the

[1] Sauger, 78-80.

same family as the Roman Emperor Galba, were ousted from Astypalaia; and the terrible corsair Giovanni de lo Cavo freed his native island of Anaphe from the Foscoli. Two dynasties alone—the Sanudi and their vassals the Ghisi, remained in the whole Archipelago; and both were thankful to be included by the Venetians in the treaties of peace which the republic concluded with the Byzantine Empire in 1277 and 1285, on condition that they harboured no corsairs. In her earlier treaty of 1265 the republic had abandoned "all the islands which had been under the suzerainty of the Latin Empire or of the principality of Achaia" to the tender mercies of Michael VIII.; she now attached more importance to their preservation, and did not forget that their rulers were of Venetian origin and might further Venetian aims against her great commercial rivals, the Genoese. The latter had obtained from the Greek emperor by the treaty of Nymphaion[1] in 1261 the right to establish commercial factories at Lesbos and Chios—the commencement of the famous connection between Genoa and the rich mastic island.[2]

The growing desire of Venice to acquire direct authority over the duchy was now shown by her attempt to claim the suzerainty over it—a claim repudiated strongly and successfully by Duke Marco II. An excuse for the Venetian pretensions was afforded by the affairs of Andros. On the death of Marino Dandolo, the first baron of that island, without direct heirs, Duke Angelo, in strict accordance with the feudal code of Romania, had left half of the barony to the widow and had invested Geremia Ghisi with the other half. But Ghisi was a powerful man without scruples—in fact, the greatest filibuster in all the Archipelago; he made himself master of the whole island, and hoisted his pennant over the castle. The widow, in her despair, sought the aid of the gallant Jacopo Quirini of Astypalaia, an influential Venetian in whom she found both a second husband and a warm advocate. Quirini appealed to Venice, which peremptorily ordered Ghisi to surrender the island to a plenipotentiary of

[1] Sanudo and Magno, *apud* Hopf, *Chroniques*, 123-5, 127, 132, 181-2; N. Gregorâs, i., 98; Pachyméres, i., 204-5, 209; *Fontes Rerum Austriacarum*, part ii., xiv., 68-9, 80, 138, 326, 344; Zabarella, *Il Galba*.

[2] Hopf, *Les Giustiniani*, 5, 6.

the republic. But Ghisi, too, had friends at court; for his daughter was married to a son of the doge; so matters were delayed in the usual dilatory style of Italian justice, till at last both Ghisi and the Lady of Andros were both dead. Upon this, Marco II., who was now Duke of Naxos, assumed possession of the whole island, as no claimant had made his appearance. Two days, however, before the period of two years and two days allowed by the feudal code had expired, there landed at Naxos Niccolò Quirini, son of the Lady of Andros by her second marriage, and demanded his mother's share. The duke might have imitated Geoffrey I. of Achaia, and have dodged the claimant among the bays of his islands for a couple of days, till the full term was expired. But he was sufficiently conscientious not to avail himself of this quibble, and expressed his readiness to abide by the decision of the feudal court of Achaia, of which state he was the vassal. This did not satisfy the claimant, who, like his father, appealed to Venice, hoping that she would support the cause of one who had been her representative in the Holy Land. After a further long delay, Marco II. was at last cited in 1282 to appear before the doge. To this summons the duke replied in a very able state paper, in which he pointed out by irrefragable historical evidence that Venice was not his suzerain, and had therefore no jurisdiction over him. It was true that the deed of partition, upon which the Venetians based their claim, had assigned Andros to the republic. But his grandfather had conquered it and the rest of the duchy at his own cost; he had been invested with his island domain by the Emperor Henry, and that sovereign's successor, Baldwin II., had transferred the suzerainty over the duchy to the Prince of Achaia. In 1267, by the treaty of Viterbo, Baldwin II. had ceded the suzerainty over that principality and all its dependencies, of which the duchy was one, to Charles of Anjou, and had expressly bestowed upon that monarch "all the islands belonging to the Latin Empire," except four outside the limits of the Cyclades. Accordingly, on the death of Prince William of Achaia in 1278, Marco II. had done homage to King Charles, who was his legal suzerain, and had commanded three galleys in the fleet which that sovereign despatched to attack the Greek

Empire. It was, therefore, to the feudal court of the latter, and not to Venice, that an appeal from the ducal court should be referred. At the same time, he gave Venice a significant hint not to cross the path of so mighty a sovereign as the King of Naples, then at the height of his power. The republic thereupon dropped the matter; Marco was wise enough to pacify Quirini, who enjoyed great influence at Venice—it was he who built the still existing Palazzo Quirini-Stampalia in that city—by a money payment; no more was heard of a case which had lasted over half a century; the Sanudi retained possession of Andros as long as their dynasty existed, and they added its name to the ducal title, styling themselves "Lords of the duchy of Naxos and Andros," and residing at times in Marino Dandolo's wave-beat castle.[1]

The campaign of Licario in the Archipelago had another effect, more disastrous even than the loss of the islands. Piracy has in all ages been the curse of the Ægean, and at this time the corsairs of every nation infested that beautiful sea. Skopelos and Keos, the volcanic bay of Santorin, and the fine harbour of Ios, were favourite lairs of the pirates; they infested the terrible Doro channel between Andros and Eubœa, and robbed one of the island barons in the haven of Melos. The Greek governors, who were appointed to administer the conquered islands, connived at the doings of the corsairs, who might even fly the imperial flag and style themselves "Lord High Admiral," like Giovanni de lo Cavo of Anaphe, while the reduction of the imperial navy by Andrónikos II. converted swarms of half-breed sailors into pirates. The exploits of these men have already been described, and the terrible devastation which they wrought on the smaller and more defenceless islands may easily be imagined. Sometimes the more remote consequences of their raids were worse than the raids themselves. Thus, in 1286, on one of these expeditions, some corsairs carried off a valuable ass belonging to one of the Ghisi, and sold it to Duke Marco II.'s son William, who was baron of Syra. The

[1] Hopf, *Andros* (tr. Sardagna), 36-52, 161-70; *Veneto-Byzantinische Analekten*, 462-4; Ducange, *Histoire de l'Empire*, i., 455-63; Buchon, *Recherches et Matériaux*, i., 32, 33; Sanudo, 130.

purchaser was under no illusions as to the ownership of the ass, for it was marked with its master's initials, but was perfectly aware that he was buying stolen goods. Seeing this, Ghisi invaded Syra, and laid siege to the castle. But the fate of the ass had aroused wide sympathies, and was agitating all the small world of the Archipelago. Just at this moment it chanced that the admiral of Charles II. of Naples, who was now the suzerain of the Sanudi, had put into Melos for provisions. Feudal law compelled him to assist the son of his master's vassal; the prayers of the fair *châtelaine* of Melos, Donna Cassandra Sanudo, conquered any hesitation that he might have felt; so he set sail for Syra, and with the aid of the ducal troops, forced Ghisi to raise the siege. The great ass case was then submitted to the decision of the Venetian bailie in Eubœa, who reconciled the two great families of the Archipelago and restored the peace of the duchy, but only after "more than 30,000 heavy *soldi*" had been expended for the sake of the animal, which had probably died in the interval.[1]

A fresh disaster fell upon the Archipelago in 1292, when the Aragonese admiral, Roger de Lluria, arrived on his punitive expedition against the Greek Empire. Latin or Greek was all the same to this licensed freebooter, when plunder was to be had. Andros, Tenos, Mykonos, and Thermia were all ravaged by his sailors, who thus gave Greece a foretaste of Catalan cruelty.[2] Yet, if we may credit a later historian, even at this very period, Naxos was a flourishing island. We are told that the fertile plain of Drymalia then "contained twelve large villages, a number of country houses, and more than 10,000 inhabitants"—a total doubtless partly due to the immigration of the population of Amorgos half a century earlier. Yet towards his orthodox subjects Marco II. was by no means so conciliatory as his two predecessors. There was in the island an altar dedicated to a portly man of God, St Pachys, or "the fat," who was believed by the superstitious Naxiotes to possess the power of making their children stout, and consequently comely, according to Levantine ideas. Fond mothers accordingly flocked to his altar with their skinny offspring, and pushed

[1] Sanudo *apud* Hopf, *Chroniques*, 113-14. [2] Muntaner, ch. cxvii.

their children's bodies several times through a perforated stone still preserved as a curiosity in the seventeenth century, and similar to those which have been found in Cyprus and Ireland. If Marco II. had been a wise statesman, he would have allowed the Naxiote matrons to offer up prayers to the "fat" saint as long as they pleased. But he was either too bigoted, or too sceptical, to tolerate this harmless exercise, which savoured of paganism and had doubtless originated in classical times. He smashed the altar, and thereby so greatly excited the Greeks, that he had to build a fortress to keep them in order. The double walls and the round tower of this stronghold, Castel d'Alto, or Apanokastro, as it was called, still stand on a mountain commanding the plain of Drymalia—a warning to those who would interfere with the beliefs of the people.[1]

Towards the end of his long reign, Marco II. had the satisfaction of seeing the recovery of several of the lost islands. During the seven years war between Venice and Andrónikos II., supported by the Genoese, which began in 1296, the republic of St Mark repeated the tactics of ninety years earlier, and let loose a new swarm of privateers upon the Archipelago. The bailie of Negroponte was ordered to fit out vessels to prey upon the Greeks, and as that official happened to be one of the Barozzi, the dethroned barons of Santorin, he naturally carried out his orders with the utmost zeal. Other dispossessed island lords joined in this filibustering expedition, the Ghisi, the Michieli, and the Giustiniani, while a new and *bourgeois* family from Venice, the Schiavi, recaptured the island of Ios for the Duke of Naxos and received it as a fief from his hands. The patrician exiles were equally successful; the Barozzi recovered Santorin and Therasia, the Ghisi and their fellows Amorgos, Keos, and Seriphos, and these five islands were specially confirmed to the conquerors in the treaty which Venice concluded with the Greek emperor in 1303. But the feudal relations of these barons no longer remained on the old footing. It was under Venetian auspices and by Venetian diplomacy that they had regained and retained their lost islands, and it was thence-

[1] Sauger, 65-8; Buchon, *Les Cyclades* in *Revue de Paris* for 1843, vol. xvi., 350; xvii., 269.

forth Venice, and not the Duke of Naxos, whom they regarded as their suzerain. Such an attitude of independence naturally provoked ill-feeling and led to disputes between him and them, and thus destroyed the unity of the Latin duchy. Moreover, the long war, successful though it had been, had added yet another scourge to the Archipelago, and all the islanders were not so fortunate as those of Keos, who received compensation from the Genoese republic for the damage inflicted by its subjects upon that most convenient maritime station, where galleys could obtain provisions on their way to the East.[1] But the Catalans were less scrupulous than the Genoese; their leader, Roger de Flor, ravaged Keos in 1303, carried off many of the islanders, and inflicted damage, against which remonstrances were idle.[2]

Marco II. seems to have died in that year, and was buried in the church of St Catherine in the plain outside the town of Naxos, which served as the ducal chapel, and in which his tomb was afterwards found, marked by an inscription and the arms of his family.[3] William I., his eldest son, the hero of the famous War of the Ass, followed him as fourth duke, and endeavoured to compel the reinstated barons of the other islands to return to their old allegiance to the duchy. As might be inferred from his former exploit, he was not likely to be hampered by scruples. Accordingly, when Jacopo Barozzi, lord of Santorin, was traversing the Archipelago, he had him seized by corsairs and flung him into the dungeons of Naxos. This was, however, more than Venice could stand, for the kidnapped baron had been her bailie at Negroponte and her governor in Crete. An ultimatum was, therefore, sent to the duke, bidding him send his captive to Negroponte within a week, under pain of being treated as an outlaw. This message had the desired effect; the duke let his prisoner go, and men saw that the name of Venice

[1] Hopf, *Veneto-Byz. Analekten*, 502; Navagero *apud* Muratori, xxiii., 1009, 1011; Thomas, *Diplomatarium*, i., 15, 18; Sanudo, in *op. cit.*, 131; Predelli, *Commemoriali*, i., 36, where the Michieli and Giustiniani write in 1303, that *essi avevano riconosciuto la sovranità feudale di Venezia sopra quei luoghi*. George I. Ghisi even issued coins.

[2] Thomas, *Diplomatarium*, i., 138, 149.

[3] Buchon in *Revue de Paris*, xvi., 348; William I. is first mentioned in a document of 1303, alluded to below.

was more powerful than that of Sanudo in the Ægean. But William was not easily baffled. He despatched his faithful vassal and admiral, Domenico Schiavo of Ios, against the Ghisi's island of Amorgos in an unguarded moment and reunited it with his duchy.[1] Thanks, too, to the feeble policy of Andrónikos II., the Greeks continued to lose the ground which they had acquired under the energetic rule of his predecessor. In 1307 a whole batch of islands was recovered by the Latins. John, or Januli I. da Corogna, whose name indicates that his family had come originally from Coruña, and who belonged to the Knights of St John, seized Siphnos, threw off his allegiance to his Order, and declared himself a free and independent sovereign, in spite of the protests of the Sanudi, who still considered the island theirs. At the same time, his namesake, Januli Gozzadini, a member of that ancient and only just extinct family of Bologna, a branch of which had been settled in Greece for the past half century, recaptured the distant island of Anaphe, or Namfio, of which he became the petty sovereign. Thus, exactly a century after the Latin Conquest, two new Latin families, one Spanish, one Italian, established themselves in the Archipelago. The Gozzadini still ruled there in the seventeenth century, while the ruined "chancery" of the castle of Siphnos still bears a Latin inscription of Januli II. da Corogna, dated 1374, and the family still flourishes in Santorin.[2] Finally, in 1310, the Quirini, aided by another Venetian family, the Grimani, recovered their lost island of Stampalia, for which they did homage to Venice and which was too remote from Naxos to be molested by the jealous duke.[3] Thus, Greek rule had once more been eliminated from the islands, but the place of the Byzantine governors had been taken by Venetian vassals or independent lords.

Outside the frontiers of the duchy the Latin cause in the Levant was at this time strengthened by two important

[1] Hopf, *Veneto-Byzantinische Analekten*, 388, 454.

[2] *Ibid.*, 466, and *apud* Ersch und Gruber, lxviii., 306, 307 ; lxxvi., 415, 416 ; Buchon, *Recherches historiques*, ii., 475-6 ; Tournefort, *Voyage du Levant*, i., 68. He, Ross (*Reisen*, i., 1, 43), and Hopf misread the date, which Mr Wace has copied for me on the spot.

[3] Piacenza, *L'Egeo Redivivo*, 241 ; Zabarella, *Il Galba*, 82.

conquests. In 1304, Benedetto Zaccaria, the rich Genoese who already owned the valuable alum mines of Phokaia and had married a sister of the late Emperor Michael VIII., occupied the island of Chios, nominally as a vassal of the Greek Empire, really as an independent prince. Five years later, the Knights of St John, in quest of a new home, now that they had been driven from the Holy Land, conquered Rhodes from the Turkish corsairs, who had made themselves its masters. We are specially told by the elder Sanudo that the Duke of Naxos sent his dashing son Nicholas with a fleet of galleys to assist them in this conquest. It was perhaps at the duke's suggestion that they occupied the classic island of Delos, where the Emperor Cantacuzene describes them as settled twenty years later, and where the remains of their castle have been traced by some archæologists on the top of Mount Kynthos, by others on Rheneia.[1] The duke was naturally pleased to see the warrior Knights established at Rhodes, and the Zaccaria at Chios, for they were likely to defend the Archipelago against the Turkish pirates from the coast of Asia Minor, who had now begun to make their appearance. In 1318 we find them ravaging the rich island of Santorin, and already some of the Cyclades had been almost depopulated by their raids.[2] Yet Marin Sanudo wrote in 1321 that Melos could provide mill-stones and the other Cyclades plenty of large and small cattle, as well as wood and straw for his projected crusade.[3]

Both William Sanudo and his eldest son Nicholas were adventurous men, leading figures in the critical period which saw the establishment of the Catalans in the duchy of Athens. William was one of those invited to the grand tournament on the isthmus of Corinth in 1305; and, as we saw in a former chapter, his heir, who was married to the half-sister of Walter of Brienne, commanded a Naxian contingent at the great battle of the Kephissós, where he received two wounds in the face and hand, and was among

[1] Cantacuzene, i., 380, 476-78, 485; *Journal of Hellenic Studies*, i., 38; *Revue de Paris*, xvi., 339.

[2] Hopf, *Les Giustiniani*, 14; Sanudo, *Ep.*, vii., *apud* Kunstmann, 810; Pachyméres, ii., 344; Thomas, *Diplomatarium*, i., 107, 108, 110.

[3] *Secreta Fidelium Crucis*, 67.

the few Latin nobles who were taken alive, while another magnate of the Archipelago, George Ghisi of Tenos, was among the slain. Undeterred by this experience of Catalan warfare, he went to the aid of his father's suzerain, Princess Matilda of Achaia, in 1316, when that principality was invaded by the Infant of Majorca, and at the battle in Elis he was again taken prisoner. In revenge for these two acts of hostility against the Company, Alfonso Fadrique overran the island of Melos, and carried off about 700 captives; and, when the Venetians remonstrated with King Frederick II. of Sicily at this invasion, the latter replied with perfect correctness, that in feudal law the Duke of the Archipelago held his islands as a fief of the Princess of Achaia, so that "the republic had no jurisdiction" in any of them. Duke Nicholas, who succeeded his father in 1323, continued scrupulously faithful to this feudal tie, and we find him assisting John of Gravina, his suzerain, in his campaign against the Greeks of the Morea. Together they attempted in vain to capture the strong castle of Karytaina, and when the Prince of Achaia returned to Italy, the warlike Duke of the Archipelago was left behind as commander-in-chief of all his forces. In that capacity he routed the Greeks with great loss in the plain of Elis below the castle of St Omer, not far from the place where he had once been taken prisoner.[1] Old Marin Sanudo was horrified at these proceedings; he pleaded his kinsman's youth as an excuse for what he had done, and promised to persuade him to be a good servant of the Greek emperor, as his father had been before him, and at the same time to give him some good advice for the preservation of his duchy.

So restless a personality could not be expected to acquiesce in the continued independence of the former vassals of the duchy. Like his father, but with more success, Nicholas attacked the Barozzi of Santorin and Therasia, in spite of their appeals to Venice and their high-sounding title of "Lord High Admiral" of the paper Empire of Romania, extracted a reluctant pledge of homage, and in 1335 wrested their two valuable islands from them and

[1] *L. d. C.*, 271, 465; X. *τ*. M., ll. 8032-5; *C. d. M.*, 461; *L. d. F.*, 88, 99, 120, 144-6; Predelli, *Commemoriali*, i., 111-12.

united them with his own possessions. The Barozzi never regained the barony of their forefathers, which remained united with the duchy for over a century; they retired to Crete, and thence emigrated, after the Turkish conquest of that island, to Naxos, where the author has seen their tombs and where they were still extant at the close of the eighteenth century. The Sanudi did not neglect their new acquisition; they encouraged cotton-planting on the volcanic soil of Santorin, they strengthened the fortifications; and, for the greater security of the island, Nicholas, in 1336, conferred the fortress of "La Ponta," or Akrotiri, as it is now called, upon the Gozzadini, who had recently established themselves with his consent in the island of Kythnos, or Thermia, which formed a portion of the duchy. So strong was this castle, as its ruins still testify, that it remained in the hands of the Gozzadini long after the Turkish Conquest. It was not till 1617 that it at last succumbed to the crescent.[1] As the plebeian Schiavi, of Ios, had been induced to resign it to their lord, the duchy was now more important than it had been since the early days of Marco II., and for the first time had a currency of its own. The duke now had in his immediate possession the richest and largest islands—Naxos, Andros, (where he sometimes resided), Paros and Antiparos, Melos and Kimolos, Santorin, Syra, and Ios, while the Gozzadini of Thermia and the Schiavi and Grimani, upon whom the late duke had bestowed the island of Amorgos (the latter a Venetian family engaged in the alum trade), were his vassals. His hereditary rivals, the Ghisi, however, still held Tenos and Mykonos under Venetian suzerainty; the Quirini and Grimani looked to the republic to protect their island of Stampalia; newcomers, like the Premarini[2] of Keos and the Bragadini of Seriphos, were Venetian by race, and as much bound to their old home as the Giustiniani and Michieli, who divided those islands with them; the Knights of Rhodes had

[1] Hopf, *Analekten*, 391-8, 505, 515-16. The Gozzadini had taken Thermia from the Castelli (a family from Treviso, connected with, and attracted to Greece by, the Catalans of Attica), on whom Nicholas Sanudo had conferred it about thirteen years earlier. Like the Schiavi, they were one of the two or three middle-class families which became barons in the Cyclades, and their sway was even shorter.

[2] *Ibid.*, 443. A coin of one other Duke, John I., is in the Museo Correr.

a garrison at Delos; while at Anaphe the Gozzadini, and at Siphnos the Da Corogna, asserted their independence, alike of Venice and of the duke.

At such a critical period, when the Turks were rapidly advancing, it was most important that the minor luminaries of the Archipelago should rally round the duke. The historian, Sanudo the elder, considered that his ambitious relative ought to sink his ancient feud with the Ghisi and unite with them in keeping up one galley, while the Genoese barons of Chios should maintain another, against the common foe of Christendom. "The Turks," he wrote in 1326, "specially infest these islands, which are appurtenances of the principality of the Morea" (that is to say, the duchy of Naxos); "and if help be not forthcoming, they will be lost. Indeed, if it were not for the Zaccaria of Chios, and Nicholas Sanudo of Naxos, and the Holy House of the Hospital, who have hitherto defended and still defend them, those islands could not exist. Nor do I believe," concludes the pious Venetian, "that they will continue to exist, without the help of God and the pope."[1] Two years earlier the Turks had ravaged Naxos during the absence of the duke in Achaia; two years later the Venetian bailie of Negroponte wrote that the whole Archipelago threatened to fall into the hands of these corsairs, who had dragged away from the islands some 15,000 men in a series of raids; on one of these terrible visitations, no less than 380 Turkish vessels with 40,000 hands on board plied their deadly trade in the fair Ægean, and carried off more than 10,000 souls. But even these severe lessons failed to make any permanent impression on the jealous Latins of the Levant. At one moment we find Nicholas Sanudo joining Ghisi and the Knights of Rhodes in a league against the Turks; at another we hear that he has attacked Mykonos in his colleague's absence, and carried off his wife. He even sends six vessels and 100 horsemen to assist the Greek Emperor Andrónikos III. in capturing Chios from the bold Genoese, Martino Zaccaria, titular "King of Asia Minor," in the heraldry of the phantom Latin Empire, who had killed

[1] Sanudo, *Secreta Fidelium Crucis*, 2, 30, 294, 300, 302; Villani *apud* Muratori, xiii., 723; *Arch. Veneto*, xx., 86-9.

or captured no fewer than 10,000 Turks in his fifteen years' tenure of that island, and he showed his friendship to the emperor by appearing in person to pay his respects, and to offer him gifts. His relative, Marin, explains that he had been compelled to act thus by the apathy of those from whom he had a right to expect aid in recovering and preserving his dominions—an excuse usually made for unnatural alliances in the Near East to-day. Yet the duke was quite ready to join the Knights of Rhodes and Cattaneo, the lord Phokaia, in attacking the Greek island of Lesbos when opportunity offered. On this occasion, however, Nicholas was well served by Cattaneo, who prevented his allies from plundering and dividing the island between themselves. The result of these animosities among the Christians was seen in 1341, the last year of the duke's reign, when Omarbeg of Aidin, the same satrap who was pleased to style himself "Prince of Achaia," or Morbassan, ravaged the islands of the Archipelago with a large fleet, and forced them for the first time to pay an annual tribute.[1]

Nicholas's brother and successor, John I., took an active part in all the stirring events of a period which saw the Turks cross over into Europe and the Genoese establish themselves in the Ægean. He contributed a galley to the allied fleet, which, under the auspices of Pope Clement VI., attacked and took Smyrna in 1343. In the following year, a body of Turks, led by a Genoese pirate, occupied the lower town of Naxos, plundered the island, and carried off 6000 of his subjects into slavery. Two years later, the "Black Death" traversed the Archipelago in its course across Europe, and animals as well as human beings perished in its embrace. His fidelity to Venice, which had assisted him with arms against the Turks, involved him in the great war between the Venetian and Genoese republics, of which the Levant was the theatre in the middle of the fourteenth century. So zealous was he to aid his old home, that he at once joined his flotilla to the Venetian fleet, and was about to proceed in person to Venice to offer his aid, when the Genoese squadron of fifteen galleys appeared off his capital. The town of

[1] N. Gregorâs, i., 438, 523-7, 597; Cantacuzene, i., 385; *Secreta Fidelium Crucis*, 315; Buondelmonti, *Liber Insularum*, ch. xviii.

Naxos surrendered, and, in 1354, the duke was taken away as a captive to Genoa. Keos was ravaged; Melos and other islands fell a prey to the Genoese; but at the peace of 1355 the duke was released, and they were restored to him.[1] The critical circumstances of the time taught him the wisdom of securing unity in his island domain; he, therefore, pacified the Ghisi by conferring upon them the island of Amorgos, which his father had taken from them, as a fief of his duchy, and bought off any claims of the Barozzi to Santorin by a money payment. The Ghisi did not, however, long retain the island of fair women; the baron of Amorgos was so rash as to take part in the great insurrection of the Venetian colonists of Crete against the mother country in 1363; he atoned for this act of treason on the scaffold, and Venice took possession of his island. But the Cyclades were no longer desirable acquisitions, for there was a complete dearth of labour to cultivate the land. We are told at this time that the serfs had fled from Anaphe, Amorgos, and Stampalia to Crete, because they did not think it worth while to sow, in order that Turks and Catalans might reap. The one exception to this general state of desolation was the island of Seriphos, a rugged rock, possessed, however, of mineral wealth, which is still exploited. A large share of this island had passed to Ermolao Minotto, a Venetian noble, who worked the iron mines and made it one of the richest spots in the Archipelago. The serfs had saved enough money to purchase their enfranchisement, and the importance of the place may be judged from the fact that Gregory XI. included Minotto among the dignitaries whom he summoned to the congress at Thebes in 1373.[2]

John I. of Naxos died[3] in 1361, leaving an only daughter, Fiorenza, an extremely eligible young widow, for she was not only Duchess of the Archipelago, but had been married to one of the great Dalle Carceri clan, who owned two of the three big baronies of Eubœa, and by whom she had

[1] Lichtle, *Histoire de Naxie;* N. Gregorâs, ii., 797; L. de Monacis, 222; Romanin, *Storia documentata di Venezia*, iii., 194.

[2] Ersch und Gruber, lxvi., 338, 343; Hopf, *Analekten*, 438.

[3] Predelli, *Commemoriali*, II., 327, whence Count Mas Latrie (*Les Ducs de l'Archipel*, 8) infers that he was already dead.

had one son, still a mere child. It was the first time that this romantic duchy had been governed by a woman, and needless to say, there was no lack of competitors for the hand of the fair Fiorenza. Over her second marriage there now raged a diplomatic battle, which was waged by Venice with all the unscrupulousness shown by that astute republic whenever its supremacy was at stake. The first of this mediæval Penelope's suitors was a Genoese, the most important of the merchant adventurers, or *maonesi*, who held the rich island of Chios much as modern chartered companies have held parts of Africa under the suzerainty of the Home Government. Venice had viewed with alarm the recent establishment of Genoese influence at Chios and Lesbos, and she was resolved that no Genoese citizen should be installed at Naxos and in Eubœa as Fiorenza's consort. The lady was therefore solemnly warned not to bestow her hand upon an enemy of the republic, when so many eligible husbands could be found at Venice or in the Venetian colonies of Crete and Eubœa. At the same time, the bailie of Negroponte was instructed to hinder the Genoese marriage by fair means or foul. The beauteous Fiorenza's mother meekly replied that her daughter had never dreamt of marrying anyone unacceptable to the most serene republic; but soon afterwards the young widow showed a desire to accept the suit of Nerio Acciajuoli, the future Duke of Athens, whose family had long had her in view as a desirable match for one of its members. This alliance the republic vetoed with the same emphasis as the former; but the Acciajuoli had much influence at the Neapolitan court, and Nerio was therefore able to obtain the consent of Robert of Taranto, who, as Prince of Achaia, was suzerain of the duchy. To his letter requesting Venice not to interfere with the matrimonial arrangements of his vassal, the Venetians replied that Fiorenza was also a daughter of the republic, that her ancestors had won the duchy under its auspices, had been protected by its fleets, and owed the continued existence of their dominions to its diplomacy. Simultaneous orders were sent to the commander of the Venetian fleet in Greek waters to oppose, by force if necessary, the landing of Nerio in the Cyclades.

The Venetian agents in the Levant had, however, no need of further instructions. They knew what was expected of them, and were confident that their action, if successful, would not be disowned. Fiorenza was kidnapped, placed on board a Venetian galley, and quietly conveyed to Crete. There she was treated with every mark of respect, but was at the same time plainly informed that, if she ever wished to see her beloved Naxos again, she must marry her cousin Nicholas Sanudo "Spezzabanda," the candidate of the republic and son of a large proprietor in Eubœa. The daring of this young man, which had gained him his nickname, "the disperser of a host," may have impressed the susceptible duchess no less than the difficulties of her position. At any rate, she consented to marry him; the republic expressed its complete satisfaction, and pledged itself to protect the duchy against all its enemies. "Spezzabanda" showed his gratitude to his Venetian patrons by going with a flotilla to assist in suppressing the great Cretan insurrection of this period, and loyally administered, with the title of duke,[1] the dominions of his wife till her death in 1371. As his stepson was still not of age, he continued to govern the duchy in his name, as *avogier*, or tutor. It was to his influence in this capacity that we may attribute the grant of Andros, the second island of the Archipelago, as a fief to his little daughter Maria Sanudo—an act which weakened the state at a moment when it needed a centralised administration.[2] Andros had been an immediate possession of the dukes for over a century; it never again enjoyed personal union with Naxos.

When young Niccolò dalle Carceri came of age, he proved to be the worst ruler who had ever reigned over the Archipelago. Hitherto, the dukes had had no interests outside their duchy, and had always resided in it, either at Naxos or at Andros. But their successor was, unfortunately, a great baron in Eubœa as well, and lived most of his time in the latter island, for which he cared more than for his ducal throne. Leaving one of the Gozzadini of Anaphe to

[1] All the documents are given by Gerland, *op. cit.*, 138-49. *Cf.* also Buchon, *Nouvelles Recherches*, II., i., 175.

[2] Magno, 182; Sáthas, i., 204.

act as regent for him at Naxos, he schemed to extend his possessions in Eubœa, and in 1380, while Venice was at war with Genoa, he plotted the capture of the city of Negroponte with the assistance of the Navarrese Company, which had then entered Attica. While this act of treachery irritated Venice, which had helped him with a galley against the Turks, he aroused the strongest resentment among his subjects by his extortion, and they found a ready leader in an Italian who had recently become connected by marriage with the Sanudo family. This man, Francesco Crispo—a name which suggested to biographers of the late Italian Prime Minister a possible relationship—belonged, like the Dalle Carceri, to a Lombard family from Verona, which had settled in Negroponte, where Francesco, or Franguli, as the Greeks called him, held the barony of Astrogidis. A few years before he had married the daughter of Marco Sanudo, brother of Duke John I. and baron of Melos, which would seem to have prospered greatly under his rule. Crispo had succeeded his father-in-law as baron of that island, but aimed at being something more than a vassal of the young Duke of Naxos. He sounded the discontented in several of the islands, and set out for Naxos, where Niccolò chanced to be. According to one story, the duke met his fate in his capital; according to another, a ducal hunting-party in the interior of the island gave Crispo an opportunity for carrying out his plan. The merry band of huntsmen set out for the lovely valley of Melanes, a paradise of oranges and lemons, where the duke had a villa, still called *Aphentikó*, "the lord's domain." After the luncheon, they proceeded to a spot where game was plentiful, Crispo leading the way with the duke's most trusty friends, so that his unsuspecting host was left with his own minions. Suddenly, on the mountain-side the duke's companions fell upon him; in vain he tried to defend himself; a sword-cut laid him dead on the ground. The murderers, carefully instructed by their employer, hastened after him, and told how the duke had been attacked by a body of strange horsemen, who had either killed or carried him off—which of the two they had not stopped to enquire. Crispo feigned amazement and indignation at his kinsman's fate; he was for returning at once to the scene of the murder, but allowed himself to be dissuaded by his partisans, who begged him not to expose his life also to an ambuscade. Two horsemen, sent back to investigate, reported that they had found the duke lying in his blood; one of Crispo's intimates urged him to seize the fortresses of the island at once, in order to prevent the designs of the mysterious assailants of the unfortunate Niccolò. Crispo at once occupied the ducal castle of Naxos; and the Naxiotes, glad to be freed from their tyrant, unanimously accepted him as their duke, for, in virtue of his wife, he was the next-of-kin to the late ruler, with the exception of Niccolò's two step-sisters. Thus, in 1383, a new dynasty arose in the Archipelago, which lasted for nearly two hundred years. The Sanudi disappeared from Naxos; but illegitimate descendants of the Dalle Carceri lingered on there as late as the seventeenth century, and their arms still adorn the pavement before the door of the Greek cathedral.[1]

Even in our own time, the assassination of a sovereign has not prevented Christian Europe from recognising his successor, and the Venetians were avowedly politicians first and Christians afterwards. They had no reason to love the murdered duke, who had plotted against them, while his assassin was a man of energy, who could defend the duchy against the Turks, and, being an usurper, would be more amenable to Venetian influence than the legitimate dynasty. Like his modern imitator, Francesco Crispo found a high ecclesiastic to act as his apologist; the bishop of Melos went as his envoy to obtain the consent of Venice to his usurpation, and to prepare the way for a visit from himself. Everyone wrote in his favour—the Latin nobles of the Archipelago and the Duke of Candia alike; of all the barons of the Cyclades, Januli Gozzadini, the late duke's viceroy, alone had the chivalry to protest against him. By a clever stroke of diplomacy, the usurper won the bailie of Negroponte to his cause by depriving Maria Sanudo, the late duke's half-sister,

[1] Magno, 182-3; Rubió, *Los Navarros*, 436; Sauger, 185-92; Lichtle; Buchon, in *Revue de Paris*, xvii., 269; *Byz. Zeitschrift*, xvi., 259; *Revue de l'Orient latin*, iii., 581. The family arms given by Turresanus are, however, quite different.

of her island of Andros, and bestowing it, combined with Syra, upon the bailie's son, Pietro Zeno, together with the hand of one of his own daughters. A proposed matrimonial alliance between one of his sons and a daughter of the doge, gained over the chief magistrate. Two voices alone were raised against him—those of Maria Sanudo and of the late duke's widow. The latter, who had trumped Crispo's cards by herself marrying a son of the doge, was ultimately pacified by a widow's portion near the hot baths of Ædepsos in Eubœa; the former, whom Crispo hypocritically pretended to "treat as his own child," received as compensation the marble island of Paros, on condition that she married Gasparo di Sommaripa, a member of a family which still flourishes in the Archipelago. Originally descended from the Marquis de Sommerive, in Languedoc, they had emigrated to Verona, whence, like the Dalle Carceri and the Crispi, they had come to seek their fortune in Greece. Various motives seem to have operated with Crispo in the choice of the man. The Sommaripa may very likely have been connected with the Dalle Carceri, in which case he would think it desirable to pacify a dangerous rival; or else he may have considered that a man who had hitherto held no position in the feudal world of Greece, would feel gratitude to his benefactor; a third reason, we are expressly told, was to neutralise the claims of Maria Sanudo by marrying her to one who was regarded in the exclusive circles of the Archipelago as a *parvenu*. In this, however, he was disappointed; she did not abandon her claim, and, though her husband appealed in vain to his relative, Giovanni Galeazzo Visconti of Milan, after a long and wearisome litigation their son regained, half a century later, his mother's island of Andros.[1]

The Venetians had every reason to be content with the usurpation of Francesco Crispo. It gave them a free hand in Eubœa, for he prudently made no claim to succeed the late duke in the two great baronies of that island, which thus

[1] Magno, 183-5; Sanudo *apud* Muratori, xxii., 779, 783; Lichtle; Sauger, 325 *et sqq.*; Hopf, *Andros* (tr. Sardagna), 78; *Codice Cicogna*, 2532, § 34. The first of these reasons seems to have been the tradition in Naxos, for Sauger makes Crispo anxious to discredit Sommaripa by accusing him of the late duke's murder.

passed under Venetian influence; it made the Archipelago much more dependent upon the good will of the republic, which henceforth took a keener interest in its preservation. In the person of Pietro Zeno, the new baron of Andros, she found the most useful diplomatist of the age, a man perfectly familiar with every phase of the Eastern question, whom she employed in all her delicate negotiations in the Levant. Moreover, in 1390, the Ghisi family, the second most important dynasty in the Cyclades, came to an end in Tenos and Mykonos, and those islands, with Delos, passed by will into her hands. There are still Ghisi in Greece—the author has met them at Athens—proud of their genealogical trees, conscious of their aristocratic past; but they never held sway again in their ancestral islands. Thus, Venice became paramount in the Archipelago; in the very year of Crispo's usurpation, Jacques de Baux, the last Angevin Prince of Achaia had died, so that the new duke had nothing to hope for from the old feudal overlords of the duchy. Venice, on the other hand, assisted him with vessels against the privateers of the Sultan Bajazet, and included him in her treaties with that sovereign and other Levantine powers, only protesting when he himself indulged in piratical expeditions as far as the Syrian coasts. There can be no doubt that the Greeks preferred the rule of Venice in the Archipelago to that of the petty barons. When Tenos and Mykonos became Venetian, the islanders implored the republic not to dispose of them, and declared that they would emigrate into some other Venetian colony rather than remain in their own island, if it were bought by Pietro Zeno of Andros.[1] "No lordship under heaven," they protested, "is as just and good as that of Venice," and this was not altogether an exaggeration, as an incident which occurred at that time in the Archipelago showed.

In the flourishing island of Seriphos, the wise rule of Ermolao Minotto had been followed by the grinding tryanny of a perfect fiend in human shape, a Venetian noble, Niccolò Adoldo Fortunately for the Seriphians, their lord was usually an absentee, preferring the delights of Venice to residence in the island, which the ancient Greeks and

[1] Predelli, *Commemoriali*, iii., 278.

Romans alike had regarded as the abomination of desolation, and which the fifteenth century traveller, Bartolomeo dalli Sonetti, calls *Serfeno de la calamitate.* But from time to time Adoldo descended upon Seriphos for the purpose of wringing more money from his unhappy subjects. On one of these occasions, he landed with a band of Cretan mercenaries—the worst species of cut-throats — invited various leading Seriphians to dinner in his castle, and then had them arrested. The most awful tortures failed to make them disclose the spot where they had concealed their money, whereupon the baffled tyrant hurled them from the castle battlements to death on the stones below. Seriphos was a remote island in 1393—it is not very accessible now—but in course of time the news of this massacre reached Venice, for the Venetian families of Michieli and Giustiniani had also shares of Seriphos, and Adoldo had encroached upon their rights. He was accordingly put on his trial for cruelty and murder, sentenced to two years' confinement "in the lower prisons," and forbidden ever to revisit his island, his share of which was sequestered by the republic. Thus, the islanders had an object-lesson in the vengeance which Venice meted out to tyrants who happened to be her citizens. As for Adoldo, he died at a ripe old age in the odour of sanctity; his remains were interred in the church of S. Simeone Piccolo, which he endowed, and a splendid tomb was erected over his unworthy ashes.[1]

Francesco Crispo died in 1397, leaving a large family of sons, and the necessity of providing for them led to the further sub-division of the duchy into baronial fiefs. Thus, while his eldest son, Giacomo I., succeeded him as Duke of Naxos, another of his children received Melos and Kimolos, a third Anaphe, a fourth Syra, and a fifth Ios. Giacomo, though he gained the epithet of "the Pacific," was none the less ready to join the other Christian powers of the Levant in defending their common interests against the Turks, whose great defeat by the Mongols at Angora had given the Archipelago a merely temporary respite from attack. Thus, he was a member of the Christian League, on whose behalf his brother-in-law and vassal, Pietro Zeno

[1] Ersch und Gruber, lxvi., 344.

of Andros, concluded the very advantageous treaty of 1403 with the new Sultan Suleyman.[1] A year later he even visited England to invoke the aid of Henry IV. Our enterprising sovereign was not able to assist him, though he had at one time intended to lead an army "as far as to the sepulchre of Christ"; but, when Henry Beaufort, bishop of Winchester, made a pilgrimage to Palestine in 1418, he was conveyed back to Venice on one of Pietro Zeno's galleys—the only connection, so far as we have been able to discover, between England and the duchy.[2] The duke was ready, too, to join his galley to those of the Venetian colonies in a campaign against the Turks on the coast of Asia Minor, and Venice not only described him as her "good and dear friend," but used her friendly offices with the sultans Musa and Mohammed I., and with Elias Bey, the ruler of Caria, to preserve the Archipelago from depredations, besides allowing her *protégé* to buy arms from her arsenal and to export cypress wood from Crete for the fortification of his islands. None the less, however, did the duchy suffer from the raids of the inevitable Turks, which, as Zeno told the Venetian Government, were of daily occurrence. In 1416, the tactless omission of the duke to salute Mohammed I. at Smyrna brought a large Turkish fleet down upon the Cyclades, which carried off many of the inhabitants of Andros, Melos, and Paros, and did a vast amount of damage. Venice avenged this attack upon one who, in the words of the Byzantine historian, "had long been her vassal and flown her flag," by the naval victory of Gallipoli,[3] but the injury inflicted on the islands was so great, that some of them were almost depopulated. The Florentine priest Buondelmonti, who spent four years at this time, "in fear and great anxiety," travelling among the Cyclades, of which he has left us one of the earliest accounts composed by any writer during the Frankish domination, depicts life in the Archipelago in gloomy colours. At both Naxos and Siphnos there was such a lack of men, that many women were unable to find husbands; in fact the small

[1] Thomas and Predelli, *Diplomatarium*, ii., 290-3.

[2] Sáthas, ii., 125; Sanudo *apud* Muratori, xxii., 923; Antonio Morosini, *Chronique*, ii., 164.

[3] Doúkas, 109; Sáthas, ii., 174; iii., 92-3, 112.

and wretched population of the latter island, still the absolute property of the Da Corogna, who had a tower there in a lovely garden, was mainly composed of females, who were zealous Catholics, though they did not understand a word of the Latin language, in which their services were held. At Seriphos, so rich forty years earlier, the cultured Florentine found "nothing but calamity"; the people passed their lives "like brutes," and were in constant fear, day and night, lest they should fall into the hands of the Infidels, though Venice had the island included in her treaties with the Turks, like so many others of the Cyclades.[1] Syra, destined in modern times to be the most flourishing of all the islands, was then "comparatively of no account"; the islanders fed on carobs and goats' flesh, and led a life of continual anxiety, though a strong sense of clannishness bound them to their poverty-stricken home. The people of Paros were in the same plight, the principal town of Paroikia had few citizens, while pirates frequented the big bay of Naoussa. Antiparos and Sikinos were abandoned to eagles and wild asses, and most of the islets were deserted. Compared with the other islands, Andros had suffered least, owing no doubt to the energetic personality of Zeno, the "Duke of Andros," as he was sometimes called,[2] and the vigour of Januli della Grammatica, his henchman. But even Zeno found it politic to harbour the dreaded foes of Christendom in his island, just as the duke of Naxos gave shelter to corsairs from Cataluña and Biscay.[3] The one place in the Ægean which the Mussulmans never molested was the monastery of Patmos, whose monks were on the best of terms with them. In order to repair the ravages made by the Turkish raids, several of the island barons took steps at this time to repopulate their desolate possessions. Thus, Marco Crispo colonised Ios with Albanians from the Morea, and strengthened the defences of the place by building a castle and a town at its foot, the remains of which may still be seen.[4] To this castle the peasants used to climb up every

[1] Thomas and Predelli, *Diplomatarium*, ii., 295, 320.

[2] Sanudo, xxii., 896.

[3] Sáthas, ii., 255; iii., 158; *Revue de l'Orient latin*, iv., 319.

[4] Sauger, 214-15; Tournefort, i., 95-6; Pasch von Krienen, *Breve Descrizione*, 31.

evening from their plots of land in the rich plain below, nor did they dare to open the gates in the morning and sally forth, till the old women whom they had sent out as spies before dawn, reported that the coast was clear and no pirate craft was careening in the fine harbour. In 1413 Giovanni Quirini of Stampalia, who was also administering Tenos and Mykonos for the Venetians, proceeded to repopulate his own island, which had never recovered from the great raid of Omarbeg Morbassan seventy years before, at the expense of the two Venetian colonies committed to his charge. This wholesale emigration of Teniotes to Stampalia attracted great notice throughout the Archipelago. An inscription, together with a stone escutcheon quartering the three lilies of the Quirini, and his wife's nine counters, in the chapel of the castle at Stampalia which he restored, still reminds us that the "Count of Tenos," as he styled himself, began the importation of the colonists on 30th March 1413, the feast of the translation of his patron saint, S. Quirinus, and almost every successive traveller in the Cyclades alludes to it. But Venice naturally objected to the depopulation of her two islands; Quirini was ordered to return thither with all the people whom he had transported, and not to move more than twenty-five miles from his office.[1] Similarly, the Gozzadini repopulated the town of Thermia, which the Turks had taken by treachery, and it was probably at this period that the Albanians crossed over from Eubœa to settle in the north of Andros—the only island of the Cyclades which still retains an Albanian population. Under these circumstances, the mineral resources of the islands, except the Parian marble quarries, could not be exploited. The gold found in some parts of Naxos was left unworked, and the emery mines of that island, which Buondelmonti mentions, and which are now so profitable to the Greek Government, do not seem to have been a source of revenue to the duke, who was obliged to raise money for the payment of his liabilities by the sale of horses and mules at Candia, just as, even then, the cattle of Tenos were highly esteemed.[2] Buondelmonti mentions the sulphur

[1] Buchon, *Atlas*, xlii., 2, 3; Sáthas, iii., 4; Buondelmonti, ch. xviii.; Bartolomeo dalli Sonetti, 12; Boschini, *L'Archipelago*, 20; *B. S. A.*, xii., 152.

[2] Sáthas, ii., 129, 130, 279; Hopf, *Andros* (tr. Sardagna), 177.

springs and the millstones of Melos, and alludes to an unsuccessful experiment made by Duke Giacomo to plumb the unfathomable depths of the crater which forms the harbour of Santorin.[1]

Giacomo I. died of a flux at Ferrara in 1418 on his way to meet Pope Martin V. at Mantua.[2] He had played a considerable part in the Levantine politics of his time; he had been instrumental in arranging the retrocession of Corinth to the Greeks by the Knights of St John;[3] his possession of his father's usurped throne was little disturbed by the continual appeals for pecuniary compensation, which the widow of the last legitimate duke made against him at Venice, and to which he opposed the usual dilatory tactics of Italy, supported by the normal impecuniosity of the Levant. By his will he appointed his brother John as his successor, thus for the first time in the history of the duchy setting aside the usual custom of the Empire of Romania, according to which one of his daughters should have succeeded him. It might have been well for the rest of Greece, had this frank recognition of the advantages of the Salic law in troublous times been generally accepted; certainly the history of the Frankish states would have been more pacific, if less picturesque. At any rate, Giacomo I. thus set a precedent, which was subsequently followed; no woman sat again on the sea-girt throne of the Archipelago.

The Venetian Government, long anxious to obtain a hold over the duchy, thought that the time had come for a decisive step. It was accordingly proposed to occupy the late Duke's dominions in the name of his widow and her mother, and to confirm all his brothers in their respective fiefs, on condition that they paid the same homage as before. In that case, the republic would be willing to put the castle of Naxos into thorough repair. A Venetian ambassador was to convey these proposals to Niccolò Crispo of Syra, who was acting as regent in the absence of the late duke. But more prudent counsels prevailed. Niccolò, it was pointed out, was not only an adversary of Venetian rule, but had a Genoese wife—according to another account she was a

[1] Buondelmonti, chs. xviii.-xx., xxiv.-vi., xxviii.-xxx., xxxii.-iv., xxxvii., xl., xlix., lxxix.
[2] Sáthas, i., 96.
[3] Bosio, pt. ii., 121.

Princess of Trebizond—while his brother John, the late duke's heir, was fond of Venice. He was in the habit of residing there for months at a time; he was at that moment staying with his sister-in law at the convent of S. Maria delle Vergini, now used as a magazine; and he chose his wife, not from Genoa or Trebizond, but from among the daughters of the republic.[1] It was therefore decided to recognise him as duke, provided that he took an oath of obedience to Venice and acknowledged his duchy to be a Venetian dependency. A Venetian galley was accordingly made ready to conduct him either to his capital or to his own island of Melos. He had the sense to meet any possible opposition from his brothers by increasing their already considerable appanages, bestowing Santorin, which had been united with Naxos for over eighty years, upon Niccolò of Syra, and Therasia upon Marco of Ios—an arrangement which, though doubtless inevitable, tended to weaken the unity of the State. But where there was a large ducal family, subdivision was the only alternative to civil war.[2] On the other hand, the new duke acted with a complete lack of chivalry towards his sister-in-law and her mother, Maria Sanudo, reducing them to penury and exile by depriving them of their islands of Paros and Antiparos, valuable possessions which each furnished thirty sailors to the ducal galleys, and restoring them to the unfortunate ladies only after strong and repeated remonstrances from Venice, backed by force.[3]

John II., though he had succeeded to the duchy with the full approval of Venice, found that, in that time of stress, she was not always able to protect her distant nominee. Occasionally she would give him a galley for his defence against the Turks; and in her treaties with Mohammed I. and Murâd II. in 1419 and 1430, she inserted a clause to the effect that he and his brothers should be included in the terms of peace, treated as Venetians, and exempted from

[1] Sanudo *apud* Muratori, xxii., 923; Antonio Morosini, *loc. cit.*; Cicogna, *Iscrizioni Veneziane*, v., 92, 629 (whose quotation from the chronicle of the convent obviously refers to this duke); Sáthas, i., 96-101; Sansovino, *Cronologia del Mondo*, f. 184.

[2] Sauger, 213.

[3] Sáthas, i., 124, 129-33; iii., 220, 223-4, 283; *Revue de l'Orient latin*, v., 137.

tribute and other molestation. Indeed, in a schedule of the former treaty, the sultan expressly stated that he reckoned "Santorin, Anaphe, Therasia, Astypalaia, Thermia, Amorgos, Ios, Paros, Naxos, Syra, Melos, Siphnos, Keos, Seriphos, Tenos, Mykonos, and Andros" as all Venetian. But, in 1426, the proud republic frankly confessed that she could not help him, and was content that he and Zeno of Andros should make the best terms they could with the Turks, so as to save their islands, provided only that they neither received nor victualled Turkish ships, nor in any way aided those foes of Christendom. The duke, however, not only agreed to pay tribute and to open his ports to the Turks, but inflicted an even greater injury on Venetian interests by omitting from that time to light the usual signal fires to warn the bailie of Negroponte of the approach of an Ottoman fleet.[1] His connection with Venice proved, at times, to be an actual source of danger to himself; for, when the Venetians ravaged the Genoese colony of Chios in 1431, the Genoese admiral, Spinola, took revenge by seizing Naxos and Andros, and all the diplomacy of the Crispi was required to prevent their islands from becoming Genoese possessions. Great was the disgust of Venice when she heard that her "dear friends" had made a treaty with, and paid blackmail to, her deadliest rival; none the less, they continued for some years to be adherents of Genoa.[2] But then, as now, the small states of the Levant could retort with some truth that, if their natural protectors in Europe neglected them, they must fend for themselves.

John II. would seem to have died[3] in 1433, leaving an

[1] Thomas and Predelli, *Diplomatarium*, ii., 318-19, 345; Predelli, *Commemoriali*, iv., 164; Sáthas, i., 179; iii., 304, 372; *Revue de l'Orient latin*, v., 320, *n.* 3.

[2] *Ibid.*, vi., 124, 130; Foglietta, *Historia Genuensium* (ed. 1585), p. 208; Predelli, *Commemoriali*, iv., 208.

[3] Not in 1437, as Hopf and Count Mas Latrie assume from the Venetian document of that year addressed to him and printed in Sardagna's translation of Hopf's *Andros*, p. 171, where, as Jorga has pointed out (*Revue de l'Orient latin*, vi., 383 *n.*), "Johanni" must be a mistake for "Jacopo," who is obviously "the duke" alluded to in another Venetian document, issued the same day, as having "made a marriage-contract with the daughter of the late lord of Andros." A document from the ducal chancery at Naxos, dated 26th December, 1433, speaks of John as dead (*Byzantinische Zeitschrift*, xiii., 143). *Cf.* Magno 186.

only son, Giacomo II., still a minor, under the guardianship of a masterful woman, the dowager Duchess Francesca; while the child's three uncles, Niccolò of Syra and Santorin, Marco of Ios, and William of Anaphe, were appointed their brother's executors, and the first of the trio regent of the duchy. Giacomo II.'s reign was chiefly remarkable for the final settlement of the claims of the Sommaripa family to the island of Andros. Maria Sanudo had never abandoned her rights to that valuable island, which the first of the Crispi dukes had bestowed, as we saw, upon Pietro Zeno. That famous diplomatist, so long the leading figure of the Latin Orient, who, if his lot had been cast on a bigger stage, might have left a great name in history, had died in 1427; and, as his son and successor, Andrea, was delicate, and had an only daughter, Venice early made preparations to occupy Andros on his death, lest it should fall into undesirable hands, and decided that his daughter should be under the tutelage of the republic till her marriage. News of these plans, however, leaked out; and, when Andrea really died in 1437, the Venetian bailie of Negroponte, who had been ordered to seize the island in the name of the republic, found himself forestalled and his envoy refused admittance by the young duke's uncles, who had imprisoned the late baron's widow in the old castle at Andros and forced her to sign a document, promising the hand of her little daughter, still a mere child, to their nephew within the next five years, together with Andros as her dowry. The Venetian Government was naturally indignant at this frustration of its long-cherished scheme by the petty lords of the Archipelago; a Venetian noble, Francesco Quirini, was sent to Naxos; backed by a Cretan galley, and the threat that the duke would be treated as the enemy of the republic, he obtained the cession of the island to himself, as Venetian governor, pending the decision of the question. For three years he and his successor administered Andros in the name of the republic, which protested that she merely wanted to assert her jurisdiction in the Archipelago, while all the claimants were being heard at Venice. Finally, in 1440, the Venetian court decided that the lawful baron of Andros was Maria Sanudo's son, Crusino I. Sommaripa, lord of Paros and triarch of Eubœa; Crusino agreed to pay indemnities to the members of the Zeno family, and thus, after more than half a century, Andros returned to its legal possessor.[1]

Installed in this valuable island, which it retained till the Turkish Conquest, the Sommaripa clan now occupied the position formerly held by the Ghisi—that of the second most important family in the duchy. Crusino was, moreover, a man of culture as well as a man of affairs. He had excavated marble statues at Paros, and was delighted to show them to Cyriacus of Ancona, who visited him more than once and inspected the quarries of that island, whence marble was still exported. The antiquary found a ship laden with a cargo of the polished Parian stone lying in the harbour ready to sail for Chios, whose rich Genoese colonists had ordered the material for their villas, and Crusino allowed him to send the head and leg of an ancient statue to one of his friends there. When, therefore, archæologists blame the Latin rulers of the Cyclades for destroying classical temples in order to build their own castles out of the marble fragments—an example of which may be seen at Paros itself—it is well to remember that some of them, like Crusino, did something for archæology—more, perhaps, than archæologists have ever done for the remains of the Middle Ages. Cyriacus himself mentions that he saw at Mykonos marble fragments of statues, which had been brought from Delos.[2] Buondelmonti, a quarter of a century earlier, had noticed more than a thousand scattered on the ground of the sacred island, whence he had in vain tried to raise the colossal statue of Apollo.[3]

The installation of the Sommaripa at Andros was not the only dynastic change in the Archipelago at this period. Crusino's son-in-law, a Loredano, received from him the island of Antiparos, and thus a fresh great Venetian family obtained a footing in the Cyclades. This infusion of new blood was of great benefit to the island, which had long been

[1] Hopf, *Andros* (tr. Sardagna), 171-9; *Revue de l'Orient latin*, vi., 379, 383, 388; Sáthas, i., 199-208; Magno, 185-93; Predelli, *Commemoriali*, iv., 224.

[2] Tozzetti, *Relazioni di alcuni viaggi*, v., 423; *Bulletino dell' Istituto* (1861), 187.

[3] *Ibid.*, 181; Buondelmonti, ch. xxxii.

uninhabited: for the energetic Venetian repopulated it with new colonists, and built and resided in the castle, whose gateway, now fallen, still preserved, in the eighteenth century, his coat of arms.[1] At the same time, another Venetian coloniser, Giovanni Quirini of Stampalia, acquired the whole of Amorgos, and this increased stake in the Levant might perhaps warrant the title of "Count," which he and all his descendants bore.[2] A third Venetian family, the Michieli, now owned all Seriphos, and set up their arms with the date of 1434 over the castle gate. Even non-Venetian dynasties, such as the Gozzadini of Thermia and Keos, and the Spanish Da Corogna of Keos and Siphnos, were glad to be regarded as Venetians, whenever the republic concluded a treaty of peace with the Turks, although Januli da Corogna proudly asserted that he owned allegiance to no man for his rock of Siphnos,[3] over which the Dukes of Naxos still claimed a shadowy suzerainty, and of which their vassals, the Grimani, long pretended to be the rightful lords.[4]

The fourteen years' reign of Duke Giacomo II. was a period of peace for the Archipelago. The energies of the Turks were temporarily diverted to Hungary, and their crushing defeat by John Hunyady at Nish emboldened the Venetians to send a fleet to the Ægean under Luigi Loredano, father of the new baron of Antiparos. In these circumstances, we are not surprised to find the islands of Andros and Naxos, which had just strengthened its flotilla, contributing galleys to the Venetian squadron; but the overthrow of the perjured Christian host in the great battle of Varna led Venice to make peace with the sultan in 1446, including the Naxian duchy in the provisions of the treaty.[5] The following year the duke died,[2] leaving his wife *enceinte* with a son, who was

[1] Magno, 194; Pasch von Krienen, 128; Sauger, 346.

[2] Magno, 195; Predelli, *Commemoriali*, iv., 299; Zabarella, *Il Galba*, 82; Hopf, *Analekten*, 524-6.

[3] "Esse liberum dominium insule Siphani," in a document of 1434, *apud* Ersch und Gruber, lxviii., 307.

[4] Hopf, *Andros* (tr. Sardagna), 185.

[5] Sáthas, i., 208; Thomas, *Diplomatarium*, ii., 368; Predelli, *Commemoriali*, iv., 296.

[6] The doge of Genoa wrote to him in 1447 (*Giornale Ligustico*, iii., 315)—the last allusion to him; Magno (p. 196) says he died "in 1450 or thereabouts."

born six weeks after his father's death, and received the name of Gian Giacomo. The two strongest members of the family, Niccolò of Syra and Santorin and William of Anaphe, the same who had acted as regents of the late duke, once more assumed the government with the assent of Venice, and imprisoned the child's grandmother, the dowager Duchess Francesca, who had exercised great influence during the late reign, and who claimed the regency. Niccolò soon died, and we then find the Duchess Francesca, the archbishop, and the citizens of Naxos, electing his son Francesco in his place, and begging the Venetian Government to ratify their choice—an interesting fact, which shows that the people had a voice in the selection of a regent, and that the duchy was more than ever dependent upon Venice. The republic accordingly again included the two regents in the treaties of peace which she made with Alfonso I. of Naples and Mohammed II. in 1450 and 1451—the last agreement which she concluded with the Turks before Constantinople fell.

In 1452 the little duke died,[1] and a disputed succession at once ensued. Had females been allowed to succeed, the next-of-kin was the boy duke's aunt, Adriana, wife of Domenico Sommaripa, son of the baron of Andros, and it had been stipulated in her marriage-contract, that if her brother Giacomo II. died without heirs, she should succeed him. But there was already a precedent in the Crispo dynasty for the exclusion of women, and this afforded a pretext to the two regents, old William Crispo of Anaphe, the late duke's great-uncle, and Francesco of Santorin, his cousin, for claiming the duchy as the nearest agnates. At first, the Venetian Government, by a decree of March 1452, excluded both these rival candidates, and it might have been possible for the Sommaripa family, had they taken the trouble to canvass at once in person at Venice, to secure the succession.[2] But William Crispo, though he was old, was ambitious; he had twice acted as regent of the duchy, and was in no mood to end his days in the castle which he had built on his island of Anaphe, the most remote of all the Cyclades. He

[1] Magno, 196-98; Thomas and Predelli, *Diplomatarium*, ii., 383-4; Predelli, *Commemoriali*, v., 56, 65; *Revue de l'Orient latin*, viii., 42, 76.

[2] Sauger, 214, 226, 343, 348; Lichtle.

came to terms with his nephew Francesco, which seemed to be favourable to both of them. He was to be duke for the rest of his life; and, as he had only one legitimate child, and that a daughter, the duchy was to pass at his death to his nephew, his daughter was to inherit distant Anaphe, while lands and female serfs in Naxos were the portion of his bastard Giacomo.[1] Civil war was, above all else, to be avoided, for by this time the Turks were masters of Constantinople, and a scare of Turkish and Catalan corsairs had lately frightened the islanders, who fled in numbers at the bad news from the great city. Accordingly, before the end of 1453, William II. was proclaimed duke: and though Venice cited him to appear before the senate to answer the plaint of the Sommaripa, she at last wisely acquiesced in the succession of so experienced a man, who was ready to place his naval resources at her disposal, and allowed his chancellor to accompany her fleet.[2] The domineering dowager, Francesca, who had so long exercised influence in the affairs of the duchy, had now retired to her native lagoons, so that there was no one at the ducal court to dispute his supremacy. The memory of the Duchess Francesca is, however, still preserved at Naxos by the little church of S. Antonio on the shore, part of the monastery which she had built, and which she bestowed on the Knights of St John in 1452, in order that she might obtain the jubilee indulgence of the *anno santo*, which Pope Nicholas V. had proclaimed two years before. From that time Naxos became one of the bailiwicks of the Order, paying no less than 51,000 florins a year to the grand-master at Rhodes. The arms of the Knights still adorn the little church; on the right of the altar are the tomb and escutcheon of Giovanni Crispo, who was commander of the Order; and hard by are the remains of the arsenal, where they kept some half-dozen galleys.[3] It was, indeed, the era of pious foundations in Naxos. This was not the only

[1] Sauger, 227; *Byzantinische Zeitschrift*, xiii., 150. This deed, dated 9th November 1453, is his first known act as duke.

[2] Predelli, *Commemoriali*, v., 92; Magno, 200; Chalkokondýles, 400.

[3] Magno, 199-200; Bosio, II., 239; Sauger, 220; Lichtle; Buchon in *Revue de Paris*, xvi., 343; *Atlas*, xl., 33. The church was built before 1440, for in that year Niccolò Gozzadini of Thermia left it a legacy (Ersch und Gruber, lxxvi., 419). There are no arms at St Elias now.

church built by the Duchess Francesca, and the piety of her son, Duke Jacopo II. and his wife is said to have been recorded by their armorial bearings on the church of St Elias.

During the reign of Duke William II. occurred one of those tremendous phenomena which have conferred world-wide notoriety upon an island of the Cyclades. For more than seven centuries, ever since the year 726, the volcano of Santorin had been silent, though the lava rocks and the strong wine may have reminded the islanders of its origin. But, in 1457, the sea murmured as if in agony, the rocks of Old Kayméne, "the Burnt Island," which had arisen in the harbour 200 years before Christ, were cleft asunder with a groan, and a fresh mass of rock, black as a coal, was thrown up from the deep to fill the gap. The "birth of this memorable monster," the third accretion to the islet, was commemorated in a set of detestable Latin hexameters inscribed on a slab of marble at the castle of Skarós and addressed to Francesco Crispo, "true descendant of heroes," who was at that time baron of Santorin and who was soon to be Duke of Naxos, and two centuries later the offspring of this upheaval could be clearly distinguished by its burning sand from the older portions of the "burnt" rock.[1] For more than a hundred years no further eruption disturbed the "magnanimous" rulers of Santorin.

But the political cataclysms of the time were more serious than those of nature. It was reserved for old William of Naxos to witness the disappearance of one Christian state after another before the advancing Moslem. In the year of his accession the Byzantine Empire had fallen; in his reign fell, too, the Byzantine principality in the Morea, the Florentine duchy of Athens, and, still nearer home, the island state which the Genoese Gattilusii had ruled for over a century in Lesbos. Of all these calamities, the fall of the Gattilusii must have affected him most, for his family was connected with them by ties of matrimony, and when Dorino Gattilusio was driven by the Turks from Ænos, he settled in exile at Naxos, and married the grand-niece of the duke.[2]

[1] Pègues, *Histoire de Santorin*, 138; Casola, *Viaggio a Gerusalemme*, 96; Bartolomeo dalli Sonetti, 5.

[2] Kritóboulos, ii., 16.

It was now, too, that the islands of Skyros, Skopelos, and Skiathos offered themselves to the Venetians. More clearly even than their fellows of the Northern Sporades, the islanders of the Cyclades saw that Venice was now their only possible protection against the Turk—for what would the 2000 horsemen of the duchy avail against the hosts of Islâm? On her side, Venice did not forget "the Duke of Naxos, his nobles and their men, with their places and all that they have," in the treaty which she made with Mohammed II. in 1454, and which specially exempted them from "tribute or any other service," and gave them the status of Venetians,[1] with the right to hoist the lion banner of St Mark from their castles. Yet the duchy was only saved by one of those sudden storms so common in the Ægean from an attack by a large Turkish fleet under Junis Beg in the very next year—an attack justified in the eyes of the irate sultan by the hospitality and shelter which pirates had received in the harbours of Naxos, Paros, and Rheneia. Warned by the fate of the Lesbians, and by a fresh Turkish raid, the duke thought it advisable to ensure his possessions by paying tribute to the all-powerful Mohammed.[2] He felt himself terribly isolated from the rest of Christendom since the Turkish conquest of the Greek continent; he must have realised that sooner or later a similar fate awaited his own dominions, and that the highest form of practical statesmanship was to supplement the paper safeguards of Turco-Venetian treaties by the more durable cash *nexus* with the sultan.

[1] Sanudo *apud* Muratori, xxii., 1155.
[2] Kritóboulos, ii., 3; iii., 10; Doúkas, 331, 340.

CHAPTER XVIII

THE DUCHY OF THE ARCHIPELAGO (1463-1566)

WILLIAM II. died in 1463, and, in virtue of the arrangement made at his accession, his nephew, Francesco II. of Santorin, succeeded him. But the new duke did not long enjoy this coveted dignity; afflicted with a serious malady, he went to seek the advice of a doctor at the Venetian colony of Coron, and died there the same year. His son, Giacomo III., was proclaimed duke by the people, under the regency of the late duke's widow,[1] though it seemed doubtful at first whether the lad's uncle, Antonio of Syra, would not usurp the throne.[2] Coinciding as it did with the long Turco-Venetian war, which lasted from 1463 to 1479, the reign of Giacomo III. could not fail to be affected by the further disasters befalling the Venetian possessions in the Levant. In 1468 four Turkish vessels attacked Andros; Giovanni Sommaripa, baron of the island, lost his life in defending his home; and the invaders withdrew, after ravaging the place, with numerous prisoners and booty to the value of 15,000 ducats. Two years later, after the crowning disaster of the war—the capture of Negroponte—the Turkish fleet landed at Andros again on its way home, and carried off so many captives that the population was reduced to 2000 souls. Despite the reassuring visits of Venetian fleets, almost all the islands suffered in greater or less degree from Turkish raids at this terrible period. Paros retained no more than 3000 inhabitants; Antiparos, repopulated a generation before by Loredano,

[1] The doge wrote to her in 1464 as *Gubernatrici Egeopelagi.* Cornelius, *Ecclesiæ Venetæ*, viii., 272.

[2] Magno, 204-5.

was reduced to barely a hundred persons; despite the previous efforts of Giovanni Quirini to colonise Stampalia, the carelessness of his son, an absentee, allowed the colony to dwindle down to 400, while the rich island of Santorin, though now a direct possession of the Duke of Naxos, nourished only 300 inhabitants, and yielded the duke no more than 500 ducats. Still smaller was the population of Keos and Seriphos, while the two Venetian islands of Tenos and Mykonos had long complained of the devastation wrought by the Turks—to which must be added the drain of men enlisted in the Archipelago for service in the Venetian navy, which put in there on the way to attack Smyrna in 1472. Delos, which the Venetian admiral, Mocenigo, visited at this time, was quite deserted; but the remains of the temple and the theatre, the colossus of Apollo, the mass of pillars and statues, and the cisterns full of water are described by his biographer.[1] Naxos was visited by the Turkish fleet in its turn in 1477, and two years later the Naxian diocese, which had for some time been very poor, is described as being largely in the occupation of the Turks.[2] Happily, the peace of 1479 at last terminated the long contest between Venice and the sultan; the Duke of Naxos and his subjects were treated as Venetians, and three years later the new sultan, Bajazet II., repeated his predecessor's compact.[3]

The restoration of peace was naturally a subject of rejoicing to the sorely tried Archipelago, and the marriage of his daughter at the Carnival of 1480 gave the duke an opportunity of giving vent to his own and his people's feelings. He had chosen as his son-in-law, Domenico Pisani, son of the Duke of Candia and member of a very distinguished Venetian family, and he bestowed upon him, as his daughter's dowry, his own native island of Santorin, on condition that Pisani should restore it in the event of a son being born to the ducal donor. Never had there been such splendid festivities in the history of the duchy. The castle

[1] Magno, 205, 207; Rizzardo, *La presa di Negroponte*, 24; Sáthas, i., 244; Predelli, *Commemoriali*, v., 230; Cippico, *P. Mocenigi Gesta*, 341, 344.

[2] Eubel, ii., 221.

[3] Predelli, *op. cit.*, v., 228, 241; Miklosich und Müller, iii., 295, 314; Malipiero, *Annali*, 121.

at Melos, where Giacomo III. was then residing, rang with the mirth of the wedding guests; and the merriment was renewed when the young couple landed with the duke in their new domain. Giacomo, we are told, "danced every day, leaping for joy and singing," while the islanders shouted *Viva Pisani!* in honour of their baron. In the old castle of the Barozzi at Skarós, the chief of the five fortresses of the volcanic island, whose ruins still look down on the bottomless harbour far below, Pisani knelt down with his wife before their lord the duke, and received from his hands the keys of the castle, the rod which betokened their feudal rights, and the scroll, drawn up by the chancellor, which set out the conditions of their investiture. Then, in the tower of the lower castle, the vassals were ushered in to do homage to their new lord, foremost among them the two great families of Santorin, the Gozzadini and the Argyroi, or D'Argenta, Latinised Greek *archons*, who boasted their descent from one of the Byzantine emperors, but did not scorn to hold the castle of S. Niccolò from the lord of Santorin. When the ceremony was over, the flag of the Pisani was run up on the upper castle; the new dynasty was officially recognised in the motley heraldry of the Archipelago. Then the duke returned to his residence at Melos, and the new lord of Santorin set out to survey his island domain, too long neglected by its absentee ruler. Pisani showed all the energy of a king upon his coronation day. He planted vines and olives, sowed cotton, and consulted how he could best benefit the traders of the community. A new era seemed to have opened for the depopulated island; wherever the baron went, the church bells rang a merry peal to greet him; whenever he lay down to rest, the governors of the castles laid the keys in his chamber. Anxious for the spiritual welfare of his subjects, he appointed a new bishop; desirous to secure them against attack, he placed his island under Venetian protection, hoisted the banner of the republic beside his own, and journeyed with his wife to Venice to obtain confirmation of his possession. Naturally, Venice granted the request of so desirable and so well-connected a ruler.

But the idyll of Santorin did not last long. While Pisani was still in Venice, his father-in-law died. Giacomo III. had left no son, so that, by virtue of the marriage-contract, Pisani was entitled to retain his island; indeed, had not the Salic law been adopted, as we saw, in the Crispo dynasty, his wife would have succeeded as Duchess of the Archipelago. But the late duke's brother, John III., not content with succeeding to the duchy, landed in Santorin, occupied Skarós, pulled down the Pisani flag, and hoisted the lozenges and two crosses of the Crispi. Pisani's father complained at Venice of this act of violence, and the Venetian Government ordered the admiral of the fleet to compel restitution of the island. But when his emissaries arrived at Santorin, they found that John III. had strengthened the defences of Skarós, and were compelled to retire ignominiously under a heavy shower of stones. This was more than the Venetian authorities could endure. They ordered the erring duke, in a most peremptory letter, to appear at Venice to answer the charges against him. His reply was to instruct his brother-in-law, then in Venice, to act on his behalf. The whole question was then investigated, and as important points of feudal law were involved, the judges ordered a clerk to make a fresh copy of the *Book of the Customs of the Empire of Romania*, and to draw up a genealogical tree of the Dukes of Naxos—the oldest pedigree of the Sanudi and Crispi, with which we are acquainted. After opposite opinions had been expressed by the Court, a compromise was at last agreed upon, that the duke should keep Santorin on payment of compensation to Pisani and his heirs. John III., having obtained what he wanted, now humbly replied that he "was ready to live or die for Venice"; while the Pisani family ere long had the doubtful satisfaction of reigning over three of the smaller islands of the Archipelago.[1]

The peace concluded between Venice and the Turk did not ensure the security of the Levant. During Mohammed II.'s operations against Rhodes, the Ægean was beset with Turkish pirates, who were a continual dread to the more or less pious pilgrims on their way to the Holy Land, and

[1] Magno, 209; Sáthas, vi., 225, 233; Hopf, *Analekten*, 404-13, 517; *Andros* (tr. Sardagna), 185; Predelli, *op. cit.*, v., 305; Feyerabend, *Reyssbuch*, f. 371; Canciani, *Barbarorum Leges*, iii., 485. The author published the genealogical tree in *Byz. Zeitschrift*, xvi., 258.

it was no uncommon thing to find the hold of a Turkish corsair filled with prisoners dragged away from their homes in the Cyclades.[1] Bajazet II., the new sultan, in spite of his pledge to Venice that the duchy should not be asked for tribute, demanded arrears of payment, and complained that the Duke of Naxos and the baron of Paros harboured pirates who preyed upon the Turkish dominions. He followed this complaint by preparing a small fleet to drive the latter offender from the marble island. The republic ordered her admiral to protect him, and the Archbishop of Paros and Naxos took the opportunity of his presence in the Archipelago to suggest that the offer of an annuity might induce the rulers of those islands to make over all their rights to Venice. Neither the duke nor Sommaripa were, as a matter of fact, willing to abdicate, though the latter was glad to fly the Venetian flag beside his own. But the tyrannical conduct of John III. soon brought about a Venetian occupation. That headstrong ruler exasperated his subjects by his exactions to such a pitch, that, led by a Greek veteran, they besieged him and the nobles in the castle, whence he was only rescued by the timely arrival of a fleet belonging to the Knights of Rhodes. Even this lesson did not make him mend his ways. The execution of the rebel leader rekindled the enmity of the people against the duke, and, when he died, in 1494, many of his subjects wagged their heads and spoke of poison.

Though he had left two children, a son and a daughter, both were minors and both illegitimate, so that the moment was favourable for Venetian intervention. It was perhaps not a mere chance that the Venetian admiral with six galleys was in the harbour, and his appearance inspired the popular party to advocate annexation to the republic. The chief men, however, favoured the claims of the children's mother; and the most energetic member of the Crispo family, Giacomo, bastard of the old Duke William II., assumed the title of Governor of Naxos on their behalf and issued official documents in that style. Meanwhile, however, the people, accompanied by their wives holding their children in their arms, approached the Venetian

[1] Bartolomeo dalli Sonetti, 36; Faber, *Evagatorium*, i., 37.

admiral with cries of "we want to be governed by Venice! we submit to her!" The admiral, who had probably suggested this demonstration, received them well, appointed a Venetian governor of Naxos, and despatched officers to occupy and administer the other islands which had belonged to the late duke—Santorin, Syra, Nio, and Melos. At the same time, an envoy of the Naxian people was sent to Venice to announce the news, followed by their archbishop and a formal embassy. It was then proposed in the senate that the republic should accept the duchy, after making due provision for the late duke's widow and children, in order to relieve the people from tyranny, and to prevent the islands from becoming a nest of corsairs and a part of the growing Turkish Empire. It was, however, decided that the administration of the island revenues should be left to the ducal family; but that a Venetian governor should be appointed for a term of two years with residence at Naxos and a salary of 500 ducats payable out of those funds; Naxian citizens were to be sent to govern the dependent islands. As first Venetian governor of Naxos, Pietro Contarini was elected. Thus, in 1494, Venice at last became mistress of the duchy of the Archipelago.[1]

The acquisition was not perhaps of great economic value. We are told that of the five islands which the late duke had held under his immediate sway, Santorin and Nio contained 800 souls, and Syra half that number. Both Nio and Melos had fine and frequented ports, but the fortifications of the latter harbour were in ruins, and the Milanese canon Casola, who put into Nio just before the duke's death, likened the mountain castle of the Crispi there to "a pigstye," where the inhabitants were crowded together for fear of pirates, but where the food was good and the women beautiful. Melos and Naxos were the most flourishing of the Cyclades; the former was rich in saltpetre, pumice, and mill-stones; and its hot baths, which had proved fatal, so it was said, to old Duke William II., were second only to those of Thermia, which the enthusiastic Venetian mariner, Bartolomeo "dalli

[1] Magno, 209; Sáthas, vi., 241; Navagero, xxiii., 1203; Bembo, *Historia Veneta* (ed. 1809), i., 73, 101-2; Casola, *Viaggio*, 96; *Archives de l'Orient latin*, i., 614.

Sonetti," as he called himself, declared to be superior to the baths of Padua. Of the other Cyclades, where Venetian influence was now predominant, though the island barons were nominally independent of her, the two most prosperous were those of the Sommaripa—Paros and Andros. The German pilgrim, Father Faber, who was in the Archipelago eleven years earlier, tells us that Parian marble was exported to Venice, and that the island produced another stone, better even than marble.[1] The lord of Andros, who was recognised by Venice as quite independent of the duchy of Naxos, seems even to have styled himself "Duke" of his own island,[2] as Pietro Zeno, a much more important man, had done. All the other islands, except three and part of a fourth, now belonged to Venetian families—Amorgos and Stampalia to the Quirini; Seriphos to the Michieli; Antiparos to the Loredani; part of Keos, whose harbour could hold a great fleet, to the Premarini. The daughter of old William Crispo, Fiorenza, still held her isle of Anaphe; and the Gozzadini ruled over Siphnos, Thermia, and part of Keos. Seeing that Venice was absolute mistress of Tenos and Mykonos, as well as of the Northern Sporades, and had acquired Cyprus five years before, she still possessed a considerable stake in the Levant, despite the loss of Negroponte.

The Cyclades were all fortified, as we can see from the plans of each island, which the Venetian mariner, Bartolomeo dalli Sonnetti, has inserted in his quaint metrical account of his many voyages among them.[3] Santorin and Keos boasted five castles apiece; Paros four (among them the strong fortress of Kephalos, which Niccolò Sommaripa had recently erected as his residence on a high rock above the sea); Naxos and Amorgos three each; Melos two; and

[1] Sáthas, vi., 241; Casola, 39, 96; Faber, *Evagatorium*, iii., 299, 301, 319-21.

[2] Hopf, *Andros* (tr. Sardagna), 135, 185.

[3] The author's surname is unknown, but he dedicated his book to Mocenigo, the doge who held office from 1478-85. The only historical allusions in it are to Fiorenza, Lady of Melos (fl. 1376); to the recolonisation of Astypalaia by Quirini in 1413; to the eruption of Santorin in 1457; to the dismantling of Tenedos in 1384; and (perhaps) to the loss of Negroponte. Much of the book is not original, being merely copied from Buondelmonti; hence it must be used with caution; but the plans are very accurate, as I have found from personal observation.

Syra and most of the other islands one. Such was the condition of the Archipelago when the first Venetian governor landed at Naxos.

The Venetian administration, brief as it was, seems to have been beneficial to the islands. For a moment corsairs were wiped from the sea, and the frequent presence of a Venetian fleet in one or other of the harbours gave the inhabitants a sense of security. "They look upon our admiral," so runs a Venetian report, "as the Messiah." But these benefits were only temporary. The pirates returned to their favourite hunting-ground as soon as the Venetian admiral had sailed, and two of them in particular, Paolo de Campo of Catania, half-corsair half-hermit, and his rival, Black Hassan by name, did much damage. Moreover, the renewal of hostilities between the sultan and the republic in 1499 alarmed the islanders. The Venetian governor of Naxos wrote that he had no powder; a Venetian ambassador, who paid a passing visit, reported that the fortifications were weak, and suggested that the governor should be recalled and his salary devoted to strengthening them. This policy received powerful support at home from the Loredano family, one of whose daughters, "a lady of wisdom and great talent," had married Francesco, the son of the late Duke of Naxos; accordingly, as the latter was now of age, the senate decided, in October 1500, to restore the duchy to him, on condition that he promised not to take his father as his model. And thus, in an evil hour, a youth who turned out to be a homicidal maniac, took the place of Venice.[1]

The change was in every way unfortunate for the people of the Cyclades. The continuance of the Turco-Venetian war exposed Naxos to two attacks in successive years, in the course of which the lower town was taken and sacked, and many Naxians carried off as prisoners. So savage were the feelings of revenge which such deeds caused, that a celebrated Turkish corsair, driven ashore at Melos, was slowly roasted for three hours by the infuriated people. The peace of 1503, as usual, included the Archipelago, but the petty lords of the

[1] Sanudo, *Diarii*, i., 204, 463, 739, 744, 815; ii., 130, 630, 662-3, 701; iii., 23, 85, 971; Bembo, i., 324 (f. 115, Latin ed.); E. A. C., *Cenni storici intorno Paolo de Campo.*

Ægean were at this time often more oppressive to their subjects than the Turks themselves. The Sommaripa of Paros were at war with the Sommaripa of Andros; the hapless Andrians wrote in Greek to Venice complaining that many of their fellow-countrymen had been borne off to the marble island, while their own "Duke" Francesco was so cruel a tyrant that they actually thought of calling in the Turks. Rather than allow such a calamity to happen, the republic removed the oppressor to Venice, and for seven years, from 1507 to 1514, Andros was ruled by Venetian governors and the lion banner floated over the wave-beat castle of her feudal lords.[1] Meanwhile, the capital of the Archipelago, the fairest isle of the Ægean, had been the scene of one of the most ghastly tragedies in the history of the duchy. Francesco III. had for long been ailing, but it was not till 1509, when he was engaged with the ducal galley in the Venetian service at Trieste, that we first hear of his madness. So violent was his conduct, that his men vowed they would rather serve the Turk, and the duke was put in custody at San Michele di Murano,[2] the present cemetery island. Thence, however, in accordance with a practice still common in Italy, he was released, and thus given the opportunity of committing an atrocious crime. On 15th August 1510, he managed, "by songs, kisses, and caresses," to entice his wife to his couch with the object of murdering her. For the moment, the duchess succeeded in escaping from the maniac's sword by fleeing, just as she was, in her nightdress, to the house of her aunt, the Lady of Nio, Lucrezia Loredano. Thither, however, on the night of the 17th, her husband pursued her, burst open the doors and forced his way upstairs, where he found the Lady of Nio in bed. Meanwhile, on hearing the noise, the terrified duchess had hidden under a wash-tub; but a slave betrayed her hiding-place; the duke struck her over the head with his sword; and, in a frenzied attempt to ward off the blow, she seized the blade with both hands, and fell fainting on the floor at his feet. Even then the wretch's fury was not appeased; he gave the prostrate

[1] Sanudo, *Diarii*, iv., 40, 178, 205, 310; v., 1007; vii., 159, 683, 717; *Relazioni degli Ambasciatori Veneti*, Series III., iii., 14, 15.

[2] Sanudo, *Diarii*, viii., 328, 337, 355, 366.

woman a thrust in the stomach, and then left her to die. Meanwhile, the whole town was on its feet; the duke fled to his garden, and was thence induced by the people to return to his palace, where he vainly endeavoured to prove that his wife's wounds were the result of playing with a knife. A meeting was now held, at which it was decided to depose the murderer, to proclaim his son Giovanni, then not more than eleven years of age, and to elect as governor of the duchy Giacomo Gozzadini, baron of Keos, who resided in Naxos and had already held that office once before. The news of his deposition reached Francesco as he sat at meat in the palace with his son; so great was his fury that he seized a knife to slay his heir, and had not the palace barber caught his arm, a second murder would have been committed. Fortunately, the lad escaped by leaping from the balcony; the people rushed into the palace, and after a fierce struggle, in which the duke was wounded, he was seized, and sent off to Santorin in safe custody.[1]

The Naxiotes lost no time in reporting what had occurred to the nearest Venetian authorities, and the question was brought before the Republican Government. The latter decided to send out Antonio Loredano, the brother of the murdered duchess, as governor of Naxos, with a salary of 400 ducats a year, payable out of the ducal revenues, and to remove the maniac to Candia. There, in 1511, on the anniversary of his crime, he died of fever. For four and a half years Loredano remained in office, and thus for the second time Naxos enjoyed a brief Venetian protectorate.[2] As Andros was also under the administration of the republic, pending the settlement of the various claims to that island, the shadow of the winged lion had fallen over the whole Archipelago. Nor were the Venetian governors by any means to be pitied, for life was taken easily in the Ægean when there was no fear of plague and when there was a temporary lull in the raids of corsairs. We have an interesting account of the amusements organised for one of the Venetian ambassadors who stopped in the islands at this period. "Naxos and Paros," we are told, "are places of much

[1] Sanudo, *Diarii*, xi., 393-4, 705.
[2] *Ibid.*, xii., 22, 175, 503; xx., 354, 356, 376.

diversion, whose lords honoured his Excellency with festivities and balls, at which there was no lack of polished and gracious ladies." The rector of Skyros reported that his island would be most productive, if only the Greeks could be induced to cultivate it assiduously. But there were only two working-days in the week; day after day the people were keeping some festival, gazing with awe at the famous miracle-working eikons in the church of St George, which even Turks thought fit to propitiate with offerings, or dancing the picturesque country dances that have now all but gone. "So passes our life," the rector, evidently a serious man, sadly wrote. Under these circumstances, it is no wonder that no revenues were ever seen at Venice from the Venetian islands of the Ægean.[1]

The Venetian administration of Naxos ceased when the young Duke Giovanni IV. came of age,[2] and as Alberto Sommaripa had at last been recognised as rightful lord of Andros and clad in scarlet at Venice in token of his succession,[3] the Cyclades were once more left to the government of the local dynasties. The reign of Giovanni IV. was the longest of any Duke of the Archipelago, and, with one exception, the most unfortunate. He had not been long on the throne, when he was surprised while hunting, by a Turkish corsair, and carried off as a prize. Venice at once ordered her admiral in Greek waters to ransom her *protégé*, and the Venetian ambassador at Constantinople spoke so strongly on the subject, that the sultan promised to issue a letter "marked with the corsair's head." The duke's imprisonment was brief, but his capture, as he plaintively said, had so bad an effect on his finances that he could not pay his liabilities.[4] Possibly he was not sorry of an excuse for shirking them, as a Venetian commissioner found his revenues to be 3000 ducats and his expenditure 1300. "The young duke," wrote this authority, "is surrounded by evil counsellors; his island is weak, his castle strong, but badly armed." Sanudo, who met him in Venice, describes him as "a very inexperienced

[1] Sanudo, *Diarii*, xvii., 35; xviii., 359-60; xxvi., 457.

[2] From Sanudo, *Diarii*, ii., 701, and xxvi., 457, it seems that he was born in 1499; he is first mentioned as duke in May 1417.

[3] *Ibid.*, xviii., 358, 361.

[4] *Ibid.*, xxiv., 467, 471, 596, 645; xxv., 158, 185.

youth," but none the less the proud republic treated him with the utmost consideration. Not only did she include "Naxos and the islands appertaining to it" in her treaty with Selim I. in 1517, but she bestowed many marks of honour upon the ducal visitor, which show how high was the social status of the ruler of the Archipelago. Four nobles in scarlet and many more in black were sent by the doge to escort him from the house where he was staying, six trumpeters and the men of the ducal galley preceded him, and when he appeared clad in crimson velvet with a gold chain round his neck, the doge embraced him and bade him be seated at his side.[1]

Like most of his race, however, Giovanni IV. did not scruple to defy the republic when it suited his purpose. Soon after his accession, the Sommaripa dynasty became extinct in Paros, by the death of the last baron without issue. Several claimants at once arose; for Paros, though its revenues were then small, was one of the most important islands. Of these claimants the most active was the young Duke of Naxos, who captured the castles of Kephalos and Paroikia, and installed his own officials in both of those fortresses. Meanwhile, the Venetian Government, in its capacity of the late baron's residuary legatee, and in virtue of the general powers of arbitration which it had long claimed in such cases, ordered a commissioner to occupy Paros in its name, pending the decision of the dispute. The Naxian garrison, however, forcibly repulsed his overtures, and it was necessary to make a naval demonstration before the duke was brought to reason. The question was then submitted to a committee of experts in Venice, and the senate decided in favour of Fiorenza Venier, who, as sister of the late baron, was the legal heiress, according to the statutes of the Empire of Romania, and who, as widow of a Venetian noble, was the most desirable candidate. Thus, in 1520, the marble island, like the island of Venus, passed to the Venieri. But they had little time to leave any mark upon their new domain, for their dynasty too became extinct at Paros eleven years later, when a fresh dispute arose as to the succession. On this occasion, the Duke of Naxos, now grown wiser, did not interpose; a Venetian commissioner was sent to govern the island in the

[1] Sanudo, *Diarii*, xxv., 416; xxvi., 457; xxxiv., 245, 246, 259, 260.

interim, and in 1535 the republic decided in favour of another woman—Cecilia, sister of the last baron and wife of a brave Venetian, Bernardo Sagredo, whose heroic defence of the island against the Turks is one of the last and brightest pages in the history of the Archipelago.[1]

The accession of Suleyman the Magnificent renewed and increased the dangers to which the petty lords of the Ægean, as the advanced guard of Christendom, were peculiarly exposed. Any advantages which they might gain from his treaty with Venice were more than balanced by his capture of Rhodes—a feat of arms facilitated by the indifference of the most serene republic. But the Duke of Naxos was not indifferent to the fate of the warrior Knights, a branch of whose Order existed in his capital, and who had held for the last forty years the neighbouring island of Nikaria. He prayed God to help them in this, their hour of need, and incurred the censure of Venice and the risk of a Turkish attack by furnishing them with provisions. It seems, indeed, to have been thought that after the fall of Rhodes they would ask his permission to make Naxos their headquarters. Such an act of generosity would, however, have been fatal to the duchy; for either the newcomers would have made themselves its masters, or the sultan would have annexed it without delay, rather than allow so central a position to fall into the possession of his deadly foes. The popes had, however, long ago transferred Lindos and two Asian bishoprics to the metropolitan see of the Archipelago at Naxos, and now endowed the archbishop with the goods of the Order there.[2]

During the next ten years we hear little of the duchy; Venice was at peace with the great sultan, so that her *protégé* was able to leave his island state for the purpose of paying a vow at Loreto and Rome, undisturbed except by the visit of some dangerous Turkish corsair. His weakness was, however, clearly displayed in 1532, when Kurtoglu, one of the worst of those sea-robbers, suddenly appeared at Naxos with twelve sail, and was only bought off by a gift of

[1] Sanudo, *Diarii*, xxv., 259, 264, 281, 282, 421, 422; xxvi., 24, 160, 161; xxvii., 482; xxix., 52, 55, 57, 64, 68, 507; Sauger, 344.

[2] *Ibid.*, xxxi., 59; xxxiii., 362, 375; Sauger, 286; Lichtle, *op. cit.*; Reg. Av., clxvii., f. 441.

money and refreshments. Both the Venetian governor of Paros and the petty seigneur of Sifanto had to pay blackmail to this ruffian, who levied 30 ducats from the exiguous finances of the latter island. "It would make the very stones weep," wrote the Venetian rector of Mykonos, "to see the ruin" which another of these pirates caused.[1] Meanwhile, the nephew of a famous corsair compiled a Turkish account of the Cyclades to facilitate their conquest.

The long-threatening storm at last burst over "the isles of Greece." In 1536 France and the sultan made an unholy alliance for the purpose of driving Venice from the Levant, and in the following year the war broke out, which was destined to deprive the republic of her last possessions in the Morea.[2] The Turkish attack upon Corfù failed, as we saw; but a fleet of seventy galleys and thirty smaller vessels appeared in the Ægean under the command of Khaireddîn Barbarossa, the terrible corsair, himself an islander from Lesbos,[3] who had risen to be the Turkish admiral. His first attacks were directed against the two Venetian islands of Cerigo and Ægina, whose terrible sufferings at his hands have been described in previous chapters. From Ægina the red-bearded commander sailed to the Cyclades, where one petty Venetian dynasty after another fell before him. The castle of Seriphos, where the Michieli had lorded it for over a century, could not save their diminutive barony from annexation; the group of three islands, Nio, Namfio, and Antiparos, which had passed by marriage or inheritance a few years before from the ducal family to the Pisani,[3] now became Turkish; the Quirini lost their possessions of Stampalia and Amorgos, whose inhabitants fled to Crete. These six islands never again owned the Latin sway. Abandoned by Venice in the shameful treaty of 1540, their Venetian lords in vain attempted to recover them by negotiations with the Porte. The Pisani pleaded for the restitution of little Namfio, but the Venetian bailie at Constantinople

[1] Sanudo, *Diarii*, xxx., 450; lvi., 882; *Mitteilungen* (*Athen*), xxvii., 417-30.

[2] Haji Kalifeh, *History of the Maritime Wars of the Turks*, 28.

[3] Hopf, *Analekten*, 419; Sanudo, *Diarii*, lvii., 472; Pasch von Krienen, 31.

replied that all the inhabitants had been removed, and that the islet had been left a mere barren rock. The Quirini were willing to acquiesce in the loss of Amorgos, if they could but retain Stampalia, the island whose name they had incorporated with their own. But there, again, the sultan was inexorable.[1] The escutcheon of the Michieli over the castle gate at Seriphos alone preserves the memory of their rule there; but the connection of the Quirini with Stampalia survives in their arms and superscription in that island, and in the name of the square, street, bridge, and palace in Venice, where they long resided, and where the last of their race only recently died. But few who enter the library, into which the Palazzo Quirini-Stampalia has now been converted, realise the historic meaning of its double name.[2]

Having thus made an easy conquest of the smaller islands, Barbarossa appeared at Paros, and ordered it to surrender. But Bernardo Sagredo, the baron of the marble island, was resolved not to relinquish his newly-won possession without a struggle. Abandoning the fortress of Agousa to the enemy, he shut himself up with the small forces at his command in the strong castle of Kephalos, where, with the aid of a Florentine outlaw, he not only held out for several days, but made effective sorties against the besiegers. Want of powder, however, forced him to yield; his wife, Cecilia Venier, was allowed to withdraw to Venice, and Sagredo himself was soon released from captivity, thanks to the gratitude of a Ragusan sailor who had once rowed in a galley under his command. The Parians, some 6000 in number, were treated as the other islanders had been; the old men were butchered, the young men were sent to serve at the oar; the women were ordered to dance on the shore, so that the conqueror might choose the most pleasing for his lieutenants; the boys were enrolled in the corps of the janissaries.[3] Though Sagredo tried to recover his lost island

[1] A. Maurocenus, *Historia Veneta* (ed. 1623), 182; Paruta, *Historia Venetiana* (ed. 1703), 382; Predelli, *Commemoriali*, vi., 236, 238; Hopf, *op. cit.*, 417, 476; *La Vidade Barbaroxa* in *Arch. Stor. Sicil.*, xi., 105-9.

[2] Pasch von Krienen, 110.

[3] Maurocenus, *loc. cit.*; Paruta, *loc. cit.*; Buchon, *Recherches*, ii., 468; Hopf, *Andros* (tr. Sardagna), 148-50; Pasch von Krienen, 119; A. Cornaro, "Historia di Candia," ff. 93, 94.

by the offer of tribute, it was abandoned to the sultan by the treaty of 1540. But the latter would seem to have given it to the Duke of Naxos, among whose possessions we find it included some twenty years later, while at the same time, a Greek named Eraclídes Basilikós, one of those adventurers so common in the Levant, who boasted that he was descended from the rulers of Moldavia, was pleased to style himself Margrave Palatine of Paros![1]

From Paros the Turkish fleet sailed across to the capital of the Cyclades. We have from the pen of the duke himself a graphic account of this dreaded visitation. As soon as the fatal galleys were sighted, the inhabitants fled from all parts of the island to take refuge in the city, leaving in their haste their heavy goods and chattels behind them. The Turks had no sooner landed than they forced their way into the tower near the sea and the adjoining houses, and, in their rage at finding no one there, destroyed all those buildings and broke open the cellars, where corn, wine, and oil were stored. Meanwhile, a Christian emissary of the Turkish commander sought an audience of the reluctant duke in his palace in the upper town. "If," he said, "you will voluntarily submit yourself and your islands to the emperor, already master of Asia and ere long of all Europe too, you may easily obtain his favour. If not, then I bid you expect his hatred and indignation." The envoy continued in the same strain: "If you surrender, all your possessions shall be saved; but if you refuse, we will send you, your wife and children, your fellow-countrymen and subjects, to destruction together. We have a powerful fleet, a vigorous and victorious soldiery, and an admirable siege equipment. Take warning and counsel, then, from the Æginetans, the Parians, and the other lords of the Cyclades. You are fortunate to be able, if you choose wisely, to profit by the misfortunes of your neighbours." The duke begged the envoy to withdraw, while he took counsel with his advisers. The trembling council hastily met, and, as the ducal resources were inadequate to the task of resisting and there was no hope of help from Western Christendom, it was decided to accept the Turkish terms, rather than expose the

[1] Gratiani, *De Joanne Heraclide Despota*, 6.

duke and his subjects to the certainty of death or slavery. Accordingly, on 11th November, Giovanni IV. surrendered, promising to pay an annual tribute of 5000 ducats,[1] and paying the first year in advance, in order to mollify his threatening adversary. The sum, he plaintively says, was beyond the means of a poor duke and an exiguous state, but the loss of the money was a lesser evil than the loss of his dominions. Yet, with all these concessions, he could not prevent the Turks from ravaging "the Queen of the Cyclades" and carrying off more than 25,000 ducats' worth of booty, and he already foresaw that, unless Christendom would unite against the Turk, in a few years' time he would share the same fate which had, eighty years before, befallen the last Greek emperor of Constantinople.

With the forlorn hope of making Christendom forget its quarrels and combine against the common foe, the duke addressed his memorable letter to "Pope Paul III.; the Emperor Charles V.; Ferdinand, King of the Romans; François I. of France; and the other Christian kings and princes." In this curious document he bade them "apply their ears and lift up their eyes, and attend with their minds, while their own interests were still safe," lest they, too, should suffer the fate of the writer. He reminded them of the wealth and strength of the magnificent sultan, which, even if united by some miracle, they would find it hard to resist. He pointed out that Suleyman's policy was to separate them, so as the easier to destroy one while cajoling another, and that by this means ere long the whole earth would be the sheep-fold of Mahomet. He emphasised these admirable truisms, which might have been addressed to the Concert of Europe at any time during the last thirty years, by a well-worn tag from his ancestor Sallust—Sallustius Crispus "the author of our race"—and urged his correspondents to wake up and invade the Turkish Empire while the sultan's attention was distracted by the Persian war.[2] But neither his platitudes nor his allusion to his distinguished

[1] In 1553 and 1554 the tribute for the Cyclades was 6000 ducats; *Relazioni degli Ambasciatori Veneti*, Series III., i., 39, 150.

[2] Buchon, *Recherches*, ii., 464-72; Charrière, *Négociations de la France dans le Levant*, i., 373.

ancestry, which he might have had some difficulty in proving, availed the unfortunate duke with the selfish powers of Europe.

Meanwhile, Barbarossa went on with his career of conquest; Mykonos, so sorely tried sixteen years before, now succumbed, never to become Venetian again, though the rector of Tenos might still pretend to jurisdiction over the sister island and for half a century longer bear its name in his commission. Many of the inhabitants were carried off; the rest fled to Tenos. The people of the latter island, despite their devotion to Venice, yielded at once to the summons of the terrible admiral; at the suggestion of a treacherous Melian, who, as a subject of the Duke of Naxos, was no friend of the Venetians, they handed Dolfino, the rector, to Barbarossa. They soon repented their precipitate surrender, sent to Crete for aid, and once more hoisted the lion banner. So ashamed were the Teniotes of their disloyalty, that later travellers were told that their ancestors had merely thought for a moment of surrender, and that they had not only routed the forces of Barbarossa, but had thrown down from the battlements of the castle the officer whom he had sent to arrange the terms of the expected capitulation.[1] Keos, then divided between the Premarini and the Gozzadini, was captured, but bestowed by the sultan on the duke in the following year.[2] Crusino Sommaripa lost Andros, but managed to regain possession of his island, thanks to the intervention of the French ambassador at Constantinople, to whom he doubtless emphasised his own French descent. It was arranged that he should pay an annual tribute of 35,000 *aspers* to the Bey of Negroponte, and a firman of the sultan specially allowed the Andrians to defend themselves against the violence of the janissaries.[3] The other islands received similar capitulations.[4]

In 1538, Barbarossa made a second cruise in the Ægean

[1] Cornaro, *op. cit.*, ff. 94, 95, 99; Maurocenus, *loc. cit.;* Tournefort, *Voyage du Levant*, i., 139. *Cf.* the author's article on Mykonos in the *English Historical Review*, xxii., 307.

[2] Haji Kalifeh, *op. cit.*, 58; Mar., xxvi., f. 48 (mistranslated by Hopf, *Analekten*, 451.)

[3] Sauger, 349-51; Pègues, *Histoire de Santorin*, 609.

[4] Sanudo, *Diarii*, lv., 458-9, 472-6.

with a fleet of 120 sail, received the tribute due from the Duke of Naxos, and put an end for ever to the rule of Venice in the Northern Sporades. Though at times oppressed by their Venetian rectors, the Greeks of those islands had often sought and found justice from the Home Government. Only a few years before their capture by the Turks, they had taken the opportunity of the visit of a Venetian commissioner to complain of the tyranny of their rectors. Sanudo has left us a picturesque account of the scene—how the people of Skyros, men and women alike, came down to the shore, crying "Mercy, mercy upon us!" how the commissioner bade the town-crier summon all who had any grievance against the rector to appear before him, and how they told him the piteous tale of their woes. Their rector, said their spokesman, the Greek bishop, had "cornered" all the corn of the island, and had prevented the importation of more by asking the neighbouring Turkish governors to send none to Skyros. Then, despite the express clause in their capitulations forbidding the rector to engage in trade, he had sold them his whole stock at his own price, and allowed no one to bake bread except from his corn, so that many had fled to Turkey. Similarly, the people of Skiathos had complained that there was such insecurity that they must perforce remain shut up in the castle "like a bird in its cage." In both these cases the rector was removed, and Venetian justice was amply vindicated; it might therefore have been expected that the natives would have fought to the last for their masters. But their treachery caused the loss of both these islands. The people of Skyros at once handed over Cornaro, their rector, with his court and some Italian artillerymen sent from Candia, and offered to pay 2000 ducats tribute to the Turk. Memmo, the rector of Skiathos, knew that the lofty castle possessed great natural strength; he therefore resolved to hold out, and, as his garrison was small, armed the natives, on whom he thought he could rely. Unhappily, an arrow wounded him at the first attack; as he lay wounded in his litter, the traitors in the castle fell upon him and slew him; whereupon they let down ropes from the rocks and drew the Turks up into the citadel. Barbarossa was so indignant at the murder of his brave opponent, that he ordered the instant beheadal of the men who had betrayed their commander, and carried off the rest of the inhabitants into slavery. When Baron Blancard, the French admiral, passed soon afterwards, he found Skiathos and Skopelos both deserted.[1]

Like the islands of the dispossessed barons of the Archipelago, the Northern Sporades and the much older Venetian colony of Mykonos were retained by the sultan at the peace of 1540, despite the efforts of the Venetian plenipotentiary. Five years later we find Venice still in vain trying to obtain the restitution of little Mykonos.[2] Only the non-Venetian dynasties of the Ægean—the Crispi, the Sommaripa, and the Gozzadini—survived the two fatal visits of the red-bearded admiral. Even the lord of little Siphnos was glad to pay tribute, "not wishing to appear either wiser or more foolish than his neighbours."[3] They well knew, however, that they only existed on sufferance. Venice could no longer afford them protection, nor had she the same interests as before in a sea where Tenos was now her sole possession.

Her shameful neglect of even so important an outpost as Tenos was shown from the fact that no *sindici* visited the island to redress the grievances of the Greeks for over thirty years. It is to the visit of one of these officials in 1563 that we owe a most interesting account of the state of the Cyclades on the eve of the Turkish Conquest. "Tenos," he wrote, "is the richest and most populous of all the Ægean islands, with the exception of Chios; the fortress is almost impregnable, though the garrison consists of but twelve foot soldiers; the population is 9000, a good part of whom speak Italian and are Catholics. Such is their civilisation, that this remote island scarcely differs at all from Venetia; while the corsairs are a constant menace to the other islands, they rarely venture to molest Tenos, defended as it is by 2000 able-bodied men. Among themselves the Teniotes are peaceable; the oldest inhabitant cannot remember a murder; the rectors

[1] Maurocenus, 196; Paruta, 409; Charrière, *loc. cit.*; Cornaro, *loc. cit.*; Haji Khalifeh, 59-61.

[2] Predelli, *Commemoriali*, vi., 236, 238; Lamansky, *Secrets de l'État de Venise*, 58; Sáthas, viii., 451.

[3] Cornaro, *op. cit.*, f. 100.

find them excellent and most obedient subjects, and fines are accustomed to be paid in silk, the staple of the island. Yet some of those officials in the past have made too much out of the islanders, who have one special grievance against them. Tenos, it should be remembered, consists of two halves—one half directly administered by the republic, the other originally let by the senate to the Loredano family and disposed of by them to some citizens of the island called Scutoni, or Scutari. According to the Venetian regulations, the produce of the former half, consisting of corn and wine, should be sold every year by auction to the highest bidder; and out of the proceeds, which should average 800 ducats, the salaries of the rector and the other officials should be paid. Latterly, however, in distinct violation of the capitulations, which prohibit direct or indirect trading by the rectors, those officials have bought up all the corn at low prices, as no one dared to bid against them, especially as the governors of Tenos have more power than those of any other Venetian colony, and are less liable, from their distance from Venice or even Crete, to be called to account. This abuse is doubly bad: for not only are the natives compelled to buy corn from the rector on his own terms, as the island does not produce sufficient other grain for their nourishment, but the castle is often left without provisions. Two remedies are suggested: the increase of the rector's present miserable salary of seven ducats a month, which forces him to make money in this way; and the substitution of a cash payment by the people, instead of this *zemoro*, or tithe in kind, which they would much prefer. For humanitarian, strategic, and political reasons alike, the republic should hold this island dear. For it is the sole refuge in the Archipelago for fugitive slaves, whose surrender the other islanders dare not refuse, and it is the first point whence a Turkish fleet can be spied, and thus Candia can be warned in time. Above all, it is a living memorial of Venetian rule, which keeps ever before the eyes of the other islanders the blessings of your sway. Moreover, if the Teniotes were discontented, you could not retain them for a moment, nor are there wanting incentives to disaffection among them. Their neighbour, the Duke of Naxos, naturally an ambitious man, anxious to increase his state by hook or by crook at the expense of his neighbours, covets Tenos, and lavishes favours on its inhabitants, whenever they come to Naxos or any of his other islands, trying to persuade them that they would be better off under his rule. His argument is an appeal to their material interests. "'As my subjects,' he tells them, 'you would be Turkish tributaries, and in that capacity you would be able to purchase corn in Turkey and could more easily recover any of your friends who have been captured by Turkish corsairs.' On the other hand," added the commissioner, "I have found in the other islands, formerly under Venetian protection, incredible affection for, and devotion to, your rule. Never have those people forgotten that happy time."

It was the Venetian policy to allow the Teniotes a large measure of local government, and the local offices were held on short tenures, so that as many as possible might participate in them. Every 25th of April the rector summoned the council, composed of all the citizens of the capital, or Castello, and submitted to them the names of four different families, from one of which they elected an official, called the "bailie." Local judges, annually elected, tried small cases, with an appeal to the rector, instead of to Crete, as the journey thither was both expensive and unsafe. The republic wisely allowed the old code to continue in force—the Assizes of Romania and the statutes of Casa Ghisi, by which Tenos had been governed for nearly two centuries before her time. She had confirmed the privileges, alike of the Byzantine emperors and of the Latin barons, and her rector every two years named the headmen, or primates (*protogeri*) of the villages. Once a year, on May-day, he kept up the ancient custom of receiving the homage of the feudatories at the mountain of S. Veneranda; four times a year it was their duty to practice the cross-bow for the defence of the island. All the summer long, watch was kept day and night at the coast (the so-called *merovigli* and *nichtovigli*), and relays of peasants, called *roccari*, or "men of the fortress," had to guard the castle at night. Beacon-fires were lighted as soon as a suspicious sail was sighted; rewards were offered for every corsair's head that was brought to the rector; Turkish captains were propitiated by presents of live stock; and finally five so-called "centurions" were elected by the council to form a trainband of 100 men each, as in the Ionian islands. Such was existence in the one Venetian island of the Ægean at the time of the Turkish conquest of the other Cyclades.

The writer above mentioned then proceeds to describe the condition of the duchy. "The islands of Zia, Siphnos, and Andros," he told his Government, "have their own lords (the Sommaripa and the Gozzadini), but are tributaries of the sultan; the other sixteen islands are under the duke, but of these, only five—Naxos, Santorin, Melos, Syra, and Paros—are inhabited. The Duke of Naxos, a man of nearly seventy, is, in point of dignity, the Premier Duke of Christendom; but, despite his title, he is duke more in name than in fact; for in all things the Grand Turk and his ministers are practically supreme. Every year, when the Turkish captains arrive, the duke's subjects bring their complaints against him before them, so that he dare not punish his own dependents for their crimes, nor even for their offences against his own person. He dresses and lives like a pauper, without the least pomp or princely expenditure; for, though he raises from 9000 to 10,000 ducats a year out of his islands, he has to pay 4000 ducats as tribute to the sultan, and his sole thought is how he can save money with which to bribe the Turkish captains and ministers. Under these circumstances, his administration is rather the shadow of a principality than a government."[1]

The Venetian commissioner's report is fully confirmed from what we know of the duke from other sources. Scarcely had the peace of 1540 been concluded than he, who had so eloquently preached to the Great Powers the need of union, exemplified the insincerity of such maxims by benefiting his own relatives at the expense of his Christian neighbours. The Turks acquiesced, and the Venetians in vain protested, when he kept the Premarini out of their part of Zia, and bestowed it, together with the devastated island of Mykonos, which Venice had been forced to abandon to the sultan, upon his daughter on her marriage

[1] Lamansky, *op. cit.*, 651-60, 08-10; Sáthas, iv., 236-311. *Cf.* Count Albrecht zu Löwenstein (who visited Melos in 1562), *apud* Feyerabend, *Reyssbuch*, fol. 205.

with Gian Francesco Sommaripa, the last Latin lord of Andros, while allowing the Gozzadini, who were his wife's relatives and the traditional friends of his dynasty, to retain their share of Zia.[1] The duke might go on distributing fiefs to his friends—we have several documents bearing his name, and one bearing his ducal seal[2]—he might appoint his relatives governors of his subordinate islands; but he was under no illusions as to the security of his tenure. Every year the disaffection of his Greek subjects, who at this time formed nineteenth-twentieths of the population of Naxos,[3] increased; they saw that their Latin masters were themselves the slaves of the Turks, and when a Western nation has lost its prestige, how can it hope to govern an oriental people? Moreover, in order to raise funds for his tribute to the sultan and for bribing the Turkish officials, the duke was forced to squeeze more money than before out of his subjects. The latter, as in the other Latin states of the Levant, found leaders in the Orthodox clergy. In 1559, the duke was forced to banish the Orthodox metropolitan of Paronaxia for sedition. This divine, dabbling in politics after the fashion of his kind, had conspired with a certain Mamusso of Candia to stir up a revolt among his flock. "It was disgraceful," he said, "that so many valiant Greeks should allow their religion to be insulted and their country to be governed by a mere handful of Franks."[4] Such an incident, to which there had been no parallel in the history of the duchy since the days of Marco II., was ominous of the future. Worse still, the œcumenical patriarch asked the grand vizier to oust the Catholic hierarchy, whose scandalous conduct and great unpopularity were admitted by the duke in two letters to Rome. "I have decided," he told the Vatican, "to have no more friars or foreigners as archbishops: local people alone are popular." It was obvious that at any moment the natives might call in the Turks to

[1] Hopf, *Analekten*, 451; Sauger, 296, 352 (whose account, more trustworthy as he approaches his own time, here tallies with the fact, unknown to Hopf, that Mykonos was no longer Venetian).

[2] Buchon, *Recherches*, ii., 463, 473; *Atlas*, xlii., 14; *Byzantinische Zeitschrift*, xiii., 154-6.

[3] Lichtle.

[4] Lamansky, 064; Vat. Arch., Arm. xi., Caps. iv., 183.

put an end to the tyranny of the small foreign garrison, which still preserved its titles and dignities without the power to make them respected.

Giovanni IV., happy in the opportunity of his death, was spared the humiliation of witnessing the fall of his dynasty. He ended his long reign—the longest of any Duke of the Archipelago—in 1564, and his second son, Giacomo IV., the last Christian ruler of the duchy, reigned in his stead[1]—for his elder son, Francesco, who had shared his father's throne and had therefore acquired some experience of government, had unfortunately predeceased him. The new duke recognised that he was a mere puppet of the Turks; in a letter, written in 1565, he plaintively says: "We are now tributaries of the great emperor, Sultan Suleyman, and we are in evil plight, because of the difficulties of the times; for now necessity reigns with embarrassment and pain for her ministers; and, like plenipotentiaries or commissioners of others, we husband our opportunities as fate doth ordain."[2] But, though he saw the weakness of his position, he acted as if it were impregnable. He and the nobles of his petty court thought of nothing but their pleasures and of how to gratify them. The debauchery of the castle of Naxos utterly scandalised the temperate Greeks; the heir apparent was a notorious evil liver; and the climax was reached when the Latin clergy lived in open concubinage and a Catholic ecclesiastic publicly accompanied the body of his mistress to the grave and received the condolences of his friends on his loss. These shocks to their morality, combined with fiscal oppression, at last made the Greeks desire a change of master, such as the people of Chios had just experienced. They sent two of their number to the sultan, begging him to send them some person fitter to govern them, much as the Samians constantly do at the present day. The duke now realised his peril; he collected 12,000 ducats and sailed for Constantinople to counteract their efforts by the most convincing of arguments. But he was too late; on his arrival, he was at once stripped of all his possessions and

[1] We have a document of Giacomo IV., dated 10th December 1564, *Byzant. Zeitschrift*, xiii., 157.

[2] *Ibid.*, 138.

thrown into prison like a common malefactor, where he remained for five or six months. Meanwhile, another Christian renegade, Piali Pasha, who had driven the Genoese from Chios, returned from the Adriatic, and occupied Naxos without opposition. The Greeks of Andros, who had learnt to despise their feeble lord, seeing how successful their fellows in Naxos had been in getting rid of their duke, conspired against the life of Sommaripa. Deserted by most of the Latins of the island, who, instead of rallying round him, fled from the persecution of the Greeks, he saved his life, but lost his islands of Andros and Zia, by flight to his wife's native Naxos. At the same time, the last remaining Latin dynasty, that of the Gozzadini, was wiped from the map.[1] Thus, after having lasted for 359 years, the Latin duchy of the Archipelago ceased to exist. Tenos alone survived the wave of Turkish conquest which swept over the Ægean.

The Naxiotes and Andrians soon found that they had exchanged the rule of King Log for that of King Stork. The new sultan, Selim II., bestowed the oldest and most picturesque of all the Latin states of the Levant upon his favourite, Joseph Nasi, a Jewish adventurer, who thus, after many vicissitudes, rose from the prosaic counting-house to the romantic island-throne of the Sanudi and the Crispi. Nasi belonged to a family of Portuguese Jews, who had outwardly embraced Christianity in order to escape persecution, and had assumed the aggressively Portuguese name of Miquez, the better to conceal their Hebrew origin. Like other members of his family, João Miquez, as he was then pleased to call himself, went to seek his fortune at Antwerp, where his aunt, a rich widow, admitted him to the management of her affairs. He there won the favour of the regent of the Low Countries, Maria, sister of the Emperor Charles V., and the love of his fair cousin, with whom he eloped. His aunt sanctioned the marriage, and the whole household migrated for greater security to Italy. We next hear of Miquez founding a bank at Lyons, and becoming the creditor of the French crown to a large amount. Thence, armed with a letter of introduction from the French

[1] Sauger, 299-301, 354-5; Luccari, *Copioso ristretto degli Annali di Rausa*, 148; Conti, *Historie de' suoi tempi*, i., 475.

ambassador in Rome, he made his way to Constantinople, where Jews were well received, and where his real fortunes began. There was no longer need for disguising himself as a Christian; he returned to the faith and name of his Jewish forefathers; and, as Joseph Nasi, gained the intimacy of the future sultan, Selim II., thanks to one of his co-religionists, a Jewish doctor named Daout, and retained it by pandering to the vices of that bibulous and gluttonous ruler, to whom he presented choice wines and dainties for his table.[1] But Nasi, like the Jewish magnates of our own time, was anxious to benefit his race as well as himself. He had long cherished the idea of founding a Jewish state, and thus, in the sixteenth century, anticipated the Zionist movement. He had in vain asked Venice to give him an island for the new Zion; from Suleyman the Magnificent he obtained permission to rebuild the town of Tiberias. Startled French diplomatists, upon whom he kept pressing his claims for payment, reported that he intended to make himself "King of the Jews"; fulsome Jewish authors dedicated to him their works; the whole downtrodden race regarded him as its head. Such was the man upon whom Selim II. now solemnly conferred Naxos, Andros, and the other islands of the Archipelago, with the historic title of duke.[2]

When the islanders heard that a Jew was to be their new master, they hastened to repair the mistake which they had committed. The Greeks do not love the Catholics, but they love the Jews even less, and the latter fully reciprocate their feelings. The subjects of the dispossessed duke begged the sultan to release Giacomo IV. and restore him to his now faithful people. Selim set the prisoner free, but refused to replace him on the ducal throne. Finding that arguments were useless against the all-powerful Jew, Crispo, accompanied by his family and by his sister, the Lady of Andros, fled to the

[1] *Le Relazioni degli Ambasciatori veneti*, Series III., i., 343; ii., 66, 67, 91.

[2] Charrière, *Négociations de la France*, ii., 403, 707, 708, 735-7, 773-5; iii., 80, 84; Strada, *De bello Belgico*, i., 171-2; Reports of Venetian and Imperial Ambassadors, *apud* Hammer, *Geschichte des osm. Reiches*, iii., 564-5; Sereno, *Commentari della Guerra di Cipro*, 7; Contarini, *Historia delle cose successe*, 2; Carmoly, *Don Joseph Nassy* (a work to be used with caution); Levy, *Don Joseph Nasi*; Romanin, vi., 317, *n.* 2.

Morea, whence he proceeded to Rome to seek aid of Pope Pius V., while his wife found a refuge in the republic of Ragusa. From Rome the duke went to beg alms of Venice; and the Venetian Government, moved by the spectacle of his poverty, assisted him, as the pope had done, and thus enabled him to live in a manner more suitable to the "Premier Duke of Christendom."[1]

The Jewish Duke of Naxos never once visited his duchy during the thirteen years for which it belonged to him. Possibly he did not dare, certainly he did not desire, to quit the court of Constantinople, where he was the boon companion of Selim the Sot, for the splendid isolation of the Crispi's feudal castle at Naxos or for the island fortress of the Sommaripa at Andros. Moreover, he was engaged in larger enterprises—seizing the French ships at Alexandria, hounding the Turks against Otranto, scheming for the conquest of Cyprus. At the same time, he was anxious to make as much out of the Cyclades as possible—for his tribute to the sultan from the islands was 14,000 ducats and his personal expenses enormous—and he therefore sent there as his deputy a man in whom he had the fullest confidence, Dr Francesco Coronello, a lawyer by profession, a Christian by name, but a Spanish Jew by race, whose father, Salamon, had been governor of Segovia, but was at this time "the right eye" of Nasi at Constantinople, constantly consulted by the great financier, and together with his son Francesco—so it was said in the Cyclades—responsible for the deposition of the Crispi and the Sommaripa.[2] The Jesuit historian of the duchy, moved by the fact that a Coronello was in his time French consul at Naxos,[3] has depicted Francesco Coronello as a beloved and respected ruler; and such was the official Turkish view.[4] But the contemporary opinion of him, as held at least in the Venetian island of Tenos, was very different. The Teniotes had special reasons for disliking the change of government in the neighbouring islands.

[1] Luccari, *loc. cit.*; Conti, *loc. cit.*; Sauger, 303.

[2] Gerlach, *Tagebuch*, 426; Lamansky, *Secrets*, 82.

[3] Sauger, 302.

[4] As expressed in the capitulations of 1580 and 1640; Pègues, *Histoire de Santorin*, 609, 614.

The lords of Andros and Naxos, even when Turkish tributaries, had not ceased to be Christians, and had always secretly warned their co-religionists of any coming attack. The Jewish duke's lieutenant, on the other hand, allowed neither news nor food to reach Tenos or Crete from his islands, and sent back all runaway slaves to their masters at Constantinople. At a time of peace, this "mortal enemy of Venice" seized a Cretan brig, laden with money and powder for the garrison of Tenos, taking the cargo and enslaving the crew. In order to hound on the sultan against the republic, he sent him a specimen of the bread which the Venetians of Crete were obliged to eat in their dire extremity. Being in the adjacent island of Andros in 1570, he discovered that Tenos also had no provisions. According to a story current at the time, he had sent Selim a picture of a lovely garden, in the midst of which was one very fruitful tree. "The garden," the sultan was told, "is the Cyclades, and is all your majesty's, save this one tree, which is Tenos."[1] Sure of the sultan's approval, he therefore urged Piali Pasha, who was then at Athens, to complete his conquest of the Cyclades by capturing the Venetian island. "Tenos," he told the Turkish admiral, "is the refuge of all the fugitive slaves and of all the Christian vassals; unless you take it, the other islands will never be quiet." Piali responded to this appeal; he landed with Coronello at Tenos with 8000 men; but though he did great damage, the courage of Girolamo Paruta, the Venetian rector, saved the last Venetian possession in the Ægean. Soon afterwards, Coronello himself fell into the hands of his enemies. During a visit to Syra, even then a flourishing island with more than 3000 inhabitants, he was seized in the night by the leading men, and handed over to the commander of three Cretan vessels, then lying in the harbour. When the Teniotes heard that their arch foe, "the heart and soul of João Miquez," had been captured, they offered the ships' captain 500 sequins to put him ashore on Tenos and let them execute him with cruel tortures. Coronello, however, bid a higher sum, if the captain would take him to Canea instead, and he was accordingly put in prison there, pending

[1] Buochenbach, *Orientalische Reyss*, 39.

the decision of the Home Government. Meanwhile, the Turkish authorities despatched a commissioner to punish the people of Syra, but the latter protested that it was not they but the ships' captain who had kidnapped Coronello, and convinced the commissioner of their truthfulness by a bribe.[1]

The fatal war had now broken out which was to cost Venice the possession of Cyprus, and the republic, suspecting that Nasi had been responsible for the recent conflagration in her arsenal, and knowing that he had been largely instrumental in hounding on Selim II. against that island, whose arms he had had painted in his house, and whose king he aspired to be,[2] naturally bethought herself of the exiled Duke of Naxos. A Venetian fleet entered the Archipelago; the moment was propitious, for Nasi's lieutenant was a prisoner at Canea; and thus, in 1571, with the aid of the *provveditore* Canale, Giacomo IV. was restored to the ducal throne, and Niccolò Gozzadini recovered his island of Siphnos.[3] He does not seem, however, to have returned to Naxos, which was temporarily placed under the administration of a certain Angelo "Giudizzi," perhaps one of the Gozzadini family.[4] But he exercised his authority by nominating a new Archbishop. The duke showed his gratitude to the republic by following her fleet at the great battle of Lepanto with a force of 500 men.[5]

Meanwhile, the Teniotes had sent a secret envoy to Venice, imploring the republic not to let loose so dangerous a man as Coronello. The senate accordingly ordered the Cretan authorities to enquire into the truth of the allegations against him; if they proved to be true, then to put him to death secretly and give out that he had died of an illness; if there was any doubt about the charges, to send him to the prison at Candia for greater security.[6] The sequel of this

[1] Lamansky, *Secrets*, 80-3; Contarini, *op. cit.*, 5; Hammer, *op. cit.*, iii., 576.

[2] Contarini, *op. cit.*, 2; Charrière, *op. cit.*, iii., 88; *Relazioni degli Ambasciatori veneti*, *Appendice*, 391.

[3] Crescenzi, *Corona della nobiltà d'Italia*, ii., 159.

[4] Lichtle; Hopf *apud* Ersch und Gruber, lxxvi., 422, *n.*

[5] Predelli, *Commemoriali*, vi., 327; Theiner, *Annales Ecclesiastici*, i., 473.

[6] Lamansky, *loc. cit.*

incident is unknown; but Coronello managed to regain his freedom and his former position in Naxos, which was recovered by the Turks under Mehmet Pasha almost as soon as it had been won by Canale. At any rate, in 1572 we find Giacomo IV. begging the republic to order its fleet to aid him in recapturing his dominions,[1] and presenting them in advance to his benefactress Venice. Like other people, he was inspired with hope by the recent victory of Lepanto, in which he had borne a part; but his hopes were disappointed in the humiliating peace which the Venetians concluded with the sultan in 1573.

On the death of Selim II. in the following year, the influence of his favourite Nasi was expected to wane, especially as the grand-vizier loathed him, and the chances of the deposed duke accordingly seemed brighter. The mother of the new sultan (Murâd III.), a Baffo, was a native of Paros, and he therefore hoped that her influence with her son would be exerted in his favour. Accordingly, in 1575, he set out for Constantinople by way of Ragusa and Philippopolis, where the Ragusan historian Luccari[2] invited him to dinner and learnt from him much about the past glories of the Crispi. But his mission failed, and in the following year he died of a broken heart at Pera, and was buried in the Latin church there. Nasi, whose influence, though diminished since the accession of Murâd III., was still sufficient to enable him to retain the duchy of Naxos and the duty on wine, continued to govern the islands from his mansion at Belvedere, near Constantinople, through the faithful Coronello, whose authority was such that he is said to have styled himself officially "Duke of the Archipelago."[3] Nasi maintained the ancient customs and laws of the Latins; his other officials were all Christians; and he tried to win over some of the old families, like the Sirigo and the D'Argenta, or Argyroi of Santorin, by giving them places under his lieutenant-governor and by confirming them in their ancient fiefs. Coronello even succeeded in legitimising his own position to a certain extent by marrying one of his

[1] Haji Kalifeh, *Cronologia Historica* (tr. Carli), 150; Predelli, *Commemoriali, loc. cit.*
[2] P. 148.
[3] *Relazioni degli Ambasciatori*, Series III., ii., 166; Lichtle.

sons to a member of the old ducal family.[1] But his administration was as little able as that of the Crispi to protect the lives and property of his master's subjects from corsairs. In 1577, the D'Argenta, who had been barons of the castle of St Nicholas in Santorin for generations, were attacked by ten Turkish galleys and carried off to Syria. They managed to obtain their freedom, but not to regain their ancestral castle; for four weary years they wandered about Europe, seeking the aid of princes and men of renown, till at last, armed with a letter from Gregory XIII., they knocked one day at the hospitable door of honest Martin Kraus, Professor of Classics at Tübingen. Kraus was interested in the new Greece as well as in the old; he collected money for his two visitors, and at the same time material from them for his *Turcogræcia*. One of them described for him the present condition of the Archipelago—how Santorin still had five castles, Paros two, and Melos, Nio, Seriphos, Siphnos, Andros, Mykonos, Amorgos, Anaphe, and Astypalaia one apiece; how all these islands still possessed towns or villages; and how two of them, Paros and Melos, were episcopal sees. He told him how Tenos still kept aloft the Venetian flag; and he might have added that the Teniotes were intensely loyal to the republic, which gave them a large share in the government. Since the severe lesson which Coronello had received, he does not seem to have molested them again. They now received news and food from Syra with the more or less open connivance of Nasi's Christian officials; they continued to harbour fugitive slaves—a practice at which the Venetian rector wisely winked, and their only grievance was that the republic had issued an ordinance confiscating their property if they were absent for more than six months—a penalty which affected many breadwinners.[2]

Duke Nasi of Naxos died of stone in August 1579, and, as he left no heirs, his dynasty died with him. The Jewish poets, whom he had so liberally encouraged, lamented him as "the sceptre of Israel, the standard-bearer of the dispersed

[1] Pègues, *op. cit.*, 614; Curtius, *Naxos*, 46; Sauger, 302; Νέα Πανδώρα, vi., 572; ix., 436.

[2] Crusius, *Turcogræcia*, 206; Foscarini's Report of 1577, *apud* Lamansky, *Secrets*, 641.

Jews, the noble duke, the sublime lord." His widow, the Duchess Reina, continued to live at her husband's mansion near Constantinople for many years longer, publishing at her own cost the works of Hebrew scholars and poets; while of his mother-in-law, Gracia, we have two memorials, in the shape of the Jewish Academy which she founded at Constantinople, and in the bronze medallion of herself now in the national library in Paris. Of Francesco Coronello we hear no more; but his family became thoroughly naturalised at Naxos, and is not yet extinct in Greece.

Thus ended the brief Jewish sway over the "Isles of Greece"—not the least curious of the many strange accidents of Levantine history, where the most unlikely nations are found in the least expected situations. The experiment was bound to be a failure. A Jew was the last person calculated to make a popular ruler of a Greek state; an absentee, whose expenses, owing to his mode of life and the exigencies of *bakshîsh*, were so huge that three years after he became duke he was described as "overwhelmed with debts," and that he did not leave 90,000 ducats behind him when he died, was sure to wring the uttermost farthing out of his alien subjects. If the last Crispo had chastised them with whips, we may be sure that Nasi had chastised them with scorpions. The official view, as expressed in the capitulations of 1580, was that they had lived unmolested and unoppressed; but their desire for the reinstatement of their old masters, already once manifested, and again demonstrated on the death of the Jewish duke, proves the unpopularity of his rule.

No sooner was the news known, than several inhabitants of the Cyclades who were at Constantinople went to the Porte and begged for the restoration of their former lords of Naxos and Andros, whose children had retired to Venice. The French ambassador reported that the grand-vizier—a bitter enemy of Nasi—had expressed himself as favourable to the revival of these two ancient dynasties, but nothing came of the plan.[1] It was decided to annex the islands to the Turkish Empire, and a *sandjakbeg* and a *cadi* were sent to govern them.[2] In 1580, a deputation of Christians from the

[1] Charrière, *op. cit.*, iii., 71, 809, 931; Carmoly, *op. cit.*, 10-14; Mas Latrie, *Les Ducs de l'Archipel*, 15.

[2] Pègues, 609, 614.

islands, including a Sommaripa of Andros, appeared at the Porte, and obtained from Murâd III. extremely favourable capitulations. Their capitation tax was to be kept at its old figure; their churches were to be free, and could be repaired at their own pleasure; all their ancient laws and customs were to remain in full force; they were entitled to retain their local dress; and, as of old, silk, wine, and provisions were exempt from duty in their islands. These capitulations were confirmed by Ibrahim sixty years later, and formed the charter of the Cyclades under Turkish rule.

But, though the duchy of the Archipelago had passed away for ever, one petty but ancient Latin dynasty still lingered on in the Cyclades for well-nigh forty years longer. The Gozzadini had been restored to Sifanto, as we saw, in 1571, and in their palace in that insignificant island, and in their time-honoured castle of Akrotiri in Santorin, they continued to reside. We are not told how they managed to survive the Turkish wave, which had swept all else away; perhaps their insignificance saved them—perhaps their greater subservience to the sultan—possibly the fact that they sprang from Bologna and not from Venice. At any rate, they, who had boasted their independence of the duchy, still existed, though tributaries of the Turkish Empire. In 1607 Angelo Gozzadini sent his sons to be educated at the Collegio Greco in Rome, and on that occasion Pope Paul V. issued an appeal on his behalf to all Christendom, with special reference to the forthcoming cruise of the Venetian fleet in the Ægean. "I have heard," wrote the pope, "that my beloved son, Angeletto Gozzadini of the noble Bolognese family rules the seven islands of Sifanto, Thermia, Kimolos, Polinos, Pholegandros, Gyaros, and Sikinos, truly adhering to the Catholic faith. All Christians who arrive in his islands should therefore treat him well." In the following year, the Venetian squadron found a hospitable reception from him in his island domain, and he professed himself a loyal vassal of the republic; but, in 1617, his diminutive state was swallowed up in the Turkish Empire, at a moment when feeling ran high against the Catholics of the Archipelago. Angelo took refuge in Rome, where Cardinal Gozzadini was then influential; but in his old age he returned to Naxos, where his forbears had lived so long.

His two sons, one of whom fought for Venice in the Candian war, in vain hoped for the restoration of their seven islands, but they died, like so many dispossessed princes, in exile in Rome.[1] The family has only just become extinct at Bologna; Tournefort[2] found three of its members residing at Sifanto, and it still exists in the Cyclades, where for 310 years it had held sway. During that long period, as was natural, the proud nobles from Bologna erected monuments of their rule, some of which still survive. Their ruined castle at Sifanto is still called "the palace" (*seraglio*), and inside, on a marble pillar, could till lately be seen their arms, with the date 1465 and the initials of Niccolò Gozzadini, the first of the family who ruled there. One of the two towers of the island long bore their name, while their escutcheon still ornaments the old convent, now turned into a school; their name recurred in inscriptions on two of the now ruined churches at Zia, and their arms used to be seen on that of Palaiochora at Melos recently restored.[3] Those from "the palace" are now in Syra.

Owing to its longer duration and to the essentially aristocratic character of its constitution, the duchy of the Archipelago has bequeathed to us more heraldic memorials than the other Frankish states. While coats of arms are rarely found in the castles of feudal Achaia, with the notable exception of Geraki, there is scarcely an island in the Cyclades which has not preserved some emblem of its former lords. Two hundred years ago the arms of the Sommaripa covered the walls of Andros; and the author has seen on a tower in that picturesque town a splendid escutcheon—two heraldic monkeys supporting a shield containing two fleurs-de-lys, while the sun is represented on the stone below. Allusion has already been made to the heraldry of Naxos, the big church in the castle at Melos still bears the escutcheon and inscription of the Crispi, while two crowned lions rampant with outstretched paws—perhaps the arms of the

[1] Hopf, *Gozzadini*, apud Ersch und Gruber, lxxvi., 423; *Veneto-Byzantinische Analekten*, 398, 516; *Cod. Cicogna*, 2532, § 34.

[2] i., 68.

[3] Pasch von Krienen, 114; Piacenza, 286; Buchon, *Atlas*, xl., 26; Νέα Πανδώρα, ix., 196; Hopf, *loc. cit.* (who emends MCCCC. into MCCCCLXV. because the Gozzadini were not lords of Siphnos before 1464).

Michieli—may be seen on two slabs in the floor of the church in the ancient monastery of Our Lady at Amorgos.[1] Even when they have preserved nothing else, the descendants of the island barons have cherished these marks of nobility.

But an agency more powerful than stone inscriptions has kept alive the Latin influence, and has kept together the old Latin families in the Cyclades. In the very year that Naxos was finally annexed to Turkey, Pope Gregory XIII. confirmed the metropolitan jurisdiction of the Archbishop of Naxos over his suffragans, who in Sauger's time, a century later, were five in number; and among the bishops we find scions of the former dynasties; others of the old Italian families went over to the Greek Church, but numbers of them remained true to the faith of their ancestors; and at the present day the Catholics of the Cyclades are in many cases descendants of the Latin conquerors. In the present Greek parliament there are such names as Crispi; and the present Catholic Archbishop of Athens is a Delenda of Santorin.

Of the feudal society in the Cyclades it is possible to form some idea from the letters of the dukes which have come down to us. There, as in the rest of Frankish Greece, the Assizes of Romania were the feudal code, modified by the special usages of Naxos, of which one clause in Italian has been preserved in the British Museum.[2] The duke, as the head of the social firmament was, as we have seen, a personage of much importance, not only in his own scattered realm, but in Achaia, of which he was a peer, at the Vatican, where he insisted on his right of nominating bishops, and at Venice, where he was regarded as the premier duke of Christendom.

The republic treated him with much the same attention, and for much the same reason, which the British Government shows to Indian princes on a visit to London. Nominally independent, he was really a Venetian vassal, and as such might at any time be useful to Venetian interests in the East. In his own immediate circle of islands—those which were under his direct government—he was more autocratic than the Prince of Achaia, and the long history of both the Sanudo and the Crispo dynasties is not broken by the

[1] *Lettere edificanti*, vii., 153; Δελτίον, i., 599.

[2] *Archives de l'Orient latin*, 613-14; *Byz. Zeitschrift*, xiii., 147, 150.

appearance of those pretenders who were so common in the more important principality. It was only in the smaller islands that disputed successions sometimes arose, and then they were usually settled by Venetian intervention. More fortunate, too, than their brethren of the mainland, both the Sanudi and the Crispi produced an abundant stock of males to inherit their throne. Once only did the ducal dignity devolve upon a woman, and in the second dynasty, as we saw, the Assizes of Romania were so far modified as to exclude females from the ducal succession. Hence, with one or two rare exceptions, dynastic intrigues were avoided.

The duke in so peculiarly scattered a domain could not personally administer the affairs of all the islands which were directly subject to him, and in these he was represented by governors. In the ducal letters we read of such officials as "lieutenants," "bailies," and "ducal factors"—an office found also under the Jewish dispensation at Santorin—while there was a "captain" of the castle of Naxos. Another important post, conferred for a long term of years and extant also in Turkish times, was that of *apanochinigari*[1] of the island and city of Naxos—an official perhaps originally the "chief huntsman" of the ducal household, but later on a civil authority. Legal documents were usually countersigned by the chancellor, and the usual language of the ducal chancery was the Venetian dialect, varied by Latin. There is, however, an example of a Naxian deed drawn up in a Greek copy.

In a state where the Latins had dwelt so long, there was naturally a large number of half-castes, called *vasmuli* in the language of the islands. These half-breeds were neither wholly free, nor wholly slaves; they could acquire property, but they could not bequeath it to their heirs, and at their death all they had was their lord's; they and their animals were liable to forced service by land and sea; and, if enfranchised, they had to purchase their freedom anew from their lord's successor. As for the serfs, though they could acquire a *peculium* of their own, it was ever at their lord's disposal, and a female serf with her children yet unborn was

[1] *Byzantinische Zeitschrift*, xiii., 156.

transferred from one master to another like so much personal property. Yet, if these serfs were exclusively Greek, the dukes, with rare exceptions, treated the Orthodox Church with respect. There can, however, have been no love lost between the Greek serf, chained to the oar of the baronial galley, or labouring in the fields of his feudal lord, and the proud nobles, who traced their descent from the great families of Venice or Bologna, and who sat as of right in "the higher and lower court" of the duchy.[1]

Taxes and dues, however, do not, as a rule, appear to have been excessive. An orange at Christmas, or a fowl, was the usual equivalent of our peppercorn rent—a formal recognition of feudal ownership. Tithes and thirtieths were paid by the islanders; the Byzantine land-tax, or *akróstichon*, had survived; and there was the *turcoteli*,[2] the equivalent of our Danegeld, the blackmail levied by the Turkish corsairs on the duke, and extracted by him in turn from his subjects. Yet, as we saw, when the islands became a Hebrew possession, the natives might well have exclaimed in the language of their former dukes—*quando si stava peggio, si stava meglio.*

The Italian society of the Cyclades was by no means uncultured in the fifteenth and sixteenth centuries. We saw how Crusino Sommaripa made excavations at Paros, and how he received the travelling antiquary from Ancona. Giacomo I. Crispo, whose lovely park was a proof of his taste, made scientific experiments in the crater of Santorin, and Buondelmonti was able to buy a manuscript at Andros.[3] At the end of the fifteenth century, the old baronial castles of the islands rang with the sound of merriment; balls were of constant occurrence; and, as the Turkish peril drew nearer and nearer, the motto of the dukes seems to have been: "Let us eat and drink, for to-morrow we die."

The duchy of the Archipelago has passed away for ever —unsung, unlamented. The stern classicist regards the Italian dukes as mere interlopers on the old Hellenic soil; he would pull down their towers as ruthlessly as a Sanudo or

[1] Buchon, *Recherches historiques*, ii., 463.
[2] *Byzantinische Zeitschrift*, xiii., 152.
[3] *Ibid.*, xi., 499; Buondelmonti (ed. Legrand), 25.

a Crispo pulled down his temples, and a Venetian lion, winged and evangelised, is of less value in his eyes than a Periklean potsherd. But the romance, the poetic haze of Greece was in her middle age, rather than in her classic youth; and, as we voyage among those dream islands over a sea of brightest blue, we seem to see the galley of some mediæval duke shoot out from the harbour in quest of spoil.

TABLE OF FRANKISH RULERS

PRINCES OF ACHAIA

	A.D.
Guillaume de Champlitte	1205
Geoffroy I. de Villehardouin — Bailie 1209; prince	1210
Geoffroy II. de Villehardouin	1218
Guillaume de Villehardouin	1246
Charles I. of Anjou	1278
Charles II. of Anjou	1285
Isabelle de Villehardouin	1289
With Florent of Hainault	1289
With Philip of Savoy	1301
Philip I. of Taranto	1307
Matilda of Hainault	1313
With Louis of Burgundy	1313
John of Gravina	1318
Catherine of Valois / Robert of Taranto	1333
Robert of Taranto	1346
Marie de Bourbon	1364
Philip II. of Taranto	1370
Joanna I. of Naples	1374
Otto of Brunswick	1376
[Knights of St John—1377-81]	
Jacques de Baux	1381
Mahiot de Coquerel, vicar	1383
Bordo de S. Superan — Vicar 1386; prince	1396
Maria Zaccaria	1402
Centurione Zaccaria	1404-32

DUKES OF ATHENS

Othon de la Roche, *Megaskyr*	1205
Guy I. — *Megaskyr* 1225; duke	1260
John I.	1263
William	1280

	A.D.
Guy II.	1287
Walter of Brienne	1309
Roger Deslaur, chief of the Catalan Company	1311
Manfred	1312
William	1317
John of Randazzo	1338
Frederick of Randazzo	1348
Frederick III. of Sicily	1355
Pedro IV. of Aragon	1377
John I. of Aragon	1387
Nerio Acciajuoli	Lord of Athens 1388; duke 1394
[Venice—1394-1402]	
Antonio I.	1402
Nerio II.	1435
Antonio II.	1439
Nerio II. (restored)	1441
Francesco	1451
Franco	1455-6; "Lord of Thebes" 1456-60

DESPOTS OF EPIROS

Michael I. Angelos	1204
Theodore	1214
Manuel	1230
Michael II.	1236
Nikephóros I.	1271
Thomas	1296
Nicholas Orsini	1318
John II. Orsini	1323
Nikephóros II.	1335-58
[Byzantine—1336-49; Serb—1349-56]	
Simeon Urosh	1358
Thomas Preliubovich	1367
Maria Angelina	1385
Esau Buondelmonti	1386-1408
[Albanians—1408-18; then united with Cephalonia]	

DUKES OF NEOPATRAS

John I. Angelos	1271
Constantine	1295
John II.	1303-18
[United with Athens]	

PALATINE COUNTS OF CEPHALONIA

Matteo Orsini	1194
Richard	Before 1264

	A.D.
John I.	1303
Nicholas	1317
John II.	1323
[Angevins (united with Achaia)—1324-57]	
Leonardo I. Tocco	1357
Carlo I.	Before 1377
Carlo II.	1429
Leonardo III.	1448-79
Antonio	1481-3

DUKES OF THE ARCHIPELAGO

Marco I. Sanudo	1207
Angelo	*c.* 1227
Marco II.	1262
Guglielmo I	1303
Niccolò I.	1323
Giovanni I.	1341
Fiorenza	1361
With Niccolò II. Sanudo "Spezzabanda"	1364
Niccolò III. dalle Carceri	1371
——	
Francesco I. Crispo	1383
Giacomo I.	1397
Giovanni II.	1418
Giacomo II.	1433
Gian Giacomo	1447
Guglielmo II.	1453
Francesco II.	1463
Giacomo III.	1463
Giovanni III.	1480
[Venice—1494-1500]	
Francesco III.	1500
[Venice—1511-17]	
Giovanni IV.	1517
Giacomo IV.	1564-6
——	
Joseph Nasi	1566-79

LORDS OF CORFÙ

[Venice—1206-14]

Despots of Epiros	1214-59
Manfred of Sicily	1259-66
Chinardo	1266
Charles I. of Anjou	1267
Charles II. of Anjou	1285
Philip I. of Taranto	1294
Catherine of Valois / Robert of Taranto	1331

	A.D.
Robert of Taranto	1346
Marie de Bourbon	1364
Philip II. of Taranto	1364
Joanna I. of Naples	1373
Jacques de Baux	1380
Charles III. of Naples	1382-86

[Venice—1386-1797]

VENETIAN COLONIES

Modon, Coron	1206-1500
Argos	1388-1463
Nauplia	1388-1540
Monemvasia	1464-1540
Lepanto	1407-99
Negroponte	1209-1470
Pteleon	1323-1470
Ægina	1451-1537
Tenos	1390-1715
Mykonos	1390-1537
Northern Sporades	1453-1538
Corfù	1206-1214 ; 1386-1797
Cephalonia	1483-5 ; 1500-1797
Zante	1482-1797
Cerigo	1363-1797

Sta. Mavra	1502-3
Athens	1394-1402
Patras	1408-13 ; 1417-19
Naxos	1494-1500 ; 1511-17
Andros	1437-40 ; 1507-14
Paros	1518-20 ; 1531-36
$\frac{1}{4}$ of Amorgos	1370-1446
Maina	1467-79
Vostitza	1470

BIBLIOGRAPHY

I. Contemporary Documents.

(a) *Venetian:*

Tafel und Thomas: "Urkunden zür älteren Handels-und Staatsgeschichte der Republik Venedig (1204-1300)" in *Fontes Rerum Austriacarum*, Part II., vols. xii., xiii., and xiv.

Thomas and Predelli: *Diplomatarium Veneto-Levantinum* (1300-1454), 2 vols.

Giomo: "Le Rubriche dei Libri Misti perduti," in *Archivio Veneto*, xvii., *et sqq*.

Predelli: *I Libri Commemoriali*, 6 vols.; *Il Liber Communis.*

Jorga: "Notes et Extraits pour servir à l'histoire des Croisades, au XVe Siècle," in *Revue de l'Orient latin*, vols. iv.-viii.

Sáthas: Μνημεῖα Ἑλληνικῆς Ἱστορίας (*Monumenta Hellenicæ Historiæ*), 9 vols.

Lamansky: *Secrets de l'État de Venise.*

Relazioni degli Ambasciatori Veneti, Serie III. and Appendice.

(b) *Neapolitan:*

Del Giudice: *Codice Diplomatico di Carlo I. e II. di Angiò* (1265-8), 2 vols. (Napoli: 1863-9).

La Famiglia di Re Manfredi, 2nd ed. (Napoli: 1896).

Minieri Riccio: *Saggio di Codice Diplomatico*, 2 vols., with supplement. (Napoli: 1878-83).

Alcuni fatti riguardanti Carlo I. di Angiò, dal 1252 *al* 1270.

Il regno di Carlo I. di Angiò negli anni 1271 *e* 1272.

Il regno di Carlo I. d'Angiò, dal 2 *Gennaio* 1273 *al* 31 *Dicembre* 1283. In *Archivio Storico Italiano*, Serie III., vol. xxii.—Serie IV., vol. v

Il regno di Carlo I. d'Angiò, dal 4 *Gennaio* 1284 *al* 7 *Gennaio* 1285; *Ibid.*, Serie IV., vol. vii. *Genealogia di Carlo II. d'Angiò*, in *Archivio Storico per le Provincie Napoletane*, vols. vii., viii.

Della dominazione Angioina nel reame di Sicilia.

Nuovi studii riguardanti la dominazione Angioina nel regno di Sicilia.

Studii storici fatti sopra 84 *Registri Angioini.*

Notizie storiche tratte da 62 *Registri Angioini.*

Studi storici sui fascicoli Angioini.

Barone: *Notizie storiche di Re Carlo III. di Durazzo.*

(c) *Papal:*

Epistolarum Innocentii III., libri XVI. (ed. 1682).
Honorii III. Opera, 4 vols. (ed. Horoy, 1879-80).
Regesta Honorii III. (ed. Pressutti, 1895).
Les Registres de Grégoire IX. (ed. Auvray, 1896-1906).
Les Registres d'Innocent IV. (ed. Berger, 1884-97).
Les Registres d'Alexandre IV. (ed. Bourel de la Roncière).
Les Registres d'Urbain IV. (ed. Guiraud).
Les Registres de Clément IV. (ed. Jordan).
Les Registres de Grégoire X. et de Jean XXI. (ed. Guiraud).
Les Registres de Nicolas III. (ed. Gay).
Les Registres de Martin IV. (ed. École française de Rome).
Les Registres d'Honorius IV. (ed. Prou).
Les Registres de Nicolas IV. (ed. Langlois).
Les Registres de Boniface VIII. (ed. Digard).
Les Registres de Benoît XI. (ed. Grandjean).
Regestum Clementis V. (ed. Benedictine Order).
Lettres secrètes et curiales de Jean XXII. (ed. Coulon).
Lettres communes de Jean XXII. (ed. Mollat).
Lettres communes de Benoît XII. (ed. Vidal).
Lettres closes, patentes, et curiales de Benoît XII. (ed. Daumet).
Lettres closes, patentes, et curiales de Clément VI. (ed. Déprez).
Lettres secrètes et curiales d'Urbain V. (ed. Lecacheux).

(d) *Miscellaneous:*

Miklosich und Müller: *Acta et Diplomata Græca Medii Ævi*, 6 vols.
Exuviæ Sacræ Constantinopolitanæ (ed. 1877), 2 vols.
Lámpros: Ἔγγραφα ἀναφερόμενα εἰς τὴν μεσαιωνικὴν Ἱστορίαν τῶν Ἀθηνῶν. (The third volume of his Greek translation of Gregorovius, *Geschichte der Stadt Athen im Mittelalter*).
Ross und Schmeller: "Urkunden zur Geschichte Griechenlands im Mittelalter," in *Abhandlungen der philos.-philol. Classe der K. Bayer. Akademie*, B. II.
Atti della Società Ligure di Storia patria.
Liber Jurium Reipublicæ Genuensis.
Documenti sulle relazioni toscane coll' Oriente.
Guardione: *Sul Dominio dei Ducati di Atene e Neopatria.*
Mélanges historiques, vol. iii.
Charrière: *Negociations de la France dans le Levant*, vols. i.-iii.
Archives de l'Orient latin.

II. Contemporary Authors.

(a) *Greek:*

Μιχαὴλ Ἀκομινάτου τοῦ Χωνιάτου τὰ σωζόμενα (ed. Lámpros).
Nikétas Choniátes (ed. Bonn).
Akropolita (ed. Bonn).
Michael Palaiológos, *De vitâ suâ.*
Pachyméres (ed. Bonn).

Nikephóros Gregorâs (ed. Bonn).
J. Cantacuzene (ed. Bonn).
Laónikos Chalkokondýles (ed. Bonn).
Phrantzês (ed. Bonn).
Doúkas (ed. Bonn).
Chronicon breve (ed. Bonn).
Epirotica (ed. Bonn).
Kritóboulos *apud* Müller: *Fragmenta historicorum Græcorum*, vol. v.
Manuel Palaiológos *apud* Migne: *Patrologia Græca.*
G. Gemistòs Pléthon *apud* Migne: *Patrologia Græca.*
Bessarion *apud* Migne: *Patrologia Græca.*
Theódoulos Rhétor *apud* Boissonade: *Anecdota Græca*, vol. ii.
Mázaris *apud* Boissonade: *Anecdota Græca*, vol. iii.
Kydónes *apud* Boissonade: *Anecdota Nova.*
Θρῆνος τῆς Κωνσταντινουπόλεως *apud* Wagner: *Mediæval Texts.*
Τὸ Χρονικὸν τοῦ Μορέως (ed. Schmitt). Cited as Χ. τ. Μ.
Dorótheos of Monemvasia: Βιβλίον Ἱστορικόν (ed. 1814).

(b) *Miscellaneous:*

Le Livre de la Conqueste. (Forming vol. i. of Buchon, *Recherches historiques*). Cited as *L. d. C.*
Cronaca di Morea, *apud* Hopf, *Chroniques gréco-romanes.* Cited as *C. d. M.*
Libro de los Fechos et Conquistas del Principado de la Morea. (The Aragonese version of the above). Cited as *L. d. F.*
Benedict of Peterborough: *Gesta Regis Ricardi*, in Rolls' Series.
Matthew Paris: *Chronica Majora*, and *Historia Minor*, in Rolls' Series.
Muratori: *Rerum Italicarum Scriptores.*
Pertz: *Monumenta Germaniæ historica.*
Historiæ patriæ Monumenta. (Torino, 1854-7).
Martin da Canal: "La Chronique des Veniciens," in *Archivio Storico Italiano*, vol. viii.
Laurentius de Monacis: *Chronicon.*
Enrico Dandolo: "Cronaca Veneta." (MS. in Venice).
Amadeo Valier: "Cronaca." (MS. in Venice).
A. Cornaro: "Historia di Candia." (MS. in Venice).
Antonio Morosini: *Chronique.*
Sabellico: *Historia Rerum Venetarum* (ed. 1556).
Bembo: *Rerum Venetarum historia* (ed. 1551).
Guazzo: *Historie.*
P. Jovius: *Historiæ sui temporis.*
Cippico: *P. Mocenigi Gesta.*
Paruta: *Historia Venetiana* (ed. 1703).
A. Maurocenus: *Historia Veneta* (ed. 1623).
Sanudo: *Diarii.*
Conti: *Historie de' suoi tempi.*
Contarini: *Historia delle cose successe* (ed. 1572).
Foglietta: *Historia Genuensium* (ed. 1585).

Albericus Trium Fontium : *Chronicon* (ed. 1698).
Philippe Mouskés : *Chronique rimée*, vol. ii. (Bruxelles, 1838).
"Chronique de Geoffroy de Villehardouin" and "Continuation par Henri de Valenciennes," in Buchon, *Recherches et Matériaux*, vol. ii. ; and also editions by Bouchet and P. Paris.
Muntaner : "Cronaca," in *Cronache Catalane* (tr. Moisè) ; and also edited by Lanz (1844).
The Chronicles of Rabbi Joseph Ben Joshua (tr. Bialloblotzky).
Luccari : *Copioso ristretto degli annali di Rausa.*
Gerlach : *Tagebuch.*
Æneas Sylvius : *Europa.*
Pius II. : *Commentarii.*
Rizzardo : *La Presa di Negroponte.*
"De Nigropontis Captione," in Basle ed. of Chalkokondýles.
Pegalotti : *Della Decima.*
Barbarorum Leges Antiquæ (ed. P. Canciani, 1785).
The Itinerary of Benjamin of Tudela (tr. Asher, 1840).
Géographie d'Édrisi (tr. Jaubert).
Itinerarium Symonis Simeonis (ed. Nasmith, 1778).
Friar Jordanus : *Mirabilia Descripta* (tr. Yule).
Ludolph von Suchem : *De Itinere Terræ Sanctæ.*
Nicolaus de Marthono : "Liber Peregrinationis ad Loca Sancta," in *Revue de l'Orient latin*, vol. iii.
Faber : *Evagatorium.*
Casola : *Viaggio a Gerusalemme.*
Feyerabend : *Reyssbuch des Heyligen Lands* (ed. 1584).
Breuning von und zu Buochenbach : *Orientalische Reyss.*
Kyriaci Anconitani Itinerarium (ed. Mehus).
Epigrammata reperta per Illyricum.
Tozzetti : *Relazioni di alcuni viaggi fatti in Toscana.*
Fabricius : *Biblioteca latina mediæ et infimæ Ætatis*, vol. vi.
Colucci : *Delle Antichità picene.*
Brocquière : "Voyage d'Outremer," in *Mémoires de l'Institut.*
Τῶν ἀποδημιῶν Ἀνδρονίκου τοῦ Νουκίου (ed. M. A. Mustoxidi, 1865).
Buondelmonti : *Liber insularum Archipelagi* (ed. Sinner, 1824 ; and ed. Legrand, 1897).
Bartolomeo dalli Sonnetti : *Periplus.*
Crusius : *Turcogræcia.*
Bongars : *Gesta Dei per Francos*, 2 vols. (The second contains Sanudo : *Secreta Fidelium Crucis*).
Beugnot : *Recueil des historiens des Croisades.*
Sgurópoulos : *Vera historia Unionis.*
Sansovino : *Historia universale dell' Origine et Imperio dei Turchi. Cronologia del Mondo.*
Spandugino : *I Commentari . . . dell' Origine de' Principi Turchi* (ed. 1551).

III. Later Writers.

Ducange: *Histoire de l'Empire de Constantinople*, 2 vols. (ed. Buchon).
Buchon: *Recherches et Matériaux*, 2 vols.
Recherches historiques sur la Principauté française de Morée, 2 vols.
Nouvelles Recherches historiques sur la Principauté française de Morée, 2 vols.
Histoire des Conquêtes.
Atlas des Nouvelles Recherches historiques.
La Grèce Continentale et la Morée.
"Les Cyclades," in *Revue de Paris* for 1843, vols. xiii., xvi., and xvii.
Hopf: "Geschichte Griechenlands vom Beginn des Mittelalters bis auf unsere Zeit," in Ersch und Gruber's *Allgemeine Encyklopädie*, vols. lxxxv. and lxxxvi.
"Ghisi." *Ibid.*, vol. lxvi.
"Giustiniani." *Ibid.*, vol. lxviii. Also in French, *Les Giustiniani* (tr. Vlasto) and Italian, "Di Alcune dinastie latine nella Grecia" (tr. Sardagna), in *Archivio Veneto*, vol. xxxi.
"Gozzadini," in Ersch und Gruber's *Allgemeine Encyklopädie*, vol. lxxvi.
Chroniques gréco-romanes.
"Geschichtlicher Ueberblick über die Schicksale von Karystos," in *Sitzungsberichte der Wiener Akademie* (1853), B. XI. Also, with additions, in Italian, *Dissertazione documentata sulla storia di Karystos* (tr. Sardagna).
"Geschichte der Insel Andros und ihrer Beherrscher," in *Sitzungsberichte der Wiener Akademie* (1855), B. XVI.
"Urkunden und Zusätze zur Geschichte der Insel Andros." *Ibid.* (1856), B. XXI. Also, in Italian, *Dissertazione documentata sulla storia dell' Isola di Andros* (tr. Sardagna).
"Veneto-Byzantinische Analekten," in *Sitzungsberichte der Wiener Akademie* (1859), B. XXXII.
Emerson: *The History of Modern Greece.*
Finlay: *A History of Greece*, vols. iii., iv., v. (ed. Tozer, 1877).
Hertzberg: *Geschichte Griechenlands seit dem Absterben des antiken Lebens bis zur Gegenwart*, Bde. II. and III.
Gregorovius: *Geschichte der Stadt Athen im Mittelalter.* Also, translated, with many additions, into Greek, by Lámpros, as Ἱστορία τῆς πόλεως Ἀθηνῶν κατὰ τοὺς μέσους αἰῶνας.
"Briefe aus der 'Corrispondenza Acciajoli,'" in *Sitzungsberichte der philos.-philol. und histor. Classe der K. Bayer. Akademie* (1890), B. II.
Fallmerayer: *Geschichte der Halbinsel Morea während des Mittelalters.*
Diane de Guldencrone: *L'Achaïe féodale.*
Sir Rennell Rodd: *The Princes of Achaia and the Chronicles of Morea.*
Mas Latrie, Count: "Les princes de Morée," and "Les ducs de l'Archipel," in the Venetian *Miscellanea*, vols. ii. and iv.

Paparregópoulos: Ἱστορία τοῦ Ἑλληνικοῦ Ἔθνους, 4th ed. by P. Karolídes, 1903.
Sourmelês : Κατάστασις συνοπτικὴ τῆς πόλεως τῶν Ἀθηνῶν.
Kampoúroglos, D. G. : Ἱστορία τῶν Ἀθηναίων, 3 vols. (1889-96).
Μνημεῖα τῆς Ἱστορίας τῶν Ἀθηναίων, 3 vols. (2nd ed., 1891-2).
Philadelpheús : Ἱστορία τῶν Ἀθηνῶν ἐπὶ Τουρκοκρατίας, 2 vols. (1902).
Konstantinídes : Ἱστορία τῶν Ἀθηνῶν ἀπὸ Χριστοῦ γεννήσεως μέχρι τοῦ ἔτους 1821 (2nd ed., 1894).
Hammer : *Geschichte des osmanischen Reiches.*, Bde. I. and II.
Heyd : *Le Colonie Commerciali degli Italiani in Oriente.*
Geschichte des Levantehandels.
Daru : *Histoire de Venise.*
Romanin : *Storia documentata di Venezia.*
Cicogna : *Iscrizioni Veneziane*, vol. v.
Cornelius : *Ecclesiæ Venetæ*, vol. viii.
Schlumberger : *Les Principautés francs du Levant.*
Numismatique de l'Orient latin, with *Supplément.*
Expedition des "*Almugavares*" *ou routiers Catalans en Orient.*
Moncada : "Expedicion de los Catalanes y Aragones contre Turcos y Griegos," in *Biblioteca de Autores Españoles*, vol. xxi.
Rubió y Lluch : *La Expedicion y Dominacion de los Catalanes en Oriente.*
Los Navarros en Grecia.
Catalunya a Grecia.
Stamatiádes : Οἱ Καταλάνοι ἐν τῇ Ἀνατολῇ.
Çurita : *Anales de la Corona de Aragon.*
Rosario Gregorio : *Considerazioni sopra la storia di Sicilia.*
Bozzo : *Notizie Storiche Siciliane del Secolo XIV.*
Guichenon : *Histoire généalogique de la royale maison de Savoye* (1670).
Datta : *Storia dei Principi di Savoia del ramo d'Acaja* (Torino, 1832).
Spedizione in Oriente di Amadeo VI.
Servian : *Gestez et Chroniques de la Mayson de Savoye.*
Litta : *Le famiglie celebri italiane.*
Muratori : *Antiquitates Italiæ.*
Mazella : *Descrittione del Regno di Napoli.*
Panvinius : *Antiquitatum Veronensium.*
Turresanus : "Elogium historicarum nobilium Veronæ propaginum." (MS. at Verona).
St Genois : *Droits Primitifs des anciennes terres . . . de Haynaut.*
Lami : *Deliciæ Eruditorum.* (Vol. v. contains many documents about Corinth.)
Mai : *Spicilegium Romanum.*
Bosio : *Dell' Istoria della Sacra Religione . . . di S. Gio. Gierosol* mo.
Martène et Durand : *Thesaurus.*
Wadding : *Annales Minorum.*
Raynaldus : *Annales Ecclesiastici* (ed. 1747).
Le Quien : *Oriens Christianus*, vol. ii.
Eubel : *Hierarchia Catholica Medii Ævi* (1198-1503).
Gerland : *Neue Quellen zur Geschichte des lateinischen Erzbisthums Patras* (1905).

Schultz-Gora: *Le Epistole del Trovatore Rambaldo di Vaqueiras.*
Laborde: *Athènes aux XVE, XVIE, et XVIIE Siècles.*
A. Mommsen: *Athenæ Christianæ.*
Lámpros: Αἱ Ἀθῆναι περὶ τὰ τέλη τοῦ δωδεκάτου αἰῶνος.
Fanelli: *Atene Attica.*
Magni: *Relazione della città di Atene.*
Viaggi e dimore per la Turchia.
Spon et Wheler, *Voyage d'Italie de Dalmatie, de Grèce et du Levant*, 3 vols. (Lyon, 1678).
Guillaume: *Histoire généalogique des Sires de Salins.*
D'Arbois de Jubainville: *Voyage paléographique dans le département de l'Aube.*
Ubaldini: *Origine della famiglia Acciajuoli.*
Gaddi: *Elogiographus.*
Corollarium Poeticum.
Pouqueville: *Voyage dans la Grèce.*
Millet: *Le Monastère de Daphni.*
Schultz and Barnsley: *The Monastery of St Luke.*
Polýkarpos: Τὰ Μετέωρα (1882).
Sáthas: Χρονικὸν Ἀνέκδοτον Γαλαξειδίου.
Τουρκοκρατουμένη Ἑλλάς.
Lamprinídes: Ἡ Ναυπλία.
Marmora: *Historia di Corfù.*
A. Mustoxidi: *Delle Cose Corciresi.*
Illustrazioni Corciresi.
M. A. Mustoxidi: Ἱστορικὰ καὶ Φιλολογικὰ Ἀνάλεκτα.
Lunzi: Περὶ τῆς πολιτικῆς καταστάσεως τῆς Ἑπτανήσου ἐπὶ Ἐνετῶν. Also in an enlarged Italian version: *Della Condizione politica delle Isole Ionie sotto il dominio Veneto.*
Idroménos: Συνοπτικὴ Ἱστορία τῆς Κερκύρας.
Jervis: *History of the Island of Corfù.*
Botta: *Storia Naturale dell' Isola di Corfù.*
Saint-Sauveur: *Voyage historique, littéraire et pittoresque dans les isles et possessions çi-devant vénitiennes du Levant*, 4 vols.
Albánas: Περὶ τῶν ἐν Κερκύρᾳ τίτλων εὐγενείας.
Brokínes: Περὶ τῶν ἐτησίως τελουμένων ἐν Κερκύρᾳ λιτανειῶν τοῦ θ. λειψάνου τοῦ Ἁγίου Σπυρίδωνος. (Eng. tr. by Mrs Dawes).
Romanós: Γρατιανὸς Ζώρζης αὐθέντης Λευκάδος.
Ἡ Ἑβραϊκὴ Κοινότης τῆς Κερκύρας.
Δημοσία Κερκυραϊκὴ Πρᾶξις.
Περὶ τοῦ Δεσποτάτου τῆς Ἠπείρου.
Arabantinós: Χρονογραφία τῆς Ἠπείρου.
Meliarákes: Ἱστορία τοῦ Βασιλείου τῆς Νικαίας καὶ τοῦ Δεσποτάτου τῆς Ἠπείρου.
Γεωγραφία πολιτικὴ τοῦ νομοῦ Κεφαλληνίας.
Γεωγραφία πολιτικὴ τοῦ νομοῦ Ἀργολίδος καὶ Κορινθίας.
Ἄνδρος, Κέως.
Ἀμοργός, Κίμωλος. In Δελτίον τῆς Ἱστ. καὶ Ἐθν. Ἑτ., vols. i. and vi.
Οἰκογένεια Μαμωνᾶ.

Risposta di Jacopo Grandi . . . intorno S. Maura.
Petritzópoulos : *Saggio Storico sull' età di Leucadia* (1824).
Stamatélos : Φιλολογικαὶ διατριβαὶ περὶ Λευκάδος (1851).
Blantês : Ἡ Λευκὰς ὑπὸ τοὺς Φράγκους (1902).
Remondini : *De Zacynthi Antiquitatibus.*
Serra : "Storia di Zante." (MS. in author's possession).
Chiótes : Ἱστορικὰ Ἀπομνημονεύματα Ἑπτανήσου.
Mercati : *Saggio Storico Statistico di Zante.*
Karavías : Ἱστορία τῆς νήσου Ἰθάκης.
Stai : *Raccolta di antiche autorità . . . riguardanti l'Isola di Citera* (Pisa, 1847).
P. A. S. : Ἡ Πάργα.
Perrhaibós : Ἱστορία τοῦ Σουλίου καὶ Πάργας.
Foscolo : "Narrazione delle fortune e della cessione di Parga," in *Prose Politiche.*
Bury : "The Lombards and Venetians in Euboia," in *Journal of Hellenic Studies*, vols. vii.-ix.
Historia del Regno di Negroponte (1695).
Piacenza : *L'Egeo Redivivo.*
Boschini : *L'Archipelago.*
Porcacchi : *Le Isole più famose al Mondo.*
Tournefort : *Voyage du Levant.*
Pasch von Krienen : *Breve Descrizione dell' Archipelago.*
Sauger : *Histoire nouvelle des anciens Ducs de l'Archipel* (ed. 1699).
Lichtle : "Description de Naxie." (MS. copy in Berlin).
Zabarella : *Tito Livio Padovano.*
Il Galba.
Curtius : *Naxos.*
Carmoly : *Don Joseph Nassy.*
Levy : *Don Joseph Nasi.*
Lettere Edificanti scritte dalle missioni straniere, vol. vii.
Pègues : *Histoire de Santorin.*
E. A. C. : *Cenni Storici intorno Paolo de Campo.*
Dugit : "Naxos et les Établissements latins de l'Archipel," in *Bulletin de l'Académie Delphinale*, vol. x.
Haji Kalifeh : *The history of the Maritime Wars of the Turks* (tr. Mitchell).
Cronologia historica (tr. Carli).

IV. Periodicals.

Archivio Storico Italiano.
Archivio Veneto and *Nuovo Archivio Veneto.*
Archivio Storico per le Provincie Napoletane.
Giornale Ligustico.
Napoli Nobilissima.
Bulletino dell' Istituto.
Revue de l'Orient latin.
Bulletin de Correspondance hellénique.

Revue des Études grecques.
Revue Archéologique.
Bibliothèque de l'École des Chartes.
Mélanges de l'École française de Rome.
Académie de Besançon.
Byzantinische Zeitschrift.
Mitteilungen des k. deutsch. Arch. Instituts (Athen).
The English Historical Review.
Journal of Hellenic Studies.
Ἑλληνομνήμων.
Νέος Ἑλληνομνήμων.
Δελτίον τῆς Ἱστορικῆς καὶ Ἐθνολογικῆς Ἑταιρίας. Cited as Δελτίον.
Δελτίον τῆς Χριστιανικῆς Ἀρχαιολογικῆς Ἑταιρείας.
Παρνασσός.
Ἁρμονία.
Νέα Πανδώρα.
Βυζαντινὰ Χρονικά.

INDEX

(Except where expressly stated, the Greek names of places are used, the Frankish equivalents being put in brackets after them.)